SPORTS ETHICS

For Bernard, Lisa, and Debzita

SPORTS ETHICS
AN ANTHOLOGY

Edited by
JAN BOXILL

Blackwell
Publishing

Editorial material and organization © 2003 by Jan Boxill

350 Main Street, Malden, MA 02148-5018, USA
108 Cowley Road, Oxford OX4 1JF, UK
550 Swanston Street, Carlton South, Melbourne, Victoria 3053, Australia
Kurfürstendamm 57, 10707 Berlin, Germany

First published 2003 by Blackwell Publishers Ltd, a Blackwell Publishing company

Library of Congress Cataloging-in-Publication Data has been applied for.

ISBN 0-631-21696-0 (hardback); ISBN 0-631-21697-9 (paperback)

A catalogue record for this title is available from the British Library.

Set in 9½ /11½ pt Erhardt
by Kolam Information Services Pvt. Ltd. Pondicherry
Printed and bound in the United Kingdom
by TJ International, Padstow, Cornwall

For further information on
Blackwell Publishing, visit our website:
http://www.blackwellpublishing.com

Contents

Notes on Contributors

Peter J. Arnold was for sixteen years the head of the Education Department at Dunfermline College, Edinburgh. He is author of *Education, Physical Education and Personality Development* and *Meaning in Movement, Sport and Physical Education*. Since 1979 he has been corresponding fellow of the American Academy of Physical Education. He has served as president of the Philosophic Society for the Study of Sport.

Jan Boxill received her BA, MA, and PhD at UCLA, where she also played basketball. She taught philosophy and was head women's basketball coach at the University of Tampa, Florida, before joining the Philosophy Department at the University of North Carolina in 1985, and becoming the public address announcer for women's basketball and field hockey, and radio commentator on away basketball games. At the 1996 Atlanta Olympics, she served as public address announcer for men's and women's basketball, including the women's medal rounds and ceremonies. A lecturer and associate chair of the Department of Philosophy at UNC, Jan specializes in social and political philosophy and the philosophy of sport.

Brenda Jo Bredemeier, co-director of the Mendelson Center for Sport, Character and Culture at the University of Notre Dame, is a member of American Academy of Kinesiology and Physical Education. She gained her PhD at Temple University and was a professor for 20 years at the University of California at Berkeley. A certified sport psychologist, her research focuses on social and moral development in sport and physical education contexts. She was an intercollegiate athlete and coach, and served as a consultant for the NCAA.

W.M. Brown, a philosophy professor at Trinity College, Hartford, Connecticut, serves as the dean of the faculty. Prior to joining Trinity's faculty in 1965, he was a teaching fellow at Harvard University (1963–5) and a lecturer in French at Boston University (1960–3). He received his bachelor's degree from Amherst College and his PhD from Harvard University. He has lectured and written extensively in the areas of philosophy of science and philosophy of sport.

Robert Butcher received his PhD in philosophy (practical ethics) from the University of Western Ontario in 1992. Since 1990 he has been a partner in Foundations: Consultants on Ethics and Values, specializing in providing ethics services to the government and the health, sport, and business sectors. He teaches a variety of ethics (health, business, professional) and philosophy courses at the University of Western Ontario, and has published extensively in ethics in sport.

Nicholas Dixon, professor of philosophy at Alma College, Michigan, holds a BA, University of Leeds, and MA, PhD, Michigan State University. His work in philosophy of sport is part of his general interest in applied ethics. He has published articles on such issues as gun control, abortion, rape, physician-assisted suicide, boxing, and filial duties, in journals including *Social Theory and Practice, Philosophical Forum, Public Affairs Quarterly, Journal of Applied Philosophy, Hastings Center Report*, and the *Monist*.

Jane English was a faculty member in the Department of Philosophy at the University of North Carolina at Chapel Hill when she died climbing the Matterhorn in 1978. Prior to the fatal accident, she published several well-received articles and edited both *Sex Equality* and *Feminism and Philosophy*.

Randolph M. Feezell is a professor of philosophy at Creighton University. His areas of interest are ethics, philosophy of religion, and contemporary philosophy. He has written several articles on sportsmanship and has been a frequent contributor to the *Journal of the Philosophy of Sport*.

Liz Galst is deputy editor of *MAMM: Women, Cancer and Community* and is a writer for the *Boston Phoenix*.

Francine Hardaway, PhD, is a former college professor turned writer and coach to start-up companies. A former film reviewer and critic of popular culture, she has written and published three books on the teaching of writing, and is a regular columnist for several magazines. You may read her web log at http://www.stealthmodepart.blogspot.com.

Peter Heinegg is professor of English and comparative literature at Union College, Schenectady, NY. His interests are religion (and irreligion), the Bible, the classics, Yiddish literature, Swift, Gibbon, Proust, Woolf, tragedy, comedy, pastoral, pastoral-comical, historical-pastoral, tragical-historical, tragical-comical-historical-pastoral, etc. Recent publications include "Lessons from a Lunatic" and "God-doggerels."

Nicholas Hunt-Bull, an assistant professor of philosophy at New Hampshire College, received his BA from the University of Ontario and his PhD from the University of North Carolina at Chapel Hill. He has taught at the University of North Carolina at Greensboro, and his research interests are in the history of ethics, especially the Scottish moral sense theorists.

Carwyn Jones is a senior lecturer in the philosophy and social theory of sport at the University of Teesside. Having gained a PhD in sports ethics, he has published in the areas of sport and moral development, and moral action in professional sport.

James W. Keating, professor emeritus at DePaul University, received his PhD at the Catholic University of America.

R. Scott Kretchmar, professor of exercise sport science at Penn State University, is Penn State's faculty representative to the NCAA. He received his BA in physical education from Oberlin College and his doctorate from the University of Southern California. He was honored as the alliance scholar for the American Alliance of Health, Physical Education and Dance, the distinguished scholar for the National Association for Physical Education in Higher Education, and the Fraleigh honorary scholar of the International Association for the Philosophy of Sport. He is author of a text on the philosophy of sport and has written numerous articles on ethics, fair play, and human intelligence in physical activity

Richard E. Lapchick is the DeVos eminent scholar chair and director of the business sports management graduate program at the University of Central Florida. He founded both Northeastern University's Center for the Study of Sport in Society and the National Consortium for Academics and Sport, and is now director emeritus of the center and director of the consortium. He was recently inducted into the Sports Hall of Fame of the Commonwealth of Nations in the humanitarian category.

Michael Lavin is a psychologist in private practice in Alexandria's Old Town. A former associate professor of philosophy at the University of Tennessee, Knoxville, he received his BA in philosophy at California State University at Northridge, MA in philosophy at Claremont Graduate School, a PhD in philosophy and humanities at Stanford, and a PhD in psychology at the University of Arizona. He has published widely in philosophy and in psychology, especially on topics relating to ethics.

Robert E. Leach, MD, professor, Department of Orthopedics, Boston University School of Medicine, is a member of the American Orthopedic Society for Sports Medicine, and currently serves as editor of the *American Journal of Sports Medicine*.

Catharine MacKinnon is a lawyer, teacher, writer, activist, and expert on sex equality. She has a BA from Smith College, a JD from Yale Law School, and a PhD in political science from Yale University Graduate School. She has been professor of law at the University of Michigan Law School since 1990, and visiting professor of law at the University of Chicago Law School since fall 1997. She has taught at Yale, Harvard, Stanford, Minnesota, UCLA, University of Chicago, Osgoode Hall (Toronto), and the University of Basel (Switzerland). Beginning in the mid-1970s, she pioneered the legal claim for sexual harassment as a form of sex discrimination.

Mike Marqusee is a political journalist. He is the author of *Slow Turn, Defeat from the Jaws of Victory: Inside Kinnock's Labour Party*, and *Anyone But England: Cricket and the National Malaise*.

Mike McNamee is reader in applied philosophy at the University of Gloucestershire. He has co-edited books on the ethics of sport, the ethics of leisure, and research ethics. He co-edits

the series "Ethics and Sport" and is currently editing a book on the philosophy of sport sciences. He is immediate past president of the International Association of the Philosophy of Sport and is a former executive member of the Philosophy of Education Society of Great Britain.

Laura Morgan received her BA and is a PhD candidate at the University of North Carolina at Chapel Hill. She has taught at the University of North Carolina at Greensboro, and her research interests are in philosophy of language, epistemology, and metaphysics.

Albert Mosley, professor of philosophy at Smith College, has written extensively in African American philosophy. He received his PhD from the University of Wisconsin-Madison, and before coming to Smith in 2000, taught at Ohio University, the University of the District of Columbia, and Howard University. He is an avid musician and tennis player.

Janice Moulton, research associate in philosophy at Smith College, received her PhD from the University of Chicago. She has taught at the University of Chicago, Duke University, and Central China University. Her research interests are feminism, linguistics, and philosophical methodology. Her publications include *The Guidebook for Publishing Philosophy, Scaling the Dragon: Adventures in China* (a novel co-authored with George Robinson), *The Organization of Language*, and *Ethical Problems in Higher Education*, as well as many articles. She began running at 33, learned to play softball at 35, and fell in love with soccer at 39.

Mariah Burton Nelson, a former Stanford and professional women's basketball player, is the author of *Are We Winning Yet?*, *The Stronger Women Get, the More Men Love Football*, *Embracing Victory*, *The Unburdened Heart: Five Keys to Forgiveness and Freedom*, and *We Are All Athletes: Bringing Courage, Confidence, and Peak Performance into Our Everyday Lives*. Still an athlete, she swims two miles each morning and coaches her mother, Sarah, who holds three

Arizona breaststroke records for women aged 75–9.

Rick Reilly is in his seventeenth year as a senior writer for *Sports Illustrated*, where he writes the weekly "Life of Reilly" column. He has been voted National Sportswriter of the Year seven times, and is the author of *The Life of Reilly: The Best of Sports Illustrated's Rick Reilly* and the novel *Slo-Mo: My Untrue Story*, a farce about the NBA. He has won numerous awards in his 24-year writing career, including the prestigious New York Newspaper Guild's Page One Award for Best Magazine Story.

Angela Schneider, associate professor and assistant dean of ethics and equity, University of Western Ontario, received her PhD in philosophy (writing her thesis on doping in sport) in 1993. Since 1990 she has been a partner in Foundations: Consultants on Ethics and Values. She teaches and researches on ethics in sport and gender issues in sport. Her publications include numerous scholarly articles on ethical and gender issues in sport. She is past president of the International Association for the Philosophy of Sport, and was a 1984 Olympics silver medallist in rowing.

David L. Shields, PhD, co-director of the Mendelson Center for Sport, Character, and Culture at Notre Dame, received his training in education from the Graduate Theological Union in Berkeley, California. He has collaborated with Brenda Jo Bredemeier on numerous sport and character studies, and they co-authored the book *Character Development and Physical Activity*. In addition to his academic work, he has several years of experience in non-profit management. A former intercollegiate track and field competitor, he now serves as a consultant for the NCAA.

Robert L. Simon holds a PhD from the University of Pennsylvania. A past Rockefeller Foundation and National Endowment for the Humanities fellow, he has also served as president of the Philosophic Society for the Study of Sport. He was the beloved coach of the men's varsity golf team at Hamilton 1986–2000, and is the author of *Fair Play*. He is the recipient of numerous teaching awards and sits on the editorial board for the *Journal of the Philosophy of Sport*.

Dean Smith at age 30 became the head basketball coach at the University of North Carolina. He finished his career as the all-time most-winning coach in basketball history, with 879 victories against only 254 losses. In 36 years, he coached Carolina to eleven final fours, two national titles and thirteen ACC tournament championships. In 1976 he was named coach of the US Olympic team. He has won numerous coaching awards, including eight ACC Coach of the Year titles, and at the 2002 NCAA Final Four he and coach John Wooden were honored as the best basketball coaches in history by the National Association of Basketball Coaches. The author of three books, Dean Smith serves as a consultant for the University of North Carolina at Chapel Hill.

Michael Smith was professor of sociology and physical education at York University. He was a founding member and director of the LaMarsh Center for Research on Violence and Conflict Resolution. An athlete and a scholar, he published the leading text *Violence and Sport*. He had a special interest in hockey violence and developed an interest in studying violence toward women. Together with a colleague at the University of Michigan, he was writing a book on sexual harassment in the workplace at the time of his death in June 1994.

Christopher Wellman directs the Jean Beer Blumenfeld Center for Ethics and teaches in the Department of Philosophy at Georgia State University. He received his BA in philosophy and economics at the University of North Carolina at Chapel Hill and a PhD in philosophy from the University of Arizona. He works in ethics, specializing in political and legal philosophy.

Peter S. Wenz, Professor of Philosophy and Legal Studies at the University of Illinois at Springfield and Adjunct Professor of Medical humanities at the Southern Illinois University School of Medicine, teaches a variety of courses in applied ethics and law, including moral issues in the law, philosophy of law, biomedical ethics and the law, and environmental values. He is the author of *Environmental Justice, Abortion Rights as Religious Freedom*, and *Nature's Keeper*. He and Laura Westra co-edited *Faces of Environmental Racism*. He serves on the advisory board of *Environmental Ethics*.

Foreword

Dean Smith

Sports are all about breaking down barriers; not just the barriers of speed and scores, championships and personal bests. It's also about breaking down stereotypes and the barriers that limit opportunities and a fair playing field for all. We in sports can be the trailblazers when it comes to social justice issues. Further, there can be values learned through participation in sports, but our society's emphasis on winning, rather than participation, is a problem, a problem that creates other problems. Our society is so concerned with the "number one" syndrome that often there is nothing left for others who competed with integrity and gave their all, but came up short on the scoreboard. However, despite these problems and the fact that sports are imperfect activities, I firmly believe there is value in exploring the athletic heart on all levels. My father taught me to value each human being and to treat each person with dignity. This respect can be exemplified in the sports world; it is clear when others show respect, and it is clear when they don't. Thus, as Professor Boxill points out, sports play a significant role in our society by dramatizing both our virtues and our vices.

For several years now Professor Jan Boxill has taught a course in the ethics of sport, and I have been an invited guest lecturer. Having been associated with sports and athletics for over 60 years, I have seen a great many changes, some good, some bad. It is important to keep sports in the right perspective, but that seems very diffi-

cult. Addressing the ethics of sports in the context of their moral significance for both the individual and the society is very important. Jan has put together a collection of essays which address the main issues in sports today, including the nature of sport and competition. To keep these in perspective, all of us who love sports must teach others about the role sports play in society. It is important that sports play a role in promoting sportsmanship, friendship, and respect for others, by discouraging violence, cheating, and drugs. And it is important that these be reinforced by parents, teachers, coaches, and professors, in order that society and its members can learn from them.

Jan maintains that sports are the single most available means for self-development, self-respect, and self-esteem, when properly played, as cooperative activities. I think she is correct in this, and in my years of coaching I have tried to promote this. And basketball is the perfect game. Played the right way, basketball is the most beautiful sport of them all – the ultimate team game. Good coaching means teaching your players how to play individually and then unselfishly as a team. In this way players learn to respect one another's contributions, as well as respect the fact that our differences are what unite us rather than separate us. We owe our natural talents to our genes, and along life's journey receive help from many people in order to be successful. This is as true of a well-functioning society as it is in sports.

Preface

Twenty-five years ago, I wrote my first essay on the ethics of sports. The field was new and recognized only by those of us writing in it, among whom were Jane English, Robert Simon, and Paul Weiss. After Jane's tragic death in 1978, the Society for Women in Philosophy devoted a session at the Eastern Division of the American Philosophical Association to her contributions. Though I never met Jane, we corresponded and spoke on many occasions, sharing our thoughts on social justice and equal opportunity in general, and on equal opportunity for women in sports in particular. Her essay "Sex Equality in Sports" has been essential reading for my courses in feminism and in ethics in sports, and appears in this collection as well. I was privileged to be invited to present my first APA paper, "Sport as an Unalienated Activity," in her honor. I never published this paper, but its thesis is incorporated in my "Moral Significance of Sport," the introduction to this collection.

With the publication of Robert L. Simon's book *Sport and Social Values in 1991*, the formation of the Philosophic Society for the Study of Sport, and the appearance of the *Journal of the Philosophy of Sport*, the interest in ethics in sports has come center stage. Of course, ethical issues in sports have always been center stage, but academics left them to those in athletics, somehow feeling they didn't want to dirty their hands. But their doing so meant ethics in sports deteriorated, as did sportsmanship.

Violence, drugs, cheating, and winning at all costs took over at the college and professional levels, then found their way to the high school and children's leagues, to the point where people are shaking their heads in despair as they try to find solutions. Centers for the study of sport have sprung up, commissions have been established, universities have councils to address the problems on campus, books have been written, and anthologies have been compiled.

This collection has been a few years in the making. It contains eleven previously unpublished essays, written specifically for this collection. The remaining readings are previously published articles, mainly from the *Journal of the Philosophy of Sport*, which in my mind has been in the forefront on all the issues. In selecting the articles for this collection, I have concentrated on what I believe are the core issues: the educational value of sport; sportspersonship; competition; drug use in sports; violence in sports; sport as a source of equal opportunity; and sport and role models. It was extremely difficult to decide just what to include, especially as I wanted to support the work on philosophical issues with psychological studies and some discussion of sports in practice, as seen in *Sports Illustrated*, and by real people participating in sports, in particular Coach Dean Smith. Thus, my hope is that this collection will appeal to academics as well as people who are interested in keeping ethics in sports, by applying theory to practice. It is for this reason I approached Dean Smith to write a foreword.

Two coaches stand out as the most successful and most ethical in attaining their success: John Wooden at UCLA and Dean Smith at the University of North Carolina at Chapel Hill. Though I met Coach Wooden only once, as a UCLA basketball player I was able to watch and admire his coaching, as I could Coach Smith's at the University of North Carolina. But even more, Coach Smith has become a friend and colleague, and my students have had the good fortune to hear him speak in some of my classes. His book, *A Coach's Life*, tells us a great deal about who he is, and I have included part of chapter 12 of that book in this collection (reading 14). His class shows in everything he does.

I continue to use Robert L. Simon's book, *Fair Play: Sports, Values, and Society* (1985), now in its second edition, as the core text for my courses on ethics in sports, and Bob continues to be a friend and supporter of discussions on the topic. I am honored that he provided an essay specifically for this collection (reading 1).

In teaching my course on ethics in sports, I have assigned many of the essays I was considering for this anthology to my students, who have helped me a lot in making selections. In particular I wish to thank my Johnston Scholars Seminar and my First Year Seminar, who were very diligent in reading and active in discussing several of the readings, and who continue to be a source of support for my work. I wish also to acknowledge several other students who have worked independently with me on the topic, the first of whom at the University of North Carolina at Chapel Hill was Kit Wellman. I had just published "Beauty, Sport, and Gender,"[1] and we wanted to examine further the relationship between sport and art. Kit, now a professor at Georgia State University, and I continue to have discussions about issues in ethics in sports, and it was only natural that I

should invite him to write on any topic he wished for this anthology. Since we disagreed about the issue of athletes as role models, I was pleased that his contribution was on this area (reading 34). Two other former students whose papers I have included are Nicholas Hunt-Bull and Laura Morgan (readings 27 and 18). At a recent conference on ethics and sports at the University of South Florida where Mike McNamee and I served on panels, I asked Mike to contribute an essay, and was happy when he agreed (reading 3). Also having just read *Taboo*, it was serendipitous when I learned that Al Mosley had just completed an essay on that book, and I was delighted when he allowed me to include it in this volume (reading 31).

My mentor since I was an undergraduate at UCLA and presently my colleague at UNC, Tom Hill, always encourages and comments on my writing. At a Public Ethics Discussion group at UNC, we co-led a discussion on sports as forum for public ethics. He and his wife, Robin Hill, provide strong support for my love of sports, attending nearly every UNC basketball game, men's and women's.

I also wish to acknowledge Beth Remmes and Fiona Sewell of Blackwell Publishers; they provided stimulation and much needed prodding to finally get this completed.

Last, but certainly not least, I want to thank and acknowledge my husband, Bernard, and my daughters, Lisa and Debbie, who have always been my biggest sources of support. They have suffered through my obsession with sports, as a player, a coach, an announcer, a fan, a teacher, and a writer. March Madness has been madness in my house for well over 35 years! I can't thank them enough for their love, support, and understanding. They continue to be the most important people in my life, and so I dedicate this collection to them.

JMB

Note

1   *Journal of the Philosophy of Sport*, XI (1985), pp. 36–47.

Acknowledgments

The editor and publisher gratefully acknowledge the permission granted to reproduce the copyright material in this book:

Arnold, Peter J., "Three Approaches Toward an Understanding of Sportsmanship," reprinted by permission from *Journal of the Philosophy of Sport*, copyright 1984, vol. X, pp. 61–70.

Boxill, Jan, "The Ethics of Competition." © 2003 by Jan Boxill. Written especially for this volume.

Boxill, Jan, "Introduction: The Moral Significance of Sport." © 2003 by Jan Boxill. Written especially for this volume.

Boxill, Jan, "Title IX and Gender Equity," reprinted by permission from *Journal of the Philosophy of Sport*, copyright 1993–4, vols XX and XXI, pp. 23–31.

Bredemeier, Brenda Jo, David L. Shields, and Jack C. Horn, "Values and Violence in Sports Today: The Moral Reasoning Athletes Use in their Games and in their Lives," *Psychology Today*, vol. 19, October 1985.

Brown, W.M., "Personal Best," reprinted by permission from *Journal of the Philosophy of Sport*, copyright 1995, vol. XXII, pp. 1–10.

Butcher, Robert and Angela Schneider, "Fair Play as Respect for the Game," reprinted by permission from *Journal of the Philosophy of Sport*, copyright 1998, vol. XXV, pp. 1–22.

Dixon, Nicholas, "On Winning and Athletic Superiority," reprinted by permission from *Journal of the Philosophy of Sport*, copyright 1999, vol. XXVI, pp. 10–26.

Dixon, Nicholas, "On Sportsmanship and 'Running Up the Score,'" reprinted by permission from *Journal of the Philosophy of Sport*, copyright 1992, vol. XIX, pp. 1–13.

English, Jane, "Sex Equality in Sports," *Philosophy and Public Affairs*, vol. 7, no. 3, pp. 269–77 (Spring 1978). Copyright © 1978 by *Philosophy and Public Affairs* 7, no. 3, reprinted by permission of Princeton University Press.

Feezell, Randolph M., "Sportsmanship and Blowouts: Baseball and Beyond," reprinted by permission from *Journal of the Philosophy of Sport*, copyright 1999, vol. XXVI, pp. 68–78.

Galst, Liz, "The Sports Closet," from *Ms*, September/October 1998. © 1998 by Liz Galst. Reproduced by kind permission of the author.

Hardaway, Francine, "Foul Play: Sports Metaphors as Public Doublespeak," from *Sport Inside Out*, eds David L. Vanderwerken and Spencer K. Wertz (Texas Christian University Press, Fort Worth, 1985).

Heinegg, Peter, "Philosopher in the Playground: Notes on the Meaning of Sport," from *Sport Inside Out*, eds David L. Vanderwerken and Spencer K. Wertz (Texas Christian University Press, Fort Worth, 1985).

Hunt-Bull, Nicholas, "Why Women do Better than Men in College Basketball, or 'What is Collegiate Sport for, Anyway?'" © 2003 by Nicholas Hunt-Bull. Written especially for this volume.

Keating, James, W., "Sportsmanship as a Moral Category," *Ethics*, vol. 75 (October 1964), pp. 25–35, reprinted by permission of The University of Chicago Press.

Kretchmar, R. Scott, "In Defense of Winning." © 2003 by R. Scott Kretchmar. Written especially for this volume.

Lapchick, Richard, "Race and College Sport: A Long Way to Go," *Race and Class*, vol. 36, no. 4, 1995, reprinted by permission of Institute of Race Relations.

Lavin, Michael, "Sports and Drugs: Are the Current Bans Justified?," reprinted by permission from *Journal of the Philosophy of Sport*, copyright 1987, vol. XIV, pp. 34–43.

Leach, Robert E., "Violence and Sports," reprinted from *American Journal of Sports Medicine*, September–October 1997, p. 595, copyright © American Orthopaedic Society for Sports Medicine, 1997.

MacKinnon, Catharine, "Women, Self-Possession, and Sport," reprinted from *Feminism Unmodified: Discourses on Life and Law* by Catharine A. MacKinnon, Cambridge, Mass., Harvard University Press, copyright © 1987 by the President and Fellows of Harvard College.

McNamee, Mike, and Carwyn Jones, "Moral Development and Sport: Character and Cognitive Developmentalism Contrasted." © 2003 by Mike McNamee and Carwyn Jones. Written especially for this volume.

Marqusee, Mike, "Sport and Stereotype: From Role Model to Muhammad Ali," *Race and Class*, vol. 36, no. 4, 1995.

Morgan, Laura, "Enhancing Performance in Sports: What is Morally Permissible?" © 2003 by Laura C. Morgan. Written especially for this volume.

Mosley, Albert, "Racial Differences in Sports: What's Ethics Got to Do With It?" © 2003 by Albert Mosley. Written especially for this volume.

Moulton, Janice, "Why Everyone Deserves a Sporting Chance: Education, Justice, and School Sports." © 2003 by Janice Moulton. Written especially for this volume.

Nelson, Mariah Burton, "Stronger Women," from *The Stronger Women Get, the More Men Love Football: Sexism and the American Culture of Sports*, copyright © 1994 by Mariah Burton Nelson, reprinted by permission of Harcourt, Inc.

Pearson, Kathleen M., "Deception, Sportsmanship, and Ethics," from *Sport Inside Out*, eds David L. Vanderwerken and Spencer K. Wertz (Texas Christian University Press, Fort Worth, 1985).

Reilly, Rick, "Get the Message?," copyright © Time Inc., 1999.

Simon, Robert, L., "Good Competition and Drug-Enhanced Performance," reprinted by permission from *Journal of the Philosophy of Sport*, copyright 1985, vol. XI, pp. 6–13.

Simon, Robert L., "Gender Equity and Inequity in Athletics," reprinted by permission from *Journal of the Philosophy of Sport*, copyright 1993–4, vols XX and XXI, pp. 6–22.

Simon, Robert L., "Sports, Relativism, and Moral Education." © 2003 by Robert L. Simon. Written especially for this volume.

Smith, Dean, "Foreword." © 2003 by Dean Smith. Written especially for this volume.

Smith, Dean, "Winding Down, Looking Ahead," reprinted from *A Coach's Life*, copyright © 1999 by Dean E. Smith. Used by permission of Random House, Inc.

Smith, Michael, "What is Sports Violence?," from *Violence and Sport* (Butterworths, Toronto, 1983).

Wellman, Christopher, "Do Celebrated Athletes have Special Responsibilities to be Good Role Models? An Imagined Dialog between Charles Barkley and Karl Malone." © 2003 by Christopher Wellman. Written especially for this volume.

Wenz, Peter S., "Human Equality in Sports," from *Sport Inside Out*, eds David L. Vanderwerken and Spencer K. Wertz (Texas Christian University Press, Fort Worth, 1985).

The publisher apologizes for any errors or omissions in the above list and would be grateful if notified of any corrections that should be incorporated in future reprints or editions of this book.

Introduction: The Moral Significance of Sport

Jan Boxill

There is no doubting that sports play a significant role in the lives of many Americans and indeed of many people around the world. Millions watch not only the Olympics, soccer's World Cup, baseball's World Series, football's Super Bowl, test cricket, the college football bowl games, college basketball's Final Four, and the NBA Basketball Championships, but also games leading up to these, as well as those that never make it to that level. ESPN has afforded us the opportunity to watch sports twenty-four hours a day on not just one but two television channels; newspapers devote entire sections to sports. And while millions watch, millions more participate at their own levels of play. The engagement in sports at all levels surpasses that in any other activity, including work.

What accounts for this? It has been suggested that sports merely provide an outlet for violence in society; but this is too simplistic. Participants, spectators, writers, and even critics recognize and admire the artistry, beauty, grace, elegance, heroism, discipline, courage, and drama of sports. Human beings are moved by the discipline of the best athletes, and applaud their heroism and courage, not the violence which occasions the display of these virtues.

There is more to sport than what draws our attention to it. Because of its nature and design, it serves significant moral functions both for individuals and for societies. First, sport provides individuals with activities for creative self-expression, and means of self-respect and self-development. By extension, sport serves to form a social union in a society of social unions, "a community of people with shared ends and common activities valued for themselves, enjoying one another's excellences and individuality as they participate in the activities."[1] In this way individual development and respect are reciprocal.

Second, because sport is a microcosm of society, it dramatizes the social order. Sport represents the social order in miniature, exhibiting a "slice of life" in an exaggerated and dramatic form, much as a play dramatizes an episode from life. Sport mirrors or reflects society, its virtues and vices, but, unlike a mirror, it is active; it affects what it is a reflection of.

Finally, as an art form, as a controlled expression of emotion, sport enhances the notion of a social union, and further serves a significant moral function in its dramatization.

The Paradigmatic Form of Sport

The paradigmatic form of sport can serve to illuminate its moral significance, both negatively and positively. Four features exemplify sport in its paradigmatic form: (1) it is a freely chosen, voluntary activity; (2) it is governed by rules, of two sorts; (3) it is physically challenging; (4) it involves competition in a mutual challenge to achieve excellence.[2] These features provide neither an exhaustive nor an exclusive definition, but a model.

First, sport is a freely chosen, voluntary activity, participation in which is an expression of the individual's creativity and his or her freedom to choose. Thus, sport is an unalienated activity, and as such is in what may be called "the realm of freedom,"[3] and has as its end the activity itself. Though it may serve other purposes, it does not have to have a product or provide a service, nor is it a means to an end outside itself.

Of course, those who participate in a sport necessarily have goals. For example, to play basketball one must have the goal of scoring baskets. In stating the rules of the game, one necessarily states the goals internal to it which the participants must have. The goals are within the context of the activity itself.

In its paradigmatic form then, participation in sport is both conscious and free, and the participants know and freely abide by the rules. This voluntary cooperation is required to begin, continue, and end the activity. Thus, for example, when I play basketball, tennis, or golf, I freely choose to do so and am conscious of my freedom to participate in the activity for no end outside the activity itself. Neither my existence nor my subsistence depends on my participation in the activity. This is unlike work.

By contrast work in its paradigmatic form is non-voluntary and aims at something other than itself. Most members of society work in order to live; for them work is a means to an end other than itself. It is seen as a deliberate providing for needs or wants. As such work belongs in what may be called "the realm of necessity."

It is possible, of course, for the fortunate few to express their creativity and freedom to choose in their work; most often when work approaches the paradigm of sport, it also enters the realm of freedom. But this cannot be the case for the great many workers whose work has little or no room for creativity or self-expression. Conversely, sport, which in its paradigmatic form is in the realm of freedom, may be an individual's means of living and thus in the realm of

necessity. As I will argue, however, this is one possible source of the perversion of sport.

Now it might be objected that on my analysis, sport is no different from work, because sport is indeed a means to some ends: happiness and pleasure, health, discipline, relaxation, a sense of achievement, or money. Several points may be made here. First, when the aim is health or discipline, the activity degenerates into dull routine and quickly becomes something akin to work. When these objectives dictate what is done, efficiency becomes the concern. The question is "what is the most efficient way of obtaining these products?" This is the question one asks in work, not in sport. Examples of such activities are calisthenics, weightlifting, and jogging. These are better called exercises, not sports. They are generally designed for physical fitness and are generally subjectively different from sport, in that they are not enjoyed for themselves.

This subjective difference has an objective counterpart. They are not designed or participated in for self-expression because they are repetitive and simple. In doing sit-ups, for example, you do not try to be creative, nor do you do them for their own sake. You can concentrate on the sit-ups initially to make sure you are doing them correctly or efficiently, but after the efficiency level is reached, there is no more to think about except what end they will achieve, the "cut" abdominal muscles. "Once given a chance to train for games, students revolted against doing set exercises as ends in themselves. They found them to be tedious, repetitious and meaningless."[4] This may be further illustrated in body building. This was not satisfying in itself; the regimen had to be seen to be for something; thus, competition was devised.

Interestingly and importantly, when one participates to the fullest, the by-products of all sports are health, discipline, and a sense of achievement. These may be aimed at, as we saw, but they are better achieved when one forgets about them. This is certainly also the case with relaxation, happiness, and pleasure. These are by-products of sports, but only when they are not the aim. This is just a particular instance of the paradox of happiness. In discussing this issue, a friend commented that she jogged, "not for its own sake, but for fun, relaxation, health and a sense of achievement." But if my analysis is correct, these can best be achieved by participating without those aims in mind. A person "who wants to be refreshed through play must forget about refreshing himself and just play."[5] By participating to the fullest, that is by participating freely with no other specific aim in mind, one achieves these "products." This is not the case in work, where the end product must always be kept in mind. If I am building a house and am concerned with the end product, I must keep fully aware of that end and must be alert to all the day-to-day operations. If I "lose myself" occasionally, it could be disastrous.

When money becomes the aim, sport begins to degenerate into a means to that end, insofar as this objective dictates what is done. "How best can I command money?" becomes the question. Being good at the sport helps, but creating a spectacle or being an entertainer is often the main criterion. To this end individuals try gimmicks or antics, or go to schools with a big athletic publicity department. For example, winning the Heisman trophy means players command more money, but they are not always the best football players in the nation. Winning this most coveted award is often the result of the publicity put out by the athlete's school and by television promotions. Athletes become commodities and the "bottom line" is what matters to the owners. Further, salaries are decided relative to how high up a player is chosen in the annual draft selections of the professional leagues.

Of course, the Heisman trophy winner is still an outstanding athlete, but unfortunately there are other cases where the sport itself is incidental. How best to be an entertainer or produce a spectacle is the primary concern, since that is how to command more money. At this point sport begins to be perverted, and moral virtues are undermined. The epitome of a perverted sport is professional wrestling. Everything is done for the entertainment value, for the benefit of the spectators, or more honestly for their money. In fact there is little sport left in it.

The perversion is so pervasive that in most states professional wrestling is not even considered a sport. The participants are not athletes, but actors and stuntpeople, certainly talented in their own right. There is little resemblance between this spectacle and collegiate wrestling, which is a spectacular sport, but is far from being spectacle.

Fortunately, in most sports ability is still the primary money-maker. But because money becomes the aim, other factors are introduced, or at least encouraged; namely violence or "bad boy" behavior. Violence is encouraged, not for the good of the game, but for the good of the gate. Violence does nothing to enhance the sport performance. This can readily be seen in professional hockey. Hockey is a contact sport, but the contact is often exaggerated and violence is encouraged because it is spectacular and develops fan loyalty through hatred. This testifies to humankind's great capacity for passionate involvement and our failure to focus on the essence of the event. In this sense sport begins to parallel war. Love of one's country, or patriotism, is enhanced during war; loyalty developed through hatred of a common enemy.

We also see this in professional basketball, with some players seeing who can be the "baddest" or the most outrageous. We are all familiar with former NBA players Charles Barkley and Dennis Rodman. Spectators flocked to see their antics, encouraging others to follow in their footsteps. League officials could curtail behavior such as theirs, but it would cost the league ticket sales, and so their infractions are basically ignored. Again this attests to what is good for the gate not for the game. It is true that fines are levied for fighting in professional basketball, but given the enormous salaries players can command, this has little affect.[6] Once more the bottom line is money.

It might be claimed here that where there are spectators perversion is inevitable. It is certainly possible, in that spectators often dramatize or intensify the atmosphere so that violence is encouraged even more. But it is not inevitable. While participating rather than watching is central to sport,[7] spectators can add a new dimension by recognizing and applauding the choreographies of good play and by admiring beautiful moves. Nevertheless, I hold that everyone should participate, if she or he is able. This point I will take up in the following section.

The second feature of sport in its paradigmatic form is that it is rule governed. There are two different sorts of rules that are important to sport: rules of decency or fair play and constitutive rules. Some sports have more rules than others, and some may have only one sort. First, there are rules of decency, safety, and fair play. For example, in boxing one cannot hit below the belt; in football one cannot tackle by grabbing the face mask or tackle a non-ball carrier from behind; in baseball one cannot throw at the batsman's head; in cricket one cannot continually bowl bodyline, etc. There are very many rules for decency and safety, and when these are violated players are penalized. Rules of fair play include penalties for moves of strategy within the game. Rules of decency reflect basic moral standards. The ground rules are accepted, and while they may be manipulated for strategic advantage, they must not be overstepped without swift punishment (e.g. in the case of fighting, biting, etc.). The death of ethics is the sabotage of excellence.

Added to the rules of decency and fair play are constitutive rules which define the game and the permissible moves. Their existence comes from their acceptance. Constitutive rules are designed to develop and exhibit distinct sets of skills and talents. In combination these rules impose a discipline and create a framework for self-expression and self-development. These rules require calculations, decisions, strategies, and mental agility as well as the meeting of a physical challenge. Thus, when I agree to play basketball, I agree first of all to abide by the rules which define the game, and the rules of decency, safety, and fair play within it. Further, I use these rules as a disciplined means of self-expression and self-development. For example, I cannot put the ball in the basket any way I choose; I must put it in the basket in the ways the rules permit. I cannot stand on a ladder, knock someone out of my way, or climb on someone to reach the basket, nor can I score a basket by sending

the ball through the bottom of the net. The carefully specified rules impose a kind of discipline that requires me to devise ways of scoring a basket which require skill, bodily excellence, and ingenuity. The rules force me to use various strategies to create moves to score within them.

Now it is a fact that not all sports impose a defining set of rules. One example is mountain climbing. However, besides the rules for safety, there are impositions that require bodily excellence and ingenuity, rules that require strategies for climbing to reach the top. The goal is not just to reach the top, but to climb to reach the top, and this requires adherence to rules, or laws, of nature. No artificial rules need be imposed.

It is this rule-governing feature that differentiates sport from play, where the rules are simply the more general rules of the society. In play there is little to guide the play activity except the general rules that guide normal human behavior, in particular ones against harming others. But such rules impose no discipline for self-expression or self-development. (They do serve to develop character, however.) The rules of sport, on the other hand, provide a framework for creativity in accordance with aesthetic standards, requiring both mental and physical energies. It is this last notion which leads on to the third feature of sport.

The third feature of sport in its paradigmatic form is that sport is physically challenging. This feature differentiates sports from games. In being rule-governed, sports are coextensive with games, but games do not always emphasize a physical challenge or require bodily excellence. Thus, for example, chess is a rule-governed activity and is a game, but it does not qualify as a sport because it is not physically challenging. The rules which define the sport activity are specifically designed for displaying and expressing bodily performance and aimed at bodily excellence. Thus, these rules often create artificial obstacles for just this purpose.

Using the example of basketball again, rules and obstacles are designed so that scoring baskets requires skill, coordination, strategy, and bodily excellence. The obstacles and rules present a challenge. The size of the court forces the action into a relatively small area. The "three-second lane" forces continuous action around the basket and prevents very tall players from simply standing next to the basket for a dunk. This is why we have heard some people advocate raising the rim of the basket to 11 or 12 feet, so that the tallest players must create moves which require bodily excellence. Dunking itself displays a tremendous amount of ability – co-ordination, timing, jumping ability, and balance. It is probably one of the most beautiful moves in basketball because it requires such a combination of abilities – mental and physical.

A rule that imposes another discipline is the shot clock. In college men's basketball the shot clock is 35 seconds; in women's it is 30; and in the professional game it is 24. The shot clock requires a basket to be attempted within the time allowed. This requires not only bodily excellence but mental concentration and strategy. Interestingly the women's rules included the 30-second clock in their revision when they changed to approximate the men's rules. Professional men's basketball has required the 24-second clock since 1954. In every case the clock serves to keep the game challenging, mentally and physically, and also increases spectator appeal.

Obviously some sports impose more obstacles and discipline than others. However, as I mentioned above, not all obstacles need be artificial. The mountain itself is the obstacle in climbing, as the water is for kayaking and white water rafting. But all impose some obstacles providing a physical challenge, and forcing the participants to create ways to display their abilities. Cricket, for example, does not allow the bowler to throw the ball to the batter in the same way the pitcher throws to the batter in baseball. Also the bats are very different. But in both baseball and cricket the bats are designed to meet very definite specifications stipulated by the rules.[8] All these rules, obstacles, and equipment specifications are designed for displaying and creating bodily excellence.

What is interesting and significant is that the different sets of rules which define different sports are designed to exploit the different bodily excellences which correspond to the different body types in men. A good basketball player, for example, does not necessarily make a good football player; a good football player does not necessarily make a good swimmer, etc. There presently exist sports opportunities for nearly every male body type; though there have been great strides, this is not the case for women.

Women cannot as a rule compete in football and boxing, or compete with men in most other sports. Although there will always be exceptions, because these are exceptions there will always be societal prejudice which guarantees inequalities of opportunities. Therefore, there is a case for developing sport activities that exploit women's body types. In some cases this may simply involve revising the rules of existing sports, such as in basketball by reducing the size of the ball for college players. In other cases it may require developing entirely new activities. In any case since sport is already the single most available activity for self-expression for men, as is clear from the great variety of sports which serve most men's body types, it seems reasonable that similar activities ought to be provided for women. It is interesting to note that basketball was originally created for men to play in the winter between the fall and spring sports. This testifies to the truth that a sport can be a fresh creation made to satisfy definite purposes; other sports could be similarly created. What is also fascinating about basketball is that women played the same game as men in 1892, but due to concern for women's bodies, it did not develop as the men's game did, and only in 1976 was women's basketball made an Olympic sport.

The final feature of sport in its paradigmatic form is that it requires competition. And it is in competition that the mental and physical skills, talents, and coordination come together. Competition in sport obviously compels the players to exercise and develop their mental skills. Each must develop strategies to counter a competitor's skills and strategies. Here coaches often play significant roles; they are the skilled strategists, work with the athletes in practice, and discuss the mental aspects of the sport in the locker room. But once on the court or the playing field, it is up to the athletes to make quick calculations and decisions based on experience, since only the most basic plays and moves become automatic. The quarterback in football must be able to "read" and understand the opposing team's defense and then call the next play accordingly.[9] And if the defense shifts in anticipation or if the play does not go quite as it should, the quarterback must make a quick calculation and decision, and the other players must do the same. Good players are afflicted neither with "decidophobia" nor with rashness. In most activities challenges change in unpredictable ways and so one must be prepared to counter within the rules. Making these decisions in those circumstances can serve an important moral function. It is not only in sport that one has to make decisions quickly, but not rashly.

It should be noted here that not all sports require person-to-person competition or even team competition. There are different forms of competition. Sports such as rock and mountain climbing do not require competition between persons; rather they pit a person against nature. This may be understood as "contention" rather than competition; but the requirements are the same in that one must put one's mental and physical skills to the test. However, while this is the case, in analyzing the moral significance of sport, my discussion centers on the person-to-person aspects especially seen in organized sport.

Sport dramatizes how competition can lead to friendship, to a cooperative challenge toward a shared end. When the game is played fairly according to its rules, and when the competitors are relatively evenly matched, the participants take pleasure in a well-played game, in which they put out their best efforts in the desire to win. This requires the cooperation of all involved. The shared end is the game well played. Without the cooperative efforts of the participants, referees, etc., such an end cannot be achieved. This cooperative effort constitutes a mutual challenge: I am challenged by my competitor as she is challenged by me. I am not interested in destroying or subjugating her; I view her not as an enemy, but as a challenger, someone who by her efforts makes me work hard to develop my abilities. In this way I respect her as a person with similar abilities and virtues and also respect myself in this mutual cooperative

challenge. That competition leads to friendship is epitomized by the traditional handshake at the end of the competition. What the competitors are saying in this symbolic gesture is, "Thanks friend, I could not have done it without you. Thanks for the challenge."

Unfortunately sport also dramatizes how competition may lead to combat. But the dramatization in either case performs a significant moral function. It shows our intense passion and desire to be victorious as well as our failures. Competition as a challenge to better oneself is of value to society and to the individual. This is not unique to sport situations; it is important in all fields of endeavor. Competition is valuable when it is viewed as a cooperative challenge and not as combat, when it is viewed as a means to friendship and not as a means to alienation. In these ways competition does serve to develop citizens as well as individuals. Competition enables participants to deal properly with other realities.

Now, of course, this does not carry over into all activities and realities. It does not mean, for example, that participants then put as much energy into activities they dislike or find great difficulty doing. There are, of course, aberrations, and these are definitely dramatized in a sport context. This is especially seen when competition is viewed as combat, emphasizing the "win-at-all-costs" syndrome, and when viewed as a zero-sum game. It has been argued that these are essential features of competition. But if my analysis is correct, these "features," so far from being essential, are instead perversions.

The point of competition is not just to win, but to function at a maximum, to develop oneself to the fullest, and to do this one must compete against those who challenge. If it were simply to win, one would choose weak opponents that one could always defeat. Generally one prefers to lose against a strong opponent than win against no competition at all. This is evidenced by the expression "hollow victory." Certainly winning is part of the game (i.e. someone must win), but one sees an opponent not as an enemy to be defeated, but as one whose excellences challenge and make possible one's own best performance. This point was made clear to me in the 1993 National Indoor Tennis Championship. Roland Thornquist of the University of North Carolina disagreed with a line call that was in his favor, saying, "I'd rather lose a match and be a good sport than cheat and win the match. I think you win in the long run."[10] This epitomizes competition in sports. The goal is not to destroy, but to *achieve*, to discover how effectively one's power can be used to bring about a successful outcome under the established rules, *not* at all costs. Again here I am talking about person-to-person competition. These observations are not relevant to all kinds of competition, as I noted above. Perhaps we ought to derive our model of competition from that of the mountain climber, or kayaker, or rower, where strategy is used to challenge the mountain or the river. The point is not to subjugate, but to challenge, to achieve, where the struggle involves the *process*, the desire to be tested. The win-at-all-costs syndrome does not seem to be present in sports where the competition does not involve other persons. Much can be learned from this and transferred to the person-to-person organized sports which are the focus of this project.

To illustrate the virtue of competition as an achievement toward a shared end, let me quote David Halberstam, a noted sportswriter:

> When most oarsmen talked about their perfect moments in a boat, they referred not so much to winning a race as to the feel of the boat, all eight oars in the water together, the synchronization almost perfect. In moments like that, the boat seemed to lift right out of the water. Oarsmen called that the moment of swing. . . . it allowed you to trust the other men in the boat. A boat did not have swing unless everyone was putting out in exact measure, and because of that, and only because of that, there was the possibility of true trust among oarsmen.[11]

This same moment of "swing" can be seen in other team sports when the play works beautifully because everyone is putting out the same energy to be synchronized with each other's.

These four features constitute a schema for sport in its paradigmatic form, and it is these four that characterize the importance of sport. Sport, therefore, is an unalienated activity which is required for self-development, self-expression, and self-respect. This is part of its fascination. I do not deny that other activities provide vehicles for these goods. What I contend is that sport is the single most available means and the single most participated-in means for attainment of these goods. It is in this sense that sport is the art of the people and is therefore morally significant.

Sport and Work in a Social Union

Karl Marx argues that work is the means to self-development[12] – not, of course, work under capitalism, but unalienated work; work that is freely chosen and exemplifies human creativity requiring the energy of both the mind and the body, in accordance with aesthetic standards. And, Marx continues, given the proper setting, i.e. communism, there can be this unalienated work available to everyone. This obviously was essential for Marx's argument.

Further Marx maintained that in a communist society, we could all be not only workers, but philosophers, poets, etc.:

> In communist society, . . . each can become accomplished in any branch he wishes, society regulates general production and thus makes it possible for me to do one thing today and another tomorrow, to hunt in the morning, fish in the afternoon, rear cattle in the evening, criticize after dinner, just as I have a mind, without ever becoming hunter, fisherman, cowherd, or critic.[13]

I am not sure this is the case, but Marx is correct in emphasizing that this well-roundedness, which is necessary for self-development, requires "unalienated activities"; activities designed specifically to provide room to express and develop oneself freely and not activities that are means to satisfy needs. I have already discussed sport as an unalienated activity. I will now discuss how it also provides the basis for well-roundedness and for development of our uniquely human capacities.

I adhere to the claim that we all ought to be well-rounded and that we all ought to develop our uniquely human capacities; capacities which include the rational, aesthetic, and moral, as well as the capacities for friendship and cooperation. But Marx's claim notwithstanding, we can't all be artists, philosophers, poets, or top athletes. To be well-rounded and to develop all our faculties is impossible if it means we must attempt to perfect all our faculties. Time alone does not permit the development of all our potentialities. As Rawls puts it, "One characteristic of human beings is that no one person can do all that they might like to. . . . Potentialities of each are greater than those we can hope to realize."[14]

How then can we be well-rounded? If excellence necessarily requires specialization, it would seem that we cannot. One possible solution is for everyone to participate in as many activities as possible, but specialize in only one or two endeavors. We can't perhaps all be philosophers, but we should all philosophize. We can't all be experts in any one area, but we should participate in as many as possible. Obviously not all of us can be superior athletes, but we should all participate; and the more we participate, the more we appreciate the excellence of the best. In both cases, philosophy and sports, some must specialize so that they embody excellence in that activity. In this way we can participate in that excellence. It is in this sense that sport fulfills the requirements of Rawls's social union. The successes and enjoyments of others complement our own good. Thus, the successes and enjoyments of superior athletes and their performances complement the good of others. This justifies professional sports. The professionals display the superior talent and excellence of the best and as such enable us to participate in and appreciate their excellence. We do this as spectators. In this way we become complete vicariously.

Now it may be asked here whether participation is necessary for appreciation. The answer is yes; otherwise one runs the risk of becoming an elitist, or of focusing on the "accidents" of the activity, or of denying its significance. As a result the non-participant often fails to give respect to the superior participant. It is in this situation that spectators contribute to the perversion of sport.

Rather than perverting sports, our participation and knowledge enhance the quality of the performance. An analogy may be made with philosophy and philosophical conventions. Attending a convention are professional philosophers, students of philosophy, other academics, and professionals interested in certain areas of philosophy. Some of the performances are entertaining with little content. But these are rare, because most of the spectators at any presentation are fairly knowledgeable and are actual participants themselves, and thus "see through" such performances. Thus the quality of the convention is enhanced. And further, we as spectators appreciate the excellences of the professional philosophers through these performances (i.e. their papers).

The same can and does hold true in sports. By being a participant, or a student or a knowledgeable aficionado of a sport, a spectator enhances its quality. The more knowledgeable people become, the more they are able to see through the performers who lack ability, and the less likely to be impressed with violent displays. Such people appreciate the superior performances, the hard work, the creativity, the strategy, and the artistry involved. They need not be participants in all sports to appreciate all sports. The unique nature of sport activities inheres in any sport. So that while I may be a participant in basketball, I can appreciate the excellences of other sports because they all have similar requirements. They all, in some way, participate in the model presented in the preceding section. However, the more I know about any one sport, the more I can appreciate it.[15] And the more I participate in a variety of sports, the more I can appreciate the significance of sport in general.

To sum up: we cannot all be specialists in all areas, but because there are specialists who do achieve excellence, we can participate in excellence in the performances of others. In this way our capacities are complemented, and we become well-rounded. So, "when [we] are secure in the enjoyment of the exercise of [our] own powers, [we] are disposed to appreciate the perfections of others."[16] This is the essence of Rawls's social union.

Thus, individuals realize themselves as individuals by participating in roles and stations in the social order. "We need one another as partners in ways of life that are engaged in for their own sake, and the successes and enjoyments of others are necessary for and complementary to our own good."[17] Social institutions, and sport along with them, are to be judged by their contribution to this aim.

Sport as a Microcosm

It has been argued by many that sports mirror the society in which they operate, and I will now examine this claim in more detail. Sport is a microcosm of society,[18] complete with all its conflicts, assets, and defects. Sports serve to bring out the best and the worst in people. Just as there is corruption in society, there is corruption in sports; just as there is violence in society, there is violence in sports; just as there are drugs in society, there are drugs in sports. On the other hand, just as there are rules of conduct in society, there are rules of conduct in sport; just as there are successes and heroes in society, there are successes and heroes in sports. In all these ways and others, sports reflect the society in which they take place. But this is only part of the picture. A mirror provides a passive reflection, but sport is active and affects what it is a reflection of. Further, sport not only reflects society, it also dramatizes the social order. These unique aspects are what make clear the moral significance of sport both for the individual and for society at large.

In being a miniature of society, sport compresses and heightens certain features, much like a dramatic presentation. Aspects of society are exaggerated and dramatized, and in this way are made clear to all of us. Like drama, sport may reveal to the society virtues it has not yet recognized, or present new values and criticize old ones, or dramatize the established virtues and values. For example, in the triathlon competition perseverance is dramatized in the mere attempt to finish. We admire the finisher as well as those who push themselves to the limit in the attempt.

In all of these ways sport may spur moral change. Insofar as it declares the virtues and values of society, sport tells people when they do not live up to their ideals, chastises them for their laxity, and prods them to be better people. For example, "that's not cricket" is not said only in cricket.

We espouse the virtue of hard work. Sport does much to dramatize this, and it is with this in mind that some rule changes are made. Surely some people have more talent and aptitude than others. That is as it should be; but raw talent is usually not sufficient. No one, no matter how apt, is naturally great. To be great, an athlete must become great. This is why Michael Jordan is a great basketball player, and Tiger Woods is a great golfer. They both have talent, but they have dominated their sports because they developed their natural abilities to be the best they could be. Sport emphasizes the development of the raw talent, and this carries over into society.

We also espouse the virtues of courage, patience, sportsmanship, perseverance, and determination. These are emphasized in sports, but are also dramatized so that any undermining of them becomes more obvious and acute. And when this happens we chastise not only the violators but society itself for its laxity. This was illustrated quite well in our attitude toward John McEnroe, who in his displays on the tennis court dramatized the lack of some of our cherished values. Again some rule changes have tried to address such behavior.

Another value society holds dear is justice as fairness. Sport may serve to dramatize how justice ought to be administered and how fairness is emphasized. This is done by carefully specifying rules, both to define the game to provide for development, bodily excellence, hard work, and fairness, and to provide for proper conduct within the game. With regard to the latter, infractions are swiftly and surely dealt with. Referees and umpires mete out immediate justice.

In playing the game one agrees to abide by the rules, recognizing both their importance and their essential fairness. In this way participants are made aware of each other as individuals with shared ends. And it is in this way participants come to appreciate others as moral persons and as such constitute a moral community.

It is because sport is an art form and dramatizes our virtues and values that we are outraged at its aberrations from these. And it is therefore most important that these be corrected within sports and that this is done surely and quickly. But while this dramatization of virtues may spur moral change, it may also be the source of a great moral danger in sport. People may substitute sport for reality and in so doing be content with their cherished virtues being played out in the game and not in reality. For example, C.L.R. James, in his book *Beyond a Boundary*, gives the example of how on the playing field, racism was non-existent.[19] The important thing was the competition, the cooperation, teamwork, and friendship. But as soon as the players left the playing field the racial prejudices returned, and this the racists felt was all right. After all we treat you as equals on the playing field, what more do you want?

This situation is analogous to the effects of religion that Marx criticized. Religion, says Marx, "is the imaginary realization of the human essence."[20] Thus, to tolerate misery on earth, people live in imagination and all that is good is played out in this imaginary world. "Religion is the sigh of the oppressed creature, the feeling of a heartless world, and the soul of the soulless circumstances. It is the opium of the people."[21] Sport could represent an alienation in this sense and become the opium of the people in a similar way.[22] All the virtues could be carried out in the sport instead of in our own day-to-day lives, as C.L.R. James says. On the cricket field there was no prejudice – not on the field, a place of honor – not in heaven! Thus the players alienate their good qualities from themselves and live them out in an imaginary realm. But neither sport nor religion is wholly imaginary.

In sport the realm is not imaginary. As a matter of fact in sport the prejudices were not and are not dropped. As James shows, there were black captains in cricket, and there were indeed teamwork and friendships on the field which were not acknowledged off it; but other prejudices carried over into the sport itself. So what happened? When glaring prejudice was pointed out, people were forced to recognize what they were doing. By focusing on a specific point, they made changes. Hopefully this dramatization and change carried over into society and spurred further changes. As I have said above, sport is not a mere passive reflection, but is active in that it affects society even when this is not intended.

We can see this in the circumstances and changes in our own society and in sport in America, in particular baseball, football, and basketball. In baseball there were black and white leagues, no integrated teams. This was a glaring violation of the ideal. When dramatized with the emergence of Jackie Robinson into the Brooklyn Dodgers, it stimulated or provoked analysis and criticism of wider issues in society. More recently the issue of black managers has been raised, and when Al Campanis, then vice-president of the Los Angeles Dodgers, answered that blacks do not have the requisite abilities to manage, he was chastised and relieved of his position. And after that, we had Marge Schott, owner of the Cincinnati Reds, whose racist comments landed her a suspension. In an interview she commented that "everyone" makes these comments, so why was she singled out? The answer is that doing so serves to put people on notice to recognize these issues in society, and that people in power are most in need of this awareness because their examples may not only reflect society's prejudices, but also serve to perpetuate them. Such people, by their very positions, take on the duties attached to those positions, because they exemplify what is allowed in society. This includes owners, CEOs, public athletes, and professors, to name a few. It is through these people that society learns what is proper, what is tolerated, and is right or wrong. So Marge Schott, Dennis Rodman, John McEnroe, and Marion Jones all have duties beyond those of the general public. Once you choose to become a public figure, you also choose the duties that go along with this, because it is the nature of being a public figure that you affect others in society. Since sports have become the most public of all professions, they impose more duties. Sports figures are role models; it goes with the territory.[23]

This can be extended to other areas as well, and feminist issues in particular. The Title IX ruling of 1972 requires that schools not discriminate in their athletic programs on the basis of sex. Though even today this is met with resistance, most schools complied with this ruling and provided teams and coaches for females. Some schools did the bare minimum just to placate females and keep the law off their backs. Other schools made facilities and revenue available to provide competitive and challenging sports. Now we could stop there, claiming that the challenges have been provided, and that is enough. But because sports are viewed by many people as insignificant, sex equality in sports is tolerated, though not necessarily extended to or tolerated in society in general, in business or politics, say. But rather than permit this, sports can serve to show that many of the old ideas held about women were simply prejudices – prejudices such as women being weak, not competitive, rendered incapacitated by their biology, etc. – and in this way sport may again spur moral change. "If women's athletic potentialities are taken with as much seriousness as a man's, it will become more evident that sport concerns not only mankind but humankind and deserves to be viewed as a basic human enterprise."[24] Gender equity is presently one of the biggest issues facing the NCAA and college athletics.

This serves to strengthen the analogy between sport and religion. Both are only partially or temporarily in an imaginary realm. Prejudices carry over in both, and in this way both are reflections of the wider society. But because sport dramatizes and affects these prejudices, it turns and helps change society. Religion may serve a similar function, and often does, but only when it approaches the public dramatization that sport can perform.

Marx recommended that religion be abolished to destroy the illusion, this "holy form of self-alienation . . . to establish the truth of the here and now."[25] On the contrary, neither sport nor religion ought to be abolished; rather both should continue to dramatize our ideals and our virtues, as well as our prejudices and vices. In this way both may serve to spur on moral change. But because sports involve a more public realm, the dramatizations are more visible and prominent. And further, sports are concerned with the here and now in a way that religion is not. Sport is only "imaginary" in the sense that it is set apart from the normal everyday world, and like religion may serve to help individuals tolerate the miseries of that workaday world. But it is in the here and now that the participants are finding solace, not in any life after death. And so it is in the here and now that sports may serve to spur on moral change. This can be seen, for example, in television ads that show young girls participating in sports and how this is good for them. The television promotion of the US National Soccer Team does the same. These show that the old prejudices were just that, and that girls and women can and should participate to receive the same benefits men have so long enjoyed.

In religion it is in heaven that everything is just and good, and this goodness depends on God, not on us. We can't make it good on earth; only God can. In sport, goodness depends on us, not on God. Sport has no God; there is no pretense that the perfect realm of sport is God's. Sport is a realm of human beings and human creations. Thus for moral change no gigantic step is required. We don't have to wait for God to do it; it is within our present abilities. Sports reveal who we are and may reflect who we are in society, but it is up to us to recognize our duties to ourselves and others. In this way sport serves a different but compatible function to that of religion. And in this function lies its moral significance.

Conclusion

In this essay, I have argued that sport serves significant moral functions for both individuals and society at large. Sports, as unalienated activities, provide autonomous agents with a vehicle for self-expression, self-respect, and self-development. There are, of course, different kinds of unalienated activities, but sports are the most available of these. Further, there are all kinds of sports at all levels of participation.

Sports also perform significant moral functions in society at large. In its dramatization and active reflection, sport may spur moral change. But while sports may be the art of the people, they may also serve as the opium of the people.

Sports will continue to be discussed on television, in newspapers, and in other forms of the media including the internet. But the discussions cannot be left to these public forums if, as I have argued, sports are morally significant. This moral significance calls for academics to take part in those discussions, to which this volume is one contribution.

Notes

I have had the benefit of helpful comments and criticisms from a number of students and colleagues, most notably Bernard Boxill, Thomas E. Hill, Jr., Jacob Hale, Kit Wellman, Shirl Hoffman, participants at the Hillsdale College Conference "Who's on First? Liberal Arts, Christianity or Sports," where an earlier version of this paper was presented, the Johnston Scholars Honors, and my First Year Seminar students at the University of North Carolina at Chapel Hill.

1   John Rawls, *A Theory of Justice* (Cambridge, MA: Harvard University Press, 1971), p. 523.
2   This concept I take from Robert Simon, in *Fair Play: Sports, Values, and Society* (Boulder, CO: Westview Press, 1991).
3   For more on this see Bernard Boxill, "Sexual Blindness and Sexual Equality," *Social Theory and Practice*, 6.3 (1980), pp. 282–3.
4   Paul Weiss, *Sport: A Philosophic Inquiry* (Carbondale, IL: Southern Illinois Press, 1969), p. 225.
5   Ibid., p. 228.
6   The Latrell Sprewell situation is a case in point.
7   See James Michener, *Sports in America* (New York: Random House, 1976).
8   Recall the controversy when George Brett hit a game-winning home run with a bat with too much tar, and further controversy over "super-bats."
9   Admittedly technology has made some decision making less spontaneous.
10 Roland Thornquist went on to play professional tennis and is currently the head women's tennis coach at his alma mater, the University of North Carolina at Chapel Hill.
11 David Halberstam, *The Amateurs* (New York: William Morrow 1985), p. 40.
12 Karl Marx, "The Economics," in *Karl Marx: Selected Writings*, ed. David McLellan (Oxford: Oxford University Press, 1977), p. 368.
13 Marx, "German Ideology," in *Selected Writings*, p. 169.
14 Rawls, *A Theory of Justice*, p. 523.
15 This is why those who most respect Coach Smith are players and other coaches.
16 Rawls, *A Theory of Justice*, p. 523.
17 Ibid., pp. 522–3.
18 For example, see D. Stanley Eitzen, "Sport as Microcosm of Society," in *Sport in Contemporary Society*, sixth edition (New York: Worth Publishers, 2001), pp. 1–9.
19 C.L.R. James, *Beyond a Boundary* (New York: Pantheon, 1963).
20 Marx, "Toward a Critique of Hegel's *Philosophy of Right*: Introduction," in *Selected Writings*, p. 64.
21 Ibid.
22 See p. 2 for an analysis of this concept.
23 Kit Wellman discusses this issue in reading 34.
24 Weiss, *Sport*, p. 228. Also see Jane English's essay in this collection (reading 23).
25 Marx, "Toward a Critique of Hegel's *Philosophy of Right*: Introduction," p. 64.

PART I

Sport and Education

CHAPTER 1

Sports, Relativism, and Moral Education

Robert L. Simon

The idea that sports help build moral character is an ancient one, finding some support even in the dialogs of Plato, who declared in the *Republic* that "there are two arts which I would say some god gave to mankind, music and gymnastics...not for the soul and body incidentally, but for their harmonious adjustment." Centuries later, the existentialist philosopher Camus noted that the context in which he really learned ethics was that of sport.[1] Of course, the belief that sports are an important form of moral education is not one that is restricted to some philosophers but is widely held throughout our culture. On the other hand, many critics of contemporary sport rejoin that sport may very well promote values, but that frequently what they regard as the wrong values, such as an overemphasis on winning and consequent disrespect of opponents, are being taught.

These critics raise important issues about moral education. Who decides what values are to be promoted and what values are to be abjured, particularly in controversial cases, and on what basis should such a decision be made? Whose morals are to be taught? Moreover, is it the business of organized athletic programs within educational and academic institutions to promote a moral stance? Surely, secondary schools, colleges, and universities should educate, not indoctrinate. But isn't "moral education" simply a guise for indoctrination into the values of those who control the institutions in question? If not, how specifically can it avoid being partisan?

These are extremely difficult questions. The discussion that follows is an attempt to suggest a response to some of them and, in particular, to suggest what role sport can play in moral education. To help make our inquiry manageable, let us focus on the role of athletic programs in secondary schools and in colleges and universities. We can begin by identifying a number of concerns about the very idea of moral education.

Perhaps the most serious concern is over what values should be taught within an institutional setting. Do we want schools fostering a partisan ideology, perhaps based on the religious values of some people in the community but opposed by others? Do we want coaches imposing their own religious or political commitments on their teams? Whose values are to be taught, promoted, or expressed? To avoid these difficulties, many would argue that public schools, as well as colleges and universities, should be politically neutral and avoid taking partisan stands on controversial issues. But how can the very same institution both be neutral and promote certain values? The price of neutrality would seem to be abstinence from moral education, but to abandon neutrality would open the door to partisanship and indoctrination. Neither horn of this dilemma is attractive, but how are we to avoid one or the other of the two alternatives?

Second, what form should moral education take? Should it be explicit, as in the form of special classes or lectures? Should it involve explicit philosophical treatment of ethical issues, as in a class on ethical issues in sport, or should it be informal and implicit? Indeed, how can some form of implicit moral education be avoided in educational institutions? How could any learning even go on, for example, if students were not required to be civil? However, the more informal moral education is, the less control there would appear to be over its content. How are we to strike the right balance?

Moreover, while one segment of the population seems at least on the surface to be very clear about what moral values it favors and wants others to adopt, a significant number of students, at least in my experience, enter college already imbued with a kind of moral skepticism or crude moral relativism. This segment of the student population seems to equate making moral judgments either with dogmatism, with being judgmental or opinionated, or with what is regarded with almost as much disdain, holding an "absolute." This group of students actually may hold covert moral judgments of their own but disguise them under the cloak of skepticism or relativism to avoid appearing dogmatic or intolerant in front of their peers. Perhaps because one segment of the population often appears quite dogmatic in advancing its own moral views, it is not surprising that another segment of the population identifies advocacy of moral principles with intolerance and drops out of moral discussion entirely. An admittedly extreme case of this reluctance to make moral judgments occurred when one of my students commented on an examination, "Of course I dislike the Nazis but who is to say they are morally wrong."

Does making moral judgments commit us to a belief in "absolutes?" Is that to be avoided? But how can we support moral education without believing that at least some approaches to morality are correct? Should "absolutophobia," the fear of committing to what one regards as an objectively warranted moral judgment, prevent us from endorsing moral education?[2]

My suggestion is that approaching such questions by way of sport can not only be illuminating, but also show that commitment to moral principles need not be dogmatic or intolerant, and that "absolutes," depending upon what we mean by them, need not be avoided at all cost. The discussion that follows begins by exploring three approaches to values and sports, then examines whether moral education must necessarily be partisan or dogmatic, and concludes with some comments about implications for moral relativism, dogmatism, and moral judgment.

Values in Sport

Before exploring how sports might serve as a form of moral education, it will be useful to consider how they might be related to moral values in the first place. Although proponents of sport stress its value as a character builder and critics worry about the kind of character that might be produced, it is important to go deeper and ask what sport might primarily have to do with ethics or morality.

According to one view, sports merely reflect and perhaps reinforce adherence to the dominant values of the wider society. According to this thesis, often called the mirror thesis or reductionism, sports serve a conservative social function. They express the values of the wider culture and perhaps socialize participants and spectators to accept those values as their own. For example, advocates of the mirror thesis might argue that in a primarily capitalist society such as the United States, it is not an accident that sports are highly competitive, glorify individual stars such as Michael Jordan, and emphasize fame and fortune as rewards for competitive success. The mirror thesis is an example of what might be called an externalist theory, where *externalism* is the view that sport is not an independent source of value but borrows whatever normative or moral force it has from outside sources.[3]

Other observers of sport, however, contend that sport has internal connections to certain values. These internal values can often conflict with those of the wider society. If these *internalists* are correct, sport can be an independent basis for criticism of the wider culture and, depending upon the morality dominant in the rest of society, can be a force for social change.

One version of internalism is known as formalism. "Formalism" is the name given to a position or, more accurately, a family of positions that characterize games, and such game-derivative notions as "winning a game" or "making a move or play within a game," in terms of the formal structure of games, particularly their constitutive rules.[4] Thus, an act counts as a move or play within a game only if it is allowed by the constitutive rules. For example, hitting a pitch with a bat in a manner allowed by the rules is part of baseball but running over the opposing pitcher in an armored personnel carrier is not. Formalists tend to see the point of the rules of games to be the creation of worthwhile challenges, and hence conformity to the rules is required if the challenge is to be truly met.

Let us assume for our purposes that sports primarily are games of physical skill and ask what normative implications formalism has for how sports should be played. Perhaps the most important normative implication of formalism is what is often called the incompatibility thesis. According to this, it is logically impossible for cheaters to win at competitive games or sports. Since cheaters violate the rules, they fail to make moves within the sport and hence fail to play it. Since cheaters aren't playing the game, and one can only win the game if one plays it, cheaters can't win. Formalists also tend to view sportspersonship primarily in terms of conformity to the letter and perhaps the spirit of the rules, and fairness in their application.

Formalism, however, has problems dealing with ethical issues in sports that go beyond the application of current rules. Consider, for example, whether a team that is winning easily against a much weaker opponent should deliberately "run up the score" against the opposition. Opponents of running up the score argue that such a tactic humiliates opponents and hence disrespects them as persons. However, such an orthodox view has been questioned

lately by Nicholas Dixon, who asks whether athletes ought to be humiliated as persons by the result of a sports contest, and points out that running up the score sometimes can serve important functions such as demonstrating athletic excellence to the spectators.[5] Which position is correct? What does sportspersonship require in such cases? Whatever the answer, it is far from clear that a formalistic emphasis on the rules provides the intellectual resources to resolve such issues of sportspersonship, which, at least on the surface, seem to go beyond mere conformity to the constitutive rules of the sport.

Formalism also may have difficulty assessing the desirability of proposed changes in the rules. What makes a change in the rules desirable from the perspective of improving the sport rather than, say, making it more entertaining to casual spectators? Formalists may suggest that since the point of the rules of the game is to provide a challenge to competitors, who in turn seek excellence in trying to overcome that challenge, we can ask whether rule changes improve the challenge the sport provides. Such a reply is a fruitful one but, as will be argued below, it seems to go beyond pure formalism. It requires that we formulate and act upon an account, not just of the rules, but of their point or purpose. This suggestion, as we will see, is well worth pursuing, but whether or not we recognize it as an extended form of formalism, it certainly is conceptually richer than a primary focus on the actual constitutive rules themselves.

Consider also the ethics of the strategic foul in athletic competition. Strategic fouls are those that are committed with the intent of gaining a competitive advantage in the contest. To take a common example, the losing team in a basketball game may foul late in the game in order to stop the clock and provide a chance for a comeback in case the team with the lead misses its foul shots. Is this practice ethical?

On an analysis that seems closely tied to the formalist emphasis on constitutive rules, some writers maintain that since the players who foul are intentionally violating the rules (unlike players who foul while making legitimate defensive moves while trying to steal the ball or block a shot), they are cheating. In reply to the claim that strategic fouling is part of the game because the rules prescribe penalties, one writer has stated that this is as absurd as arguing that murder is permitted by law because the law contains rules for its punishment.[6]

However, the claim that strategic fouling in basketball is a form of cheating is rejected by many other theorists as well as by many if not most players and spectators. After all, each team commits strategic fouls and all teams know other teams will foul to stop the clock when they are losing at the end of the game, so the behavior is not covertly practiced by the few to the disadvantage of the many. Rather, it is an accepted part of practice.

At this point, many readers may conclude that formalism is too removed from reality and that its "purist" vision of sport is too ideal to be of much help in practice. Some theorists who are dissatisfied with formalism agree, and suggest that the formalists have ignored actual practice by not paying attention to the implicit conventions that participants accept as applying to their sport. These conventions sometimes are referred to as "the ethos of the game."[7] For example, with respect to strategic fouling in basketball, conventionalists may argue that there are conventions accepted by basketball players according to which such action is permissible. Strategic fouling is not cheating, on this view, but is legitimized by widely accepted social conventions which apply within the game. This form of conventionalism, I would suggest, is a kind of externalism, since the conventions are thought of as social norms arising from the social context surrounding sport and hence are not necessarily tied to the internal logic or nature of sports themselves.

However, it is far from clear that social conventions associated with a game or sport can provide a basis for ethical values. To say that conventions exist is to claim sport can provide a basis for ethical values. To say that conventions exist is to claim that they are followed, but values are concerned with what behavior is justified, or with what sorts of acts ought to be prohibited, required, allowed, or encouraged. Conventions describe *accepted* behavior but ethics is concerned with what behavior is

acceptable or *ought* to be encouraged or condemned.

In fact, conventionalism in sport has some resemblance to the position in ethical theory sometimes called normative cultural relativism, which claims that we ought to follow the moral code of our own society or culture. This view seems unacceptable for reasons that also undermine the idea that social conventions surrounding sport can by themselves provide a basis for a justifiable ethic of sport. Both positions imply that the existing social order ought to be followed and that those who would reform or change it always are in the wrong. But surely we cannot decide in advance of even knowing the issues that we ought always to follow dominant codes or conventions no matter what. Moreover, dominant social codes and conventions may be arbitrary and in some cases involve great damage to important human rights and liberties. A similar problem can arise in sport. For example, suppose the dominant set of social conventions surrounding a particular sport implies that it is permissible for competitors to try to seriously injure star players on the opposing side. Would that make it morally right?

Rather than simply accept existing conventions and practices uncritically, we can instead be more critical and return to the suggestion of the formalists that the rules of sports have a point; namely to provide good competition. This leads us to an extension of formalism, or perhaps just a broader interpretation of it, that I have called *broad internalism*. This view suggests that there are values internal to sport and these values are supported by a broad understanding of the purposes and point of athletic competition, including an interpretation of the point of the constitutive rules on which formalism places such emphasis.

Formalists see the point of the constitutive rules of games and sports as creating challenges simply so that participants will have worthy challenges to face. Broad internalism extends this idea by providing an overall theory of the nature of those challenges and of how the challenge created by a sport is best understood, and, most important for our purposes, makes explicit the values presupposed by the activities in question. For our purposes, it makes no difference whether broad internalism is viewed simply as a fuller version of formalism or, as I would suggest, as a distinct approach which encompasses formalistic elements but goes beyond formalism in its scope and purposes.

Consider, for example, the application of broad internalism to the question of strategic fouling in sports such as basketball. One approach, which I have defended elsewhere, maintains that it is a mistake to view all penalties within a sport as analogous to sanctions or punishments for wrongdoing.[8] That is, not all penalties fit the model of punishments within the criminal law. Consider, for example, the unplayable lie rule in golf. According to the rules of golf, when a player hits a shot into a position where no subsequent shot is feasible, as for example when the ball is lying in the middle of a large, thick bush, the player is given various options for dropping the ball for a next shot, subject to accepting a penalty stroke for moving the ball. For example, the player may drop a ball within two club lengths on either side of the position of the original ball at the cost of a one-stroke penalty. Clearly, the point of this rule is not to punish the player for an infraction but to allow the player an option which may be exercised at the cost of "paying" the penalty stroke, so that the player gets no competitive advantage over others. The penalty in this case seems much more like the price of exercising an option, or perhaps the payment of compensation to the other players, rather than a punishment for a crime or infraction.

Similarly, it is arguable that strategic fouling to stop the clock in basketball is an option allowed by the rules. The foul shots awarded to the other team are not punishment for breaking the rule against fouling but are the price the other team must pay for stopping the clock (or the compensation the team receives for being fouled). If the price is a fair one, a good team would be indifferent between possessing the ball and running out the clock or having the foul shots and a chance to increase its lead. (Of course, a poor foul-shooting team might prefer not to be fouled, but that does not show the penalty is an unfair price; rather, the team should work to improve its free-throw shooting.)

Whether or not such an analysis of the strategic foul in basketball is correct, it provides an example of a broad internalist analysis. In particular, it places the act of strategic fouling within the broad context of a theory of basketball which is claimed to make good sense of the game and to provide a perspicuous account of the challenges it involves. Such a theory sees basketball as a sport, embodying the mutual quest for excellence among competitors through the challenge one side provides to the other, and then tries to give an account of the particular features and nuances of basketball within this broader account of the point and purpose of competition in sports and athletics.

But what has all this to do with moral education? For one thing, a full understanding of sport along lines of broad internalism includes commitment to fundamental moral values. Thus, as a number of writers I would classify as broad internalists have maintained, sport presupposes a commitment to such values as fairness, liberty, and equality. For example, equality and fairness are guaranteed not only by the commitment to following the rules, but also because the rules themselves must be equitable and not favor competitors on grounds irrelevant to the basic skills and virtues called forth by the challenges of the sport. Moreover, if we view the sports contest as a mutual challenge acceptable to all the competitors, we can view sport as a freely chosen and unalienated activity in which the competitors are committed to viewing their opponents as fellow persons equally engaged in meeting the challenge set by the contest itself. This does not necessarily mean that competitors must like each other, but it does imply that each should be committed to seeking a good contest in which each participant plays at his or her best in order to bring out the best in the opponents.

This suggests further that while winning is an important goal of the sports contest, since it is a primary way in which a competitor meets the challenge of the sport, it is far from everything. After all, even an undefeated season achieved through scheduling only competitively inferior opponents might lack significant value. In fact, it may be of less value than an outstanding but losing performance against an especially worthy opponent. For example, I am now the best basketball player in my neighborhood, mainly because all the other players are less than 8 years old. I win every game, but since my opponents are too small to even reach the basket, is that an achievement of any note?

Accordingly, then, certain values seem inextricably involved in the idea of a sporting contest as a mutual quest for excellence through competitive challenge. Sport is not a value-free activity. Moreover, as Peter Arnold has emphasized, these values are not relativistic but are involved at all levels of serious sport, in the sense that violation of them normally is a justifiable ground for criticism throughout the now virtually world-wide sporting community.[9] For example, bribing an official to insure the victory of a team in a soccer competition is not seen as "unfair for us" but "fair for them," but is universally regarded as a violation of the ethics of sporting competition. On the broad internalist analysis suggested above, this is because the major point of a sporting contest is to test the skills and character of the competitors according to the challenges presupposed by the formal rules; bribing an official removes the challenge and so defeats the point of the contest before it even gets off the ground.

What, then, are the implications of this analysis for moral education? After all, even if sports are a value-laden activity, it does not follow that those values can or should be taught or promoted in the schools. In particular, isn't the promotion of any set of values in educational institutions highly partisan? After all, who is to say what values should be promoted and in what manner?

Sports, Morality, and Inquiry

Even if there is what might be called an inner morality of sport, focused on such values as fairness, respect for the opponent as a facilitator in a mutual quest for excellence, and dedication and commitment to meeting challenges, why should that morality be favored by educational

institutions? There are other conceptions of sport, such as the belief that winning is either everything in sport, or at least the predominant value that ought to be emphasized. Which view of sport should be taught? Second, why should *any* moral values be taught? Why is it the school's job to endorse one conception of morality, perhaps a highly partisan one, over other conceptions? After all, shouldn't we just be tolerant of moral differences rather than simply impose one morality on everyone?

Let us begin with the question of tolerance. First of all, those who maintain that we should avoid making moral judgments about the behavior of others, particularly about the moralities of other cultures, out of concern and respect for differences among peoples, are themselves making a moral judgment. Rather than avoiding ethical judgment, they are committing one. For their claim is that we *ought* to be tolerant of and respect differences, including cultural differences in ethical belief and judgment. But that itself is an "ought" claim which purports to be morally justified. The advocates of tolerance are claiming it is better to be tolerant than intolerant. If they did not believe such a view, they would have no basis for condemning invidious discrimination, racism, or sexism, or even Nazi genocide. One cannot have it both ways by denying that we ought to make moral judgments and asserting that the stance of tolerance and respect for difference is morally best.

A related point is that moral judgments need not be made in a dogmatic or intolerant way, any more than, say, scientific judgments ought to be made dogmatically or without regard for evidence. Rather, in making a moral claim, one can and should be open to discussion of the issue and consideration of arguments for other positions, and should be willing to revise one's position if that is what the evidence suggests is warranted. A participant in a discussion of an ethical issue normally can and should take the stance of a discussant in a form of inquiry designed to elicit the most justified view. Discussants, if inquiry is to be effective in eliciting justified views and avoiding unjustified ones, must be open to dialog with others and consideration of objections to their own positions. Dogmatism and unwillingness to consider criticisms of one's own position simply make it less likely that one's own views are justified. Discussants who are not open to intellectual challenges are like sports teams that never play worthy competitors; just as the latter have little or no basis for asserting that they have achieved excellence by meeting challenges, so the former have no sound basis for claiming their views are justified, for they have never considered or responded effectively to worthy criticisms that might show just the opposite.

This point has an important implication for moral education. It suggests that there are fundamental moral values which must be in place for education and discussion to even take place. For example, participants in inquiry must be free to make critical points and engage in discussion, canons of rational inquiry and logic must be observed, and persons may not be excluded from the conversation simply because we don't agree with their views. If such requirements are not observed, rational discussion either cannot take place or can occur only in an attenuated and impoverished form, which is far less likely to arrive at truth or justification than a more robust version which accepts the status of others as interlocutors or fellow discussants in dialogic inquiry.

In fact, our discussion suggests that there is a close connection between what might be called the internal morality of sport and the morality of intellectual inquiry and discussion. Just as good sport requires seeing competitors as fellow facilitators engaging in a mutual quest for excellence, so rational inquiry, if it is to be carried out effectively, requires us to regard others as fellow discussants.[10] Both, in other words, require respect for others as persons and so stand in contrast to both personal selfishness and the kind of limited sympathy which regards only those like me (my team or my group) as worth full moral consideration. Moreover, just as competitors in sport must subject themselves to the discipline of the rules of the game, so participants in intellectual inquiry must subject themselves to the requirements of evidence and good reasoning. Parallels such as these are not just coincidental, and as we will see provide the basis for the role that sport can and should play in moral education.

Before turning directly to implications for moral education, we need to address the issue of partisanship. Consider, first, the kind of values that are presupposed by intellectual inquiry. Although these are values, and hence inquiry is not a value-free activity, they are non-partisan, in that anyone committed to genuine inquiry and to dialog on the issues with others is committed to these values, for they are presuppositions of critical investigation itself.[11] They are non-partisan or neutral, not in the sense of being value free, but in the sense that anyone committed to inquiry is committed to them.[12] That is, if someone whom we can call "the dictator" claimed to be committed to inquiry but arbitrarily silenced others, refused to listen to criticism, or excluded positions from discussion on grounds irrelevant to their merits, then the dictator would be in a very weak position to claim that her own views were justified. As noted earlier, she would be in a position like that of a team that claimed to be excellent at a sport but never played a worthy opponent.

Couldn't an elitist group conduct inquiry among its own members but exclude others who were not group members, perhaps because those excluded were members of the "wrong" ethnic group, race, gender, or religion? Such an exclusionary policy, however, would be open to the charge of arbitrariness. Moreover, it would be self-defeating. The exclusion would be arbitrary because those excluded might be, or could be if provided with fair opportunities, as effective contributors to dialogic inquiry as those included. It would be self-defeating because the insights those excluded might have provided would have made inquiry more thorough and comprehensive. In effect, by limiting access to the playing field, the participants have unjustifiably protected themselves from possible challenges and from the positive insights that might have been provided by those left out of the activity. The participants would be like athletes who thought of themselves as competing at the highest levels but who did not actually do so because whole groups, such as African Americans in the days of racially segregated sports, were excluded from the playing field, thereby lowering the overall level of the competition.

Schools, then, are not acting in a partisan way when they require that students be civil, listen to the positions of others, respond to criticism and evaluation through rational discussion, and respect the status of other students as fellow participants in a common endeavor. Although these are values, they are not partisan values. Rather, they provide the framework within which partisan positions can be debated and examined. By promoting, encouraging, and endorsing such a framework for dialog, discussion, and inquiry, the schools are not acting as political agents in any narrow sense but are promoting and preserving the arena in which reasoned political discourse and intellectual inquiry can take place.

The internal morality of sport also can be regarded as non-partisan for similar reasons. That is, if the broad internalist argument is correct, this morality will include values that are presupposed by a commitment to sport and so can be presumed to be acceptable to all athletes. Thus, the ideal of the good sports contest between worthy opponents seems inextricably involved with the idea of sports as a framework within which challenges are addressed. Dedicated athletes should be committed to pursuing excellence through meeting the challenges set by the formal rules of the sport in which they are participating. Of course, individual athletes may have other goals as well. Professional athletes, for example, may have the goal of earning a good living through their play. The point is, however, that competitive sport would not be a good way of earning a living if the players did not try to meet the challenge set by the sport, because it would not generate the same interest and excitement. Michael Jordan, Mia Hamm, and Tiger Woods are great athletes because they meet the challenges set by their sport with style, grace, dedication, and courage, and for that reason fans are eager to pay to see them play. So external goals, such as making money from sport, are parasitic on the internal goals of sport in at least the sense that the external goals can be achieved precisely because the internal ones are honored and achieved. When critics argue that much of contemporary sport has become corrupt, what they seem to be suggesting is that the pursuit of such external goals as fame and fortune have undermined the structure of meeting worthy challenges within a fair framework of competition.[13]

Our discussion suggests, then, that certain activities, including both sport on the one hand and intellectual inquiry and dialog on the other, can be value laden without being partisan. That is because the values involved are not highly partisan but are presuppositions of the activities themselves. This does not mean that all participants share the exact same conception of either sport or inquiry. Some of the values alleged to be presupposed by each activity may be contested or controversial. Surely, there can be different but related conceptions of each area, and dispute about contested areas can be healthy and constructive. However, individuals who reject core aspects of either activity face a heavy burden of proof if they still claim to be participants in it. It normally would be absurd, for example, for someone to claim to be engaged in intellectual inquiry on an issue if he refused to even consider evidence that might count against his view or excluded any possible critics from stating objections through the use of force. Similarly, it normally would be absurd for anyone to claim to be playing a sport if she intentionally violated rules whenever she felt like it, and excluded worthy opponents from competition by physically barring them from the field.

Thus, we can distinguish between a partisan use of values within sport, as when coaches require their team members to say a prayer before contests regardless of the religious views of the players, and relatively non-partisan uses of values, as when coaches emphasize the value of competing hard so as to provide a good contest for the opponent. In the latter case, but not the former, the values at stake are required by our best understanding of what athletic competition requires and so involve values internal to athletic competition itself. How, then, does this bear on sport as a form of moral education?

Sport and Moral Education

Consider the claim that schools ought not to be involved with, endorse, or teach morality, in order to avoid indoctrination or imposition of highly partisan ideas on relatively powerless students. Such concerns may have considerable force when applied to the imposition of specific highly controversial values and principles. For example, secular colleges and universities almost surely should not adopt official stances on such topics as abortion.

However, it does not follow that educational institutions can or should be totally value free. The proper kind of neutrality for educational institutions is not total value freedom but non-partisanship on controversial issues which have no direct tie to the educational mission of the institution itself. However, schools, including colleges and universities, must insist on civility in the classroom so that learning can take place, respect for evidence and rational canons of inquiry and investigation, and willingness to consider rather than suppress the points made by others. Thus, in training students in the techniques of inquiry and discussion, in teaching them how to test their views through discussion with others, schools are engaging in an important and indeed crucial form of moral education. Moreover, although various elements of the idea of inquiry may be contested at any given time, as when protesters assert that their demonstrations are a contribution to dialog while others view them as disruptive of learning, core values at the heart of inquiry do seem to have presumptive universal force. Thus, if proponents of a position in a debate refuse even to hear objections to or criticisms of their view, then they justifiably can be accused of being dogmatic. Even worse, they are not in a good position to claim their view is justified, since they have not shown it can meet objections.

In teaching the fundamental values of inquiry and discussion, schools are creating the moral climate in which views can be discussed, debated, and evaluated. This function, of course, is crucial for democracy, since democratic government presupposes examination of important issues so that citizens and their representatives can vote on the basis of reasoned opinions, not blind loyalty or ignorance.

One kind of moral education which is clearly proper for the schools to engage in, then, is

training in the process of inquiry and discussion, which involves such values as respect for evidence and reasoning, recognition of the rights of other inquirers, and the benefits of engaging in dialog with adherents to alternate perspectives. Training in the nature of inquiry and rational dialog is not indoctrination but rather is a prerequisite for the kind of liberation that the ability to think critically for oneself involves.

But what has all this to do with sport and the role it might play in moral education? What I want to suggest is that training in and involvement with the internal values of sport is an important element of the kind of moral education with which schools are properly involved. That is, sport, when uncorrupted by over-emphasis on external values such as fame and fortune or a win-at-all-costs mentality, provides lessons in respect for others, meeting challenges, facing difficulties, and engaging in dialogic activity that supplement and reinforce similar values that should be emphasized in class.

A number of scholars have emphasized that the internal values of sport support and reinforce other educational values as well as those of equality, fairness, and respect for others that are so central to the proper functioning of a liberal democracy. As Peter Arnold points out, "democracy as a way of ordering and living our lives is dependent upon the social principles of freedom and equality, and . . . it is these same principles that underpin in turn what it is to be liberally educated as well as the idea of sport as fairness."[14] Moreover, as Arnold also maintains, sport is a major social practice in our culture (and in most cultures throughout the world), and learning how to engage in it appropriately or appreciate and criticize sporting activities intelligently is an important part of being an educated person in our society.

These points, while true and important, may not do enough to bring out the special features that make sport such an excellent tool of moral education. These features, in my view, are (1) the accessibility of sport, (2) the dialogic structure of sport, and (3) the related characteristic that sport is a critical activity. Let us consider all three in turn.

First, sport is a widely recognized and followed cultural practice or set of practices. Different sports have wide followings ranging from fans of professional sport, to serious amateur participants, to recreational players and their families. Critics of sport understand what it is they are criticizing, while, in our culture at least, even those who are not interested routinely employ the vocabulary of sport in everyday activities, as when one may be told by one's friends to "hit a home run" when leaving for a job interview. That is, sport is accessible to and understood by a wide segment of our population, so that the values sport might express or presuppose are out in the open for all who approach sport with some understanding to appreciate.

Second, and more important in my view, I suggest that the structure of competitive sport is dialogic in a way that resembles the dialogic structure of intellectual inquiry. Just as the latter involves criticism and reply, so sport involves moves and countermoves among the participants. In each case, this involves considering the opponent (or critic) as a person whose choices must be responded to within a framework of rules and principles that provide fairness and promote the point of the activity (a mutual quest for excellence through challenge in sport, and justification and the pursuit of truth in inquiry). Sport, then, because of its accessibility, provides an excellent context for introducing people to the structure of dialogic activity and encouraging them, through participation, to internalize its ethic.

For example, no serious competitor likes to lose a sports contest but, as I believe every successful athlete would acknowledge, losing provides a significant opportunity to analyze one's performance and learn from one's mistakes. The good competitor's attitude to a loss is to see what can be learned from it. Similarly, participants in intellectual inquiry normally do not enjoy having their pet theories devastated by criticism, but a good inquirer still welcomes criticism and tries to learn from it when it is cogent or sound. Sport, because most of us lose at least some of the time, can at its best teach us a useful way to deal with failure as well as to

understand and respect the achievements of our fellow competitors. Participation and understanding of competition in sport, then, is participation in a kind of give-and-take of dialog that also characterizes intellectual inquiry and democratic discussion.

This in turn suggests that sport is a kind of critical activity. Participants learn to have game plans, to analyze their own weaknesses and strengths and those of their opponents, and to devise programs for improvement. This requires an objective analysis of one's abilities and those of others, and the willingness to revise that analysis when it turns out to be inaccurate or incorrect.

It is important to be clear about what is and what is not being suggested here. I am not claiming, for example, that there is a direct causal link between becoming a good competitor in sport and becoming a good scholar in the domain of intellectual inquiry or a good participant in democratic debate. Extreme versions of the thesis that sport builds character are no doubt grossly overstated. More modest versions, however, may have some degree of plausibility. It probably is no more unreasonable, for example, to think that learning to be a good competitor in sport may *tend to promote* carryover effects in the other areas than it is for advocates of liberal arts education to believe that the traits they value among their students, such as intellectual openmindedness, may also tend to promote similar values in other areas, such as in the workplace or in civic affairs.

What I most want to suggest, however, is that in addition to tendencies to develop or reinforce desirable character traits that sport may promote, the *understanding* of the structure of competition in sport can help promote *understanding* of parallel underlying values presupposed by both intellectual inquiry and democratic debate. Sport, on this view, is an excellent tool of moral education, because understanding the internal values and structure of sporting competition at its best is a way of understanding broader values that apply in a variety of other important contexts as well.

This is not to imply that sport simply is a means for promoting certain values in other more important contexts. Sport is an important practice in its own right and it flourishes in great part because of our concern with the value, much of which is intrinsic, of meeting the unique challenges to mind and body presented by the good athletic contest. Nevertheless, sport has an underlying internal normative structure which encompasses broad values of wider concern, which we would do well not to ignore. But the way to promote these values is not to use sport as a platform for preaching, but to promote understanding of its internal morality and its relationship to broad ethical principles that apply across a variety of domains and activities.

While the exact form that moral education in sport should assume is debatable, I doubt that simply preaching is what is needed. Rather, at all levels of sports, parent, coaches, and players need to discuss and examine actual sporting practices. Within educational institutions, this might involve formal classwork parallel to courses already offered in many institutions on medical and business ethics. Within the arena of sport itself, a beginning could be made if coaches were judged as much on their ability to articulate the values implicit in sporting competition and to criticize excesses taken in the pursuit of victory as on their won-and-lost record. Coaches, for example, can teach much of value in ways appropriate to the age, maturity, and level of competition of their players, in getting their athletes to view opponents as persons and to appreciate the achievements of others, even when performed by the other side. Opponents are to be viewed, on this account, as facilitators in a mutual quest for excellence, not simply obstacles to be beaten down and defeated.[15]

Unfortunately, much sporting practice in our culture, particularly at the higher levels of many sports, is open to severe moral criticism. The cult of victory at almost any cost has been widely criticized, as has the tendency of sport to degenerate into a form of entertainment, as when subtle elements of a sport are replaced by features that make it more intelligible or entertaining to a mass audience at the price of removing nuances of the game and reducing the variety of skills that are required for success. However, by understanding the internal structure and values of sporting practice, and engaging in critical dialog about them, we can become better able to distinguish the best in sport from corruption of what sport should be, and make intelligible the moral standards that should apply both within sport and, if what I have suggested is right, across critical inquiry and dialog as well.

Sport, Relativism, and the Refutation of Absolutophobia

Does our discussion have implications for the views of those individuals who, when confronted with a moral issue, respond by dismissing the possibility of rational discussion, because moral issues, they assume, cannot be rationally adjudicated? "Who is to say?" is their response to moral issues, implying, often without argument, that no one is ever in a better position than anyone else to offer a reasoned defense of a position on a moral controversy.

While nothing said here implies moral conclusions can be "proved" in any mathematical sense, my discussion does support the view that, at least on many moral issues, some positions are more reasonable than others. Thus, a team which claimed that the rules of a sport ought to be changed simply because such a change was to its competitive advantage but not those of opponents would be holding an arbitrary position. Unless a relevant consideration was provided as to why its competitive interests should outweigh those of opponents, or the interests of the athletic community in having the sport be appropriately challenging, such a claim should be rejected. Likewise, someone who claimed her interests always ought to take precedence over those of others, regardless of the circumstances, surely would have the burden of proof on her to show why she was so special that her interests ought always to be assigned priority over anyone else's.

While many moral issues are highly controversial, and reasonable people can be found taking opposing positions, not all moral issues are of that kind. Moreover, inquiry into complex moral issues can often suggest that not all views are equally reasonable, or at least advance the discussion to a new level of thinking. Thus, the view that at least some penalties for strategic fouls in sport are prices for an allowable option rather than punishments for prohibited behavior calls into question the formalist view that strategic fouling is a form of cheating. Formalists, of course, may be able to effectively criticize the view that such penalties often are prices rather than punishments, but if, as I would suggest, the discussion has been moved to a new level, then a response is clearly required. Moral issues, then, are not best approached by dogmatic assertions but can be investigated and sometimes resolved or advanced through inquiry and reasoned dialog among proponents of different views.

Perhaps a feature that makes sport such a useful medium for moral education is that many of the values presupposed by or involved with sporting practices are not relative to a particular perspective or culture, and can be supported or justified by strong reasons. While cultural differences may affect styles of play, or the importance assigned to a given sport within a broad social context, core values of sport do not seem to be culturally variable in the same way. The American and Chinese women were playing the same game in the finals of the 1999 World Cup Soccer Tournament. Moreover, this is not only a descriptive point but also a normative one. Cheating, attempts to intentionally injure opponents, or bribing officials to influence the outcome, had no moral place in the game regardless of other cultural differences that may have existed between the teams.

Similarly, lying about one's score on a hole in a golf tournament surely cannot be justified. The whole idea of a golf tournament is to see which of the competitors best meets the challenge set by the golf course and the pressure of keeping pace with the performances of the other players. It provides a context for seeing if one can meet the physical and mental challenges set by the sport of golf. Lying about one's score may, if undetected, allow one to win a trophy or prize money, but it does not show that one has met the challenge of the sport. Moreover, it shows disrespect for the other competitors, since cheating gains one an advantage only if others don't cheat. The cheater, therefore, arbi-

trarily assigns to himself or herself a superior position that takes advantage of the compliance of the other players with the rules of the game, and so cannot be justified.[16]

Sport, then, provides an arena which illustrates a framework of universal values within which competition takes place. These values can be given rational support, and as players are socialized into the game, they tend to internalize them as their own. Of course, there can be cultural differences between the styles in which a game is played and strategies that tend to get employed, but the basic ethic of meeting challenges within a mutually acceptable framework of rules and the principles they presuppose is a constant. Some aspects of sport will be controversial and some issues in sport may be difficult to resolve reasonably. Different sides may each hold plausible views. This no more suggests that all values in sport are arbitrary than the fact that some theories in science are debatable suggests that no scientific theory is any more justifiable than any other. Rather, education about a subject, whether it is sport or chemistry, should help us distinguish areas that are controversial from those that are not, and promote the habits of inquiry and dialog that allow us to build upon what is basic to make progress in resolving disagreements over what is not.

What I hope our discussion suggests, then, is not that players, spectators, or others ought simply to be told how to behave morally in sport. Although beginners need to become immersed in the practices and traditions of sporting communities, and may properly be required to conform to appropriate standards of behavior, moral education as presented here is in a particularly important form a kind of inquiry, involving reasoned dialog with others. Moral education in sport would require teachers, coaches, players, and observers to become more cognizant of the structure of sport as a quest for excellence through challenge, and conversant with and articulate about the values and principles presupposed by such an activity. It would involve emphasis on reasoned inquiry and dialog, rather than dogmatic pronouncement, as a means of resolving controversies. This does not mean that sports teams should be run as direct democracies. After all, even philosophy classes require direction and decision making, for example in the choice of texts, by the instructor. It does imply, however, that coaches proceed as educators and try to promote understanding of the underlying principles and values of the sport with which they are involved, as well as of its strategies and techniques.

Moreover, educational institutions need to stress the affinities between sporting activities and intellectual inquiry and scholarship that were emphasized earlier. Although it is at best unclear whether participation in sports makes athletes more moral (of course it is doubtful if participation in corrupted versions of sport would have such a positive effect), sport *at its best* expresses and illustrates important values and norms that can be of educational value to the whole community. Sport, when properly practiced, can be an important medium for transmitting values of fundamental moral worth and for enhancing our understanding of them. The beauty of sport as a form of moral education is that for sport to serve this function, it cannot be reduced simply to a means or mechanism for promoting good behavior. Rather, if sport is valued on its own terms, as a challenge and as a test of our minds and bodies, then we already are immersed in a framework of fundamental values.

Proper understanding of sporting activity, then, involves us in a moral framework that encompasses the thrills and excitement of competitive athletics. If the argument suggested here is sound, crucial elements of that framework apply not only to the realm of sport but also more broadly to the pursuit of the examined life itself.

Notes

1   The quotation from Plato is from *The Republic*, book III, section 412. Albert Camus, "The Wager of Our Generation," in *Resistance, Rebellion, and Death*, trans. Justin O'Brien (New York: Vintage Books, 1960), p. 242.

2   I discuss student relativism and "absolutophobia" in my article, "The Paralysis of Absolutophobia," *Chronicle of Higher Education*, XLIII, 42 (June 27, 1997), pp. B5–B6, and draw on the discussion there throughout the present article.

3   My discussion of internalism and externalism in this section draws heavily on my Presidential Address to the International Association for the Philosophy of Sport (formerly the Philosophic Society for the Study of Sport) entitled "Internalism in Sport." I discuss these views more extensively in that paper, which is to appear in the *Journal of the Philosophy of Sport*. I thank the editors for permission to use some of that material here.

4   For such a characterization of formalism, see, for example, Fred D'Agostino, "The Ethos of Games," *Journal of the Philosophy of Sport*, VIII (1981), p. 7, and William J. Morgan, "The Logical Incompatibility Thesis and Rules: A Reconsideration of Formalism as an Account of Games," *Journal of the Philosophy of Sport*, XIV (1987), p. 1.

5   Nicholas Dixon, "On Sportsmanship and 'Running Up the Score'," *Journal of the Philosophy of Sport*, XIX (1992), pp. 1–13 (reprinted here as reading 9).

6   See Kathleen M. Pearson, "Deception, Sportsmanship, and Ethics," *Quest*, XIX (January 1973), p. 118 (reprinted here as reading 8).

7   See D'Agostino, "The Ethos of Games," pp. 7–18.

8   What follows is a summary of the position I defended in *Fair Play: Sports, Values, and Society*, (Boulder, CO: Westview Press, 1991), pp. 48–9.

9   See Peter Arnold, *Sport, Ethics and Education* (London: Cassell, 1997), particularly chs 1 and 2.

10   These standards may be positive as well as negative. For example, in sport, participants may not only be required to refrain from certain actions, such as bribing officials or deliberately injuring opponents, but also be encouraged to perform acts of good sportspersonship. Similarly, participants in dialogic inquiry may not only be prohibited from silencing critics by force but also be encouraged to support institutions, such as schools, which are necessary for the development and support of other inquirers.

11   Of course, there might be different conceptions of what constitutes inquiry, as well as dispute over what methods of participation, e.g. forms of civil disobedience, are contributions to it. But while

there is much room for debate in this area, it is doubtful if any activity would qualify as a form of inquiry if it allowed participants to be silenced on grounds irrelevant to the intellectual merits of their position or if it abandoned canons of reasoning and respect for evidence altogether.

12   For a fuller discussion of the forms neutrality can take in educational contexts, and of the distinction between neutrality as value freedom and more robust forms of neutrality, see my *Neutrality and the Academic Ethic* (Lanham, MD: Rowman and Littlefield, 1994), especially chs 2 and 3.

13   See, for example, William J. Morgan, *Leftist Theories of Sport: A Critique and Reconstruction* (Urbana: University of Illinois Press, 1994), particularly ch. 5.

14   Arnold, *Sport, Ethics and Education*, p. 90.

15   Professional and high-level amateur golf is perhaps the best example among popular contemporary sports of an athletic practice most closely combining intense competition with mutual respect for opponents, the rules of the game, and the internal values of the sport. Top-level players frequently call penalties on themselves and enforce among themselves the courtesies, traditions, and internal values of the game.

16   More precisely, cheating cannot be justified in the absence of some overriding justification. For example, if the cheater must win to avoid having his family assassinated by criminals who have bet on the game, cheating presumably would be justified, or at least excusable.

Why Everyone Deserves a Sporting Chance:
Education, Justice, and School Sports

Janice Moulton ————————————————————————

At a college athletic banquet, Donald Kennedy, the former president of Stanford University, spoke about when he had been a college athlete 30 years earlier:

> It occurs to me to wonder: what would the reaction have been if I had predicted that soon women would run the Boston Marathon faster than it had ever been run by men up to that point? There would have been incredulous laughter from two-thirds of the room, accompanied by a little locker-room humor.
>
> Yet that is just what has taken place. My classmates would be astonished at the *happening*, but they would be even more astonished at the *trends*. If we look at the past 10 years of world's best times in the Marathons for men and women, it is clear that the women's mark has been dropping over the decade, at a rate about seven times faster than the men's record.

While Kennedy was in school, the swimming teams of Harvard and Yale were the best in the country. He used them for comparison:

> What would have happened if you had put this year's Stanford women into the pool? *Humiliation* is what. Just to give you a sample, *seven* current Stanford women would have beaten my friend Dave Hed-

berg, Harvard's great sprint free-styler, and *all* the Yalies in the 100. The Stanford women would have swept the 200-yard backstroke and breast-stroke, and won *all* the other events contested.
>
> In the 400-yard freestyle relay there would have been a 10-second wait between Stanford's touch and the first man to arrive at the finish. Do you know how *long* 10 seconds is? Can you imagine that crowd...seeing a team of *girls* line up against the two best freestyle relay groups in the East, expecting the unexpected, and then having to wait *this* long for the men to get home?[1]

Kennedy's anecdote asks us to re-examine assumptions about male–female differences that are based on past performance. Short-distance swimming and long-distance track records of men are better to date than those of women, but the rate of improvement for women is far better than the rate of improvement for men. What has changed is the opportunity for women to participate and train in these sports, because about ten years before Donald Kennedy spoke, Title IX, the federal legislation prohibiting sex discrimination in school programs, was passed. The lesson is that we must be careful about attributing differences in sports ability to sex differences: opportunity produces far greater improvement in performance than anyone would have predicted.

Equal opportunity is an important value in our society. It is often invoked to support controversial positions because everyone agrees that it is good. But it is not always clear what or how much should be done to achieve this goal, or how to provide equal opportunity for people who are not equal at the start. In sports, there is a special problem: sports are physical, and females and males are different physically. Some of the physical differences are the result of different experience. Some differences in stamina, flexibility, or strength are assumed to be innate. But how do we handle such differences if our goal is to provide equal opportunity in sports?

Should equal resources be provided for male and female football teams? Should males and females compete together or separately in particular sports? Are there some sports that females should not play? Some that males should not play? Should the rules of some sports be changed to promote equal opportunity? If so, why? And if not, why not?

This essay attempts to provide a means to answer these questions by comparing sports with education, recommending that our experience in trying to increase equal opportunity in education be applied to opportunities in sports.

Recommendations for improving sports opportunities for females have met with opposition. Title IX has been obeyed slowly and begrudgingly in the area of sports. Portions of the legislation allowing sex separation in certain sports have been used to continue sex inequalities. Institutions claim to comply with the legislation with unequal facilities because fewer females participate in sports. Yet in other areas of education, attempts to provide equal opportunity have resulted in programs designed to increase interest and ability: "Head Start" preschooling, special training for parents, attempts to connect education with more popular activities such as sports and television, special training in math and science. Even though the success of these programs may be modest, they have not been resisted the way proposals for changing school sports have been.

In the first half of this essay I will compare sports with education. To the extent my analogy is successful, it will follow that beliefs we have about equal opportunity in education also apply to the goal of equal opportunity for participation in sports. Then I will examine proposals for changing school sports to foster equal opportunity.

Why Equality Matters

First, we need an explanation of why equality in sports for women is important. In what follows, I argue that access to sports is like access to education, and therefore the arguments for equal opportunity in education hold for equal opportunities in sports. And the very solutions that provide equal opportunity in education for people with different abilities also work for sports.

The use of analogy

I am going to explain why I believe sports opportunities should be treated like educational opportunities. Such an analogy says: "A is like B." Of course no A is ever exactly like a B. But if A is a controversial topic and no one knows exactly how to handle it, then an analogy can help. If B is better understood and less controversial, thinking of problem area A as if it were B may lead to a better understanding of A.

Let us look at one well-known analogy. We have been told that alcoholism is a disease and should be treated like one. That is, it is *like* a disease. Those who make the analogy want us to think of the way we treat people who have diseases – with sympathy and understanding and special care, with government money and foundation grants to search for cures and remedies, with hospital care and sick leaves if necessary. If people get pneumonia, we do not usually fire them from their jobs, denounce them from pulpits, or laugh at them on street corners. A person cannot help getting pneumonia; at least he or she cannot control the disabling consequences. So also, the analogy tells us, for alcoholism: alcoholics need special treatment, as if they were sick; they should not be blamed and punished by society.

If the analogy is accepted, certain actions are called for, certain things become clear. The analogy helps us focus on some issues and rule out others. For example, we might suppose that people who become alcoholics have weak constitutions, that perhaps they are genetically disposed to be that way. But with the disease analogy, we can see that even if this is true, becoming an alcoholic is not inevitable or disgraceful, any more than getting pneumonia or breast cancer is. Given the analogy, having a "weak constitution" is not reason for blame or shame. Most of us have inherited predispositions for some illnesses or weaknesses; most of us have some kind of weak constitution.

If the analogy is not accepted, then it is up to the rejecter to show what is wrong with the comparison, to show how the differences between alcoholism and cancer or pneumonia are significant and relevant enough that what we say about one does not apply to the other.

Some might think the example does not go far enough. Alcoholism is not *like* a disease, they would argue; it *is* a disease. If the analogy with sports and education works the same way, people might begin to think the same thing – sports participation is not *like* education; it *is* education, an essential part of it.

If the analogy of sports with education turns out to be a good one, it will help us when we define the issues, recommend solutions, and talk about equal opportunity in situations where abilities may differ. While it may not necessarily help us find solutions or decide between alternative proposals, it will help us focus on the important dimensions of the problem.

Our view of education

Let us look first at education. In the United States we think that education is a right. Everyone should receive an education, whether or not that person is going to appreciate it, benefit from it, or use it later, whether or not that person is any good at learning. No one would say, "I don't really believe in education for boys. Everyone knows that boys lag behind girls in learning

ability and many of them are not really interested, so there's really no point." Education is too important to deny to the unskilled or uninspired.

When it comes to education we have a better idea of what equal opportunity means. It does not mean only that there are no legal barriers preventing people from learning some sorts of things. And it does not mean merely that everyone has an equal chance at the start. Nor does it mean that everyone is given instruction in everything, or allowed to attend any school whatever. Our experience with education has taught us that providing equal opportunity requires much more than allowing everyone to try out and excluding those who do not make it. We have to provide extra teaching, eyeglasses, hearing aids, or Braille lessons for some. We do not exclude people from education because they cannot see or hear or are slow to learn. We try to provide role models of different sorts, educational television programs, earlier preschooling, extra tutoring, and incentives for the unmotivated. We do more than give people an equal opportunity for learning; we try to make sure they do learn.

Even higher education of some sort is available to nearly everyone who has graduated from high school and to many who have not. There are adult education classes for people who want extra education, literacy courses for people who missed out when they were younger, and special education for those with mental or physical disabilities. Up through high school and in many colleges and universities, the primary responsibility of the institution is to provide a basic education for everyone. The resources go first to basic courses for the majority and then to special classes for the gifted.

Equal opportunity is taken seriously even where the educational opportunities are restricted. For example, Smith College, one of the few remaining institutions reserved (at the undergraduate level) for women, defends its restriction by arguing that in this society men dominate to such an extent that even in education women tend to be ignored, women's interests tend to be given second place, women students tend to be given less attention. Smith therefore provides an opportunity for women to be educated in a setting where *they* are the more important gender, where they are not discouraged from areas of study that are dominated by males. Perhaps the best arguments for Smith College's policy are the statistics it cites about the percentage of math, science, and computer science majors it produces, far in excess of coed universities with larger facilities and Nobel laureate science teachers. Smith argues that by reserving its undergraduate education for women, it contributes toward equal opportunity on the larger scale.

Our view of sports

When it comes to sports, equal opportunity does not play the same role. People rarely talk about a certain basic level of athletic proficiency being achieved by all, or about special training programs for the athletically disadvantaged, at least not in the United States. We do not hear about recruitment of minority coaches or players, or attempts to get girls interested in sports by associating sports with other things they are interested in. In contrast to the educational rationale for Smith College, many sex-segregated sports provide benefits for males that are not offered to females.

Unlike education, in sports resources are provided mainly to the elite. The vast majority is neglected. Only if the resources are plentiful do secondary teams receive support. If there are cutbacks, it is the less skilled who suffer.

Many have argued that to provide sports opportunities for everyone would require an enormous increase in funding. There is not enough money available. Therefore sports opportunities are treated as a scarce resource. No attempt is made to distribute them evenly. Instead, they are reserved for the few who can benefit most, or can provide the most glory or money for the institution.

The same argument could be made for education. We *could* provide a much better education to the especially talented by depriving the majority. We could treat education as a scarce resource to which only a given amount of time and money can be dedicated, and give it out only to the specially deserving, the privileged few

who would really benefit the most. But this does not seem either wise or fair.

There are countries where education *is* treated as a scarce resource. Until recently, the British and Chinese systems of higher education were reserved for the privileged few, those who show an aptitude early in life. But, as the quotation from Donald Kennedy at the beginning of this essay shows, increased access to sports can produce successes not previously imagined. The changes in women's participation in basketball and soccer, the success of the WNBA and the World Cup soccer win by American women, would not have happened without that Title IX legislation enacted nearly 30 years ago.

The US attitude toward education, and increasingly the British and Chinese attitude as well, is that everyone can benefit, and that the country as a whole, including the specially talented, would benefit more from distributing educational benefits widely than from reserving them for the elite.

If we treated sports resources the way we treat educational resources, we would distribute them more widely to include more people. We would not reserve them for the few who "make the team." We would make sure there were teams, coaching, and facilities for everyone. We could still give out trophies, medals, and high scores to the best, just as we can give out As to the best students or limit enrollment in some schools to the academic elite. We could still have some teams and games and tournaments reserved for advanced players, just as certain courses, certain types of laboratory equipment, and rare book collections are reserved for advanced students. But the basic resources of sports – instruction, coaching, team and tournament organization, supplies, and whatever else is necessary for participation and the achievement of a certain level of proficiency – would not be denied anyone just because he or she is not exceptionally talented.

Why we might think sports and education are different

Let us look at why we think education is a basic benefit that should not be denied to anyone, and why we think sports are not.

Some people may resist the analogy of sports and education because they think the skills acquired are quite different in nature and importance. The education one receives in school, they would claim, is about thinking – mental activity, part of our work, our career, something that is the essence of what it means to be human – while sports are merely recreational, a physical activity, and therefore less important.

One might point out that to be human is to have both mental and physical abilities. To encourage equal opportunity in the development of mental abilities while denying equal opportunity in the development of physical abilities is analogous to encouraging equal opportunity in literary education while denying equal opportunity in math education.

However, it is not clear that the difference between education and sports can be characterized as a difference between mental and physical activity. Sports require mental activity to learn the rules and strategies of the games. And many school subjects require physical activity in the form of practice and hands-on experience. Some obvious examples are courses in art, theater, and music. Language learning is another area where physical as well as mental activity is needed. Students have to practice forming the sounds, listening, and imitating the phrases of the language over and over to begin to master it. In the sciences, collecting specimens, using laboratory equipment, and conducting experiments all require physical activity. Medical students need to practice before they can perform even routine examinations. The list could go on.

While a distinction between the physical and the mental may not serve to separate sports and education, some would say the two are distinct in other ways. Getting an education is important, while playing a sport is merely recreational, a leisure activity. An education is necessary for full participation in civilization. In many cases an education is necessary for getting and keeping a job or for getting a promotion. And without the ability to read, write, and do basic math, one cannot understand much of the society, acquire new information, and use it to work with others. Education helps people understand their world, to get along in a changing and complex society, to appreciate its benefits and recognize its dangers. We may think of education as a means and participation in civilization as the end. The more education you have, the more you can participate. That is why we think that everyone should have access to an education, and that if they are not quick to learn they deserve more resources.

In contrast, people usually think of the benefits of sports differently. Sports provide personal pleasure, enjoyment of the game and the pleasure of competence, camaraderie with other players (including opponents), and sometimes the exultation of winning. Where education is thought to be necessary, sports are thought to be optional.

Opponents of equal opportunity in sports are likely to reason thus: sports may provide pleasure, but there is no special reason why a society has to try to provide such pleasures for everyone. People ought to be free to seek such pleasures, but there are different ways of having fun, and if some people cannot participate in sports, they should look for another way to enjoy themselves – listen to music or take up knitting, for example.

Therefore, in order to argue for equal sports opportunities on the model of equal opportunity in education, we need to show that sports participation is like education in its importance, that it should not be considered just an optional activity for some students to enjoy and excel in, any more than math and literacy should be considered optional activities.

There is no doubt that sports are important in our culture. Sports professionals become famous and are highly paid. Sports are highly valued and receive attention, even devotion from many people. Still we might think its importance is essentially different in kind from the importance of education.[2] Yet there are ways in which the importance of sports is very much like that of education.

How sports are like education

Review for a minute why education is important, and why we think that equal opportunity in education is important. It provides the tools for success in our culture. It gives people the opportunity to use and contribute to the benefits of our culture. It gives people the means to participate fully in the world.

But these benefits are just what many people claim about sports, even those who would reserve the greater portion of sports resources for males.

For many, sports participation is seen as more than just fun, more than optional recreation. It helps to build character. It teaches leadership. One learns to try harder when things get tough instead of giving up, to persevere, to concentrate, to practice. One learns how to compete with friends,[3] to play with people one does not like, to consider game strategies, even to sit on the bench. One learns the capabilities of one's body, to have a positive self-image, to have greater self-confidence.[4] The clichéd metaphors about being "team players," about "playing ball," "touching base," having a "field sense," "playing by the rules," "running interference," even "knowing the score" all testify to the value of sports participation in learning to flourish in our society.[5]

Someone might argue that the important things that can be learned through sports might be taught in other ways. However, the same thing might be said about formal education. Perhaps the things one learns in classrooms can be taught in other places, by informal conversations or on-the-job training. Perhaps. But just as the possibility of outside training does not diminish our belief in the goal of equal opportunity in education, the possibility of learning by other means some of the things sport teaches should not diminish our belief in the goal of equal opportunity in sports.

Even if one denies the particular values claimed for sports participation, there are other reasons to distribute access to sports more widely. Mary Anne Warren has pointed out that school sports function now to identify *who* is valuable.[6] The attention and prestige given to school sports leaders make them heroes. To the extent that students learn that only boys can be heroes, they are learning that boys are going to become the dominant people and girls are not. And Warren thinks this is a bad thing to learn.

There *are* other outlets for leadership in school, so Warren's point may not be as strong as she would like it to be. The best scholars, the class presidents, the leads in school plays, the students with musical talent, all are possible school heroes, possible school stars. While the relative value of these different abilities may vary from school to school, excellence in sports is only one way to become a hero.

But Warren's idea that school sports teach something about roles in life is a good one. We learn in school which sports are interesting, what kinds of players are interesting, and what we are going to play or watch later in life. Playing a sport makes it much more likely one will be a spectator of that sport. Most importantly, as Warren says, we learn whether we are going to be included in this aspect of civilization.

This aspect of civilization – sports – involves an immense amount of time and energy and resources: sporting events garner more television viewers and more advertising money than any other event. There are sports facilities in cities, in private clubs, in backyards; sports equipment in stores; television, newspaper, and magazine space; the time and money devoted to reporting scores, gossip, highlights of sports events; Olympic games, "battles of the stars," football games on television that sometimes delay all the later shows; the time people spend reading about, watching, and discussing games; statistics and predictions; the teaching of sports to children; the organizing of sports events. If some people are deprived of sports opportunities when they are young, they are less likely to develop the interest or the knowledge needed to participate in this aspect of their culture.

A society comes with rituals and activities and organizations that constitute its civilization. Barring people who live in that society from important aspects of the civilization is unjust, whether or not what they are excluded from has particular value. It is unjust if those activities, as Warren points out, are used as symbols of power, signs of who is allowed to have power. It is also unjust because those people are excluded from an important aspect of the civilization, denied a chance to fully participate in the society, denied these common interests and common experiences with other members of their society, deprived of a chance to learn about those aspects of the society.

Compare sports with subjects taught in schools. One could argue that although literature and history, for example, may be interesting, they are not important for daily life. However, it would be harder to deny their value in allowing people to participate more fully in our culture and civilization. People who do not learn about the Civil War or Tom Sawyer or Romeo and Juliet will not have that information in common with other members of their culture and will not be able to appreciate or understand references to these subjects.

The importance of being able to jog or play softball or tennis with co-workers or to converse intelligently about baseball and football should not be underrated. People who have not played sports are less likely to follow them, which can be a cultural disadvantage as great as if they had never learned any history or literature.[7] It does not matter whether we think sports are culturally worthwhile or not. Merely because sports *are* valued in our society, it is important that people not be denied access to them.

We measure a civilization in terms of the education of its people. And it is not just the number of Nobel laureates who are measured, but the education of all its citizens. A growing illiteracy and school drop-out rate in the United States or a poor performance by US students in world-wide science and math tests are causes for everyone's concern because they indicate a downturn for our society.

Countries are also evaluated by the physical abilities of their citizens. It is a source of pride and patriotism to produce world champions, and it is women who have produced the biggest international wins for the US recently. While this argues for increased opportunity for women athletes, still, unlike the case in education, it is mostly the stars that boost national pride, not the athletic ability of the general population. Increased opportunity for all would increase the pool of potential stars and improve eventual quality. It might also change our criteria for comparing and evaluating other cultures.

Because we do not think of sports participation the way we think of education, we do not value it in the same way. But maybe we should. Consider our concern about poor performance by American children on physical tests, a problem that could be solved by making sports participation more attractive and more widespread, as we try to do with science and math education. Consider our worry about the increasing obesity of US residents. Instead of looking primarily at the eating habits of other countries to try to improve our own, we might do better to increase the sports opportunities and enjoyment for everyone.

By thinking of sports in terms of education, we can benefit from what we have learned about working toward equal opportunity in education to promote equal opportunity in sports. The comparison will help us to evaluate the proposals for providing more sports opportunities for females. For example, many of the educational programs have been attempts to motivate – to get educationally deprived children to want to learn. Perhaps we should spend more energy doing the same in sports – getting sports-deprived children, especially girls, to want to play sports.

Fine, some might say. Equal opportunity is a good thing, but what more do you want to do? We already have Title IX legislation that has led to astonishing increases in women's sports. Since this legislation, the number of high-school girls playing interscholastic sports increased eight times to more than 2.4 million. While the ratio of males to females on athletic scholarships was once 1,000 to 1, it is now roughly 2 to 1.[8] Yet males still participate in sports more, and get more opportunities and encouragement to participate, than do females. How do you change that?

Proposals to Increase Equality

In what follows, we will look at proposals to encourage equal opportunity for sports. On the model of equal opportunity for education, a 2 to 1 ratio of participation by different groups should be cause for alarm, and other programs to encourage the less involved group need to be considered. In what follows, I hope to show that the proposals designed to encourage more girls to play do not require radical changes, nor do they threaten the quality of sports – at least no more than changes and variations that routinely occur in sports.

Allow females access to more kinds of sports

This proposal would go farther than the federal legislation designed to provide equal opportunity for females in school sports. The legislation allows exceptions for certain college sports in the distribution of resources, allowing sex segregation in sports that involve bodily contact and then providing no team organization or coaching for female football, ice hockey, or wrestling, claiming lack of interest. This proposal would merely allow females to participate in all the sports that are now restricted to males, allowing the possibility that a new generation of women skilled in those sports might achieve the same earning power and star power, and become the kind of role models that men in those fields now have. It would remind those who consider female participation in some sports to be inappropriate that before Title IX legislation it was thought inappropriate to have women run the New York City Marathon and inappropriate to let girls play in Little League Baseball. Allowing females access to these sports has changed those beliefs.

Change the rules

Some sports emphasize physical activities that males are more likely to excel in. In order to allow females full participation in such sports – that is, to allow females to participate in those sports even though they may not be as good as the males they play with – some have proposed restructuring scoring techniques and team composition.[9] Unfair, defenders of the status quo would say, forgetting that such scoring techniques already exist – handicaps in golf, for example. Relay races in running, cycling, and swimming add the scores of individual perform-

ers, so that the less skilled members of a team participate with the more skilled to do the best they can. Coed softball and volleyball usually require a certain minimum number of players to be female. Municipal softball leagues have all-female, all-male, and mixed-sex leagues.

Rules of sports are constantly undergoing revision in order to make the games more challenging for players and more interesting to spectators, and in order to better exhibit the skills of the players. The rules of men's lacrosse have changed through the years so that it is more like American football than the original sport. Women's lacrosse remains closer to the original, emphasizing skill in handling the ball and flexibility rather than physical strength and mass. Some children's soccer leagues reduce the number of players and the size of the field to help children learn soccer skills. The height of basketball hoops has been changed through the history of the game. The introduction of the shot clock changed the pace of play. Someone might even want to reconsider the special rules in wrestling and boxing that are designed to protect males' more delicate parts – rules that females would not need.

As it is now, athletes are used to adjusting their play to rule changes, and systems of scoring now exist to allow players at different levels to compete together. Informal games of many kinds are played with whoever shows up, and every school athlete has played in such games. The rules are freely revised to take into account the number of players, the playing field ("If it hits the tree it's a foul"), the level of skill, and anything else that is considered important. People who object to making changes in the standard rules may not realize how very often such rules are altered in practice.

Change the coaching

Some people believe that it is not just the access to sports but the present emphasis on aggression and competition and winning that prevents equal opportunity.[10] As long as sports training emphasizes traits that females are socialized to avoid, they will be at a disadvantage. In order to promote equal opportunity, sports training should emphasize skill and teamwork and personal achievement. Usually this position also argues that it is not just females, but males and the world of sport itself, that would be better off. (This explanation might also claim that a more equal allotment of sports opportunities in the first place would have produced a better attitude about sports – that it is the absence of females from sports that has resulted in this biased emphasis on aggression.)

It is not always easy to recognize how coaching in sports is affected by socialization. I learned through experience that the different expectations we have about boys and girls affect the way they are taught to play games. One season I coached first-, second-, and third-grade girls in soccer. In our town the boys' league did not want to allow girls to play, so the girls formed their own league. In a nearby town that was even smaller than ours, the girls and boys played together, a few girls on each team. At the end of the season, we arranged to play our girls' team against the girls from the teams in the neighboring town, an exhibition game. Our girls won, with the highest score they had had all year. We expected to win, given the magnificent coaching they had received. What surprised us was the difference in the way the two teams played. The girls from the next town were rough, often fouled our players, and broke all sorts of rules. We were astonished and talked to their coaches, people just like us who volunteered to teach kids soccer, some of whom we played soccer with ourselves. We had similar beliefs about how the game should be played. But we had emphasized the rules to our all-girls' team, made sure they knew the proper behavior, been quick to correct them when they were too rough or did something illegal. In contrast the coaches of the teams in the neighboring town, where most of the players were boys, had not been picky about the rules. They thought that these kids were so little they could hardly hurt each other. There were so many things to teach that conveying what counts as a foul could be done later. If we had been coaching boys, we probably would have done the same thing. But we were not coaching boys, so the girls we coached learned to play a different game than the ones who played with boys. We did not do it consciously. We saw little girls tripping and pushing each other as abnormal behavior and corrected it. But our friends in the next town did not see it as abnormal when their little kids, who just happened to be mostly boys, tripped and pushed each other, so they let it go. And since these coaches were *not* sexists, they did not correct the little girls on their teams either. (Interestingly, at a more advanced level, in college soccer, the reverse seems to be true. Referees who are used to male players hardly ever call the fouls that occur in games between females. Perhaps they do not see how these slimmer, smaller bodies can really hurt each other.)

You might think that we, the Northampton coaches, were the sexists, teaching little girls to be too proper and making them unable to adjust to the "real" world of sports, where well-placed fouls are part of game strategy. Don't be too sure that the real world is like that. Remember that our team won. And they won because they learned to pass and dribble around their opponents instead of pushing through them. And if these children grow up to play in the weekend games that we play in, they will all have to learn to play more like our little girls' team. For we adults play without referees and do not want to risk injury, so we stop rough play and call fouls that referees might let go by. Everyone who plays with us learns to play more carefully. Sometimes high-school boys have had trouble adjusting to sports in this real world.

Adding new sports

Some people have proposed that even the sports be changed. Develop new sports that have less emphasis on height and muscle mass and physical brutality and more emphasis on flexibility and skill and endurance.[11] This proposal to develop sports that emphasize women's superior physical abilities seems the most radical and the most difficult to realize. If we have to invent new sports, new forms of physical prowess, just so women can have equal opportunity in sports, such equality is not in the foreseeable future.

At least that is what I thought before I spent a year in China. There I learned that many games and sports in other countries count flexibility and grace more important than stopping power and size. In China students regularly had "slow races" on their bicycles to see who could take the longest time to travel a distance without falling off – once an important skill in the crowded streets of China. And such races elicited the same sort of wild cheers and shouts of encouragement that "fast races" and combat sports do in the United States. Chinese physical education universities train future Olympic hopefuls – in volleyball, crew, swimming – along with participants in sports that would not be seen outside Asia were it not for Kung Fu movies. The fighting and weapons-wielding shown in those movies are learned and practiced at a very early age through elaborately choreographed routines and treated as sports in China.

Eight-year-old girls and boys participate in contests of sword play and martial arts acrobatics, performing feats that seem to require trick photography. The grace and flexibility required for these martial arts are certainly not less difficult to master or less impressive to watch than the field goals and slam-dunks of our popular sports.

If we look around to other countries where women do much or most of the physical labor, it is not hard to find physical skills in which women excel. Remember those pictures of women carrying huge loads on their heads?

Studies have shown that these women expend far less energy and use up fewer calories and so can carry heavier loads farther than even the strongest men. It would not be hard to work that skill into a game or a contest, one in which those women, because of their daily activities if nothing else, would have an advantage. New sports would not be hard to find.

Summary

I have compared sports with education, citing the benefits of sports to the development of the individual, the full participation in a country's culture, and the evaluation of a culture. I have claimed that knowledge and interest and basic ability in sports are as important for getting along in daily life in our society as knowledge and interest and basic ability in many academic subjects. The purpose of the analogy was to help us see the many values in sports participation and encourage us to think of sports participation as something that everyone, and not just the talented few, should enjoy.

People resist making changes, and without good reasons to change, they would rather keep things the way they are. The ideal of equal opportunity works as a good reason for changes in education. Similarly, the ideal of equal opportunity can be used to motivate changes in sports in order to increase participation for everyone.

Notes

An earlier version of this paper was given as a talk and published in *Rethinking College Athletics*, eds Judith Andre and David N. James (Philadelphia, PA: Temple University Press, 1991), pp. 210–20. The revisions were prompted by comments from Bob Cohen and George Robinson, for which I thank them both.

1   Donald Kennedy, quoted in Douglas Hofstadter, "Metamagical Themas: 'Default Assumptions' and their Effects on Writing and Thinking," *Scientific American*, 247 (November 1982), p. 36.

2   Bob Cohen pointed out that entertainment is very important in the US, its stars are well paid, etc., but it does not follow that acting lessons should be provided for everyone. If people without acting experience were unlikely to enjoy performances, then perhaps we would have to consider this suggestion.

3   G. Ann Uhlir, "Athletes and the University: The Post-Woman's Era," *Academe*, 73 (July–August 1987), pp. 25–9.

4   Judith Andre and David James, editors of *Rethinking College Athletics*, mentioned these benefits.

5   *Newsweek* reports that Jack Nassar, a top executive at Ford Motor Company, said "that playing sports as a kid – particularly Australian 'football' with its loose rules – prepared him well for the top

job. 'It's a very practical education system for growing potential leaders,' he said" (January 17, 2000, p. 52).

6 See Mary Anne Warren, "Justice and Gender in School Sports," in *Women, Philosophy, and Sport: A Collection of New Essays*, ed. Betsy C. Postow (Metuchen, NJ: Scarecrow Press, 1983).

7 A qualification to this claim: as long as a subculture of our society, such as that of women, is denied access to sports, then sports will be unimportant for participation *in that subculture*. But the same holds true for education: illiteracy and undereducation create a subculture that one does not need an education to belong to.

8 "Achieving Success under Title IX" at: http://www.ed.gov/pubs/TitleIX/part5.html (June 1997).

9 Warren, "Justice and Gender," pp. 12–35.

10 See Mary A. Boutilier and Lucinda SanGiovanni, *The Sporting Woman* (Champaign, IL: Human Kinetics, 1983).

11 See Jane English, "Sex Equality in Sports," *Philosophy and Public Affairs*, 7, 3 (Spring 1978), pp. 269–77 (reprinted here as reading 23); and J. Theodore Klein, "Philosophy of Education, Physical Education, and the Sexes," in Postow, *Women, Philosophy, and Sport*, pp. 207–30; also Betsy C. Postow, "Women and Masculine Sports," *Journal of the Philosophy of Sport*, 7 (1980), pp. 51–8.

CHAPTER 3

Moral Development and Sport: Character and Cognitive Developmentalism Contrasted

Carwyn Jones and Mike McNamee

Introduction

The relationship between playing sport and the development of a sound moral character is about as old a chestnut as any educator is likely to find. And time itself has seen no conclusive answers to the issue. In this reading, we discuss critically a recent and growing trend in social scientific research that has marshaled empirical evidence to make the case for the educational value of sporting engagement. We offer a critique of the methodological and moral commitments it makes within the research particularly relating to its picture of character and virtue. In contrast, we offer an older, unscientific, account of sport's potential to develop characters of virtue rather than vice.

Contextualization: Education, Moral Development, and the Value of Sports

Both education and sports serve a variety of goals and purposes that may either be inherent, instrumental, or relational. That is to say, we may think of the purposes of education and of sports as relating to their very nature, to external things beyond those natures, or to both. Liberal educators have argued that educational activities and processes are by definition inherently valuable and intellectual in character. Sports, taken

as paradigms of bodily activity, are thought to have little or no educational value in themselves but may be valued only as a means to other "serious" ends such as health, socialization, group cohesion, identity formation, and, of course, moral development (McNamee, 1998; McNamee and Jones, 1999). Characteristically, the nature of this relation is seen as one of instrumentality: sports are just one means among others to achieving these goals. And we should be clear that to value sports as mere instruments is to relegate that value; to make it conditional upon successful, effective, and economic criteria by which success or failure would be measured. Now sports may be valued and valuable in precisely this instrumental manner, but to consider them under that description is to ignore two important dimensions of an argument that requires some clarification before we proceed. While we do not aim to demonstrate here the educational value of sports (cf. Carr, 1998; McNamee, 1998), it is worth observing that to consider whether sports are educational, morally educational, or morally developmental,[1] by their very natures or merely as neutral means to an end, is to ignore the dimension of the subject who plays them. Sports can be played and taught badly or well according to the motives, aspirations, and character of those who play, teach, and coach them.

If we agree in principle that sports may have moral developmental potential inherently, instrumentally, or relationally, it would be as well to ask what kind of tasks and achievements we could think of as educational. For, in education, a variety of aims may legitimately be sought: from blind to critical habituation, simple and complex attitude formation, basic and advanced knowledge and skill development, character development, and beyond to wisdom and understanding things in the round. Moral development, as one of a family of educational processes, could therefore aim at any (and presumably) all of these states of affairs. Characteristically, moral educators have been persuaded by the dominance of one of these models at the expense of others. That model revolves around the development of knowledge and understanding of moral rules to govern actions that are thought to be universalizable, action-guiding, and impartially applied. This common and commonsensical approach might be criticized by persons other than philosophers or educators: "What place should be given to feelings and emotions?", a parent or coach might ask. Are moral knowledge and understanding to be tied only to acts of cognition? Understanding moral rules is one thing, the parent or coach might say; caring about and acting on them is quite another. A picture of moral development arising from the questions asked above, will be developed in the course of this reading. For the moment, it is important to bear in mind the diversity these questions point toward, since they are easily forgotten when one moves from the practical affairs of moral development to their supporting or justifying moral theoretical positions. Proponents are apt to argue that moral development is essentially about cognitive development, or essentially about affective or character development, and so on. The debate amongst educators, professional and lay, is easily polarized and made dichotomous. In contrast, we will argue for a moderately eclectic position that makes central the development of virtue, thought of as a combination of emotional, cognitive, and deliberative capacities which are the bases of moral development in and through sports.

Having set out a picture of the bases of moral development, however brief, we have assumed thus far that the object of such development, the "moral," is unproblematic. Yet this assumption is itself problematical. A few words of clarification are all that will be permitted here. For precisely how we are to think of ethics, conceived of as the systematic enquiry into morals, is largely a function of a particular perspective or group of them. An especially brutish way of separating the items on the spectrum might be to think of a classification against which one thought moral action and character to be governed either by rules (of a special kind) or by the context or situation. There is an all-too-obvious relation between the former view of ethics and a widespread understanding of sports as a paradigm of rule-governed activities. But there is an equally widespread view of sports as a universal situation or context for character development. How are we to think of their relations, or to characterize an accommodation of these views without a loss of integrity?

Sports Ethics

Ethical sports as ethical rule following

Suits'(1988) classic essay attempts to elucidate the necessary and sufficient conditions of sport. He identified a number of elements that if collectively present in an activity would allow us to confidently call that activity "sport." To begin with, Suits argued that all sports are particular types of games. Games qualify as sports if they involve physical skill and achieve a certain level of institutional stability. His account of games is particularly informative in the present context. Games, Suits suggests, all have a certain specifiable goal, whether it be to get a ball in a goal in soccer, or bankrupt your opponents in Monopoly. Unlike other activities such as cleaning, getting to work on time, and writing book chapters, the goal in a game is achieved in a peculiarly specific way. The means employed are restrictive and always complicate the task by making the achievement of the goal more difficult. It is in the prescription of allowable means that the rules play their primary role: "The rules of a game are, in effect, proscriptions of certain means useful in achieving pre-lusory goals"

(Suits, 1988, p. 41). Suits calls these rules "constitutive rules" because they constitute or define the game, telling competitors what to do and the limits within which they can do it. Given the central definitive nature of rules, Suits (1988, p. 41) argues that "to break a constitutive rule is to fail to play the game at all." To play a game according to Suits is therefore to volunteer to try to achieve a certain goal in accordance with certain specified rules that restrict the legitimate means for its achievement. Given this, there is a school of thought that argues that certain moral implications arise from playing games. On the one hand, certain rules prohibit dangerous behavior in sports, such as high tackles in rugby and two-footed lunges in soccer. On the other hand, the decision to play the game engenders in itself a tacit obligation to abide by its rules. The obligation is grounded in either or both of the following:

1   The rules of sport are premised on the principle of fairness. Breaking the rules, therefore, changes the balance of the game illegitimately, violating the principle of fairness; all competitors are afforded fair and equal treatment in the pursuit of victory.
2   The decision to play is seen as a kind of tacit promise to the sporting community as a whole to abide by the rules. To break the rules, therefore, is to renege on this promise. To break the rules is to violate moral principles and/or break a promise, both of which are morally inappropriate. Playing sport on this account is minimally an exercise in moral development.

Sports as virtue developing

The formal properties of sport, however, are not as important as the way it is practiced. Sport is a complex cultural practice that is neither entirely synonymous with the rest of society nor separate from it. In recent years it has become fashionable for philosophers of sports to think of them not in a purely analytical fashion as activities to which criteria such as being rule-governed, play, and competitiveness apply (cf. Suits 1988). Many philosophers of sport (Burke, 1997;

Butcher and Schneider, 1998; Gibson, 1993; McNamee, 1995) have come to appreciate the analysis of the concept of sport in terms of broader social and historical evolutions. That is to say, they have socialized and historicized their conceptual analyses of sports. Most recently, and following the work of Alisdair MacIntyre (1986), they have come to think of sports as paradigmatic examples of "practices." To do so is to recognize the essentially social character of the activities in and through which goods definitive of the activity (speed, skill, strength, tactical imagination, and so on) and consequent upon it (money, status, peer esteem, and so on) are required and developed. In that development, the cultivation of certain virtues, such as trust, courage, and fairness, is paradoxically both a necessary condition and a consequence of proper engagement. In such an account we can think of sports in terms of a human, or moral, or character laboratory (McFee, 2000; Parry, 1988) where one tests oneself and one's competitors in order to find one's limitations in pursuit of the ends of the game. Having sketched out a contrastive model of these two bald possibilities for moral development in sports, it is necessary to dig a little deeper to find their theoretical roots.

Moral Development: The Cognitivist Tradition

Moral development as cognitive development

Academic debates in moral development have until recently been conducted almost exclusively from within the cognitive developmental tradition of psychology. The epistemology and methodology that Kohlberg (1981), its chief architect, constructed on firm experimental footings achieved and maintains hegemonic status, especially in the United States. Kohlberg proposed a theory of moral development that brought together the moral insights of the great eighteenth-century German philosopher Immanuel Kant and the British philosopher Richard Hare with the Swiss genetic psychologist Jean Piaget's account of cognitive development. The result is a comprehensive and empirically supported theory of moral development that purportedly avoids the antagonistic educational heresies of indoctrination and subjectivism.

Prior to Kohlberg's celebrated research, Piaget (1932) as part of his general investigations into child development examined the development of moral judgment. Piaget believed that morality consisted of a system of rules. Moral development therefore was closely related to both the obedience to, and understanding of, moral rules. Piaget observed children playing marbles in order to comprehend their understanding of these rules. From his observations he found that immature children believed that a higher authority constructs rules. The rules of the game, like moral rules, must be obeyed to avoid incurring punishment. Mature children, however, were more autonomous, engaging in rule construction and adherence to create fair contests. Moreover, mature rule adherence was based on an understanding of the importance of fairness rather than avoidance of censure. Piaget thus defined moral maturity in terms of the understanding of, and autonomous obedience to, moral rules. Given these findings, moral development for Piaget is essentially a process of getting children to obey, by understanding the sanctity of moral rules.

In keeping with the Piagetian paradigm, Kohlberg (1981) similarly proposed that the defining feature of moral maturity is autonomy. Kohlberg, however, talked less about rules and more of moral principles. A person's understanding of these principles is revealed by the quality of the moral judgments he or she makes. Autonomous or mature judgments are characteristically impartial; they give equal consideration to the feelings, wants, and desires of all that may be affected by the judgment. In essence, morally mature judgments are paradigmatically fair or just. As mentioned, such views are firmly located in the broad deontological (duty-based) tradition of moral philosophy. Moral goodness is reducible to doing the "right thing," which is defined by moral rules or principles. For both Kohlberg and Piaget, moral development is a species of cognitive development that deals with moral propositions and problems rather than problems of time, space, and causality.

Piaget and Kohlberg believed that there were identifiable and sequential stages to moral development. Immaturity characterized by an egocentric perspective may develop, given the right circumstances, sequentially into a fully differentiated perspective. Piaget (1932) described the development in two distinct stages. Kohlberg's (1981) more discerning analysis comprised a six-stage sequence. Moral development was essentially a process whereby simple cognitive structures from which immature egocentric judgments result, given conducive conditions, are supplanted by complex and differentiated cognitive structures capable of mature, autonomous moral judgments. It is important to note that moral development is not the simple acquisition of moral knowledge. Development is defined by a structural difference in the mode of understanding revealed in judgment. It is not the particular issue addressed by a judgment that gives it its moral status. It matters not whether the judgment is made in respect of an act of cruelty or loyalty. Rather, what does matter is the form of the judgment. Kohlberg argues, in characteristic deontological fashion, that it is the universalizable, action-guiding, and impartial nature of the judgment that qualifies it as moral, and not the particular issue that it addresses. Given Kohlberg's epistemological commitments, any given person's moral maturity is to be gauged by examining the form that her or his judgments take. This in turn indicates the individual's stage of moral development. Moreover, Kohlberg (1981) argued that researchers could reliably assess moral maturity vis-à-vis moral judgments in response to hypothetical moral dilemmas.

The cognitivist tradition and moral development in sport

At first sight, and for many at second, third, and fourth visits, Kohlberg's (1981) theory provides an excellent implement for defining and measuring moral maturity and development. As such it was employed by Bredemeier and Shields (and their various co-researchers) to shed light on the issue of sport involvement and moral development. In their early research they remained loyal to Kohlberg's methodology, using it to compare and contrast athletes' and non-athletes' reasoning about sport-specific and non-sports moral dilemmas. Bredemeier and Shields (1984) found that judgments made in response to sport dilemmas were characteristically egocentric and less mature than reasoning about non-sports dilemmas. Moreover, in certain cases, those who spend much of their time playing sport exhibit this moral immaturity in their everyday lives. These initial results did not bode well for sport. They suggest that playing certain sports, rather than contributing to the development of a more mature moral judgment, may detract from such development: "In summary, results generally confirmed the hypothesis that hypothetical sport dilemmas would elicit lower levels of moral reasoning than dilemmas presented within an everyday life context" (Bredemeier and Shields, 1984, p. 355). Bredemeier and Shields (1984) concluded that the rule-governed nature of sports serves to create a special context that was typically detrimental to the exhibition of moral maturity. Rather than encourage autonomy, sport engagement discourages it, at least whilst playing sport. It is thought that the strict rule-governed nature of sport, the role of the umpire, referee, or officials in determining lawful behavior, and the instrumental nature of sport encourage a kind of arrested sense of responsibility. Rules are to be obeyed to ensure victory and/or avoid censure.

Rather than naively condemning sports, Shields and Bredemeier (1995) came to question the efficacy of their adopted methodology. From their observations and from conversations with athletes, they realized that the moral engagement and interaction involved in sport are not simply reducible to moral judgments, and particular nuances of the sports' context may inhibit moral action in a number of ways. The researchers therefore moved to a more comprehensive account of morality that focused on character rather than moral maturity to investigate sport and moral development.

Shields and Bredemeier's model of moral action

Although Shields and Bredemeier's definition of character has a firm footing in the cognitive tradition of Piaget and Kohlberg, it has a more eclectic flavor and draws on influences from diverse psychological traditions. The researchers' definition of character is constructed around a complex model of moral action influenced by Rest (1984). According to Shields and Bredemeier (1995), there are four important processes to examine. These are not definitive psychic processes that occur necessarily in a strict temporal sequence. Rather, they are best viewed as a heuristic analytical sequence. Shields and Bredemeier (1995, p. 85), however, argue that "there is a kind of logical progression among the processes so that it makes sense – for the purposes of analysis – to divide the processes leading to moral action in the manner described." The four processes in question are: (1) "interpretation," (2) "judgment," (3) "value selection," and (4) "implementing action." Thus:

1   Interpretation is the process in which a person identifies the important moral cues present in the situation. Certain manifest features frame, define, or characterize the given situation as being of moral significance.
2   The second process is a cognitive one of making a moral judgment. The kind of moral judgment made depends on the moral maturity of the person.
3   The third process involves choosing a value that will reflect the moral judgment and guide action.
4   The final process is implementation of a moral response, to act in a way that reflects the judgment made and the value chosen.

The four processes Shields and Bredemeier articulate are the backbone of the model. They form the first of three tiers of a complex model of moral action. The second tier aims to encapsulate the various contextual and psychological capacities that impact each of the steps in moral action. These are introduced in order to explain the discrepancies in moral reasoning between athletes and non-athletes, within and outside the sports context. These variables are classified under one of the following three categories: context, personal competencies, and ego processes. In this model, contextual factors refer to the qualities of the given situation, for example the composition of the team, the perceived goals, the prevailing "moral atmosphere," and so forth. The "personal competencies" refer to the qualities of the agent that will allow him or her to either interpret, judge, select a value, or act. Essentially, the "personal competencies" to which Shields and Bredemeier refer are those which under-gird general maturity and complexity of moral understanding. These first two variables are fairly straightforward. The final category of variables, "ego processes," is a psychoanalytic feature first seen in Haan's (1978) theory of morality. These variables deserve a special mention in this context.

Haan's theory, although heavily influenced by Kohlberg, differed in certain important ways. First, she argued that moral maturity was characterized by the ability to construct fair and impartial solutions in a process of moral dialog. Moreover, Haan argued that moral judgment was a far more context-sensitive construct than Kohlberg suggested. She believed that it was to be expected that intersubjective moral maturity scores would vary depending on the context. This difference in the quality of a given person's moral judgments is explained by Haan with reference to certain psychic capacities or "ego processes." Haan argues that different situations, especially unfamiliar or new ones, may lead to stress. The "ego processes" describe the way in which contextually induced stress is managed and how it affects moral judgment. Stress is dealt with by employing either "ego defensive" or "ego coping" techniques. Both are made use of in order to preserve, maintain, and sustain one's self-image or ego. However, coping strategies are conducive to morally mature judgments, whereas defending strategies are often deleterious to such judgments. The use of defensive strategies such as denial and repression often results in less adequate moral reasoning.

Conversely, someone who remains in control or "coping" is more likely to reason consistently, unhampered or unhindered by the contextual factors. Shields and Bredemeier embrace the importance of "ego processes" in explaining moral action, suggesting that they play a key role in the consistent and mature display of morally mature action in sport. "Ego processes" are therefore incorporated into the model of moral action. To summarize, the second tier is a categorization of the factors distinct from (but including) cognitive capacities that work to affect the maturity of moral action.

The last tier is peculiar inasmuch as it deviates from cognitive developmental tradition by outlining a supplementary account of virtues. These function to facilitate mature moral action through the model. Talk of virtues was anathema for Kohlberg (1981) in formulating his theory of moral development, which was constructed partly in response to the fatal flaws he saw in the traditional virtue approach. Kohlberg (1981, p. 9) referred to character development in terms of cultivating certain virtues as the "relativistic bag of virtues approach." He rejected this approach on two grounds. First, he argued that it was unduly subjective and therefore fatally compromised its use in any formal educational sense. "One difficulty with this approach is that everyone has his own bag," he argued (ibid.). Second, there is no real consensus as to the actual meaning of trait names such as integrity: "What is one person's 'integrity' is another person's 'stubbornness'" (ibid.). Kohlberg (1981) craved a single ideal moral standard that served as the goal for moral education and the basis for moral evaluation.

It is significant, therefore, that Shields and Bredemeier (1995) should look to certain virtues to supplement Kohlberg's original theory. The main role of the virtues, however, is to ensure, or increase the likelihood, that any given person acts in a morally mature way despite all the possible distractions; problems and factors that have been described or categorized above. The virtues they describe are "compassion," "fairness," "sportspersonship," and "integrity." They take their definition of virtues from Erikson (1964) and define them as strengths that animate moral principles. These four, if present, according to Shields and Bredemeier (1995, p. 192), "facilitate the consistent display of moral action." Shields and Bredemeier (1995, p. 198) summarize moral character as a composite of four virtues, namely compassion, fairness, sportspersonship, and integrity. Moreover, "each virtue is premised on a set of psychological competencies, some of which develop through a regular, age-related sequence of stages or phases. Each virtue extends the underlying competencies by placing them in the service of moral action" (ibid.).

A person's moral responses reflect the co-operative employment of these virtues. Those who favour a cognitivist explanation characterize morally mature sportspersons as players who are capable of acting in a fair way. The virtues are an additional requirement that facilitate morally mature action even in difficult circumstances. Shields and Bredemeier argue that sport necessarily contributes to character. They suggest that a person exhibits her or his character in the process of playing. Moreover, every display of character contributes to character: "When action is taken, the consequences of that action provide feedback to the actor and other observers of the act. The feedback then informs future action" (1995, p. 217). The important issue for the development of moral character is the nature and quality of this feedback. As far as moral development is concerned, a positive sporting experience is fundamental. The provision of this positive experience essentially involves a two-pronged attack. The first aims at developing the required moral maturity necessary to make judgments that instantiate the principle of fairness. The second aims to develop the executive virtues of compassion, fairness, sportspersonship, and integrity that mediate the appropriate response in the often ambiguous context of sports.

Although this model marks a significant move away from Kohlberg's original theory, it remains faithful to it in an important way. The cornerstone of moral character is the impartial application of moral rules. There is a supplementary but severely truncated account of virtues, four of which are instrumental for

mature action. We hope to illustrate the deficiencies of such an account in the next section.

Moral Development as the Development of Character

The goal of moral development

Character has traditionally been discussed in the vocabulary of virtues and vices. Laymen and women, irrespective of Piaget and Kohlberg's discoveries, still describe their friends and heroines as kind and generous, their enemies as mean and cruel. Modernity, however, has seen the constriction of this vocabulary, and character has been redescribed in terms of moral judgment. In Kohlberg's (1981) cognitive development theory, this reduction reaches its climax, where character is essentially defined in terms of a singular virtue, namely justice or, more precisely, "justice reasoning." This clearly identifies an objective and standard moral minimum by which all can be judged. There are a number of good reasons to expand the vocabulary once more and add to (rather than subtract from) the palette available for character assessment. In the previous section we noted how Shields and Bredemeier (1995) in particular saw the need to expand upon, but remain faithful to, Kohlberg's cognitive development account by supplementing it with virtues. In this section we examine an account which has a more plural view of moral values and a less reductive one of moral character. The account is firmly located in the neo-Aristotelian tradition.

One significant difference in this tradition is the rejection of a singular, overarching concept of the morally right, howsoever it is defined.[2] Attempts at characterizing moral goodness in this reductive way are numerous. Utilitarians have defined moral goodness in terms of happiness. Persons are therefore praised or derided with respect to the contribution their actions make to the promotion of happiness. A person who gives to charity is commended because his actions increase the happiness of all by relieving the misery of those in need. A person who is fair is commended because her actions contribute to the happiness of those subject to discrimination, and so on. Deontologists, as we have noted, exalt persons who dutifully live according to the requirements of moral principles. Both these theories aim to provide rational, action-guiding maxims that transcend all particularities, whether of contexts or of persons. They tell us what we should do, or what we ought to do, in the complex moral milieu of everyday life.

It is clear why moral judgment takes center stage as the most important capacity for moral agents. Good judgment is what is required when attempting to arrive at a solution to a moral dilemma or moral problem. It is knowledge of moral rules and principles and the application via good judgment that inform the deontologist of what ought to be done in the particular situation at hand. It is the same for the utilitarian. It is knowledge and good judgment, therefore, that are most commonly the focus of moral development theorists.

Virtue-based accounts of moral character and moral education will differ significantly from that outlined in the previous section. Moral goodness is not defined in relation to a system of rules or principles. Standards of moral goodness are deeply entrenched in institutions and social practices. It is the rules, conventions, traditions, and ethos of these practices that, to a large extent, define moral goodness. It is in the context of social practices like sport, rather than in universal principles from which systematic action can be deduced, that character is developed and displayed. The idea is at least as old as Aristotle. The position, and its disavowal of the universalized rule approach, are caught well in a celebrated essay by McDowell:

> The best generalizations about how one should behave hold only for the most part. If one attempted to reduce one's conception of what virtue requires to a set of rules, then, however subtle and thoughtful one was in drawing up the code, cases would inevitably turn up in which a mechanical application of the rules would strike one as wrong – and not necessarily because one had changed one's mind; rather, one's mind on the

matter was not susceptible of capture in any universal formula. (1989, p. 93)

As we have noted, Shields and Bredemeier display some sensitivity to this difficulty but fail to address it head on. We will argue that sports are special contexts, which, though not excusing vicious or violent acts, can allow us to accommodate norms of acceptable conduct and character that might not hold in other spheres of life. And these will become apparent when we foreground the notion of characters in contexts. So, an appeal to character as a fundamental component of moral development is based on both negative and positive reasons. The negative critique rests on the inadequacy of universalized moral prescriptions for behavior that fail to take account of the particulars of situations and how these are to be accommodated in action. More positively, a focus on character traditionally speaks to two lacunae of moral cognitivism. First, some people genuinely do not perceive the salient characteristics of situations; some features just do not register on their horizon of significance. Second, cognitivism is standardly criticized for saying nothing regarding the problem of the weakness of will: many a time sportspersons *know* what they should and should not do; they merely do not possess the character to do it or not do it. It is clear that Shields and Bredemeier's model attempts to address these issues from one direction, namely the addition of the four virtues understood in an executive mode. We shall try another.

The nature of moral character

Explanations of vicious or virtuous sporting action in mass media rarely rise above empty or banal generalizations. Sport in particular is a context where reaction is as prominent as action. There is often little time for considered judgment. Shields and Bredemeier's model does not sufficiently acknowledge this fact. Although the four processes are separated for analytical purposes, they fail heuristically to capture the nature of moral action in sports. Other aspects of a person's character must figure more prominently. Shields and Bredemeier (1995) recognize that good judgment is not a sufficient condition for good character, and they import the four virtues that purportedly buttress this cognitive capacity. These four virtues, however, only serve to paper over the cracks in Kohlbergian theory. Their description as mediating capacities is significantly deficient in ways revelatory of a limited conception of virtue and character. Specifically, there is a need to revisit the concept of character in order to contextualize a preferred alternative.

First, we should say that the terms "character" and "trait" are close relations. Both terms have their home in cognate fields; "character" is drawn from the practice of engraving, while "trait" derives from drawing (Peters, 1981). While cognitivists tend, like rule-based moral theorists, to focus on moral and immoral action, a focus on character and virtue leads us to consider wider questions about the self and identity that are wrapped up in a person's sense of who she or he is and what he or she aspires to be (however critical or uncritical that may be). So the significance of character traits, some though not all of which are virtues, is primarily adverbial. Terms like "conscientious," "careful," "callous," or "courageous" tell us how a person pursues certain goals or ends. Of course, there are different and perfectly natural ways of talking of character. We talk of character fairly descriptively as the sum of a person's traits; of being in and out of character; of being a "bit of a character"; of being a weak or a strong character. The sense that we wish to draw attention to here is that wherein the notion of character plays a critical integrating and coherency function in a person's life and especially within the practices of sport.

Thus, it cannot merely be the case that we wish to have strong characters. Mussolini and Hitler had no deficiencies in this respect. Strength and goodness of character are independent. But there is a point at which in our moral development of the young, through sports and other practices, we must draw this out. For it is not possible, as Kupperman (1991, p. 15) points out, to have a strong character and to blow with the wind; to abandon one's projects and commitments at the drop of a hat. There is a

close resemblance between this point and the characteristic picture of the moral agent in Aristotle; one who acts in accordance with his nature, which is productive of a firm and unchanging character already charged with moral force. But this is to jump ahead of ourselves. More needs to be said about virtuous character.

The specific nature of the dispositions we call virtues is both heterogeneous and complex. What is clear is that the virtues are not simply executive in nature. They are not limited to the functions of correct interpretation in preparation for judgment, or merely to the facilitation or implementation of that judgment in action. Different kinds of people experience different kinds of moral problems depending on the type of people they are and the kinds of values they cherish. Those who value honesty characteristically recognize breaches of honesty and act in order to remedy these, while those who do not value it fail even to see a potential dishonesty (and therefore necessarily fail to remedy the situation). Lying is a concern for honest, truthful people, deception is an issue for fair people, and cowardice is problematic for the courageous. These moral problems commonly fail to register with the cruel, vengeful, and deceptive. Similarly, violent play rarely troubles the reckless as it does the considerate. A person's character therefore defines what she or he perceives, feels, and thinks, as well as how she or he acts. The virtues are not just instrumental in fulfilling *a priori* obligations in problematic situations. They do not simply help us to choose the fair act over the selfish, to obey rather than break the rules. Such questions only arise for certain kinds of people. It would be counterintuitive to praise someone who valued honesty, had a mature and autonomous appreciation of honesty, and yet could never bring himself to act honestly. So in sport we are wary of players who maintain in principle that their play is fair but who continually break the rules and have a poor disciplinary record. Claims that action was accidental or unintentional must be weighed against the players' clumsiness, recklessness, and overenthusiasm; their characteristic modes of action.

A central point about virtue, then, is that it is a *disposition* to act in a certain way. It is a special kind of *habit*; one difficult to obtain and to break. Using a virtue vocabulary, as we have seen, provides us with a wider range of ascriptions for people's moral and immoral action. Virtues are not, however, habitual in the sense of rubbing one's nose when tired or biting one's nails when nervous. They are complex, partly open-ended dispositions, not mere physical reactions. They are both cognitive and affective in nature; they facilitate action both from good sound reasons and from strong passions. Rorty and Wong (1997, p. 26) argue that virtues:

> affect what is (perceptually, imaginatively, emotionally and cognitively) salient to an agent. In directing interpretations of situations and affecting the associations that such interpretations generate, central identity traits form (what might be called) the problematics of an agent's experience. They propel an agent into certain sorts of situations and problems, and they provide a relevant selector among a relatively indefinite number of action routines that might be elicited in any given situation.

Given this heterogeneity there is a plethora of virtuous and vicious responses that may or may not be elicited.[3] The appropriateness of the response is partly determined by the social context *and* by the person who offers it. Careful consideration of the contours of a given situation must feature in a moral evaluation. Moral evaluation is more complicated under the auspices of virtue ethics because there are neither rules nor clear-cut guidelines.

Moral development as the cultivation of character

Given the nature of moral character, its development can be viewed as a parallel process. There are two important components to character development: imitation and initiation. The first concerns how a child starts to learn the simple and basic conventions of the world into which it has been born. This is essentially a process of simple imitation:

one learns to be virtuous the same way one learns to cook, dance, play football and so forth, and that is by imitating people who are good at those sorts of things. Since being moral means learning how to do the right thing, it seems to me not at all logically odd to argue that learning how to be moral is strictly analogous to all other cases of learning how to ... moral agents learn best when they act like people who exemplify what is expected of them. (Alderman, 1997, p. 156)

As the child grows, however, the conventions become more complex. Nevertheless, the process of education is similar: one observes and attempts to emulate experienced practitioners. The experienced practitioner initiates the novice into the practice, introducing its conventions, norms, values, and traditions. When entering a practice, one subjects oneself to its authority and standards. Moreover, as MacIntyre (1986) argues, one enters a relationship with those that have practiced before and shaped the moral and technical excellences of the practice. It is both from current exemplars and from the tradition of the practice that one must learn appropriate conduct. The development of moral character occurs in social situations, including practices, in much the same way.

The experienced practitioner, therefore, adopts the mantle of the moral exemplar, and through observing and interacting with a moral exemplar one begins to develop similar characteristics. By observing the moral exemplar, one experiences appropriate moral responses in appropriate situations; it is partly within and in relation to the social practices that such appropriateness is defined and necessarily born of (often bitter) experience. Trait names, such as integrity, responsibility, and reliability, and their appropriateness in our evaluations of persons must be defined partly in relation to the conventions and traditions of the practice. In sport a player is not called a cheat or a bad sport simply in reference to moral principles. Unsporting conduct is conduct unbecoming one who plays sport. So, in golf it is distracting a player who is taking a shot; in tennis it is delaying the play by changing rackets constantly; in almost all sports disputing the official's decision is condemned, but officials are more tolerant in soccer than in rugby. The point is that such evaluations are made against an understanding of the formal and informal norms and traditions that are meaningful in given sports.[4]

Moral Development in Sport

One can see that what we will require of the young is that they become committed to sports *as moral practices*. We want them to become, and only to become, developed persons of virtuous character who become initiated and committed to those practices only as they ought to be played, and not in the shabby ways that they are often portrayed by the various institutions that would corrupt them for external ends. And how is this to be achieved? This is, of course, *the* question. What will have emerged here is merely suggestive of a picture of engagement, development, and education that is based not simply upon consideration of moral rules to be rationally discerned, to be effected in the face of our desires or inclinations, impartially and with universal application. Attention must be paid to the here and now, which is at the same time a product of history, tradition, and initiation.

Scruton (1986) captures the point of critical initiation into a practice through received traditions, which serves as a perfect starting point for the ethical potential of sports. Though he speaks of the rule-governed and governing nature of legal action, we do well to remember that human action in sport is both constrained *and* enabled by its very rules, in their letter and their spirit:

It is of the essence of a tradition that it is alive, that it grows, develops and declines, in obedience to the inner determination of its nature. A tradition exploits the freedom of its participants: they grow into it, but adapt it through their participation. A model for this kind of development is provided by the tradition of common

law, which is neither a habit, nor merely a custom, and still less a body of rules. It is a developing way of seeing the social world, and redefines the place of the individual in that world by responding to and influencing his [*sic*] own image. (Scruton, 1986, p. 221)

Within this picture of the importance of practices and traditions we have begun to adumbrate here, there is a picture of virtue as a way of orienting oneself in the (sports) world; of standing for, and on, what one feels and how one sees sports *as* moral enterprises. The *moral* virtues that are often referred to under the umbrella of sporting behavior are revealed in acts of fair play. Such virtues as magnanimity, fairness, politeness, respect for rules, and cooperation are the qualities of character displayed and developed by those who play well. Often these virtues and their exhibition are the hardy perennials that have become embedded in and partly define the traditions of sport that are produced and reproduced by those who play. The codes of conduct in cricket, for example, have been observed for over a century. The tradition of walking from the crease when one knows that one has touched the ball into the wicket-keeper's gloves, despite the umpire's not knowing, the paradigmatic exhibition of sportsmanship, is only now under threat from the corrupting influence of the media and the commercialization of the game. And it is this picture of a practice suffused with ethical notions at its core that is the one to be celebrated, imitated, and emulated by players, coaches, teachers, maybe even the cynical media, if sports are to flourish.

The ability of sport to function as a nursery to cultivate these other moral virtues depends significantly on the health of particular practices. If sport is more a brutal battle than robust rivalry and the players are sworn enemies rather than rivals, then there is some doubt about the validity of the old adage about learning the lessons of life on the playing field. If, however, the practice is followed in a way that allows these virtues to flourish, and practitioners set good examples rather than bad ones, there is no *prima facie* reason to reject the old adage. It is the health of the values, virtues, and traditions that are produced and reproduced, the actual playing of the game rather than its formal structure defined by its rules, that will tell us if it's good for us. Practices that characteristically call for vices rather than virtues for successful participation are unlikely to promote positive attributes. Activities such as torture require undesirable traits in those who excel. In sport, however, if the ethos of the activity is characterized by egoism, unfairness, malice, aggression, and violence, and it is engaged in by persons who exhibit these vices, then similarly such a practice is unlikely to be a fertile ground for character development. Edmund Pincoffs (1986) once remarked that moral development might largely consist in not becoming a person with these and other vices. Keeping the rules of sport, playing the game both literally and metaphorically, can be thought of as a valuable first step in this direction.

Notes

1   We will here draw no hard and fast distinctions between moral education and moral development, though for other purposes that might be important. See instead Peters (1974). We will refer throughout predominantly to moral development.
2   Critics sympathetic and antipathetic to virtue theory might dispute the particular account of virtue theory espoused here. Some will argue that the virtues can all be characterized under a single super-virtue such as wisdom, while others focus on their sometimes oppositional nature. Time and space, however, do not permit further comment here.
3   For an example of what this might entail see McNamee (2002).
4   For an account of how formal norms and the less formal ethos of sports can support fair play therein, see Loland and McNamee (2000).

Bibliography

Alderman, H. (1997) "By Virtue of a Virtue," in D. Statman (ed.), *Virtue Ethics: A Critical Reader.* Edinburgh: Edinburgh University Press.
Bredemeier, B.J. and Shields, D.L. (1984) "Divergence in Moral Reasoning about Sports and Everyday Life," *Sociology of Sport Journal* 1: 348–57.
Burke, M. (1997) "Drugs in Sport: Have they Practiced Too Hard?," *Journal of the Philosophy of Sport* XXIV: 47–66
Butcher, R. and Schneider, A. (1998) "Fair Play as Respect for the Game," *Journal of the Philosophy of Sport* XXV: 1–22
Carr, D. (1998) "What Moral Educational Significance has Physical Education? A Question in Need of Disambiguation," in M. McNamee and J. Parry (eds), *Ethics in Sport.* London: Routledge.
Erikson, E. (1964) cited in D.L. Shields and B.J.L. Bredemeier (1995) *Character Development and Physical Activity.* Champaign, IL: Human Kinetics.
Gibson, J. (1993) *Performance Versus Results: A Critique of Contemporary Values in Sport.* New York: SUNY.
Haan, N. (1978) "Two Moralities in Action Contexts: Relationship to Thought, Ego Regulation, and Development," *Journal of Personality and Social Psychology* 36: 286–305.
Kohlberg, L. (1981) *Essays on Moral Development. Vol. 1: The Philosophy of Moral Development.* San Francisco: Harper and Row.
Kupperman, J. (1991) *Character.* Oxford: Oxford University Press.
Loland, S. and McNamee, M. (2000) "Fair Play and the Ethos of Sports: An Eclectic Philosophical Framework," *Journal of the Philosophy of Sport* XXVII: 63–80.
McDowell, J. (1989) "Virtue and Reason," in S.G. Clarke and E.E. Simpson (eds), *Anti Theory in Ethics and Moral Conservativism.* Brockport: SUNY.
McFee, G. (2000) "Spoiling: An Indirect Reflection of Sport's Moral Imperative?," in T. Tannsjo and C. Tamburrini (eds), *Values in Sport.* London: Routledge.
MacIntyre, A. (1986) *After Virtue.* London: Duckworth.

McNamee, M.J. (1995) "Sporting Practices, Institutions and Virtues: A Critique and Restatment," *Journal of the Philosophy of Sport* XXII: 61–82

McNamee, M.J. (1998) "Education, Philosophy and Physical Education: Analysis, Epistemology and Axiology," *European Physical Education Review* 4.1: 75–91.

McNamee, M.J. (2002) "Hubris, Humility and Humiliation: Vice and Virtue in Sporting Communities", *Journal of the Philosophy of Sport* XXIX.1: 38–53.

McNamee, M.J. and Jones, C. (1999) "Value Conflict, Fair Play, and a Sports Education Worthy of the Name," in M. Leicester, C. Modgil and S. Modgil (eds), *Education, Culture and Values. Vol. 4.* London: Cassell.

Parry, J. (1988) "Physical Education, Justification and National Curriculum," *Physical Education Review* 11.2: 106–18.

Peters, R.S. (1974) "Moral Development: A Plea for Pluralism," in *Psychology and Ethical Development.* London: Unwin.

Peters, R.S. (1981) *Moral Education and Moral Development.* London: George, Allen and Unwin.

Piaget, J. (1932) *The Moral Judgment of the Child.* London: Routledge and Kegan Paul.

Pincoffs, E. (1986) *Quandaries and Virtues: Against Reductivism in Ethics.* Kansas: Kansas University Press.

Rest, J. (1984) cited in **D.L.** Shields and B.J.L. Bredemeier (1995) *Character Development and Physical Activity.* Champaign, IL: Human Kinetics.

Rorty, A. and Wong, D. (1997) "Aspects of Identity and Agency," in O. Flanagan and A. Rorty (eds), *Identity, Character, and Morality.* London: MIT Press.

Scruton, R. (1986) "Freedom and Custom," in S.G. Clarke and E.E. Simpson (eds), *Anti Theory in Ethics and Moral Conservatism.* Brockport: SUNY.

Shields, D.L., and Bredemeier, B.J.L. (1995) *Character Development and Physical Activity.* Champaign, IL: Human Kinetics.

Suits, B. (1988) "The Elements of Sport," in W. Morgan and K. Meier (eds), *Philosophic Inquiry in Sport.* Champaign IL: Human Kinetics.

CHAPTER 4

Philosopher in the Playground: Notes on the Meaning of Sport

Peter Heinegg

Down through the ages the athlete and the philosopher have never had much to say to each other. In 1970 half a billion people watched the final match of the World Cup soccer championship, but the intelligentsia must have missed the show. Nobody noticed that history's biggest experiment in simultaneous mass consciousness had just taken place – during a *game*. A casual glance at pro sports[1] might lead anyone not hopelessly naive to write the whole thing off as simply organized childishness or another phase of the quest for the almighty dollar. But there's more to it than this.

Of course, sports in this country *are* big business, a highly popular, handsomely packaged, and increasingly expensive consumer item. Players, as their annual wage disputes and occasional strikes remind us, are only members of a glamorous labor union, their inflated wages compensated by bruises, exhaustion, and merciless competition. Professional teams come equipped with a bristling array of bureaucrats, PR men, and capitalist owners, who sell stock in their enterprise, trade players, etc.

But if the people who make their living through sports are trapped in the gears of economic determinism, there is no reason why this should bother the spectator, least of all the living-room contemplative watching the game for free. Insulated from the struggle for survival and success that racks the participants, he can give himself up to purer pleasures. And yet, why

does he, why do they, sit there by the tens – or hundreds – of millions staring at the tube? It is time for philosophy to break her silence and say something about this puzzling phenomenon.

Called upon to justify the hours spent indulging his vice, the literate fan might take an aesthetic tack: professional athletes perform with fabulous strength, speed, grace, and coordination. A well-executed power play, fast break, or kick-off return can be awesome.

Even the anti-fan will sometimes stop in his tracks in front of the TV set and admire despite himself. Talented players, clearly, go about their work with as much precision and brio as ballet dancers or violinists.

Actually, athletes have an evolutionary superiority over artists. Poetry and French horn playing do not necessarily improve with time, but thanks to better nutrition, coaching, and equipment, players continually surpass their predecessors. The record-book, out of date as soon as published, shelters in its banal pages the myth of infinite perfectibility. Any middle-aged fan can testify that linemen and linebackers are not only bigger and stronger than their counterparts of a generation ago, they are even faster off the mark.

There are a handful of activities, such as dance and gymnastics, where art and sport seem to converge, but such analogies deceive as much as they enlighten. Art is a heightened form of life. Although it ushers us into a realm of fantasy, it always brings us back to earth, to the "real world." Sport, for all its simple-minded concreteness, is essentially a mode of escape from life. Great art inevitably turns to tragedy. Sport is utopian and comic.

One reliable touchstone to test the unreality of sport is sex. We may muse over the phallic quality of billiard cues or the symbolism of "stuffing" in basketball, but sport remains basically sexless. Relationships between men and women create tension and conflict (the very stuff of art), which is too serious for sport to cope with. Institutions that exclude or ignore sex, such as prisons, reform schools, army bases, or seminaries, encourage sports to distract their horny inhabitants. The locker room survives as one of the last unprofaned sanctuaries of maledom, i.e., where grown men can in good conscience behave like boys.

If art reveals the serious, sexually charged world to us by transforming it, sport sets out to build another world altogether. Observe the structure of most games. There is first of all an ideal space, the playing field or court. Here we have a tidy microcosm, carefully lined and ordered, set off from its workaday environment: nature humanized. While real life muddles along in opaque confusion, the ongoing action of sport is luminous, especially for the TV viewer with the advantage of instant replay. The home audience can analyze key plays at its leisure, in slow motion, and from more than one angle. The feeble human eye is suddenly divinized. Video tape fixes what might have flashed by in a peripheral blur, so that the Olympian spectator can pass judgment on it. The beauty and elegance of the fleeting moment are recalled, enjoyed, and then gratefully dismissed.

The soothing clarity of sport comes from its strict adherence to the rulebook. An elaborate system of regulations attends to every imaginable contingency and produces a state of utopian justice. For example, it was recently estimated, on the basis of game films, that calls made by N.F.L. officials were correct 98% of the time. Could any civil judiciary dare to claim such accuracy? And if, *per impossibile*, it did, how could it prove its case? Where else can one find such a flawlessly clear legal code, such quick and distinterested decisions? Where is there less bias, secrecy, or wire-pulling? Sport eliminates the suffering caused by the randomness of existence – the loose ends and ragged edges, the imbalances and anticlimaxes of everyday life. All men are aesthetes to some extent: they fly from the messiness of sick room, bedroom, factory, and market place to the artificial neatness of the playground.

Because of all the improvisation in sport there is enough room for novelty, upsets, flukes, and long shots – and without novelty deadly boredom would ensue. But sport restrains within reasonable bounds the chances that tyrannize human life. Real life may move the bases farther apart while you run them, or let your opponent field twice as many as your side, but sport does not. All in all, the playing field is probably the best place in the world to look for fair play.

Sport, then, is a flight from the pain of existence. As life is perpetual motion – change, growth, and decay – under the rule of time, sport is an attempt to fashion a world of stasis, or ecstasy, a standing apart from the river of time. Sport is a separate universe with a fully articulated structure which is a comic imitation of the real one; an ersatz Creation with both design and purpose (wholly arbitrary, yet consistent). Once you accept a few absurd axioms, everything else follows. Sport of necessity works with the raw materials of everyday life, its desires, energies, and obstacles, but it detoxifies them and renders them pleasurable. Take aggression, for instance. Sport is, among other things, a form of war. In games players can unleash and satisfy the lust for violence that the human race is so far from outgrowing. The spectators share vicariously in this instinctual release. Sport fulfills a perpetual masculine wish: a state of total war without death or serious injury. There are, to be sure, many degrees in the spectrum, from boxing to ping-pong, but violent conflict is always there, expressed or implied.

Sport is a pointless partisan struggle. (What does Green Bay have against Detroit?) It involves a sympathetic identification by the crowd or solitary viewer that can reach the point of frenzy, the end, as Nietzsche might put it, of the principle of individuation. Once again the flight from stern reality, from the shackles of the self to union with the corporate ego of the Home Team. Even when watching a game between unknown teams, the fan willy-nilly takes sides.

The fan roots out of anxiety over the outcome. The equivalent in "reality" to rooting is our concern with the endless cycle of worldly cares and crises. In the outside world we may win or lose any given contest, but new ones supervene to keep us agitated. A similar syndrome occurs in sport, inning after inning, game after game, but most fans feel no real pain, since the outcome makes no difference beyond the stadium walls. Once the score is final, the game has no more interest than an old newspaper. One may wish to review a few highlights, but no more.

The game exhausts itself in the playing. It is, like music, pure act, and produces no artefact. It is, and then is not. But in most concerts the player merely interprets the music of another man, the composer, whereas in sport he is a true innovator, responding to each situation as it comes along. Since this prevents any completely prepared patterns from arising, as in a rehearsed performance, the absorbing question is always "What next?" and the best game is the one which piles up the most brilliant, exciting *coups de théâtre*. But both the joys and the agonies of sport are shortlived (except for the players), which is as it should be. Sport generates a welter of vehement emotions, easily purged (a much better catharsis than tragedy) because they are so insubstantial.

The hero of Sartre's *Nausea* is oppressed and at times sickened by the maddening givenness of reality, its total factitiousness. Reality is *de trop*, a pointless, hypertrophied, overwhelming viscous chaos. To escape this meaningless monster, Roquentin has the habit of playing jazz records, but he might just as well have gone to a soccer match. The cheering throngs there undoubtedly contained many inarticulate sufferers from the same malaise. They (and the radio audience, if any) instinctively sought liberation in sport, and who can say who, the intellectual or the mob, made the better choice?

Note

1 And these days high quality in sports and professionalism are all but synonymous: you cannot field a first-rate team without paying it, one way or another. Consider the farce of the "amateur" Soviet national hockey team or the recruiting tactics of American college coaches.

Foul Play: Sports Metaphors as Public Doublespeak

Francine Hardaway ————————————————————

Nobody would argue the place of sports in American life; they are big business. And they are big business because they fit philosophically with the widely accepted American dream of open competition in a free market economy. Americans believe in competition, foster it, and encourage it. They live by its rules. No wonder the language of athletic competition has found its way as metaphor into every aspect of American life. If we are at a disadvantage, we say we've "got two strikes against us," things have "taken a bad bounce," or we're "on the ropes." If we are being aggressive, we "take the ball and run with it," "take the bull by the horns," "come out swinging," or "make a sweep." If the fates still conspire against us, we "take it on the chin," "throw in the towel," or "roll with the punches" until we're "saved by the bell."

It's worth taking some time to think about how these sports metaphors, so ubiquitous and so ignored until Watergate brought them to our attention, describe the quality of life in America.

The purpose of such metaphors is to explain unfamiliar or difficult concepts in terms of familiar images. But recently there have been some changes in our national self-concept and these changes are duly reflected in sports metaphors. We seem to have changed drastically from a society in which "it isn't whether you win or lose, but how you play the game," to one in which, to use Vince Lombardi's words, "winning isn't everything, it's the only thing." And

our sports metaphors have changed with us. "The good fight" and "the old college try" have given way to the more sophisticated "game plans," "play-calling," and quarterbacking rhetoric of Vietnam and Watergate. Sports metaphors now often function as public doublespeak: language meant to manipulate its audience unconsciously. Analyzing sports doublespeak reveals some scary truths about how we Americans look at life. In John Mitchell's words, "when the going gets tough, the tough get going," and we turn out to be a society in which "nice guys finish last," and everybody wants to "be on the winning side."

The rhetoric of the playing field appears in advertising, business, and government. Let's take an obvious example first. President Ford, in publicizing his economic strategies when he first took office, devised the W.I.N. button. An offshoot of Ford's other unfortunate sports metaphor, the promise to "hold the line" on inflation, the W.I.N. button was meant to appeal by familiarity to the sports-minded American who will "get up for the game," and "tackle the job" if the coach just tells him what to do. Ford hoped that the "win" mentality was so strongly ingrained in America that the very word would alter attitudes and behavior.

With the W.I.N. button, Ford hoped to make use of a sports metaphor the way advertising does. He wanted to make the analogy from athletic success to success in other fields. We all expect to be manipulated by advertising, so it is no surprise to see professional athletes advertising hair tonic, shaving cream, even frozen pizza or panty hose. The doublespeak is implicit: use this product, and you will enjoy the same success as Frank Gifford, Arthur Ashe, Joe Namath. Associating the athlete with the product, however, makes another claim for the athlete: it extends his expertise beyond the playing field. Ad agencies hope we will take the advice of these "pros" about shaving cream, hair tonic, frozen pizza, or panty hose; after all, the pro wouldn't make a wrong choice about these products any more than he would throw the ball away at a crucial moment of the game. So the athlete is an expert, as well as a hero. His ability to "score" carries over into financial and sexual arenas as well; there is even a product named "Score."

Since it has been established by advertising that the athlete is both hero and expert, sports metaphors are used more subtly to sell products. In the MGB ad that reads "MGB. Think of it as a well-coordinated athlete," we can see how much athletic ability is admired. No longer do we compare the good athlete or the good team to a well-oiled machine: now we're comparing the machine to the good athlete. Like a well-coordinated athlete, you'll "score" in your MGB.

But advertising is an easy target for doublespeak analysis. More complex by far is the way sports metaphors function in business, where their analysis leads to crucial revelations about American ethics. Business has always been fond of the football analogy, as William H. Whyte, Jr. points out:

> No figure of speech is a tenth as seductive to the businessman. Just why this should be – baseball curiously is much less used – is generally explained by its adaptability to all sorts of situations. Furthermore, the football analogy is *satisfying*. It is bounded by two goal lines and is thus finite. There is always a solution. And that is what makes it so often treacherous.[1]

Business uses the team philosophy, says Whyte, to hedge on moral issues. By making analogies to sports, business convinces the outside world that its decisions aren't truly consequential: they are "games" executed by good "team players." The fact that dollars and human lives may also be involved is not included when the sports metaphor is used, for the sports metaphor imposes automatic limits on the way business activity is seen.

> The goal of sports activity is always unambiguous and non-controversial; participants do not come together to discuss or debate the ends for which the activity has been established, but rather take this end for granted and apply themselves in a single-minded fashion to the task of developing the most efficient means to achieve the predetermined unchanging and non-controversial end: winning.[2]

So the sports metaphor precludes thought; it operates on unconscious and irrational levels, manipulating its users as well as its audiences. Perhaps its use in business, where the idea of competition in the free marketplace still carries moral force, has something to do with man's aggressive nature; what sports and business have in common that allows the sports metaphor to be drawn so often and so successfully by American businessmen is aggressiveness. Sports are an acceptable form of releasing aggressive impulses; if business uses the sports metaphor, isn't the aggressiveness of business automatically acceptable?

> . . . [the] same aggressive impulse which can lead to strife and violence also underlies man's urge to independence and achievement. Just as a child could not possibly grow up into an independent adult if it were not aggressive, so an adult must needs continue to express at least part of his aggressive potential if he is to maintain his own autonomy.[3]

No wonder the Duke of Wellington was able to observe that "the battle of Waterloo was won on the playing fields of Eton." The skills learned on the playing field by the child are translated into the battles of the adult.

But there is also a certain cynicism associated with the use of the sports metaphor by business.

> What happens to some guys is – well, I'll draw the analogy to sports again. Baseball has its hot players and the next year the hot players cool off, and what happens is that their salaries drop and they get optioned out to Toledo.[4]

In Jerry Della Femina's description of what happens to advertising men who don't produce, the sports metaphor obscures the human position of the advertising executive, the man who has a good year followed by a bad year and suddenly finds himself nursing an ulcer and out of a job. Like most sports metaphors, this one permits the reader to ignore the ethical implications of cut-throat competition among advertising agencies for top talent.

But business still isn't the "Big Game" – that's government. And, as we might now expect, the bigger the game, the more prevalent the sports metaphor as doublespeak. Watergate revealed the wholesale use of the sports lexicon by politicians, but Watergate was neither the beginning nor the end of the sports metaphor. As William Safire points out in his excellent book *The New Language of Politics*,[5] Shakespeare may have been the first to use these comparisons. King Henry V told his troops before Harfleur "I see you stand like greyhounds in the slips, straining upon the start. The game's afoot..." But Safire also notes that Shakespeare wasn't the last; the section on "Sports Metaphors" in *The New Language of Politics* is a wonderful compendium of quotations from past political greats beginning with Woodrow Wilson's "I have always in my own thought summed up individual liberty, and business liberty, and every other kind of liberty, in the phrase that is common in the sporting world, 'A free field and no favor,'" and stopping at JFK's "Politics is like football. If you see daylight, go through the hole."

Amusingly enough, politics doesn't content itself with the football metaphor so favored by business. Instead, it inadvertently reveals its seamier side by the frequent use of the horse race analogy. There are front-runners and dark horses, long shots and shoo-ins. The winner takes the reins of government, while the loser is an also-ran who was "nosed out." Harry Truman said, "I am trying to do in politics what Citation has done in the horse races. I propose at the finish line on November 2 to come out ahead...." It seems that in politics, more than in advertising or in business, the use of the sports metaphor reveals more than gamesmanship, competition, or vicarious aggression; it also reveals an affinity with gambling.

But Safire's compendium, while amusing and instructive, is pre-Watergate and he therefore views the sports metaphor as innocuous. He says,

> Sports metaphors relate closely to many people, which is why politicians spend the time to create them; at other times they are tossed off without thinking because they are already a part of the language. After a Kennedy aide appeared on Lawrence Spivak's television panel show *Meet the Press*, the President called to say "They never laid a glove on you." It is the classic remark of a trainer to a prizefighter who has been belted all over the ring. (pp. 421–22)

Since Watergate, we have become more attuned to the way sports metaphors are often used to make big decisions involving all our lives seem trivial and inconsequential.

> Nixon's "jocko-macho" talk (as Nicholas von Hoffman called it) was amply demonstrated; the limited supply of tough-guy metaphors, akin to verbal locker room swaggering muscle-flexing *machismo* at the beach:... Years earlier, some critics had felt that Nixon's overt enthusiasm for spectator sports (shaking hands with athletes, telegrams and phone calls to coaches) was simply a calculated ploy ("a grandstand play") to win the favor of certain voters, to create the illusion that he was "just one of the guys." It was no illusion. Nixon was not the first politician

to use the imagery of athletics ... but the transcripts reveal that the traditional emphasis on "fair play," "following the rules," and "good sportsmanship" had been replaced by a "win at all costs" mentality.[6]

One need hardly comment further on what Watergate did to the language; its only good effect was to alert many Americans to the way language does both form and corrupt thinking. For that, we should probably be grateful.

Unfortunately, the effects of Watergate aren't longlasting. In the midst of the recent New York City financial crisis, the *Wall Street Journal* carried the following story:

> After a seven-month game of political brinkmanship, the Ford administration has browbeaten New York City into "fiscal responsibility" and the city has pressured Washington into limited federal help.
>
> But the path to that outcome proved to be far different than either side had expected, and the ultimate results happier than either would have predicted just a short time ago. There seems to be no clear winner in the long struggle – just losers of varying degrees. . . .
>
> The reconstruction of these events leading up to the Wednesday statement discloses basic miscalculations by every player in the game. . . .
>
> The city's fiscal crisis, surfacing last May, rapidly developed into a high-level game of political chess – played out in Washington and New York and Albany, full of bluff and bombast, maneuver and surprise.[7]

Only the name of the game has changed; the article goes on to discuss how New York's crisis

developed into a standoff between Ford and the city, in which participants in the negotiations between New York and Washington felt that "it was hardball both ways, and nothing was spared." The "hardball season" of negotiations ran from September through November, when Ford and New York City finally reached a compromise.

The story illustrates very well the dangers of relying too heavily on sports metaphors. Here a genuine crisis has been reduced for readers to a game in which participants are trying to out-bluff and out-maneuver each other while New York and perhaps the rest of the nation await the consequences. And the crisis is portrayed as a strategy problem, rather than a human problem or a problem in responsible government.

What is the lesson to be learned from looking at our culture's continuing use of sports metaphors to render important situations innocuous in advertising, in business, and in government? If it is true, as Walker Gibson said to the NCTE Convention in 1973, that "learning to read is learning to infer dramatic character from linguistic evidence," then examining the metaphors used in popular culture provides good insight into our character as a nation. And if it is also true, as Orwell remarked in *Politics and the English Language*, that "language can corrupt thought," then sports metaphors become not merely ways of revealing our adolescent preoccupation with aggressiveness, with winning, with games, but also ways of perpetuating those concerns, of glorifying them, of passing them on unexamined to our children through our national culture. It is at least worth a few minutes of our time to wrestle (there it is again) with the decision of whether we really want to see ourselves forever as a nation of teamplayers and sports fans.

Notes

1   William H. Whyte, Jr., "The Language of Business," in *Technological and Professional Writing*, ed. Herman A. Estrin (New York: Harcourt, Brace & World, 1963), p. 83. In this part of the paper, I am indebted to an unpublished paper on "Sports Metaphors in Business" by John Driscoll.

2   Ike Balbus, "Politics as Sports: The Political Ascendancy of the Sports Metaphor in America," *Monthly Review*, March 1975, p. 30.

3   Anthony Storr, *Human Aggression* (New York: Atheneum, 1970), p. 59.

4   Jerry Della Femina, *From Those Wonderful Folks Who Brought You Pearl Harbor* (New York: Simon & Schuster, 1971), p. 124.

5   New York: Random House, 1968, p. 421.

6   Hugh Rank, "Watergate and the Language," in *Language and Public Policy*, ed. Hugh Rank (Urbana, Ill.: NCTE, 1974), pp. 7–8.

7   November 28, 1975.

PART II

Sport and Sportspersonship

CHAPTER 6

Sportsmanship as a Moral Category

James W. Keating

Sportsmanship, long and inexplicably ignored by philosophers and theologians, has always pretended to a certain moral relevancy, although its precise place among the moral virtues has been uncertain. In spite of this confusion, distinguished advocates have made some remarkable claims for sportsmanship as a moral category. Albert Camus, Nobel Prize winner for literature in 1957, said that it was from sports that he learned all that he knew about ethics.[1] Former President Hoover is quoted as saying: "Next to religion, the single greatest factor for good in the United States in recent years has been sport."[2] Dr. Robert C. Clothier, past president of Rutgers University, paraphrased the words of Andrew Fletcher and commented: "I care not who makes the laws or even writes the songs if the code of sportsmanship is sound, for it is that which controls conduct and governs the relationships between men."[3] Henry Steele Commager, professor of history at Columbia University, has argued that it was on the playing fields that Americans learned the lessons of courage and honor which distinguished them in time of war. Commager sums up: "In one way or another, this code of sportsmanship has deeply influenced our national destiny."[4] For Lyman Bryson, of Columbia University, sportsmanship was of extraordinary value:

> The doctrine of love is much too hard a doctrine to live by. But this is not to say that we have not made progress. It could be established, I think, that the next best thing to the rule of love is the rule of sportsmanship.... Some perspicacious historian will some day write a study of the age-old correlation between freedom and sportsmanship. We may then see the importance of sportsmanship as a form of enlightenment. This virtue, without which democracy is impossible and freedom uncertain, has not yet been taken seriously enough in education.[5]

Pope Pius XII, speaking of fair play which is widely regarded as an essential ingredient of sportsmanship, if not synonymous with it, has said:

> From the birthplace of sport came also the proverbial phrase "fair play"; that knightly and courteous emulation which raises the spirit above meanness and deceit and dark subterfuges of vanity and vindictiveness and preserves it from the excesses of a closed and intransigent nationalism. Sport is the school of loyalty, of courage, of fortitude, of resolution and universal brotherhood.[6]

Charles W. Kennedy was a professor of English at Princeton University and chairman of its Board of Athletic Control. His small volume,

Sport and Sportsmanship, remains to this day probably the most serious study of sportsmanship conducted in America. Kennedy's commitment to sportsmanship was not merely theoretical and scholarly. As chairman of Princeton's Board of Athletic Control, he severed athletic relations with Harvard when unsportsmanlike conduct marred the relationship.[7] For Kennedy it was not sufficient that sportsmanship characterize man's activities on the athletic field; it must permeate all of life.

> When you pass out from the playing fields to the tasks of life, you will have the same responsibility resting upon you, in greater degree, of fighting in the same spirit for the cause you represent. You will meet bitter and sometimes unfair opposition.... You will meet defeat (but) you must not forget that the great victory of which you can never be robbed will be the ability to say, when the race is over and the struggle ended, that the flag you fought under was the shining flag of sportsmanship, never furled or hauled down and that, in victory or defeat, you never lost that contempt for a breach of sportsmanship which will prevent your stooping to it anywhere, anyhow, anytime.[8]

Similar eulogies by other distinguished men with no professional or financial interest in sport or athletics could be multiplied without difficulty, but perhaps the point has already been made. The claims for sportsmanship as a moral category deserve some investigation. It is surprising that the experts in moral theory, the philosopher and the theologian, have seen fit to ignore so substantial an area of human conduct as that occupied by sport and athletics.

Three interrelated problems will be considered in this study: (1) the source of the confusion which invariably accompanies a discussion of sportsmanship and the normal consequences resulting from this confusion; (2) the essence of genuine sportsmanship, or the conduct and attitude proper to sport, with special consideration being given to the dominant or

pivotal virtues involved; (3) sportsmanship as applied to athletics – a derivative or analogous use of the term. Once again special attention will be directed to the basic or core virtues which characterize the conduct and attitude of the well-behaved athlete.

The Source of Confusion and Its Consequences

What is sportsmanship? William R. Reed, commissioner for the Big Ten Intercollegiate Conference, is most encouraging: "It [sportsmanship] is a word of exact and uncorrupted meaning in the English language, carrying with it an understandable and basic ethical norm. Henry C. Link in his book 'Rediscovery of Morals' says, 'Sportsmanship is probably the clearest and most popular expression of morals.'"[9] Would that this were the case. Reed, however, does not define sportsmanship or enumerate the provisions of its code, and the briefest investigation reveals that he is badly mistaken as to the clarity of the concept. The efforts of no less a champion of sportsmanship than Amos Alonzo Stagg presage the obscurities which lie ahead. In addition to a brilliant athletic career at Yale and forty years as head football coach at the University of Chicago, Stagg did a year of graduate work in Yale's Divinity School and would thus seem to have the ideal background of scholarly training in moral theory and vast practical experience to discuss the problem. Yet his treatment leaves much to be desired. He defined sportsmanship as "a delightful fragrance that people will carry with them in their relations with their fellow men."[10] In addition, he drew up separate codes of sportsmanship, or Ten Commandments of sport, for the coach and for the football player and held that both decalogues were applicable to the business world as well. The second, and by far the most unusual, commandment contained proscriptions seldom found in codes of sportsmanship. "Make your conduct a worthy example. Don't drink intoxicants; don't gamble; don't smoke; don't use smutty language; don't tell dirty stories; don't associate with loose or silly women."[11] Stagg's position is undoubtedly an extreme one, but it calls attention to a tendency all too common among the champions of sportsmanship – the temptation to broaden the concept of sportsmanship until it becomes an all-embracing moral category, a unique road to moral salvation. As always, there is an opposite extreme. Sportsmanship, when not viewed as the pinnacle of moral perfection, can also be viewed as a moral minimum – one step this side of criminal behavior. "A four point program to improve sportsmanship at athletic events has been adopted by the Missouri State High School Activities Association."[12] The first and third provisions of bylaw No. 9 detail penalties for assaults or threats upon officials by players or fans. Such legislative action may be necessary and even admirable, but it is a serious error to confuse the curtailment of criminal activities of this sort with a positive promotion of sportsmanship.

What, then, is sportsmanship? Another approach is by way of the dictionary, everyday experience, and common-sense deductions. Sportsmanship is conduct becoming a sportsman. And who is a sportsman? One who is interested in or takes part in sport. And what is sport? Sport, Webster tells us, is "that which diverts and makes mirth"; it is an "amusement, recreation, pastime." Our problem, then, is to determine the conduct and attitude proper to this type of activity, and this can be done only after a more careful consideration of the nature of sport. Pleasant diversion? Recreation? Amusement? Pastime? Is this how one would describe the World Series, the Masters, the Davis Cup, the Rose Bowl, the Olympic Games, or a high-school basketball tournament? Do the "sport" pages of our newspapers detail the pleasant diversions and amusements of the citizenry, or are they preoccupied with national and international contests which capture the imaginations, the emotions, and the pocketbooks of millions of fans (i.e., fanatics)? It is precisely at this point that we come face to face with the basic problem which has distorted or vitiated most discussions of sportsmanship. Because the term "sport" has been loosely applied to radically different types of human behavior, because it is naïvely regarded as an apt description of (1) activity which seeks only pleasant diversion and, on the other hand, (2) the agonistic struggle to demonstrate personal or group excellence, the determination of the conduct proper to a participant in "sport" becomes a sticky business indeed. Before proceeding with an analysis of sportsmanship as such, it is necessary to consider briefly an all-important distinction between sport and athletics.

Our dictionary definition of sport leans upon its root or etymological meaning. "Sport," we are told, is an abbreviation of the Middle English *desport* or *disport*, themselves derivatives of the Old French *desporter*, which literally meant to carry away from work. Following this lead, Webster and other lexicographers indicate that "diversion," "recreation," and "pastime" are essential to sport. It is "that which diverts and makes mirth; a pastime." While the dictionaries reflect some of the confusion and fuzziness with which contemporary thought shrouds the concept of athletics, they invariably stress an element which, while only accidentally associated with sport, is essential to athletics. This element is the prize, the *raison d'être* of athletics. Etymologically, the various English forms of the word "athlete" are derived from the Greek verb *athlein*, "to contend for a prize," or the noun *athlos*, "contest" or *athlon*, a prize awarded for the successful completion of the contest. An oblique insight into the nature of athletics is obtained when we realize that the word "agony" comes from the Greek *agonia* – a contest or a struggle for victory in the games. Thus we see that, historically and etymologically, sport and athletics have characterized radically different types of human activity, different not insofar as the game itself or the mechanics or rules are concerned, but different with regard to the attitude, preparation, and purpose of the participants. Man has probably always desired some release or diversion from the sad and serious side of life. This, of course, is a luxury, and it is only when a hostile environment is brought under close rein and economic factors provide a modicum of leisure that such desires can be gratified. In essence, sport is a kind of diversion which has for its direct and immediate end fun, pleasure, and delight and which is dominated by a spirit of moderation and generosity. Athletics, on the other hand, is essentially a competitive activity, which has for its end victory in the contest and which is characterized by a spirit of dedication, sacrifice, and intensity.

When this essential distinction between sport and athletics is ignored, as it invariably is, the temptation to make sportsmanship an all-embracing moral category becomes irresistible for most of its champions. In 1926 a national Sportsmanship Brotherhood was organized for the purpose of spreading the gospel of sportsmanship throughout all aspects of life, from childhood games to international events.[13] Its code consisted of eight rules:

1. Keep the rule.
2. Keep faith with your comrades.
3. Keep yourself fit.
4. Keep your temper.
5. Keep your play free from brutality.
6. Keep pride under in victory.
7. Keep stout heart in defeat.
8. Keep a sound soul and a clean mind in a healthy body.

The slogan adopted by the Brotherhood to accompany its code was "Not that you won or lost – but how you played the game." In giving vigorous editorial support to the Sportsmanship Brotherhood, the *New York Times* said:

> Take the sweet and the bitter as the sweet and bitter come and always "play the game." That is the legend of the true sportsmanship, whether on the ball field, the tennis court, the golf course, or at the desk or machine or throttle. "Play the game." That means truthfulness, courage, spartan endurance, self-control, self-respect, scorn of luxury, consideration for one another's opinions and rights, courtesy, and above all fairness. These are the fruits of the spirit of sportsmanship and in them ... lies the best hope of social well-being.[14]

Dictionaries that have suggested the distinction between sport and athletics without explicitly emphasizing it have remained relatively free from this type of romantic incrustation and moral exaggeration in their treatment of sportsmanship. Beginning with nominal definitions of sportsmanship as the conduct becoming a sportsman and of the sportsman as one who participates in sport, they proceed, much more meaningfully, to characterize the sportsman by the kind of conduct expected of him. A sportsman is "a person who can take loss or defeat without complaint or victory without gloating and who treats his opponents with fairness, generosity and courtesy." In spite of the limitations of such a description, it at least avoids the inveterate temptation to make sportsmanship a moral catch-all.

The Essence of Genuine Sportsmanship

Sportsmanship is not merely an aggregate of moral qualities comprising a code of specialized behavior; it is also an attitude, a posture, a manner of interpreting what would otherwise be only a legal code. Yet the moral qualities believed to comprise the code have almost monopolized consideration and have proliferated to the point of depriving sportsmanship of any distinctiveness. Truthfulness, courage, spartan endurance, self-control, self-respect, scorn of luxury, consideration for one another's opinions and rights, courtesy, fairness, magnanimity, a high sense of honor, co-operation, generosity. The list seems interminable. While the conduct and attitude which are properly designated as sportsmanlike may reflect many of the above-mentioned qualities, they are not all equally basic or fundamental. A man may be law-abiding, a team player, well conditioned, courageous, humane, and the possessor of *sangfroid* without qualifying as a sportsman. On the other hand, he may certainly be categorized as a sportsman without possessing spartan endurance or a scorn of luxury. Our concern is not with those virtues which *might* be found in the sportsman. Nor is it with those virtues which *often* accompany the sportsman. Our concern is rather with those moral habits or qualities which are essential, which characterize the participant as a sportsman. Examination reveals that there are some that are pivotal and absolutely essential; others peripheral. On what grounds is such a conclusion reached? Through the employment of the principle that the nature of the activity determines the conduct and attitudes proper to it. Thus, to the extent that the conduct and attitudes of the participants contribute to the attainment of the goal of sport, to that extent they can be properly characterized as sportsmanlike. The primary purpose of sport is not to win the match, to catch the fish or kill the animal, but to derive pleasure from the attempt to do so and to afford pleasure to one's fellow participants in the process. Now it is clear that the combined presence of such laudable moral qualities as courage, self-control, co-operation, and a spirit of honor do not, in themselves, produce a supporting atmosphere. They may be found in both parties to a duel or in a civil war. But generosity and magnanimity are essential ingredients in the conduct and attitude properly described as sportsmanlike. They establish and maintain the unique social bond; they guarantee that the purpose of sport – the immediate pleasure of the participants – will not be sacrificed to other more selfish ends. All the prescriptions which make up the code of sportsmanship are derived from this single, basic, practical maxim: Always conduct yourself in such a manner that you will increase rather than detract from the pleasure to be found in the activity, both your own and that of your fellow participants. If there is disagreement as to what constitutes sportsmanlike behavior, then this disagreement stems from the application of the maxim rather than from the maxim itself. It is to be expected that there will be differences of opinion as to how the pleasurable nature of the activity can best be maximized.

The code governing pure sport is substantially different from a legalistic code in which lawyers and law courts are seen as a natural and healthy complement of the system. In fact, it is in direct comparison with such a system that the essence of sportsmanship can best be understood. In itself, sportsmanship is a spirit, an attitude, a manner or mode of interpreting an otherwise purely legal code. Its purpose is to protect and cultivate the festive mood proper to an activity whose primary purpose is pleasant diversion, amusement, joy. The sportsman adopts a cavalier attitude toward his personal rights under the code; he prefers to be magnanimous and self-sacrificing if, by such conduct, he contributes to the enjoyment of the game. The sportsman is not in search of legal justice; he prefers to be generous whenever generosity will contribute to the fun of the occasion. Never in search of ways to evade the rules, the sportsman acts only from unquestionable moral right.

Our insistence that sport seeks diversion, recreation, amusement does not imply that the sportsman is by nature a listless competitor. It is common practice for him, once the game is under way, to make a determined effort to win. Spirited competitor that he often is, however, his goal is joy in the activity itself and anything – any word, action, or attitude – which makes the game itself less enjoyable should be eliminated. He "fights" gallantly to win because experience has taught him that a determined effort to overcome the obstacles which his particular sport has constructed adds immeasurably to the enjoyment of the game. He would be cheating himself and robbing the other participants of intense pleasure if his efforts were only halfhearted. Yet there is an important sense in which sporting activity is not competitive but rather co-operative. Competition denotes the struggle of two parties for the same valued object or objective and implies that, to the extent that one of the parties is successful in the struggle, he gains exclusive or predominant possession of that object at the expense of his competitor. But the goal of sporting activity, being the mutual enjoyment of the participants, cannot even be understood in terms of exclusive possession by one of the parties. Its simulated competitive atmosphere camouflages what is at bottom a highly co-operative venture. Sport, then, is a co-operative endeavour to maximize pleasure or joy, the immediate pleasure or joy to be found in the activity itself. To so characterize sport is not to indulge in romantic exaggeration. It is indisputable that the spirit of selfishness is at a very low ebb in genuine sport. Gabriel Marcel's observation concerning the relationship of generosity to joy may even have a limited applicability here. "If generosity enjoys its own self it degenerates into complacent self-satisfaction. This enjoyment of self is not joy, for joy is not a satisfaction but an exaltation. It is only in so far as it is introverted that joy becomes enjoyment."[15] In comparison with sport, athletics emphasizes self-satisfaction and enjoyment; sport is better understood in terms of generosity, exaltation, and joy.

Although there is no acknowledgment of the fact, the concern which has been shown for sportsmanship by most of its advocates has been almost exclusively directed to its derivative meaning – a code of conduct for athletes. To the extent that the Sportsmanship Brotherhood was concerned with athletics (and their code of conduct would indicate that was their main concern), their choice of a slogan seems singularly inappropriate. "Not that you won or lost – but how you played the game." Such a slogan can be accommodated in the world of sport, but even there the word "enjoyed" should be substituted for the word "played." Application of this slogan to athletics, on the other hand, would render such activity unintelligible, if not irrational.

"Sportsmanship" in Athletics

Careful analysis has revealed that sport, while speaking the language of competition and constantly appearing in its livery, is fundamentally a co-operative venture. The code of the sportsman, sportsmanship, is directed fundamentally to facilitating the co-operative effort and removing all possible barriers to its development. Mutual generosity is a most fertile soil for co-operative activity. When we move from sport to athletics, however, a drastic change takes place. Co-operation is no longer the goal. The objective of the athlete demands exclusive possession. Two cannot share in the same victory unless they are team mates, and, as a result, the problems of competition are immediately in evidence. "Sportsmanship," insofar as it connotes the behavior proper to the athlete, seeks to place

certain basic limitations on the rigors of competition, just as continual efforts are being made to soften the impact of the competitive struggle in economics, politics, international relations, etc. But we must not lose sight of an important distinction. Competition in these real-life areas is condoned or encouraged to the extent that it is thought to contribute to the common good. It is not regarded as an end in itself but as the only or most practicable means to socially desirable ends. Friedrich A. Hayek, renowned economist and champion of competition in economics, supports this position:

> The liberal argument is in favor of making the best possible use of the forces of competition as a means of co-ordinating human efforts, not an argument for leaving things just as they are. It is based on the conviction that, where effective competition can be created, it is a better way of guiding individual efforts than any other. It does not deny, but even emphasizes, that, in order that competition should work beneficially, a carefully thought-out legal framework is required and that neither the existing nor the past legal rules are free from grave defects. Nor does it deny that, where it is impossible to create the conditions necessary to make competition effective, we must resort to other methods of guiding economic activity.[16]

A code which seeks to mitigate the full force of the competitive conflict can also be desirable in athletics. While an athlete is in essence a prize-fighter, he seeks to demonstrate his excellence in a contest governed by rules which acknowledge human worth and dignity. He mistakes his purpose and insults his opponent if he views the contest as an occasion to display generosity and magnanimity. To the extent that sportsmanship in athletics is virtuous, its essence consists in the practice of fairness under most difficult conditions. Since the sportsman's primary objective is the joy of the moment, it is obvious from that very fact that he places no great emphasis on the importance of winning. It is easy for him to be modest in victory or gracious in defeat and to play fair at all times, these virtues being demonstrated under optimum conditions for their easy exercise. The strange paradox of sportsmanship as applied to athletics is that it asks the athlete, locked in a deadly serious and emotionally charged situation, to act outwardly as if he were engaged in some pleasant diversion. After an athlete has trained and sacrificed for weeks, after he has dreamed of victory and its fruits and literally exhausted himself physically and emotionally in its pursuit – after all this – to ask him to act with fairness in the contest, with modesty in victory, and an admirable composure in defeat is to demand a great deal, and, yet, this is the substance of the demand that "sportsmanship" makes upon the athlete.

For the athlete, being a good loser is demonstrating self-control in the face of adversity. A festive attitude is not called for; it is, in fact, often viewed as in bad taste. The purists or rigorists are of the opinion that a brief period of seclusion and mourning may be more appropriate. They know that, for the real competitor, defeat in an important contest seems heartbreaking and nerve-shattering. The athlete who can control himself in such circumstances demonstrates remarkable equanimity. To ask that he enter into the festive mood of the victory celebration is to request a Pagliacci-like performance. There is no need for phony or effusive displays of congratulations. A simple handshake demonstrates that no personal ill-will is involved. No alibis or complaints are offered. No childish excuses about the judgment of officials or the natural conditions. No temper tantrums. To be a good loser under his code, the athlete need not be exactly gracious in defeat, but he must at least "be a man" about it. This burden, metaphorically characterized as sportsmanship, bears heavily upon all athletes – amateur or professional. But there are added complications for the professional. Victories, superior performances, and high ratings are essential to financial success in professional athletics. Too frequent defeat will result in forced unemployment. It is easy, therefore, for a professional athlete to view his competitors with a jaundiced eye; to see them as men who seek to deprive him of his livelihood. Under

these circumstances, to work daily and often intimately with one's competitors and to compete in circumstances which are highly charged with excitement and emotion, while still showing fairness and consideration, is evidence of an admirable degree of self-mastery.

Attempts have been made to identify sportsmanship with certain games which, it is contended, were the private preserve of the gentleman and, as a result, reflect his high code of honor.

Bullying, cheating, "crabbing" were all too common in every form of sport. The present movement away from muckerism probably should be attributed in large measure to the growing popularity of golf and tennis. Baseball, boxing, and many of our common sports trace their origin to the common people who possessed no code of honor. On the other hand, golf and tennis, historically gentlemen's games, have come down to us so interwoven with a high code of honor that we have been forced to accept the code along with the game ... The effect of the golf code upon the attitude of the millions who play the game is reflected in all our sports.[17]

It is true that in England the terms "gentleman," "sportsman," and "amateur" were regarded as intimately interrelated. The contention that the common people, and consequently the games that were peculiarly theirs, had no comparable code of honor may be correct, but it awaits the careful documentation of some future social historian. One thing is certain, however, and that is that there is nothing in the nature of any game, considered in itself, that necessarily implies adherence to a moral code. Some games like golf and tennis in which the participants do their own officiating provide greater opportunity for the practice of honesty, but if a high code of honor surrounds the "gentleman's games," it is due principally to the general attitude of the gentleman toward life rather than to anything intrinsic to the game itself. The English gentleman was firmly committed to sport in the proper sense of that term and eschewed the specialization, the rigors of precontest preparation, the secret strategy sessions, and professional coaching which have come to be regarded as indispensable for the athlete. "The fact that a man is born into the society of gentlemen imposes upon him the duties and, to some extent, the ideas of his class. He is expected to have a broad education, catholic tastes, and a multiplicity of pursuits. He must not do anything for pecuniary gain; and it will be easily seen that he must not specialize. It is essentially the mark of the bourgeois' mind to specialize."[18] Moreover, "too much preparation is contrary to all English ethics, and secrecy in training is especially abhorrent. Remember that sport is a prerogative of gentlemen. And one of the ear-marks of a gentleman is that he resort to no trickery and that he plays every game with his cards on the table – the game of life as well as the game of football."[19]

It is the contestant's objective and not the game itself which becomes the chief determinant of the conduct and attitudes of the players. If we take tennis as an example and contrast the code of conduct employed by the sportsman with that of the athlete in the matter of officiating, the difference is obvious. The sportsman invariably gives his opponent the benefit of the doubt. Whenever he is not sure, he plays his opponent's shot as good even though he may suspect that it was out. The athlete, however, takes a different approach. Every bit as opposed to cheating as the sportsman, the athlete demands no compelling proof of error. If a shot seems to be out, even though he is not certain, the athlete calls it that way. He is satisfied that his opponent will do the same. He asks no quarter and gives none. As a result of this attitude and by comparison with the sportsman, the athlete will tend toward a legal interpretation of the rules.

The athletic contest is designed to serve a specific purpose – the objective and accurate determination of superior performance and, ultimately, of excellence. If this objective is to be accomplished, then the rules governing the contest must impose the same burdens upon each side. Both contestants must be equal before the law if the test is to have any validity, if the victory is to have any meaning. To the extent that one party to the contest gains a special advantage, unavailable to his opponent, through an unusual interpretation, application, or circumvention of the rules, then that advantage is unfair. The well-known phrase "sense of fair play" suggests much more than an adherence to the letter of the law. It implies that the spirit too must be observed. In the athletic contest there is a mutual recognition that the rules of the game are drawn up for the explicit purpose of aiding in the determination of an honorable victory. Any attempt to disregard or circumvent these rules must be viewed as a deliberate attempt to deprive the contest of its meaning. Fairness, then, is rooted in a type of equality before the law, which is absolutely necessary if victory in the contest is to have validity and meaning. Once, however, the necessary steps have been taken to make the contest a true test of respective abilities, the athlete's sole objective is to demonstrate marked superiority. Any suggestion that fair play obliges him to maintain equality in the contest ignores the very nature of athletics. "If our analysis of fair play has been correct, coaches who strive to produce superior teams violate a fundamental principle of sportsmanship by teaching their pupils, through example, that superiority is more greatly to be desired than is equality in sport.... But who today would expect a coach to give up clear superiority – a game won – by putting in enough substitutes to provide fair playing conditions for an opposing team?"[20] Thus understood, sportsmanship would ask the leopard to change its spots. It rules out, as illegitimate, the very objective of the athlete. Nothing shows more clearly the need for recognition of the distinction between sport and athletics.

Conclusion

In conclusion, we would like to summarize our answers to the three problems set down at the outset.

1   The source of the confusion which vitiates most discussion of sportsmanship is the unwarranted assumption that sport and athletics are so similar in nature that a single code of conduct and similar participant attitudes are applicable to

both. Failing to take cognizance of the basic differences between sport and athletics, a futile attempt is made to outline a single code of behavior equally applicable to radically diverse activities. Not only is such an attempt, in the nature of things, doomed to failure but a consequence of this abortive effort is the proliferation of various moral virtues under the flag of sportsmanship, which, thus, loses all its distinctiveness. It is variously viewed as a straight road to moral perfection or an antidote to moral corruption.

2   The goal of genuine sport must be the principal determinant of the conduct and attitudes proper to sporting activity. Since its goal is pleasant diversion – the immediate joy to be derived in the activity itself – the pivotal or essential virtue in sportsmanship is generosity. All the other moral qualities that may also be in evidence are colored by this spirit of generosity.

As a result of this spirit, a determined effort is made to avoid all unpleasantness and conflict and to cultivate, in their stead, an unselfish and cooperative effort to maximize the joy of the moment.

3   The essence of sportsmanship as applied to athletics can be determined by the application of the same principle. Honorable victory is the goal of the athlete and, as a result, the code of the athlete demands that nothing be done before, during, or after the contest to cheapen or otherwise detract from such a victory. Fairness or fair play, the pivotal virtue in athletics, emphasizes the need for an impartial and equal application of the rules if the victory is to signify, as it should, athletic excellence. Modesty in victory and a quiet composure in defeat testify to an admirable and extraordinary self-control and, in general, dignify and enhance the goal of the athlete.

Notes

1   *Resistance, Rebellion and Death* (New York: Alfred A. Knopf. Inc., 1961), p. 242.
2   In Frank Leahy, *Defensive Football* (New York: Prentice-Hall, Inc., 1951), p. 198.
3   "Sportsmanship in Its Relation to American Intercollegiate Athletics," *School and Society*, XLV (April 10, 1937), 506.
4   Henry Steele Commager, in *Scholastic*, XLIV (May 8–13, 1944), 7.
5   Lyman Bryson, *Science and Freedom* (New York: Columbia University Press, 1947), p. 130.
6   Pope Pius XII, *The Human Body* (Boston: Daughters of St. Paul, 1960).
7   "Athletic Relations between Harvard and Princeton," *School and Society*, XXIV (November 20, 1926), 631.
8   Charles W. Kennedy, *Sport and Sportsmanship* (Princeton, N.J.: Princeton University Press, 1931), pp. 58–59.
9   William R. Reed, "Big Time Athletics' Commitment to Education," *Journal of Health, Physical Education, and Recreation*, XXXIV (September, 1963), 30.
10   Quoted in J.B. Griswold, "You Don't Have To Be Born with It," *American Magazine*, CXII (November, 1931), 60.
11   Ibid., p. 133.
12   "Sportsmanship," *School Activities*, XXXII (October, 1960), 38.
13   "A Sportsmanship Brotherhood," *Literary Digest*, LXXXVIII (March 27, 1926), 60–61.
14   Ibid., pp. 60–61.
15   Gabriel Marcel, *The Mystery of Being, Vol. II: Faith and Reality* (Chicago: Henry Regnery Co., 1960), pp. 133–34.
16   Friedrich A. Hayek, *The Road to Serfdom* (Chicago: University of Chicago Press, 1944), p. 36.
17   J.F. Williams and W.W. Nixon, *The Athlete in the Making* (Philadelphia: W.B. Saunders, 1932), p. 153.
18   H.J. Whigham, "American Sport from an English Point of View," *Outlook*, XCIII (November, 1909), 740.
19   Ibid.
20   Frederick R. Rogers, *The Amateur Spirit in Scholastic Games and Sports* (Albany, N.Y.: C.F. Williams & Son, 1929), p. 78.

CHAPTER 7

Three Approaches Toward an Understanding of Sportsmanship

Peter J. Arnold

It is strange, but true, that few recent attempts to analyze and clarify the concept or nature of sport make any significant reference to sportsmanship. Despite this neglect, however, few people would wish to deny that the connection of sportsmanship to sport is an important one. Certainly in the games-playing ethos of the 19th century English Public Schools the use of one term without the other would barely have been conceivable. The same can be said of such terms as "amateurism" and "Olympism." Today, it would seem, especially if contemporary philosophy of sport literature is anything to go by, the matter is quite different. As far as I know, no serious endeavour has been made to look at the phenomenon of sportsmanship for nearly twenty years.[1] Even McIntosh (18: p. 1), who in his book *Fair Play* sets out "to link an analysis of the ethics of sport with the theory and practice of education," makes only passing comment on it. What follows, therefore, is an attempt to help rectify what I see as a neglected dimension in contemporary debate in the general area of ethics and sport.

Sportsmanship, although most readily associated with particular types of commendatory acts done in the context of sport, is sometimes extended to apply to other spheres of life and living, especially those which are concerned with competing fairly and honestly as well as with good humor. I do not propose to embark upon these latter applications, but to concentrate upon what I see to be its central cases, all of which are to do with the actions and conduct of sportsmen and sportswomen when engaged in sport. There are, it seems to me, essentially three different, if related, views about sportsmanship and I propose looking at each of these in turn. They are:

1 Sportsmanship as a form of social union,
2 Sportsmanship as a means in the promotion of pleasure, and
3 Sportsmanship as a form of altruism.

It should be made clear that, although I shall be looking at each of these views separately and in turn for purposes of exposition, I do not necessarily wish to maintain that they are not to some extent overlapping. In any one person, at different times (and maybe even at the same time), all three views can be partially represented.

First, I would like to make a preliminary comment. The idea of sport as justice maintains that when a player enters into the institutionalized social practice of a sport he tacitly agrees to abide by the rules which characterize and govern it. It implies that sport involves a proper understanding of and a commitment to the two principles upon which it is based, namely freedom and equality.[2] The idea of sport as a social union reflects these same undertakings and values. It recognizes that if the practice of sport is to be preserved and flourish, a great deal is dependent upon the players, and officials, understanding and acting in accord with what is fair. They will accept and realize that breaches of the rules, especially if flagrant and deliberate, will destroy the very activity that they have agreed to participate in and uphold. They will appreciate further that if "fairness" is interpreted too contractually or legalistically there is always the danger that the aspect of sport known as "sportsmanship" will be construed as being concerned only with these acts which demonstrate a ready acceptance of the rules and a willingness to abide by them. It will be seen, however, that this is a reasonable expectation of all players and the notion of sportsmanship connotes something more. What must be emphasized is that fairness, if understood only in a legalistic or formal rule-following sense, can only be regarded as a necessary condition of sportsmanship, but by no means a sufficient one. This point applies to all three views of sportsmanship I intend to outline.

Sportsmanship as a Form of Social Union

The idea of sport as a social union takes into account, but goes beyond, an agreement to willingly abide and play by the rules in the interests of what is fair. It is also concerned with the preservation and continuation of its best traditions, customs, and conventions so that the community which makes up the social union cannot only cooperatively participate in sport, but successfully relate to one another as persons through an understood, shared, and appreciated mode of proceeding. "The Sportsmanship Brotherhood" (22) which was founded in 1926, while itself indebted to the English Public School ethos of games playing, may be regarded as a forerunner to this view. Its aim was to foster and spread the spirit of sportsmanship throughout the world which it saw, in part at least, as a form of social and moral well-being. By adopting the slogan "Not that you won or lost – but that you played the game," it brought home the point that the *manner* in which sport

is conducted is no less important than its outcome, if amicability and brotherhood are to be encouraged and upheld. Rawls (19: pp. 525–26), in speaking of games as a simple instance of a social union, suggests that in addition to it being concerned with its rules, it is also concerned with an agreed and cooperative "scheme of conduct in which the excellences and enjoyments of each (player) are complementary to the good of all." The idea of sport as a social union, then, is not just concerned with getting players to accept and abide by the rules but also with the maintenance and extolling of a way of life in which sportsmen find value, cooperation, and mutual satisfaction. If this view of sportsmanship is to flourish and be furthered, it is not a matter of merely adopting a particular code of etiquette or set of shibboleths, but of having a genuine commitment to the values of fellowship and goodwill which are held to be more important than the desire to win or the achievement of victory. The central purpose of the social union view of sportsmanship is to preserve and uphold fraternal relationships that can arise in and through a participation in sport. More than this, it sees this purpose as being intrinsically involved with the nature of sport itself. Any attempt, therefore, to characterize the nature of sport without reference to it would leave the conceptual map of sport incomplete and considerably impoverished.

It is important to stress that the social union view of sportsmanship is not to be seen merely as a socially cohesive device in order to help regulate and oil the institutional practice of sport, though this effect may well come about. Rather it should be perceived as a community of individuals united by a particular practice in which the arts of chivalry are practiced in the interests of mutual affection, comradery, and fellowship. It is seen by the participants as the kind of practice which places a high premium upon those qualities and forms of conduct such as good humor, respect, politeness, and affability which are conducive to, rather than destructive of, good interpersonal relations and cooperative, if competitive, endeavor. In other words, the idea of sport as a social union is a particular kind of social system in and by which players and officials come together in order to share a commonly valued form of life, a part of which is concerned with the manner in which one should ideally participate if the system is to flourish.[3] An example of this is provided by an incident at the French Tennis Championships of 1982 when Wilander, a Swedish player, was awarded match point against his opponent Clerc on the grounds that a drive down the line was out. Wilander, instead of accepting the umpire's decision, as the rules state, asked for the point to be played again because he thought the ball was "good and that he didn't have a chance." Mr. Dorfman, the referee, at some risk to his official position, but conscious of the good of the players and game alike, agreed (3: p. 10).[4] Another example comes from the World Athletic Championships of 1983, when Banks, the American world triple jump record holder, was defeated in the last round by the Pole, Hoffman. Instead of being grieved and withdrawn, as is often the case when victory eludes an athlete by a hair's breadth, Banks demonstrated his delight at Hoffman's success by running around the track with him as an act of respect and comradery. For both, a moment between them had been forged. The system requires of all members a commitment to live out the ideals cherished by the union in a way that predisposes towards its convivial continuance. When sport is viewed in this way, sportsmanship can be seen as an evaluative term which is attributed to those who not only uphold and play according to the rules, but keep faith with their spirit by acts and forms of conduct which are not required by the rules but which are freely made in accordance with the best traditions of competitive, but friendly, rivalry. The social union view of sport then, apart from a ready acceptance of what is fair, sees acts of sportsmanship as chiefly having to do with maintaining the best traditions of sport as a valued and shared form of life. In this view, sportsmanship is more in keeping with a particular kind of socialization or ideology which predisposes group members to act in ways that are supported and admired by the social union of which they are an integral part. Because of this, the social union view of sportsmanship is best understood as having more to do

with an idealized form or model of group mores rather than as an individual and principled form of morality.

Sportsmanship as a Means in the Promotion of Pleasure

Keating's (12: p. 265) analysis of sportsmanship, although it has some things in common with the idea of sport as a social union, arises more from the etymological meaning of sport. In essence, he maintains sport is "a kind of diversion which has for its direct and immediate end fun, pleasure and delight and which is dominated by a spirit of moderation and generosity." He contrasts sport with athletics which he says "is essentially a competitive activity, which has for its end victory in the contest and which is marked by a spirit of dedication, sacrifice and intensity" (12: p. 265).

What it is important to realize is that when Keating speaks of "sport" and "athletics" he does not necessarily have in mind a difference between particular activities (i.e., field games and track and field) so much as an attitude or motivation towards them (13: p. 167). With the term "sport," he associates the notion of play and the doing of something for its sake, and with "athletics" he associates the notion of contest and the struggle for victory. I do not intend to dwell upon the difficulties of holding such a simplistic either/or position. Nonetheless in the interests of clarity a few brief comments seem desirable. First, while it may be true that play is more readily associated with some activities than with others, it should not be assumed that play is confined to them or that play can be adequately expressed only in terms of them. Play can enter "serious" activities, like war, just as it can enter "nonserious" ones like games.

Second, the fact that an activity is "competitive" does not necessarily preclude having a play attitude towards it. This point holds true even when recognizing that a preoccupation with winning can sometimes inhibit, even neutralize, a play spirit. To acknowledge this however, is not to say, as Keating suggests, that if an activity is competitive it *necessarily* follows that a given attitude accompanies it.[5]

Third, it is needlessly confusing to imply, as Keating does, that "athletics" is concerned with competition whereas "sport" is not. The fact is most, if not all, physical activities commonly known as sports are competitive in one sense or another. This is a logical, if trivial point, about them. In view of this it might have been said less perplexingly that the "sportsman's" attitude towards that family of physical activities known as sport differs from that of the "athlete's." This difference in attitude, however, stems not from the constitutive nature of the activities themselves, as Keating (12: p. 266; 13: p. 170) suggests,[6] but rather from the way they are viewed by those who participate in them. Fourth, it does not follow either, as is suggested by some other writers,[7] that because an "athlete" is concerned with "victory" rather than with "pleasure" his motives are necessarily undesirable or immoral in some way. There is a big distinction, for example, between a contestant setting out to gain an honorable victory and a contestant setting out to defeat at all costs (and maybe to humiliate) an opponent.[8]

At this point, I wish to examine and comment upon – accepting for the moment Keating's two ways of regarding competitive activities – what amounts to two ways of looking at sportsmanship. It would seem that for the "athlete," given his goal of "exclusive possession" rather than cooperative endeavor, sportsmanship can never be much more than a means of taking some of the rawness out of competitive strife. Its purpose is to mitigate the effects of what is seen as a confrontation and challenge between two adversaries. Sportsmanship in these circumstances, Keating seems to be saying, can only ease, soften, and in some way make more civilized what is essentially a contest between two prize fighters. Athletes will see the need for disciplined conduct and self-control, even courtesy, but they will not be inclined towards expressions of cordiality or generosity. Sportsmanship for the athlete above all means achieving victory in a dignified and honorable way. They will see the need for "an impartial and equal following of the rules" and the need for "modesty in victory and

quiet composure in defeat," but that is all. "Fairness or fair play," says Keating (13: p. 170), is "the pivotal virtue in athletics." His chief and driving motive, however, will be the outcome of "winning" rather than amicability or joy. In summary, Keating's presentation of sportsmanship in athletics seems pretty commensurate with the idea of sport as justice, which, as I suggested, should be an expectation of all participants. It should not perhaps, therefore be regarded as a genus of sportsmanship at all. It meets minimal requirements, but no more than this.

For the *"sportsman,"* on the other hand, sportsmanship becomes something more expansive. Here sportsmanship is more than simply following a legislative code (which the justice theory of sport might be wrongly accused of being); nor is it best understood as being represented by those virtues which often accompany the admired player such as courage, endurance, perseverance, self-control, self-reliance, sangfroid, and self-respect (with which the character theory of sport is largely associated). Rather it is concerned with those "moral habits or qualities" which essentially and characteristically have to do with generosity and magnanimity (12: p. 266). Unlike the merely "just" player, the true sportsman adopts a cavalier attitude towards his/her rights as permitted by the code. Instead he prefers to be magnanimous and self-sacrificing if, by such conduct, "he contributes to the fun of the occasion" (12: p. 266). It is important to see in Keating's account of sport that competition is not seen in logical terms of "exclusive possession," by one or the other of the vying parties, but more in terms of a cooperative enterprise, which is seen to be a potentially shared source of pleasure. For Keating then, sportsmanship for the sportsman is essentially a desirable or efficacious manner or way of acting in sport which is in keeping with the promotion of pleasure and the spirit of play.

From the moral point of view at least three questions arise from Keating's account of sportsmanship. The first question is: can sportsmanship in relation to sport be considered moral if it is seen only as a *means* or as an instrument in the promotion of pleasure? The answer to this question is very closely related to whether or not he is taking a utilitarian stance towards moral issues and he does not make this clear.

The second question is concerned with the sense in which Keating uses the phrase sportsmanship as a "moral category." If he means it in the sense of being "self-contained"[9] then it cannot properly be said to be moral since it is inapplicable to life outside of sport. Similarly, if he wants to regard it as a form of play, as he seems to, then at least at one level of analysis, it is "nonserious" as opposed to "serious" and therefore nonmoral in consequence. If, on the other hand, he is intending that sportsmanship is concerned with the type of actions that fall within the general category of the moral and therefore somehow related to the "business of life," this should have been stated more explicitly. If this is the case, however, the problem remains as to how this interpretation is to be reconciled with the notion of play. One way around this dilemma might be to say that although play is generally regarded as a nonserious affair, this is not to say that players cannot take what they are doing seriously (in the psychological sense) or that serious incidents (e.g., death, injury, or acts of malevolence) cannot occur. To say, in other words, that play as a category is nonserious and therefore nonmoral is to say that this is the way it is best understood, but recognizing, at the same time, things occasionally occur that transform it momentarily into something else, which may or may not have moral significance.

The third question is related to the first one. Even if utilitarianism is adopted as a general ethical theory, it is not clear why conduct that is conducive to fun is necessarily more pleasurable and therefore more moral than conduct that is conducive to "honorable victory." One is tempted to ask here, is it not the case that the best examples of sportsmanship in terms of generosity and "magnanimity" arise out of the pursuit of "honorable victory?" A case which gives some support to this thesis is when Brasher, at the Melbourne Olympic Games in 1956, was disqualified from winning the 3000 meters steeplechase for allegedly hindering his opponents. The point here is that it was these same

athletes (Larsen, Loufer, and Rozsnyói) who protested on Brasher's behalf and got the decision reversed, thus sacrificing the medals they would otherwise have won.

All in all Keating's attempt to look at sportsmanship in terms of "athletics" and "sport" by reference to competition, or its relative absence, it not altogether clear or helpful. It does, however, emphasize the importance of the play spirit of sport and the desirable attributes of magnanimity and generosity.

Sportsmanship as a Form of Altruism

It should be apparent by now that the term sportsmanship and its relation to sport and morality is a more complex and subtle one than is commonly supposed. In the social union view of sportsmanship it was suggested that sportsmanship largely has to do with the preservation and exemplification of a valued form of life which puts a premium upon an idealized and amicable way of participating. The pleasure view of sportsmanship sees sportsmanship as being chiefly and characteristically concerned with generous and magnanimous conduct that is conducive to the promotion of fun and pleasure. The view of sportsmanship I shall now present takes a different stance. This view is concerned more with seeing sportsmanship as a form of altruistically motivated conduct that is concerned with the good or welfare of another. Again it should be stressed that I do not see these three views of sportsmanship as mutually exclusive. I see them rather as providing a different focus or perspective on a form of social phenomenon which is essentially both recognizable and understood.

What then, more precisely, is the altruistic view of sportsmanship and how and in what way, if at all, can it be considered as a moral form of conduct? In order to look at the second part of the question first I propose to contrast the Kantian view of morality with what I shall call the altruistic view. For Kant, morality is primarily a matter of reason and rationality. It resides in and is based upon the adoption of principles which are universalizable, impartial, consistent, and obligatory. It emphasizes choice, decision, will, and thoughtful deliberation.[10] Williams, in writing of Kantian tradition, points out that:

> The moral point of view is specially characterised by its impartiality and its indifference to any particular relations to particular persons and that moral thought requires abstraction from particular circumstances and particular characteristics of the parties, including the agent, except in so far as these can be universal features of any morally similar situation. (24: p. 198)

Williams continues:

> The motivations of a moral agent, correspondingly, involve a rational application of impartial principle and are thus different in kind from sorts of motivations that he might have for treating some particular persons differently because he happened to have some particular interest towards them. (24: p. 198)

It will be seen that the Kantian view of morality has a lot in common with the justice theory of sport as well as with those preconditional features of sportsmanship which are to do with fairness. In stressing the universal and impartial, however, the Kantian view seems to overlook or disregard some aspects of interpersonal relations which are as morally important in sport as in other spheres of life. I refer to such virtues as sympathy, compassion, concern, and friendship. What needs to be clarified is that the 'moral point of view', while it is importantly connected with the impartial and obligatory, is by no means totally taken up by them. In speaking of sportsmanship then as a form of altruism, I am particularly concerned to show that sportsmanship in this sense, while obligated to the following of impartial rules which govern play, at the same time gives moral scope to go beyond them. In order to say more about this and at the same time point up the differences between the Kantian view of morality and those aspects of morality and sportsmanship that place greater emphasis upon the importance of personal and particular relationships, I propose to look now at sportsmanship as a form of altruism. At the same time I shall indicate that acts of supererogation are more in keeping with the Kantian view than with the altruistic view.

Altruism is perhaps best understood as having to do with those forms of action and conduct that are not done merely because of what is fair and just in terms of playing and keeping to the rules but because there is a genuine concern for and interest in one's fellow competitors, whether on the same side or in opposition. At first sight it may seem as if sportsmanship in this altruistic sense has to do with supererogatory acts in that they go beyond duty or what the rules expect. In common with other forms of supererogatory acts, these acts in sport are to do as Hare (10: p. 198) puts it with those acts which are "praiseworthy but not obligatory." Stated another way, to say that an act in sport is supererogatory is to say two things about it. First, the sportsman is not morally (or by role) obliged to perform it. He is, in other words, permitted not to perform it. Second, the action is morally praiseworthy; it would be commendable if it were performed. Urmson, in speaking of the need to make room for the moral actions which lie outside the realm of obligation, could well be speaking of the kinds of situation with which the sportsman is confronted. He argues that there is a large range of actions whose moral status is insufficiently expressible in terms of the traditional classification of actions into morally impermissible, morally neutral, and morally obligatory and that it is necessary to allow "for a range of actions which are of moral value and which an agent may feel called upon to perform, but which cannot be demanded and whose omission cannot be called wrongdoing." (23: p. 208)

There seem to be at least two ways in sport in which an act can go beyond duty (or demands of fair play). The first way is by acting out of concern for the other or at some risk, cost, or sacrifice to oneself. An example here might be the marathon runner who, at the cost of victory, stops to help a fellow runner in a state of distress. The second way is by acting on behalf of another so that more good is brought about than if one had merely acted out of duty or in accordance with the rules. An actual case is provided by Meta Antenan, who, although leading in a long jump competition against her great German rival, asked of the presiding jury that her opponent have a longer rest period than is provided by the rules, because of her having just taken part in another event (6: p. 8).[11]

Such examples of sportsmanship, it might be thought, are both supererogatory and altruistic in that they go beyond what is required by duty or a proper observance of the rules, but it should be pointed out that although acts of supererogation and altruism have certain things in common – namely that they have moral value and that they are not morally obligatory – they also have certain important differences which prevent one being assimilated to the other. Whereas supererogatory acts tend to stem from a traditional framework dominated by the notions of duty and obligation, and by some writers (9: Chapter 4) are even spoken of as "doing more than duty requires" in a sacrificial or enobling sort of way, altruistic acts are prompted by various forms of altruistic emotion. Whereas "supererogatory" sportsmen may be prompted into acts which, to them, have the force of duty, but they would not recognize as being encumbent on others, "altruistic" sportsmen may be prompted into acts by the emotions of concern and care.[12]

In referring to the two examples of the "going beyond duty" forms of sportsmanship cited above, it will be seen that either or both could be considered "supererogatory" or "altruistic." The correct interpretation would depend upon the considerations or states which prompted them. Moral actions in sport, like other actions, cannot be properly understood only by reference to their external form.

It will be seen then that supererogatory or altruistic forms of sportsmanship are essentially different from those forms which are to do with a conventional set of values to do with preservation of amicability and group harmony or with the successful pursuit of pleasure.

What characterizes altruistic forms of sportsmanship particularly is that sympathy, compassion, and concern are directed towards the other in virtue of his or her suffering, travail, misery, or pain. The altruistic sportsman not only thinks about and is affected by the plight of the other, but acts in such a way that is directed to bring help or comfort in some way. Altruistic acts of sportsmanship stem from a desire for the other's good. This sometimes leads to impulsive or spontaneous forms of conduct that arise from the sporting contest as when, for example, Karpati, the Hungarian fencer, reached out and tried to console a defeated and disappointed opponent. Such acts, it will be seen, are not motivated by such Kantian virtues as obligation and duty so much as by a perceptive and human response to another's plight. On the rationalistic Kantian view such acts based on altruistic emotions would be considered unreliable as moral motives because they are too transitory, changeable, maybe emotionally charged, and not sufficiently detached, impartial, and consistent. Yet the question arises are they less moral on account of this? Blum (5: p. 93), who has addressed himself to this very problem, argues, for instance, "that the domain in which morally good action takes the form of universalizable principles of obligation does not exhaust the areas of morally good action." He argues further that there are different kinds of virtues. Some are articulated by the Kantian view such as justice, impartiality, conscientiousness and so on while others, such as kindness, concern, and compassion, are articulated better by the altruistic view.

Whereas the Kantian view is predominantly concerned with what is right and what is just for all, the altruistic view is more concerned with the good of the other, even if this sometimes means acting particularly and personally rather than objectively and impartially and/or in a strict accordance with what the rules decree. All in all, the altruistic view of sportsmanship, in contrast to the social union view or the pursuit of pleasure view, arises not from a concern for the preservation of a valued and particular form of interpersonal life or the promotion of pleasure as an ethic, but rather from a particular and genuine concern for another's welfare. When acts in sport go beyond that which is expected of players generally and are done only out of concern for another's good and for no other reason, they are not only altruistic, but exemplify the best traditions of sportsmanship.

Notes

1   J.W. Keating's article (12: pp. 264–271) first appeared in *Ethics*, 75 (1964), pp. 25–35.
2   For an interesting article along these lines see Keenan (14: pp. 115–119).
3   This conception of the way sport can (or should) be conducted is not out of keeping with what some writers have referred to as the "radical ethic" which recognizes "the excellence of the outcome as important, but holds equally important the way that excellence is achieved." See Scott (20: pp. 75–77). It also holds that "the winning of the game is subservient to the playing of the game" in which such qualities as "corporate loyalty and respect for others" are encouraged. All in all "The game is viewed as a framework within which various aims may be realized, qualities fostered, needs met, and values upheld." See Kew (15: pp. 104–107).
4   Two points can be made about this incident. The first is that Wilander, on being asked about why he had challenged the umpire's decision, replied that he could not accept a win "like that" by which he was taken to mean not only unfairly but in a way which would have brought dishonor to himself, and discredit from his opponent, who also thought his drive was in, as well as from his fellow circuit players.
5   See Gallie (8: pp. 167–198), who argued that competition is a normative concept and as such is open to being contested since the evaluative frameworks surrounding it (e.g., a 'Lombardian ethic', where winning is everything, as opposed to the 'radical ethic', referred to in Note 3 above) are sometimes irreconcilable.
6   Fraleigh (7: pp. 74–82) has touched upon some of the complexities of this issue.
7   Bailey (2: pp. 40–50) argues that since competitive games are concerned with winning, especially when they are made compulsory, they are not only morally questionable but morally undesirable in those behaviors and attitudes that are conducive to the defeat of the other side and all that this implies for both the winner and loser.
8   Arnold (1: pp. 126–130) attempts to refute Bailey's view of competition and point out the difference between 'trying to win' when competing and the attitude and outcome of 'winning at all costs'. He also points out the intrinsic values of competitive games.
9   For an explication of play seen in this way see Huizinga (11: p. 32), Lucas (16: p. 11) and Schmitz (21: pp. 22–29) among others.
10 Consult Beck (3) for a good statement of the Kantian position.
11 As a result she lost the competition by one centimeter.
12 Lyons (17: pp. 125–145), in keeping with the points I am making, speaks about a "morality of response and care." This she contrasts with a "morality of justice," which stems more from the Kantian tradition, grounded in obligations and duty.

Bibliography

1   Arnold, P.J. "Competitive Games and Education." *Physical Education Review*, 5, No. 2 (1982), 126–130.
2   Bailey, C. "Games, Winning and Education." *Cambridge Journal of Education*, 5 (1975), 40–50.
3   Beck, L.W. *Immanuel Kant: Foundations of the Metaphysics of Morals*. Indianapolis, IN: Bobbs-Merrill, 1959.
4   Bellamy, R. "Wilander: A Winner and a Gentleman." *The Times* (June 5, 1982).
5   Blum, L.A. *Friendship, Altruism and Morality*. Boston: Routledge and Kegan Paul, 1980.
6   Borotra, J. "A Plea for Sporting Ethics." *Bulletin of the Federation Internationale D'Education Physique*, 48, No. 3 (1978), 7–10.
7   Fraleigh, W.P. "Sport-Purpose." *Journal of the Philosophy of Sport*, 2 (1975), 74–82.
8   Gallie, W.B. "Essentially Contested Concepts." *Proceedings of the Aristotelian Society*, 16 (1955–56), 167–198.
9   Grice, G.R. *The Grounds of Moral Judgment*. New York: Cambridge University Press, 1967, Chapter 4.

10 Hare, R.M. *Moral Thinking*. New York: Clarendon Press, Oxford, 1981.

11 Huizinga, J. *Homo Ludens*. Boulder, CO: Paladin, 1970.

12 Keating, J.W. "Sportsmanship as a Moral Category." *Sport and the Body. Second Edition*. Edited by Ellen W. Gerber and William J. Morgan. Philadelphia: Lea and Febiger, 1979, [reprinted here as reading 6].

13 Keating, J.W. "The Ethics of Competition and its Relation to Some Moral Problems in Athletics." *The Philosophy of Sport*. Edited by R.G. Osterhoudt. Springfield, IL: Charles C. Thomas, 1973.

14 Keenan, F.W. "Justice and Sport." *Journal of the Philosophy of Sport*, 2 (1975), 115–119.

15 Kew, F.C. "Values in Competitive Games." *Quest*, 29 (1978), 103–113.

16 Lucas, J.R. "Moralists and Gamesman." *Philosophy*, 34 (1959), 1–11.

17 Lyons, N.P. "Two Perspectives: On Self, Relationships and Morality." *Harvard Educational Review*, 53 (May, 1983), 125–145.

18 McIntosh, P. *Fair Play: Ethics in Sport and Education*. Heinemann, 1979.

19 Rawls, J. *A Theory of Justice*. New York: Oxford University Press, 1973.

20 Scott, J. "Sport and the Radical Ethic." *Quest*, 19 (January, 1973), 71–77.

21 Schmitz, K.L. "Sport and Play: Suspension of the Ordinary." *Sport and the Body. Second Edition*. Edited by E.W. Gerber and W.J. Morgan. Philadelphia: Lea and Febiger, 1979.

22 "A Sportsmanship Brotherhood." *Literary Digest*, 88 (March 27, 1926).

23 Urmson, J.O. "Saints and Heroes." *Essays in Moral Philosophy*. Edited by A.I. Melden. Seattle: University of Washington Press, 1958.

24 Williams, B. "Persons, Character and Morality." *The Identity of Persons*. Edited by A.O. Rorty. Berkeley: University of California Press, 1976.

CHAPTER 8

Deception, Sportsmanship, and Ethics

Kathleen M. Pearson

Physical educators, if they are to go beyond the lay person's grasp of their profession, must be willing to undertake the task of dissecting and analyzing the many concepts they employ. Some of the most common concepts with which we deal are only dimly understood. Worse yet, we seem content to live in this twilight world. Status as a profession demands that we make every effort to shine the light of analysis on the many fuzzy concepts with which we constantly must deal.

One of the more troublesome areas with which we struggle is the domain of ethics, and this seems particularly acute for those who work in athletics. I believe that some of the confusion surrounding the nature of ethical conduct in sport can be cleared up through an analysis of the concept of deception in athletics.

At the heart of every athletic activity is the attempt to successfully deceive one's opponent. The thesis presented here is that deception in athletics is not a simple, unitary event. Deception can be analyzed into at least two types: (a) Strategic Deception and (b) Definitional Deception. Finally, a rule of thumb can be established for deciding on the ethics of acts of deception which fall into those two categories.

Strategic Deception

Strategic deception occurs when an athlete deceives his opponent into thinking he will move to the right when he actually intends to move left – that he will bunt the baseball when he intends to hit a line drive – that he will drive the tennis ball when he actually intends to lob it. Examples of this sort of deception are replete in athletic events and need not be elaborated here. The important question is whether these acts of strategic deception are ethical or unethical.

In order to deal with this question, we need a rule of thumb for deciding on the ethics of an act. A standard for deciding if an act of deception is unethical is as follows: If an act is designed by a willing participant in an activity to deliberately interfere with the purpose of that activity, then that act can properly be labeled unethical.

What is the purpose of athletic activities? Why even have such things as basketball games, football games, tennis games? I suggest that the purpose of these games, in an athletic setting, is to test the skill of one individual, or group of individuals, against the skill of another individual, or group of individuals, in order to determine who is more skillful in a particular, well defined activity.

How is any particular game defined? A particular game is no more (in terms of its careful definition) than its rules. The rules of one game distinguish it as being different from all other games. Some games may have quite similar rules; however, there must be at least one difference between the rules of one game and those of all other games in order for that game to be distinguished from all other games. If we were to find another game with exactly the same rules between the covers of its rulebook, we would naturally conclude that it was the same game. Thus, problems of identity and diversity of games are decided by the rules for each game. Identical games have identical rules and diverse games have differing rules. A game is identified, or defined, as being just that game by the rules which govern it.

If the purpose of athletics is to determine who is more skillful in a particular game, and if an unethical act is one which is designed to deliberately interfere with that purpose, it is difficult to see how acts of strategic deception could be called unethical. In fact, this sort of deception is at the heart of the skill factor in athletic events. It is the sort of activity which separates the highly skilled athlete from the less skilled athlete, and therefore, is the sort of activity that makes a significant contribution to the purpose of the athletic event. Strategic deception is in no way designed to deliberately interfere with the purpose of athletics.

Definitional Deception

Definitional deception occurs when one has contracted to participate in one sort of activity, and then deliberately engages in another sort of activity. An example of this sort of deception might occur if one were to sign a contract to teach political science, be assigned to a political science class, and then proceed to campaign for a particular political candidate.

How does this parallel an act which might be committed in an athletic setting? The paradigm used here suggests that: (*a*) Under certain circumstances, the commission of a foul in a game falls into the category of definitional deception; (*b*) Under certain circumstances, the act of fouling can be labeled as unsportsmanlike; and, (*c*) Certain kinds of fouls can be linked to acts which can be properly labeled as unethical.

It was established earlier that a game is identified, or defined, as being just that game by the rules which govern it. Furthermore, we are all familiar with the fact that it is in compliance with the rules of a particular game that we commit certain acts, while it is against the rules to commit other acts. When one commits an act that is not in compliance with the rules he is said to have committed a foul, and a prescribed penalty is meted out in punishment for that act. The ways in which fouls are committed in athletic contests can be separated into two categories. The first category consists of those fouls which are committed accidentally, and the second is composed of those fouls which are committed deliberately.

Let us first consider the case of accidental fouls. According to our rule of thumb, an act must be designed to deliberately interfere with the purpose of the activity in order for that act to be labeled unethical. Since the criterion of intentionality is missing from the accidental foul, that act has no ethical significance. We would ordinarily expect a person to accept the penalty for that foul, but we would not place moral blame on him.

Next, let us turn to the person who deliberately commits a foul while participating in an athletic contest. If the purpose of the contest is to determine who is more skillful in that game we can say that a player has entered into a contract with his opponent for the mutual purpose of making that determination. In other words, he has contracted with his opponent and the audience (if there is one) to play football, for instance, in order to determine who is more skillful in a game of football.

I have argued earlier that a particular game is defined by its rules – that the rules of a game are the definition of that game. If this is the case, a player who deliberately breaks the rules of that game is deliberately no longer playing that game. He may be playing "smutball," for instance, but he is not playing football. This is a case of deliberate definitional deception. These kinds of acts are designed to interfere with the purpose of the game in which they occur. How can it be determined which of two players (or teams) is more skillful in a game if one of the players (or teams) is not even playing that particular game? If the arguments presented here are correct thus far, we can conclude that the intentional commission of a foul in athletics is an unethical act. Ordinarily, when we refer to un-ethical acts on the part of athletes, we call these acts unsportsmanlike.

Someone might argue, at this point, that the penalties for fouling also are contained within the rulebook for a particular game, and there-fore, fouls are not outside the rules for the game. The obvious rebuttal to this position is that penalties for breaking the law are contained within the law books, but no sensible person concludes, therefore, that all acts are within the law. If this were the case, there would be no sense in having laws at all. Similarly, if this were the case with games, there would be no sense in having rules for games. However, since the def-inition of a game is its rules, if there were no rules for that game there would be no game. Therefore, even though the penalties for fouling are contained within the rulebook for a game, the act of deliberate fouling is, indeed, outside the rules for that game.

When a teacher or coach has contracted with an institution and with individual students to teach those students how to play a particular game, he is violating that contract when he encourages deliberate definitional deception. The purpose of teaching or coaching a game is to help persons learn to play that game. An act which is deliberately designed to interfere with that purpose is an unethical act. It has already been argued that when a player commits an intentional foul in a game, he is no longer playing that game. Similarly, when a teacher or coach instructs players to commit an intentional foul, he is no longer teaching that game. He is committing an act which is deliberately designed to interfere with the purpose of the contract into which he has entered, i.e., to help students to learn to play that game. Thus, according to our rule of thumb, his conduct is properly labeled as unethical.

A variety of elegant arguments can be pro-duced to indict the deliberate foul. It violates the ludic spirit, it treats the process of playing as mere instrument in the pursuit of the win, and it reflects a view of one's competitor as both enemy and object rather than colleague in noble contest. All of these pleas, however, fall short of the ultimate and most damaging testimony; de-liberate betrayal of the rules destroys the vital frame of agreement which makes sport possible. The activity even may go on in the face of such fatal deception, but neither the logic of analysis nor the intuition of experience permit us to call whatever is left a game – for that is shattered.

CHAPTER 9

On Sportsmanship and "Running Up the Score"

Nicholas Dixon

I wish to argue against a widely-held view concerning sportsmanship.[1] I call this view the *Anti-Blowout* thesis (AB):

AB: It is intrinsically unsporting for players or teams to maximize the margin of victory after they have secured victory in a one-sided contest.[2]

Having elaborated on the thesis in Section I, I present my main arguments against it in Section II. Section III is devoted to showing that none of several currently favored theories of sportsmanship supports the AB thesis. Section IV is a qualified conclusion.

I

The sporting community (players, coaches, and journalists) seems almost unanimous in condemning the pursuit of lopsided victories, which is described in such derogatory terms as "running up the score" and "showing up" the losing team. For instance, the University of Michigan's 61–7 defeat of Houston's football team in 1992 was greeted with howls of delight that Houston had been given a taste of its own medicine. The "grossly classless behavior" which, according to a Detroit sports journalist, earned Houston such heavy retribution was its own habit of running up the score against outmatched opponents. Similarly, in the early 1980s, a Big Ten football coach was outraged when the opposing team, already ahead by several touchdowns, scored another touchdown on a long passing play in the game's closing moments. After the play, the coach led his entire team onto the field and drew its attention to the scoreboard, which indicated the few seconds remaining to play. They stood there for several seconds contemplating the scoreboard, presumably vowing bloody revenge for this humiliation when the teams met the following season.

Apparently the sporting thing for victorious teams to do on such occasions would be to "go easy" on their opponents. They should insert second- and third-string players, and mercifully run out the clock with time-consuming running plays, gracefully coasting to victory without compounding the losers' suffering.

The AB thesis is widely held in both college and professional sport, especially football. It is also applied to some extent in basketball, and even in baseball. For instance, eyebrows would be raised if the visiting team, already ahead 12–0 in the top of the ninth inning, attempted to pad the lead by bunting and stealing bases.

The few passing references to this issue that I have been able to find by philosophers indicate that they share the AB view, albeit in a less extreme form. For instance, Randolph M. Feezell (2: p. 2) states that "running up the score on an opponent . . . is bad form, somehow inappropriate because it violates the nature of what sport is about." He considers the fictitious coach Smith, who intimidates both players and referees, ruthlessly pursues victory by all means short of cheating, believes that the only thing wrong with cheating itself is being caught, *and would willingly run up the score if it improved his team's rating and tournament seeding*: "Smith has an impoverished view of sport, an impoverished experience of sport, and it is just such views and attitudes that tend to generate unsportsmanlike behavior in sport" (2: pp. 4–5).

Warren P. Fraleigh (3: pp. 180–190) discusses what he calls "the problem of right action in the uneven contest" at considerable length, showing the complexity of the moral considerations that are relevant to this matter. However, he does not attempt to defend a position on this issue, since his goal is rather to use this example to illustrate a *method* of dealing with value conflicts in general. A virtue of his analysis is that he shows that many options are open to the team leading by a wide margin, ranging from actually allowing the losing team to score a few "consolation" points, to aggressively pursuing an even greater margin of victory. Intermediate tactics include substituting less competent players, or trying out new tactics and strategies (3: p. 181). What is of most interest for my discussion is that Fraleigh (3: p. 184) includes as a reason against tactics that increase the chance of a lopsided victory the fact that "such action would be viewed by other sports agents and spectators as 'running up the score,' intentionally, which is a negatively sanctioned act and contrary to courtesy."

Finally, in a discussion of Fraleigh's views, R. Scott Kretchmar (8: p. 28) suggests in passing that Fraleigh may have to defend the view that, even when a team has an invincible lead, its players are obligated to play their hardest until the end of the game. This is because Fraleigh believes that the central nonmoral value involved in all sporting contests is "knowledge of relative abilities to move mass in space and time in the ways prescribed by the rules" (8: p. 28). Such knowledge is possible only if both teams play to the maximum of their abilities for the duration of the contest. Kretchmar suggests that other nonmoral values may deserve consider-

ation alongside, even in opposition to, the acquisition of knowledge. In the context of uneven contests, one such value would be avoiding the "psychically painful embarrassment" experienced by those who suffer heavy defeats (8: p. 28).[3] Though Kretchmar does not directly raise the issue, this value could be used in support of the AB view.

II

I agree that it *would* be churlish to refuse to relent in a friendly, recreational racquetball game against a completely outmatched opponent. What was meant to be fun would be turned into an exhausting, frustrating ordeal for the other player. In contrast, holding off would help her to improve her game and would lead to longer rallies, making the game more enjoyable for both players. In the same way, an experienced adult chess player should not repeatedly overwhelm a young child whom she is teaching how to play. This might fuel the adult's ego, but would also very likely discourage the child to the point of destroying her interest in chess. Deliberately making weak moves, and even allowing the child to win occasionally, would be a far more appropriate way to help the child to enjoy and improve her game. In both cases, "going for the jugular" would destroy the purpose of the game: recreation and nurturing, respectively.

In contrast, my main thesis in this paper is that there is absolutely nothing intrinsically wrong with pressing for a lopsided victory in a *competitive* game, whether it be football, basketball, soccer, or any other sport. While values such as mercy and mutual enjoyment are also relevant to competitive sport, the introduction of the element of competition makes complaints voiced by proponents of the AB view inappropriate. The distinction I draw between recreational and competitive sports parallels that made by James W. Keating (7) between sport and athletics,[4] though in Section IIIB I will consider an objection to his distinction.

It might be *unwise* for a coach to risk injuries to key players and waste a golden opportunity to give second-string players some playing time and perhaps try out novel plays and strategies in a low-risk setting. However, I reject the received wisdom among AB advocates that winning a game by a wide margin is not just unwise, but positively *unsporting*.

One line of argument for this mistaken belief is a rather distasteful attitude toward sport: Winning is the only thing that matters. If this were so, it would indeed be gratuitous to continue to score points long after victory, the game's only goal, has been secured. However, the premise is false: Winning is *not* the only thing that matters. Players who win blowouts can be justly proud of their display of athletic excellence, the personal and team records they have set, and the excitement provided for fans.

Even if it is granted that there is more to sport than winning, the feeling persists that there is still something cruel in inflicting one-sided defeats. Underlying this feeling is an attitude toward sport that can be used to mount a second, more plausible argument for the AB thesis: Players who suffer lopsided defeats have been humiliated and diminished as human beings. The fact that the AB thesis is most often cited in football and basketball, both of which involve considerable contact, suggests that the macho notion of sport as a test of manhood is also involved.[5]

This attitude has lost sight of the element of play in all sports, at whatever level, and regardless of their business aspect.[6] Moreover, even on a view such as Fraleigh's (3), which regards the determination of athletic superiority as the essential value of sport,[7] there is absolutely no disgrace in suffering a heavy defeat by a far stronger team. While they do indicate athletic ability, neither victory nor defeat affects one's worth as a human being. What *does* reflect players' character is how hard and fairly they play, and how they conduct themselves in defeat and victory.

It might be countered that a lopsided defeat does humiliate the loser, not as a human being, but *as an athlete*, and that this is why it is unsporting to inflict such defeats. Athletes take pride in their ability and effort, and blowouts are an affront to this pride.

My response involves distinguishing between weak and strong humiliations. In the weak sense of "reducing to a lower position,"[8] any defeat, not just a blowout, is by definition a humiliation of the loser qua athlete. Inflicting humiliation in this harmless sense is the inevitable outcome of most competitive activities. Only in the strong sense of causing shame or disgrace does humiliating someone become a moral issue. And it isn't clear that an athlete is humiliated qua athlete in this stronger sense by the fact that her opponent is far stronger. The only cause for shame after a heavy defeat would be knowing, for example, that I did not play to the best of my ability, or that I gave up trying. A heavy defeat is in and of itself no cause for shame.

More appropriate occasions for feelings of strong humiliation would be the revelation of a moral fault (e.g., cheating), a nonmoral character fault (such as the lack of persistence I show if I give up too easily in my defeat), or an act of gross stupidity or incompetence. Suffering a heavy defeat to a far stronger athlete or team reveals no such failing. In general, the fact that someone else is far better than me at x-ing strongly humiliates me neither qua x-er nor as a human being. Why should sport be regarded differently than other activities? Even if one confines attention to the person *qua athlete*, then, the claim that she is strongly humiliated by a heavy defeat indicates an inflated estimate of the importance of the outcome of sporting contests.

The AB thesis seems to require that a team which is far stronger should *conceal* the extent of its superiority by easing up. An analogy from the academic world may be helpful. When a student makes a comment in class that indicates a misunderstanding of an elementary point, the sensitive instructor will give the comment the most favorable reading possible and gently lead the student to a better understanding. At a professional meeting, in contrast, an academic will not hesitate to point out an error made by a peer. This can be done in a respectful, nonconfrontational way, just as a team can win a contest by a wide margin while still showing respect for its opponents. The suggestion that an academic should diplomatically try to conceal the error made by her peer is condescending. A vastly superior team should treat its opponents just as an academic would treat a colleague, not as she would treat a student.

None of this is to deny that malevolent coaches and players may maximize the margin of victory precisely in order to humiliate their opponents. The wrongness of such actions consists in the *intention* to harm, since, if my analysis is correct, such defeats do not actually humiliate the losers in the strong, harmful sense. Such behavior is just as reprehensible as any deliberate attempt to humiliate others, and may justly be called "running up the score." My point is that one can also pursue a lopsided victory *without* any intention to humiliate one's opponent, and that there is nothing wrong with such victories. Heavy defeats are not intrinsically humiliating in the strong sense that is prima facie morally wrong.

However, partly because some teams arguably do intend to humiliate the opponents they beat by a wide margin, a connection has been forged in American sporting consciousness between lopsided victories and humiliation. Even if the winning team has no such malevolent intentions, the losers are likely to *infer* them, and to *feel* humiliated, anyway. Consequently, an objection to my view is that respect for the feelings of opponents should prevent teams from pursuing victory by a wide margin, however innocent the motives behind the victory would have been.

Certainly the way an action will be perceived is one of the factors that should be considered in evaluating that action. However, if people's negative perception of the action is based on a misconception – as I claim is the case with the view that lopsided victories strongly humiliate the opponent – it carries little weight as an objection to the action. For instance, the fact that interracial relationships would have shocked and even offended people in southern states in the 1950s sheds more light on the prejudice of the offended people than it does on the morality of interracial relationships. Those who lose sporting contests by a wide margin may *feel* humiliated, but, if my argument in the last few paragraphs is sound, they have not *in fact* been strongly humiliated, either as human beings or as athletes. Consequently, the existence of such feelings does not justify moral condemnation of

teams pursuing victory by a wide margin. We might hope that, as a less inflated estimate of the importance of the outcome of sporting contests prevails, such groundless feelings of humiliation will become less and less common. Consequently, malicious athletes and teams will be less and less tempted to inflict heavy defeats in a misguided attempt to harm their opponents.

When one strips away these two mistaken attitudes toward sport – winning is the only thing that matters, and heavy defeat is a serious affront to one's humanity or to one's status as an athlete – there remains no good reason to criticize teams for pursuing high scores in one-sided victories. As long as the winning team shows respect for the losers (which is perfectly compatible with winning a soccer game by 10 goals, or a football game by 50 points), no apology is needed for an exciting display of skill and athleticism. What *does* show a lack of respect for outmatched opponents is mocking and taunting them, and this will often be a distinguishing feature of the deliberate attempts to humiliate opponents that I do condemn.

An unlikely source of support for my view was provided by the opponents of the U.S. "Dream Team" in the 1992 Olympic basketball tournament. Despite being thoroughly outmatched, they played with great enthusiasm and spirit, clearly enjoying every minute they shared the court with the NBA legends. They understood, far better than proponents of the AB thesis, that a lopsided defeat in sport need mean no more than a lopsided difference in ability.

What *was* distasteful was the jingoistic buildup to the Olympics, fueled by NBC's promotional "spots" for the Dream Team's imminent display of American superiority. This chauvinism has nothing to do with sportsmanship, and everything to do with the mistaken view that sport is a test of the worth of a human being or a nation.

III

My concern in this section is not to propose a new analysis of sportsmanship. Instead, my purpose is to show that my view comports far better than the AB thesis with the most plausible models of sportsmanship that have been proposed.

A

I will consider first an influential account of sportsmanship developed by Keating (7). His view is best understood in contrast to a model of sportsmanship that *would* condemn lopsided victories: the "Eton" view of sport prevalent in English public (i.e., exclusive and private!) schools in past centuries.[9] Sport was played by gentlemen for the intrinsic pleasure of playing, rather than for the purpose of winning. Amateurism was encouraged, excessive preparation for a sporting event was considered bad form,[10] and players and coaches were expected to value a "good game," an equal contest, as more important than achieving superiority. Since even strenuous efforts to win a game were frowned upon, this model would clearly not tolerate the pursuit of victory by a wide margin.

Keating's account of sportsmanship is based on the distinction between recreational ("sport") and competitive ("athletics") contests. The different purpose of each of these two activities gives rise to a different conception of sportsmanship. Since the purpose of recreational sport is "pleasant diversion – the immediate joy to be derived in the activity itself – the pivotal or essential virtue in sportsmanship is generosity" (7: p. 34). While generosity does not require the adoption of the Eton model, it calls for moderation on the part of the person or team with an insurmountable lead in a friendly game. Such moderation will help "to avoid all unpleasantness and conflict and to cultivate, in their stead, an unselfish and cooperative effort" (7: p. 34). This insight underlies my own support for the AB thesis in purely recreational sport. What little plausibility the Eton model has is confined to recreational sport. It is wholly inadequate, however, when applied to competitive sport, and hence cannot be used to undercut my arguments against the AB thesis in the context of this type of sport.

Competitive sport (athletics), according to Keating (7: p. 33), has the different purpose of "the objective and accurate determination of superior performance and, ultimately, of excellence." The corresponding concept of sportsmanship is hard but fair play. A similar view of the purpose of competitive sport is expressed by Warren P. Fraleigh: "to provide equitable opportunity for mutual contesting of the relative abilities of the participants to move mass in space and time within the confines prescribed by an agreed-upon set of rules" (3: p. 41).

While this paradigm clearly excludes cheating, in no way does it deem lopsided victories as unsporting. If anything, if the runaway winner eases up in the later stages of the game, the purpose of determining athletic excellence is *undermined*. It is true that the contestants' "relative abilities" have already been determined by this stage in the sense of a *rank ordering*. However, an eight-goal margin of victory may more accurately reflect, for instance, the relative abilities of two soccer teams than a still-comfortable three-goal difference. The margin of victory gives a tangible *quantitative measure* of the relative abilities of the teams. Those who complain that continuing to score goals long after victory has been achieved is gratuitous and unsporting are guilty of a simplistic reduction of the comparative purpose of competitive sport to the categories of "winners" and "losers." Moreover, the interest of competitive sport goes beyond a comparison between the contestants. We are also interested in assessing their abilities in comparison with other athletes and teams, both past and present, as is evidenced by the assiduous attention given to sporting records. The attempt to make quantitative comparisons between contestants, and to maintain the integrity of sporting records, would be sabotaged if easing up in a sporting event once victory is secured were to become common practice.[11]

In defense of the AB thesis, it might be objected that the actual context of many blowouts is far removed from the accurate measure of athletic ability that Keating and Fraleigh believe is central to sport. In college athletics, lopsided victories often result from a team's desire to "pad" its record, and thus improve its national ranking, by deliberately scheduling weak opponents. Such blowouts are meaningless as a measure of the ability of the winning team, since the outmatched losers present no serious challenge. Since the goal of measuring athletic ability is not met, the charge remains that lopsided victories involve the gratuitous infliction of suffering.[12]

I have three responses. First, this objection is confined to the Fraleigh/Keating view of the purpose of competitive sport discussed in this subsection. Lopsided victories may serve *other* goals of sport, such as providing excitement for fans, and hence may avoid being gratuitous.

Second, I reject the assumption that a lopsided victory over an outmatched opponent gives no measure of athletic excellence. While the superior team's victory may never be in doubt, its manner of victory can be most revealing. Even when the opponent is weak, an exciting display of offensive firepower, full of skill and imagination, can be a testament to a team's strength. By the same token, a narrow, lackluster victory over a clearly inferior team will often justifiably result in a lower national ranking for the winning team. Throughout the world of soccer, including the World Cup, "goal difference" is used as a tie-breaker. Of all the methods of tie-breaking, this is the least controversial, since people recognize that the ability to score and prevent goals over a series of games, especially over a whole season, is a reliable measure of excellence in soccer. More generally, as pointed out previously, the practice of record keeping in sports reflects the belief that scores in a game, season, or career are a meaningful basis for comparison between athletes and teams.

Third, and most important, the objection is addressed primarily to the *scheduling* of contests that are known in advance to be uneven, not to lopsided victories themselves. This type of scheduling may result in an unrealistically inflated win–loss record for the stronger team, and hence undermine the reliability of national standings (although those responsible for the standings may be able to take into account the quality of a team's opponents when they decide on its ranking). However, the arguments I have presented so far indicate that once a contest has been scheduled, there is nothing unsporting about pursuing victory by a wide margin, as long as respect is shown for the losing team.

In sum, if the primary purpose of competitive sport is to determine relative athletic ability, then the pursuit of emphatic victories may be not only compatible with sportsmanship, but even required by it. However, we now need to consider rival models of sportsmanship based on different views of the purpose of sport.

B

Randolph Feezell (2) rejects the sharp distinction between recreational and competitive sport (sport and athletics) that underlies Keating's two-level theory of sportsmanship. Whereas Keating excludes keen competition from his account of recreational sport, and playfulness from his account of competitive sport, Feezell argues that both the serious desire to win and a sense of playfulness are involved, in varying degrees, in all sport. The person who engages in sport

> is simultaneously player and athlete. His purpose is to win the contest *and* to experience the playful and aesthetic delights of the experience. His attitudes are at once both playful and competitive, and these color his relationship with his fellow participants. He sees his opponent as both competitor and friend, competing and cooperating at the same time. (2: p. 6)

Keating's account of sportsmanship in *competitive* sport, which is my main concern in this paper, is inadequate, Feezell argues, because it would sanction brutal, no-holds-barred competition, as long as one stays within the letter of the rules of the game. Such an attitude is actually more like an instance of bad sportsmanship, since it "ignores the unwritten rules of playing ... and tends to destroy the spirit of play" (2: p. 7).

Once we recognize that "sport is a formal, competitive variety of human play" (2: p. 7), a more appropriate model of sportsmanship would accommodate the playfulness that Keating confines to purely recreational sport. At the same time, the person whose attitude is so playful that she makes no serious effort to win the game is being unsporting in a completely different way: failing to respect the importance of trying one's hardest in competitive sport. Feezell's model of sportsmanship is an Aristotelian mean

> between excessive seriousness, which misunderstands the importance of the play-spirit, and an excessive sense of playfulness, which might be called frivolity and which misunderstands the importance of victory and achievement when play is competitive. (2: p. 10)

A certain degree of seriousness is needed in order to experience the pleasure of competition, but at the same time this very seriousness creates the danger of alienating, unsporting behavior.[13]

In defense of Keating, Feezell's accusation that Keating's account of sportsmanship in competitive sport would permit an unsporting obsession with winning within the letter of the rules may be unfair. After all, Keating (7: p. 35) bases his account of sportsmanship on his belief that *honorable* victory is the goal of participants in competitive sport. The player who constantly badgers the referee, and who rudely but legally tries to "psych out" her opponent, may not violate the purpose of an "objective and accurate determination of superior performance," but her victory is certainly not honorable. However, Keating's account of sportsmanship may be circular, in that exactly what kind of behavior *is* honorable is the very point in question in explaining sportsmanship.

At first blush, Feezell's account of sportsmanship, which includes playfulness as well as competitiveness, would be less tolerant of one-sided victories than would the Keating/Fraleigh model, which puts primary emphasis on sport as a fair and accurate assessment of the relative ability of the contestants. Shouldn't the competitive urge to achieve a high score be tempered by a generous desire to ease up and soften the impact of defeat on the losers? As we saw in Section I, Feezell himself believes so. However, I have two arguments that show why Feezell's account of sportsmanship does not support the AB thesis.

First, the value of generosity that calls for easing up in one-sided games is a moral value more germane to the model of sportsmanship, to be discussed in the next subsection, based on altruism. Playfulness is a more aesthetic, even hedonistic concept, which does not clearly require generosity. This is not to suggest that the spirit of playfulness places no moral demands on competitors. Not only cheating, but any form of disrespect for opponents, is directly contrary to the spirit of playfulness. The trash talking and taunting of opponents practiced by some basketball players and admired by some sports journalists and fans are clearly ruled out by Feezell's account of sportsmanship. However, as I argued in Section II, beating an outmatched team by a wide margin is in itself not in the least disrespectful. The belief that it is disrespectful is based on the mistaken notion, criticized previously, that a heavy defeat diminishes losers as human beings, or disgraces them as athletes.

Second, continuing to play strenuously even after victory has been secured is actually more congruent with the spirit of playfulness than is easing up. There is nothing in the least bit playful when the football team that is ahead by five touchdowns devotes the entire fourth quarter to grinding out time-consuming, conservative running plays, motivated by the desire to avoid "showing up" the outmatched opponents. Such time-wasting would be openly booed by soccer fans. It reinforces the distinctly *un*playful attitude that the game is effectively over once the sole goal of winning has been guaranteed. Genuine playfulness would consist of continuing to entertain the fans with exciting, innovative plays, taking advantage of the freedom that is provided by having already secured victory. Not only would this enable the winning team to celebrate its excellence, it would also give the opponents the opportunity to demonstrate their pride and character by continuing to compete hard and fairly against superior opponents, and to score "consolation" points. The opponents of the U.S. basketball team in the 1992 Olympics were especially gracious in this regard.

None of this is to deny the value of substituting backup players for starters in uneven contests. Aside from the prudence of not risking injury to key players, team morale will be improved by sharing the fun, and these values may well outweigh the importance of creating scoring records and giving an objectively accurate measure of the winning team's superiority. In any event, inserting second-string players does not guarantee that the margin of victory will be minimized. They are perfectly justified in taking advantage of their rare minutes of playing time by playing hard. It would be unfair to demand that they refrain from inflicting heavy defeats, and thus deny themselves the opportunity to showcase their abilities.[14]

My point in this subsection has been that neither starters nor backups are required to ease up in uneven contests by Feezell's model of sportsmanship as a mean between competitiveness and playfulness.

C

The strongest support for the AB thesis comes from models of sportsmanship that put more explicit emphasis on moral values.[15] Peter J. Arnold (1: p. 66) has developed a model of sportsmanship "as a form of altruistically motivated conduct that is concerned with the good or welfare of another." He argues that there is more to sportsmanship than the mere observance of the rules of the game or the unwritten rules of fair play. The paradigm case of sportsmanship is the athlete who acts altruistically, even if this action diminishes her chance of victory, for instance, the runner who stops to help a badly injured competitor (1: pp. 67–69).

Arnold does not characterize such sportsmanlike acts as supererogatory, since this is the language of duties, albeit "imperfect" ones, based on universal principles.[16] Instead, he puts altruism and sportsmanship in the context of an ethic of care, based on the sympathetic responses we have to particular individuals.[17]

Arnold's view makes more stringent demands on the athlete than any of the other models of sportsmanship we have considered. The sporting athlete not only facilitates a fair contest that accurately reflects the participants' abilities, and behaves in the spirit of playfulness; she also responds altruistically to her rival should the

need arise, even if this impairs her chance of victory. The question before us is whether the altruistic athlete will take pity and refrain from lopsided victories over outmatched opponents. In other words, does Arnold's model of sportsmanship support the AB thesis?

In considering this question, we should first note that Arnold's account of sportsmanship differs from the others we have examined in one crucial respect. These other models present sportsmanship in the form of mandatory moral prescriptions. For instance, the person who cheats, or who violates the playful spirit of sport, exhibits the vice of bad sportsmanship. Arnold, in contrast, regards sportsmanlike acts as those that go beyond the call of duty (though, for reasons already explained, he prefers to characterize them as altruistic, rather than as supererogatory, a term which belongs to the ethics of duty). His examples of sportsmanship are heroic acts of altruism, where an athlete jeopardizes her own chances of victory out of sympathy for the plight of a rival. While few would deny Arnold's claim that such actions "exemplify the best traditions of sportsmanship," the competitor who does *not* perform them is guilty of no moral failing.[18] Viewed in this light, the practice of easing up on outmatched opponents is at best an optional act of mercy, and players who do not do so are innocent of bad sportsmanship.

Moreover, the account of victories by a wide margin that I have developed throughout this paper indicates that suffering a heavy defeat is hardly the kind of disaster that calls for spontaneous acts of altruism by the victor. To paraphrase a point made earlier, a lopsided defeat need reflect only a lopsided difference in performance, and in no way disgrace the loser. Heroic acts of altruism are better reserved for athletes who are genuinely in need of help, such as Arnold's (1: p. 67) example of the marathon runner who, "at the cost of victory, stops to help a fellow runner in a state of distress." Though he uses it to illustrate a different model of sportsmanship, another of Arnold's (1: p. 63) examples also indicates a more appropriate occasion for the altruism which he endorses: Tennis player Mats Wilander corrected a call made by the umpire in the French Open in

1982, even though the call had been in his favor and had given him match point.

The exercise of altruism in the case of the bad tennis call would also be endorsed by the Keating/Fraleigh view of sportsmanship as facilitating a fair and accurate measurement of the rivals' abilities. Wilander's sportsmanlike intervention ensured that the game's outcome depended on a fair application of the game's rules, and not on an error by the umpire. In contrast, when the reason for a one-sided victory is nothing other than a vast difference in ability, there is no need to "go easy" on the losers in the name of the Keating/Fraleigh view of sportsmanship.

Arnold's model of sportsmanship fails to support the AB thesis. First, it relegates sportsmanship to the status of optional acts of altruism, making it inappropriate to condemn the failure to perform such acts as easing up on outmatched opponents. Second, even within the realm of optional acts of altruism, they are better reserved for fellow competitors who are genuinely in need of help than extended to people whose only misfortune is to be losing a competitive sporting contest by a wide margin.

IV

This paper should not be construed as endorsing the obsessive pursuit of massive victories in competitive sport. The value of resting key players, giving second-string players valuable and enjoyable game experience, and trying out untested strategies may often outweigh the value of pursuing victories that accurately reflect the full extent of the winning team's superiority. Even less should it be construed as endorsing the cruel, contemptuous attitude toward the losers exhibited by the team that runs up the score in a deliberate (but misguided) attempt to humiliate its opponents. Any plausible model of sportsmanship, including all those examined here, requires that all competitors show mutual respect at all times. Mocking, taunting, and gloating at outmatched opponents is despicable.

The sportsmanlike victors should thank the losers for the game, and console them for their obvious disappointment.

My only goal has been to show that no sound arguments, including those based on the models of sportsmanship currently in favor, give any good reason for condemning the pursuit of victory by a wide margin as intrinsically unsporting. It might be objected that this only shows the inadequacy of current models of sportsmanship, and that we should develop a new model that *does* condemn the pursuit of runaway victories. However, the models considered here are all supported by careful theoretical arguments and produce plausible analyses of sporting behavior in a wide variety of situations. To reject them, and to build an ad hoc theory, all in the name of the unshakable intuition that lopsided victories are unsporting, creates the suspicion that the intuition is no more than a prejudice.

Interesting though it is in its own right, discussion of the AB thesis is most valuable for the light it sheds on prevailing American attitudes toward sport. While the thesis is ostensibly offered as a merciful corrective to ruthless competition, further analysis has revealed, ironically, that it presupposes views that are ill suited to the spirit of sportsmanship.

First, the AB thesis may be based on the view, condemned by all plausible accounts of sportsmanship, that winning is the only thing that matters in sport. Second, it assumes that suffering a heavy defeat is an affront to one's status as an athlete, if not as a human being. While this mistaken attitude is in itself inoffensive, it reflects a gross overestimation of the importance of the outcomes of sporting contests, and this overestimation may well be associated with unquestionably unsporting behavior. Huge financial incentives already exist for cheating, illicit drug use, and other violations of sportsmanship in both college and professional athletics. To add to these financial incentives the view that defeat brings disgrace on the loser only increases the temptation to resort to unsporting means to achieve victory.[19]

Notes

1 To conform to standard usage, and to avoid unwieldy expressions, I have reluctantly used the term *sportsmanship*. I trust that my routine use of *she* as a generic personal pronoun will allay any concerns that my use of *sportsmanship* has a masculinist intent.

2 I add the qualifier *intrinsically* because, as I explain in Section II, I do condemn those who pursue lopsided victories *in order to* humiliate their opponents. If my main argument is sound, however, even these deliberate attempts do not actually humiliate the losers in a morally objectionable way.

3 One wonders why Kretchmar classifies this as a nonmoral value. Minimizing suffering is very much a moral value, at least on a utilitarian approach.

4 See Section IIIA for more detail on Keating's view.

5 It may be no coincidence that both football and basketball are time-based sports, in which the contest continues for a specified time, regardless of the score. A point may be reached, well before time expires, when one team has no realistic chance of winning. The AB thesis is most plausible in precisely such situations in time-based sports. In score-based sports such as tennis, on the other hand, play continues until a certain score has been reached, regardless of the time elapsed. In such sports, dramatic comebacks are feasible until the final point has been played, and we are unlikely to criticize as unsporting the behavior of a player who pads her lead in order to reduce the likelihood of such a comeback.

   What this shows is that there is a reason for trying to maximize the margin of victory in score-based sports that does not exist in time-based sports. I maintain, however, that in neither case is it unsporting to pursue one-sided victories. I am grateful to Michael Meyer for the distinction between these two kinds of sport.

6 See Section IIIB for a more detailed discussion of the role of play in sport.

7 See Section IIIA.

8 *Webster's Ninth New Collegiate Dictionary* (Springfield, MA: Merriam-Webster, Inc., 1990), p. 587.

9 See Arnold (1:p.62), and Keating (7:pp.32–34).

10 British disdain for what was considered as excessive American zeal for training is given a remarkably favorable portrayal in the 1981 film *Chariots of Fire*.

11 I do not mean to suggest that sporting scores are "transitive," in the sense that if A beats B by x points, and B beats C by y points, it follows that A will beat C by $x + y$ points. The value of keeping records, rather, is that figures such as the total points or goals scored by a player or team over a season can provide a meaningful measure of excellence and basis for comparison with other players and teams, both past and present.

12 I am grateful to a reviewer of the *Journal of the Philosophy of Sport* for this objection.

13 See Hyland (5: pp. 68–69).

14 I am grateful to a reviewer of the *Journal of the Philosophy of Sport* for this point.

15 *All* theories of sportsmanship are evaluative, in that sportsmanship is an inherently normative concept. Sportsmanship is by definition a virtue, and being a bad sport is by definition a moral failing. I distinguish Arnold's view because he defines sportsmanship in terms of the moral virtue of altruism, whereas the other views define it in terms of facilitating the nonmoral goals of sport.

16 For the distinction between perfect duties ("duties of justice") and imperfect duties ("duties of benevolence"), see Kant (6: pp. 191–195).

17 For two formulations of an ethic of care, see Gilligan (4) and Manning (9).

18 A more comprehensive account of sportsmanship would combine mandatory requirements of the kind explained by Keating, Fraleigh, and Feezell, along with Arnold's insight that the highest level of sportsmanship is exemplified by optional acts of altruism that exceed these minimal requirements. Developing such an account is beyond the scope of this paper.

19 I am grateful to the reviewers of the *Journal of the Philosophy of Sport* for helpful suggestions, to Sterling Harwood for encouraging me to write this paper and for extensive written feedback, and to Mike Meyer for his incisive and generous criticisms.

Bibliography

1 Arnold, Peter J. "Three Approaches Toward an Understanding of Sportsmanship." *Journal of the Philosophy of Sport*, X (1984), 61–70 [reprinted here as reading 7].

2   Feezell, Randolph M. "Sportsmanship." *Journal of the Philosophy of Sport*, XII (1986), 1–13.
3   Fraleigh, Warren B. *Right Actions in Sport: Ethics for Contestants*. Champaign, IL: Human Kinetics, 1984.
4   Gilligan, Carol. *In a Different Voice: Psychological Theory and Women's Development*. Cambridge, MA: Harvard University Press, 1982.
5   Hyland, Drew A. "Opponents, Contestants, and Competitors: The Dialectic of Sport." *Journal of the Philosophy of Sport*, XI (1985), 63–70.
6   Kant, Immanuel, *Lectures on Ethics*. Translated by Louis Infield. New York: The Century Company, 1930.
7   Keating, James W. "Sportsmanship as a Moral Category." *Ethics*, LXXV (October 1964), 25–35 [reprinted here as reading 6].
8   Kretchmar, R. Scott. "Ethics and Sport: An Overview." *Journal of the Philosophy of Sport*, X (1984), 21–32.
9   Manning, Rita C. *Speaking From the Heart: A Feminist Perspective on Ethics*. Lanham, MD: Rowman & Littlefield, 1992.

CHAPTER 10

Sportsmanship and Blowouts: Baseball and Beyond

Randolph M. Feezell

As a player and a coach, I've been on both sides in blowouts, games in which a team won by a lopsided score. If my team was crushed, I felt worse than I would have had our team been more competitive. If I was fortunate to be on the winning side, I attempted to be gracious in closing out the game and relating to opponents after the game. I assumed that such graciousness was an important part of sportsmanship. As a player, I learned to be gracious. As a coach, I've insisted that my players behave this way. In contrast, attempting to "run up the score" to beat an opponent as badly as possible was, I thought, a clear example of bad sportsmanship. Silly me. If Nicholas Dixon is right (3), I have been fundamentally misguided by the acceptance of a common but mistaken part of the moral framework of the sports world.

There are others who have rejected this piece of supposed moral wisdom associated with the language and traditions of sportsmanship. The most notable recent example is Billy Tubbs, current Texas Christian University basketball coach. During the 1997–1998 season, as he had in the past, Tubbs took pride in crushing his opponents as badly as possible. In a 138–75 blowout of noted basketball power Delaware State, he not only kept his starters in until late in the game, he also was still using a press with 4 minutes to go. Tubbs is quoted in *Sports Illustrated* (January 1998) as saying: "Our job as coaches is to make our team look as good as

it possibly can and the other team as bad.... That's called winning."

To give Tubbs some credit, he does offer a reason for his view, although his reason isn't a very good one. To defend the traditional view of what might be called "blowout ethics," we will need to do more than simply respond to Tubbs's seemingly thin view of what he's about as coach. His position, that there's nothing really wrong with "running up the score," is interestingly and powerfully defended by Nicholas Dixon. Dixon is no smirking curmudgeon, poking fun at the sentimentality of common views of sportsmanship. His case against what he calls the "Anti-Blowout thesis" is a strong challenge to one of the central assumptions associated with sportsmanship. His arguments show why the issue is important. It involves basic views about the nature of sport and our attitudes toward competition, the pursuit and display of excellence, and the importance of victory.

As I have said, my own intuitions are contrary to Dixon's position. He believes that no current model of sportsmanship, including my own (4), can show that pursuing a blowout is unsporting. If he is right, then, he says, my "intuition is no more than a prejudice" (3: p. 11). I believe Dixon is wrong and that there are good arguments to show why such behavior is unsporting. If this is the case, the traditional view is no mere prejudice. However, I do want to qualify what I am arguing. I am most familiar with the particularities of baseball, having played and coached this sport at virtually all levels for many years. Hence, my examples and my arguments will be directed in a sport-specific manner. I believe analogous arguments are effective for most other sports, but I'm convinced that good judgments about sportsmanship often require an insider's understanding and appreciation of the particularities of a sport and its relevant customs and traditions. I leave it to others to extend these arguments in obvious ways to other sports.

Part I: Formulating the Thesis

Nicholas Dixon argues against what he takes to be a widely-held view of sportsmanship and blow-outs. He calls this the Anti-Blowout thesis (AB):

AB: It is intrinsically unsporting for players or teams to maximize the margin of victory after they have secured victory in a one-sided contest. (3: p. 1)

Let's call a person who supports the traditional view of the relationship between sportsmanship and blowouts a "traditionalist," and let's call a person who rejects this view a "critic." Must the traditionalist support Dixon's formulation of the AB thesis?

First note that the AB thesis stresses the "intrinsic" nature of the actions at issue. This is an important aspect of Dixon's criticism of the traditional view. For example, he restates his thesis in this way: "There is absolutely nothing intrinsically wrong with pressing for a lopsided victory in a *competitive* game" (3: p. 3). Later he insists that lopsided defeats "are not intrinsically humiliating in the strong sense that they are prima facie morally wrong" (3: p. 4). One can anticipate where the argument is heading. If pressing for a lopsided victory always expresses a morally bad intention – for example, wanting to humiliate an opponent – then such an action would be "intrinsically wrong." But it may not express such an intention, and the action's wrongness would then depend on the relevant intention. Hence, it wouldn't necessarily be "intrinsically wrong" to "run up the score." More-

over, on consequentialist grounds, if such actions do not, in fact, humiliate opponents, then the actions would not be "intrinsically wrong."

Whether an action is taken to be intrinsically wrong will depend on the moral theory one holds. For example, a particular action might be judged to be wrong just because it is an instance of some action-type that is taken to be intrinsically wrong. Consider an instance of lying. A deontologist of some sort might hold that an act of lying is wrong just because it is an instance of a type of action: lying. A Kantian deontologist might further explain that an act of lying is absolutely intrinsically wrong because such an act could not be an expression of a good will, or the intention to act from duty, insofar as the moral rule (or maxim) describing the action could not be universalizable.[1] A virtue theorist of some sort might hold that lying is intrinsically wrong because it is always an expression of dishonesty, a vice, rather than the virtue of honesty.[2]

On the other hand, the act consequentialist evaluates an action in terms of the goodness or badness of the consequences that arise as a result of the action.[3] For the act consequentialist, there are no intrinsically wrong actions, since the moral evaluation of the act depends on factors that are not intrinsic to the act.

Must the traditionalist hold that it is "intrinsically wrong" to attempt to maximize the margin of victory after victory has been secured? Not necessarily. It will depend on the moral theory held by the traditionalist. Such a theory would explain what makes actions right or wrong, or it would offer some account of the basis and nature of the virtues.

Consider again the example of lying. Kant's ethical theory was forced to confront one notorious problem: the possible conflict of two absolutely binding or exceptionless moral duties. In the standard textbook example, how could Kant's ethics give coherent guidance to a person hiding a Jewish family in Nazi-occupied Holland, when the commandant comes to the house inquiring whether Jews are being harbored there? Kant holds that it is absolutely wrong to lie – no exceptions. In this situation, however, the duty to help persons fleeing Nazi oppression is stronger than the duty to tell the truth. But to say that it is not "absolutely intrinsically wrong" to lie, or that it could on occasion be morally permissible to lie, does not deny that it is prima facie morally wrong to lie. This is the language that W.D. Ross introduced to argue that lying is typically wrong.[4] We have a duty to tell the truth unless some more important duty overrides truth-telling in a particular situation. To say that we have a prima facie duty to tell the truth is to hold that in any situation, there is a strong moral presumption against lying.

Likewise, a virtue theorist recognizes that honesty is a morally praiseworthy trait of character. But the Aristotelian emphasizes that honesty is not simply the strict adherence to an absolutely binding moral rule.[5] It is a developed disposition to make wise choices in a whole range of situations that require not only resisting the temptation to tell outright lies. Good moral character may be expressed in situations in which it would not be virtuous to be *too* honest, as, for example, when Aunt Alice asks what you think about her beautiful new hat.

The view that lying is prima facie wrong, not absolutely wrong, or that the honest person may on occasion not tell the truth, squares well with our common moral consciousness. To recognize the moral importance of truth-telling or honesty, one need not be forced to defend the kind of absolutism characteristic of Kant's ethics. Nor does one need to agree with certain contemporary defenders of absolutism who believe that there are types of conduct that are "really right and wrong." Therefore, they must defend the view that it could *never* be right to engage in certain kinds of action.

Now we are in a better position to formulate the traditional view of the relationship between sportsmanship and blowouts. Dixon believes that the traditionalist must embrace the AB thesis as he formulates it. But the defender need not be saddled with this absolutist view. The traditionalist may admit that there are occasions when maximizing the margin of victory might be called for. For example, there might be a situation in a tournament where one of the tie-breakers for advancing to the championship is total runs scored. This might reasonably call for pursuing

a lopsided victory. But such situations are relatively rare – or so the traditionalist maintains. Usually it's unsporting to attempt to "run up the score," and that's the view that is widely and plausibly held in the sports community.[6] Finding a plausible counterexample to the AB thesis need not defeat the traditional view. I will call this view the Revised Anti-Blowout thesis (RAB):

RAB: It is prima facie unsporting for players or teams to maximize the margin of victory after they have secured victory in a one-sided contest.

One of the strengths of Dixon's paper is his attempt to force the traditionalist to think about the reasons for the traditional point of view of blowout ethics. I believe the critic is right that one can imagine situations in which maximizing the margin of victory is not unsporting. But the traditionalist maintains that these situations are relatively rare, and for a variety of reasons, pressing for blowouts will require quite strong overriding factors. In most cases, the traditionalist insists, these overriding factors are absent, and thus it is typically unsporting to "run up the score."

Part II: Arguments For the Revised Thesis

What can be said in support of the RAB thesis? First, it seems natural to locate the unsportingness of "running up the score" in relationships to opponents. But it is important to describe in a psychologically appropriate manner the reactions of opponents to being blown out. It is sometimes said that the attempt to beat an opponent as badly as possible expresses the desire to humiliate him, since he will in fact be humiliated when he is badly beaten. However, that seems much too strong for a number of reasons. (I will discuss Dixon's treatment of what I will call the "Humiliation Argument" later.) It is more appropriate to say that suffering a lopsided loss is often embarrassing for obvious and natural reasons. To lose is to fail, and to lose badly is to fail badly. Sport is an arena in which there are standards of excellence, and the desire to be good is at the heart of the competitive athlete's participation in sports. Being good qua athlete may not be as important, in some sense, as being good qua human being or being good qua physician, teacher, or scientist, but it is a legitimate and strongly desired kind of goodness.[7] To lose is to fail to be as good as one wants to be in a certain situation, so losing badly normally carries with it the pain of recognizing the significant gap between one's desires and the reality of one's actual talents and abilities. "Pouring it on" or "rubbing it in," however one might describe the phenomenon, is rubbing the opponent's nose in his failure and, at least momentary, badness. To do so is typically an expression of a lack of graciousness and respect for others' feelings or emotions, just as it would be if Jill kept reminding Jack of how miserably he failed the scholarship exam. Hence, it is prima facie unsporting to attempt to crush the opponent as badly as possible because it fails, in a significant way, to respect one's opponent. It is analogous to situations in everyday life in which one person occasions in another, in an insensitive and sometimes callous manner, natural negative psychological reactions to loss and failure.

Of course, it's difficult to know what the reaction of opponents will be. But you can be certain of your own reactions, and because of this you are in a position to make use of one of the great principles of ethical life. To be a good sport in particular, as well as to be a good person in general, often requires that we consider the perspectives of other people and attempt to see things from an impartial perspective. R.M. MacIver has spoken of the "deep beauty of the Golden Rule" (10) which encourages such impartiality as the key to morally appropriate conduct. For our purposes, the so-called "Silver Rule" – "Do not do to others what you do not want them to do to you" – is a particularly useful guide.[8] You may confront an opponent who both pursues blowouts and consistently accepts them without reproach, but in my experience, such people are rare in sports. In most cases, the Silver Rule would prohibit a competitor from wanting to crush an opponent as badly as possible, because of the competitor's own reactions to opponents who seek to do this to him and the moral appropriateness of impartiality.

A second important line of argument supports the RAB thesis. Sport is by its very nature competitive. But there are two different senses in which a game or a match might be said to be competitive. In the weak sense, if I play against any opponent who literally *opposes* me and makes it possible to have a game or match, then the activity is competitive. In the strong sense, a game or match is competitive if it involves opponents whose skills or talents are relatively equal, where the game or match is a *good* one. It's good, because the outcome is a result of opponents whose talents are tested by the other, where dramatic tensions create uncertainty about the outcome (at least at some point after the game has begun), and where excellence is a result of being challenged to perform at one's highest level. In this sense a coach may thank his defeated, weaker team for being "competitive" against a stronger team, or he might offer consoling remarks that his weaker team made the stronger one "work" for victory. His remarks indicate another way to explain the distinction. The weak sense of "competition" simply makes a descriptive claim: As a matter of fact, a contest occurs in which there are opponents, rules, and the possibility of victory. The strong sense of competition carries some evaluative weight. To say that a game or match is competitive in the strong or evaluative sense indicates "successful" or "good" competition, hence, the subject of possible praise.

What happens in a blowout? One of the following conditions obtain: (a) The opponents are mismatched, in the sense that one is much stronger than the other, so the winner does not face a worthy or "competitive" opponent; (b) a usually worthy opponent plays unusually poorly; (c) a player or team plays unusually well; (d) one of the participants in the competition is either unusually fortunate or unusually unfortunate; or (e) some combination of these factors occurs. Since the issue of winning has already been resolved in a blowout, the outcome is not in doubt. The game is no longer – and perhaps was not from the start – competitive in the strong sense. In fact, competition in this sense has broken down. If players or teams attempt to maximize the margin of victory after they have secured victory in a one-sided contest, I believe they fail to respect "true" or "real" competition. True competition, good competition, requires being challenged or tested by worthy opponents. In a blowout this factor is at least momentarily absent.

Moreover, good competition often occasions excellence, the best performances that players and teams can achieve. These performances are expressions of the best things a sport has to offer, rare and wonderful moments amidst intense competition. In respecting good competition, players and teams show respect for the very sport in which they are engaged. This leads us to a more sport-specific understanding of the ethics of blowouts. Let's call this aspect of sportsmanship "respect for the game."[9] Consider a baseball game between a very good team and a very bad team (or a team having an unusually terrible game). Suppose the team being blown out makes numerous errors (both physical and mental). The pitcher is wild and has mediocre stuff, the catcher has bad hands and a weak arm, and so forth. Suppose the score is 18–0 by the third inning. The coach of the winning team is relentless in scoring more runs. He avoids substitutions and continues to steal bases, hit and run, bunt, and take extra bases when possible, although the run-rule (the "mercy" rule) does not take effect until the fifth inning. One who loves baseball and respects its highest possibilities might say this isn't "real" baseball, by which he appropriately judges that the winning coach fails to "respect the game."

In fact, respect for the game of baseball requires respect for its traditions and customs, not just its central formal rules.[10] Knowing and understanding these customs is an important part of sportsmanship in baseball. Knowing how to act in light of these customs is not always easy. It requires experience and good judgment. In addition, customs change. In baseball it's now more acceptable than in the past to steal bases when significantly ahead. Aluminum bats have made large leads more unsafe in high school and college baseball. So it's now more acceptable than it was in the past for a team to aggressively

attempt to score more runs even when it has a large lead. But there is still some point at which it is judged to be unsporting in baseball to steal bases when ahead. It is permissible to throw inside, step out of the batter's box to disrupt the rhythm of a pitcher, quick-pitch, slide hard to break up a double play, and steal signs. On the other hand, blowout ethics is a central aspect of sportsmanship in baseball. When a team has a huge lead, players should not steal, bunt for a hit, squeeze, or do anything that they would normally do strategically in order to score more runs.

Does this mean that baseball players and coaches are required to "ease up" in blowouts, and wouldn't that be contrary to the duty to respect competition and opponents by playing as hard as one can at all times? Here I would make another important distinction. In one sense, to ease up might be to play less hard, to expend less effort. In another sense, to ease up involves strategy, not effort. In the second sense, to ease up is to avoid strategies that are usually taken to score runs. In a baseball blowout, it is appropriate to ease up in the strategic sense, not in the sense of effort. All players are required to play hard, even in a blowout. But one of the obvious things coaches can do to hold down the score is to put in backup players who will play hard but not be as effective in scoring runs. On the other hand, even backup players might be able to steal bases at will, but stealing bases in blowouts is strategically inappropriate.

The problems with such appeals to tradition in a moral argument is that they can always be undermined, in principle, by the normative question: "Well, I know it's a tradition (or custom), but why should I accept the tradition? Perhaps there are good reasons to reject the tradition." I recognize that there is a certain autonomy to such a normative query,[11] but the fact that some norm or kind of behavior is part of an established tradition grounds a presumption. The attempt to build a prima facie case against the pursuit of blowouts has moved from our relationship to opponents, to the nature of competition, and finally to the traditions specific to baseball. I suspect the tradition in baseball that judges as unsporting the pursuit of lopsided victories is grounded in the very concerns that we have been discussing. To respect baseball is to respect one's opponents and the specific competitive aspects of the game. When coaches or teams "run up the score" in baseball, they are judged to be in the business of embarrassment and shallow self-glorification; they are not in the business of what baseball is about.

It's also important to note that athletic accomplishments in at least certain kinds of blowouts are tainted or at least undervalued by the sports community. Players or coaches who attempt to "pad statistics" in blowouts show no respect for displaying excellence and no respect for the game. Significant athletic excellence requires worthy opponents who can challenge a team or player. Suppose the coach plays the star for the entire game in the first round of a tournament against an extremely weak team. The coach, let's suppose, is a critic of the AB thesis and is committed to the "display of excellence" in a game, even a blowout. The star goes five for five, hits two home runs, drives in eight runs, and gets the post-game interview as "star of the game." In the remaining games of the tournament, he is hitless in 10 at bats. In the championship game, he leaves eight runners on base, and his team loses. He finishes the tournament hitting .333, leading all players in home runs and runs batted in. Big deal. Did he have a good tournament? Should he be placed on the all-tournament team? Of course not.

Part III: Arguments Against the Thesis and Replies

We are now in a position to evaluate Dixon's case against the AB thesis. He believes there are no good arguments for this thesis. and there are important considerations that positively count against it. First, let's consider what he takes to be two central lines of argument for the AB thesis. We'll call these the Gratuity Argument and the Humiliation Argument.

The Gratuity Argument goes like this:

1 In sport the only thing that matters is winning.

2 If the only thing that matters in sport is winning, then running up the score after victory is secured is gratuitous.
3 Persons ought to avoid gratuitous actions.
4 Therefore, persons ought to avoid the attempt to maximize the margin of victory after they have secured victory in a one-sided contest. (3: p. 3)

Dixon reasonably rejects the first premise because there are other important aspects in sports: "Players who win blowouts can be justly proud of their display of athletic excellence, the personal and team records they have set, and the excitement provided for fans" (3: p. 3).

The first odd thing about the Gratuity Argument involves what to make of the kind of prescription it offers. Perhaps from some point of view we ought to avoid unnecessary or groundless actions, but it's not clear what is the moral force of this "ought" in the argument. If winning is the only thing that matters in sport, then maximizing the margin of victory may be gratuitous, but why would such conduct then be unsporting? Rather, it would seem to be "unreasonable" or "irrational" or "unnecessary." I'm uncertain why Dixon thinks this is an argument for the "intrinsically unsporting" nature of pursuing blowouts.

Moreover, I agree with Dixon that there's more to sport than winning or that winning is not the only thing that matters in sport. But given the arguments in the last section, appealing to the "display of athletic excellence," "records," or "excitement for fans" would not lead one to reject the AB thesis. As I have argued, crushing a weak opponent or beating up a normally worthy opponent who is having a bad day is not an adequate measure of athletic excellence, nor are such "records" achieved against weak opponents particularly noteworthy. In responding to this kind of argument, Dixon says this: "While the superior team's victory may never be in doubt, its manner of victory can be most revealing" (3: p. 7). But beating a weak opponent by 20 runs in baseball reveals little more than beating the opponent by 10 runs. It often indicates more about the weakness of the opponent than the excellence of the winner.

And the appeal to the "excitement of the fans" is irrelevant. The reaction of the fans is extrinsic to the essential elements involved in sports: competing with opponents, pursuing excellence and victory, and having fun. These are the key elements that ground our judgments about sportsmanship. There are other things besides winning that matter in sport, and it is reflecting on these things that leads one to *accept* the RAB thesis.

Dixon spends much more time examining what I will call the Humiliation Argument.

1   If players or teams maximize the margin of victory after they have secured victory in a one-sided contest, then the opponents who suffer such defeats are humiliated and diminished as human beings.

2   Persons ought not to humiliate other human beings.

3   Therefore, persons ought not to maximize the margin of victory after they have secured victory in a one-sided contest. (3: p. 3)

Unlike the Gratuity Argument, the Humiliation Argument clearly has moral force, since the actions in question supposedly harm or inflict a kind of cruelty on the defeated opponent. Dixon rejects the first premise of this argument, because he denies that losing badly in a sporting contest humiliates the defeated: "Neither victory nor defeat affects one's worth as a human being" (3: p. 3). Nor is one humiliated as an *athlete* rather than as a human being, because such a claim "indicates an inflated estimate of the importance of the outcome of sporting contests" (3: p. 4). Even if opponents *feel* humiliated, we need not be morally concerned about such reactions, since these negative perceptions would be based on a "misconception" (3: p. 5) about the importance of the outcome of sporting contests.

I agree with much of what Dixon says here, but his objections to the Humiliation Argument leave untouched the strength of the considerations I have previously offered. Losing badly may not diminish one's worth as a human being, nor humiliate one in a strong sense, but it is the experience of loss and extreme failure, made

public, hence the actual occasion for quite "negative perceptions." On the one hand, Dixon is right that sensitivity to "negative perceptions" need not always be respected. One need not respect the reactions of racists to interracial relationships nor the Philistine's reactions to Michaelangelo's "David." On the other hand, embarrassment or psychological pain does morally count in our deliberations, especially when such reactions are not based on "misconceptions" or some kind of shallowness. The opponent who is crushed need not be suffering from any kind of intellectual or moral deficiency when he reacts negatively.

Dixon insists that he is not defending coaches and players who do want to humiliate their opponents, since the "wrongness of such actions consists in the *intention* to harm" (3: p. 70). He simply denies that pursuing blowouts does harm, in the strong sense of humiliate, and one may have morally permissible intentions in pursuing blowouts, insofar as players or teams may desire the display of excellence, setting records, and exciting fans. But if I am right, blowouts do typically embarrass. They also fail to respect both competition and, in the case of baseball, the game and its traditions.

Dixon also argues that "none of several currently favored theories of sportsmanship supports the AB thesis" (3: p. 1). He discusses the view I have defended (4), in which I primarily counter James Keating's well-known account of sportsmanship (8). My view, Dixon believes, does place moral demands on competitors. To see sportsmanship as a mean between the excessive seriousness of the ruthless competitor and the excessive playfulness of one who is frivolous and doesn't care about excellence and victory rules out cheating and "any form of disrespect for opponents" (3: p. 9). I agree. Dixon denies that pursuing blowouts disrespects opponents. As I have argued, I believe such behavior typically does fail to respect opponents, but in a sense weaker than humiliation. So even my earlier account leads to the RAB thesis. I have recently offered a much more extensive account of sportsmanship based on the foundation I had previously offered (2). This book attempts to explain more fully the principles of respect, including "respect for opponents" and "respect for the game" (2: pp. 26–38, 59–72) that are important expressions of sportsmanship so conceived. The arguments I have offered here and in the book are based on my earlier model of sportsmanship, so I would deny Dixon's claim about the relationship between at least one "currently favored" theory of sportsmanship and the traditional view of blowout ethics.

Dixon also seems to believe that my view wouldn't entail "easing up" in an uneven contest (assuming that the AB thesis does require players or teams to ease up), because a sense of playfulness seems more compatible with "continuing to entertain fans with exciting, innovative plays, taking advantage of the freedom that is provided by having already secured victory" (3: p. 9). In response, I have two points. My view requires that players or teams "ease up" only in the strategic sense, not in the sense of effort. Playing hard shows respect for opponents; pursuing blowouts doesn't. Second, Dixon seems to misunderstand at least part of my emphasis on the playful character of sport. To stress that sport is competitive *play* is to emphasize the intrinsic value of the activity and the experiences and values associated with human play. Play has no essential connection to "entertainment," and the competitive play of sports offers its primary values to participants, not spectators. Playfulness does not entail a commitment to "entertain fans." The deep paradox of sport involves the conjoining of the seriousness of competition with a sense of playfulness that recognizes and affirms the ultimate triviality of these concerns.[12] This paradox is the basis for attempting to judge what kind of behavior is appropriate for such activities. The spirit of play is important for sportsmanship, because it infuses the pursuit of victory and relationships to opponents with a sense of realism or clear vision about the relative unimportance of sports and the inappropriateness of the "winning is the only thing" view of sports.[13] Such a view often leads to bad sportsmanship. However, sport is competitive, so the good sport must respect the conditions of competition: fair play and pursuit of excellence and victory.

Conclusion

There's much to admire in Nicholas Dixon's criticism of the AB thesis. Like Dixon, I believe that winning is not the only thing that matters in sport. I also agree that losing need not humiliate a person, since the outcome of relatively trivial activities like sporting contests is not as important as many persons seem to believe. He's right that overestimating the importance of victory often leads to cheating, drug abuse, and scandal (3: p. 11). But such reflections need not lead to the rejection of the traditional view of blowouts. A deep concern for the value of sportsmanship supports the tradition in holding that it's usually unsporting to "run up the score."

Notes

1   See Kant (7). For a lucid discussion of Kant's account of universalizability, see Feldman (6).
2   See Mayo (11).
3   See Smart (15) for an important discussion of act consequentialism.
4   See Ross (14).
5   See Aristotle (1: Book II).
6   I would not deny that there are other situations in which pursuing blowouts might be justified. For example, blowouts might have some strategic significance for future games played in a series. In professional basketball or baseball, a blowout in the first game of a playoff series might shake the opponent's confidence. On the other hand, soundly thrashing an opponent and then easing up, in a strategic sense, usually would seem to have the same effect on the opponent's confidence. It's interesting that a friend of mine, a former major league baseball player, used precisely the same example – pursuing a blowout against an opponent you would play in the future – to argue that "running up the score" is a bad idea because it causes your opponent to be more highly motivated in the rematch. I thank a reviewer for calling attention to the possible strategic significance of

pursuing blowouts. Since my view is that such behavior is prima facie wrong, the factors involved in each particular situation are relevant. Still, my arguments show why the overriding factors must be quite strong in order to pursue blowouts.

7   MacIntyre distinguishes between the internal goods associated with human practices, including sports, and external goods (9: chapter 14). To desire to become excellent in a particular sport is to desire to achieve various internal goods in that sport. For example, becoming an excellent hitter is an internal good in baseball. If a player becomes excellent enough, he may have the opportunity to acquire external goods like money and fame when he becomes a professional player.

8   See Clifford and Feezell (2: pp. 36–37) for a brief discussion of applying the Silver Rule as a practical guide to "respect for opponents."

9   For a more extensive discussion of "respect for the game" as an important principle of sportsmanship, see Clifford and Feezell (2: pp. 59–70).

10 See Clifford and Feezell (2: pp. 68–70).

11 See Nagel (13: chapter 6) for a penetrating discussion of what I have called the autonomy of normative query. Nagel speaks of "the more general truth that the normative can't be transcended by the descriptive" (13: p. 105).

12 See Feezell (5).

13 Iris Murdoch (12) connects virtue with "seeing the way things are."

Bibliography

1   Aristotle. *Nichomachean Ethics* (Martin Ostwald, Trans.). New York: The Library of Liberal Arts, 1962.

2   Clifford, C., and Feezell, R. *Coaching for Character: Reclaiming the Principles of Sportsmanship.* Champaign, IL: Human Kinetics, 1997.

3   Dixon, N. "On Sportsmanship and 'Running up the Score'." *Journal of the Philosophy of Sport.* 19:1–13, 1992 [reprinted here as reading 9].

4   Feezell, R.M. "Sportsmanship." *Journal of the Philosophy of Sport.* 12:1–13, 1986.

5   Feezell, R. "Play and the Absurd." *Philosophy Today.* 28:319–329, 1984.

6   Feldman, F. *Introductory Ethics.* Englewood Cliffs, NJ: Prentice-Hall, 1978.

7   Kant, I. *Foundations of the Metaphysics of Morals and What is Enlightenment?* (L.W. Beck, Trans.). Indianapolis, IN: Bobbs-Merrill, 1959.

8   Keating, J.W. "Sportsmanship as a Moral Category." *Ethics.* 75:25–35, 1964 [reprinted here as reading 6].

9   MacIntyre, A. *After Virtue.* Notre Dame, IN: University of Notre Dame Press, 1981.

10 MacIver, R.M. "The Deep Beauty of the Golden Rule." In: *Vice and Virtue in Everyday Life*, C. Sommers and F. Sommers (Eds.). Fort Worth, IN: Harcourt Brace, 1997.

11 Mayo, B. *Ethics and Moral Life.* New York: St. Martin's, 1958.

12 Murdoch, I. "The Sovereignty of Good Over Other Concepts." *The Sovereignty of Good.* New York: Schocken, 1971.

13 Nagel, T. *The Last Word.* New York: Oxford University Press, 1997.

14 Ross, W.D. *The Right and the Good.* Oxford, UK: Clarendon Press, 1930.

15 Smart, J.J.C. "Extreme and Restricted Utilitarianism." *Philosophical Quarterly.* 6:344–354, 1956.

Sport and Competition

CHAPTER 11

The Ethics of Competition

Jan Boxill

One of the most controversial features of our society is competition. It is condemned by Marxists, is championed by capitalists, is deemed a necessary evil in education, and is necessary to and dramatized in sport. In this paper I analyze the concept of competition as it is dramatized in sport, with an eye to elucidating the moral dimensions of competition as it applies to various endeavors in our society.

Objections to competition are two-fold. First, it may be argued that the intrinsic nature of competition is immoral. Competition is selfish and egoistic, and it involves treating others as means, as enemies to be defeated, or as obstacles thwarting one's victory or success, to be removed by any means possible.

Second, it may further be argued that the consequences of competition are harmful. In aiming for success, competitors view their opponents as enemies, and focus on winning by whatever means possible, including cheating, using drugs, and harming their opponents. These harmful consequences of competition are of two sorts, to the body and to the character. These are especially clear in the extreme in the "win-at-all-costs" syndrome usually found in professional and bigtime college sports. But there may be less extreme cases of fostering selfishness, glory, and aggressive behavior and, while winning within the rules, using morally questionable means short of outright cheating. It is no accident that these are dramatized in

sport, but they are also present in many other practices in our society in both extreme and less extreme forms – in business and industry, and in education.

Thus, it is argued that competition is a vice, and is the very antithesis of cooperation, a virtue. Indeed the criticisms of our education system often center on these two seemingly opposed practices, and one does not have to look very hard to find educational psychologists advocating the replacement of the ethic of competition by one of cooperation and community.[1]

Now, while sports may not hold a monopoly on the "win-at-all-costs" syndrome or on the harmful effects of competition, because competition is dramatized and exaggerated in sport, and because that may be the arena where the competitive spirit is first fostered, publicly reinforced, and approved, it is in that context that the characteristics of competition are best seen.

Hence, it is in the sport context that I will argue, first, that the intrinsic nature of competition is not immoral, that it need not involve treating others without equal respect; second, that when competition has harmful effects, these are due either to accident, to a deviation from the ideal of competition, or to circumstances outside the competition itself, e.g. the professionalization of sport; third, that competition is the surest means of maintaining and/or raising standards and of achieving excellence in any field; and fourth, when viewed as a challenge to achieve excellence[2] and, when it involves others, as a "mutual challenge to achieve excellence," competition leads to friendship rather than enmity, to mutual respect and esteem rather than mutual disrespect. It is in this sense that it becomes clear that far from competition and cooperation being mutually exclusive, they are complementary.

Essentials of Cooperation and Competition

In analyzing the intrinsic character of competition I will begin by looking at its apparent opposite, cooperation. In cooperation individuals work together to produce a desirable outcome. There is no rivalry; there is no zero-sum game to win or lose; all benefit from the outcome.

Sometimes a cooperative process toward an outcome is valued for the cooperation itself, the outcome being only secondary; or the process and outcome may be valued on a par. And insofar as all the participants can recognize their contributions to the outcome, they are all winners. The result is a *team* effort, stressing that it is important for individuals to work in concert with others for a common goal, that each participant is valuable as a member of that team, and that each person's value derives from the interdependence. Selfishness and aggression toward others are not only minimized but discouraged as being immoral.

Now whereas cooperation involves a striving *with*, competition involves a *striving* against. Competitors necessarily strive against something or someone. When they strive against someone, competition involves comparisons with others and success is achieved by doing better than all the rest in that activity.

Thus, competition inevitably produces winners and losers (even when the outcome is a tie, this is seen by most as a failure to achieve the ideal outcome). Further, the competition is always open and never predetermined. The outcome may be predictable, but no one has won or lost until the game is played. At its clearest, competition in sport is an attempt to secure victory within the appropriate constitutive rules

defining the contest and within the rules of decency and fair play. And since such competition involves winners and losers, it involves participation in the goal of defeating opponents in a zero-sum game. In economics, competition may be described as an attempt according to agreed-upon rules to get or keep any valuable thing either to the exclusion of others or in a greater measure than others.

Thus, competition involves striving and comparing; striving toward an outcome which is not predetermined; striving to do better than others, or perhaps striving to do better than one's former self. Competition involves both a process, striving, and a product (or outcome), victory or loss, and both are important. Further, since success is measured in terms of comparisons, one obvious implication of this conception of competition is that while there may be equality of opportunities, there must be inequalities of outcome.

Characteristics of Competition in Sports

Sport in its paradigmatic form is a freely chosen, voluntary activity that is rule governed and requires bodily excellence, which is highlighted in competition. Sport is an activity which need have no end outside itself; it is complete in itself, although it may serve other purposes.

Sport by definition is agonistic, a term derived from the Greek *agonia* (contest). The original Greek concept embodied the notions of struggle, toil, hardship, and risk in striving for victory. In any contest there was a qualitative victory embodied by the triumph of the cause, of the struggle within oneself and against one's competitors. To merely overcome was not enough; one must internally deserve the victory if there was to be a true victory. Process and product, or outcome, were inseparable.

Unfortunately our contemporary practice of sports often fails to adhere to the Greek ideal. In emphasizing the victory, which is identified with the prize or reward, an external outcome becomes the symbol of success and the importance and the significance of the process are deemphasized. As a result opponents are often seen as obstacles blocking one's path to success rather than partners in challenge.

To illustrate both the basic essentials and the ideal of competition in sport, and to show how the contemporary practice of sport departs from the Greek ideal, I will set out several characteristics of competitive sports. These characteristics may also serve to classify sports, since some exhibit only one of the aspects while others exhibit many of them.

First, there are competitions that are individual pursuits against nature, such as mountain climbing, skiing, kayaking, white water canoeing, and hang gliding.[3] In these activities there need be no other person to be defeated; it is the individual against nature and natural obstacles. At the heart of these challenges are what we may call "natural encounters." "Winning" or success in these endeavors implies a strong consciousness of the struggle they involve; the struggle not to subjugate but to achieve, not to dominate but to master the ability to work with nature. It is against the mountain, the river, or some natural obstacle that one tests oneself, that one risks one's capabilities. There is no other will to contend against.

Encounters involve strategies requiring mental and physical energies. Further, because nature is unpredictable, athletes must continually adjust their strategies. One cannot anticipate every facet of the endeavor; one may try to minimize the risks, but one must constantly be on the alert for the unexpected. Still, however one plans, the outcome is not predetermined, i.e. it is not artificially fixed by factors independent of one's efforts, skills, etc. Indeed, because of the radical uncertainties of nature, the outcome may not even be predictable. Thus, encounters can be, and often are, risky and dangerous.

Then there are other competitive activities, which are still individual pursuits and based on encounters; here, though, the encounters are not with nature but with others, and involve a comparison with others or with established criteria of excellence. Sports such as gymnastics, figure skating, and field events like high jumping and long jumping are clear examples.

Sometimes participating in these sports may simply involve a striving to see just how much the body can achieve. Competing against others may not be absolutely necessary, but unless there are comparisons with others it may be difficult to establish independent criteria of excellence. Further, unless one is challenged by the best it is difficult to know what standard of excellence one is trying to achieve. Of course, you could simply be striving to improve your own score, height, or distance, but without competitions it is unlikely you will achieve a high standard, or come close to your potential.

In these human encounter competitions there is certainly an "other", an "other" that opposes and contends, but the "other" is not an "enemy" to be destroyed. He or she is simply a means of challenging another to achieve excellence. Thus, competitors test their capabilities against each other in a mutual challenge to achieve. The emphasis is not on defeating the opponent, but on striving for excellence, even if this requires that competitors strive to win.

It is in these kinds of encounters that competitors often help each other on techniques and strategies to enable them to push to a higher level of achievement. Dwight Stones, a former Olympic high jumper, gave us a good example of this. During a competition, Stones recognized a possible flaw in an opponent's approach to the high-jump bar and pointed it out to him. On this particular occasion, Stones lost to his competitor. He still helps out his competitors, because he says it pushes him to do better. Sometimes you "win" and sometimes you "lose", but in pursuit of excellence nobody really loses. Thus Stones first of all wanted to be challenged by the best to do his best, to reach his potential, and second wanted to strive to be the best.

When encounters involve striving to be the best, another characteristic of human competition is added, ranking. In these endeavors, a different strategy emerges, one which involves another person's will. So not only do you have the strategies of a physical nature, but also one of a psychological nature. For example, if you are the last in the competition, you must calculate to see what is needed to win or place. If you are behind, you may need to make some more risky and more difficult moves; whereas if you are ahead, you may decide to play it safe and just do what you feel comfortable doing, and do that as well as you can. This is often shown in the Olympics.

There can be two kinds of ranking competitions; those that require intermittent revisions of strategy where the competitors perform one at a time, as in gymnastics and figure skating; and those that require continuous revisions of strategy where the competitors perform at the same time and side by side, as in racing events.

In competitions that feature ranking, competitors coordinate all their mental and physical capabilities to do their best, to perform without error, sometimes emphasizing beauty and grace along with technical skill. The outcome is not predetermined, or not fixed, and while it may at times be predictable, there are always the uncertainties: mental lapses, a slight mistiming, the ice, or the feel of the bar, to name a few.

Ranking competitions may be further subdivided in such a way as to cut across the previous subdivisions. Some rankings may be decided by esthetic criteria, others by non-esthetic ones, and others again by both. For example, rankings in events like gymnastics, diving, and figure skating are in part decided by an aesthetic criterion. On the other hand, track and field events are decided by purely non-esthetic criteria. This does not mean, however, that these latter do not display an esthetic element.

Another set of individual activities that involve others, such as tennis, features another aspect which may be termed "face to face." Here competitors face their opponents across the net; the human element is essential, for one cannot achieve excellence in tennis without another person to challenge and strive against. Nature may still play a part in the outcome, e.g. a sudden gust of wind might make the difference between victory and defeat, but it is mainly the human element that players must contend with.

In rankings competitors do not manipulate the physical world outside their bodies in order to win. For example, Bannister tried to beat Landy with his strong kick at the end of the mile race; Landy tried to counter that strategy by burning out Bannister with a fast overall pace. But neither changed the track or the distance over which they ran. However, in face-to-face competition, such as tennis, the opponents try to place the ball where the other cannot get it, on both service and volley. This strategy elevates the human element as a decisive factor in deciding the outcome.

Because competitors must compete against each other and use strategy to contend against an opponent's will, there may be some room for viewing the opponent across the net as a combatant to be dominated and destroyed. But this is not necessarily the case, and destruction can hardly be literal in tennis; there is little room for inflicting physical harm, and the competitors are separated by a net. There may be a different kind of destruction in that a competitor may render her opponent so helpless that her struggle is to no avail, that her skills and strategies are ineffective and of no use in achieving her goal. In this case we would say that one competitor is dominating another. This can be avoided if the competitors are relatively evenly matched, and even when they are not, if each is trying to win, one need not humiliate the other.

However, in games where there is a possibility of contact, we begin to see more occasions for deviations from the ideal of competition. One does not only try to win but also to avoid contact, and when there is contact, the likelihood of anger increases. In baseball, as in tennis, contact is not necessary to the game; it is usually incidental, but when it is intentional, the likelihood of anger is increased.

Other team face-to-face competitions include cricket, soccer, and basketball. While cricket, like baseball, involves rare occasions of contact, soccer has more and basketball more again. Their effect is heightened by the fast pace of both sports, especially basketball because it is played in such a confined area. In both soccer and basketball, the continuous changes in mental and physical strategies are more demanding. Competitors must make quick calculations and adjustments to counter each other's strategies, but all toward winning in the context of the rules. The human element is clear and absolutely essential. The problem of anger, violence, and cheating is further increased here because of the fast pace of the game, the confined space, the elaborate set of rules, the contention of wills, and the possibility of contact.

In basketball especially, it is difficult to see violations. Rule changes have helped, and maybe more rule changes are necessary, but seldom do players set about to destroy their opponents. It is relatively easy to injure opposing players, and some players do. But fortunately there are few of these and most competitors do not support them.

Basketball has a significant amount of contact, as I have said, partly because of the fast pace, and partly because it takes place in such a confined area, which leads into my final aspect of competitive activities as "head to head." Sports that typically exhibit this feature are football, boxing, and perhaps ice hockey. Here, almost constant contact is prescribed by the rules. Football and boxing require much brute strength and aggression in striving toward success. The obstacles to success involve other persons' bodies, which must be moved or incapacitated if there is to be a victory. But there is much more to these activities than violence, brute strength, and aggression. As in the other contests, mental and physical strategies are required to win within the context of the rules. You want to avoid contact from your opponent, while you try to hit him. It is a strange kind of strategy, but it is the strategy nonetheless; one which requires much concentration, discipline, skill, and physical and mental agility.

It is in contests which exhibit this feature that most deviance is noticed. Here there is almost constant contact, and aggression can mean there is even more. Because of the danger of contact, there is more frustration, more anxiety, and so more cause to treat your competitor as an enemy.

But the competitors even in these sports need not treat each other as enemies to be destroyed. They agree to abide by the rules and for the most part do. For those who do not, officials are present to keep order. The participants do not usually reject their authority. Competitors may challenge a call, but they do not usually challenge the officials' authority to make the calls.

I am not claiming in this analysis that these characteristics or aspects are exhaustive or exclusive. There are many others. They do, though, serve to point out some of the essential features of competition and both its intrinsic and its extrinsic values.

Thus, competition of whatever form is a striving to achieve an outcome that is not predetermined, or fixed. There is both a process and a product which are linked by skill or ability. The process of competition emphasizes the struggle. It is the pursuit of excellence, the desire to become what one is capable of becoming. It is this challenge to achieve excellence that is the source of the need to compete. The outcome, or product, is the achieved excellence or the success defined within the context of the rules.

In natural encounters, there is a strong consciousness of the struggle against nature; there are no contentions of wills, and therefore little likelihood of anger; one must contend against the natural elements.

In activities that exhibit the ranking characteristic, because there is a comparison you add a new dimension to the competition, an "other." Now one begins to need a different kind of strategy. Sometimes the strategy needs to be revised intermittently, sometimes almost continuously.

In face-to-face contests the string is tightened. The other person attempts to alter the physical world in order to win – not, of course, the *real* physical world, but the one created by the rules of the game. And in head-to-head contests, the string is tightened to the breaking point. In addition to adjusting your strategy to meet the continuing strategy of your opponent, you must take care to avoid physical contact which may be painful or even harmful.

Thus the more strategies involve contending against others' strategies, the more chance there is for treating others as enemies. It is another's will that one is contending against, and so frustrations and anxieties are directed toward the other. This has both negative and positive effects. First, it forces you to put your skills to the test; you cannot predict another's strategies, and she cannot predict your counter-strategies. Each must always be prepared to revise her strategies. The more complex the game, the more your mental and physical energies are taxed.

Because it is another person, you in your anxiety and frustration begin to view the strategist as an enemy to be countered; you want to destroy her *strategy*, and you may come to picture this as destroying her. Now when you add not only strategy but contact, there is more frustration and anxiety involved, and so more cause to treat your competitor as an enemy. Thus, head-to-head competitions present the ultimate challenges to one's moral being.

All of these characteristics may be present in various activities in society. In education, in studying physics for example, the "natural encounter" aspect may appear – it is only nature that one is contending against. However, when you enter into classroom situations, a new dimension is added, the ranking. Grades are forms of rankings; some in comparison to others, and some applied to an objective standard. The justification for competitions in ranking in education is to achieve excellence. But, because of rewards outside the achievement of excellence itself, deviations begin to emerge – such as cheating. An activity which features the face-to-face aspect is debate. Debaters must counter each others' moves and points; one cannot always anticipate and predict every move. One must always be prepared to revise one's strategy or position during, and perhaps after, the debate itself. In the broader society, the head-to-head aspect occurs only in survival on the streets and in war.

Contrast with Cooperation

Using the above analysis, I now want to make clear the nature of competition, as I set out to do in the beginning. The first point I want to elucidate and which should be obvious from my analysis is that cooperation and competition are not opposites. If my analysis makes any sense at all, it should be clear that in participating in any sport, cooperation is required to begin, continue, and end the competitive activity. In individual pursuits, because they involve a mutual challenge, each participant must cooperate in accordance with the rules defining the activity and those which define success or winning. Further, the mutual challenge ideally involves a commitment by the challengers to put out their best efforts in the desire to win. The

mutual challenge leads to the shared end of the game well played. Because of this commitment and desire competitors treat each other not as enemies, but as persons whose abilities each respects; not as objects to be destroyed, but as persons who challenge each other to work harder. In this way the competitors respect each other's abilities and also respect themselves in this mutual cooperative challenge. In this way the participants recognize each other as complementary, as partners in a certain relationship which requires a striving together.

In team sports it is even more clear that cooperation and competition are not opposites. The participants, of course, agree to the rules and cooperate in the way discussed above, but further cooperation is required. The participants on a team cooperate with each other to work together for shared success, or a shared win within the rules. The synchronization is the essence of the game well played.

In either case, whether one is involved in a team sport or an individual sport, there is cooperation. The cooperative efforts take on different forms in different sport activities, but such efforts constitute a mutual striving for achievement or success. In that it is mutual, all involved participate in the shared end and recognize each other as partners in a certain relationship. This is seen in the requirements of strategies essential to competitive activities, as described above.

Thus the cooperation required in sports may be described as a mutual challenge to achieve excellence. This is the ideal of competition, not only in sports, but in society. Since it is mutual it is by definition a cooperative endeavor. The fact that someone wins and someone loses does not render the activity non-cooperative or immoral. It cannot be immoral to strive to achieve excellence.

Several objections must now be considered. First, exception may be taken to my last remark on the ground that it is immoral to strive to be an excellent rapist, or an excellent assassin. But it is strange to add the word "excellent" to "rapist," or to "assassin." One may be an expert assassin, which indicates that a certain skill is perfected, but skills are not in themselves excellences. The concept of excellence is valuative, and this excludes bad achievement; an excellence is in itself worthy of achievement. However, skills may be developed for good or for ill. A person skilled in the use of knives may use this skill to harm others or to help others, as in surgery.

This leaves the question open whether the skills and dispositions developed in sport are really excellences. If they are not, I cannot claim that in sports people pursue excellences, even if they acquire skills.

But sports do develop excellences. In conjunction with skills, which are disciplined within the constitutive rules, sports do serve to develop courage, perseverance, honesty, and cooperation, and these certainly do seem to be excellences, at least in a conditional sense. That is, they count to your credit if combined with certain other basic moral virtues.

Further, this kind of competition leads to friendship, which is often characterized by the traditional handshake after a game or match. Symbolically what is being said is: "Thanks, friend, for the challenge; I respect you for the challenge." When the game is played fairly according to its rules, and when the competitors are relatively evenly matched, the participants take pleasure in a well-played game, in which the participants put out their best efforts in the desire to win. As good competitors they try their best to win; as it is a cooperative challenge, however, they may value the competition not only for the outcome, but for the process of testing themselves against others. In this way individual conflicts of interests do not completely define the activity. There is a shared end which gives meaning to the activity and which provides the basis of friendship. But this is exactly the nature of competition. Consequently, competition is a perfect vehicle for friendship.

If sound, these considerations block any proposal to eliminate competition from society. This is not impossible. I have argued that competition involves cooperation; but not that cooperation involves competition. Conceivably there could be a purely cooperative society. But, while possible, such a society is not practicable. A purely cooperative society is possible only where there is abundance or where there is pure benevolence. But no such situation prevails. For economic goods there is competition, mainly because of the scarcity of such goods, coupled with our lack of benevolence. But even if such goods were abundant, my previous argument shows that competition should not be ruled out.

As long as individuals strive for honor, personal excellences, and achievements, there will always be competition, for these things are best developed and tested in competition. For example, honesty and other virtues are best developed when there is an incentive to be, or interest in being, dishonest. There need be no virtue in honesty when honesty pays. If a person is honest and gives the exact change because it is good business, that does not necessarily show she is honest; what would do so is if she were honest when honesty did not pay. In sports competitions, for example, there is an interest in cheating to win, so individuals who do not cheat can know they are honest. Sports competitions serve as tests giving people a kind of knowledge of themselves, of their abilities and virtues.

Given the equality of human beings, you can best test yourself and discover your powers when you are challenged by another equal. Human beings introduce a qualitatively distinct element of uncertainty and unpredictability that is not present in nature. This qualitative difference is rooted in reason.

In the short story "The Most Dangerous Game" by Richard Connell, a big game hunter, in his quest for self-realization and self-knowledge, found that big game was not enough of a challenge. "No animal had a chance with me any more," the hunter lamented. "It is a mathematical certainty. The animal had nothing but his legs and his instinct. Instinct is no match for reason."[4] He therefore contrived to hunt the animal with reason, the human animal. Only that animal could offer a challenge. But for the ultimate challenge, the other human had to be another big game hunter equal to him; only such a being could fully test his abilities. And he rejoiced when chance sent such an opponent his way. Of course, I am not recommending this activity; this shows how conditional virtues so developed can make a person worse. In the development of courage, for instance, your goodness is conditional on your having other virtues. Or as Kant would claim, courage enhances one's worth only if one has a good will. Without other virtues, or a good will, courage, or any other conditional virtue, could make a bad person worse.

A final objection is that although the qualities developed in competition are indeed excellences, competition is still tainted because it involves using other people to achieve these excellences. This objection depends on the assumption that it is always wrong to use other people. But this assumption is false. It is *sometimes* wrong to use other people, but not always. In a society where people need each other to carry out their plans of life, are we using each other or treating each other as means? We do, of course, use each other's services, etc., but that does not mean we deny their providers respect. Students use teachers to learn, consumers use store-owners to obtain supplies, etc. But is there a denial of respect? On the contrary, because they need each other as partners in a certain relationship, because they recognize this complementarity, they treat each other with equal respect. This is not only true in society, it is also the case when sport is viewed as a mutual challenge to achieve excellence. In both cases there is a community of people with shared ends and common activities enjoying one another's excellences and individuality as they participate in the activities. This epitomizes respect for persons.

Consequences of Competition

I consider now the issue of the harmful consequences of competition in sport. Probably the most significant source of problems is *money*. Where money becomes the aim, one's perspective on the competition is blurred. The focus is on the outcome only and on a "benefit" outside the competition itself. But this is certainly not unique to competition in sports.

If money is one's aim, the defeat of another for a prize outside the competition becomes essential, and this leads to a desire for superiority and to the "win-at-all-costs" syndrome. But the person who has internalized the ideal of competition could not possibly try to win at all costs, for example to win by cheating. Winning by cheating is often referred to as a "hollow victory"; it is indeed self-contradictory, since to *truly* win requires that one win within the rules of the game and the rules of decency. This doesn't remove the factual point that people do in fact cheat to win. When this is the case it is the external factors which divert people from what the competition in sport tells them. The aim is for scarce benefits external to the competition itself: money, fame, glory, lionizing, etc. These are what make people want to cheat.[5]

This is not, however, to depreciate the necessity of the desire to win. Both the desire to win at all costs and the lack of a strong desire to win are fatal to the ideal of competition. The importance of "how you play the game" cannot mean a lack of a desire to win.

People who say that winning is not important are simply preparing for failure in whatever the activity might be. Further, people who say that winning is more important then decency, honor, integrity, etc. are a disgrace to sports and a disgrace to the human race. However, if one views the competition as a struggle to achieve, one must have the *desire* to achieve, and in most game contexts this means winning within the rules. One is not being challenged, nor is one challenging, if one lacks the desire to achieve. This may be described by Simon's concept of a mutual challenge to achieve excellence. This is the ideal of competition, not only in sports, but also in society. Since it is a mutual, it is by definition a cooperative endeavor. The fact that someone wins and someone loses does not render the activity immoral. Only when the loser is seen as an object to be destroyed without compassion, honor, or decency is the activity immoral. But again, *in itself*, it cannot be immoral to achieve excellence.

Conclusion

Competition as a mutual challenge to achieve excellence is of course an ideal and actual practices may deviate from it. This is so most often when competition is viewed as combat, and when the competition is seen as a means to an end external to the competition itself, namely when the reward of money is the aim. While the internal benefits of competition are what may be called "basic benefits," the external rewards are "scarce benefits."[6] These include money, fame, glory, and media attention. These are by-products of competition and are incidental to the process of competition itself, which is often perverted in the pursuit of these ends. It is in striving for these scarce benefits that deviations become obvious, winning is over-emphasized, and the spirit of selfishness reigns supreme. But we must look at the consequences of competition and examine whether the bad outweighs the good. This is, in part, an empirical issue.

We certainly have many examples of what appear to be evils in sports competition: drug abuses, "battleground" mentalities, arrogance in superior athletes, cheating, etc. And these are readily obvious, dramatized, and exaggerated in sports. One ready reason is because bigtime sports are public, there for everyone to see. We are familiar with these athletes, if we choose to be. Unfortunately those who reject sports in competition recognize only these deviations, focusing only on the "accidents" of the activity. It is partly for this reason that I recommend, as do others, that participation is important, and perhaps even necessary, to appreciate the value of sports in competition, participation in a competitive activity which involves what I have been advocating, a mutual challenge to achieve excellence or a cooperative challenge.

These notions are dramatized in sport, and this is what makes sport morally significant. It is not only that sport mirrors the society in which it operates, it compresses and heightens aspects of that society. It is that society in miniature, exaggerating and dramatizing aspects of it, much like a theater production does. Like drama, sport may reveal to the society virtues it has not yet recognized, or present new values to the society and criticize old ones, or dramatize the established virtues and vices in the society. Insofar as it declares the values of the society, sport tells people when they do not live up to their ideals, chastises them for their laxity, and prods them to be better people.

Sport emphasizes and dramatizes the virtues and values of the society so that when they are undermined they become more obvious and acute. And in so doing it chastises not only the violators but society itself for its laxity.[7]

Deviations from the ideal in sports are exaggerated versions of what is present in the society in which the sports operate. Competitive sports do not have a monopoly on these deviations, and these deviations are not essential to them. It is for this reason that sport is morally significant. Competition when viewed as a mutual challenge to achieve excellence, no matter the field, leads to progress, to respect for others, to friendships, and to excellence. This is the essence of competition.

Notes

I wish to thank Bernard Boxill and Thomas E. Hill for comments on earlier drafts of this paper.

1   See for example, Alfie Kohn, *No Contest: The Case Against Competition* (Boston: Houghtin Mifflin, 1986).

2   This concept is first used in Robert Simon, *Fair Play: Sports, Values, and Society* (Boulder, CO: Westview Press, 1991).

3   Some of these may also be forms of competition with others as well.

4   Richard Connell, "The Most Dangerous Game," in *Stories for Men* (New York: Garden City Publishing, 1944), p. 96.

5   Of course, in the marketplace, competition aims directly for the reward of money, which complicates the issue. The justification for competition, however, remains the same.

6   For more discussion about benefits, see Jane English, "Sex Equality in Sports," in this volume (reading 24).

7   This has become quite evident in the recent developments regarding racism in the European soccer league, where racist taunts and remarks within the game are made by the fans.

CHAPTER 12

On Winning and Athletic Superiority

Nicholas Dixon

How do we decide which team or player is better in a competitive sporting contest?[1] The obvious answer is that the winner is the superior team or athlete. A central purpose of competitive sport is precisely to provide a comparison – in Kretchmar's terms (7), a contest – that *determines* which team or player is superior. However, we can easily find undeserved victories in which this purpose is not achieved – in other words, contests in which the player or team that wins is not, according to both our intuitions and plausible accounts of the goal of competitive sport from the philosophy of sport literature, better than the losing player or team.[2] This paper is an examination of several such situations in which competitive sport fails to provide an accurate measure of athletic superiority. For brevity's sake, I will at times refer to such events as "failed athletic contests," meaning contests that have failed in their central comparative purpose, even though they may have succeeded in other goals like entertaining spectators.

My purpose is threefold. First, studying various ways in which athletic contests fail to achieve their central comparative purpose is intrinsically interesting. While the philosophy of sport literature is replete with discussions of the purpose of competitive sport, it does not, to my knowledge, address the question of how well athletic contests fulfill that purpose. An instrumental benefit of

this discussion is that a clear delineation of the wide variety of sources of unjust outcomes in sporting contests, showing that winning is not the be all and end all of athletic superiority, may help to weaken the motivation to resort to morally objectionable means to secure victory. Second, in the process of examining unjust victories, we will deepen our understanding of the concept of athletic superiority. More specifically, we will be forced to confront the issue of how much weight we should give to such psychological traits as guile and poise in our determinations of athletic superiority. Third, consideration of how much weight we should give to one particular psychological trait – the ability to perform well under pressure – in our judgments about athletic superiority will lead to the conclusion that the "playoff" system by which championships are determined in American team sports is a relatively inefficient method of determining which team is best.

For the first four sections, I will use "the better team" as interchangeable with "the team that deserves to win." Both expressions refer to the team that performs better (however we choose to define superior performance) in a particular athletic contest. In Section 5, the two concepts diverge, as I discuss the possibility that the team that performs better and deserves to win may still not be the better team.

Refereeing Errors

Suppose that a soccer referee is either incompetent or openly biased in favor of the home team. He or she disallows as offside three perfectly good goals for the away team, even though replays clearly indicate that all the attacking players were onside. The home team wins by a single goal after the referee awards a "phantom" penalty, even though replays conclusively show that no contact was made with the attacker who slumped to the ground in the penalty area. Furthermore, the away team was constantly on the attack, pinning the far less skillful home team in its own half throughout the entire match. In this case, I suggest, the home team did not deserve to win. The better team did not win.[3] Several different views on the goal of competitive sport support this claim, assuming that the team or player that best meets this goal is the better one and deserves to win. For instance, Robert Simon's view that competitive sport is "the attempt to secure victory within the framework set by the constitutive rules" (11: p. 15) indicates that the away team is superior, since, had the referee applied the rules of the game correctly, it would have won. The injustice of the home team's victory follows from another of Simon's views, namely "the idea of the sports contest as a test of skill, a mutual quest for excellence by the participants" (11: p. 50), since the away team displays more skill and excellence. For the same reason, the away team's superiority also follows from Kathleen M. Pearson's view that the purpose of competitive sport is

> to test the skill of one individual, or group of individuals, against the skill of another individual, or group of individuals, in order to determine who is more skillful in a particular, well-defined activity. (10: p. 183)

But let us pause to consider some objections that would deny that refereeing errors lead to undeserved victories and, hence, to failed athletic contests.

First, we might insist that the referee's word is final and that, as long as no cheating occurs, any results based upon the referee's decisions are just. As a long-serving baseball commentator in Detroit was apt to point out, when people challenged an umpire's calls, tomorrow morning's box scores will always prove that the umpire was right after all. The problem with this argument is that it clumsily conflates power with infallibility. The jury in the first trial of the LAPD officers who assaulted Rodney King certainly had the power to acquit them. Those of us who disagreed with the verdict believed that, even though the correct *procedures* for a jury trial may have been followed, the *outcome* was unjust. Similarly, even though the procedural rules of soccer do indeed give the referee the final word, this in no way guarantees that the referee's calls will be correct. And referees' errors can lead to unjust results.

Second, and rather more plausibly, some people argue that a great team should be able to overcome bad calls by the referee and win anyway. There may be some truth to this claim, but it does not undermine my thesis, which is that the *better* team can be prevented by refereeing errors from winning, not that great teams can be. The away team in my example may not be good enough to overcome the referee's poor calls, but it is certainly the better team, and deserved to win, according to the rules of the game.

A third objection takes a very different tack. Rather than denying that the winning team (in my example, the home team) is superior, this final objection consists in arguing that the home team does not win at all. For instance, Suits (12: p. 9) argues that "a player who does not confine himself to lusory means may not be said to win, even if he achieves the pre-lusory goal." Thus the home team's alleged victory, which has been achieved by methods that violate the permitted lusory means, even though the referee negligently failed to punish these violations, is not a victory after all. This approach has an interesting parallel in natural law theory's treatment of unjust laws. In justifying his violation of segregation laws, Martin Luther King cited St.

Augustine's view that "an unjust law is no law at all" (6: p. 89). Just as an unjust law, according to natural law theory, is superseded by the moral law that it violates, so an apparent victory by illicit means is nullified by the very rules that have been violated.

A problem with this approach is that, in preserving the justice of the outcome of sporting contests by legislating out of existence victories by inferior teams due to refereeing errors, it creates the suspicion of an ad hoc maneuver designed to respond to a troubling objection by stipulation rather than by argument. More important, in considering the analogy with natural law theory, we need to examine a rival theory, that of legal positivism. According to legal positivism, [to determine] whether a statute is indeed a valid law, we need only consider its "pedigree" (that is, whether it was enacted in accordance with the constitution or whatever other "rule of recognition" is operative) without deciding on its moral justifiability. So a bad law is still a law. The problem with natural law theory, according to legal positivists, is that it conflates the concepts of "law" and "good law," and fails to allow for the very possibility of a bad law. We would do better, they suggest, to focus our attention on moral evaluation and criticism of immoral laws than to dispute their status as law.[4] The implication of legal positivism for our debate over refereeing errors is that, rather than disputing the fact that the home team won the game, we should instead concentrate on describing the injustice of this victory. Ordinary usage has a meaning for the expressions "hollow victory" and "undeserved victory," and we should be suspicious of an approach that would render these concepts meaningless by fiat.

Showing that refereeing errors can lead to undeserved victories by inferior teams has not required us to make any controversial assumptions about our criteria for athletic superiority. The fact that the visiting team was far superior in terms of physical skills and performance seems sufficient, in our example, to identify it as the better team. In the next section, however, we will have to broaden our concept of athletic superiority beyond mere physical prowess.

Cheating

My purpose in this section is not to offer a comprehensive account of cheating, a complex topic that deserves a much more detailed discussion than is possible in the confines of this paper. I offer instead what I hope will be an uncontroversial sufficient condition for cheating – namely, an attempt to break the rules of a game while escaping detection and punishment. Whatever else may count as cheating, we can be sure that anything meeting this description does. My goal is to explore the implications of this minimal definition for my topic of the relationship between victory and athletic superiority.

A victory that depends in large part upon cheating seems neither deserved nor a sign of athletic superiority. This is, presumably, why Ben Johnson was stripped of his gold medal in the 1988 Olympic Games after he tested positive for illegal steroids. Granted, Johnson did outperform his rivals. But he would also outperform them if he spiked their food or drink with a performance-impairing drug. In neither case does Johnson's victory prove him to be a superior athlete, because his violation of the rules gives him an unfair advantage over his opponents, thus subverting the race as a legitimate test of athletic excellence. Cheating can also occur *during* a game: A golfer may move the ball from a bad lie when her opponent is not looking, a pitcher may doctor the baseball, or a player in a tennis match without an umpire may wrongly call a ball out. An especially infamous act of cheating was committed by Diego Maradona, one of the most gifted soccer players of all time, who illegally punched the ball into the net to score a goal for Argentina against England in a 1986 World Cup quarterfinal. The referee did not spot the infraction that replays revealed, and Maradona afterwards boasted that the "hand of God" had scored his goal. In general, the reason why cheats do not deserve to win is that their victories are due not to their athletic superiority, but to their violation of rules which their opponents, in contrast, obey. This claim is based on the assumption that the athlete who deserves to win is the one who performs better *within the game's rules* and *under conditions of equality*.

However, we need to consider an audacious defense of cheating as playing a legitimate role in competitive sport. Oliver Leaman (8) describes cheating as the use of "wits" in addition to skill and strategy and suggests that it adds a new dimension that makes sport more interesting. As long as cheating occurs in the context of *overall* obedience to the rules by the cheater and other competitors, it will not result in anarchy, and the overall character of games will be preserved. Moreover, if we were to recognize cheating as a *legitimate* tactic for athletes to use, then the cheater would no longer have an unfair advantage, since *all* athletes would feel free to cheat. Indeed, the ability to cheat without being detected might even become a prized aspect of athletic skill. So, if Leaman is correct, even the orthodox view that the best athlete, the one who deserves to win, is the one who displays most skill does not necessarily preclude cheating. Perhaps Maradona's ability to deceive the referee into believing that he had used his head and not his hand to score the infamous goal against England is itself evidence of his genius. Machiavellian conflict between ruthless competitors would be the best test of this new, broader concept of athletic prowess.

Regardless of the merits of Leaman's defense of cheating, he has said enough to indicate that we need to broaden our concept of athletic superiority to include more than mere physical prowess. An excellent athlete must not only have superior physical skills but also the acumen to use them wisely, employing shrewd tactics and strategy that are designed to maximize the benefits of his or her skills while simultaneously neutralizing those of opponents. A soccer team that has exquisite ball control skills, but unwisely commits all 11 players to a constant onslaught on the opposing team's goal, will often leave itself vulnerable to fast breaks from the opposition. Should the opponents win the game by virtue of a goal scored during just such a fast break, the technically-superior losers cannot justly claim to be the superior team, since they have failed to exhibit an integral part of athletic excellence. If, as Leaman argues, the ability to cheat is itself a legitimate component of the "strategy and tactics" dimension of athletic excellence, then perhaps the cheating winners listed at the beginning of this section did after all deserve their victories.

Of course, moral condemnations of cheating in sport are easy to formulate.[5] However, Leaman's point is precisely that athletes are protected by a kind of moral immunity to the criticisms that would rightly be directed at them were they to cheat outside the context of sport.[6] We might compare this immunity to that enjoyed by defense attorneys in the U.S. Even when an attorney is convinced that her client committed a despicable crime, she is professionally obligated to mount a zealous defense, trying to get key evidence excluded on constitutional grounds, challenging truthful prosecution witnesses, and trying to persuade the jury of alternative possibilities that she herself believes did not happen. The end product of the attorney's actions may be the acquittal of a dangerous, factually guilty defendant.

Now the attorney's moral immunity is an essential part of the legal adversary system, which is itself justified by the belief that even the most despicable defendant deserves a loyal ally to protect his or her rights. Whether or not Leaman's argument for the moral immunity of athletes succeeds depends on the existence of a similar rationale for allowing cheating in sport. Is cheating essential to sport in the way that an attorney's loyalty to clients is essential to the legal adversary system? The answer seems to be no. Granted, widespread cheating would add an extra layer of intrigue and excitement to sport, but it hardly seems to further any of sport's central values. On the contrary, it sabotages one of competitive sport's least controversial goals: to determine which team has most athletic skill, including, as we have just seen, mental abilities like shrewd tactics as well as physical prowess, *as permitted by the rules of the game.* Certainly, successful cheating requires some skill and cunning and even, in some cases, considerable physical ability, but this is very different from the kind of legitimate use of tactical and physical prowess that competitive sport aims to test.[7]

My goal in this subsection is not morally to condemn cheating, even though good reasons exist for doing so. It is, instead, to evaluate the relationship between cheating and athletic superiority. However, for the same reason that teams cannot claim moral immunity for their acts of cheating – that is, they subvert the test of athletic skill that is a central goal of competitive sport – the claim that the team that uses cheating to win is *ipso facto* the best team and deserves to win is unconvincing. This judgment is reflected in the heavy penalties that sporting federations have imposed on athletes whom they catch cheating. More than the long-term suspension that was imposed on Ben Johnson for his illegal drug use, the fact that his Olympic gold medal was taken away from him indicates the belief that he did not deserve to win. In terms of the abilities that competitive sport is designed to test, Johnson was *not* the best athlete. So, at least in some cases, cheating can prevent competitive sport from providing an accurate measure of athletic superiority.

Gamesmanship

Gamesmanship is a slippery concept that is hard to define. Unlike cheating, it does not involve violating the rules of the game in the hope of avoiding detection. Examples include using legal but morally dubious designed tactics to unsettle opponents: trash-talking, taking an inordinate amount of time between points in a tennis match, and so on. A different kind of gamesmanship is the so-called "professional foul," which is committed in order to prevent an opposing player from scoring an easy goal or lay-up. Unlike outright cheating, such fouls are committed openly, in the expectation that a penalty will be imposed. Perhaps what all gamesmanship has in common is an apparent violation of the *spirit* of a game[8] My purpose here is not morally to assess gamesmanship. It is, rather, to argue that an athlete or team that successfully uses gamesmanship as a major weapon in securing victory may not deserve to win in the sense of being the best athlete or team. Gamesmanship, then, provides another

category of situations in which athletic contests can fail in their aim of accurately determining athletic superiority. We should note that at this stage we may only call gamesmanship an *apparent* violation of the spirit of a game. Should we conclude that successful use of gamesmanship is one sign of a good athlete, then we must withdraw the judgment that it violates the spirit of competitive sport.

I begin by considering the professional or "strategic" foul. Some philosophers of sport outright condemn such fouls,[9] while Robert Simon has given a nuanced, qualified defense of professional fouls in some circumstances (11: pp.46–49). He points out that in basketball, for instance, the intentional foul is widely regarded as a legitimate strategy. The only issue, on Simon's view, seems to be the prudential one of whether preventing an easy lay-up is worth the penalty incurred for intentional fouls. For the sake of argument, I will grant Simon's point that a professional foul is sometimes a legitimate strategy. My goal in this section is to show that sometimes it is *illegitimate* and subverts the goal of measuring the relative athletic ability of the contestants.

For such an example, let us consider a soccer game that has been dominated by the home team but that remains scoreless going into the final few minutes. The home team finally mounts a decisive attack, and one of its players is about to tap the ball into an empty net when he is brutally rugby-tackled by an opponent, preventing him from scoring. The goalkeeper then saves the resultant penalty. In the final seconds of the game, the away team mounts a similar attack. The home team, in contrast, refrains from resorting to a professional foul to prevent the attacker from scoring, and the away team scores the winning goal with the last kick of the game. In such a case, I suggest, the away team did not deserve to win, because it did not demonstrate superior athletic skill. Its victory is due, instead, to its cynical willingness to exploit the rules of the game that "permit" the professional foul to teams willing to incur the resultant free kick or penalty. The recent (but unevenly enforced) decision by FIFA (the Federation of International Football Associations) to automatically penalize the professional foul by ejection from the game (without substitution) indicates that soccer's highest governing body regards it as a violation of the game's spirit.

How we view a professional foul may depend on the type of foul involved: we naturally view hard fouls more harshly that risk injuring opponents. Especially in basketball, we are more apt to condemn such fouls when they occur late in the game, since they are more likely to determine its outcome than those that occur earlier. The difference in attitude to the professional foul in basketball and soccer is arguably attributable to the vastly different impact that it can have in each sport. Basketball is a high-scoring sport, in which preventing a lay-up and requiring the offensive player to earn points from the free throw line normally has a minimal impact on a game's outcome. Soccer, in contrast, is a low-scoring sport, in which a single professional foul can prevent what would have been the decisive winning or equalizing goal. In such sports, a team that wins as a result of a professional foul is not necessarily the best team, in terms of the criteria we have so far allowed as relevant for athletic excellence: physical skill and tactical acumen, both exercised within the rules of the game.

The use of psychological tricks – for example, trash-talking or delaying the game – to try to unsettle opponents is a very different kind of gamesmanship that forces us to confront another dimension of our concept of athletic excellence. We have already widened the concept to include mental as well as physical attributes. We now need to consider whether the mental element of athletic superiority should include such emotional characteristics as coolness under pressure, in addition to the cognitive abilities (for instance, strategy) that we have already added. In favor of such a widening of our understanding of athletic excellence is the view that players who allow themselves to be distracted by such tactics do not deserve to win. Truly great players, one might argue, will use their vastly superior skill to compensate for whatever loss of composure they suffer as a result of opponents' psychological tricks. However, we need to remember that the question here is not whether

great players always win but, rather, whether the *better* player wins when gamesmanship is a decisive factor. And we can easily imagine examples in which a clearly superior, but not great, player is so rattled by her opponent's gamesmanship that she loses her cool and the game. According to the uncontroversial view that the primary purpose of competitive sport is to determine which team or player has superior athletic skill (understood as including both physical ability and astute strategy as permitted by the game's rules), players who use this kind of gamesmanship to win do not appear to deserve their victory.

In response, apologists for gamesmanship will respond that it *is* a legitimate strategy in competitive sport. If the ability to use gamesmanship (and to remain impervious to opponents' use of it) is part of athletic excellence, then the technically superior player who allows herself to be unsettled by her opponent's psychological tricks is deficient in one of the mental elements of athletic excellence and is not, after all, the better athlete. The issue, which we may safely leave unresolved at this stage, hinges on whether we include "psychological coolness" or temperament as part of the mental element of our definition of athletic excellence. In Section 5, I will discuss in more depth the relationship between temperament and athletic excellence. I will conclude there that, while repeated defeats due to extreme nervousness may disqualify a team's claim to be the best, we must also allow for the possibility that a team that loses a big game due to nervousness may nonetheless be the better team. What has already emerged from this section is that at least one kind of gamesmanship – the professional foul in low-scoring games like soccer – can result in undeserved victories in which the better team does not win, and the athletic contest has failed.

Bad Luck

The next set of putative failures of athletic contests to accurately measure athletic superiority involves neither mistakes by referees nor misconduct by players. It arises, rather, in games in which one team dominates the other but still manages to lose the game, because of a succession of strokes of bad luck.[10] The distinction between high- and low-scoring games is relevant here. In a high-scoring game like basketball, a few unlucky breaks are unlikely to sway the outcome. In contrast, in a low-scoring game like soccer, a small number of unlucky breaks can be decisive. Nor do we have to resort to thought experiments: most soccer fans have seen games dominated by one team that hits the woodwork several times and still ends up losing to a single goal scored on one of its opponents' few serious attacks. Suppose further that the dominant team has several goal-bound shots deflected by erratic gusts of wind, others stopped by thick mud on the goal line, and others still inadvertently stopped by a poorly-positioned referee. When, moreover, the winning goal is caused by a freakish deflection by a defender, the dominant team may justly claim that it was the better team and deserved to win. Unlucky losers appear, therefore, to provide another category of failed athletic contests. Let us pause to consider some objections.

First, mirroring an argument we have already considered, one might insist that a great team makes its own luck, and teams that fail to do so do not deserve to win. But this argument is vulnerable to a response already given: While a truly great team may indeed be able to salvage victory despite horrendously bad luck, a less talented team may be unable to do so, while still being clearly the better team and deserving to win. Granted, if a team with a long-term poor record claims that its losses were all due to bad luck, we would suspect self-deception and suggest that its players take a little more responsibility for their performances. Luck does tend to even out in the long run. However, in the short run – for instance, an individual game – we may plausibly say that a team was unlucky and did not deserve to lose.

A second objection reminds us that the purpose of any competitive game is to score more points than opponents. When a team dominates the action, keeping the opponent pinned in its own half, yet still manages to lose, it may be the lack of two legitimate considerations in determining athletic superiority, a killer instinct and good strategy, not bad luck, that accounts for its losses. Such charges were made, for instance, against the French soccer team in the 1982 World Cup, when it played beautiful, crowd-pleasing soccer but was eliminated in the quarter-finals. However, even granting for the sake of argument that some dominant teams do not deserve to win, we can still produce cases in which a team loses undeservedly due to bad luck. In the hypothetical case at the beginning of this section, the dominant team did not play pretty but innocuous soccer. It employed shrewd strategy and displayed a killer instinct, translating its dominance into several accurate shots on goal that were stopped only by the woodwork and by aberrational interventions by the wind, the mud, and the referee. Had these interventions not taken place, had any one of these shots gone just a few inches inside, and had the freakish deflection not occurred, the team would have won. Under these admittedly far-fetched circumstances, the better team did not win. However, more mundane examples of unlucky losses do occur in the real soccer world. Even the best players cannot direct their shots to the nearest inch, and the precise placement of any shot is partly a matter of luck. When a team repeatedly hits the goalpost without scoring, it is usually unlucky.

A final objection draws a line in the sand and insists that, no matter how close a team may have been to scoring several goals, it does not deserve to win if it does not score. According to this defense, the team that wins by a freakish goal on an isolated attack, despite several lucky escapes, including having its own goal's woodwork rattled repeatedly throughout the game by opponents' shots, deserves to win. The problem with this impregnable-sounding argument is precisely that it is *too* impregnable. Instead of honestly confronting the role of luck in sport, it tries to legislate it out of the picture by simply *defining* the best team as the one that scores most points. Arguments, not question-begging stipulative definitions, are needed to decide the question. And the arguments that I have presented in this and previous sections indicate that refereeing errors, cheating, unacceptable gamesmanship,[11] and bad luck can all result in undeserved victories by inferior teams.

Before moving on to a different aspect of the relationship between winning and athletic superiority, I pause to consider an argument that stipulative definitions of the kind I have just criticized are not necessarily question-begging. According to this argument, winning is an *operational definition* of the concept *the better team* in the same way that a score on an IQ test is an operational definition of the everyday concept of intelligence, and a legal verdict of guilty is an operational definition of the intuitive concept "that guy did it!" Operational definitions generally provide clear, objectively-ascertainable criteria for concepts whose everyday usage is more ambiguous and complex. (Legal guilt is an exception, in that rules of evidence and burden of proof requirements may make determinations of guilt appear more complex than the intuitive sense of "he did it!" Nonetheless, like all operational definitions, it provides an objective decision procedure – in this case, has the prosecution proven beyond a reasonable doubt that the defendant performed the *actus reus* with the requisite *mens rea*? – for determining a question that might otherwise be subject to arbitrary personal preference.) Since operational definitions do not claim to capture all the connotations of the everyday concepts that they replace, we should not be surprised by divergences between the two. People whom we judge very intelligent may perform poorly on IQ tests, and people who we know committed the act of which they are accused may be *correctly* found legally innocent. These divergences need reflect no fault in the operational definitions but, rather, the mere fact that they are operational definitions.

In support of viewing winning as an operational definition of athletic superiority, one goal of athletic contests is precisely to *determine* which team is better, and they have been designed to provide an accurate measure of excellence. Moreover, we sometimes modify rules in order to make contests a more accurate test of athletic superiority, for instance the offside rule in soccer, which prevents the tactic of booting the ball upfield to strikers who are permanently camped in front of the opposing goal, and en-

courages teams to play a more skillful passing game. To the extent that winning the contest is an operational definition of athletic superiority that has evolved over the years in the sporting world, it appears to be immune from the critiques that I have made, since my critiques are made from the point of view of the intuitive, everyday concept of athletic excellence. As we have seen, operational definitions do not claim to coincide with the everyday concepts that they are designed to replace.

In response, I do not deny that regarding winning as the criterion for athletic superiority is, *qua* operational definition, irreproachable. However, critiques of operational definitions from the point of view of intuitive concepts still perform two useful functions. First, too great a divergence between an everyday concept and its operational definition casts doubts on the adequacy of that definition. This is precisely what has happened with the concept of IQ, which has been criticized because of major discrepancies between it and intuitive judgments about intelligence. Victories by inferior teams or athletes, on the other hand, are sufficiently rare to indicate that this particular criticism is not applicable to regarding the winner as the better athlete, which remains a workable operational definition. Second, and most important, "external" critiques from the point of view of everyday concepts serve to remind us that such concepts as legal guilt *are* only operational definitions. They remind us that a defendant may really have "done it," even though he was correctly found legally innocent. And, in the case of the intuitive concept of athletic superiority,[12] they remind us that, while regarding the winner as the better athlete is generally a harmless convention, on some occasions it leads to inaccurate judgments of athletic superiority. I intend this paper, in part, as just such a reminder.

Inferior Performances by Superior Athletes

Steffi Graf dominated women's tennis for several years from the late 1980s until the mid-1990s. Suppose that in the middle of her period of dominance, she plays devastating tennis to reach the final at Wimbledon without losing a set. Her opponent is an unseeded player who has battled her way to the final by means of a series of gutsy three-set victories over technically superior players. And suppose, finally, that the unseeded player continues her string of upsets with a famous victory over Graf in a long, desperately close game. Her victory is fair and square. It involves no refereeing errors, no cheating, no gamesmanship, and no notably good luck. She deserves her victory because, on that day, she is the better player. However, in another sense, she is not the better player. Steffi Graf, who would almost certainly beat the player nine times out of ten, is the better player. She just had an off-day.

So we appear to have found another sense in which an athletic contest can result in an inaccurate measure of athletic excellence: The winning player can deserve to win and yet still be an inferior athlete. Superior athletes do sometimes have bad days and lose. Few people would deny this claim in the case of my Steffi Graf example, but when it comes to other sports, some sectors of the sporting community are surprisingly reluctant to concede the possibility of this source of failed athletic contests. Concurrent with discussing their obvious relevance for my central topic of the relationship between winning and athletic superiority, I will point out the implications of such inaccurate measures of athletic superiority for the playoff system used in the U.S. to determine the winners of team sports championships.

According to a popular approach in the U.S. sporting community, a football team with the best record during the National Football League's regular season and playoffs, winning all its games easily but losing the Superbowl, is not after all the best team in the NFL. The surest sign of the best team, the view continues, is the ability to save its best performances for the biggest occasions, and this is precisely what the winning team does, despite its indifferent play during the regular season and the playoffs. Evidence of the prevalence of this view is provided by the astonishing scorn directed at the Buffalo Bills football team in the U.S. for a series of Superbowl losses in recent years. Even though it had the best record in American football for several years and was agonizingly close to winning one of its Superbowl games, the mere fact that it lost several of these finals not only prevented it from being considered the best team but also made it a despised laughing-stock among many sport journalists.

Michael Jordan's status as an all-time great was secured in the opinion of many American basketball fans the first year he led the Chicago Bulls to a National Basketball Association championship, even though his play, both quantitatively and qualitatively, may have been just as outstanding in previous seasons. Once again, the underlying belief is that the best players, especially great ones, are those who come through to achieve victory when it matters most: post-season playoff games.

More generally, the playoff system in the best-known professional team sports in the U.S. – baseball, basketball, football, and hockey – clearly presupposes that victory in the biggest games is the best measure of athletic superiority. The championship is awarded not to the team with the best regular-season record but rather to the team that excels in a relatively brief playoff tournament involving some of the teams with the best regular-season records. Athletic excellence is understood as the ability to perform well under pressure, when the stakes are highest, rather than as the ability to perform well over the course of an entire season.

As a matter of contingent fact, the two rival criteria for athletic excellence – performance over an extended period (a season) versus performance in a brief, high-pressure playoff tournament – usually point to the same player or team. With rare exceptions, playoff winners tend to have very strong regular-season records, if not the best. Strong teams win most of their games, including high-pressure playoff games. The most interesting cases from the point of view of our discussion of athletic superiority, though, are those where a team with a mediocre regular-season record wins the playoffs, for example a wild-card team winning the Superbowl. What reasons exist for the belief that this Superbowl winner is, *ipso facto*, that season's best NFL team? Think back to the example about Steffi Graf, where a single defeat in a major tournament to an unranked player would not have dislodged our belief that she was the best women's tennis player in the world during her years of dominance. By analogy, why don't we also believe that the team with a perfect regular-season record, which has dominated its opponents throughout the regular season and playoffs, is still the best team in the NFL, despite its subpar performance in its Superbowl loss to a wild-card team? Certainly, a difference of degree exists between the two situations. Whereas a single loss in a major tournament is relatively insignificant in the context of Steffi Graf's dozens of victories in many other tournaments, the Superbowl is clearly the most important game in a very brief NFL season, consisting of a *single* tournament with a maximum of only 20 or so games. However, this difference in degree seems insufficient to support the view that the team that wins the playoffs for the championship is necessarily the best team. My scenario in which the season's dominant football team has an off-day and loses the Superbowl makes a strong enough *prima facie* case that it is still the best team in the NFL to require in response an *argument* for, and not just an assertion of, the accuracy of the playoff system in measuring athletic excellence.

And perhaps such an argument is not too hard to find. The ability to perform well under pressure, so the argument goes, is a sign of *psychological toughness*, which is an essential ingredient of excellence in competitive sport. We have already encountered in Section 3 one element of psychological toughness, namely the ability to remain impervious to opponents' gamesmanship. Now little doubt exists that psychological toughness is an important quality for winning athletic contests. The key question is how much weight we assign to it in assessing athletic excellence.

I agree that a claim to athletic excellence would be hollow in the case of an athlete who *always* choked in any competitive game, not just big games in big tournaments. We would suspect that a general lack of athletic ability, and not just a suspect temperament, is responsible for the repeated losses. Furthermore, we could

even require a baseline of psychological toughness as a prerequisite for athletic excellence, and concede that, however gifted an athlete may be, repeated losses in major tournaments due to nerves, undue sensitivity to opponents' gamesmanship, or a failure to be "up" for the occasion preclude us from considering her as the best athlete in her field. However, we also need to avoid the danger of setting our standard for psychological toughness so high that only actually *winning* the tournament or playoff series or Superbowl qualifies us as mentally strong enough to be the best athlete or team. In other words, we should leave conceptual space for regarding the team that has shown supreme skill, strategy, *and* psychological toughness throughout the entire regular season and playoffs, before losing the final game in the playoffs in a subpar performance, as nonetheless the best team. If we fail to allow for this possibility, the belief that the best team always comes through on the big occasions has become an article of faith rather than a hypothesis that is open to confirmation or falsification by open-minded examination of our concept of athletic excellence.

To further challenge the centrality of psychological toughness to athletic excellence, consider, by analogy, the importance that we place on the ability to perform well under pressure in other activities. For instance, is excellence in teaching best judged by a job candidate's classroom performance during a one-day campus visit, or by observing her classes for an entire semester? While we admire the candidate who rises to the occasion to deliver a dynamic guest lecture, most search committees recognize that nerves caused by the momentousness of the occasion can obscure the ability of even excellent teachers. A far better, but logistically impractical, way to evaluate a candidate's teaching ability would be to observe her over a longer period of time in a more relaxed setting. Why should we regard performance under pressure as so much more important in judging athletic excellence when in other fields we regard pressure as a factor that can *obscure* excellence? Of course, important disanalogies exist between teaching and sport, which is by its very nature competitive and tense. However, this does not explain why people regard performance under the greatest pressure as *the best* indicator of athletic excellence.

One reason for this may be that we in the U.S. are accustomed to the playoff system, which puts a premium on performing well in a small number of high-pressure games. And the very fact that we do have such a system may cause teams to approach the season in such a way that does indeed make the playoff system a reasonably accurate measure of excellence. In other words, professional teams in the U.S. recognize that reaching and sustaining a peak level of performance during the playoffs is far more important for winning the championship than compiling the best regular-season record. They may, therefore, regard the regular season primarily as a training period of little intrinsic importance, the main purpose of which is to allow them to fine-tune their skills and strategy for the playoffs for which they reserve their maximum effort. Given that we have such a system, the best teams will successfully channel their talents into developing the ability to produce excellent performances under extreme pressure in the brief playoff period.

However, we should not let this blind us to the more fundamental question of whether the playoff system is the best way of measuring talent in the first place. The force of my arguments in this section is that it is not. We seem to have fetishized the ability to perform well under pressure and given it far more importance as a criterion of athletic excellence than it deserves. It is instructive to compare the playoff system with the organization of professional sports in other countries. For example, in professional soccer leagues in Europe and South America the most prestigious trophy goes to the team with the best record at the end of the season. No post-season or playoffs exist. Single-elimination cup tournaments also exist, but they run concurrently with and independently of the so-called league championship. The underlying belief is that the most accurate measure of athletic excellence is performance against all rival teams over an entire season. Why does the introduction of the high pressure that accompanies playoff series provide a better measure? A further advantage of the "over the entire season" method of evaluation is that it minimizes the impact of refereeing errors, cheating, gamesmanship, and luck, much of which will tend to even out over the length of a season, whereas any one of them may be decisive in a playoff tournament.

In the case of international tournaments such as the soccer World Cup or the Olympic Games, simple logistics require a brief, high-pressure "knockout" or single elimination tournament. A season-long series of games or track meets would not be feasible for such international competitions. And doubtless powerful financial considerations underlie the American playoff system, in that it sustains fans' interest and attendance at games far deeper into the season than does the league table approach, which can effectively eliminate most teams from contention well before the season ends. None of my arguments in this section are intended to diminish the value of success in such tournaments or in post-season playoff series in American professional sports. The ability to rise to the occasion and succeed in competition against the best athletes in the nation or the world is indeed a sign of athletic excellence. In the absence of crucial refereeing errors, cheating, unacceptable gamesmanship, and exceptional luck, winners of these tournaments are fully deserving of our admiration. They are indeed the best athletes and teams, in the sense that they performed best on the days of the tournament and deserved their victories. In most cases, they are also the best athletes and teams, judged on their form throughout the current or past season.

My objections have been directed solely at the view that insists that the winning team or athlete in a playoff or a similar tournament is *by definition* the best one, not just on the day but for the entire season or year. My point has been that a subpar performance resulting in a loss, whether due to nerves, insufficient motivation, or some other psychological factor, does not necessarily negate an athlete's or a team's claim to be the best. Psychological toughness is a legitimate component of the mental element in athletic excellence, and a serious deficiency in it greatly weakens an athlete's claim to athletic superiority. But we should beware giving psychological toughness so much importance in our understanding of athletic excellence that it eclipses all other elements.

The most important consequence of my reasoning in this section is that we should reexamine our attitude toward the playoff system in American professional sport. The best way to measure relative ability in domestic professional sport is the system used in European countries for such sports as soccer: a league championship, which is awarded to the team with the best record after an entire season of play. This system minimizes the impact of unjust results in individual games due to such factors as poor refereeing, cheating, gamesmanship, and bad luck. And while end-of-season games will sometimes involve enormous pressure, and while the ability to perform well under this pressure is a legitimate aspect of athletic excellence, the over-a-season method of evaluation is superior to the playoff system in not placing an inordinate weight on this ability in determining which team wins the championship. Unlike international tournaments like the Olympics and the World Cup, logistics do *not* demand that we base championships in American professional sport on brief tournaments. If we persist in using the playoff system, we need to acknowledge that this is a choice, not a necessity. And this choice involves sacrificing a more accurate measure of athletic excellence – the season-long championship – in order to enjoy the financial benefits of the playoff system. By choosing this system, we decrease the probability that the best team wins the championship.

Justice and Results in Sport

Despite the relatively uncontroversial nature of the list of situations I have described in which a sporting contest fails to provide an accurate measure of athletic superiority (Sections 1–4), we are reluctant to concede that sometimes sporting contests may have unjust results. We like to think of sport as a supremely democratic arena where ability and dedication are the only determinants of success, at least in those sports that do not require expensive equipment and

country club memberships. And there is some truth in this belief: A child from the shantytowns around Rio may face insurmountable socio-economic obstacles that prevent him from any realistic chance of becoming a lawyer, but exquisite soccer skills may by themselves be sufficient to raise him to fame and fortune with the Brazilian national team. My conclusion that even sport is not a pure meritocracy may, therefore, appear to tarnish its image. However, the fact that a conclusion may disappoint us is not a good reason for rejecting it.

A helpful parallel to my thesis about sporting results exists in ethics. A venerable tradition associated with Kant holds that I am morally responsible only for what is within my control. I am not responsible for any consequences of my actions that I did not intend and had no reason to foresee. Strictly speaking, the only human actions that are subject to moral evaluation are our *intentions*, which, unlike the consequences of our actions, seem to be fully within our control. However, in the last 25 years or so, philosophers have realized that *moral luck* may play a significant role in determining our moral "record."[13] Factors beyond our control, including genetics, upbringing, and even where and when we happen to be born, influence what kind of people we become and even what kind of intentions we form. Nor does recognizing the role of moral luck require that one make controversial metaphysical assumptions about the absence of free will. Even if we grant that people have free will, we must concede that two people with exactly similar moral character may be faced with vastly different challenges and obstacles during their lives, resulting in one's leading an unobjectionable life, while the other becomes a moral monster. But for the historical accident of living in Germany during Hitler's rise, a Nazi war criminal might well have led a morally innocuous life, while his morally innocuous counterpart who spent his entire life as a farmer in South America might have played a gruesome role in the Holocaust had he lived instead in Nazi Germany.[14] Yet if we were to try to strip away the unfair influence of these external factors and confine our moral evaluation to the part of ourselves over which we have complete control, we would be left with no subject for our ethical judgments.[15] If we are to have moral assessment at all, we have to concede the role played by moral luck.

Similarly, my arguments show that displaying superior athletic skill, strategy, and mental toughness to those of our opponents – in other words, doing everything that is within our control while obeying the rules and spirit of the game – does not guarantee victory. Poor refereeing decisions, cheating, gamesmanship, and bad luck can all deny us the victory that we deserve. Perhaps the realization that morality itself is sometimes unfair, in the sense that we are not in complete control over our moral record, will soften the blow of the unfairness that sometimes arises in sporting results.

In contrast, my discussion of inferior performances by superior athletes (Section 5) does not indicate any unfairness in the results of sporting contests. After all, the team that plays better on the day against superior opponents *deserves* to win. What my arguments in that section do show is that even a just result is sometimes not an accurate indicator of the relative athletic excellence of the teams. The only sense in which such a result is unjust is reflected in the statement that the losing team did not do justice to itself.

So we have seen many factors that can prevent the better team from winning. Bad refereeing decisions, cheating, gamesmanship, and bad luck can result in a loss for the team that performed better and deserved to win. And a subpar performance can result in a deserved loss by a team that is better than its opponents. The concept of athletic superiority that has emerged from our examination of these situations includes not only physical prowess but also mental attributes. And relevant mental attributes include not only cognitive skills like astute strategy but also affective qualities like poise and toughness. However, we should beware of placing undue stress on these affective qualities in our determinations of athletic superiority. A welcome consequence of our realization that a wide range of situations exists in which the better team or player does not win may be to weaken the obsession with winning that exists among some athletes, especially in the U.S. Putting winning and losing in a saner perspective may reduce the motivation to resort to cheating, distasteful forms of gamesmanship, and trash-talking and other forms of taunting. And, while the desire to win is a necessary ingredient of competitive sport, realizing that winning is not the be all and end all of athletic excellence may help to foster the cooperation that is part of healthy competition and prevent it from degenerating into alienation.[16]

Acknowledgments

An early draft of this paper was presented at the Philosophic Society for the Study of Sport conference in Clarkston, WA, on Oct. 3, 1996. This final draft has greatly benefited from suggestions by the editor of the *Journal of the Philosophy of Sport* and three anonymous referees, to all of whom I am most grateful.

Notes

1   For the sake of convenience, I will refer throughout most of this paper to the "better" team or player. While the comparative "better" applies most naturally to contests between pairs of players or teams, I also intend my discussion to include competitions involving several players or teams. Understanding "better" in such contexts to mean "better than the rival(s)" will enable me to avoid the cumbersome construction "better or best."

2   For the sake of brevity, I will henceforth usually refer only to the better team, except when explicitly discussing individual sports, in which case I will refer to the better player. The reader should understand, however, that my entire paper pertains to both team and individual sports.

3   An actual example of a victory resulting from a refereeing error was the University of Colorado football team's infamous "5th down" win over the University of Missouri in 1990.

4   For an excellent summary of this central tenet of legal positivism, see Hart (4: sec. 1).

5   See, for example, Edwin J. Delattre's critique (2).

6   "Cheating in sport need not be compared morally to cheating in our everyday affairs since sport is 'just a game' and not simply a reflection of our everyday behavior. It may be morally acceptable to do certain things in sport which are not acceptable in everyday life" (8: p. 196).

7   See Simon (11: pp. 37–51) for a very perceptive analysis of the incompatibility between cheating and sport as a test of athletic skill.

8   Fine questions arise concerning whether a professional foul can be such a violation of D'Agostino's concept of the ethos of a game (1) that it constitutes an outright act of cheating rather than gamesmanship. Such questions, while of great intrinsic interest, are beyond the scope of this section. My concern is with whether such acts, *however* we characterize them, can result in an undeserved victory by an inferior team, and with what implications this has for our concept of athletic superiority.

9   See Warren Fraleigh (3) for a persuasive example of such critiques.

10   By luck I mean factors that are beyond the control of either team and that have, hence, no bearing on the teams' athletic ability, whether understood in purely physical or psychological terms. Uncontroversial examples of bad luck are being on the wrong end of a net cord in tennis or losing a golf game when one's opponent's tee shot on the final hole rebounds freakishly from a tree into the hole.

11   I add the qualifier "*unacceptable* gamesmanship" to allow for my concession to Simon, for the sake of argument, in the previous section – namely, that some gamesmanship may be permissible. By implication, a team that succumbs to opponents who use *legitimate* gamesmanship may have lost the right to call itself the better team.

12   I remind the reader that what I refer to as the "intuitive" concept of athletic superiority is not a blind appeal to intuition. The account developed in this paper is based on uncontroversial views on the purpose of competitive sport by such philosophers of sport as Kretchmar, Simon, and Pearson, and modified in the light of Leaman's radical critique.

13   Two ground-breaking articles are Thomas Nagel (9) and Bernard Williams (13).

14   This is a variation on an example that Nagel gives (9: p. 26).

15   Nagel: "The area of genuine agency, and therefore of legitimate moral judgment, seems to shrink under this scrutiny to an extensionless point" (9: p. 35).

16   For an excellent account of healthy, non-alienated competition in sport, see Drew A. Hyland (5).

Bibliography

1   D'Agostino, F. "The Ethos of Games." *Journal of the Philosophy of Sport*. 8: 7–18, 1981.

2   Delattre, E.J. "Some Reflections on Success and Failure in Competitive Athletics." *Journal of the Philosophy of Sport*. 2: 133–139, 1975.

3   Fraleigh, W. "Why the Good Foul Is Not Good." *Journal of Physical Education, Recreation and Dance*. 53(1):41–42, 1982.

4   Hart, H.L.A. "Positivism and the Separation of Law and Morals." *Harvard Law Review*. 71:593, 1958.

5   Hyland, D.A. "Opponents, Contestants, and Competitors: The Dialectic of Sport." *Journal of the Philosophy of Sport*. 11:63–70, 1984.

6   King, M.L. "Letter from a Birmingham Jail." In: *I Have a Dream: Writings and Speeches that Changed the World*. San Francisco: HarperCollins, 1992.

7   Kretchmar, R.S. "From Test to Contest: An Analysis of Two Kinds of Counterpoint in Sport." *Journal of the Philosophy of Sport*. 2:23–30, 1975.

8   Leaman, O. "Cheating and Fair Play in Sport." In: *Philosophic Inquiry in Sport* (2nd ed.), W.J. Morgan and K.V. Meier (Eds.). Champaign, IL: Human Kinetics, 1995.

9   Nagel, T. "Moral Luck." In: *Mortal Questions*. Cambridge, UK: Cambridge University Press, 1979.

10   Pearson, K.M. "Deception, Sportsmanship, and Ethics." In: *Philosophic Inquiry in Sport* (2nd ed.), W.J. Morgan and K.V. Meier (Eds.). Champaign. IL: Human Kinetics, 1995 [reprinted here as reading 8].

11   Simon, R.L. *Fair Play: Sports, Values, and Society*. Boulder, CO: Westview Press, 1991.

12   Suits, B. "The Elements of Sport." In: *Philosophic Inquiry in Sport* (2nd ed.), W.J. Morgan and K.V. Meier (Eds.). Champaign, IL: Human Kinetics, 1995.

13   Williams, B. "Moral Luck." In: *Moral Luck: Philosophical Papers 1973–1980*. Cambridge, UK: Cambridge University Press, 1981.

CHAPTER 13

In Defense of Winning

R. Scott Kretchmar

Competitive behaviors in the workplace, during social interactions, in education, and in other common day-to-day settings have received mixed reviews by ethicists. (See for example Frankena [5] and Singer [9].) In sport, judgments are sometimes even less supportive. Two recent articles by Carr [1] and Dixon [3] are cases in point. Neither author takes on competition per se. Their complaint is more about the significance we attribute to its successful outcome – namely, winning or victory. Competition, as a result of their arguments, is lowered in value more by inference than by direct assault. If winning is not as significant as many people think it is, and if competition is what is required to produce such ends, then competition itself loses a bit of stature.

Carr's and Dixon's arguments are clear and forceful. To my knowledge, nobody has shown weaknesses in the lines of reasoning they employ. I too think they are generally sound, as far as they go. However, I believe that their analytic approach leaves much unsaid and leads to unnecessarily pessimistic conclusions about competition and the importance of winning. My own conclusions are more compatible with commonsense views that hold winning in very high esteem and, at the same time, better support full-blooded competitive activity.

I begin with a very brief review of Carr's argument. Natural endowment, he asserts, is a threat to the assignment of merit in sport. We cannot take credit, of course, for that over which we have no control and for which, therefore, we have no responsibility. Nobody deserves credit or merit, says Carr, for being 7 feet 2 inches tall, or for the victories that can be traced back to that genetically programmed condition. He reminds us, however, that rules have been written that would minimize or neutralize natural endowment – rules, for example, that specify weight categories in wrestling or height allowances in some junior basketball leagues. This, presumably, would allow the spotlight of merit to shine, once again, on displays of superior skill.

Of course, as Carr points out, it does not work this way. First, these rules are not entirely successful. While certain physical attributes may be neutralized, others are not. In addition, Carr argues, capacities for learning motor skills quickly and effectively are themselves part of our endowment. Therefore, genetic dispositions toward being tall and learning motor skills at uncommonly high levels complicate the assignment of merit for precisely the same reasons.

Carr proceeds to look for other grounds on which merit in sport might be assigned – for instance, greater effort and superior moral qualities – but rejects them for a variety of reasons including the fact that they deflect attention from what we want merit to be about in sport, namely, the display of superior skill. Carr concludes that competitors cannot take full credit for athletic success. Because of this, he recommends that informed participants take a "disinterested attitude" into competition, one that focuses more on the aesthetic values of play and less on winning and its extrinsic spoils.

Dixon also argues that winning does not signify as much as many people think it does, but for reasons that are very different from the ones provided by Carr. Dixon suggests that victory is not a foolproof indicator of superiority, as a sign of either who played better that day or, more importantly for Dixon, who the superior performer is overall.

Dixon offers three arguments to support his case for victory as an imprecise, often misleading measure of superiority. The first suggests that accurate assessments of superiority are often frustrated by refereeing errors, cheating, gamesmanship, and bad luck. Second, he notes that, in the short run, superior athletes do not always produce superior performances. In contemporary professional baseball and basketball, for instance, an interest in increased revenues has produced multiple team playoff schedules, where early rounds are often no more than best-of-five series. This, says Dixon, increases the likelihood that the best team will not win. To the counter-argument suggesting that superior competitors are precisely those individuals or teams who can produce top performances on command in short tests, he offers a third argument. Sport is about superior athletic skill. To require a top performance on any single occasion places too much emphasis on psychological traits and, in addition, is an unreasonable expectation.

Dixon's bottom line is this: victory is not necessarily an accurate measure of superiority. To the extent to which a display of superiority is the intended end of competition, its achievement is often compromised. If people understood this, they would not put so much stock in this outcome. Like Carr, Dixon prefers a sporting public that understands that winning is not all it is cracked up to be. A corollary would be that defeats are not as devastating as they are often regarded. In fact, Dixon [2] argued previously that part of the supposed harm in running up the score would disappear if people only understood what winning and losing really mean.

I think that Carr and Dixon are right, at least as far as they take their arguments. Winning is overvalued and otherwise misunderstood for the reasons they state. However, the conclusions drawn by Carr and Dixon are bothersome. They believe that competitors should treat winning and losing more ironically, less passionately, with a "disinterested aesthetic attitude." Once athletes are disabused of their false beliefs, they suggest, winning and losing will not matter so much. But this is not the only conclusion that can be drawn from their analyses. The limitations they place on the significance of winning are still compatible with the investment of considerable meaning in victory. This deep concern over victory, moreover, better squares with commonsense attitudes toward competition.

I plan to sketch out three arguments against Carr and Dixon's attack on winning and competition. Others are available, but these three should be sufficient to raise doubts about the adequacy of their critique and the direction in which they think it leads us.

The first issue might be called the problem of the uncertain target. Is it really sport or a much larger swath of life? While Carr and Dixon limit their comments to sporting competition and the excessive significance we attach to winning games, their arguments seem to apply just as well to all forms of striving – whether competitive in nature or not, whether in games or some other endeavor. Carr's question about where the merit is if the best man wins in sport can actually be asked of any of us when we succeed in most any sphere of life. Where is the merit if the genetically blessed researcher turns out a fine article? Where is the merit if the inherently brilliant student receives a high grade? Where is the merit if the ethicist who is predisposed to act kindly and who is also socially advantaged acts with generosity?

The target identified by questions about relationships between achievement and merit would appear to far transcend the domain of sport and its victories. Any time we attempt to solve problems without comparative scores (alone at work, in leisure at the piano keyboard, in our marriages or relationships), any time we aim at achievement or success or simply doing tolerably well, we venture forth on the foundation of our natural endowments. Therefore what started as a critique of merit related to winning in sport ends up subtracting merit from most everything we accomplish.

Likewise with Dixon's arguments about confounding factors that complicate measures of superiority: analogies to his concerns about umpiring errors, cheating, gamesmanship, and bad luck can be found without difficulty in everyday life – that is, in non-competitive and non-sport situations were we are attempting to succeed and where no comparative scores are at stake. Should Clinton get credit for succeeding in producing a robust economy during his eight years at the helm? Should Bush receive blame for the economy turning south? Were Eisenhower's war successes primarily the result of his own clear thinking or a combination of many factors that are, even now, difficult to untangle? Serendipity, political gamesmanship, "umpiring errors" by commentators, and a whole host of other complicating factors make it difficult to say.

It appears then that non-competitive achievements fall to the same criticisms as those leveled by Carr against sport and competition. In addition, successes in many walks of life carry ambiguous meanings of just the sort Dixon has shown relative to winning in sport. At a minimum, this revelation that most all human achievements and successes can be questioned takes some of the sting out of the critique of sporting competition. Sport, to put the point another way, finds itself in pretty good company. But there is yet a further problem. What if Carr and Dixon were to respond that they are indeed willing to extend their arguments to the entirety of life? What if they were to agree that merit for virtually all achieving is compromised and that the assessment of success is almost always complicated? They might conclude that they were indeed right about sport . . . and much else besides!

This conclusion, however, should give us pause. After all we commonly assign merit to our everyday problem-solving activities, and we do so with a great deal of confidence. Moreover, many of us are convinced that at least some of our achievements are not hopelessly compromised by serendipity, cheating, or "umpiring" errors.

Finally, very few straight-thinking people would want to take a "disinterested attitude" into all of life or approach serious matters at work from a detached "esthetic" perspective that focuses strictly on labor's intrinsic values. In truth, this broader application of Carr and Dixon's critique shows just how counter-intuitive their claims are.

The second argument I offer examines the positive case that can be made for the assignment of merit and for the use of competitive verdicts as good measures of superiority. Carr is certainly aware of the fact that natural endowments do not necessarily determine later behaviors or successes, least of all victory in sport. Being 5 feet 11 inches or 7 feet 2 inches certainly influences and constrains my choices and opportunities, but arguably it does not determine them in any strong sense.

I like Frankena's [5] metaphor for describing the ambiguously free and constrained situation in which we find ourselves as human beings. He says we are far more like a bus than a tram. As a bus, we cannot go everywhere. But because we are not a tram, we come to intersections where a right or left turn are both possible – given our genetic and other endowments. Because of that existential choice, we are responsible for the turn. In sport, while we are never free of these endowments that influence everything from the speed at which we learn motor skills, to our strength, to our ability to focus and expend effort, we still encounter numerous intersections. The number of intersections we meet and their impact on sporting outcomes would affect the degree of merit that can be assigned. Common sense suggests that this degree is relatively high. It is what we do with our tendencies, our genes, our socialization, our history, we might say, it is the turns we take with choices about practice and strategies and diet and coaches, that provide a foundation for the assignment of merit. I do not know if we encounter more intersections in sport than other places, or if those intersections are of greater consequence than in other life situations. What is important is that the intersections exist, much as they do in most other walks of life.

A stronger objection, however, might be raised in relationship to Dixon's argument. Sport may well be superior to other walks of life in providing one of the better venues for determining excellence or superiority. To be sure, sport is not immune from the ills identified by Dixon, but in contrast to other life settings it seems to enjoy some advantages. Precisely because sport is a contest built on gratuitous tests, it can be designed to promote certain ends. One of those ends is presumably the accurate measurement of non-comparative performances in tests and comparative performances in contests. Thus, most of our games specify dos and don'ts to standardize the problem faced by different individuals or teams, and they include multiple testing events. In basketball, for example, rules indicate how baskets may be scored, and each team is given numerous chances to show what it can do. Across the course of a game, each side tests the other one again and again, and then again. This redundant testing, of course, better assures that the final score will accurately reflect greater and lesser performances.

In many life circumstances, of course, we do not have the freedom to design repetitive tests to better assure accurate attributions of achievement. In business, for example, a decision must be made about a billion-dollar advertising campaign. The stakes are tremendously high. The executive decides in favor of the expenditure and, months later, profits increase. Was the executive brilliant? Or was he or she simply lucky on this one-time test? And given the uniqueness of his or her particular business, how would we ever compare this executive to others in different industries who make similar decisions? Who really is better? Executives, in contrast to athletes, do not begin at the same starting lines; they do not have rule books that explicitly identify what is and is not allowed; and they lack common finishing lines. Moreover, their tests are often one-time events, and this raises serious questions about the significance of successes or failures.

Eleanor Metheny [7] pointed out another difference between sport and life that is relevant here. As she wrote almost forty years ago, "The rules of sport provide each performer with a rare opportunity to concentrate all the energies of his being in one meaningful effort to perform a task of his own choosing, no longer pushed and pulled in a dozen directions by the many imperatives he may recognize in his life" (p. 63). That is, there is less confusion about what we are trying to accomplish, less confusion about how we are allowed to go about it, and perhaps too then, less ambiguity about what a superior score means. Sporting competition, in short, may actually provide exceptionally good venues for the determination of superiority. If winning means anything anywhere in life, it may be most poignant in the repetitive, intentionally crafted tests of sport where competitors are often free to focus on just how well they can perform – and little else.

The final argument is related to the work of Alisdair MacIntyre [6]. Here I depart from Carr's and Dixon's arguments to venture one claim in support of the value of winning. This argument depends on our ability to see two things – first, that winning is a process that is distinct from achieving; and second, that this process has excellences associated with it that are, once again, distinct from the excellences that are tethered to achieving. The first distinction, I believe, is not particularly controversial. It has been discussed by myself and others in the literature before. (See for example Kretchmar [8] and Fraleigh [4].) It seems clear that a person could be doing poorly on the test (achieving very little) and still – if the opponent is faring even less well – comparing favorably in the contest, that is, winning. Of course, the opposite is possible too: an Olympic sprinter, for example, may achieve excellence by setting a world record but still lose the contest because an opponent broke the record more convincingly.

The second distinction about excellences of winning in contrast to the excellences of achieving, to my knowledge, is not well represented in the literature. Whenever MacIntyrian excellences are cited, they involve the skills, tendencies, and knowledge related to the practice, the sport, the profession, the testing arena. Thus, there are excellences surrounding a variety of problem-solving communities – the fine skills, understanding, and capacities associated with teaching, lawyering, playing football, and any number of other endeavors that fit MacIntyre's notion of practices. However, what happens when such practices are converted into contests? Does this not introduce a host of additional excellences related to the processes of winning – such as, leading, taking the lead, holding a lead, gambling for a lead, delaying strategically for a reversal late in the contest, intentionally forfeiting a lead, mustering resources that would not be needed just to do well on the test, intentionally and skillfully deceiving an opponent into thinking that a lead has been lost when it has not? Arguably, these processes involve a second group of excellences, a group that has been missed or ignored by most commentators, including the critics of competition like Carr and Dixon.

If the existence of this second set of excellences is still not clear, the following might be considered: we know that individuals can be good at the practice itself – say, running long distances in unreasonably short periods of time – but still be mediocre when it comes to comparative standings, such as pacing oneself relative to the field, deciding when to make a move, choosing to draft at the right times or take the lead, intuiting when one is actually winning even though he or she is literally behind, or simply producing the concentration and effort that is needed to provide that whisker of a difference that results in victory. In short, to take a test successfully involves one set of capabilities or excellences. To take that same test in a competitive environment, where a new comparative objective is present and where the progress of one's opponent is now crucial, seems to demand additional perceptions, motivations, strategies, and skills. On MacIntyrian grounds then, contesting excellences might demand the same respect usually accorded testing capabilities. When we compliment an athlete by noting that this individual is an excellent marathon distance runner *and* a remarkable competitor, we are not being redundant. The running and the competing involve different sets of challenges and, correspondingly, different sets of capabilities.

If this argument is at all persuasive, winning takes on a different life than the one often associated with it. It is not simply a crass product or end state associated primarily with extrinsic goods like fame and fortune. Rather, it is an ongoing process that requires its own set of excellences. It is not just a zero-sum outcome or product, a treasure that is eventually possessed by only one individual or team. Rather, winning involves a series of relationships where the excellences related to superiority can be (and usually are) shown by both teams on the way to the final verdict. And finally, winning is not just a possession whose luster often wears off soon after it is gained. Rather, it embodies excellences that can be appreciated and valued long after the event.

Conclusions

Carr and Dixon were right: winning is not a foolproof indicator of merit or superiority. Perhaps it is misunderstood and overrated, by some, for that very reason. But these concerns, I have argued, are not sufficient to recommend that winning be approached with a disinterested, ironic, or esthetic attitude, or that winning does not really deserve the significance many give it.

I would prefer a more modest conclusion about the limits of winning. Here is one possibility: winning and the display of excellences that go with it should always be accompanied by a degree of humility. This humility would be a signal that serendipity, endowment, and other factors forever play a role in our testing achievements and our contesting victories. But humility, importantly, does not require disinterestedness or esthetic distance. Our acknowledgement that we cannot take credit for everything, that we are not responsible for everything, that luck and umpiring errors preclude perfect measurement, does not force us to take less ownership of the process or results. We *are* the authors of our sporting actions, albeit constrained ones. And winning and losing *do* describe us and our actions, if only imperfectly. We can experience human excellence *twice* – first by testing well and then, in partly different ways, by contesting with distinction. This gives us sufficient warrant to grow passionate about our sporting projects and to care deeply about how well they proceed.

Bibliography

1   Carr, David (1999) "Where's the Merit if the Best Man Wins?," *Journal of the Philosophy of Sport* XXVI: 1–9.
2   Dixon, Nicholas (1993) "On Sportsmanship and 'Running Up the Score,'" *Journal of the Philosophy of Sport* XIX: 1–13 (reprinted here as reading 9).
3   Dixon, Nicholas (1999) "On Winning and Athletic Superiority," *Journal of the Philosophy of Sport* XXVI: 10–26 (reprinted here as reading 12).
4   Fraleigh, Warren (1984) *Right Actions in Sport: Ethics for Sport Contestants.* Champaign, IL: Human Kinetics.
5   Frankena, William (1973) *Ethics* (2nd edn). Englewood Cliffs, NJ: Prentice Hall.
6   MacIntyre, Alasdair (1984) *After Virtue: A Study in Moral Theory* (2nd edn). Notre Dame, IN: Notre Dame University Press.
7   Metheny, Eleanor (1965) *Connotations of Movement in Sport and Dance.* Dubuque, IA: Wm C. Brown.
8   Kretchmar, R. Scott (1975) "From Test to Contest: An Analysis of Two Kinds of Counterpoint in Sport," *Journal of the Philosophy of Sport* II: 23–30.
9   Singer, Peter (1995) *How are We to Live? Ethics in an Age of Self-interest.* New York: Prometheus Books.

CHAPTER 14

Winding Down, Looking Ahead

Dean Smith

It's difficult for me to speak impartially when the subject is college basketball. Our game, played the right way, is the most beautiful sport of them all. We're the perfect game for television. The big ball is easily followed by the camera and the eyes of the viewers. The raging emotion of the sport – the highs and the lows – is written on the faces of the players. There are no protective face guards, no helmets to shield their feelings. Fans see this and identify with their favorite team in a way that isn't possible in any other team sport.

Our game is unique and has so much intrigue that I don't agree with those who fret because some of our players leave college basketball early in order to play in the NBA. We've gone through that since 1972 at North Carolina, involving some excellent players, and we survived it. There are plenty of good players to go around. And I'm not just talking about enough good players for Carolina, Kansas, Duke, Kentucky, UCLA, and Indiana either, although, with their success, they do have some recruiting advantages. Still, it's necessary for those schools to make good recruiting decisions. At North Carolina we played several players in big NCAA tournament games who weren't offered Division 1 scholarships. While most male youngsters from my generation dreamed of playing major league baseball, basketball is clearly the game of choice now. College basketball will always have stars. Instead of dwelling

on those who leave early, we should spend our time talking about the ones who are still playing. After all, there are approximately four thousand players in Division 1 basketball. Fewer than twenty underclassmen are drafted each year. Why so much attention on the ones who leave?

With all due respect to the NBA, in many ways its game can't match the college game. They are two entirely different games, with different rules. The biggest difference might be the quality of the rivalries, some of which date back to the turn of the century. Rivalries such as Carolina–Duke, Indiana–Purdue, Kansas–Missouri, and Kentucky–Louisville are hard to match. College basketball has a pageantry that is unique, and it all adds up to sights and sounds that television loves. The NBA is terrific in its own way, but I just don't see it as a threat to our game, as some argue.

But just because college basketball is healthy and popular doesn't mean we don't have problems. We do, and they need to be addressed. Billy Packer likes to say that he's often wrong but never in doubt. With that in mind, let me take a crack at what I see as some of our game's pressing concerns.

Excessively rough play: Basketball was meant to be a game of finesse, speed, quickness, and agility. I'm afraid we've come near the point where we've made weight lifting almost as important to college basketball as jumping, running, moving the feet, ballhandling, and shooting.

In my opinion, we should reverse this unfortunate trend before it hurts our game more than it has already. How did this rough play evolve? Maybe some of it trickled down from the NBA game to ours. Some of the post play in professional basketball resembles Saturday-night wrestling. I watched an NBA play-off game last spring between Utah and Portland in which a Utah player locked arms with a Portland player, then pulled his opponent's arm toward him and flopped, as if he were the victim. Thank goodness Joey Crawford, a veteran official, saw the fakery for what it was and called the foul on the Utah player. But plays such as that, even when they're detected, are harmful to the sport. High school and college coaches see it, often hear a commentator talk about the player's savvy in making such an illegal move, and then choose to teach it themselves. To the NBA's credit, it realizes its game is too rough and is moving in a direction to clean it up.

While I'm quick to point out that television is one of the main reasons college basketball became so popular, it might also have played a role in making the game as rough as it is. Commentators and producers don't like to see trek after trek to the foul line, so they sometimes come down hard on officials who call fouls. No official wants to be criticized on television. He can be sure that he won't be criticized if he doesn't call fouls away from the ball – and this is where most of the rough, illegal play exists: away from the ball. My good friend Bill Raftery, who does a splendid job commentating on college basketball on CBS and ESPN, likes to refer to fouls as "nickel-and-dimers." Bill and I disagree here. After all, it might be a "nickel-and-dimer" if a defender flicks the elbow of a shooter, but that's all it takes, a little flick, to send the shot astray. These little tricks that some players use – and are sometimes coached to use – to get away with fouls are a pet peeve of mine. We had a player in the ACC who was unbelievable with his feet. People who were guarded by him fell like ducks in a shooting gallery. His trick was to get his feet entangled with his opponent's and trip him. He was good at it, I'll give him that. A Georgia Tech fan sent me a tape of the player doing it or I wouldn't

have noticed (it wasn't a Georgia Tech player), and when you looked for it, it was easy to see what he was doing. I'm sorry to say he usually got away with it.

It's my feeling that we must stop players from committing fouls (and coaches from encouraging them) under the assumption the officials won't call all of them. I know of a West Coast team in the 1970s that felt if they fouled on every possession, the result would be what the coach called excellent defense. The coach bragged about it. His reasoning was that only so many of the fouls would be called. Unfortunately, he was right. Somehow, there's a prevailing notion on the part of fans that fouls called on each team should be about equal, even though one team might be taught to do its best not to foul while the other has fouling as a cornerstone of its defensive philosophy. The best officials won't be swayed if one team has many more fouls than the opponent, but others might. Officials shouldn't even know the number of fouls against a team except to know when to shoot the bonus.

Most veteran coaches I know are alarmed with the roughness of the game today. Two of the greatest names in basketball history – John Wooden and Bill Bradley – not long ago were asked what they see as current trends in basketball, and what worries them most about the game's future. They each said they are alarmed at how much the officials let go in today's game.

Now, no one is suggesting that we want to turn college basketball into a foul-shooting contest. Far from it. But if the officials were instructed by their supervisors to call the fouls, the game would clean up. Also, the supervisors would have to penalize the officials who don't. It would also become more exciting for fans, because these great athletes would be allowed to demonstrate their skills. There's one thing that every basketball player in the United States – from church league to the NBA – shares, and that's a desire to stay in the game. They're not going to continue to foul if they know the officials are going to call them, thereby dispatching them to the bench for excessive fouls.

What can be done to clean up the game? Here are some suggestions:

• Reduce the number of fouls needed for disqualification in high school and college basketball from five to four. We once had a rule in college and high school basketball that a player would be disqualified after four fouls. Fewer college players are fouling out of games in the 1990s than in the 1970s. I think it would help our game now to return to the old way, although I don't expect many to agree.

A way to ruin the game would be to increase the number of fouls allowed. Back in the 1960s, John Nucatola, a Hall of Fame official, served with me on the Basketball Rules Committee. He convinced the committee to conduct an experiment in high school basketball in New York City in which a player would be granted unlimited fouls. I was present for one of those games. Any foul after the fifth personal on a player was treated as a technical foul – free throws and possession of the ball. This particular game featured two star players – Jim McMillan, of Jefferson High in Brooklyn, who was recruited by us and would play at Columbia University, and Solly McMillen, of Erasmus High, who went to DePaul. Talk about a trek to the foul line! As I recall it, Jim McMillan had eight fouls in that game and Solly had twelve or thirteen. It was a mess. The coaches wanted their best players to stay in the game, even at such a high cost. The parade to the foul line resulted in a high school game that took over two hours to play.

• Call intentional fouls against players who grab jerseys or who interlock their arms and fake being fouled. The ACC player who made an art out of tripping opponents should have been called with some intentional fouls as a deterrent. These so-called cute tricks really bother me. Sadly, it is extremely hard for teams to lose games with this type of play, and some coaches feel forced to teach this rough stuff.

• Widen the three-second lane to make it conform to international standards. The fight for low-post position is ferocious in today's game because most college players will score or get fouled when they catch the ball that close to the basket. If the lane is widened, the defensive player may be more willing to let the post man catch the ball, because it would be harder to score, and we might not have so much wrestling for position.

• Call fouls away from the ball. I recall when I used to argue at our ACC meetings to have three officials rather than two calling our games. Norm Sloan and Lefty Driesell opposed me, arguing that we had a hard enough time finding two good officials to work a game, so finding a third one who was competent would be a real challenge. We did go to three officials, and we did get better full-court coverage, so that fouls away from the ball were more often detected and called. Still, even with three officials, too many fouls are uncalled. Certainly, an official must watch the ball, but with three officials there is no excuse not to see the illegal screening or offensive pushing away from the ball. And if it is seen, it should be called! At least one official is assigned coverage of illegal activity off the ball, but very few fouls away from the ball are called in a game, and this is where the illegal activity is happening. It should be emphasized that when we allow the game to get as rough as it's become, we make the officials *too important*. They begin to pick and choose what to call, which is not fair to them, and certainly not fair to the players.

Full-time officials for college basketball: To get the college game called consistently and correctly, maybe we need to go to full-time officials as the NBA has. Such a system would give supervisors control over their officials. If officials didn't call the game the way it was meant to be called, the supervisors could dismiss them, and the officials would be out of their full-time job. Most of the men officiating Division I basketball have full-time jobs outside of refereeing. I can hear the outcry against this now: It would cost too much money; it would harm the amateur status of the college game and make us too much like the pros; the best officials in college basketball would not give up their chief professions to referee full-time.

On the other hand, if we had full-time officials, that would be the job they worked at twelve months a year. They would attend clinics and small study sessions on a regular basis, watch tapes with their supervisors, be instructed on the rules on a year-round basis. They would devote forty hours a week to basketball officiating. If they continued to make mistakes, they could be subject to fines or the eventual loss of their position. Officiating basketball is about as close to an impossible job as a person could have. Given the difficulty of it, devoting full time to the profession would provide us with better officiating. I don't see how anyone could argue with that. The new TV contract for the NCAA tournament is being discussed now. In all probability, the money will be substantially increased, so Division I basketball could afford full-time people.

NCAA: College basketball, even with our problems, is a special game. The NCAA men's basketball tournament creates so much interest, and with it revenue, that it finances about 85 percent of the NCAA's annual budget. When we signed our latest contract with CBS to show the men's tournament, we insisted that the network also telecast the women's Final Four. The women's Final Four was helped tremendously by getting that exposure, and now its tournament is shown on ESPN. We could do even more to help the women's game if we followed the plan of Terry Holland, the excellent former coach and now athletics director at Virginia. Terry says we shouldn't be marketing men's and women's basketball at the same time so that they compete for viewers and ticket sales. He suggests moving the women's schedule to September, October, and November, with the national tournament to take place before Christmas. I think it would create tremendous interest in women's basketball. A true basketball fan would enjoy watching basketball in September, and as we know, television can create interest in going to the game.

The 1972 NCAA convention – known as the "cost-saving convention" – resulted in changes to college athletics that in my opinion have been harmful to student-athletes. This was the convention that, among other things, made freshmen eligible for varsity competition, took school-bought blazers away from players, many of whom couldn't afford to own a sport coat, and abolished the $15-a-month portion of the full scholarship that had for decades given players their so-called laundry money. The convention was all about saving money, and the best interests of the student-athletes were trampled. Shortly thereafter, another awful decision was made. The NCAA abolished the four-year scholarship and made each grant for one year. In other words, the governing body for college athletics made it legal for colleges to renege on agreements made with student-athletes during recruitment.

How should we go about undoing some of the harm caused by these changes in NCAA bylaws?

● All athletic scholarships should be for four years, not one. Just last spring a prominent Southeastern Conference university saw its football coach in effect "fire" six of his players. How an institution of higher learning could stand by and allow this to happen is beyond me. That the NCAA could pass legislation that encourages this type of behavior is disgraceful. What kind of message are we sending to young people when we show them by our actions that universities can treat student-athletes this way? Some have suggested that basketball players who leave school early for the NBA are somehow not living up to their scholarship agreement. The truth is, their scholarship was only year-by-year, and the players who decide to leave early for the pros certainly aren't breaking any contract.

● To help basketball players with financial need, as determined by the Pell Grant process that is already in place, we should give those on full scholarship $2,000 a school year in money earned from NCAA men's basketball tournament television revenues. Some of these students don't have the money to go out for a pizza with their friends or to go to a movie. We need to do more for these needy student-athletes to make them feel as if they're a real part of the student body. The present scholarship does not provide the full cost of attendance, which some academic scholarships do. This additional money would match that of the best academic grants. The NCAA recently said that student-athletes on scholarship could work during the school year. This is a good rule for nonrevenue sports that have many athletes on partial scholarships, but dangerous, because it opens the door for boosters to offer jobs to football and basketball players. This would be a mistake. We know full well that many such jobs would be phantom jobs, in which the athlete is paid for doing very little work. We should learn from experience; this has been a problem since the 1930s. This additional $2,000 stipend that I'm suggesting would prohibit football or basketball players from holding a job during the school year. After all, the demands of schoolwork, practice time, games, travel, and dealing with the media don't leave players from those two sports enough time to have jobs during the school year.

• Football, with its eighty-five scholarships, should be excluded from gender equity considerations under Title IX. Please don't get me wrong. I'm all for women's athletics, and Title IX has forced many universities to offer women a chance to compete in athletics. It was, and is, the right thing to do. But there is no women's sport that gobbles up eighty-five scholarships, as football does. By keeping football in the equation, many universities are having to drop sports that have been important to men on campus for generations. It was sad that when Providence lost in the NCAA baseball play-offs last May the defeat not only ended its season but was the last game ever for Providence baseball. It was dropped for financial reasons. I think it's bad that some colleges can have a women's golf team but not one for the men, for example. Sports are helpful in the development of all college students. It is too bad that golf is the only game that is played by the honor system, where you call the penalty on yourself.

• If we took a poll of chancellors and university presidents, most of them would say that the most serious problems on campus are alcohol related. Alcohol is the leading cause of death on college campuses and for all persons under twenty-five. Most of the rapes and assaults on campuses across the United States are alcohol related.

We all know this, yet we encourage the sale of beer. We do it by allowing the beer companies to place ads on the telecasts of men's basketball and football games. I've debated this issue since

1986. I wish I could say I'm winning. I'm not. However, some progress is being made. North Carolina and Wisconsin are two universities on record as not accepting beer advertising in university-related activities that the schools control. There are no beer commercials in the radio broadcasts of our sporting events, no beer ads in our game programs, and no beer ads in arenas. Since Carolina and Wisconsin took this stand, twenty other universities across the country have adopted similar policies. I call that progress.

It's important to understand that North Carolina does not have institutional control over the advertising sold in our ACC television package for football and men's basketball. We have a vote, but we're only one of nine members. We have been promised by the ACC that it will revisit this business of allowing beer commercials on league football and basketball telecasts before the next contract is signed. We have had some other minor victories. On ACC basketball telecasts, the announcers used to "throw" to a commercial by saying: "We'll be back after this from our good friends at Budweiser." It wasn't enough that we allowed Budweiser to advertise on our basketball telecasts; we also introduced them as "our good friends." Now the announcers just say they'll be back "after this from Budweiser." The beer ads are still there, and the ACC continues to collect the money. But at least they are not "our good friends" anymore, at least not publicly.

We need to understand that children start following athletics at the age of nine or ten. These beer ads are highly appealing to them. When beer companies say their ads aren't directed at young people, I find it hard to believe. Do you think the kids don't like the lizards on the Budweiser spots? How about the frog that would get his tongue stuck to a beer can? Beer companies are in business to make a profit, and these television commercials are designed to help them sell beer. Over twenty years ago, when the legal drinking age in North Carolina was eighteen, it's little wonder that when my son, at age eighteen, went to the beach the first thing he wanted was a beer. The commercials showing volleyball, pretty girls, the beach, and the beer all appealed to him. He thought it was the thing to do. He'd been fed the message for years, and our universities serve as the willing vehicle.

There's another glaring truth about many of the beer spots: They highlight outright dishonesty, stealing, and lying. The man sitting in the back of the limousine lies about his name to get a beer. The pretty girl befriends a boy on the beach and covers him with sand so she can steal his beer. The beer ads always feature pretty women and handsome men, and happiness seems to come from drinking. That's the message.

Bubba Smith, the former NFL football star, was featured in Miller Lite commercials in the days of the "tastes great, less filling" debate. He quit the role when he spoke at a junior high school and learned that was what he was becoming known for in the minds of the students – as a salesman for beer. Beer lobbyists are careful not to tell us that the ethanol content in a can of beer is the same as in a shot of liquor. In North Carolina, we can buy beer at any corner convenience store, but have to go to a liquor store to buy liquor. Ask yourself this question: If aspirin were the leading cause of death on college campuses, do you think chancellors, presidents, and trustees would allow aspirin commercials on basketball and football telecasts? They wouldn't, not for a minute.

Virtually every high school in America has at some time suffered the tragedy of alcohol-related deaths. Young people die in automobile accidents because of drinking and driving. Young girls are raped in alcohol-related assaults. College students under the influence of alcohol fall to their death before they reach age twenty-one. Congress made a good decision many years ago when it disallowed tobacco advertising on radio and television. And in print ads now the tobacco companies are forced to display in large type the dangers of their product. If Congress can do the right thing in the case of cigarettes and chewing tobacco, why are the politicians so reluctant to treat beer advertising, whose product kills thousands of young people each year, just as firmly? It's a blemish on our society, and it's a shame that we allow it to go on. It is also puzzling to me that the liquor companies are not

winning the right to advertise on TV if beer ads are allowed.

Surgeon General David Satcher recently said, "Alcohol abuse kills and injures more of our young people and costs our society more than all the illegal drugs put together. The misuse of alcohol is a major problem among college students."

When I testified in 1993 before a joint Senate–House committee that was studying the effects of advertising by companies that produce alcoholic beverages, Senator John Danforth of Missouri, a Yale Divinity School graduate, asked me if I thought tobacco use was "inherently wrong." I told him I was a former smoker and I guessed it was. I wasn't as prepared as I should have been; I wish I had debated him more. After all, a smoker does harm only to him- or herself, and might die of lung cancer at age sixty, instead of living to seventy-two. But alcohol abuse is an overwhelming menace to our society. Look at the number of broken homes caused by alcoholics, the number of women who have been battered and raped in alcohol-related incidents, the number of people killed and maimed on our highways each year by drunken drivers, the loss of production in our workforce because of alcohol-related problems. We really have to struggle to rationalize that beer advertising is harmless. The evidence points the other way.

There's been some publicity about my wife, Dr. Linnea Smith, and her work to call foul on some truly unsporting practices. Unfortunately, much of that publicity is inaccurate: It's either misinformation spread by the commercial sex industry or misrepresentation published in unauthorized biographies of me. I'd like to set the record straight.

We in sports can be the trailblazers when it comes to social justice issues. I'm lucky to work in a field that transcends barriers, opens doors for people based on nothing more than their amazing athletic abilities rather than the conditions of their birth, like skin color. Sport is blind in that respect, thankfully. And yet it has some blind spots in other respects.

For instance, the *Playboy* All-America list is an annual event that named me its inaugural basketball Coach of the Year in 1976. Linnea and I went to that first *Playboy* awards weekend, an all-expense-paid gala at Lake Geneva, Wisconsin. Like most of you, we were influenced by today's culture; we didn't want to seem like prudes. So we went and were feted and I was photographed with basketball players who were also on an all-expense-paid trip for the magazine.

But after we came home, Linnea did some research. She got more information and decided not to play ball with *Playboy* again. After looking at research material, so did some of our players. It was hard for Linnea to do the research and a hard decision to go public with it, but she chose to do that when faced with the facts.

Some may wonder why a stand against *Playboy*, when it is mild in comparison to the ever-escalating explicit and dehumanizing pornography available today. *Playboy* is the prototype of commercial sex magazines and is perceived by many to be mainstream and legitimate. It is the so-called men's magazine that most consistently uses college sports and athletes to further legitimize its publication and attract young readers. Because the magazine is perceived by many as being legitimate, and because of its widespread distribution, it is more insidious, and the potential for negative impact may be greater.

Also, *Playboy* is a nonsports publication with an unorthodox (and arbitrary, at best) selection process, so really, how much validity can its All-American Team truly have? Plus, it's a preseason designation, not a post-season merit-based award. Again, where's the validity except using popular collegiate athletes as a marketing tool for the magazine?

And last, it's not a real award like an Associated Press All-American: If you turn this down, your name is simply taken off the list and the "award" goes to the next person . . . who agrees to travel to a place and be photographed for the magazine.

Most important of all, Linnea pointed out that it seemed that the message of *Playboy* was to make sport of women. How could we support this? How could we, as members of a community that believes in raising people up, close our eyes to a practice that seemed to be aimed at

holding certain people down? Linnea and I are pleased with Kenny Smith, J.R. Reid, Eric Montross, and a few other players from Carolina and other schools across the nation who have declined *Playboy*'s invitation through the years. These athletes have minds of their own and, after careful consideration, chose not to participate. Certainly those who chose to be on the *Playboy* All-American Team had that choice also. I laughed when Tommy Amaker, a good friend and former Duke player and assistant, said he accepted the award in 1986 since "it was the only train at my station."

Also, coaches John Thompson, Roy Williams, Bob Knight, Tom Osborne, and other college football and basketball coaches have declined *Playboy*'s invitation to be its Coach of the Year after seeing Linnea's research results.

After a few years of research and discussion, Linnea formally took her concerns about *Playboy* and a list of recommendations for consideration to the NCAA. With the support of some influential coaches, long-standing NCAA director Walter Byers, in a letter to me and his top-level staff, made a statement about the lack of value of preseason awards such as *Playboy*'s except for the commercial promotional value to the magazine and not the college players. The paper also called into question the validity of awards such as *Playboy*'s which have no sanctioned merit-based selection process.

But the story doesn't end there. In 1993, the prestigious Knight Commission on Intercollegiate Athletics made its final report to those of us in sports. It counseled that we place a premium on fairness, equality, competition, and recognition of merit for *all* student-athletes, both men and women. The Knight Commission called it "keeping the faith." Linnea took the message to heart and took on what she considered the discriminatory practices of *Sports Illustrated*. She asked the tough question: How can a magazine that publicly supports what the Knight Commission stands for publish an annual swimsuit issue? Thanks to those in the ongoing national grassroots campaign with whom Linnea and others joined ranks, there was an enormous turnover in advertisers. They were also concerned about the unsportsmanlike image the magazine portrayed with that issue, which also reflects poorly on the magazine's own standards for serious sports journalism. A wave of public support moved *SI* to create a separate sports-free men's magazine to feature swimsuits, to offer a swimsuit issue-free subscription rate for those interested in sports and sporting news, and most important of all, to remove images of children from the swimsuit issue. We applaud *Sports Illustrated* for its efforts.

But trust me, not all of Linnea's efforts have paid off. She's had her share of spectacular failures. After years of fashion show luncheons, the National Association of Basketball Coaches, at the Final Four in 1986, decided to schedule a meaty program for the wives. Linnea jumped at the chance to promote her cause to the group. To her dismay, many in the audience walked out during the explicit slide presentation. Only two out of the hundreds attending signed up for more information. The bottom line: The timing, venue, and expectations were all wrong. The issue was controversial. But it was still important for people in sports to hear the message.

Through the years, Linnea has been just one of the messengers speaking out against discrimination against women and exploitation of children. A researcher, educator, lecturer, consultant, and author, she has developed educational materials and conducted workshops about pornography as a public health and safety problem as well as a social justice and civil rights issue.

So, the naked truth about my wife, sex, and centerfolds? It all comes down to this: Sport is all about breaking down barriers. But not just the barriers of speed and scores, championships and personal bests. It's also about breaking down stereotypes and the barriers that limit opportunities and a fair playing field for all. Sports are the embodiment of good health, fair competition, mutual respect, cooperation, and character development. Linnea's work is the work of sports, to lift up *all* people.

CHAPTER 15

Personal Best

W.M. Brown

In this paper I will explore the Kantian notion of duties to oneself, that is, duties owed not to other persons but rather to oneself as a person. It is a problematic notion; indeed many philosophers since Kant have doubted that there are any such duties at all. Kant mentioned several, distinguishing between perfect duties and imperfect ones. By perfect duties Kant roughly meant those that are narrowly conceived and that allow for no arbitrary exceptions because they are so focused and specific that they require particular actions or tasks. Imperfect duties, in contrast, are wider or more general, allow for exceptions, and consist in our adoption of maxims regarding morally obligatory ends that relate to ourselves and to others and that we can comply with in a variety of ways. In short, imperfect duties give us a wide degree of freedom in deciding what to do to fulfill them. Perfect duties are most easily expressed as negative duties; imperfect ones as positive ones.[1]

Among our perfect duties to ourselves, Kant mentions the obligation not to violate one's own moral integrity or autonomy by disobeying the moral law or by refusing to curtail tendencies toward self-love by lying, avarice, or servility. This is a basic duty to promote one's own virtue, to achieve what Kant calls self-mastery (7: p. 138ff). In addition, as a moral and physical being, one must develop those natural perfections necessary to be virtuous. Accordingly one may not neglect one's self-development, misuse

sex, or injure oneself by drunkenness or gluttony, by lust, or by self-mutilation or suicide.[2] Each of these duties involves, given our imperfect natures, an objective constraint on conduct by our rational appreciation of the moral law and our willingness that it be the basis of our actions.

On the positive side, Kant mentioned several imperfect or broad duties to ourselves. In general, of course, one must increase one's own moral perfection by striving always to act according to the moral law, that is, from duty, not just in conformity with it. In our striving to achieve this state, because of the frailty of human nature there will be many tries and many failures. So we have, wrote Kant, only an imperfect duty to be perfect (8: p. 242). Beyond this, however, we are obliged in a variety of ways not specifiable in advance to cultivate our natural talents and capacities of spirit, mind, and body, since these natural perfections are necessary in order to perform other duties to oneself and others. These duties are imperfect or wide because there is no specific way in which they may be fulfilled: they enjoin a wide range of possible actions for an obligatory end.[3]

When he stressed systematic aspects of his work as in the *Metaphysics of Morals*, Kant relegated perfect duties to the doctrine or domain of right (which includes civil law) and imperfect duties to the doctrine or domain of virtue.

I want, in particular, to examine Kant's claim that we have an imperfect duty to ourselves to develop our own talents. Since athletic abilities and talents are among those that would fall under this rubric, if Kant is right, we may have a broad duty to develop our athletic talents[4] in the pursuit of those moral ends that Kant argues should govern our lives as moral agents. And indeed, we often do speak of talents in the way Kant seems to suggest.

Consider what I shall call the case of the phlegmatic athlete. Coaches frequently encounter such cases in the persons of athletes of considerable talent who manage to do well in sports without developing their skills to their highest degree in ways clearly within their capacity. Such athletes give the impression of laziness, of overconfidence in what they can achieve with minimum exertion, or of indifference to or disdain for the effort and rewards of further development of their skills. One may have a variety of responses to such an athlete. One may feel that the athlete owes it to the team to hone and polish the skills needed to have a winning season. Or, one may believe the athlete will reap the acclaim and rewards of a more successful athletic career through this attitude. However, the first appeal is directed to others, and though we may indeed have a duty to others to develop ourselves in ways that will contribute to our ability to share with them in mutual enterprises, this is not the ground of duty to oneself. The second appeal is surely self-regarding; it is an appeal to the athlete's interests and prospects; but it is a prudential appeal, a call to look to one's own happiness. Kant believed that we are naturally inclined to do this in any case and that it is not therefore a specifically moral matter, though it is certainly a permissible area of human concern for each of us and one of life's basic goods. So we may resort to a final appeal: The athlete owes it to herself or to himself. One owes it to oneself, we say, to develop one's own skills and talents. And now we seem close to what Kant had in mind when he discussed self-regarding duties. I will return to the question of which talents, and how many, such a duty may require to be developed.

Kant's illustration of this is the well-known third example of the use of the categorical imperative in the *Groundwork*:

A third finds in himself a talent whose cultivation would make him a useful man for all sorts of purposes. But he sees himself in comfortable circumstances, and he prefers to give himself up to pleasure rather than to bother about increasing and improving his fortunate natural aptitudes. Yet he asks himself further, "Does my maxim of neglecting my natural gifts, besides agreeing in itself with my tendency to indulgence, agree also with what is called duty?" He then sees that a system of nature could indeed always subsist under such a universal law, although (like the South Sea Islanders) every man should let his talents rust and should be bent on devoting his life solely to idleness, indulgence, procreation, and, in a word, to enjoyment. Only he cannot possibly *will* that this should become a universal law of nature or should be implanted in us as such a law by a natural instinct. For as a rational being he necessarily wills that all his powers should be developed, since they serve him, and are given him, for all sorts of possible ends. (9: p. 90)

What makes this an imperfect duty is that one cannot consistently, as a rational being, will that the opposite – not developing one's talents – be a universal law: It is inconsistent with the very nature of rationality. In the *Groundwork*, however, Kant usually maintained the distinction between duties that allow for exceptions and those that do not. Later in the *Metaphysics of Morals*, Kant gave other grounds for making the distinction (2: pp. 259–62).

Let me mention briefly two more cases. The second case is the case of the callow youth. Here we may be tempted also to appeal not just to self-interest or to beneficence to others in order to persuade a child to develop various talents, but rather to the child's self-regarding duty to do so. Often, of course, when we make such an argument, we do have in mind the child's happiness, believing that human happiness is connected with the flourishing of talents and capacities. But sometimes, too, we seem to insist that the duty is moral. What is owed to oneself in this case is a moral duty, not just a prudential one.

Finally, my third example is a desert island case, that of Robinson Crusoe. Does Crusoe have a duty to himself to develop his talents? Does it matter at all to him, since he is, so far as he knows, alone and with no prospects to find himself in a community of other like persons with whom he will need to exercise his practical reason and employ his talents? Why should he bother if there will be no occasion for him to act in any other respect as a moral agent?

Kant himself offered the major objection to the whole concept of duties to oneself, suggesting that "the concept of a duty to oneself contains (at first glance) a contradiction" (8: p. 214). The contradiction arises because a duty constrains one to act often contrary to one's desires or inclinations. So one is, Kant wrote, "bound" to act in a certain way. Yet if the duty is to oneself, one also is doing the binding or constraining. But it seems self-contradictory to be both the constrainer and the constrainee, the binder and the bound. Modern commentators have constructed a similar argument in different terms. As Marcus Singer argued: "(1) If A has a duty to B, then B has a right against (or with respect to) A; (2) if B has a right against A, he can give it up and release A from the obligation; and (3) no one can release himself from an obligation" (11: p. 133).[5] If one has a duty, Singer claimed, it is precisely something one cannot release oneself from because a duty is an imposed obligation imposed on oneself by someone else, binding and constraining in a way that is not one's own to remove. So one cannot have a duty to oneself. In both cases, the self-referring character of the duty seems to involve a contradiction.

Kant himself tried to resolve the contradiction by arguing that the person bound is one's phenomenal self; the person doing the binding is one's noumenal self (8: p. 215). He also insisted that we not construe such duties as "juridical" or contractual ones: "I have no legal obligations towards myself" (7: p. 117). Rather, our self-regarding duties arise out of our "moral worth...the worth of our humanity" (7: p. 121). I will return to Kant's rationale for such duties later. But is his and Singer's sense of a

contradiction in such duties warranted? Contractual obligations do seem to involve reciprocal rights, but both Kant and Singer deny that they are concerned exclusively with legal-like contracts or promises. So we need to ask whether there can be a duty *to someone* that does not entail that one can be released from that duty. If we could make sense of this, the contradiction would disappear. The problem is that duties *to someone* seem to be perfect duties, whereas imperfect duties, such as that of developing one's talents, are not usually considered as being owed to anyone specifically, let alone oneself.

But there are some cases that suggest that the concept of duty is not so narrow as the objection above suggests. For example, duties to one's parents, or parental duties to one's children, do not seem to entail the same kind of corresponding right or power of release. It is not clear that parents or children can release each other from their respective duties (10: p. 225; 11: p. 141). Or consider the case of a promise to do something after someone's death. A promises B to do *x* after B's death. Here B, now deceased, can hardly release A from the promise. Or A may have promised something to B and B gives C the right to release A. The obligation is to B, but B does not have the power of release (6: p. 155; 11: pp. 133–135). Finally, there are surely moral duties from which one cannot be released because of their general and fundamental character. Kant's second version of the categorical imperative is an instance of one: We have the duty to treat others only as ends, never as means to ends that exclude their interests (11: p. 137). Is this a duty *to* anyone? It surely involves rights on the part of others. Everyone has the right to be treated as an end, as persons with rights. I owe this duty to each and every person I encounter, as well as to people in general. So this seems to be a duty I owe to someone or everyone and yet cannot be released from it (4: pp. 4–18). I conclude that the concept of a duty to someone from which one cannot be released is not incoherent or self-contradictory.

Nevertheless, there may be no duties to oneself of the kind in which we are interested. Kant frequently referred to such duties as "self-regarding" and there is an ambiguity in this expression that many commentators have noted. It may mean that some duties are only in regard to, or related to, oneself, but not owed to oneself. So it might be that what appear to be duties that are owed to oneself are actually duties that only *involve* oneself but that are *owed* to others. If I promise my colleague to read and comment on the final draft of her book, the (perfect) duty I have is in regard to me, the person who made the promise, but only in the sense that the action called for by the promise is mine. However, the duty is owed to my colleague.[6] Of course, in this sense, all my duties involve me and are thereby, trivially, self-regarding. So we need to show further that there are self-regarding duties in a stronger sense, namely, that they are duties owed to oneself and not just ones that involve oneself.

Kant does give several arguments for such duties, though they are not entirely convincing. The first is that one has a duty to oneself if it promotes one's own perfection, one of the two obligatory ends that constitute the *summum bonum*, the system of pure rational ends (8: pp. 195–197). His rationale here seems to be that such a duty fulfills a necessary condition "to realize any ends you might encounter" (8: p. 196). With regard to others, my duties to them entail a corresponding right on their parts, as we have seen, to require compliance. But other people have no such right when their interests are not affected by the performance or nonperformance of my duty. Hence any such duty is owed not to them, but to me.[7]

Second, Kant also argued, as I previously indicated, that we have duties to ourselves by virtue of our humanity, our possession of pure practical reason, which makes all of us ends in ourselves, beings of supreme worth or value, rather than means only. It would be wrong therefore to treat oneself as a means because of one's own humanity or worth. One, accordingly, has a duty to oneself never to treat oneself as a means only, and this in turn entails a variety of particular duties that preclude various ways of violating one's humanity. Again the reason such duties are owed to oneself rather than to no one or to any others is that a violation of them does not affect others directly.

Kant seems to have another argument, or argument sketch, that defends duties to oneself as preconditions to the realization of one's autonomy and self-respect, and therefore of one's capacity to fulfill one's duties to others. In *Lectures on Ethics*, he wrote, "Our duties towards ourselves are of primary importance...; it is obvious that nothing can be expected from a man who dishonours his own person. He who transgresses against himself loses his manliness and becomes incapable of doing his duty towards his fellows" (7: p. 118).

Kant's argument can be elaborated on as follows. Moral obligations arise out of conflicts between one's inclinations and one's duty as indicated by the categorical imperative. In particular cases, these duties require that one rein in various inclinations and desires such as those manifested by drunkenness, lust, or other forms of self-destructive behavior. A failure to control these natural desires is a failure of will, a failure of one's own freedom or autonomy, one's self-mastery, and is thereby a fundamental loss of self-respect or self-esteem. Such a failure threatens to incapacitate one as a moral agent, to threaten one's inner freedom to act morally, and since this inner freedom is a necessary condition for moral behavior toward others, failure to cultivate it undermines one's performing duties to others.[8]

But this argument does not clearly show that one owes the self-regarding duties to oneself rather than to others who share one's moral community and depend on one to exercise moral agency in an effective way. How Kant would answer this is not clear. But he did write that

> a man who performed his duty to others badly...but who nevertheless did his duty to himself...might yet possess a certain inner worth; but he who has transgressed his duty towards himself, can have no inner worth whatsoever...[and] loses his worth absolutely; while a man who fails in his duty to others loses worth only relatively. It follows that the prior condition of our duty to others is our duty to ourselves; we can fulfil the former only in so far as we first fulfil the latter. (7: p. 118)

The key to Kant's view here is that failure to develop one's own moral worth, that is, failure to develop one's sense of inner freedom through the exercise of practical reason, or to allow inclinations in conflict with that exercise to override it, is in general, and in the specific ways specified by all the duties to oneself, self-destructive. It causes a fundamental injury to oneself, indeed an injury to one's basic interests as a moral agent, to what Kant calls the "humanity in our own person" (7: p. 121). We can construe Kant as arguing, then, that the duties in question are owed to whomever is most injured when they are not performed. One has a *prima facie* duty not to cause injury to anyone, and the duty is owed *to* that person. When that person is *oneself*, one has a duty not to injure oneself, and the duty is owed *to* oneself.[9]

Conflicts of duties to oneself and to others might seem to be possible, but Kant denied that such conflicts can arise. It is possible for there to be conflicts between moral rules, but these can be resolved by careful reflection on the "grounds of obligation" (8: p. 50). It might seem that conflicts can arise between such imperfect duties as those of beneficence (to others) and duties to oneself (5: pp. 152–153), but Kant does not call for us to sacrifice everything to the needs of others, even though we have an imperfect duty to help others achieve their (morally permissible) desires. One need not impoverish oneself to aid others, or deprive oneself of advantages to help others gain their own. Nor need we act benevolently toward everyone equally (8: pp. 245–246, 260). Such judgments on our part that involve beneficence to others are essentially prudential and depend on empirical information, facts about our resources, the needs of others, and the likely consequences of alternative courses of action.

This interpretation of Kant, if it succeeds in showing the plausibility of the notion of duties to oneself, works primarily for perfect duties to oneself, those that enjoin specific kinds of acts such as suicide, drunkenness, or lust. Will it work also for imperfect duties to oneself, those wide, positive duties that allow great latitude in their fulfillment? Certainly it will work with little modification for the general duty to in-

crease one's moral perfection.[10] But what about the duty to develop one's talents, one's natural perfections?

Kant often wrote about such talents as if they were only of prudential value "since they serve ... for all sorts of possible ends" (9: p. 90). And of course talents do serve us in that fashion as I noted in the three cases outlined previously. But here, too, the development of our talents and capacities, however we choose to do it within the wide range of this imperfect duty, may be a condition for the development of our self-esteem and our moral autonomy because it is another way to achieve what Kant called self-mastery (7: p. 138ff; 4: pp. 43–51).

Is this true? One way to argue for this is to note the connection between the development of our talents and the community of others, which is the main source of the standards and evaluations that enable us to understand our own development. Comparison of ourselves with others is a fallible, but necessary, corrective to the pitfalls of self-love, smugness, and narcissism against which Kant inveighs in *Lectures on Ethics* (10: p. 232). The development of one's talents, then, is closely related to one's acquiring self-knowledge about one's exercise of autonomy, in particular, and the maintenance of self-respect.

One further argument of Kant's may be effective here. Kant holds that among the variety of goods that are the ends of moral reasoning, persons, or rational agents, are of intrinsic and unconditional, or absolute, value. This view is expressed in the second formulation of the categorical imperative that we treat ourselves and others always as ends, never simply as a means. However, the talents and capacities that contribute to our natural perfection as it promotes our moral virtue are also ends (8: p. 195). In this case our duty arises from the intrinsic worth of those features of us as moral and physical beings that contribute to our status as persons. We have a duty to ourselves to develop our talents because these talents have an intrinsic worth to us as moral agents. As Kant wrote,

Hence there is also bound up with the end of humanity in our own person the rational will, and so the duty, to make our-selves worthy of humanity by culture in general, by procuring or promoting the *capacity* to realize all sorts of possible ends.... But this duty is ... a duty of wide obligation. No rational principle prescribes *how* far one should go in culti-vating one's capacities.... [T]here is only a law for the maxims of actions, which runs as follows: "Cultivate your powers of mind and body so that they are fit to realize any ends you might encounter," however uncertain you are which of them could sometime become yours. (8: pp. 195–6)

So the development of one's talents is even necessary for a rational being, given the contin-gent limitations and circumstances of one's par-ticular life.

It should be clear that the duty to develop one's talents as an imperfect duty is a wide one that does not specify any particular talent that must be developed or any particular ends that one might encounter. Rather, Kant's point is that we must look to developing our talents in general, as it were, picking the particular ways in which this duty is to be fulfilled according to the varieties of choices we make as we naturally seek to promote our own happiness.[11] The guiding idea is that doing so will enhance ourselves as persons and thereby not just enable us to pursue our own happiness more efficiently and effect-ively but, more importantly, it will allow us to develop habits of virtue and fulfill our duties to others in the community of rational persons, in what Kant calls "the kingdom of ends" (9: p. 100). According to Kant, "Man has a duty to himself to be a useful member of the world, since this also belongs to the worth of humanity in his own person, which he ought not to de-grade" (8: p. 240). So no particular talent is in question. No specific project or end is man-dated, save the general end of increasing our natural perfection or moral character. For, "which of these natural perfections should take *precedence*, and in what proportion ... are matters left for him to choose in accordance with his own rational reflection about what sort

of life he would like to lead and whether he has the powers necessary for it" (8: p. 240).

Let me now return to the cases I previously outlined. First, let's consider the case of the callow youth. When we urge a child to develop her or his talents, we are surely motivated by a concern that the child achieve what modicum of happiness is possible, a practical and prudential counsel. But especially for the young we hope to promote the development of precisely that kind of moral perfection of which Kant wrote. And insofar as the development of talents, any talents, contributes to the self-esteem, self-respect, and self-mastery that lead to autonomy, we want that, too. It is important to note that this does not mean that we are looking to pro-mote the isolation or radical independence of the child. To the contrary, since autonomy and self-mastery are necessary conditions to the fulfill-ment of one's duties to others as well, we also seek to enable the child to participate morally in various communities (e.g., families, organiza-tions, cities, etc.) and even more generally with all people.

The case of the phlegmatic athlete is more complicated. Even if we do agree that the devel-opment of talents is an imperfect duty to one-self, it is not evident that that is what is at issue in this case. Our primary concern seems to be the athlete's duty to others, to teammates, to the coach, or to the school, for example. Sport is a community enterprise and participation often involves an explicit or tacit promise to share, to excel, and to try to fulfill various expectations of the activity. It is the athlete's failure to fulfill these duties that is so troubling. The athlete has already, so it seems, chosen to develop some talents. What duty is there to do more, save insofar as it is owed to others as the result of mutual agreements? Further, if the athlete does fulfill all of the appropriate duties to others, what is there left to anyone else to complain about? Fulfilling one's duties to others is, more-over, a manifestation of an autonomous and virtuous person, so any concern with an athlete's developing talents as a way to increase his or her own moral perfection is beside the point. Be-cause the duty to develop one's talents is imper-fect, virtually any talent will do (depending on various contingencies of one's life). The athlete may choose to develop a talent for business rather than for sports or work, or skills for rock climbing rather than for swimming. So an appeal to such a duty is problematic in any case.

Of course, it may be that the athlete fulfills all the expectations solely from self-interest or prudence (what Kant called self-love), which is a strong motive. In that case, what is left to regret in regard to sports? It is not, for Kant, a moral motive, which can only be to act out of respect for the moral law. But we could just as well appeal to such natural tendencies as to duty in order to encourage greater achievement from the athlete. In this case, the consequence will not be, as it would be in the fulfillment of duty, an increase of self-esteem or autonomy, but it will have as a natural outcome more vigorous participation.

Still, perhaps we could argue in the following vein. If self-interest or prudence does not motivate the athlete, we may well point to the athlete's moral conduct, his or her fulfilling of obligations to others. On Kant's view, fulfilling duties to oneself has a kind of prior claim on us since it is a prior condition to our moral conduct toward others. "The first command of all duties," according to Kant, is "to oneself," above all to develop what he calls "moral self-knowledge" and "self-mastery" (8: p. 236). So the best way to encourage the fulfillment of duties to others is to encourage the fulfillment of duties to oneself. The phlegmatic athlete's manifestation of laziness and self-indulgence is a possible sign of a failure of one of those duties. Our urging that one owes it to oneself to develop one's talents is then an appeal to an imperfect duty to oneself and therefore for the development of moral character or perfection. However, this will not reflect specifically on the athlete's involvement in sports, and so is less than we might have wanted for this case. The athlete may choose to develop very different talents, to pursue other activities, to relegate sports to a minor, recreational, or occasional pursuit, and in doing so still fulfill the duty to develop one's talents. The wide latitude for choice in complying with imperfect duties leaves open

how anyone may seek to develop moral virtue through the cultivation of talents. The athlete, accordingly, has no self-regarding duty to develop athletic talents as opposed to other kinds of talents.

As a final tack, we might reflect on the relation between the development of talents and their exercise. It might seem that it is only the development of talents that is a moral imperative, and that the exercise of them is a matter of prudence. However, perhaps we can make the following case. Kant argued that our duty to develop our talents is to prepare ourselves for "all sorts of possible ends," including, surely, the general end of moral conduct and the fulfilling of our other duties. Even the exercise of our talents, therefore, may have a moral aspect. And so, the athlete has a duty to develop those talents that contribute to the fulfillment of commitments to team, school, coach, or whomever. But now, the development and exercise of talents become instrumental choices in the fulfilling of duties to others. That we must will the means to our moral ends, Kant argued, is analytic (9: pp. 84–5). The moral quality of the means in such cases derives from the ends they subserve. Our athlete owes it to others to choose the means necessary to carry out the chosen ends.

Poor Robinson Crusoe has been sitting on his island too long, but I confess I am hard pressed to see how to rescue him. He has no duties to others because there are (before the arrival of Friday) no others, no community, for him to encounter. Kant believed that he had a perfect duty to himself not to commit suicide or otherwise damage himself. Prudence accounts for much of his conduct. We can imagine him honing certain skills in order to survive, but what (imperfect) *duty* (to himself) does he have to develop these talents? In such isolation, what sense can be made of moral perfection? Crusoe, like Kant's South Sea Islanders, could let his talents rust and "devote his life to idleness, indulgence,... and enjoyment" (9: p. 90). Cannot he, or the last man on earth, will that this should become a universal law of nature? Kant, I believe, must say no. Even here we have a duty to develop those capacities that are the foundation of moral character. Our duty is never to be done for the sake of something else, happiness, or other people, but out of what Kant called "reverence for the law," which is a kind of moral feeling generated within us by practical reason itself (9: p. 69).

Still, I cannot make much sense of this. It is only a contingent fact for Crusoe that he is alone; others were soon to arrive, and might arrive even for the last man on earth. Perhaps it is important to maintain one's moral sensibility in the eventuality that one will once again be in a moral community where a full range of duties will be engaged. But I have argued that such moral sensibility cannot be sustained outside such a community. The development of talents and capacities is meaningless without the constraints, not of our wills, but of the socially constructed standards and activities within which they will be exercised in the achievement of our moral ends. Crusoe has only the echo of such community, a mere semblance of society, to measure his natural perfection; so there is a question of whether he can sustain his moral equilibrium. Nevertheless, to the extent that one could survive outside a human community, one might seek to perpetuate a complete moral character as a way of asserting and preserving one's integrity as a rational being, and the continued development of one's talents, no less than for the callow youth or the phlegmatic athlete, is one way to that end.[12]

Notes

1 Kant makes several attempts to draw this distinction in as many different books. I have combined some of his different versions here. It may be that finally Kant provides only a rough continuum of duties along a spectrum of width (see 2 and 3: pp. 147–175).

2 Kant's views of such activities now often seem peculiar and unacceptable. For example, he held that virtually any sexual activity not linked to procreation was misused. On the other hand, he rejected sexual conduct that treats others as means or otherwise demeans them.

3 Earlier, in the *Grundlegung* or *Groundwork* (9), Kant argued that these duties arise because we cannot will their opposites without violating the categorical imperative as indicated by self-contradiction.

4 This is stretching the point a bit. So far as I know, Kant had nothing to say about sports, and I doubt he had any conception of athletic talents. But physical and mental skills are the general focus of his argument.

5 This is the second of Singer's essays on this topic. The first (12) appeared several years earlier in *Ethics* and was followed by several replies. Articles on self-regarding duties seem to appear in clusters. Another bunch appeared in *Analysis* 23–24 at about the same time.

6 Or, to use an example of an imperfect duty, my (imperfect) duty to promote the happiness of others (given whatever are the constraints of my resources) clearly *involves* me, is to be discharged by me, in an unspecified range of activities, but is *owed* to others.

7 Kant ruled out owing such a duty to God (8: p. 237).

8 Paul Eisenberg worked out a version of this argument in "Duties to Oneself: A New Defense Sketched" (1). See also Thomas E. Hill, Jr., "The Importance of Autonomy" (4: pp. 43–51).

9 As Paul Eisenberg put it, "one must say only that in some cases the person to whom a duty is owed and the person with regard to whom it is owed are identical" (1: p. 631). This is an effective reply to Singer's effort to show that self-regarding duties are never duties to oneself (12: p. 204).

10 But how am I to fulfill this duty? What should I do to develop my autonomy or maintain my moral character? Kant deplored an obsessive preoccupation with developing one's moral perfection, what he called "fantastic virtue." But the wide latitude allowed in observance of this duty seems to allow for considerable arbitrariness. Kant mentioned cultivating one's capacity to understand, to exercise one's will, to diminish one's ignorance (8: p. 191). See also Mary Gregor's *Laws of Freedom* (3: pp. 95–112).

11 One's duty to oneself is not to promote one's own happiness. Kant held that everyone seeks happiness as a natural tendency ("by virtue of the impulses of his nature"). One's duty to oneself is rather to promote one's own perfection. But one does owe to others a duty of beneficence to promote their happiness (8: pp. 190–196).

12   My thanks to my colleagues Howard DeLong and Richard Lee for their helpful comments on earlier drafts of this paper.

Bibliography

1   Eisenberg, Paul D. "Duties to Oneself: A New Defense Sketched." *Review of Metaphysics*, 20 (1967), 602–634.
2   Eisenberg, Paul D. "From the Forbidden to the Supererogatory: The Basic Ethical Categories in Kant's *Tugendlehre*." *American Philosophical Quarterly*, 3:4 (October 1966), 255–269.
3   Gregor, Mary. *Laws of Freedom*. Oxford: Blackwell, 1963.
4   Hill, Thomas E., Jr. *Autonomy and Self-respect*. New York: Cambridge University Press, 1991.
5   Hill, Thomas E., Jr. *Dignity and Practical Reason in Kant's Moral Philosophy*. Ithaca: Cornell University Press, 1994.
6   Kading, Daniel. "Are There Really 'No Duties To Oneself'?" *Ethics*, 70 (January 1960), 155–157.
7   Kant, Immanuel. *Lectures on Ethics*. Translated by Louis Infield. Indianapolis: Hackett Publishing Company, 1963.
8   Kant, Immanuel. *The Metaphysics of Morals*. Introduction, translation and notes by Mary Gregor, New York: Cambridge University Press, 1991.
9   Kant, Immanuel. *Groundwork of the Metaphysics of Morals*. Translated by H.J. Paton. New York: Harper & Row, 1964.
10 Paton, Margaret. "A Reconsideration of Kant's Treatment of Duties to Oneself." *Philosophical Quarterly*, 40 (1990), 222–233.
11 Singer, Marcus G. "Duties and Duties to Oneself." *Ethics*, 73 (January 1963), 133–142.
12 Singer, Marcus G. "On Duties to Oneself." *Ethics*, 69 (April 1959), 202–205.

CHAPTER 16

Fair Play as Respect for the Game

Robert Butcher and Angela Schneider

Despite the prevalence and intuitive force of the term *fair play*, its precise content is much debated. Most historical introductions to the idea trace its roots to 19th century British Public Schools and the "Muscular Christianity" movement that, in turn, claim roots in classical Greek sport. In the mid-19th century, the term did not need much in the way of detailed explanation. Because sport was the preserve of an homogeneous elite (i.e., moneyed, educated, aristocratic, leisured males), their shared values spilled over into their sporting practices. Any decently brought up young man simply knew that certain things were "not cricket." But things rapidly began to change. McIntosh, in *Fair Play: Ethics in Sport and Education* (15), quotes contemporary 1891 discussions around the introduction of the penalty kick in soccer:

> It is a standing insult to sportsmen to have to play under a rule which assumes that players intend to trip, hack, and push their opponents and to behave like cads of the most unscrupulous kind. I say that the lines marking the penalty area are a disgrace to the playing field of a public school. (15: p. 80)

The reasoning behind the statement is interesting. A player might trip, hack, and push his opponent by accident or by design. If it occurred by accident, no penalty was required. No gentleman sportsman would ever intentionally consider such behavior. Sport was played by gentlemen, so either way, the penalty kick and penalty area were clearly unnecessary and insulting.

The democratization of sport, itself a good thing, admitted players from a far wider variety of backgrounds. Indeed, even women were permitted to participate in sport! The old certainties were no longer shared, and assumptions made in the offices and boardrooms of sport governing associations were sometimes not reflected in the practices of athletes. This broadening of the base of participation in sport was both positive and healthy, but it carried a price: What was once taken for granted had now to be explained, debated, and justified.

Fair play has always been an applied concept. Many treatments of fair play were, and still are, motivated more by the desire to use sport to teach some set of positive values than by the goal of understanding the nature of the concept itself. It is generally agreed that sport teaches values, but the content of those values – indeed whether the values are good or ill – depends upon the way in which sport is played, taught, and practiced. *Fair play* is often the phrase used to capture the view that sport *should* be used to teach positive social values, with the chosen values forming the content of the concept. On this view, fair play forms a subset of general moral or social values applied to, and taught through, sport and physical activity.

We begin this paper with a survey and analysis of the contemporary debate on fair play. We will map out and examine five different philosophical treatments of fair play and show how they are each intellectually unsatisfying. The approaches we will examine may be summarized as follows: (a) fair play as a "bag of virtues"; (b) fair play as play; (c) sport as contest and fair play as fair contest; (d) fair play as respect for rules; and (e) fair play as contract or agreement.

We will then present our own positive approach. We will argue that seeing fair play as "respect for the game" provides both philosophical grounding and intellectual coherence while fitting neatly with general intuitions. We will argue that the notion of fair play has its grounding in the logic of sport itself. This approach has a number of advantages:

1   Sport forms the conceptual grounding for fair play;
2   Fair play is a conceptually coherent concept;
3   The motivation for acting fairly will thus be found in the activity (sport) itself; and
4   There is a logical framework for discussions of the fairness of particular practices.

Naturally, there are some drawbacks to this approach. Fair play does not turn out to be the sum total of morality, nor does it answer all questions about the applicability of general moral concepts to sporting situations. What it does provide, however, is a method for determining right conduct in sport which refers directly to sport itself and not to a set of external, culturally determined, and variable values. In the final section, we will summarize our conclusion on fair play as respect for the game.

The contemporary debates around fair play have focused on a number of related issues: (a) content of the concept – what fair play is; (b) grounding of the concept – how to justify the claim that some action is and is not fair; (c) definitions of cheating and sportspersonship; and (d) the moral status of rule-breaking and cheating. A discussion of the different methods of grounding the concept of fair play will be our route to an examination of the varied approaches to the other issues. By and large, the philosophical grounding adopted for fair play dictates what can then be said about the other issues.

Bag of Virtues

The bag-of-virtues approach takes a list of not necessarily related virtues, praiseworthy attributes, or behaviors and associates them with, or applies them to, sport. It is easy to see how this method is derived from research in the social sciences. Here the need is to operationally define measurable behaviors so that data can be collected and analyzed. For the purposes of social scientific research, *fair play* has been defined positively, as handshaking with opponents, congratulating team-mates, or negatively, as penalty minutes, incidence of violence, or verbal intimidation.

An additional impetus to this approach comes from the desire to use sport to teach social values. On this model, sport is the vehicle by which a set of approved values can be efficiently delivered.

The most developed contemporary work, from this perspective, has been conducted by Bredemeier and Shields, whose 15 years of work are brought together in *Character Development and Physical Activity* (1). They propose four elements of character – compassion, fairness, sportspersonship, and integrity – that can be taught through properly structured sports programs (1: pp. 193–194). These elements of character are derived from their developmental model of moral reasoning, then applied to sporting situations.

A similar practical motivation lies behind Lumpkin, Stoll, and Beller's four fundamental moral values or principles that, when taken together, are proposed as the basis of a reasoning strategy for fair play behavior (13). They propose justice, honesty, responsibility, and beneficence as their four fundamentals. These are selected on the grounds that they can all be found in historical guides such as "the Bible, the Pali Cannon [sic], the Book of Koran, and most societal ethics" (13: p. 21). Fair play thus becomes the application of these general moral principles to sporting situations. Different theoretical (or cultural) models of morality thus generate different conceptions of fair play.

The drawbacks of this approach are apparent. While *justice* (or fairness) is common to both lists and *responsibility* and *honesty* could be collapsed into *integrity*, the lists, while compatible, are not identical.[1] Different views of ethics as such translate into different characteristics as the foundations of fair play, and just as we have no good method of arbitrating between the competing claims of different moral systems, we have no corresponding way of adjudicating between rival claims concerning fair play. Similarly, it is always open to the relativist to claim that a culturally grounded conception of fair play is not relevant to the enterprise upon which he or she is embarked. In the world of international and intercultural relations, these difficulties also arise and, depending on the task at hand, are either dealt with, glossed over, or avoided altogether. In sport, the situation is interestingly different. The very nature of a sporting contest requires that the participants be engaged in the *same* activity. If fair play can be grounded in sport itself, we have the ideal method for claiming the allegiance of all sportspeople.[2]

The bag-of-virtues approach is discussed, and consequently dismissed, by both Keating (8) and Feezell ([6] although neither of them recognizes it as such an approach). It is dismissed, as argued above, because it offers no defensible method of deciding which characteristics or actions should fall within the relevant definitions and no method of arbitrating between competing claims. The approach that is the standard for philosophical writers has been, not surprisingly, a conceptual analytic approach that looks first to the nature of sport and seeks to generate from that nature the moral ideals of fair play and sportspersonship.

Before we turn to these other, sport-based analyses of fair play, it is worth pointing out the difficulties highlighted by Bredemeier and Shields (1), and Lumpkin et al. (13). Because sport is conducted by human beings, it falls within the realm of morality. That is, the general rules of moral life apply to sport. Sport and any action which occurs within sport is, thus, amenable to moral discussion and analysis. However,

what would count as a violation of the moral order is determined both by the nature of sport itself and the agreement of the competitors to modify or suspend the scope of general moral rules.

The most obvious examples of the modification of normal moral rules comes in the area of violence. In everyday life, pushing, shoving and diving into people is generally prohibited. However, on the rugby field those actions are constitutive of the game. One could not play rugby without engaging in those activities. By agreeing to play rugby, one accepts that one will be subjected to and must inflict actions that would be both illegal and immoral in other contexts. So in rugby, a morally culpable act of violence might be a punch or a kick but not a crushing tackle. (And, of course, this is true even if the tackle causes more physical harm than the punch.) What is true of violence is also true in other areas. Various forms of deception are game related skills in most sports. As such, those acts (referred to as "strategic deception" by Pearson [18]) are not morally wrong. Lying about a line call in tennis, however, would be.

The observation that participation in sport modifies general moral rules raises two issues. The first issue concerns just what it is that one agrees to when one decides to participate in a sport. One certainly agrees to accept actions that are permissible within the rules of the game. One also agrees to accept accidents that are a foreseeable consequence of the game. What is less clear is whether one also agrees to accept actions which, while against the rules, are common practice in a given game. (We will look at this issue of agreement in more detail below.)

Second, we might, on moral grounds, wish to limit the possible content of the sorts of "agreements to compete" into which people can enter. Bare-knuckle boxing is currently banned in many countries (despite the argument that it is, in fact, safer than boxing with protective equipment because there is less brain damage, because the boxers cannot sustain as many blows to the head). That is, on moral grounds, we do not allow willing competitors to suspend the usual social rules against this form of violence to the extent bare-knuckle boxing would require. (Whether we should ban bare-knuckle boxing is, of course, subject to debate. The point to be made here is that the general requirements of morality can be brought to bear to limit actions in the realm of sport.)[3]

The relationship between general morality and fair play in sport is, thus, complex and nuanced. Although general moral rules still apply, they are limited and modified by the nature of the game that defines the ways in which one can do wrong and may even create new possibilities to act immorally. The nuanced nature of this relationship also provides further reasons for rejecting the view that fair play in sport can be understood simply as a subset of general moral values.

Fair Play as Play

In broad terms, much of the philosophical analysis of sport and its relationship to fair play has focused on the ideas that sport is play and sport is a contest. On the sport-is-play approach, the central feature of sport is its nature of being set apart. Sport is not a part of everyday life; it is freely chosen and entered into for its own sake. The appropriate attitude is, therefore, one of playfulness.[4] Keating (8) takes this to mean that the purpose of sport is the creation of enjoyment of the activity and that to do this, the appropriate attitudes are generosity and magnanimity. Keating claims that *sport* can be radically distinguished from *athletics*, the purpose of which is victory in a contest.

This distinction has been soundly criticized and rejected by Feezell (6) and others as unworkable, unhelpful, and false to the facts. On Feezell's Aristotelian account, sportspersonship is a mean, the balanced recognition and acceptance of the essential non-seriousness of sport combined with the utmost dedication and commitment in its pursuit.

While Feezell's objections to Keating's distinction are sound, it would be a mistake to reject out of hand Keating's emphasis on the freely-chosen nature of sport participation along with his distinction between sport and athletics. We will argue below that Keating

has, in effect, missed a step in his argument. He moves directly from the set-apart, freely-chosen nature of sport to the conclusion that enjoyment is the goal. The step he misses is an understanding and explanation of just why it is that sport is both freely-chosen and enjoyable. That is, he argues as if the pleasure or enjoyment of sport was somehow separable from the practice of sport itself. On Keating's account, it is not clear why a person who sought enjoyment through the practice of some sport wouldn't just switch to stamp collecting – or indeed take a good drug – if they held out the prospect of greater enjoyment. We will argue that it is the activity of sport itself that bring its own rewards and pleasures. It is through commitment to a sport and the standards and skills it requires that we gain enjoyment in its practice. We do not seek pleasure, then plug in means to that end. Rather, we commit to activities, then derive pleasure from them.[5]

Sport As Contest: Fair Play as Fair Contest

An alternative approach is to look at sport as a test or contest and try to derive fair play or sportspersonship from that. Within this general approach, the greatest debate has centered on the precise definition of the nature of the test or contest in which competitors are engaged. Most approaches start with the analysis that sports competitions are examples of games. Because they are games, they are created and defined by their rules, as are the permissible means of scoring goals or runs, and hence, winning. Athletes agree to test their skill against each other at a sport. The sport defines the nature and limitations of skill. If an athlete breaks the agreement to compete, he or she ceases to compete, and so, can no longer be in a position to win. That is, if one cheats one cannot win.[6] This is an essentially negative conception of fair play and sportspersonship, one which starts from a definition of cheating, then proposes that fair play and sportspersonship are the absence of cheating. This has two problems, the first definitional and the second evidential. The definitional problem concerns the nature of cheating. If we accept that cheating is the breaking of an agreement, we need to identify precisely the content of the agreement. Some authors (7, 18) argue that the agreement is defined by the rules of the sport. If one breaks a rule (especially if one intentionally breaks a rule), then one has broken the agreement to compete to test skill, so one has cheated, and hence, cannot win.

This position is viewed as too restrictive by both Lehman (12) and Leaman (11), who argue that the nature of the agreement must make some reference to the way the game is, as a matter of fact, played. If the game is generally taken to include the possibility of a "professional foul," then a player will not have cheated, or ceased to compete, if he or she commits a professional foul (11, 12).

The moral status of cheating flows from its definition. If cheating is all rule-breaking or even all intentional rule-breaking, then not all cheating is morally wrong.[7] However, if cheating is breaking one's agreement, then all cheating is morally wrong, but not all rule-breaking is cheating.

The evidential problem is that we tend not to view fair play or sportspersonship as the mere absence of cheating. While we may reject the overblown excesses of the early part of [the twentieth] century, fair play certainly has positive rather than merely negative connotations. To say that someone exhibits fair play seems to say more than: he or she clearly follows the rules or keeps to his or her agreements.

Just as Keating's analysis, while inadequate, stressed the important points that sports are participated in for their own sakes and bring enjoyment, the analysis of sport as contest, while also inadequate as an account of fair play, stresses the essential point that agreement must lie at the heart of contest.

In what follows, we will look in a little more detail at two common conceptions of fair play that develop the idea of sport as an agreement based on rules. We will argue that neither approach captures our positive sense of what constitutes fair play or sportspersonship. We will then move to our own positive conception of fair play as "respect for the game."

Fair Play as Respect for Rules

The International Council for Sport and Physical Education (ICSPE) defines *fair play*, first and foremost, as respect for the rules of the game. Fair play "requires, as a minimum, that [the competitor] shows strict, unfailing observance of the written rule" (1: p. 23). This is glossed by the suggestion that respect is due the spirit rather than the letter of the rules, but the intent is the same. This understanding of fair play is important in that it draws attention to the rule-governed and defined nature of sport. Games exist and are defined by their rules. This position is also important, because it acts as the foundation of the logical incompatibility thesis, the thesis which demonstrates that one cannot win if one cheats (21).

Fair play as respect for rules is, however, an inadequate formulation for capturing some of our intuitions about the idea. For example, we sometimes want fair play to apply to situations within sport but outside of the rules of the sport. For instance, Lumpkin et al. (13) pose the case of Josie, the squash player. Josie is your opponent in an important match and has arrived (not to her fault) without a racquet. She will forfeit the game. You use the same kind of racquet and grip as she, and you have a back-up racquet. She is the only competitor at this event who could seriously challenge you and without her, you would almost certainly win the championship. The game against her will be tough, and you are far from certain you can win. What should you do?

The fair play answer seems clear. Indeed one of the earliest fair play awards (to bobsledder Carlo Monti in 1952) was presented in a similar case. Monti loaned another team his brake when theirs was inoperable. The other team went on to beat Monti. You should lend Josie your racquet. But why?

Respect for rules does not help. You break no rule in declining to lend Josie your racquet. Lumpkin et al. (13) use the case as an illustration of the principle of beneficence. This is a standard moral notion, the idea that one ought, generally, to do nice things for people. As a general moral principle it certainly applies here. Anyone who could should lend Josie a racquet. But you are in a special position – you are her opponent – and as such, have better reasons than generalized beneficence for lending her your racquet. (Although, at first glance, it appears that it is in your self-interest not to lend her your racquet.) As we will argue below, a formulation of fair play as respect for the game will show just why it is you would want to give Josie your racquet.

As an aside, the general applicability of beneficence to sport is unclear. While fair play dictates that you must let your opponents play and that you will only use legal means to stop them, there is no compulsion to be nice to them, for instance, by allowing them to make their best shots or play to their strengths.

Fair play as respect for rules cannot account for actions we take to be required by fair play but which are not directly covered by any rule.

The rule-based conception can also err in the opposite direction. As Lehman (12) has argued, before one can make judgments of cheating or unfairness, one must consider more than just the rule book and should look at the context in which the game is played.[8] If the contestants agree that, for instance, undetected spitballs are an accepted part of modern professional baseball, then "Spitball Perry" did not cheat.[9] Similarly so for the so-called "professional foul" when a player performs an illegal act and willingly accepts a penalty, because it would seem to create a competitive advantage to do so. While we can argue with Lehman about the best approach to take to the rules of a game – should one play to their spirit, to their letter, or to what one can get away with undetected or insufficiently punished – he makes an important point, similar to D'Agostino's (4): Games are played in a context, a context that uses more than just the rule book to define cheating. Fair play as "respect for rules" – which is primarily derived from what D'Agostino has referred to as a "formalist account of games" – does not take into account the variety of sport as played and practiced.

Fair Play As Contract or Agreement

It could be argued that fair play can be seen and explained on the model of a contract or agreement. While this is an interesting and important component of fair play, it is insufficient to characterize the concept fully. Fair play as contract starts from the position, mentioned above, that games are created by their rules. A sporting competition is, thus, a test of skill within the parameters prescribed by the rules. When athletes enter a contest, they agree, and form a tacit contract, to test their skills in the ways permitted by the game concerned. On this account, unfairness or cheating is wrong, because it breaks the agreement. Fair play as contract is open on the content of the agreement. On some versions of this view, the content of the contract is created solely by the rules. In other versions, it is the rules as practiced and understood by the athletes.

This approach is important, because it shows the athlete's own role in accepting the rules of his or her own sport. By making an agreement to compete, the athlete binds him- or herself with self-imposed conditions. This approach does not permit the athlete to view the rules (and the officials who enforce them) as somehow "out there" imposing rules against the athlete's will and interest. The contest is defined by the rules, and in entering the contest, the athlete agrees to measure skill, defined by the rules, against competitors doing the same.

Because this account leaves open the exact content of the agreement, it is flexible enough to account for the variability in the way in which the same sport is played in different places and at different competitive levels. Here the agreement to compete would be framed by the rules but with the added clause "as defined or interpreted" at the relevant level (4). On this account if, for instance, the game is played to the referee – that is, one is expected to break certain rules if the referee is not looking – then the two opponents could agree to a match played in this way, and it would be fair.

This method of viewing things accounts for a number of problems. Athletes often dismiss calls for fair play with the derisive response that "the game is not played that way." Their claim is that their agreement defines what is fair, not simply the rules. Some competitive discrepancies can also be accounted for by the tacit nature of the agreement. If one team is playing the game one way, for instance to the referee, and the other practices a different ethos, for instance, playing to the spirit of the rules, then they may well not have agreed to compete in the same way. This inevitably leads to bitterness and charges of unfairness. This problem could be solved by making as public as possible the nature of the tacit agreement to compete. Note, however, that the central idea is still one of agreement. This rules out the possibility of one team, or player, playing fairly, but operating by a different set of rules from their opponents.

The alternative view would rule out consideration of the ethos of the game by insisting that the content of the agreement be taken as the rules of the game and nothing more. This renders the fair-play-as-agreement position very similar to fair play as respect for rules, with the added benefit of emphasizing the athlete's role in accepting and living up to his or her part of the agreement.

Fair play as agreement is an important further step, but it does not go far enough. The idea of governing sport by contract reduces fair play to an essentially negative concept. Fairness is the absence of unfairness, and unfairness is defined by the breaking of one's word or contract. So fair play is merely doing no less than you said you would do. Without wishing to get overly romantic about the concept, fair play is generally taken (and sportspersonship is always taken) to be something positive, something that cannot be fully explained by mere adherence to one's word, although that is certainly required. When we talk of fair play, the standard we tend to adopt is one that refers to the spirit of the game, rather than the letter of its rules.

For example, some sports still carry rules against "unsportsmanlike conduct" or "bringing the game into disrepute." These rules go undefined, and of course, they can readily be abused to punish people unfairly. However, despite their lack of clarity, we will argue that these sorts of rules can not only be rendered coherent and justified, but they carry an important concept, a concept we should do our best not to lose.

The Josie-the-squash-player example from the last section is again useful here. Your contractual agreement with Josie is to play fairly, to keep to the rules of the game. You break no rule, and hence, break no promise, by declining to lend her your racquet. Yet we want to say that fair play dictates that you lend her your racquet. So, fair play cannot be reduced entirely to keeping an agreement. It may be a necessary condition but not a sufficient condition.

In the next part of this paper, we will examine fair play as respect for the game and argue that this idea builds on the nature of the sporting agreement and provides the positive structure of our concept of fair play – a structure that will give a logical account for the intuitions in Josie's case.

Fair Play as Respect for the Game

We wish to defend the position that fair play in sport can be understood as respect for the game. As we unpack this idea, we will see the behavioral implications that flow from this central attitude. We will argue that the standard intuitive ideas of fair play are linked, and conceptually grounded, in the idea of "fair play as respect for the game."

There are two commonly used and rather similar senses of respect. In the first, weaker sense, one can respect merely by observing or following. In this sense, we respect the rules of the road by adhering to the speed limit, stopping at stop signs, and so on. The second sense of respect is stronger and carries connotations of honoring, holding in regard, esteeming, or valuing.

It is this second sense of respect that is operative in moral discussions of respect for autonomy, or equal respect for persons. Here, the idea is that one should, from a moral point of view, value the interests, rights, preferences, and so on, of others as one values one's own.

In the context of sport, it is easy to run the two senses together. Because sports are games made up by their rules, there is the requirement that we respect the rules of the game. This could mean that we treat the rules of the game in the same way we treat the rules of the road. We observe or follow them, perhaps for the sake of expediency or as a courtesy. However, it is not obvious how one could honor or esteem traffic regulations. But it is precisely in this latter sense that we wish to defend the idea that fair play can be understood in terms of respect for a game. We will argue that if one honors or esteems one's sport, not only will one wish to exhibit fair play, but one will also have a coherent conceptual framework for arbitrating between competing claims regarding the fairness, or otherwise, of actions.

We will argue below that sports are practices and that practices are the sorts of things that can have interests. Respect for the game will thus entail respect for the interests of the game (or sport) as a practice.

Sports are games

As we accepted earlier, sports are games. This means they are artificially constructed from their rules. Participation in a game takes one outside of everyday life. A game creates its own world with its own standards of excellence and its own ways of failing. What counts as skill and what counts as winning and losing are defined through its rules within the game.

Respect for the game, therefore, entails respect for the rules of the game. The rules of a sport make the activity itself possible. Because participation in a game is chosen, because the activities of sports are inherently worthwhile,[10] the rules that make those activities possible are due honor and respect.[11] But respect is a critical and reflective notion. One can criticize while still respecting. In fact, if one respects, one has a duty to criticize. But the criticism must be open and public and should be constructive rather than destructive.

Sports are contests

As noted above, although fair play cannot be straightforwardly derived from sport-as-contest, the test and contest nature of sport are import-

ant components of our approach. As Kretchmar points out, a contest is always against another and consists in the competitors trying to do the same thing better than each other (9). That the competitors are engaged in the same activity is crucial. If two people are engaged in different activities, there is no one activity they can be competing in. This begs questions about the identification, and identity, of actions or activities. In the sports context, we support the view that contests are defined by a combination of rules and ethos. The rules, constitutive and regulative, form the basis of an agreement that can then be modified by practice and further agreement – the ethos of the game. The fluid nature of the ethos of a particular game played at a particular level reinforces the necessity of agreement between the competitors. Because there are choices to be made about the way the game is to be conducted, we need to agree on what will count as fair in the contest and what will not. Otherwise we run the risk of engaging in different enterprises and thus failing to contest at all. If players wish to contest, they must agree on the precise nature of the contest.

Sports are practices

MacIntyre in *After Virtue* defines a *practice* as:

> any coherent and complex form of socially established co-operative human activity through which goods internal to that form of activity are realized in the course of trying to achieve those standards of excellence which are appropriate to and partially definitive of that form of activity, with the result that human powers to achieve excellence, and the human conceptions of the ends and goods involved, are systematically extended. (14: p. 187)

He then goes on to cite chess and football as examples of practices in the sense he intends. What practices do is create opportunities to pursue goods and to extend, expand, and realize our conceptions of what is worthwhile in life. MacIntyre makes the (by now) commonplace distinction between internal and external goods. Internal goods are those benefits or goods only available through the practice concerned. External goods, such as money or fame, can be pursued through a variety of means.

Being engaged in a practice means standing in a particular relationship to the practice itself and to other practitioners:

> A practice involves standards of excellence and obedience to rules as well as the achievement of goods. To enter into a practice is to accept the authority of those standards and the inadequacy of my own performance as judged by them. It is to subject my own attitudes, choices, preferences and tastes to the standards which currently partially define the practice. (14: p. 190)

This should not be taken to mean that a practice requires slavish and unquestioning obedience. MacIntyre stresses that practices have histories and traditions and form living, vibrant, and changing entities. Practices change – they must – but the change comes from within and operates inside the context formed by tradition.

It is the latter part of that last quotation – the idea that, as a practitioner of a practice, one's preferences, tastes, attitudes, and choices are partially shaped by the practice – that is most significant for our present purposes. We will argue that "respecting one's game" requires that one takes on or assumes the interests of that game.[12]

Respect for the game as an assumption and transformation of interests

If you are engaged in a practice, if you respect a practice, you acquire and assume a new set of interests – those of the practice itself. It may seem a little odd to speak of the interests of a practice, but we think the idea can be made clear enough. Let us take the practice of philosophy as an example. It is in the interests of philosophy for there to be innovative scholarship, lively and vigorous debate on contested issues, the study and analysis of historical work, a vibrant community of scholars (highly paid tenured faculty?), broad teaching of the concepts and techniques of philosophy, and so on. Philosophy should make a difference in people's lives. It is not in the interests of philosophy for its research to become sterile, its teaching stale, or its issues irrelevant. And, of course, philosophy being what it is, there should continue to be a lively debate about just what should constitute the interests of philosophy.

As philosophers we take on those interests as our own. If we care about philosophy, we care about our own roles and performance within the practice. We take on the interest in creating innovative scholarship, engaging in debate, teaching, and so on. We wish to add our own little brick to the philosophical edifice. Excellence in philosophy is in our interests, just as it is in the interests of philosophy itself.

This acquisition of interests has important consequences. To continue the philosophical example, as philosophers, we are committed to the quest for truth – wherever that might lead. That means that we are committed to following the argument, even if the argument runs against our most cherished positions. It is in the interests of a philosopher, as a philosopher, to see his or her own positions demolished in the name of truth.

The same principle holds good for other practices. To return to sport, the athlete takes on the interests of his or her sport. Those interests become the interests of the athlete. If you respect the game, you honor and take seriously the standards of excellence created and defined by that game. For example, an athlete who respected the game of soccer would take seriously its requirements and standards. Such an athlete would care about soccer skills and tactics. He or she would accept the fitness requirements of the game of soccer and would strive to meet them. Because such an athlete accepts the standards of soccer excellence, he or she would work to acquire and exhibit soccer skills. This general point is true whatever one's level of ability or commitment to training. Even if we can commit only small periods of time to our game, or even if we recognize that we will never have the skill to be truly great, the person who respects a game will still accept the standards imposed by the sport. (Naturally, one can also respect a game one does not play, for instance, as a spectator or official – but in all cases the same point applies: One accepts the standards of the game concerned and acts accordingly.)

The idea of the interests of the game provides a means of judging one's own actions in relation to the sport. We approach any activity with mixed motivations and interests. Taking the interests of the game seriously means that we ask ourselves whether or not some action we are contemplating would be good for the game concerned, if everyone did it.[13]

The transformation of interests that occurs when we take on the interests of a game has a second important consequence. Because the interests of the game are now our own interests, we have a motivation for striving for the good of the game. As we will see, this means we have a motivation both to play fairly and strive for excellence.

Respect for the game and intrinsic motivation

The connections between fair play, respect for the game, intrinsic motivation, and the internal goods of a practice really require a paper of their own. The association of respect for the game and intrinsic motivation offers rich practical and conceptual implications that warrant detailed analysis. However, for our present purposes, it is sufficient to introduce the ideas and draw the conceptual connections. It is a commonplace observation that people participate in sport for an enormous range of reasons. A very few participate because they are paid. Many participate for fitness and companionship or to achieve the respect and admiration of others. But for the great mass of people, the reasons for participating in sport lie within sport itself: People play games because they are fun. For many, perhaps most, participants in sport, its activities are intrinsically rewarding. They bring a feeling of pleasure and provide experiences that are enjoyable and worthwhile.

In the literature of the psychology of sport, the phenomenon of performing an action or

activity for its own sake has been studied as an issue of *intrinsic motivation*. What follows is a brief synthesis and review of that literature, which is necessary to defend the premises of our argument on fair play as respect for the game.

The standard contrast in discussions of motivation is between intrinsic and extrinsic motivation. Extrinsic motivation is available for a variety of activities. For instance, one can acquire money or fame in a variety of ways. One might become a lawyer or a pop star, so, insofar as one wants fame or money, one is motivated to be a lawyer or a pop star. If one is motivated by the desire for fame or money, the question one faces is merely of the most efficient means of achieving those ends. For those who are physically gifted, professional sports may well provide the means to both money and fame. But extrinsic motivation is more pervasive than that. The admiration that comes from one's peers for outstanding athletic performance or for the beauty of one's body are extrinsic motivations for pursuing sporting achievement. This is similarly true for "most valuable player" awards, trophies, and the like. Engaging in sport to prove one's own self-worth is also a form of extrinsic motivation (23).

In contrast, an action or activity is intrinsically motivated if it is engaged in for its own sake. This idea has been operationally defined in the psychological literature in two quite different ways: (a) actions or activities engaged in, in the absence of external rewards, or (b) activity in which participants express an interest or enjoyment (5). The difference between the two definitions is important. In the first, one cannot be intrinsically motivated if one receives any extrinsic reward for the activity in question. This begs the question of the relationship between intrinsic and extrinsic rewards. At this stage, we would like to leave open the interchange and relationship between intrinsic and extrinsic motivation.[14]

So far we have merely contrasted intrinsic and extrinsic motivation and suggested that intrinsic motivation is connected to performing an activity for its own sake. But what is it about an activity that makes performing it for its own sake worthwhile? There seem to be four key components for an activity to be experienced as sufficiently worthwhile to be intrinsically motivating.

1   The activity must be interesting. There must be room for the individual participant to express creativity, to experiment (perhaps within limits) with new ways of performing the task;
2   It must be challenging. That is, the task the person is presented with must extend, but not over- or under-extend, the person's competence to perform the required action. If the task is too simple, it will be boring, and if it is too difficult it will be stressful. This notion of challenge embraces the possibility of mastery. If the activity is appropriately challenging, the person will feel that he or she has the prospect of meeting and mastering that challenge;
3   The activity must provide feedback. The person needs to be able to assess how well or badly he or she is performing the task at hand;
4   The activity must be freely chosen. Participation should be uncoerced or voluntary (5, 23, 24).

The perfect example of the effects of deep intrinsic motivation can be found in the experience first described by Czikszentmihalyi (2, 3) over 20 years ago as "flow." When one is in flow, all of one's energies and attention are focused on the task at hand. Time seems to stop moving as one is absorbed in the activity. Czikszentmihalyi has researched this phenomenon in a number of sport and nonsport settings. For the flow experience, one should be engaged in a task that is interesting and challenging but within one's capabilities.

As it stands, this is dry and uncompelling. Flow, in fact, is the pinnacle of sporting experience. Flow is the joy of sport distilled. It is the experience felt when one's self and one's environment are one, when the plays are flowing as they should, when one's teammates are moving with almost mystical grace and ease, when one's whole being is focused on the moment, the

movement, when the ball or the puck moves as if on wires, when everything in the game is right. The flow experience is highly variable and highly prized. It can also be had at any level of sport. Because an activity that permits the flow experience must be challenging, the level of the game required to create the flow experience will improve as the player becomes more and more skilled.

Flow is the experience one has as one is achieving the internal goods of a sport. As can probably be detected from the above, discussions of flow are notoriously difficult. While the features of flow – focus, attention, absorption, and so on – are common to all flow experiences, the feelings will be different for the flow experience of the basketball player, the chess player, and the surgeon.

Interaction Between Intrinsic and Extrinsic Motivation

The obvious assumption, when one considers motivation, is that motivations would be additive. If you have one reason for doing something, then two reasons would motivate you even more. The relationship is not this straightforward. Several studies show that the presence of extrinsic motivations, such as money, food, and good player awards, all tend to decrease intrinsic motivation (5, 23).[15] It would be premature, however, to assume that extrinsic rewards automatically decrease intrinsic motivation. In another study on scholarship athletes, it was found that those in high profile sports, like basketball and football, showed decreased intrinsic motivation in the presence of extrinsic rewards, whereas those in low profile sports, such as wrestling, and women with scholarships did not (5).

The theoretical explanation for these differences, and the complexity of the interaction between intrinsic and extrinsic motivation, lies in the way the extrinsic rewards are perceived. If the extrinsic rewards are seen as controlling or coercive, they will tend to diminish intrinsic motivation. Typically, extrinsic rewards are used to pressure or coerce people into doing things they do not otherwise wish to do. By association, therefore, extrinsic rewards can be seen as coercive and controlling. But this result is not logically necessary. It is suggested that women athletes, and those in low profile sports, do not tend to view scholarships as controlling but rather see them as informational feedback and a recognition of competence and skill.

An essential component of intrinsically motivated activity appears to be that it is freely chosen. Conversely, if people perceive their actions to be controlled, they are less likely to be intrinsically motivated to perform the actions concerned (even when the same, inherently interesting tasks are examined [23]).

Although there is relatively little research on the direct effects of intrinsic motivation on sport performance and perseverance, the general position on intrinsic motivation is that people who are intrinsically motivated to perform an action, or engage in an activity, get more enjoyment from the activity and persevere longer than those who have been extrinsically motivated (23). People who are intrinsically motivated also tend to be more creative in their approach to the tasks at hand, whereas those who are extrinsically motivated tend to do the minimum required in order to receive the reward.

The connection between intrinsic motivation and internal goods of a practice should be obvious. In effect, internal goods and intrinsic motivation are the philosopher's and the psychologist's view of the same phenomenon. The substance of intrinsic motivation is the internal goods of a practice.

The psychological literature of intrinsic motivation, how it is enhanced and nurtured, and how it is affected by different treatments of opponents, competition, and so on offers a rich source for practical approaches to teaching fair play. For our purposes right now, intrinsic motivation emphasizes the achievement of internal goods that, in turn, reinforce a commitment to the process of playing a game. A commitment to the process of playing the game is a commitment to, and respect for, the game itself, with all that that implies. Because respect for the game requires respect for its rules and traditions, intrinsic motivation is its natural practical ally and support.

Practical Implications

We can think about the implications of viewing fair play as respect for the game at two levels. At the personal level of the individual athlete, fair play as respect for the game will provide guidelines as he or she considers what ought to be done. At this personal level, respect for the game will influence actions on the field of play, attitudes toward one's opponents, and even one's own level of commitment to the game. Fair play as respect for the game also has implications for actions and decisions at the level of policy. Most sports have, in MacIntyre's sense, institutions. These institutions are comprised of sports governing bodies, rule committees, administrative superstructures, and so on. At this level, too, fair play and respect mandate particular decisions – decisions that refer to the best interests of the game concerned.

For any game or sporting contest, it is possible to describe an ideal against which other contests might be measured.[16] While the particular description will naturally vary from sport to sport, we can identify some necessary conditions. Each item on the list can be justified and explicated in terms of promoting the interests of the game.

1   The contestants should be evenly matched. The ideal contest requires that the contestants be at comparable levels of skill and fitness;

2   The contestants should play at or near their best;

3   The outcome of the contest should be in doubt until the end. (This should be guaranteed by having evenly matched contestants playing at their best.)

4   The outcome of the contest should be determined by sporting skill or ability, not extraneous factors such as egregious luck or errors in officiating. Conditions of play, such as weather, may create additional obstacles but must not be so severe as to undermine the exhibition of skill;

5   The match must be fairly contested, that is, played within the rules of the game;

6   For an ideal match, the contestants must
     have a high degree of skill. Good contests
     can, however, take place between evenly
     matched opponents at any level of skill.[17]

The structure of sports and games is such that
skills cannot be tested or demonstrated in isolation. The interests of both athletes and the
game itself lie in excellent competitions. Athletes who respect and honor their sport have an
interest in participating in good sporting contests. One shows and measures one's sporting
skills in competition against others seeking to do
the same. For the athlete, a competition is a
chance to show and test his or her skills, to
play the best game that he or she is capable of.
In this case, the interests of the athlete are in
producing the best possible game. But the best
possible game, from a sporting point of view, is
not a lop-sided contest where one player or team
demonstrates its skill while the other helplessly
looks on. In the best possible competition, excellent, evenly matched competitors push each
other to the limits of their ability.

The competitive interest of an athlete who
honors his or her sport is to play the best possible game against evenly matched opponents
playing their best possible game. This interest
dictates an important attitude toward one's opponent. The best possible game requires not
only that you play to your best, but also that
your opponent does. It is not, therefore, in your
interest to have your opponent play below his or
her best, except where your methods of bringing
that about are part of the game itself. For instance, it is part of basketball to pressure a player
as he or she attempts to shoot – defensive skill
is all about creating such pressure, and shooting skill is about dealing with it – but it is
not permissible to cough while your opponent
serves in tennis.

Respect for the game, thus, creates important
behavioral consequences in competition. The
athlete who respects the game wishes to play as
well as possible against a worthy opponent
playing as well as possible. The only legitimate
reason for wanting your opponent not to show
his or her skill to its best advantage is where the
limitation is imposed by your sporting skill.

This means that you allow your opponent
every opportunity – as defined by the game –
to play his or her best.

If you ask athletes what their goal is in playing
sport, they may say "winning." This appears to
describe the athlete's interest in sport as winning and makes no reference to the manner in
which the victory is achieved. Without question,
any athlete who respects his or her sport will try
his or her best to win whenever he or she plays.
However, respect for the game requires that the
athlete view winning only as a good if it comes as
a result of a particular process: the well-played,
well-matched game.

The athlete who honors the game has taken
on the interests of the game as his or her own. It
is not in the interests of sport to have undeserv-
ing competitors win. If it is not in the interests
of sport, it is not in the interests of athletes who
respect sport.

Winning is important only if it comes to the
player or team that has played best on a given
day. (And even then, it may be tainted if the
teams or competitors are unevenly matched or if
one team plays well below its capabilities.) If
winning comes as a result of a well-played,
evenly-matched game, both the victor and the
vanquished can view the win as providing important performance feedback, an essential part
of intrinsic motivation.

Because respect for the game entails an
understanding of the relationship between a
game and its rules, the athlete who respects the
game realizes the truth of the logical incompatibility thesis. If one cheats one ceases to play, and
if one does not play one cannot win. Because
such an athlete values the process of playing, he
or she has no motivation to cheat and would not
value a victory awarded as a result of any unfairness.

A victory won through cheating is worthless.
While a certain amount of luck is part of
any sporting contest, there are some situations
where the luck all seems to run one way. In such a
case the winners would feel that the outcome was
not a true representation of the display of skill in
the contest. The further a contest is from the
model of the ideal described above, the less satisfaction is available for the victor.

The attitude of respect for the game can be seen to lead readily to an attitude toward one's opponents. If one values and seeks the well-played game, one cannot view one's opponents as an obstacle to be overcome in one's drive for victory. Rather, one's opponents are an essential part of one's quest for the well-played game. Not only can an athlete not get what he or she wants without opponents, what is desired cannot be achieved without those opponents playing as well as they are able. Opponents must therefore be seen as co-questors for excellent sport (in Fraleigh's term, *facilitators*). One's competitors share the same goals and hold the same game in the same respect. They must therefore be seen as colleagues and compatriots, not enemies.

Violence outside of the rules is a form of cheating and so would be avoided by any athlete who honors or respects his or her game. Violence within the rules is more difficult. Many games make a virtue of physical strength and power. In these contact sports, an important part of the game may be to inhibit your opponent's actions and movements by means of your physical strength. The critical issue has to concern injury and potential injury. It cannot enhance the game to take an opponent out of the game by injuring him or her (which is, as a matter of fact, precisely the goal of boxing). Intending to injure would thus be unfair and should be avoided. Causing pain is a different matter. It is perfectly legitimate, for instance, to try to disrupt a quarterback's play by tackling him hard but fairly. If his fear of a legitimate but painful tackle causes him to rush his game, your team has fairly gained a tactical edge. Football (and rugby and hockey and wrestling and boxing and many other sports) test physical courage and strength as part of their tests of skill. Fairness as respect for the game does not rule out as unfair games that permit the infliction of pain.

While it could be argued that such sports are barbarous and should be banned or seriously modified, that moral claim operates from outside of the sport rather than from within. As such it is not really an issue of "fair play" at all. The claim would thus need to be made on moral or social policy grounds rather than fair play. This indicates the limitations of the view that fair play is respect for the game. The concept of fair play should not be expected to provide an answer to any and every moral problem that arises in or around the practice of sport. What our approach can do is provide a framework for settling fair play issues that is grounded in the nature of sport itself.

Intimidation needs sport-by-sport analysis. It may be argued that verbal intimidation may have a place in physical sports such as those listed above. Where the intimidation takes the form of boasting about one's physical prowess and the vigorous things you intend to do, and where it takes place within or around the game, it may be unpleasant but not morally reprehensible. Where it takes place outside of the game, or in the context of noncontact sports, it seems far less appropriate. Lumpkin et al. (13) recount the case of a football coach who used to send dead flowers and obituary notices to his team's opponents and another case of tennis players coughing during the opponent's serve or deliberately failing to let their opponents warm up properly. Both examples seem somewhat pathetic, as well as inappropriate. The respect for the game model of fairness can be used to support this feeling. Do these practices enhance the playing of the game? Do they make for better sport? Do they test game-related skills? Quite obviously not, so on the grounds of fair play, they should be avoided.

It is possible to take two quite different views of rule infractions and their penalties. One view says that a rule against, for instance, handling the ball in soccer means that handling the ball is prohibited, then dictates a penalty (a direct free-kick) if the rule is broken. On this view, a player should not handle the ball. Another view says that handling the ball is generally imprudent (in sporting terms) because the cost – a direct free-kick – normally outweighs any possible benefits. But this is a defeasible condition. In some circumstances, for instance to stop a certain goal near the end of a vital game, the cost, the free-kick, may be worth paying. Such offences, as we discussed earlier, are usually referred to as "professional fouls," and the view that gives rise to them is one that values the outcome over the process of playing.

In effect these two views describe different games. In one game (soccer 1) the players do not consider handling the ball. In the other (soccer 2) handling is always an option to be assessed in light of its consequences. The two games would measure and test different skills, one of which (soccer 2) would be the tactical skill of assessing consequences of rule infractions. (For if this attitude is taken to the rule against handling the ball, it could, presumably, be taken for any rule.) Is the latter game, soccer 2, better, more skillful, more interesting to play and watch than soccer 1? Respect for the game will not dictate an answer, only a process for reasoning. Rules and our attitude toward them are constructed and can be changed. What is required is a debate and a decision that refer to the interests of the game of soccer.

While we cannot lay out this debate in its entirety, we can point to the sorts of arguments that might be raised. Soccer is a game where, relatively speaking, the play is continuous. Allowing players to constantly consider the relative cost of breaking the rule is likely to result in more rule-infractions and hence more stoppages. This would change the nature of the game for the worse. Soccer skills include dribbling the ball with the feet and beating opponents. If handling the ball is a constant option (especially outside of the penalty area), traditional soccer skills will become of less value. This will make for less skillful soccer and would be a bad thing. Of course, proponents of soccer 2 may wish to argue that the new attitude will permit the development of new skills – strategic penalty evaluation, for instance – and they will further have to argue that these developments make soccer better. As the debate gets deeper, we will come closer to the heart of what makes soccer the game that it is. We cannot specify the outcome of this debate in advance, but the ground rules for discussion are the nature and interests of soccer itself. The outcome of the debate will be a decision.

Once that decision is made, we have the content of the agreement we enter into when we play. If the soccer community decides soccer 1 is better and promulgates that view, introduces harsher penalties for relevant infractions, and

so on, it will not then be open to a player or team to play soccer 2, for that would constitute a breach of the agreement.

Respect for the game and racquetless Josie

In our analysis of the inadequacy of the rule-and agreement-based conceptions of fair play, we made use of the example of poor racquetless Josie. By now, it should be obvious that the notion of respect for the game provides ample reasons for lending Josie the racquet. At the personal level, if you respect the game, you enjoy the process of playing, competing, and testing your skills. You are intrinsically motivated to compete at your sport. You would forego a valuable experience and personal test if you decline to play Josie. At a more general level, the sport of squash is enhanced by people playing and competing at their best whenever possible. Squash at the institutional level would not be served by neglecting to play a possible and scheduled match. You should want to lend Josie your racquet.

Unfortunately, we do not have the time in this paper to explore in any depth the connections between our view of fair play and sportspersonship. (While we feel the connections are interesting, we do not feel that our account of fair play stands or falls on its relation to the concept of sportsperson.) In the context of sporting activity itself, we feel that fair play as respect for the game captures the attitude of the sportsperson. Such a person will be committed to the highest possible standards of play – or both himself or herself and his or her opponents. The attitude of the sportsperson is one that subsumes personal interest under the interests of fair and excellent play. This attitude is clearly grounded in our notion of fair play as respect for the game.

But there is more to the concept of the sportsperson than mere fair play and conduct within games. A person may be called a good sport for importing the general claims of morality into a sporting situation and for exporting a game-playing attitude outside of sport.

In the latter case, we might call someone a sportsperson if he or she demonstrated the characteristic sporting attitude in situations outside of sport. In this type of case, the person may subsume personal interests under a broader commitment to the task at hand. For instance, to return to the academic example we used above, it would be sporting for someone to pass on information about a job or position to a potential rival. The concern that any qualified person be considered and the hope that the best person get the job is an obvious extension of the principles of fair play as respect for a practice applied outside of sport.

But there is an additional use of the concept of sportsperson that does not obviously fit with our model. In cases of this type, the term is applied to someone who imports the general requirements of morality into a sporting situation. For example, in the 1988 Olympics in Seoul a Canadian yachtsman abandoned his race (when, apparently, he had an excellent chance of winning a medal) to save another yachtsman in distress. If it was indeed the case that the other man would have died without the intervention, then the action is hardly one of moral heroism. We would all agree that it is right to save a life over completing a race. However, the more likely scenario is that many of us would judge that someone else could have completed the rescue, while we go on. Our hero's actions are good sporting behavior precisely because he was not willing, even in a situation as dramatic as an Olympic final, to allow the increased risk of waiting for someone else to make the rescue. What such a person appears to have is a fine sense of the relative importance of sport. Sport can be all-absorbing, and great sport is always pursued with the utmost dedication and commitment. But in the end, it is not worth a life. It is not clear to us how this sense of sportsperson fits within our model. We do not, however, take this use of sportsperson as a counter-example to our position that fair play can best be understood as respect for the game.

Conclusion

We set out to argue that standard views and treatments of fair play were incoherent and in-

defensible. Rather than presenting a unified conception of fair play, they either present a shopping cart of miscellaneous values or fail to capture our intuitions.

Respect for the game is a rich and powerful conception of fair play. It captures our intuitive understanding of the concept while providing a fully worked-out philosophical foundation for those intuitions. Respect for the game, rather than presenting ready-made solutions to the issues of fair play, provides a process – a process that is grounded in sport – for working out what we should do.

Because of the connection between respect for the game and intrinsic motivation, the concept has its own, sport-based motivations for fairness. Teaching fair play as respect for the game increases intrinsic motivation, and teaching intrinsic motivation enhances fair play. The result is a philosophically credible and practically effective approach to fair play. Fair play as respect for the game is applicable at all levels of sport and readily lends itself to adaptation and implementation in education programs.

One could object that fair play as respect for the game preaches only to the converted. That is, it is applicable only to those who antecedently participate in sport for its own sake. It is true that fair play as respect for the game will resonate most clearly with those who already see sport in this way. We believe, however, that the approach is important even for those who do not currently have this view of sport. Our argument is both moral and psychological. On the moral side we are happy to argue that sport should be participated in for its own sake. Sport is only coherent if it is taken seriously on its own terms. The claims of fair play, however construed, will always be unheeded by those who insist on viewing sport instrumentally. (If one is not interested in sport itself, only the rewards that come from being hailed as the winner, there is no possible reason not to cheat if one thinks one can get away with it.)

From a psychological perspective and as a matter of fact, not only do people typically come to sport for intrinsic reasons, people who continue to play for intrinsic reasons have more fun. Those of us who care about sport and who care about fairness have an obligation to promote a view of sport that sees it practiced for its own sake.

Fair play as respect for the game is philosophy in action. It is an attempt to ground the treatment of actual sporting concerns and issues on philosophically sound foundations. As such it lays itself open to criticism from the members of two practices: sport and philosophy. As practitioners of both disciplines and, as we hope, good sports, we invite your criticism and collaboration as we attempt to make the world a slightly better place – through sport and through philosophy.

Acknowledgment

The authors would like to thank the Canadian Centre for Ethics in Sport for funding the research for this article.

Notes

1   Although we do not support this method of understanding fair play, one could certainly do worse than apply the four cardinal virtues – wisdom, courage, justice, and self-control (temperance) – to sporting situations.

2   We have made a similar point elsewhere. In *The Ethical Rationale for Drug-Free Sport* (19), we distinguish between arguments for banning doping that work from the "outside-in" and those that work from the "inside-out." The former rely on general moral principles and apply them to the specific issue of doping, while the latter work from principles found in sport itself. There, as here, we prefer the latter.

3   It could also be argued that games not only modify the scope of moral rules by limiting their applicability, but they also create new ways in which one can do moral wrong. On this view, intentionally handling the football during a game of soccer (assuming one is not the goalkeeper) and concealing that one did so would constitute a moral wrong, one only possible given the rules of the game of soccer. We think that what would constitute the immorality of handling the soccer ball lies in the nature of the agreement of the players to compete. As such, the immorality would come from the general prohibition against breaking one's agreements rather than from soccer, which merely provides the context and content of the agreement.

4   Suits refers to this attitude as *autotelicity* (21).

5   This argument has a long history in ethical discussions of the self-defeating nature of simplistic views of hedonism. See *Reason at Work* (3).

6   Suits refers to this as the "logical incompatibility thesis" (21).

7   We can illustrate this with an example from golf. If, when playing alone, I throw my ball out of the rough, I break a rule of golf but do no moral wrong. (Although we could say that I stop playing golf and start playing my own, modified version of golf.) If, however, I then tell others what my score was, or if I were playing against other people, without indicating my modification of the rules of golf, I would have committed the moral wrong, in the former case, of misrepresentation, or, in the latter, of breaking my agreement to compete.

8   D'Agostino refers to this as the *ethos* of the game (4).

9   For a full account of this kind of discussion see Morgan (15).

10   It could be objected that sports are, in fact, paradigm examples of activities that are inherently worthless. In the grand scheme of things, it is irrelevant whether one can adequately perform a layup or put topspin on a backhand. This debate turns on what one takes to be worthwhile. We accept the position that activities that bring pleasure or meaning to lives (provided they are not ruled out on the basis that they cause harm to others) are candidates for being classified as worthwhile. Sports are often such activities.

11   This point applies particularly to the constitutive (and regulative) rules of a sport.

12   It could be objected that only individuals capable of having experiences or sensations are capable of interests at all. In what sense, then, could a practice have interests? At best, on this account, the interests of a practice would be the aggregate of the interests of its practitioners. Obviously we reject this view. The interests of a practice in one sense do derive from the interests of persons. Practices are human enterprises. There would be no such practice if human needs, desires, or

preferences were not somehow behind the practice. But a practice takes on a life of its own and has the power to transform the lives and interests of those who participate. When this happens, the practitioner takes on the interests and values of the practice, to the extent sometimes of neglecting or abandoning other aspects of regular human life. A devotee can even sacrifice himself or herself to the practice he or she loves. In this context it is natural and helpful to talk of the interests of a practice.

13   The requirement of universality is included for two reasons. First, if we are considering the good of the game we must assume that innovations be accessible to all practitioners. Second, the contested nature of sport requires that each competitor be permitted to use the same means to achieve the goal of the game.

14   We argue elsewhere (20) that the mere presence of payment does not necessarily obliterate intrinsic motivation.

15   Similar results are also found for college athletes with scholarships. Athletes who were on athletic scholarships listed more extrinsic reasons for playing and expressed less enjoyment of their sports than did college athletes without scholarships.

16   See, for example, Fraleigh's description of a good badminton match (7: pp. 30–33).

17   This list owes much to discussions by both Fraleigh and Kretchmar.

Bibliography

1   Bredemeier, B., and D. Shields. *Character Development and Physical Activity*. Champaign, IL: Human Kinetics, 1994.

2   Czikszentimihalyi, M. *Beyond Boredom and Anxiety*. San Francisco: Jossey-Bass, 1975.

3   Feinberg, J. "Psychological Egoism." In: *Reason at Work*, S.M. Cahn, P. Kitcher, and G. Sher (Eds.). San Diego, CA: Harcourt Brace Jovanovich, 1984, pp. 25–35.

4   D'Agostino, F. "The Ethos of Games." In: *Philosophic Inquiry in Sport*, W. Morgan and K. Meier (Eds.). Champaign, IL: Human Kinetics, 1988, pp. 63–72.

5   Deci, E., and R. Ryan. *Intrinsic Motivation and Self-Determination in Human Behavior*. New York: Plenum, 1985.

6   Feezell, R. "Sportsmanship." In: *Philosophic Inquiry in Sport*, W. Morgan and K. Meier (Eds.). Champaign, IL: Human Kinetics, 1988, pp. 251–262.

7   Fraleigh, W. *Right Actions in Sport: Ethics for Contestants*. Champaign, IL: Human Kinetics, 1984.

8   Keating, J. "Sportsmanship as a Moral Category." In: *Philosophic Inquiry in Sport*, W. Morgan and K. Meier (Eds.). Champaign, IL: Human Kinetics, 1988, pp. 241–250 [reprinted here as reading 6].

9   Kretchmar, S. "From Test to Contest: An Analysis of Two Kinds of Counterpoint in Sport." In: *Philosophic Inquiry in Sport*, W. Morgan and K. Meier (Eds.). Champaign, IL: Human Kinetics, 1988, pp. 223–230.

10   Kretchmar, S. *Practical Philosophy of Sport*. Champaign, IL: Human Kinetics, 1994.

11   Leaman, O. "Cheating and Fair Play in Sport." In: *Philosophic Inquiry in Sport*, W. Morgan and K. Meier (Eds.). Champaign, IL: Human Kinetics, 1988, pp. 277–282.

12   Lehman, C. "Can Cheaters Play the Game?" In: *Philosophic Inquiry in Sport*, W. Morgan and K. Meier (Eds.). Champaign, IL: Human Kinetics, 1988, pp. 283–288.

13   Lumpkin, A., S. Stoll, and J. Beller. *Sport Ethics: Applications for Fair Play*. St. Louis, MO: Mosby, 1994.

14   MacIntyre, A. *After Virtue* (2nd ed.). Notre Dame, IN: University of Notre Dame Press, 1984.

15   McIntosh, P. *Fair Play: Ethics in Sport and Education*, London: Heinemann, 1979.

16   Morgan, W. "The Logical Incompatibility Thesis and Rules: A Reconsideration of Formalism as an Account of Games." *Journal of the Philosophy of Sport*. 24: 1–20, 1997.

17   Morgan, W., and K. Meier. *Philosophic Inquiry in Sport*. Champaign, IL: Human Kinetics, 1988.

18   Pearson, K. "Deception, Sportsmanship, and Ethics." In: *Philosophic Inquiry in Sport*, W. Morgan and K. Meier (Eds.). Champaign, IL: Human Kinetics, 1988, pp. 263–266 [reprinted here as reading 8].

19   Schneider, A., and R. Butcher. *The Ethical Rationale for Drug-Free Sport*. Ottawa, Canada: Canadian Centre for Drug-Free Sport, 1993.

20   Schneider, A., and R. Butcher. "For the Love of the Game: A Philosophical Defense of Amateurism." *Quest*. 45:460–469, 1993.

21   Suits, B. "Words on Play." *Journal of the Philosophy of Sport*. 4:117–131, 1977.

22   Suits, B. *The Grasshopper: Games, Life and Utopia*. Toronto: University of Toronto Press, 1978.
23   Vallerand, R., E. Deci, and R. Ryan. "Intrinsic Motivation in Sport." In: *Exercise and Sport Sciences Reviews* (Vol. 15), K. Pandolf (Ed.). New York: Macmillan, 1987, pp. 398–425.
24   Weiss, M., B. Bredemeier, and R. Shewchuk. "An Intrinsic/Extrinsic Motivation Scale for Youth Sport Settings: A Confirmatory Factor Analysis." *Journal of Sport Psychology*. 7:75–81, 1985.

PART IV

Sport and Drugs

CHAPTER 17

Good Competition and Drug-Enhanced Performance

Robert L. Simon

Competition in sport frequently has been defended in terms of the search for excellence in performance.[1] Top athletes, whether their motivation arises from adherence to the internal values of competition or desire for external reward, are willing to pay a heavy price in time and effort in order to achieve competitive success. When this price consists of time spent in hard practice, we are prepared to praise the athlete as a worker and true competitor. But when athletes attempt to achieve excellence through the use of performance-enhancing drugs, there is widespread condemnation. Is such condemnation justified? What is wrong with the use of drugs to achieve excellence in sport? Is prohibiting the use of performance-enhancing drugs in athletic competition justified?

The relatively widespread use of such drugs as anabolic steroids to enhance performance dates back at least to the Olympics of the 1960s, although broad public awareness of such drug use seems relatively recent. Anabolic steroids are drugs, synthetic derivatives of the male hormone testosterone, which are claimed to stimulate muscle growth and tissue repair. While claims about possible bad consequences of steroid use are controversial, the American College of Sports Medicine warns against serious side effects. These are believed to include liver damage, artherosclerosis, hypertension, personality changes, a lowered sperm count in males, and masculinization in females. Particularly frightening is that world-class athletes are reportedly taking steroids at many times the recommended medical dosage – at levels so high that, as Thomas Murray (4: p. 26) has pointed out, under "current federal regulations governing human subjects . . . no institutional review board would approve a research design that entailed giving subjects anywhere near the levels . . . used by the athletes."

The use of such high levels of a drug raises complex empirical as well as ethical issues. For example, even if steroid use at a low level does not actually enhance athletic performance, as some authorities claim, it is far from clear whether heavy use produces any positive effects on performance. At the very least, athletes who believe in the positive effects of heavy doses of steroids are not likely to be convinced by data based on more moderate intake.

As interesting as these issues are, it will be assumed in what follows that the use of certain drugs does enhance athletic performance and does carry with it some significant risk to the athlete. Although each of these assumptions may be controversial, by granting them, the discussion can concentrate on the ethical issues raised by use of performance-enhancing drugs.

I   What is a Performance-Enhancing Drug?

If we are to discuss the ethics of using drugs to enhance athletic performance, we should begin with a clear account of what counts as such a drug. Unfortunately, a formal definition is exceedingly hard to come by, precisely because it is unclear to what substances such a definition ought to apply.

If it is held to be impermissible to take steroids or amphetamines to enhance performance, what about special diets, the use of coffee to promote altertness, or the bizarre practice of "blood doping," by which runners store their own blood in a frozen state and then return it to their body before a major meet in order to increase the oxygen sent to the muscles?

It is clear that the concept of an "unnatural" or "artificial" substance will not take us very far here, since testosterone hardly is unnatural. Similarly, it is difficult to see how one's own blood can be considered artificial. In addition, we should not include on any list of forbidden substances the use of medication for legitimate reasons of health.

Moreover, what counts as a performance-enhancing drug will vary from sport to sport. For example, drinking alcohol normally will hurt performance. However, in some sports, such as riflery, it can help. This is because as a depressant, alcohol will slow down one's heart rate and allow for a steadier stance and aim.

Rather than spend considerable time and effort in what is likely to be a fruitless search for necessary conditions, we would do better to ignore borderline cases and focus on such clear drugs of concern as amphetamines and steroids. If we can understand the ethical issues that apply to use of such drugs, we might then be in a better position to handle borderline cases as well. However, it does seem that paradigm cases of the drugs that are of concern satisfy at least some of the following criteria.

1   If the user did not believe that use of the substance in the amount ingested would increase the chances of enhanced athletic performance, that substance would not be taken.
2   The substance, in the amount ingested, is believed to carry significant risk to the user.
3   The substance, in the amount ingested, is not prescribed medication taken to relieve an illness or injury.

These criteria raise no concern about the normal ingestion of such drugs as caffeine in coffee or tea, or about medication since drugs used for medicinal purposes would not fall under them (1). The use of amphetamines and steroids, on the other hand, do fall under the criteria. Blood doping seems to be a borderline case and perhaps this is as it should be. It is employed only to enhance performance, is not medication, is not part of any normal training routine, yet seems to pose no significant risk to the user.[2]

However, the important issue for our purposes is not the adequacy of the three criteria as a definition, for, as I have suggested, any search for a definition in the absence of the correct normative perspective will likely turn out to be a fruitless hunt for the nonexistent snark. Rather, the major concern is not with defining performance-enhancing drugs but with evaluating their use. In particular, it is one thing to claim that the three criteria (or any other proposed set) are satisfied to a particular degree. It is quite another to make the normative claim that use of the substance in question is morally questionable or impermissible.

Why should the use of possibly harmful drugs solely for the purpose of enhancing athletic performance be regarded as impermissible? In particular, why shouldn't individual athletes be left at liberty to pursue excellence by any means they freely choose?

II   Performance-Enhancing Drugs, Coercion, and the Harm Principle

One argument frequently advanced against the use of such performance-enhancing drugs as steroids is based on our second criterion of harm to the user. Since use of such drugs is harmful to the user, it ought to be prohibited.

However, if we accept the "harm principle," which is defended by such writers as J.S. Mill, paternalistic interference with the freedom of others is ruled out. According to the harm principle, we are entitled to interfere with the behavior of competent, consenting adults only to prevent harm to others. After all, if athletes prefer the gains that the use of drugs provide along with possible side effects to the alternative of less risk but worse performance, external interference with their freedom of choice seems unwarranted.

However, at least two possible justifications of paternalistic interference are compatible with the harm principle. First, we can argue that athletes do not give informed consent to the use of performance-enhancing drugs. Second, we can argue that the use of drugs by some athletes does harm other competitors. Let us consider each response in turn.

Informed consent

Do athletes freely choose to use such perform-ance-enhancing drugs as anabolic steroids? Con-sider, for example, professional athletes whose livelihood may depend on the quality of their performance. Athletes whose performance does not remain at peak levels may not be employed for very long. As Carolyn Thomas (6: p. 198) maintains, "the onus is on the athlete to ... consent to things that he or she would not otherwise consent to ... Coercion, however, makes the athlete vulnerable. It also takes away the athle-te's ability to act and choose freely with regard to informed consent." Since pressures on top amateur athletes in national and world-class competition may be at least as great as pressures on professionals, a comparable argument can be extended to cover them as well.

However, while this point is not without some force, we need to be careful about applying the notion of coercion too loosely. After all, no one is forced to try to become a top athlete. The reason for saying top athletes are "coerced" is that if they don't use performance-enhancing

drugs, they may not get what they want. But they still have the choice of settling for less. Indeed, to take another position is to virtually deny the competence of top athletes to give consent in a variety of sports-related areas in-cluding adoption of training regimens and scheduling. Are we to say, for example, that coaches coerce athletes into training and profes-sors coerce students into doing work for their courses? Just as students can choose not to take a college degree, so too can athletes revise their goals. It is also to suggest that *any* individual who strives for great reward is not competent to give consent, since the fear of losing such a reward amounts to a coercive pressure.

While the issue of coercion and the distinc-tion between threats and offers is highly com-plex, I would suggest that talk of coercion is problematic as long as the athlete has an accept-able alternative to continued participation in highly competitive sport. While coercion may indeed be a real problem in special cases, the burden of proof would seem to be on those who deny that top athletes *generally* are in a position to consent to practices affecting performance.

Harm to others

This rejoinder might be satisfactory, critics will object, if athletes made their choices in total isolation. The competitive realities are different, however. If some athletes use drugs, others – who on their own might refrain from becoming users – are "forced" to indulge just to remain competitive. As Manhattan track coach Fred Dwyer (3: p. 25) points out, "The result is that athletes – none of whom understandingly [*sic*], are willing to settle for second place – feel that 'if my opponent is going to get for himself that little extra, then I'm a fool not to." Athletes may feel trapped into using drugs in order to stay compe-titive. According to this argument, then, the user of performance-enhancing drugs is harming others by coercing them into becoming users as well.

While the competitive pressures to use per-formance-enhancing drugs undoubtedly are real, it is far from clear that they are unfair or improperly imposed. Suppose, for example, that some athletes embark on an especially heavy program of weight training. Are they coercing other athletes into training just as hard in order to compete? If not, why are those athletes who use steroids "coercing" others into going along?[3] Thus, if performance-enhancing drugs were available to all, no one would cheat by using them; for all would have the same opportunity and, so it would be argued, no one would be forced into drug use any more than top athletes are forced to embark on rigorous training programs.

Perhaps what bothers us about the use of drugs is that the user may be endangering his or her health. But why isn't the choice about whether the risk is worth the gain left to the individual athlete to make? After all, we don't always prohibit new training techniques just because they carry along with them some risk to health. Perhaps the stress generated by a particularly arduous training routine is more dangerous to some athletes than the possible side effects of drugs are to others?

Arguably, the charge that drug users create unfair pressures on other competitors begs the very question at issue. That is, it presupposes that such pressures are morally suspect in ways that other competitive pressures are not, when the very point at issue is whether that is the case. What is needed is some principled basis for asserting that certain competitive pressures – those generated by the use of performance-enhancing drugs – are illegitimately imposed while other competitive pressures – such as those generated by hard training – are legitimate and proper. It will not do to point out that the former pressures are generated by drug use. What is needed is an explanation of why the use of performance-enhancing drugs should be prohibited in the first place.

While such arguments, which describe a position we might call a libertarianism of sports, raise important issues, they may seem to be open to clear counter-example when applied in nonathletic contexts. Suppose for example that your co-workers choose to put in many extra hours on the job. That may put pressure on you to work overtime as well, if only to show your employer that you are just as dedicated as your colleagues. But now, suppose your fellow workers start taking dangerous stimulants to enable them to put even more hours into their jobs. Your employer then asks why you are working less than they are. You reply that you can keep up the pace only by taking dangerous drugs. Is the employer's reply, "Well, no one is forcing you to stay on the job, but if you do you had better put in as many hours as the others" really acceptable?

However, even here, intuitions are not a particularly reliable guide to principle. Suppose you have other less stressful alternatives for employment and that the extra hours the others originally work without aid of drugs generate far more harmful stress than the risk generated by the use of the stimulant? Perhaps in that case your employer is not speaking impermissibly in telling you to work harder. If not, just why does the situation change when the harmful effects are generated by drugs rather than stress? Alternatively, if we think there should be limits both on the stress generated by pressures from overtime *and* the risks created by drug use, why not treat similar risks alike, regardless of source? Similarly, in the context of sport, if our goal is to lower risk, it is far from clear that the risks imposed by performance-enhancing drugs are so great as to warrant total prohibition, while the sometimes equal risks imposed by severe training regimens are left untouched.

Harm and the protection of the young

Even if athletes at top levels of competition can give informed consent to the use of performance-enhancing drugs, and even if users do not place unfair or coercive competitive pressures on others, the harm principle may still support prohibition.

Consider, for example, the influence of the behavior of star athletes on youngsters. Might not impressionable boys and girls below the age of consent be driven to use performance-enhancing drugs in an effort to emulate top stars? Might not high school athletes turn to performance-enhancing drugs to please coaches, parents, and fans?

Unfortunately, consideration of such remote effects of drug use is far from conclusive. After all, other training techniques such as strict weight programs also may be dangerous if adopted by young athletes who are too physically immature to take the stress such programs generate. Again, what is needed is not simply a statement that a practice imposes some risk on others. Also needed is a justification for saying the risk is improperly imposed. Why restrict the freedom of top athletes rather than increase the responsibility for supervision of youngsters assigned to coaches, teachers, and parents? After all, we don't restrict the freedom of adults in numerous other areas where they may set bad examples for the young.

III Drugs and the Ideal of Competitive Sport

Our discussion so far suggests that although the charges that use of performance-enhancing drugs by some athletes harms others do warrant further examination, they amount to less than a determinative case against such drug use. However, they may have additional force when supported by an account of competitive sport which implies a distinction between appropriate and inappropriate competitive pressures. What we need, then, is an account of when risk is improperly imposed on others in sport. While I am unable to provide a full theory here, I do want to suggest a principled basis, grounded on an ethic of athletic competition, for prohibition of paradigm performance-enhancing drugs.

My suggestion, which I can only outline here, is that competition in athletics is best thought of as a mutual quest for excellence through challenge (2: pp. 133–139). Competitors are obliged to do their best so as to bring out the best in their opponents. Competitors are to present challenges to one another within the constitutive rules of the sport being played. Such an account may avoid the charges, often directed against competitive sports, that they are zero-sum games which encourage the selfish and egotistical desire to promote onself by imposing losses on others.

In addition, the ideal of sport as a *mutual* quest for excellence brings out the crucial point that a sports contest is a competition between *persons*. Within the competitive framework, each participant must respond to the choices, acts, and abilities of others – which in turn manifest past decisions about what one's priorities should be and how one's skills are to be developed. The good competitor, then, does not see opponents as things to be overcome and beaten down but rather sees them as persons whose acts call for appropriate, mutually acceptable responses. On this view, athletic competition, rather than being incompatible with respect for our opponents as persons, actually presupposes it.

However, when use of drugs leads to improved play, it is natural to say that it is not athletic ability that determines outcome but rather the efficiency with which the athlete's body reacts to the performance enhancer. But the whole point of athletic competition is to test the athletic ability of persons, not the way bodies react to drugs. In the latter case, it is not the athlete who is responsible for the gain. Enhanced performance does not result from the qualities of the athlete *qua* person, such as dedication, motivation, or courage. It does not result from innate or developed ability, which it is the point of competition to test. Rather, it results from an external factor, the ability of one's body to efficiently utilize a drug, a factor which has only a contingent and fortuitous relationship to athletic ability.[4]

Critics may react to this approach in at least two different ways. First, they may deny that drug use radically changes the point of athletic competition, which presumably is to test the physical and mental qualities of athletes in their sport. Second, they may assert that by allowing the use of performance-enhancing drugs, we expand the point of athletic competition in desirable ways. That is, they may question whether the paradigm of athletic competition to which I have appealed has any privileged moral standing. It may well be an accepted paradigm, but what makes it acceptable?

Drugs and tests of ability

Clearly, drugs such as steroids are not magic pills that guarantee success regardless of the qualities of the users. Athletes using steroids must practice just as hard as others to attain what may be only marginal benefits from use. If performance enhancers were available to all competitors, it would still be the qualities of athletes that determined the results.

While this point is not without force, neither is it decisive. Even if all athletes used drugs, they might not react to them equally. The difference in reaction might determine the difference between competitive success and failure. Hence, outcomes would be determined not by the relevant qualities of the athletes themselves but rather by the natural capacity of their bodies to react to the drug of choice.

Is this any different, the critic may reply, from other innate differences in athletes which might enable them to benefit more than others from weight training or to run faster or swing harder than others? Isn't it inconsistent to allow some kinds of innate differences to affect outcomes but not the others?

Such an objection, however, seems to ignore the point of athletic competition. The point of such competition is to select those who do run the fastest, swing the hardest, or jump the farthest. The idea is not for all to come out equally, but for differences in outcome to correlate with differences in ability and motivation. Likewise, while some athletes may be predisposed to benefit more from a given amount of weight training than others, this trait seems relevant to selection of the best athlete. Capacity to benefit from training techniques seems part of what makes one a superior athlete in a way that capacity to benefit from a drug does not.

Competition and respect for persons

At this point, a proponent of the use of performance-enhancing drugs might acknowledge that use of such drugs falls outside the prevailing paradigm of athletic competition. However, such a proponent might ask, "What is the *moral* force of such a conclusion?" Unless we

assume that the accepted paradigm not only is acceptable, but in addition that deviance from it should be prohibited, nothing follows about the ethics of the use of performance-enhancing drugs.

Indeed, some writers seem to suggest that we consider new paradigms compatible with greater freedom for athletes, including freedom to experiment with performance-enhancing drugs. W.M. Brown seems to advocate such a view when he writes,

> Won't it [drug use] change the nature of our sports and ourselves? Yes . . . But then people can choose, as they always have, to compete with those similar to themselves or those different . . . I can still make my actions an 'adventure in freedom' and 'explore the limits of my strength' however I choose to develop it. (1: p. 22)

I believe Brown has raised a point of fundamental significance here. I wish I had a fully satisfactory response to it. Since I don't, perhaps the best I can do is indicate the lines of a reply I think is worth considering, in the hope that it will stimulate further discussion and evaluation.

Where athletic competition is concerned, if all we are interested in is better and better performance, we could design robots to "run" the hundred yards in 3 seconds or hit a golf ball 500 hundred yards when necessary. But it isn't just enhanced performance that we are after. In addition, we want athletic competition to be a test of *persons*. It is not only raw ability we are testing for; it is what people do with their ability that counts at least as much. In competition itself, each competitor is reacting to the choices, strategies, and valued abilities of the other, which in turn are affected by past decisions and commitments. Arguably, athletic competition is a paradigm example of an area in which each individual competitor respects the other competitors as persons. That is, each reacts to the intelligent choices and valued characteristics of the other. These characteristics include motivation, courage, intelligence, and what might be called the metachoice of which talents and capacities are to assume priority over others for a given stage of the individual's life.

However, if outcomes are significantly affected not by such features but instead by the capacity of the body to benefit physiologically from drugs, athletes are no longer reacting to each other as persons but rather become more like competing bodies. It becomes more and more appropriate to see the opposition as things to be overcome – as mere means to be overcome in the name of victory – rather than as persons posing valuable challenges. So, insofar as the requirement that we respect each other as persons is ethically fundamental, the prevailing paradigm does enjoy a privileged perspective from the moral point of view.

It is of course true that the choice to develop one's capacity through drugs is a choice a person might make. Doesn't respect for persons require that we respect the choice to use performance enhancers as much as any other? The difficulty, I suggest, is the effect that such a choice has on the process of athletic competition itself. The use of performance-enhancing drugs in sports restricts the area in which we can be respected as persons. Although individual athletes certainly can make such a choice, there is a justification inherent in the nature of good competition for prohibiting participation by those who make such a decision. Accordingly, the use of performance-enhancing drugs should be prohibited in the name of the value of respect for persons itself.

Notes

1 This paper was presented at the Olympic Scientific Congress in Eugene, Oregon (July, 1984) as part of a symposium, sponsored by the Philosophic Society for the Study of Sport, on the use of performance-enhancing drugs in sport. Some of the material in this paper is included in Robert L. Simon, *Sports and Social Values* (Englewood Cliffs, NJ: Prentice-Hall, 1985), and published by permission of Prentice-Hall.

2 The ethical issues raised by blood doping are discussed by Perry (5).

3 The charge of coercion does seem more plausible if the athlete has no acceptable alternative but to participate. Thus, professional athletes with no other career prospects may fit the model of coercion better than, say, a young amateur weight lifter who has been accepted at law school.

4 Does this approach have the unintuitive consequence that the dietary practice of carbohydrate loading, utilized by runners, also is ethically dubious? Perhaps so, but perhaps a distinction can be made between steroid use, which changes an athlete's capabilities for athletically irrelevant reasons, and dietary practices, which enable athletes to get the most out of the ability they have.

Bibliography

1 Brown, W.M. (1980). "Ethics, Drugs and Sport." *Journal of the Philosophy of Sport*, VII, 15–23.

2 Delattre, Edward (1975). "Some Reflections on Success and Failure in Competitive Athletics." *Journal of the Philosophy of Sport*, I, 133–139.

3 Dwyer, Fred (1982). "The Real Problem: Using Drugs to Win." *The New York Times*, July 4, 2S.

4 Murray, Thomas H. (1983). "The Coercive Power of Drugs in Sports." *The Hastings Center Report*, 13, 24–30.

5 Perry, Clifton (1983). "Blood Doping and Athletic Competition." *International Journal of Applied Philosophy*, 1, 39–45.

6 Thomas, Carolyn E. (1983). *Sport in a Philosophic Context*. Philadelphia: Lea & Febiger.

CHAPTER 18

Enhancing Performance in Sports: What is Morally Permissible?

Laura Morgan

The use of some alleged "performance-enhancing" drugs and practices in sports raises a number of surprisingly complex ethical problems.[1] These problems are complicated by ethical concerns about the procedures and policies for banning substances and for enforcing such bans. My belief is that certain performance-enhancing drugs and practices do not belong in competitive sports.[2] Unfortunately, this is not an argument. It is a mere statement of my belief and nothing more. The trouble is that the existing arguments for banning certain performance-enhancing drugs do not provide adequate justification for the positions they recommend. These arguments are often inconsistent or vague, or fail to engage the important issues. So even though I agree with their conclusions, I cannot endorse them on the basis of the justifications offered thus far. In this paper, I will discuss some arguments that rely on a notion of *harm* as a way of justifying a ban on some drugs in sports. I will show that these arguments use different notions of harm, and none of them is sufficient to support its conclusion. I will then give a new argument to show that some drugs (especially anabolic steroids) ought to be banned in sports based on a notion of *harm to sport itself*. At a minimum, steroids ought to be banned because their use is in direct conflict with the ethical requirements of competition in sport.

The first step in addressing the use of performance-enhancing drugs and practices in sports is to determine which substances and practices are acceptable and which are not.[3] The target of drug bans in sports is not on all and only performance-enhancing drugs. I do not want to ban all drugs use in sports. Furthermore, I do not want to ban all performance enhancers. Some drugs and practices that enhance performance appear to be perfectly acceptable while others do not. We need a way of distinguishing the good from the bad. Several distinguishing features have been offered as candidates, but unfortunately all are inadequate in one way or another. One of the most common distinctions put forth focuses on whether or not a performance enhancer is natural. However, this dividing line does not work. Anabolic steroids are a derivative form of testosterone, which is natural, but steroids are at the top of the list for banning. On the other hand, some synthetic drugs are acceptable. Trying to draw the line on natural levels in the body does not work either, even if we set aside the difficulty associated with deciding what the standard levels should be.[4] We allow for extreme levels for some substances but not for others. For example, I can take 1,000 mg of vitamin C every day. Such a dose is far beyond any natural level in my body, but my intuitions (and current drug policies) tell us there is nothing wrong with doing this. However, if an athlete's testosterone levels are beyond a certain level, the athlete is disqualified.

The principle for distinguishing the acceptable from unacceptable must be tied to the justification for banning. For any *x*, we must ask why we want to ban *x*. This way we do not arbitrarily ban anything. Of course, we must then ask *what makes* a drug (or practice) unacceptable. The most plausible answer so far proposed is that such drugs and practices are harmful. Hence, I will focus my discussion on these arguments. However, basing justification for bans only on certain notions of harm is an inadequate approach. In discussing this approach, I will set aside the problem of developing a principled distinction between acceptable and unacceptable drugs and practices. This is because *even if* we can formulate a principled distinction, it is far from clear that we can adequately justify banning certain performance enhancers in sports. As a starting point, let me just take a substance most agree is problematic in competitive sports – anabolic steroids. From this example, I will show that there are many fatal flaws in the common harm-based arguments given for banning such drugs in sports.

Harm-based arguments can be sorted into different categories based on different senses of *harm*. Advocates for banning steroids typically rely on one of the following senses of harm in their arguments: (1) steroids are harmful to the athlete who uses them; or (2) steroids cause harm to others (other athletes, future athletes, impressionable spectators, etc.). I propose to add a third sense of harm: steroids harm the sport itself. It is this sense of harm that I will use in my argument for banning steroids in sports. By 'sport', I intend organized sports including, but not limited to, professional sports. I do not have in mind casual recreational sport. In this paper I am presupposing Jan Boxill's model of sport in its paradigmatic form.[5] On this model, sport is a voluntary activity that participants freely choose to engage in; it must be rule governed, physically challenging, and competitive.

If we accept the first sense of harm, steroids ought to be banned because these drugs result in physical harm to the athlete who takes them. For his own good, we should prohibit any athlete from using steroids. We are initiating a policy to protect the athlete from harm or danger. There are a number of problems with this justification. First of all, an argument of this nature is paternalistic; adopting a policy on these grounds would violate the autonomy of rational adults. Rational agents have the right to evaluate risks and decide for themselves whether or not they want to take on such risks. Given that people have such rights in general, they ought to have these rights in sports as well. Perhaps we could justifiably ban steroid use in children's competitive games because of harm, but such an approach is not compelling for rational adults. We do endorse paternalistic considerations for adults in certain circumstances, but it is not clear that sports competition in general could justifiably be made to fit with such situations. I do not think there are compelling reasons for protecting an athlete from such harm as steroid use for his own good. Furthermore, reasons must be offered and carefully evaluated, and I have yet to see such arguments.

Even if solid justification could be developed for overriding the autonomy of athletes in sports, there is a further problem. This does not give us reason to limit autonomy *only* during athletic contests. Steroid use is not an intrinsic feature of any sport. The dangers or harms associated with steroids really do not have anything to do with the constitutive rules of the game. Constitutive rules are the rules that define the game itself, and there is nothing in the constitutive rules that could be modified to protect an athlete from the dangers of using steroids. Harm does not result from one player doing something to another *within* the constitutive rules of the game. Steroids have nothing to do with defining the sport itself, so a ban on drugs in sports cannot be a part of the constitutive rules. Regulative rules, on the other hand, are instituted for two reasons: to promote safe play and fairness. Such rules are supposed to keep competitive play from becoming overly harmful and promote fairness in competition. The problem is that while regulative rules are supposed to promote safe *play*, steroid use is *not* a part of play itself. Steroid use is more accurately described as a *training practice*. There may be effects in the competitive game, but these effects do not directly relate to the notion of harm in this argument.[6] There is no reason to think that regulative rules must make for safe individual training. The question then becomes whether regulative rules *ought* to be construed broadly enough to apply to training practices. If so, it seems these rules must apply to any and all training practices that have risks of harm. Now our use of paternalism is getting completely out of hand. Proponents of this line of thinking are committing themselves to regulating the individual training practices of an athlete for her own good. Where is this going to stop? Can we tell an athlete she can only run a certain number of miles per week or do a certain number of sit-ups? To do so is not only absurd; it contradicts the deepest reasons we have for participating in sports. It is too much of an infringement on autonomy to be justified. We do not think anyone should be able to *control* our right to drink alcohol, eat fatty foods, sky dive, etc. Such choices are up to the individual. We should not monitor the lives of rational adults and restrict their freedom and autonomy *for their own good*. As long as another person's acts do not harm or constitute a threat to the welfare of others, we ought not to interfere.[7]

Paternalistic arguments are unpalatable mainly because we do not find it permissible to interfere in another's self-regarding acts *unless* those acts constitute a threat to the welfare of others.[8] Perhaps there is a sense in which steroid use is harmful to the welfare of others. If so, a different sort of argument can be offered with its justification invoking use of the second sense of harm. Steroids ought to be banned because they are harmful to others. There are two sub-categories of 'harm' here. In the first sense, steroid use in sports causes one athlete to harm another. This does not seem at all relevant. An athlete does not directly harm another athlete just by taking steroids. Rather, the harm is indirect. It is more accurate to go with the following kind of harm: steroids ought to be banned because allowing their use may coerce others into using steroids. The justification is not merely paternalistic; there is harm to others being considered. The problem is, this does not

seem to be our normal conception of "coercion" at all. This notion fails to distinguish an offer from a threat. In a normal coercive situation, the person would be worse off if she failed to act in the suggested way. But if an athlete chooses not to take steroids, she does not lose her property or health or basic rights. One might argue that she has a basic right to play sports and this is lost if she refuses to take steroids. It is not clear that this consequence follows, but even if it did, it is not a real moral problem. She does not have to play *this* sport at *this* level *with these particular people*. If steroids were not banned, she would have the option of playing a sport with others who did not use performance-enhancing drugs. What an athlete *might* lose if she refused to take steroids is, in the worst case, the opportunity to gain an extraordinary honor (a medal, a commercial endorsement, a large cash prize, fame, etc.). But this fails to distinguish potential loss from actual loss.[9] If a robber holds a gun to my head and says, "your money or your life," the money I lose is actually mine. This is an actual loss. But what the "coerced" athlete loses is an opportunity that is not a basic right in the first place. Great opportunities are often accompanied by great risks of one kind or another. Steroid use is just one of many risks in top-level sports competition. So it seems a ban cannot reasonably be based on the notion of coercion since the sense of coercion being used here is not morally problematic. A ban would still be paternalistic; it would seek to protect athletes for their own good and make decisions for them so they were not faced with such choices themselves.

Paternalism is only one flaw in arguments based on these senses of harm. Even if such paternalistic approaches were justifiable, other significant problems remain to be addressed. In particular, it seems that banning steroids on the basis of harm is disingenuous in some ways. There are all sorts of risks associated with sports. Obvious examples leap to mind in football, hockey, rugby, and boxing, just to name a few. No boxer steps in the ring without risking bodily harm, possibly quite severe bodily harm.[10] Risk of injury is not limited to head-to-head contact sports. There are risks of bodily harm in just about every sport – ligaments can tear in arms and legs, unintentional contact can lead to broken bones or concussions, intense activity can lead to exercise-induced asthma, and so on.[11] If the only concern about steroids is really about possible physical harm to athletes, then it seems that our approach is terribly inconsistent and ad hoc when placed against the backdrop of all risks of such harm in sports. Genuine concern about harm to athletes requires consistency in sports policies, which would require us to take a careful look at all the harmful risks that go hand in hand with sports. Accordingly, we should then adopt rules to modify all risks of equal harm consistently. Steroid use should not be singled out as a special harm without good reason to justify such an approach. We also need more information on the risk level. Suppose an athlete has a 40 percent risk of paralysis in football but only a 10 percent risk of developing liver cancer from steroid use. Which, if either, should be banned or regulated? Why focus on steroids if the risks of injury are greater from simply playing a sport in accordance with its constitutive rules? A further problem with this argument is that the concept of *harm* itself is rather vague. We do not have a clear sense of what is meant by "harm" or "danger" and therefore need to define such terms more clearly. It is often pointed out that hair growth is an adverse side effect of steroid use; however, this certainly is not harmful or dangerous in any normal sense of these terms. Liver cancer, on the other hand, is an example of a significant harm. But there is a lot of room in the middle of these effects. We need a way of comparing risks and ranking them. For example, which is a greater harm – brain damage in boxing or prostate cancer from steroid use? Non-arbitrary criteria are needed to answer such questions.

This brings me to the third sense of harm. My argument rests on this sense and is, I believe, the only plausible justification for banning steroids. If we accept this sense of harm, steroid use harms the sport itself. I have in mind at least two different ways in which this harm occurs: (1) steroid use alters the nature of sport in a negative way, and (2) steroid use violates the ethics of competition in sports. I will argue

that steroid use harms sport in both ways. Some argue that steroid use in sports is wrong because it is a form of cheating. There is a sense in which it is only cheating because we have a ban on such drugs. This is circular reasoning and not what I mean by cheating. The presumed purpose for banning steroids is to prevent an athlete from gaining an unfair advantage over others (by taking something to boost performance levels that others do not have access to). This sort of gaining an unfair advantage over one's opponent *is* a kind of cheating. We have two options: we could ban steroids or we could eliminate the unfair aspect of steroid use by making the same drugs equally available to everyone. To justify the former approach over the latter, we must look at the ways in which steroid use might be harmful to sport itself.

In looking at the nature of sport, I do not want to beg any questions. Steroid use may alter the nature of sport in ways that are morally permissible. We should not presuppose that any alteration to the nature of sport is bad or wrong. The first step is to determine that steroid use would change the nature of sport and then evaluate that change to see if it is positive, negative, or neutral. There is nothing sacred about the rules of any particular sport. Rules change all the time in various sports – to make the game more competitive, more challenging, safer, more interesting to fans, and so on. If steroids were available to all athletes, what, if anything, would change about the game itself? What are the positives of such an approach? These can be weighed against the negative risks of steroid use. If the benefits or gains are not enough to override the risks, then we ought to institute a regulative rule banning steroid use. On the other hand, if the risks are outweighed by benefits gained from allowing steroid use, then we ought to allow it and just let each athlete decide for himself whether or not he wants to use these drugs. If the outcome of positives to negatives is even, then we should allow steroid use given the ways in which a ban violates autonomy.[12]

It is not immediately obvious what improvements would be made to any sport that would offset the dangers that accompany steroid use. Do these additional risks really enhance the game in a significant way? This naturally leads to the question of what the purpose of competitive sports is. Arguably, we engage in and observe competitive sports for many reasons, which include (among other things) the following: to push the body to its limits; to have fun; to be entertained; to win; to make money (i.e. as a business); to exhibit an art form; to reinforce and demonstrate human virtues; to be creative; and to engage in free expression. A further distinction is worth making here. Paden distinguishes between the "goal" and the "object" of sports.[13] The object of sports is to win while the goal of sports is "to achieve the internal goods made possible through participation in sports." The constitutive rules of each sport define what counts as a win. The internal goods of a sport do not focus on winning and have nothing to do with money or fame. Instead, they are the virtues we associate with the ideal of athletic competition. The intrinsic ideal of sports is to promote virtue and human excellence through participation. As Boxill and others have argued, competition in sports is morally permissible and valuable when it is a mutual quest to overcome obstacles and achieve excellence.

Keeping this in mind, does adding the risks associated with steroid use really enhance the game? For example, suppose we decided to disallow ropes in the sport of mountain climbing. This adds a tremendous risk to the sport, but it certainly does not seem like a good idea. Perhaps spectators would find the sport more exciting and climbers would find it more exhilarating. But these benefits do not seem to offset the negatives of the added risk. Furthermore, these benefits are not intrinsic features of sport. Finally, failure to keep in mind the goal of sports takes away the justification for competitive sports at all.

The issue of health risk is not the only negative consequence to consider in evaluating changes to the nature of sport. If it were, then if a steroid could be formulated that did not have these bad effects, on this kind of argument, we could not ban it. The only restriction would be to make the drug equally available to all athletes to prevent any unfair advantage. Even if a harmless steroid could not be developed, if the only

negative is health risk, then it seems we must allow steroid use at levels that do not lead to harmful effects on the body. Of course, the level is going to differ from person to person, so some players will be allowed higher levels than others. I do not see why this should count as any kind of unfair advantage. After all, some people are stronger or faster than others. Some people digest carbohydrates more efficiently. Placing random constraints on certain genetic defects is not a morally justifiable practice.

Just making steroids available to all does not fully remove unfair advantages. Emphasis should be on well-matched contests and suitable opponents. This is why athletes are put in different weight classes in wrestling and boxing. To put athletes on a level playing field with one another, presumably all need to be taking steroids. If a certain shoe is allowed in a sport and it does improve performance, the playing field is not really even unless all participants are in fact wearing that shoe. The analogy does break down in some important ways here. In asking players to wear the improved shoe, we do not ask them to take on additional health risks or dangers; with steroids, we do.

Consideration of fairness and the ethics of competition require us to consider carefully an athlete's motives for taking steroids. The idea is to gain an advantage over someone else. An athlete takes these drugs hoping to improve his performance and chances of winning. At the same time, he hopes his opponent is not taking steroids. This form of disrespect for one's opponents is not morally defensible. Everyone should be treated with respect. Furthermore, your competitors in sports make it possible for you to play. Without an opponent, you have no game. Thus in the sphere of sports, respect for others entails significant obligations. If an athlete's motive for taking steroids is to take advantage of his opponent in some way, his act cannot be morally justified. Furthermore, he is failing to adhere to the standards for competing ethically by focusing exclusively on the outcome (winning) rather than on the process (achieving excellence cooperatively).

If steroids were used by *all* athletes in the sport, then the motivation for taking steroids would change. It would become something you were expected to do to ensure fair competition. The shift in motives is important here. The motives and outcomes are problematic in both cases but for different reasons. In the second case, I am motivated to take steroids because of my ethical obligations and commitments to standards of competition. I am not taking steroids to take advantage of my opponent. Instead, I am compelled to take steroids because the standards of ethical competition and sportsmanship require me to play to the best of my abilities and fully challenge my opponent. We are engaged in a mutual quest to achieve excellence. Proper respect for my opponent requires me to be a worthy opponent myself. This is problematic. If I am motivated to incur added risk of bodily harm *because* of my moral obligations to the ethics of competition, then it is my moral obligation to incur dangerous health risks. Using steroids is not a free choice to me but rather a moral obligation. This is more than counter-intuitive; it's wrong. Ethical competition ought not require an athlete to incur greater health risks from an activity that is not an intrinsic feature of the game itself.

Drug use runs counter to the ethics of good competition and undermines respect for persons. The principal value of athletic competition is not in winning but in the process of overcoming the challenge presented by a worthy opponent. What makes competition in sports morally defensible is seeing it as a mutual quest for excellence. Athletes have certain duties or obligations to their teammates and to their opponents. At a minimum, they have the same duties human beings have to one another in general. But there are additional duties that become binding due to the ethics of competition. Athletes ought to win (or lose) gracefully; treat their opponents with respect; have respect for the rules of the game; and challenge their opponents. Athletes are involved in a cooperative project to strive for excellence. Emphasis ought to be on that process and not simply on the outcome or the external rewards that go with it. Just as point shaving or taking a dive in boxing are wrong, not giving your best effort for any given game is wrong. This seems to require taking steroids if one's opponent is. But one who is morally committed to the ethics of competition and fair play should not be obligated to incur unnecessary health risks to fulfill her obligations of sport. Therefore, steroids ought to be banned.

Notes

1 There are additional problems that arise concerning policies for enforcing any drug bans. Determining whether or not mandatory drug testing can be morally justified is an important matter but one I will not address in this paper.

2 I want to include practices as well as drugs here. Blood doping is a practice used to enhance performance, not a drug. This practice raises the same questions and concerns that certain performance-enhancing drugs do.

3 I use the term "acceptable" here in a loose and general way. I do not want to beg the question about the permissibility of any substance or practice in sport. I simply want to set the stage here relying on some basic intuitions. In later sections of the paper, I will press much further on these intuitions and work toward clear and consistent definitions of terms.

4 Efforts to determine the natural or base line for any drug or chemical in the body raise a host of new problems. Athletes are not *normal*. They are supernormal or superhuman, compared to the rest of the population. Should an athlete with exercise-induced asthma be allowed to take steroids to return him to a baseline of what he would be without asthma, even if this is above the baseline for most people?

5 "The Moral Significance of Sport," printed here as the introduction.

6 Obviously most people believe there is a significant effect from steroid use.

7 Perhaps steroid use could be banned by regulative rules because of issues of fairness. I will address this option in assessing arguments based on harm to the sport. Fairness takes us away from the sense of harm as danger or damage to the individual and so is not the same kind of argument as I have been discussing so far.

8   For further discussion on this, see Robert Simon's discussion of John Stuart Mill's harm principle in *Fair Play: Sports, Values, and Society*. (Boulder, CO: Westview Press, 1991).

9   For an excellent discussion of this distinction, see Norman Fost's "Banning Drugs in Sports: A Skeptical View" in *Rethinking College Athletics*, eds Judith Andre and David James (Philadelphia, PA: Temple University Press, 1991).

10   Since 1945, more than 345 boxers (amateur and professional) have been killed in the ring. I am confident that the number of boxers sustaining serious (though not life-threatening) injuries is quite high.

11   Exercise-induced asthma is a complicated problem and somewhat indicative of the existing problems with inconsistent steroid policies. Medical use of stimulant inhalants is allowed in Olympic competition. Are athletes working themselves to extreme degrees and increasing asthma attacks? Or is the appeal of steroid inhalants somehow driving things? According to *Newsweek* (February 15, 1999), "Exercise-induced asthma has inexplicably stricken many Olympians, including 60 percent of the U.S. team in 1994."

12   There are further infringements of autonomy and privacy rights with respect to drug testing. Again, this is beyond the scope of this paper, but it does add further support for placing the burden on those who want to ban rather than those who do not.

13   See Roger Paden's "On Banning Performance Enhancing Drugs" in Andre and James, *Rethinking College Athletics*.

CHAPTER 19

Sports and Drugs: Are the Current Bans Justified?[1]

Michael Lavin

This paper explores some rationales for regulating drug use by athletes in order to determine what lessons the current drug crisis may have for philosophers of sport. I will proceed as follows. First, I distinguish between three classes of drugs in order to argue that only drugs in two of these classes raise special issues for sports. Second, I argue against some widely accepted distinctions regarding drugs, but argue that even if those distinctions are rejected it is still reasonable to be concerned about substances that give a player an edge or those which Robert Simon has called "paradigm" drugs.[2] Third, I discuss how edge-giving substances do raise issues of concern for philosophers of sport. I relate these issues to some arguments in favor of regulating, and even prohibiting, the use of certain substances by athletes. Finally, I reject those arguments, but conclude by offering a different kind of argument for regulation. My positive position strives to show that the failure of standard arguments for substance regulation does not force one to adopt the substance libertarianism of W.M. Brown (1, 2), even if one also rejects Robert Simon's contention (6) that regulation of substances may be justified in terms of *the* ideal of competitive sport.

To think clearly about drugs in sports, it is wise to distinguish three classes of drugs: (a) recreational drugs, (b) restorative drugs, and (c) additive drugs. Examples are perhaps the easiest way to grasp the differences between these three classes. Recreational drugs are drugs such as alcohol, cocaine, heroin, marijuana, and a host of other street drugs. Typically, recreational drugs are taken without medical supervision, and many are illegal. Restorative drugs, by contrast, are drugs such as aspirin and antihypertensive medications. These typically permit people suffering from a medical disorder to approximate their normal functioning. Additive drugs, such as anabolic steroids, are the third class of drugs. These drugs let users reach performance levels exceeding what they might otherwise reach when healthy.

Once one keeps these intuitive distinctions in mind, it should be relatively easy to see that recreational drugs pose no special problems for philosophers of sport, who presumably care about issues relating to sport itself or men and women qua athletes. But athletes abusing recreational drugs do not use these drugs to further their careers qua athletes any more than drug-abusing certified public accountants do. Recreational drug abuse may be a national tragedy; it is not peculiar to sports. So, it is of no special concern for the philosopher of sport.

If drugs raise special issues for the sports philosopher, then the issues relate to the use of restorative and additive drugs. It at least seems that real issues are lurking here. Athletes, far more than other people, have incentives to keep their bodies functioning at peak levels. For professional athletes, their very livelihood depends on being at their best. So, let me further investigate restorative and additive drugs.

Despite what conventional wisdom might think, in practice distinguishing restoratives from additives and drugs from nondrugs proves difficult. Consider these four items:

Item 1 – The International Olympic Committee (IOC) stripped Rick Demont of his 1972 Gold Medal in the 1500-meter Freestyle for swimming while under the influence of Marax, an antiasthma medication containing ephedrine. Ephedrine is a stimulant proscribed on the IOC's "dope list."

Item 2 – Bill Walton, formerly a star for the Portland Trailblazers, sued the team on the grounds that its doctor concealed the hazards of playing on a fractured foot. The doctor, evidentally complying with management's preference, prescribed analgesics. Walton's foot was further damaged.

Item 3 – A scandal occurred at Vanderbilt University when informed sources alleged that some players on the football team were using anabolic steroids in conjunction with their strength training.

Item 4 – Italian distance runners participated in the 1986 New York City Marathon though suspected of blood doping. This technique involves reinfusing athletes with their own red blood cells, previously removed and saved for this purpose. Although outlawed by the governing bodies of track, blood doping is presently undetectable.

These items should serve to induce at least a modest skepticism about the basis for distinguishing between (a) restorative and additive drugs and (b) drugs and nondrugs.

To begin with, consider what might be thought of as an obvious difference between restorative and additive drugs: Restorative drugs, unlike additives, do not take athletes beyond their natural potential. Hence, although Marax may seem to be a restorative, it is not, since the stimulant, ephedrine, would permit nonasthmatic athletes to exceed natural peaks. However, if a natural peak is to be the litmus test for distinguishing between restoratives and additives, it should be possible to determine what a natural peak is. The necessity of doing

this is most obvious if one is trying to determine whether an unfamiliar drug is a restorative or an additive. For athletes that will be no easy task. Athletes already engage in a multitude of practices specifically designed to take them beyond natural peaks. Nautilus training, high distance mileage, interval training, special diets, vitamin supplements, special equipment, and so on all converge to bring athletes far beyond anything remotely resembling a natural peak. If anything, the purpose of training is to improve what nature has provided.

Worse still, what is an athlete's peak, natural or otherwise? Athletic prowess is susceptible to myriad influences. Weather, time of day, training stage, age, emotional state, and so on vary constantly, but indisputably alter performance. Would one conclude that whenever an addition to an athlete's training program is followed by a peak performance, the addition counts as an additive? In that case far too many devices and drugs would count as additives. Moreover, distinguishing between restorative and additive drugs on the basis of their potential to alter performance for the good seems to lead to other undesirable results. It is indisputable that many restoratives could be used by healthy athletes with advantage. In the final analysis, who knows who might benefit from using a particular drug? In item 2, Walton made use of an analgesic in order to play in a championship match. Without the drug he could not have played at all. Healthy athletes could also use some analgesics to better their performance. After all, a common limiting condition on peak performance is pain.

Of course other proposals might successfully distinguish between restoratives and additives. For example, many people might not object to additives per se but to additives whose collateral effects are dangerous – without there being compensatory health benefits for the user. Hence restoratives do improve the health of an unhealthy athlete but do not improve the health of a healthy athlete. Additives of special interest to sports regulators would be those that place users at uncompensated health risk. Unfortunately, the notion of a health risk, as opposed to a nonhealth risk, is far from clear. Walton's use of analgesics made him more susceptible to injury, not less. In fact, it is safer for a noninjured player to play on painkillers than for an injured player to do so. The healthy player has no injury to aggravate. So the present proposal would yield the result that analgesics are additives when they are clearly restoratives. In the end, as Norman Fost (5) has noted, it is probably difficult to sustain a sharp distinction between restoratives and additives for superathletes.

Item 4 raises issues of a slightly different sort. Can drugs be distinguished from nondrugs? If blood counts as a drug, what does not? Attempts to make out a principled distinction do not inspire confidence. The federal Food and Drug Administration (FDA), which presumably has a passionate interest in the subject, opines that drugs are "articles (other than food) intended to affect the structure or any function of the body." Foods, one learns, are "articles used for food."[3] I presume articles other than drugs.

The FDA proposal has one feature easily overlooked. Drugs are identified not in terms of chemistry but in terms of intended effects. Specifying the chemistry of a substance will not enable one to distinguish drugs from foods. In practice, the FDA often has to list drugs. The current boom in designer drugs illustrates the difficulty. Drug peddlers produce a substance not on the FDA's list of controlled substances. The FDA then has to rush to get the new substance placed on the list. All of this suggests, but does not establish, that "drug" is a normative term used to identify what people buy from their pushers rather than their pharmacists, a term most likely to be used colloquially when one disapproves of a substance's effect. Simon (6), who defends regulating some drugs, is alert to this difficulty. He proposes to minimize it by limiting his attention to what he calls paradigm case drugs.[4] Although I believe it would be beneficial to stop talking about the regulation of drugs in sport and to start talking about what ought and ought not be regulated substances in sport, I doubt whether it ultimately matters whether one sides with me or with Simon on the seriousness of the definitional difficulty. Regulators in either case would have to keep in mind that there are no universally agreed upon objective criteria for identifying drugs and only drugs.

For Simon or me, the right question to ask is whether the traditional prohibitions against the use of substances such as anabolic steroids, amphetamines, and so on, Simon's paradigm drugs, are defensible. I contend that the traditional prohibitions are defensible, but not for either the traditional reasons or quite for Simon's reason.

Conventional wisdom recognizes a set of fairly common rationales as underwriting regulation of certain edge-giving substances in sport. Although other rationales certainly exist, the following are archetypical.

1 The argument from fairness: the substance gives the user an unfair advantage.
2 The argument from danger: the substance endangers the user to an undue degree.
3 The argument from coercion: the substance, if its use were permitted, would force athletes to use a dangerous substance that they would otherwise not genuinely wish to use.

These rationales are the common ones and are often jointly employed. They capture, I think, first-try justificatory defenses of traditional substance regulations in sport. Once the distinctions between drug and nondrug and restorative and additive substances are blurred, however, these rationales are far from compelling.[5]

The argument from fairness objects to the use of certain substances on the grounds that users secure an unfair advantage, and fails because it explains nothing. When athletes avail themselves of means that rules prohibit, they do act unfairly. Nobody doubts that. But the present demand is for a compelling rationale for making the use of certain substances against the rules in the first place. It is beside the point to say that use is against this or that nonconstitutive rule, for it is just such rules for which justifications are being requested. When people claim that using a particular drug is unfair, if they do not mean that its use is against the rules, they probably mean that it is either unnatural or secures players an advantage at grave risk to themselves or, ultimately, coerces others into taking those same risks.

I have already indicated above the appropriate reply to the claim that advantages secured by use of traditionally banned substances are unnatural. Many "unnatural" practices mark the athlete's regimen. It boggles the mind to believe that the routine or diet of a runner for Athletics West or a tackle for the Los Angeles Raiders is natural. In any case, the response leaves it a mystery as to why only some unnatural substances are banned. But the remaining two objections, which focus on dangers to the players, amount to the arguments from danger and coercion. I will now argue that they do not provide compelling rationales for current bans either.

Athletes striving for excellence incur health risks. High mileage jeopardizes the distance runner's knees. Sumo wrestlers become obese. Modern training regimens often keep players on the edge of injury. The phenomenon is an accepted part of athletic life. Traditional bans on drugs are, to be sure, often offered out of paternalistic concern. Sports regulators wish to protect athletes from undue risks. But serious reflection on the risks that regulators permit a player to run strongly suggests that risk alone does not select the present prohibitions and only the present prohibitions. Consider football. Players vary considerably in size and weight. These disparities, as many quarterbacks discover, can cause serious injuries. In principle, risks could be considerably reduced by placing size and weight limitations on players. That is not done. Now it might reasonably be claimed that most sports do not specify any limitations on who may or may not play in their constitutive rules. Competition is open to all. Suppose one accepts that. The principles for regulating what substances a player may ingest or inject are still difficult to justify if the justification is player safety.

As previously mentioned, players routinely resort to analgesics and anti-inflammatories, even though using them to play puts players at far higher risk than nonuse would. After all, without medicine's helping hand, in many cases the player could not play at all, which would indeed be the safest policy. To this the response may be made that it is up to the player to decide whether to play injured. But if that is

the response, it does not explain why players are allowed to determine what risks they wish to run in that case, but not, say, in the training case. A straightforward response would be that permitting players to make the latter judgment would force others, out of a desire to remain competitive, to resort to using whatever means, however dangerous, as are necessary to remain competitive. Although similar considerations might appear to apply to the use of painkillers during a match, the fact that matches are the goal of training justifies permitting players to run extraordinary risks. If that is so, then the present objection amounts to the third rationale for prohibition.

Ordinarily, philosophers who offer the arguments from danger and coercion do so on paternalistic grounds. W.M. Brown (2), for example, seems to think that substance control involves weak paternalism in Dworkin's sense (4), and hence requires that a judgment be defended that adult players are unfit to judge their own good. However, Brown overlooks that Dworkin himself recognizes that not all apparently paternalistic practices are paternalistic. Players themselves may have a collective interest in securing freedom from certain risks. To do this, players might have to relinquish the use of something they would gladly forego if they were confident that most everybody else would also relinquish its use. Hence football linemen might prefer to stop using anabolic steroids if they had assurance that their competitors would likewise abstain. But even if that is so, the resulting prohibitions would presumably not coincide with the traditional list of banned substances. When one remembers the amount of money involved in professional sports, it should be clear that the amount of risk that is rational for athletes to endure will depend, in large measure, on their pay.

Consequently, there would be considerable disagreement about which substances to ban as one moves from one sport to another. But that is not the case. Prohibited substances tend to be the same for all sports. I should add that many athletes might prefer not to stop using even highly dangerous substances for a simple reason: namely, their ability to participate in the sport at all depends on their use, say, of hormones and what not. And if some athletes win their advantage by running the risks of extra training, why may not others win them by ingesting or injecting what they want? It will not do to claim, yet again, that extra training is unnatural. An American athlete undoubtedly owes many of his advantages over third-world athletes to diet and even nutritional advice that may put him at risk. Body builders have long known this. Is there then no rationale for the current prohibitions? I believe there is. My solution builds on a suggestion of Robert Simon (6) but does not depend, as Simon's solution does, on spelling out the details of a particular ideal of competitive sport.

In one way or another, the previous rationales for banning certain substances in drugs focus on morally objectionable properties that those substances, unlike other substances, are alleged to have. The root idea seems to be that certain prohibitions on substance use are morally required. Not surprisingly, it has turned out to be very difficult indeed to justify prohibitions along these lines. Entirely too many substances, not to mention activities, have the relevantly objectionable properties. Simon (6) tries to avert this difficulty by proposing to segregate appropriately regulated substances in terms of the ideal of competitive sport. As Simon has it, sports involve a mutual quest for excellence on the part of the competitors. He sees this as an attempt to bring out the best in a *person*. Drugs circumvent this ideal by showing only whose body responded best to performance enhancers.[6]

W.M. Brown (3: pp. 33–34) has offered the obvious, and to my mind correct, objection to Simon's account. No account of the ideal of sport has good enough credentials to do the work Simon wants it to do. There is, though, an alternative route to prohibitions. It is mindful of Simon's suggestion to segregate objectionable substances in terms of the ideal of sports, but accepts Brown's charge that no current ideal has good enough credentials. The alternative begins by recognizing the permissibility of imposing certain prohibitions. Consider, to take one instance, the length of baseball bats. Nobody

could credibly claim that it is impermissible to limit the kinds of bats players use. Granted, that is an example involving a nonconstitutive rule of a particular game.

All the same, there is no reason to suppose that governing bodies of sport might not concur in what substances athletes may use. It is even relatively easy to discern a principle at work as soon as one forgets the traditional rationales. Prohibitions on what substances players may use typically do concern substances whose use endangers players or puts them at what most perceive, rightly or wrongly, to be an unfair advantage. But one further feature is involved. Prohibited substances share the property of being commonly, or at least publicly, disapproved of. Other substances may very well be just as dangerous as forbidden substances but fail to meet the test of pervasive disapproval. Nobody seriously maintains that playing on painkillers is a boon for players. It does endanger them. Still, there is very little agreement on the permissibility of regulating the use of analgesics. If there were agreement, then regulations could, I claim, be justified.

As I would want to put it, something approximating democracy operates to justify prohibitions. However, what might *explain* why certain substances become subject to democratic regulation and prohibition while others do not? It is implausible, for example, to suppose that prohibitions on the use of caffeine by track athletes reflect a puritan abhorrence for coffee, tea, or coke.

I propose that some core set of ideals of sport covertly operates to favor the adoption of certain prohibitions rather than others. Current prohibitions, then, do not capture a timeless ideal of sport. Nevertheless, they are explained, at least in part, if viewed as the product of covert, but quite commonly held, ideals of sport. Since those ideals may change, so may what is regulated. One might say that regulation is a democratic attempt to enforce and perpetuate widely accepted ideals. Insofar as the fostering of widely accepted and morally permissible ideals is defensible, the regulation and even prohibition of certain substances is also defensible. Hence, there being no one ideal of sport does not lead to Brown's pharmacological libertarianism. I believe Simon was on the right track, but his approach is needlessly ambitious if the goal is justifying the current prohibitions.

Some philosophers will undoubtedly have a patrician disdain for my proposal. After all, democracy poisoned Socrates, segregated schools, and prefers Rock to Bach. And so it is that no sane person equates what ought to be with what most people want. Accordingly, I might be asked to make assurances that my reliance on consensus does not pander to irrational aversions against the use of drugs. For consensus to justify an interference in the means athletes use to achieve their ends, the objection continues, it must be supplemented with good argument. However, since the arguments typically advanced to support drug regulation in sport are embarrassingly inadequate, my opponents might wonder what moral force the existence of a consensus without good arguments as a bodyguard can have.[7]

There is a sense in which I cannot give a fully satisfying response to this plea for good reasons. Let me suppose, though, for the sake of argument, that there would be a consensus on the desirability of regulating some subset of currently regulated substances. If there is no consensus, then my suggestion cannot serve to justify regulation. But given a consensus, I claim that its best explanation would refer to an unconsciously grasped ideal of competitive sport. It would of course require empirical investigation to determine the core content of the currently prevailing ideal or ideals. An example or two may help to get across what I have in mind.

In their own native tongue, people seldom have difficulty distinguishing grammatically correct from incorrect sentences. But few can articulate the rules employed to distinguish the one from the other. All the same, linguists such as Chomsky have demonstrated the fruitfulness of explaining linguistic competence with internalized rules. Similar strategies may help to explain moral competence. Americans, for example, tend to exhibit considerable agreement on what is right and wrong. It may be useful to try to explain such agreement on the basis of their having internalized many of the same

moral rules. Of course, as in the case of grammar, it will often be difficult for those who have internalized such rules to articulate them. Take an example: My students invariably think it wrong to sell huge whole-life policies to the retarded, but have trouble offering good arguments against the practice. Nevertheless they remain (to my mind, rightly) attached to their judgment even after I point out how bad their arguments for it are.

Now to return to the ideals of competitive sport, I conjecture that (a) there is a core of current ideals of competitive sport, (b) it will help explain the consensus on what substances to regulate, and (c) discovering it will reveal the ends in terms of which it is possible to develop good arguments justifying the regulatory consensus. That is my hypothesis.

To assess its plausibility, it is essential to keep one previously made claim in mind. Earlier I argued that the imposition of regulation on substance use may be no more than morally permissible rather than morally required. That that is so does complicate my argument. How? Suppose that research reveals a consensus on what substances are appropriate for regulation. Suppose further that investigation has identified a set of ideals of sport in terms of which substance regulations are justifiable. It is important to notice that my proposal does not require regulation of all similarly damaging substances. Rather, regulation *furthers* achieving the end of realizing the current ideals of competitive sport. And since it is unreasonable to expect that every morally permissible and effective means to an end must be adopted, the beginning of an explanation as to why similar substances do not have to receive the same regulatory treatment is at hand, namely, these regulations secure the end well enough. Only controversial principles that mandate adopting all the most efficacious, morally permissible means to an end would require regulation of all relevantly similar substances.

The situation might be compared to setting a college's curriculum. Although I am sure it would be mad to maintain that my university's general education requirements are the very best means for achieving the ideal of an educated citizen (students will not, alas, fail the republic if they no longer have to take Philosophy 1511 or college algebra), I maintain that universities may impose requirements that reasonably work to secure that ideal. If a current ideal of competitive sports exists, it could serve to justify regulation in much the same way that the ideal of an educated citizen serves to justify a university's general education requirements. The ideal rationalizes, without mandating, specific regulations or requirements.

At this point the importance of having a consensus on what substances to regulate in sports may be clearer. For without a consensus, individuals and groups subject to regulation will tend to view it as a capricious imposition of values alien to them. Unfortunately, I do not know how to specify what is required to establish that a consensus exists, but three features seem important.

First, consensus should involve widespread and shared opinions of diverse interest groups. It will not do to let owners, players, the IOC, fans, the NCAA, and so on singularly proclaim a consensus. A consensus should, then, invoke a pervasive opinion. Widespread disregard of a regulation, when combined with frequent criticism of it, is surely an excellent sign that a consensus is lacking. Second, as it becomes clearer what the current ideals of competitive sports are, the use of substances targeted for regulation should evoke a visceral dislike. An almost instinctive and pervasive dislike of a substance may be taken as a fallible indicator that its use does run contrary to the current ideal. Third, regulation should respect history. Generally there will be scant support for the regulation of longstanding practices. Democratic regulation requires that regulation be mindful of a sport's history. Regulations indifferent to history threaten to undermine regulatory authority. Regulators will be perceived as unmindful of what competition in that sport requires. Longstanding practices become, as it were, natural. These practices tend to become the context in which athletes pursue excellence in their chosen sports. But of course opinion can change with time on the desirability of continuing a practice. In the absence of these three features

of consensus, disillusionment with regulations will probably arise. Such disillusionment, in turn, will tend to express itself in abuse.

My discussion of ideals of competitive sport has assumed that these ideals do not involve morally impermissible ends. It seems reasonably safe to say that the ends are at least morally innocuous, being ends that some agents might wish to adopt. Consequently the only obvious objection to these ends must, I think, consist in saying that it is objectionable to impose them on all athletes. The insistence on a deep consensus is meant to meet this objection. What is more, it should be remembered that participation in professional and amateur sports is *voluntary* participation in a group activity. Those who do not share the core ideals of the group need not participate.

Still, one might grant that athletes should respect the prevailing ideals, but that they should be free to select the means for attaining those ideals. That claim, though, requires justification. Groups routinely set limitations on what means participants may employ for attaining a group end. So long as this is done democratically, it needs to be shown that such limitations are morally impermissible. This is especially so when no regulation would make the end less well achieved. If a group's end is to limit pollution, it may be necessary to specify what forms of polluting are permissible; otherwise, a failure to coordinate may result in a failure to achieve the end at all. Regulating substance choice by athletes, when in the pursuit of the current ideal of competitive sport, may make coordination possible. If it does, then the objection against restricting means has misfired.

This paper set out to identify drug issues of special interest to sports philosophers. To a large extent, the results have been negative. Recreational drug use poses no special issues. The common distinction between restorative and additive drugs, and for that matter between drugs and nondrugs, does not aid sports philosophers if they wish to justify regulating substances. And so it goes. But despite these negative results, justification is possible. Consensus often can do the work of reason. Sports philosophers do have a special interest in understanding the regulatory practices of sports bodies. Consensus, I believe, permits understanding in areas where that possibility seemed bleak. And although some philosophers may suspect that my proposal will be stillborn, I hope I have given reasons for rejecting that diagnosis. So, perhaps, regulating substances can be justified.

Notes

1   I wish to thank K.V. Meier and three anonymous referees for many helpful suggestions.
2   Simon (6: p. 7) believes that these drugs (a) increase the probability of superior performance, (b) put users at significant risk, and/or (c) are not prescribed for an illness or injury.
3   Cited in Fost (5: p. 6).
4   See Note 2 for what Simon takes the characteristic features of these drugs to be.
5   In fact writers less skeptical of those distinctions than I have rejected these rationales. See, for example, W.M. Brown (1) and Robert Simon (6). They differ over the appropriate response to the failure of the common rationales. Brown draws the skeptical conclusion. Simon seems to want to use an ideal of competitive sport to select out a class of unfair, coercive, or dangerous substances as appropriately subject to regulation or prohibition.
6   It should, in view of the arguments offered in this paper, be clear that Simon will have to put heavy stress on the possibility of distinguishing restoratives from additive substances. But even if he intends, as he does, to limit his concern to relatively uncontroversial instances of "restoratives," his regulatory justification is still open to the objections discussed above.
7   I am indebted to an anonymous referee for pressing me to respond to some variant of this argument.

Bibliography

1   Brown, W.M. "Drugs, Ethics, and Sport." *Journal of the Philosophy of Sport*, VII (1980), 15–23.
2   Brown, W.M. "Paternalism, Drugs, and the Nature of Sports." *Journal of the Philosophy of Sport*, XI (1984), 14–22.
3   Brown, W.M. "Comments on Simon and Fraleigh." *Journal of the Philosophy of Sport*, XI (1984), 33–35.
4   Dworkin, G. "Paternalism." *The Monist*, 56 (1972), 64–84.
5   Fost, N. "Banning Drugs in Sports: A Skeptical View." *The Hastings Center Report*, 16 (1986), n. 4, 5–10.
6   Simon, R.L. "Good Competition and Drug-Enhanced Performance." *Journal of the Philosophy of Sport*, XI (1984), 6–13 [reprinted here as reading 17].

PART V

Sport and Violence

CHAPTER 20 ——————————————————

What is Sports Violence?

Michael Smith ——————————————————

Scholarly articles on violence and aggression number in the thousands and are found in journals representing the spectrum of academic disciplines literally from anatomy to zoology. There are hundreds of books on the subject, most of them written in the past two decades. Russell (1983) has compiled a bibliography of over 650 books concerned with humans alone. Dozens of theories of violence and aggression vie for attention: genetic theories, neurophysiological theories, biochemical theories, sociobiological theories, frustration theories, learning theories, subcultural theories, ecological theories, structural theories, systems theories, not to mention "unifactor," "multifactor," and "polysystemic" theories. Given this vast range of materials, it is not altogether surprising that conceptions of violence and aggression are varied, to say the least.

Both terms are used to describe a very wide range of phenomena, from insect cannibalism to contact sports to international warfare. Almost any forceful, vigorous, assertive, exploitive, violative, or injurious behaviour may come under either heading. Violence and aggression may both be viewed as adaptive, constructive, and even creative and ennobling, enhancing an individual's, a group's, or an entire species' ability to cope with its environment. More often, however, they are seen as maladaptive, destructive, and dehumanizing.

The concepts have come to have so many meanings that they have lost a good deal of their meaning. One theorist defines violence narrowly as "the threat or exertion of physical force which could cause bodily injury" (Ball-Rokeach, 1972:101). Another defines it broadly as "any violation of the human rights of a person" (Riga, 1969:145). A third defines it mystifyingly as "extensive and radical changes within a short interval of time produced by given forces in the qualities and structures of anything" (Gotesky, 1974:146). Definitions of aggression are just as diverse.

Several interrelated factors account for the definitional and conceptual confusion. First, there are differences in perspective (and terminology) among the disciplines that make violence and aggression part of their domain. These disciplines examine different aspects of the phenomena, or the same aspect from different angles. A psychologist is interested in the personality profiles of violent criminals, a sociologist in the social conditions that generate criminal behaviour.

Second, it is probably a mistake to think of violence or aggression in unitary terms, as if all their forms were merely aspects of the same phenomenon. Research indicates increasingly that different dimensions of these behaviours stem from different sources, not any single source, such as instinct or frustration or culture, as has been claimed in the past. Edward O. Wilson (1978), founder of the new science of sociobiology, describes four completely different categories of aggression in rattlesnakes. Surely homo sapiens is at least as complex. If what are thought of as different forms of violence or aggression are in reality more different than alike, then the search for a single definition satisfactory for all purposes is futile.

Third, the concepts are loaded with moral, social, and political meanings. The assumptions of scholars regarding the goodness or badness of violence and aggression sometimes creep unwittingly into, and sometimes are explicitly stated in, their definitions. Defining violence as "illegitimate and unsanctioned" (Girvetz, 1974: 185) does not sit well with viewing it, at least in some circumstances, as justified (Audi, 1974). Popular usages of the terms vary similarly (Blumenthal et al., 1972).

All this is not to suggest that attempting to clarify what violence and aggression are is a waste of time. To the contrary, such an exercise underscores the complexity of the topic and at the same time discourages simplistic explanations and solutions. It helps reveal the range of associated issues. And it forces one to come to terms with how one wishes to employ the concepts.

Thankfully, there is also some agreement on definitions of violence and aggression, especially if the perspective is narrowed to the social sciences, particularly sociology and psychology. Aggression is usually regarded as the more generic concept. More often than not, aggression is defined as any behavior designed to injure another person, psychologically or physically. Malicious gossip is aggression; so is a punch in the nose. Violence, more often than not, refers to the physical side of aggression, hence the term "violent aggression." Violence is behavior intended to injure another person *physically*. These definitions are only rough approximations, but I shall adhere to their general sense in what follows.

The focus in this book is on violence, of all the manifestations of aggression, usually the most overt and arguably the most damaging. It is violence that people see as one of the pressing social problems of our time. Research and theory on other forms of aggression – verbal, for instance – are certainly relevant to the study of violence, but in the final analysis, violence is what we will seek to understand.

Violence is Physical

As already noted, some theorists seem to use the word violence more or less interchangeably with aggression; they speak of psychological violence, economic violence, political violence, and the like; any form of injustice is violence (see Audi, 1974:37–38). They argue that these less direct forms of coercive behaviour can be as painful and destructive as physical violence, if not more so. Groups who believe themselves oppressed sometimes justify their own use of physical violence on these grounds. But as Etzioni (1971) observes, physical violence does seem qualitatively different from other forms of violence. Being stabbed, beaten, or shot has a finality the other forms do not. And killing is the ultimate injury. Etzioni states that when it comes to being stabbed, beaten, or shot, the victim's freedom of choice in most circumstances has been eliminated, whereas with other forms of aggression, the victim ultimately has some recourse, some freedom of choice. He argues that most people, in fact, find physical violence more hurtful than psychological or economic pain, preferring a tongue-lashing or having their pay docked to being beaten. If this is so, physical violence represents the end point on a continuum of aggressive behavior: it is the most extreme form of aggression. The fact that physical violence is usually a means of last resort – a method of attaining some goal when other methods have failed, or seem likely to fail – reinforces Etzioni's contention. Philosopher Ronald Miller (1971:15) puts it forcefully, if perhaps dogmatically: "The phrase 'physical violence' is redundant. Violence is just the *physical* overpowering of a person or object with the intent to injure or destroy. There is no such thing as non-physical violence." For our purposes it would confuse the issue to label all injury-producing behaviors "violence," and I shall use the term only in its physical sense.

Three additional points: first, it goes without saying that psychological injury may accompany bodily injury induced through violence, as when one loses face after a public beating, but loss of face is in itself not violence. Second, although the offence of assault in the Canadian Criminal

Code, for example, includes threatened violence, threats are not violence in our definition. Threats are often implicated in violence, but threats are designed to produce psychological, not physical, harm and are not violence per se. Third, in dealing with individual violence, we shall be concerned only with persons as objects of attack, but in the chapters on collective violence [not reprinted here] we shall widen the focus to include attacks on property as well.

Violence and Intent

Even this rather narrow conception of violence requires considerable elaboration and qualification. To begin with, definitions of violence that hinge on the idea of *intent* to harm or injure – what Toch (1980) terms "process-centered" definitions – run immediately into several difficulties.

What exactly does "intent to injure" mean? Does it include cases in which a so-called aggressor makes no effort to *avoid* injuring a victim, as opposed to deliberately seeking the victim out? Cases in which a so-called aggressor passively *allows* a victim to sustain an injury, by not giving warning of an impending accident, say? In the first instance, the aggressor's intent is unclear (perhaps he or she was just lazy or careless), but in the second the nasty intent is rather more apparent. Yet the first aggressor took an active role in harming another, whereas the second was completely passive; the injury would probably have occurred in the aggressor's absence! Of course, if the second aggressor had *arranged* for the victim to have an accident, this would perhaps be a different story. Baron (1977) writes that one common criterion of intent is: did the harm-doer *voluntarily* injure the victim? But this raises the knotty philosophical question of whether or not any human behaviour, strictly speaking, is a matter of free will. These dilemmas are perhaps best left to legal or philosophical minds for solution, but they do suggest that the degree to which an alleged violence-doer's behaviour was active or passive, and whether the violence-doer used direct or indirect means, should be taken into account in ruling on intent (Buss, 1961).

In any case, intentions are private events, not directly observable, and thus often difficult to ascertain. People lie, they delude themselves, they are occasionally unsure what their intentions were. Rather than dealing with guilt, for instance, aggressors convince themselves that what happened was an accident, or that the victim deserved to be attacked. As Arendt (1970) has pointed out, violence always needs justification. Violence-perpetrators sometimes even become angry *after the fact*, working themselves into a state of moral indignation after an aggressive act in order to justify their conduct to themselves and others. Thus intentions sometimes have to be inferred from the nature of the allegedly violent act, from what happened before and after it, or from the social context in which the act occurred. When one man shoots another following an altercation in a bar, his intent to injure seems clear, compared to that of a football player who knocks an opposing player senseless with a hard tackle. The intensity or magnitude of the assault, the victim's expression of pain or injury, the social characteristics of the assailant and the assailed, are but a few other considerations used in judging intent (Bandura, 1973). In court cases, batteries of lawyers may spend weeks or months determining the extent to which a defendant accused of assault or homicide intended to do what was done. If convicted, punishment is meted out on this basis. This is the principle of *mens rea*, literally, "guilty mind."

Also, emphasis on intent to injure tends to divert attention from what is often called instrumental violence, in which harm-doing is not an end in itself, but only a means of achieving some other end, that is, when inflicting pain is irrelevant or secondary to securing some other goal or incentive; e.g., "cold-blooded" killing for money. One can even conceive of an aggressor wishing to *avoid* inflicting suffering, as when a parent spanks a child as a last resort, only when all else has failed, to dissuade the child from misbehaving in some way. ("This hurts me more than it hurts you.") The emphasis on intent to injure in definitions of violence probably results from the historical dominance of social psychological theories of aggression, like the frustration–aggression hypothesis and its derivatives, most of which seek to explain what is variously called hostile, affective, expressive, impulsive, angry, annoyance-motivated, nonutilitarian, or noninstrumental aggression, behaviour whose main goal *is* to cause suffering.

The distinction between hostile and instrumental violence is a false one, in any case, for all aggressive acts are instrumental, because all are designed to produce some end, whether a victim's expression of pain or the loss of his or her wallet. The difference is in the contrasting nature of the ends sought (Bandura, 1973). Zillmann-(1978) proposes that the terms "annoyance-motivated" and "incentive-motivated" aggression replace "hostile" and "instrumental" aggression. Annoyance-motivated acts would be those whose primary intent is the reduction of some noxious internal state, like frustration or anger. Incentive-motivated acts would be those whose primary goal is to obtain some extrinsic reward, like money, power, or status. Zillmann's terminology goes some way toward clarifying the semantic muddle, but the word "annoyance" is too weak to be paired with much of what we shall call violence.

It should be added that empirically these types of violence are not so easily partitioned. Because violence almost always produces a variety of outcomes for the aggressor, it is sometimes hard to determine whether the aggressor's act was primarily reinforced by signs of injury, by some noninjurious outcome, like the approval of another, or by both types of consequence. The athlete who, enraged, attacks an opposing player after a deliberate foul, not only vents anger, but may win the approbation of peers. When such approval is indirect and subtle, the aggressor's action is liable to be misjudged as motivated solely by anger, especially by observers not closely familiar with the social context in which the action took place. What Bandura (1973:4) calls "the pull of status rewards rather than the push of aggressive drive" often accounts for what seems on the surface purely hostile behaviour. Of course, a little "aggressive drive" helps get the job done, an insight provided by Georg Simmel (1955:34) in his classic work *Conflict*: "It is *expedient* to

hate the adversary with whom one fights, just as it is expedient to love a person whom one is tied to." Thus the football player, motivated by the spoils that accrue to the victors in an important game, generates as much antipathy as he can toward the "enemy"; it facilitates his task. "I never understood the real violence of the game until I played pro ball," says Jean Fugett, a professional player with the Washington Redskins. "I had to work very hard to be aggressive. I had to think stuff like 'This guy raped my mother' to get psyched and mad at the guy opposite" (Underwood, 1979:52). Coaches are aware of this basic psychology; so are military propagandists and the leaders of fighting street gangs.

Furthermore, in the same way that all aggression is instrumental, it can be argued that all aggression is "incentive-motivated," if incentive motivation is taken to mean the wish to obtain desired outcomes apart from hurting the victim, and to avoid undesired ones. But so-called noninstrumental theories of aggression either rule out or play down decision-making on the part of the aggressor, treating aggression as reflex-like instinctive, compulsive, or impulsive behaviour. Sociologist Desmond Ellis, in a forthcoming book on prison violence, challenges this position. He writes that if the anticipation of rewards or punishments for a violent act affects the probability that the act will occur, and how severe it will be, then the act is, to use Zillmann's term, incentive-motivated. Ellis argues that most violence falls into this category. Inmates' accounts of violent incidents in which they took part, for instance, almost invariably yield evidence that they were indeed aware of the consequences of their behaviour and modified it on the basis of this awareness. Illustration: a con savagely and apparently impulsively attacks another con with a heavy metal bar after the latter makes a rude sexual advance. Afterward, while admitting that he wanted to kill the offender, the first con concedes that in the back of his mind he knew he would be in jail for a very long time if he did, and this in fact caused him to throw down the lethal bar and finish the job with his boots. He was also aware that a passive response to the sexual advance would have marked him as a target for other prison "wolves." For Ellis, violence "whose probability cannot be influenced by the consequences that attend it" is what Zillmann calls annoyance-motivated, and others call noninstrumental, violence, but he finds it difficult to find an example of such violence, in prison or out. Even "going berserk" has strategic overtones. I shall employ the adjectives "hostile," "affective," and "expressive" in this book to refer to particular manifestations of violence having a strong emotional component, but I shall treat violence, both individual and collective, as motivated fundamentally by the desire to gain rewards and avoid punishments.

Hinging definitions of violence on *intent to injure* also renders somewhat ambiguous the status of third parties, those indirectly involved in the violence – the mafia boss who hires a hit man to do in a rival, the professional hockey coach who unleashes his "goon" to take out an opposing player. These third parties are certainly engaged in the production of violence, but they are at least once removed from the ultimate act. Some would insist that they themselves are not violent. The bullfight impresario Don Livinio-Stuyck was in a sense responsible for the death of several matadors and more than 15,000 bulls in Madrid's famous Plaza de Toros from about 1941 to 1946, yet was a gentle humanist who blanched at the sight of blood and who preferred to work in his garden rather than attend the fights he staged (Collins and Lapierre, 1969). Was his behaviour violent? If we insist that third parties implicated in violence are behaving violently, where does responsibility stop? Is the hockey coach's general manager violent? The team owner? The league president? The fans? (These questions are not as academic as they might seem. In 1980 an injured player brought a civil suit against the National Hockey League for creating an "unsafe work environment," a case examined later in this chapter.) We shall indeed be interested in third parties indirectly involved in violence, but we shall not define their behaviour as violence per se. What they do takes place before the violence occurs. Our working definition thus undergoes its first elaboration: violence is *physically assaultive behaviour designed to injure another person phy-*

sically. Admittedly this is not altogether satisfactory, for it may seem to exonerate third parties, while placing the entire onus on those who may be merely carrying out orders. However, we are merely trying to define violence as precisely as possible at this point. The assignment of responsibility is another matter. Perhaps, in summary, it can be said that violence is *observable*: it is done actively and directly by an assailant against a victim.

Violence and Outcome

Some of the problems inherent in dealing with the notion of intent can be bypassed by focusing entirely on the outcome of the act for the target-person. Such definitions Toch (1980) describes as "product-centered." Etzioni (1971:713), for instance, along with many others, defines violence as "an act that causes damage, often to a person, sometimes only to property." But this definition raises another set of problems, which then have to be explained away. As it stands, the definition would include purely accidental occurrences resulting in damage. It would also include damage-causing behaviour for almost universally agreed-upon prosocial ends, such as surgery to save a life, and for less widely accepted ends, such as abortion and euthanasia. On the other hand, it would exclude bungled and foiled attempts at violence: the baseball pitcher who throws deliberately at a hitter but misses, the "dusted-off" batter who charges out to attack the pitcher but is intercepted by other players. It seems more in keeping with what most people think of as violence to exclude accidents and helping behaviour and to include thwarted attempts. Yet by making these qualifications, as Etzioni and others do, the notion of *intent*, with its attendant complications, is implicitly reintroduced. My preference is to make clear at the outset that violence is behaviour *intended* to injure others, and then to deal with the problems this may entail. But I also see violence as product-centred; failed attempts, significant as they may be in the genesis of violence, are still not violence. Our basic definition undergoes its second elaboration: violence is *physically assaultive behaviour that is designed to, and does, injure another person or persons physically*.

Violence and Legitimacy

The problem of the social and moral judgements that play a part in determining whether conduct that in objective terms appears violent is labelled as such has been mentioned. This has to do with what could be called the legitimacy of violence: the extent to which violence is perceived as necessary, good, or justified, and hence not "violence." Conversely, that which is regarded as unnecessary, bad, or unjustified *is* "violence." Behaviour that gets labelled as "violence," in legal and scientific terminology, as well as in everyday language, seems to depend in large part (independently of intent to injure) on who is doing what to whom under what circumstances, and on who is doing the labelling (Ball-Rokeach, 1972).

Institutionalized violence – that carried out by individuals and groups, like the police, who are given a mandate by the state to do so – tends to be called "force." But not always. Monica Blumenthal and her colleagues (1972) at the University of Michigan, in a study of attitudes of American men toward violence, found that groups basically sympathetic to black or student protestors were more likely to label police actions against blacks and students "violence" than were groups unsympathetic to protestors; the latter tended to call the protestors' actions "violence." Corporal punishment inflicted by parents on children is another form of institutionalized violence, known widely as "discipline," but in some circles as "violence." Concerned citizens may call hockey fisticuffs "violence," but most professional players scoff at the idea. Nobody gets hurt in a hockey fight, they claim. Definitions of violence also change over time. The brutal, routine flogging of delinquent British soldiers in Wellington's nineteenth-century army was merely "discipline"; today it would be "violence" and as such clearly not tolerated (Stanage, 1974). "Spear" or "butt" tackling in North American football at one time

was simply sound technique; now some consider it "violence." Let us examine in detail what sports violence is and is not.

A Typology of Sports Violence

No rules or practice of any game whatever can make that lawful which is unlawful by the law of the land; and the law of the land says you shall not do that which is likely to cause the death of another. For instance, no persons can by agreement go out to fight with deadly weapons, doing by agreement what the law says shall not be done, and thus shelter themselves from the consequences of their acts. Therefore, in one way you need not concern yourself with the rules of football. (Hechter, 1977:444)

These were Lord Justice Bramwell's instructions to the jury in an 1878 British court case, *Regina v. Bradshaw*. A soccer player was accused of manslaughter after he charged and collided with an opposing player, who subsequently died, in a game played under Football Association rules. The defendant was acquitted, but the judge's pronouncement has been cited of late in North America by those who wish to make the point that sports should not be exempt from the laws that govern our behavior elsewhere.

Seventeen years later, in 1895, Robert Fitzsimmons engaged in a public boxing exhibition with his sparring mate, Riordan, in Syracuse, New York. Riordan was knocked unconscious by a punch to the head and died five hours later. Fitzsimmons was indicted for manslaughter. The judge directed the jury as follows:

If the rules of the game and the practices of the game are reasonable, are consented to by all engaged, are not likely to induce serious injury, or to end life, if then, as a result of the game, an accident happens, it is excusable homicide . . . (Hechter, 1977: 443)

Fitzsimmons was acquitted. What is noteworthy about this case is that the rules and practices of the game were taken into account in determining criminal liability, a precedent directly contrary to that established in *Regina v. Bradshaw*. It is the Fitzsimmons ruling that has more or less held ever since.

The fact is, sports violence has never been viewed as "real" violence. The courts, except for isolated flurries of activity, have traditionally been reluctant to touch even the most outrageous incidents of sports-related bloodletting; legal experts still flounder in their attempts to determine what constitutes violence in sports. The great majority of violence-doers and their victims, the players, even though rule-violating assaults often bring their careers to a premature close, have always accepted much of what could be called violence as "part of the game." Large segments of the public, despite the recent emergence of sports violence as a full-blown "social problem," continue to give standing ovations to performers for acts that in other contexts would be instantly condemned as criminal. An examination of sports violence that fails to consider these perspectives "does violence," as it were, to what most people, not to mention those involved with criminal justice systems, regard as violence.

Following is an attempt to answer the question: what is sports violence? I shall go about this task by constructing a typology. A typology is a device for categorizing a phenomenon into at least two types on each of one or more dimensions. In the present case, sports violence will be divided into four types, ranging roughly from greater to lesser, on a scale of *legitimacy*, as shown in Table 1. I shall take into account the viewpoints of the law, the players, and the public in so doing. This exercise is confined to acts performed by players during the game, or in its immediate context. [. . .]

Brutal body contact

This category of sports violence comprises all significant (i.e., high magnitude) body contact performed within the official rules of a given sport: tackles, blocks, body checks, collisions, legal blows of all kinds. Such contact is inherent

Table 1 A sports violence typology

Relatively legitimate	
Brutal body contact	**Borderline violence**
Conforms to the official rules of the sport, hence legal in effect under the law of the land; more or less accepted.	Violates the official rules of the sport and the law of the land, but widely accepted.

Relatively illegitimate	
Quasi-criminal violence	**Criminal violence**
Violates the official rules of the sport, the law of the land, and to a significant degree informal player norms; more or less not accepted	Violates the official rules of the sport, the law of the land, and players' informal norms; not accepted.

in sports such as boxing, wrestling, ice hockey, rugby, lacrosse, football, and to lesser degrees in soccer, basketball, water polo, team handball, and the like. It is taken for granted that when one participates in these activities one automatically accepts the inevitability of contact, also the probability of minor bodily injury, and the possibility of serious injury. In legal terms players are said to "consent" to receive such blows (*volenti non fit injuria* – to one who consents no injury is done). On the other hand, no player consents to be injured *intentionally*. Suppose a blitzing linebacker levels a quarterback with a ferocious but legal tackle; the quarterback is severely injured; a civil court case ensues. Theoretically, the law suggests, if it can be shown that the linebacker foresaw that his blow would severely injure the quarterback, hence *intended* to injure him, the linebacker is culpable. The probability of such a legal outcome, however, is close to zero. In effect, any blow administered within the formal rules of a sport is legal under the law of the land (Lambert, 1978).

Legal body contact is nevertheless of interest as violence when it develops (or as some might prefer, degenerates) into "brutality." A rising toll of injuries and deaths, followed by public expressions of alarm, then demands for reform, typically signal this condition. An "intrinsically brutal" sport like boxing always hovers not far from this point; for this reason, boxing is almost everywhere regulated by the state, albeit often inadequately. When body contact assumes an importance out of proportion to that required to play the game – when inflicting pain and punishing opponents are systematized as strategy, and viciousness and ferocity are publicly glorified – a stage of brutality can be said to have been reached. Such practices may strain the formal rules of sports, but they do not necessarily violate those rules.

Sports brutality is not a new phenomenon. The history of football, to take probably the best example, is in part a chronicle of intermittent waves of brutality, public censure, and reform. In 1893 indignation against alleged viciousness in American college football, smouldering for some time, erupted across the country. A campaign led by the magazines *Saturday Evening Post* and *The Nation* caused several institutions to drop the game, including Harvard, one of the first schools to play it on a regular intercollegiate basis. (Parke Davis [1911:98], then the University of Wisconsin coach and later a historian of the game, wrote that the reports of brutish play were somewhat exaggerated. Among the most hysterical must have been that appearing in a German publication, *Münchener Nachrichten*. This report, quoted by Davis, described the Harvard–Yale game of 1893 as "awful butchery," seven participants reportedly being carried in "dying condition" off the field with broken backs, broken legs, and lost eyes.) A popular vaudeville ditty of the day is revealing (Betts, 1974:244):

Just bring along the ambulance,
And call the Red Cross nurse,
Then ring the undertaker up,
And make him bring a hearse;
Have all the surgeons ready there,
For they'll have work today,
Oh, can't you see the football teams
Are lining up to play.

Antifootball sentiment swept the United States again in 1905. In a report somewhat more measured than the one above, a Chicago newspaper published a compilation for the 1905 season showing 18 players dead, 11 from high schools and 3 from colleges, and 159 more or less serious injuries. President Roosevelt called representatives of Yale, Harvard, and Princeton to the White House and threatened to ban the game unless its brutality was eliminated. Stormed Teddy "Rough Rider" Roosevelt, "Brutality and foul play should receive the same summary punishment given to a man who cheats at cards" (Stagg, 1927:253). Rule changes resulted, including the outlawing of the notorious V formation, and the furor abated.

Roughing up and intimidating opponents as a legal tactic, however, seems to have gained new life of late. Football is still in the vanguard. Consider the "hook," a sort of on-field mugging, whereby a defensive back in the course of making a tackle flexes his biceps and tries to catch the receiver's head in the joint between the forearm and upper arm. Professional player Jack Tatum (Tatum and Kushner, 1979:18), who likes to think that his hits "border on felonious assault," fondly recalls a well-executed hook (the tactic was outlawed soon after):

I just timed my hit. When I felt I could zero in on Riley's head at the same time the ball arrived in his hands, I moved ...Because of the momentum built up by the angles and speed of both Riley and myself, it was the best hit of my career. I heard Riley scream on impact and felt his body go limp.

The casualty rates, the ultimate result of this type of play, are not insignificant. The rate in the National Football League is said to be 100 per cent – at least one serious injury per player per season (Underwood, 1979). About 318,000 football injuries annually require hospital emergency room treatment in the United States (Philo and Stine, 1977). In the Canadian Football League, according to a survey conducted by the *Toronto Star* (November 25, 1981), 462 man-games were lost in the 1981 season owing to injury (down slightly from the year before). Observers seem to agree that the high injury rates at all levels of the game are attributable in significant measure to the way football is taught and played: brutishly.

Borderline violence

In this category are assaults that, though prohibited by the official rules of a given sport, occur routinely and are more or less accepted by all concerned. To wit: the hockey fist-fight, the late hit in football, the high tackle in soccer, the baseball knock-down pitch, basketball "body language," the sometimes vicious elbowing and bumping that takes place in track and road races. Such practices occasionally produce serious injuries, but these are usually dismissed as unfortunate accidents. Borderline violence is essentially the province of referees, umpires, and other immediate game officials, higher league officials and law enforcement authorities seldom becoming involved. Sanctions never exceed suspension from the game being played, and perhaps a fine.

Borderline violence is nonetheless illegal under civil law, as the U.S. *Restatement of Torts* makes clear (Rains, 1980:800):

Taking part in a game manifests a willingness to submit to such bodily contacts or restrictions of liberty as are permitted by its rules or usages. Participating in such a game does not manifest consent to contacts which are prohibited by rules or usages of the game if such rules or usages are designed to protect the participants and not merely to secure the better playing of the game as a test of skill. This is true although the player knows that those with or against whom he is playing are habitual violators of such rules.

Thus a football lineman who goes offside and injures his opposite number with a legal block has broken a rule designed to "secure the better playing of the game" and is not legally liable under civil law for his action. But a defensive back who hits a ball carrier just after the whistle

has blown has broken a safety rule, a rule designed "to protect the participants," and *is* liable on grounds of negligence or recklessness. Playing football does not, in the eyes of the law, include "consenting" to be the recipient of a late hit. Yet the law almost never intervenes in such cases, for reasons that will begin to emerge shortly.

Borderline violence is tolerated and justified on a number of grounds, most of which boil down to some version of the "part of the game" argument. Take hockey fisticuffs. A National Hockey League player, one of sixty interviewed in 1976–77 by the author (see Smith, 1979), provides this familiar (non)explanation:

I don't think that there's anything wrong with guys getting excited in a game and squaring off and throwing a few punches. That's just part of the game. It always has been. And you know if you tried to eliminate it, you wouldn't have hockey any more. You look at hockey from the time it was begun, guys get excited and just fight, and it's always been like that.

Naturally because fist-fighting is considered legitimate it is not defined by its practitioners as "violence." Also nobody gets hurt in a punch-up, players insist. (This is not precisely true. Of 217 "minor injuries" suffered by players on a Southern Professional Hockey League team over a three-year period in the mid-1970s, most involved the hand or forearm [fractures, sprains, lacerations, etc.] and were usually incurred during fights [Rovere et al., 1978:82].) To the majority of professional players interviewed by the author the periodic public fuss over hockey fighting is simply a product of the rantings of publicity-hungry politicians:

I think it's really blown out of proportion. A lot of these politicians trying to get somewhere are just trying to crack down on fighting to get their name in the paper. Most of the guys that say things like that don't know anything about hockey, and they're trying to talk about violence, and they don't even know what they're talking about. I don't think a punch in the head is going to hurt you, unless it's, you know, a sick thing where a guy pummels a guy into the ice and things like that.

There are, of course, more elaborate folk theories in circulation. Apologists are prone to claim, for example, that hockey fisticuffs are safety valves for aggressive impulses (usually described as "frustration") that inevitably accumulate due to the speed, the contact, the very nature of the game. Because these aggressive urges must be vented, the argument goes, if not one way then another, prohibiting fist-fighting would result in an increase in the more vicious and dangerous illegal use of the stick. In the words of John Ziegler, President of the NHL (*Toronto Star*, December 13, 1977:C2): "I do not find it unacceptable in a game where frustration is constant, for men to drop their sticks and gloves and take swings at each other. I think that kind of outlet is important for players in our games."

The logic is shaky. Would Ziegler argue that the pugnacious Philadelphia Flyers, NHL penalty leaders nine years in a row, get more penalties than other teams because they get more frustrated? Or that the Flyers are somehow compelled to respond to frustration with aggression, whereas other teams are not? Hockey may well have its frustrating moments (what sport does not?), but as researchers have repeatedly shown, human beings may or may not respond to frustration with aggression. Like most human behaviour, responses to frustration are shaped by culture and learning. "Frustration" seems more an excuse for, than a cause of, violence in hockey.

Belief in the inevitability of hockey violence generally is so entrenched that a judge in the famous Ted Green–Wayne Maki assault trials (stemming from a stick-swinging duel during a 1969 game in Ottawa that nearly ended Green's life) concluded that the game "can't be played without what normally are called assaults." Both players were acquitted, needless to say (*New York Times*, September 4, 1970:31).

As for public opinion, polls have revealed that substantial minorities find the hockey fist-fight

more or less acceptable. Just months after the Green–Maki episode, almost 40 per cent of the respondents in a Canada-wide survey sponsored by *Maclean's* magazine said they "liked to see fighting at a hockey game"; among males the figure was 46 per cent (Marshall, 1970). In a 1972 *Canadian Magazine* reader survey (over 30,000 questionnaires were returned), 32 per cent of all respondents and 38 per cent of the male respondents thought NHL players should *not* be given automatic game penalties for fighting (Grescoe, 1972). In the United States a state-wide survey of Minnesota residents conducted by Mid-Continent Surveys of Minneapolis, shortly after the 1975 assault trial in Minnesota of Boston hockey player David Forbes, found that 61 per cent of Minnesotans thought punishment for fighting in professional sports should be left to the leagues. Twenty-six per cent preferred court punishment, and 5 per cent preferred both (Hallowell and Meshbesher, 1977). More recently, 26 per cent of over 31,000 Ontario residents surveyed in 1979 responded "No" to the general question, "Do you feel there is too much violence in professional hockey?" (McPherson and Davidson, 1980).

Quasi-criminal violence

Quasi-criminal violence is that which violates not only the formal rules of a given sport (and the law of the land), but to a significant degree the informal norms of player conduct. It usually results, or could have resulted, in serious injury, which is what brings it to the attention of top league officials and generates public outrage in some quarters. This in turn puts pressure on legal authorities to become involved. League-imposed penalities for quasi-criminal violence usually go beyond the contest in question and range from suspensions from several games to lifetime bans, depending on the sport; each league seems to decide how much and what types of violence it will tolerate. Increasingly, civil legal proceedings follow, though perhaps less often than thought; up to 1978 only about ten civil suits involving personal injury in the National Football League took place; in the National Basketball Association, there were perhaps two (Horrow, 1980). Criminal proceedings, rare in the past, are occurring more frequently, but convictions remain few and far between. In 1976 the Attorney General of Ontario, after several public warnings, ordered a crackdown on violence in amateur and professional sports in the province. According to an internal memorandum provided by the Director of Regional Crown Attorneys, sixty-eight assault charges were laid in less than a year (sixty-seven in hockey, one in lacrosse), but only ten convictions were obtained, although sixteen cases were still pending at the time of the memorandum. Apparently all the convictions, and almost all the charges, were against amateur athletes. (Figure 1.1 lists some of the events that marked the

Figure 1   The emergence of hockey violence as a contemporary "social problem"

- 1969, The Green–Maki Fight: Boston's "Terrible" Ted Green and Wayne Maki of St. Louis engage in a stick duel during an exhibition game in Ottawa. Green is struck on the head by a full-swinging blow. His skull fractured, he almost dies. Both men are charged with assault causing bodily harm; in separate trials both are acquitted on grounds of self-defence. Later, naturally, Green writes a book about his experience.
- 1972, The First Canada–Russia Hockey Series: amid accusations and counteraccusations of dirty play, Canada's truculent Bobby Clarke eliminates the Russian star, Kharmalov, from the remainder of the series with a blatant two-handed stick-swipe across the ankle. Canada has exported hockey violence for years, but never before has it been witnessed by quite so many millions of television viewers. Reaction in the mass media is mixed: some commentators glorify Clarke for his insatiable "desire"; others express embarrassment; a handful, shame.
- 1973, The Paul Smithers Case: Smithers, a seventeen-year-old, black hockey player, engages an opposing player in a scuffle outside a Toronto arena following a raucous Midget hockey game. Kicked in the groin, the other boy collapses, chokes on his own vomit, dies. Smithers is convicted of manslaughter and sentenced to six months in jail, a decision causing bitter and prolonged public controversy.
- 1974, The Hamilton–Bramalea Game: players, officials, and spectators brawl throughout this Ontario Junior B playoff game in which 189 penalty minutes are assessed and five players and one team official are injured. Fourteen policemen finally quell the fighting. The Bramalea team withdraws from the playoffs and is promptly suspended by the Ontario Hockey Association, which finds no justification for the team's refusal to play because, it claims, the game was not as violent as many others in recent years.
- 1974, The Ontario Government Inquiry and Investigation into Violence in Amateur Hockey: Toronto lawyer William McMurtry is commissioned by the province to investigate violence in amateur hockey. In an extensive investigation, culminating in five days of public hearings and producing a 1,256-page transcript, McMurtry concludes that professional hockey is the number one cause of amateur hockey violence. His report is widely circulated and hotly debated.
- 1975, The Forbes–Boucha Case: Boston's Dave Forbes and Minnesota's Henry Boucha engage in a minor altercation for which both are penalized. Forbes threatens Boucha from the penalty box; then, leaving the box at the expiration of the penalties, lunges at Boucha from behind, striking him near the right eye with the butt end of his stick. Boucha falls to his knees, hands over face; Forbes jumps on his back, punching, until pulled off by another player. Boucha is taken to the hospital, where he receives twenty-five stitches and the first of several eye operations. Forbes is indicted for criminal assault in Minnesota, the first criminal prosecution against a professional athlete in the U.S., but a hung jury results in the case being dismissed.
- 1975, The Maloney–Glennie Fight: Toronto Maple Leaf Brian Glennie body-checks a

Detroit player. In retaliation, Detroit's quick-fisted Dan Maloney knocks Glennie down with a forearm blow, punches him repeatedly, and allegedly bounces his head several times on the ice. Glennie goes to the hospital with a concussion and other injuries. Maloney is charged with assault causing bodily harm. Hung jury, charges dropped.

– 1975, Establishment of the Ontario Hockey Council: the functions of this quasi-governmental body are to improve and over-see amateur hockey in the province. Among other steps, it forms a parents' education committee. The committee produces a book-let, *You and Your Child in Hockey*, which con-tains several antiviolence messages. *You and Your Child* goes through three revisions be-tween 1975 and 1980, as over a quarter mil-lion copies are distributed in Ontario arenas.

– 1976, The Jodzio–Tardif Beating: in a World Hockey Association playoff game, Calgary Cowboys' Rick Jodzio administers a devastat-ing beating to top scorer Marc Tardif of the Quebec Nordiques. Both benches empty, and a wild, half-hour melee ensues. Tardif, un-conscious, with a severe concussion and other injuries, is out for the season. Quebec threatens to withdraw from the series unless (1) Jodzio is suspended for life, (2) the Cal-gary coach is suspended for the rest of the playoffs, (3) the League president (the official observer at this game) is fired or resigns. The demands are met in part, and the series con-tinues. Jodzio is charged in Quebec with caus-ing bodily harm with intent to wound. He pleads guilty to a lesser charge and is fined $3,000.

– 1976, The Philadelphia–Toronto Playoff: in a brawl-filled playoff contest in Toronto (resulting in a new Philadelphia penalty record) Toronto's Borje Salming, a Swedish nonfighter, is badly beaten by Philadelphia's Mel Bridgman. Further brouhahas involving players, fans, and a policeman result in four Philadelphia players being charged – on the orders of Ontario's Attorney General Roy McMurtry – with criminal offences, from possession of a dangerous weapon (a hockey stick) to assaulting a police officer. The hockey establishment, insisting it can look after its own affairs, accuses McMurtry of headline-seeking, but considerable support for his actions is registered in other quarters. Two of the players subsequently plead guilty and are fined; the charges against the two others are dropped.

– 1977, Rapport Néron: the Quebec government conducts an investigation into violence in amateur hockey. The 325-page final report includes recommendations to remove violence from the game, including a "code d'éthique" for players, coaches, managers, parents, spec-tators, the press, and arena managers.

– 1980, The McPherson–Davidson Report: this Ontario Hockey Council-sponsored report, based on a massive mail survey and thirty-one public forums held throughout the pro-vince, contains twenty pages of recommenda-tions designed to improve youth hockey. Some of the recommendations are aimed at reducing violence on the ice and abusive be-haviour in the stands.

– 1980, No-Contact Rule for Kids: the Canadian Amateur Hockey Association bans body-checking for players twelve years and under.

– 1983, The Sports Violence Arbitration Act: this legislation, recently introduced in the U.S. Congress, seeks to establish a civil arbi-tration system "for the settlement of griev-ances resulting from violent conduct" in major professional team sports, including hockey. A similar bill, the Sports Violence Act, would make "excessive" player violence a criminal offence and is presently being con-sidered by the House Judiciary Subcommittee on Crime (see Horrow, 1982).

emergence and eventual institutionalization of hockey violence as a contemporary, albeit not a new [Hallowell, 1978], social problem.)

Still, a small number of episodes of quasi-criminal violence in professional sports have resulted in litigation, and it is these cases that have generated the greatest publicity. Several civil disputes have received continent-wide at-tention. One of the first in sport's modern era took place in baseball during a 1965 game between the San Francisco Giants and the Los Angeles Dodgers. Giant batter Juan Marichal felled Dodger catcher John Roseboro with his bat following an acrimonious verbal exchange. Roseboro sustained considerable injury; Marichal was fined $1,750 by the League and suspended for eight games. Roseboro filed a $110,000 civil suit for damages against Marichal and the San Francisco club; it was reportedly settled out of court for $7,500 (Kuhlman, 1975).

A decade and a half later, in 1979, Houston Rocket basketball player Rudy Tomjanovich was awarded the whopping sum of $3.25 million dollars in a civil suit for injuries received as a result of a single, devastating punch thrown by Kermit Washington of the Los Angeles Lakers during a 1977 game, a blow described by a Laker assistant coach as "the hardest punch in the history of mankind." Tomjanovich suffered a fractured jaw, nose, and skull, severe lacerations, a cerebral concussion, and was not surprisingly out for the season. The League Commissioner suspended Washington for sixty days and fined him $10,000. The jury, in making an award of more than half a million dollars above what Tomjanovich's attorneys had demanded, found that Washington had acted "intentionally," "maliciously," and "with reckless disregard for the safety of others." The Lakers as an organization were deemed negligent because they "failed to adequately train and supervise Washington," even though they were aware that "he had a tendency for violence while playing basketball" (nine fights in four years, according to the plaintiff's attorneys). The Lakers paid (Horrow, 1981; Rains, 1980).

A similar case is one that began in 1975, *Hackbart* v. *Cincinnati Bengals Inc.* This litigation arose out of an incident in a National Football League game in 1973 in which the plaintiff, Dale Hackbart of the Denver Broncos, was given an illegal forearm blow on the back of the head by an opposing player, Charles Clark of the Cincinnati Bengals, in a "malicious and wanton" manner five seconds after the play had been whistled dead. The referees did not see the action, and no penalty was called. Hackbart returned to the sidelines, but later discovered he had suffered a career-ending spinal fracture.

The district court ruled that Hackbart had taken an implied risk by playing a violent game and that "anything" happening to him "between the sidelines" was part of that risk. The case was dismissed. But an appeals court reversed this decision, stating that although Clark may not have specifically intended to injure, he had engaged in "reckless misconduct"; the accountability of his employer (the Cincinnati Bengals) could therefore now be legally considered (Gulotta, 1980; Rains, 1980). New proceedings have apparently been scheduled. The way now seems clear for a professional sports team, as an employer, to be held accountable under civil law for the actions of the players, its employees. (An alternative approach, the Sports Violence Arbitration Act of 1983, is now before the U.S. Congress. This act would force each major professional sports league to establish an arbitration board with the power to discipline players for using "excessively violent conduct" and to make their teams financially liable for injuries suffered by the victims.)

In none of the above cases were criminal charges laid. Why this near immunity to criminal prosecution and conviction? First, most players seem reluctant to bring charges against another athlete. Based on a mail survey of 1,400 major-league basketball, football, and hockey players (no response rate is given), Horrow (1980) concludes that professional athletes, in particular, tend to believe that player disputes are best settled privately and personally on the field of play; that team management does not appreciate "troublemakers" who go "outside the family" (i.e., the league) for justice, and contract difficulties or worse probably await such individuals; that the sheer disruptiveness of litigation can ruin careers, and so on. Bolstering these beliefs is the apparent willingness of most players to dismiss virtually and during-the-match assault short of using a gun or a knife as part of the game.

From the point of view of the law, says Horrow, based on information obtained from twenty United States county prosecutors, in whose jurisdictions most of the country's major professional teams operate, many officials are reluctant to prosecute sports violence because they believe that they have more important things to do, like prosecuting "real" criminals; that the leagues themselves can more efficiently and effectively control player misbehaviour; that civil law proceedings are better suited than criminal for dealing with an injured player's grievances; that most lawyers do not have the expertise to handle sports violence cases; and that it is almost impossible to get a guilty verdict anyway.

There are two other more subtle, nonlegal reasons for the hands-off policy of criminal justice officials. One is the "community subgroup rationale." As explained by Kuhlman (1975), this is the tacit recognition by law enforcement authorities that certain illegal activities by members of some social groups ought more or less to be tolerated because they are widespread within the group and because group members look upon them as less serious than does society in general. Moreover, it would be unfair to single out and punish an individual member when almost everyone else in the group behaves similarly. In other words, the illegal conduct is rendered less criminal because everybody does it. This rationale sometimes arises in connection with the issue of differential law enforcement for minority groups. In some tough police jurisdictions, for instance, police rarely make an arrest for felonious assault involving family members and neighbours, even though such assaults are frequent. Police in these areas tend to define domestic violence as a mere "disturbance," whereas officers in other jurisdictions are more inclined to define it as genuine violence. It seems that certain assaultive practices in sports are looked upon with the same benevolent tolerance. At the very least, the severity of the penalties for violence provided by the law are widely regarded within the legal community, as well as the sports community, as out of proportion to the seriousness of the illegal acts.

The "continuing relationship rationale" applies in assault cases where offender and victim have a ongoing relationship. Legal authorities may wish to avoid straining the relationship further by prosecuting one or both parties. Husbands and wives may wish to continue living together; neighbours may have to; athletes typically compete against each other at regular intervals (Kuhlman, 1975). Criminal prosecution in sport could exacerbate already-present hostility to the point where league harmony is seriously threatened. The 1976 prosecutions on various assault charges of four Philadelphia Flyers hockey players, arising out of a game in Toronto, caused considerable strain between the Philadelphia and Toronto Maple Leafs hockey clubs, and even a public squabble between the Philadelphia District Attorney and the Ontario Attorney General (*Toronto Star*, April 22, 1976). The assumption underlying this rationale is that society has an interest in maintaining such social relationships, that professional sport in this instance serves some socially useful purpose.

Finally there is the premise of "legal individualism" – the notion that the individual is *wholly* responsible for his or her own criminal acts – which has resulted in a virtual immunity to criminal charges of sports organizations in cases where an individual member of the organization has been indicted for assault. The leading case is *State* v. *Forbes*, apparently the only criminal prosecution ever of a professional athlete in the United States.

On January 4, 1975, during an NHL game in Bloomington, Minnesota, an altercation occurred between David Forbes of the Boston Bruins and Henry Boucha of the Minnesota North Stars. Both players were sent to the penalty box, where Forbes repeatedly threatened Boucha verbally. As they left the box at the expiration of the penalties – Boucha first and Forbes seconds later – Forbes skated up behind Boucha and struck him with the butt end of his stick just above the right eye. Boucha fell to the ice stunned and bleeding (with a badly damaged eye, it turned out). Forbes jumped on him, punched him on the back of the head, then grabbing him by the hair, proceeded to pound his head into the ice. Eventually another Minnesota player separated the two. The President of the NHL suspended Forbes for ten games, but shortly afterward a Minnesota grand jury charged him with the crime of aggravated assault by use of a dangerous weapon. Forbes pleaded not guilty. The jury, after a week and a half of testimony and eighteen hours of deliberation, was unable to reach a unanimous verdict. The court declared a mistrial, and the case was dismissed (Flakne and Caplan, 1977).

Described in law journals as a "landmark" case because it focused so much legal and public attention on the issue of violence in sports, *State v. Forbes* also raised the important and still unanswered question of legal individualism as it applies to the occupational use of violence; namely, who should be held responsible in such cases, the individual or the group? Should not only Forbes, but the Boston Bruins and even the League, have been on trial? Was Forbes merely doing his job, his duty, as a good hockey soldier? The defence counsel tried to ask these questions during the trial, to instruct the jury to consider, for example, the "context" in which the assault took place, but the judge demurred, insisting the indictment applied only to Forbes, the individual (Hallowell and Meshbesher, 1977).

The public, too, is divided on legal individualism, if an opinion poll conducted shortly after Forbes' trial, and regarding accountability in the trial of Lieutenant Calley of My Lai massacre notoriety, is any indicator. As reported by Hallowell and Meshbesher (1977), 58 per cent of the respondents in this survey disapproved of criminal sanctions being applied to an individual acting in a legitimate role and following what that individual believed to be "at least implicit orders." Are orders to perform acts of violence implicit in professional hockey? The question should be: how explicit are such orders?

As for legally raising (let alone demonstrating) criminal liability on the part of an employer in sports violence disputes, Kuhlman (1975) suggests that although problems of proof are substantial (the burden of proof on the prosecution in a criminal trial is heavier than in a civil trial), the most promising route is probably via the statutes on conspiracy; that is, the prosecution should attempt to prove that the organization and the individual conspired to commit an assault. Owners, coaches, and teammates – all members of the "system" – are thus potentially implicated; sociological reality becomes legal fact.

By way of a footnote to *State v. Forbes*, the author was engaged in 1980 by the Detroit law firm of Dykema, Gossett, Spencer, Goodnow,

and Trigg as a consultant and "expert witness" in a civil suit being brought by Boucha against the Boston Bruins and the NHL. (After several only partly successful eye operations, Boucha's career had ground to a halt.) The charge was, in effect, "creating an unsafe work environment." The case was settled out of court for an undisclosed amount two days before the trial was to begin in Detroit.

Criminal violence

This category consists of violence so serious and obviously outside the boundaries of what could be considered part of the game that it is handled from the outset by the law. Death is often involved, as in the 1973 Paul Smithers case, which received world-wide publicity. Smithers, a seventeen-year-old black hockey player, was convicted of manslaughter after killing an opposing player in a fight in a Toronto arena parking lot following a game (Runfola, 1974). Almost always such incidents, though closely tied to game events, take place prior to or after the contest itself. (One suspects that if Smithers' attack had occurred during the game he would have received a five-minute or match penalty, and the victim's death would have been dismissed as an "unfortunate accident.") On the extreme fringe of this category are assaults and homicides only incidentally taking place in a sports setting.

An extended, first-hand account of another hockey incident provides an illustration of a typical episode of criminal violence in sports, while at the same time conveying something about a social milieu that encourages such misbehaviour. This assault took place in a Toronto arena after the final game of a Midget playoff series that had been marred by bad behaviour in the stands and on the ice, including physical and verbal attacks on opposing players by the assailant in question. The victim was the coach of the winning team. He had been ejected from the game for making a rude gesture at the referee and was standing against the boards some distance from his team's bench when the assault took place. He also happened to be a student at York University. Three days after the incident he came to my office seeking some advice, his face barely recognizable. He left promising to lay an assault charge, which he had not yet done, and to write down in detail his version of what happened. He did both. (The offending player was later convicted of assault.) An excerpt from his six-page account (with fictitious names) is presented in Figure 2.

Figure 2 Criminal violence in hockey

At the final buzzer the parents applauded their sons' victory and the players of our team all left the bench to congratulate the goalie who was down at our end. Out of the corner of my eye I picked up Jones making a wide circle in our end and heading directly over toward me. My only thought was that he would skate over and continue his usual swearing and animal-like antics.

I was wrong. He let his stick drag behind him and with the stick in his left hand he took a full swing with it and made contact across my face. The force of the blow was further increased by the heavy heel-end of the stick, which made contact across my nose, just below my eyes. I went partly down against the seat. Some parents came to my aid, while others, including a couple of impartial fans, went on the ice after the boy, along with my players. Parents from both teams tangled as everyone seemed intent on getting to Jones. I was mostly concerned with the safety of my players and getting them into the dressing room. While I stood bleeding profusely from a widely gashed and multiple-fractured nose, I was approached by an impartial spectator, James Turner, who stated that he had seen the whole incident along with Al Marks and that he was going to call the police. He stated that if charges were laid he would be a witness. stating the whole story as he saw it as an unbiased observer. There is also at least one other impartial witness, along with almost all the parents and some friends of our players. A linesman saw the whole incident also, and the referee supervisor of the league told my assistant coach, who was coaching the team at the time, that it was the "most brutal thing I've ever seen."

After answering the questions of the police who arrived approximately twenty to thirty minutes after the incident, and telling my version of the incident, I was taken to North York General Hospital where I was examined first by a nurse and then by the doctor in emergency at the time. He ordered X-rays, which showed a compound fracture of the nose. After stitching the cuts across my nose and under my eye, he showed his disgust and anger at such incidents by informing me that he hoped charges were laid and law suits following. Charges of assault causing bodily harm have now been laid. He really shook me up by telling me that I was actually a very lucky person, because if I had turned my head perhaps a half-inch either way, I might very likely have been killed by such a blow to the temple or forehead. He informed me that the usual procedure for this type of fracture was to wait for three to five days for the swelling to go down and then have it set by a plastic surgeon. Later he suggested I come in that morning at 8:00 a.m. to see the head of plastic surgery. I have an appointment to see him next Tuesday, April 4th. Ever since the incident, I have had little if any sleep, a constant headache, a case of bad nerves, constant shaking, mental strain, and depression has begun to set in due to my thoughts about upcoming exams and activities at school. I have been unable to eat and at this point in time feel like a physical wreck, and the thought of almost being killed in such an incident has loomed on my mind a great deal.

The fact that no apology has been offered by the player, parents, or organization, let alone concern for my health, leaves me also with a bitter feeling for those involved or associated with this assault. I don't feel the boy is as much to blame as the coach who sanctioned and reinforced this type of behavior, the parents who didn't attempt to discourage him from playing this style of hockey, and the Wallbury organization which seems to condone this type of play throughout their organization. The fact that the boy's father was drunk at this incident only leaves me feeling more sorry for this boy and the environment he has been a product of.

Conclusion

What is called violence and what is not is no trival matter. The extent to which a behaviour is perceived as violence has a great deal to do with what people are willing to do about it. As philosopher Robert Audi (1974:38) puts it in his essay "Violence, legal sanctions, and the law": "Misnaming the disease can lead to the use of the wrong medicine or none at all." Perhaps we are close to being able to say with some clarity what sports violence is. We may soon know with greater certainty what to do about it.

References

Arendt, H. (1970) *On Violence*. New York: Harcourt, Brace and World.

Audi, R. (1974) "Violence, legal sanctions, and the law." In S.M. Stanage, ed., *Reason and Violence*. Totowa, New Jersey: Littlefield, Adams.

Ball-Rokeach, S.J. (1972) "The legitimation of violence." In J.F. Short and M.E. Wolfgang, eds., *Collective Violence*. Chicago: Aldine-Atherton.

Bandura, A. (1973) *Aggression: A Social Learning Analysis*. Englewood Cliffs, New Jersey: Prentice-Hall.

Baron, R.A. (1977) *Human Aggression*. New York: Plenum.

Betts, J.R. (1974) *America's Sporting Heritage: 1850–1950*. Reading, Massachusetts: Addison-Wesley.

Blumenthal, M.D., R.L. Kahn, F.M. Andrews, and K.B. Head (1972) *Justifying Violence: Attitudes of American Men*. Ann Arbor: Institute for Social Research, University of Michigan.

Buss, A.H. (1961) *The Psychology of Aggression*. New York: Wiley.

Collins, L., and D. LaPierre (1969) *Or I'll Dress You in Mourning*. Toronto: Signet.

Davis, P.H. (1971) *Football: The American Intercollegiate Game*. New York: Charles Scribner's Sons.

Etzioni, A. (1971) "Violence." In R.K. Merton and R. Nisbet, eds., *Contemporary Social Problems*. 3rd ed. New York: Harcourt, Brace, Jovanovich.

Flakne, G.W., and A.H. Caplan (1977) "Sports violence and the prosecution." *Trial* 13: 33–35.

Girvetz, H. (1974) "An anatomy of violence." In S.M. Stanage, ed., *Reason and Violence*. Totowa, New Jersey: Littlefield, Adams.

Gotesky, R. (1974) "Social force, social power, and social violence." In S.M. Stanage, ed., *Reason and Violence*. Totowa, New Jersey: Littlefield, Adams.

Grescoe, P. (1972) "We asked you six questions." *Canadian Magazine*, January 29: 2–4.

Gulotta, S.L. (1980) "Torts in sports – deterring violence in professional athletics." *Fordham Law Review* 48: 764–93.

Hallowell, L. (1978) "Violent work and the criminal law: an historical study of professional ice hockey." In J.A. Inciardi and A.E. Pottieger, eds., *Violent Crime: Historical and Contemporary Issues*. Beverly Hills: Sage.

Hallowell, L., and R.L. Meshbesher (1977) "Sports violence and the criminal law." *Trial* 13: 27–32.

Hechter, W. (1977) "The criminal law and violence in sports." *The Criminal Law Quarterly* 19: 425–53.

Horrow, R.B. (1980) *Sports Violence: The Interaction between Private Law-Making and the Criminal Law*. Arlington, Virginia: Carrollton Press.

Horrow, R.B. (1981) "The legal perspective: interaction between private lawmaking and the civil and criminal law." *Journal of Sport and Social Issues* 5: 9–18.

Horrow, R.B. (1982) "Violence in professional sports: is it part of the game?" *Journal of Legislation* 9: 1–15.

Kuhlman, W. (1975) "Violence in professional sports." *Wisconsin Law Review* 3: 771–90.

Lambert, D.J. (1978) "Tort law and participant sports: the line between vigor and violence." *Journal of Contemporary Law* 4:211–17.

Marshall, D. (1970) "We're more violent than we think." *Maclean's*, August: 14–17.

McPherson, B.D., and L. Davidson (1980) *Minor Hockey in Ontario: Toward a Positive Learning Environment for Children in the 1980s*. Toronto: Ontario Government Bookstore.

Miller, R.B. (1971) "Violence, force and coercion." In J.A. Shaffer, ed., *Violence*. New York: David McKay.

Philo, H.M., and G. Stine (1977) "The liability path to safer helmets." *Trial* 12: 38–42.

Rains, J. (1980) "Sports violence: a matter of societal concern." *Notre Dame Lawyer* 55: 796–813.

Riga, P.D. (1969) "Violence: a Christian perspective." *Philosophy East and West* 19: 143–53.

Rovere, G.D., G. Gristina, and J. Nicastro (1978) "Medical problems of a professional hockey team: a three-season experience." *The Physician and Sports Medicine* 6: 59–63.

Runfola, R.T. (1974) "He is a hockey player, seventeen, black and convicted of manslaughter." *New York Times*, October 17: 2–3.

Russell, G.W. (1983) *Bibliography of Human Aggression and Violence*. University of Lethbridge, Alberta, Department of Psychology.

Simmel, G. (1955) *Conflict*. (H. Wolff, Translator.) Glencoe, Illinois: Free Press.

Smith, M.D. (1979) "Towards an explanation of hockey violence." *Canadian Journal of Sociology* 4: 105–24.

Stagg, A.A. (1927) *Touchdown!* New York: Longmans, Green and Company.

Stanage, S.M. (1974) "Violatives: modes and themes of violence." In S.M. Stanage, ed., *Reason and Violence*. Totowa, New Jersey: Littlefield, Adams.

Tatum, J., with B. Kushner (1979) *They Call Me Assassin*. New York: Everest House.

Toch, H. (1980) "Evolving a 'science of violence.'" *American Behavioral Scientist* 23: 653–65.

Underwood, J. (1979) *The Death of an American Game: The Crisis in Football*. Boston: Little, Brown.

Wilson, E.O. (1978) *On Human Nature*. Cambridge, Massachusetts: Harvard University Press.

Zillmann, D. (1978) *Hostility and Aggression*. Hillsdale, New Jersey: Lawrence Erlbaum Associates.

CHAPTER 21

Values and Violence in Sports Today: The Moral Reasoning Athletes Use in their Games and in their Lives

Brenda Jo Bredemeier, David L. Shields, and Jack C. Horn

To be good in sports, you have to be bad. Or so many athletes, coaches and sports fans believe. Heavyweight champion Larry Holmes, for example, revealed a key to his success during a *60 Minutes* interview with Morley Safer. Before he enters the ring, he said, "I have to change, I have to leave the goodness out and bring all the bad in, like Dr. Jekyll and Mr. Hyde."

Even sports fan Ronald Reagan suggested that normally inappropriate ways of thinking and acting are acceptable in sports. When he was governor of California, he reportedly told a college team during a pep talk that in football, "you can feel a clean hatred for your opponent. It is a clean hatred since it's only symbolic in a jersey."

Does success today really depend on how well an athlete or team has mastered the art of aggression? The question is usually answered more by ideology than by evidence. But there is a more fundamental question that needs to be asked: Is it really OK to be bad in sports? In particular, is aggression an acceptable tactic on the playing field? If it is morally unacceptable, the debate about its utility misses the mark.

It seems odd to ask whether being bad is all right. But in contact sports particularly, acts of aggression are seldom condemned, usually condoned and often praised. Sport is a "world within a world" with its own unique conventions and moral understanding.

Lyle and Glenn Blackwood of the Miami Dolphins are nicknamed "the bruise brothers."

Their motto – "We don't want to hurt you, just make you hurt" – aptly expresses the ambiguity many people feel about sport aggression. To reduce such ambiguity, many athletes appeal to game rules, informal agreements or personal convictions to decide the legitimacy of aggressive acts. As one collegiate basketball player told us in an interview: "It's OK to try to hurt somebody if it is legal and during the game. If the guy doesn't expect it, it's a cheap shot. That's no good. You can be aggressive and do minor damage without really hurting him and still accomplish your goal."

As social scientists, we are interested in the moral meaning athletes and fans attach to aggression. Do sport participants think about aggression in moral terms? Does the maturity of athletes' moral reasoning influence their aggressive behavior? What are the unique characteristics of sport morality and how does this "game reasoning" influence the perceived legitimacy of aggression?

Most recommendations for reducing sport aggression have focused on rules and penalties against fighting, beanballs, slugging and other forms of violence. We believe, however, that reducing athletic aggression requires the transformation of both external sports structures such as rules and penalties and internal reasoning structures. To reduce aggression, we must first understand the meaning athletes attach to it.

By aggression, we mean acts that are intended to inflict pain or injury. Robust, physically forceful play not meant to harm another player is better termed assertion. Unfortunately, this distinction is often blurred on the mat, the ice and the Astroturf.

We believe that aggression is more than a convention; it is a moral issue and can be investigated as such. If this is true, there should be an inverse relationship between the maturity of athletes' moral reasoning and their acceptance of aggression. Our research [...] suggests that this relationship exists. The higher their level of moral reasoning, the less aggression athletes practice and condone.

Establishing a link between moral reasoning and sport aggression is only the first step in understanding it. It is still not clear why many people find everyday aggression objectionable but have few moral qualms when they or others hurl a beanball at a batter. We can develop a more complete portrait of athletic aggression by exploring the unique patterns of moral reasoning that sport encourages.

Some social scientists have noted a curious fact that athletes and fans take for granted: Sport is set apart both cognitively and emotionally from the everyday world. Anthropologist Don Handelman, for example, has observed that play "requires a radical transformation in cognition and perception." Sociologist Erving Goffman has described play activities as enclosed within a unique "social membrane" or conceptual "frame."

In a 1983 interview, Ron Rivera, then a linebacker with the University of California at Berkeley and now with the Chicago Bears, described the personality transformation he undergoes on the field. The off-field Ron, he said, is soft-spoken, considerate and friendly. When asked to describe the on-field Ron, he replied, "He's totally opposite from me.... I'm so rotten. I have a total disrespect for the guy I'm going to hit."

Does this personality transformation include a fundamental change in moral reasoning? To explore this possibility, we designed a study to see whether the same people would use similar levels of moral reasoning in response to hypothetical dilemmas set in sport-specific and daily life contexts. One "sport dilemma," for example, centered on Tom, a football player who is told by his coach to injure an opponent to help Tom's team win. One of the "daily life" dilemmas hinged on whether a person should keep his promise to deliver some money to a rich man or use it to help hungry kin.

We presented four dilemmas to 120 high school and college athletes and nonathletes and asked them to reason about the best way to resolve each dilemma. Most of the students clearly perceived a difference between morality in sport and in everyday life. One comment by a high school female basketball player exemplified this perspective: "In sports, it's hard to tell right from wrong sometimes; you have to use game sense." Both athletes and nonathletes used lower-level egocentric moral reasoning when thinking about dilemmas in sport than when addressing moral issues in other contexts.

These and other findings suggest that moral norms which prescribe equal consideration of all people are often suspended during competition in favor of a more egocentric moral perspective. One male college basketball player explained the difference this way: "In sports you can do what you want. In life it's more restricted. It's harder to make decisions in life because there are so many people to think about, different people to worry about. In sports you're free to think about yourself."

This theme was echoed by many others who referred to sport as a field where each person or team seeks personal triumph and where opponents need not be given equal consideration.

There are several reasons sports may elicit an egocentric style of game reasoning. The very nature of competition requires that self-interest be temporarily adopted while the athlete strives to win. In everyday life, such preoccupation with self almost inevitably leads to moral failings. But in sport, participants are freed to concentrate on self-interest by a carefully balanced rule structure that equalizes opportunity. Players are guarded against the moral defaults of others by protective rules and by officials who impose sanctions for violations. Moral responsibility is thus transferred from the shoulders of players to those of officials, the enforcers of the rules, and to coaches, whom the players learn to see as responsible for all decisions.

If the nature of competition encourages egocentricity, the "set aside" character of sport helps to justify it. Sport consists of artificial goals that are achieved through arbitrarily defined skills and procedures. Although running across a line or shooting a ball through a hoop is all-important in the immediate game context, neither has significant consequences outside sports. This lack of any "real world" meaning to sport actions helps make egocentric reasoning seem legitimate.

Not all sport goals, of course, lack real-world implications. In boxing, for example, where the goal involves damage to another person, serious injury or even death is possible. Another exception is professional sports, and even some collegiate and high school sports, where winners may receive prizes, bigger paychecks, more perks or expanded educational and professional opportunities. The moral implications of harm as a sport goal (boxing) and extrinsic rewards contingent on sport performance (in professional and quasiprofessional sports) still need to be investigated.

The dynamic of competition, the structural protection provided by officials and rules and the relatively inconsequential implications of sport intentions combine to release sport participants from the usual demands of morality. But game-specific moral understandings do not completely replace everyday morality. Just as sport exists in a unique space and time within the everyday world, so game reasoning is a form of "bracketed morality." The transformed morality that occurs in sport does not take the place of everyday morality; rather, it is embedded in the broader, more encompassing morality of daily life.

Because of this, most athletes limit the degree of sport aggression they accept as legitimate in line with their general understanding of the rights of others. Coordinating these two sets of standards is not easy. Consider, for example, how one athlete reasoned about the football dilemma in which Tom is told to injure his opponent: "If Tom looks at it as a game, it's OK to

hurt the guy – to try to take him out of the game. But if he looks at the halfback as a person, and tries to hurt him, it's not OK." Asked, "How do you decide which to go by?" the athlete explained, "When you're on the field, then the game is football. Before and after, you deal with people morally."

This man recognized that aggression can be viewed from two contrasting viewpoints but eliminated his ambivalence by subordinating everyday morality to game reasoning. For him, an opponent is a player, not a person. This objectification of opponents reduces an athlete's sense of personal responsibility for competitors.

Among some of the other athletes we interviewed, accountability was alleviated by simply "not thinking about it." As one athlete stated succinctly, "In sports you don't think about those things [hurting others]; mostly you don't think about other people, you just think about winning."

Most athletes, however, tried to coordinate game and everyday morality by distinguishing between legitimate and illegitimate aggression. As one man explained: "Some [aggressive acts] are not acceptable. The game is a game. You go out to win, but there's a line – limitations – there are rules.... You try to dominate the other player, but you don't want to make him leave the game."

Another athlete put it this way: "Tom shouldn't try to hurt him. He should just hit him real hard, stun him, make him lose his wind, make sure he's too scared to run the ball again."

Players use a complex moral logic in attempts to coordinate the goal of winning with the need to respect limits to egocentricity. Some athletes identify the rules as the final arbiter of legitimacy, but most appeal to less formal criteria. Themes such as intimidation, domination, fairness and retribution are continuously woven into participants' fabric of thought, providing a changing picture of what constitutes legitimate action.

Shifting expectations, created by the fast-paced and emotionally charged action, can readily lead to perceived violations or "cheap shots." Cheap shots, of course, are in the eye, or ribs, of the beholder. As a college basketball player explained, physical contact may be interpreted by athletes as either assertive or aggressive, depending on their perception of intent: "I've played with guys who try to hurt you. They use all kinds of cheap shots, especially elbows in the face and neck. But that's different than trying to maintain position or letting a guy know you're there. An elbow can be for intimidation or it can be for hurting. I just use elbows in the regular course of the game."

Given the complex and variable conditions of sport, it is not surprising that among the athletes we interviewed there was not a clear consensus about the line between legitimate and illegitimate aggression. Generally, we found that the more mature the athletes' moral reasoning, the less aggression they accepted as legitimate – both for the fictitious character Tom in the hypothetical football dilemma and for themselves as they reasoned about personal aggression.

Yet even the more morally mature athletes often accepted minor forms of aggression as legitimate game strategy. In fact, such minor aggression was sometimes viewed as a positive, enhancing aspect of the game. As a high school player explained: "Football is a rough game and if it weren't for rules people would get hurt real bad – even killed. Some people just want to hurt other people real bad." Asked, "Should the present rules be changed to reduce football injuries?" he replied, "No. Nobody will want to play if the rules get so uptight that you can't hit hard."

Moral research inevitably leads beyond descriptions about what people do to questions about what people ought to do. Perhaps most athletes accept some aggression as "part of the game," but should they? Should any degree of aggression be considered legitimate?

Based on what we have learned about game reasoning, we believe two criteria can be employed to distinguish morally mature athletes' judgments of aggression which they may perceive as legitimate from aggression which certainly is not. First, any act intended to inflict an injury that is likely to have negative consequences for the recipient once the game has ended is illegitimate. The legitimacy of game reasoning depends partly on the irrelevance of sport action to everyday life. Consequently, in-

flicting such "game-transcending" injuries as a broken leg or a concussion cannot be morally justified.

Second, game reasoning is also legitimated because it occurs within a situation that is defined by a set of rules that limit the relevant procedures and skills which can be used during the game. Therefore, any act is illegitimate if it occurs apart from the strategic employment of game-relevant skills, even if such an act is intended to cause only minor injury or mild discomfort. Such behavior impinges upon the protective structure that releases participants from their normal moral obligations.

The implications of our research on athletes' game reasoning may extend to other spheres of life. If game reasoning is distinct from the morality of general life, are there other context-specific moralities, such as business reasoning or political reasoning? Perhaps the list could be extended indefinitely. While every context raises unique moral issues, however, we agree with most moral-development theorists that the fundamental structure of moral reasoning remains relatively stable in nearly all situations.

Sport is employed frequently as a metaphor for other endeavors, and game language is often utilized in discussions of such diverse topics as business, politics and war. A recent book by Thomas Whisler of the University of Chicago, *Rules of the Game*, has little to do with sport and everything to do with corporate boardrooms.

The borrowing of sport images and language may reflect a tendency to transplant game morality from its native soil to foreign gardens. If this is the case, game reasoning has social implications that extend far beyond the limited world of sport. Game morality is legitimated by protections within the sport structure, but most other contexts lack such safeguards. If game reasoning leads to manipulation to gain job advancement, for example, are adequate laws available and enforced to guarantee equal opportunity? Can the dirty tricks of politics be legitimated as if they were just a game? Does game reasoning encourage a view that nuclear war is winnable, propelling us toward the "game to end all games"? And if it does, who consents to play these games?

CHAPTER 22

Violence and Sports

Robert E. Leach

This is a male athlete problem. In the middle of the summer the newspapers in my area were dominated by two stories: Mike Tyson biting Evander Holyfield's ears and allegations that Wilfredo Cordero has physically abused two of his wives. Several weeks ago the magazine *Sports Illustrated* featured a story about teenaged football players in a New Jersey town who had sexually abused a young woman. Every day one can read in a newspaper about some sports personality who has been involved in violence. Usually it is a professional athlete, but college and high school athletes also have this problem.

The apologists for professional athletes (club owners, general managers, agents, and others who make a living in one way or another related to professional sports) say that all this violence is nothing more than a mirror on society in general. They say that the high profile of the athletes brings media attention and that athletes are involved in this situation no more than others.

I don't buy it. Male athletes in our society, from an early age, are cosseted, praised, and singled out for special treatment. Early on they realize that the rules are different if you throw a football well, dunk a basketball, or hit home runs. Girls are attracted to these young athletes, and sexual possibilities are more easily come by. Problems may be ignored. Teachers and administrators alike find it easy to help these athletes along the road.

The better the athlete, which may culminate in high-profile professional athletics, the more help there is. Money and fame are certain, and societal rules are relaxed. We accept many transgressions from these sports personalities, as we do from famous rock and movie stars, yet there is a difference between the groups. Much of the background of athletics is violent. Boxing is intended to cause injury. Football is not gentle. Coaches don't say, "Please, push that fellow out of the way, John." Football, rugby, karate, wrestling, and hockey are all contact sports. Basketball at the higher levels is very physical. Knocking people down, hard, is accompanied by coach's praise, fan applause, and possibly winning. "Controlled" violence seems good.

This background of violence, present to different degrees in various sports, coupled with society's willingness to accept rule-breaking from high-profile athletes, leads to much of what we read about. Television executives say that the violence we see daily on TV doesn't cause violence in society. Be real! Television and movies have always influenced society. These ever-increasing episodes of male athletic violence toward others and themselves seems to lead the way rather than follow society.

Athletes learn at an early age that the rules are different for them. The rest of us – coaches, fans, administrators, agents – are culpable, too, in the sense that we don't make the athletes tow the line. Look at Tyson. He got a year's vacation and made 27 million dollars for biting another boxer. What did he learn? What did he and others learn? They learned that we accept violence and abusive behavior from many athletes that would result in loss of job and reputation if it occurred from a teacher, computer programmer, or doctor. Even when athletes are found guilty in court, most are sentenced to community service. Is that service cleaning the streets or planting trees? You can bet it isn't. Most of the time that service is talking to young kids.

The majority of athletes in high school, college, and professional leagues are decent people for whom violence is not a way of life. With increasing frequency we are reading about the others, and I believe that many of these athletes form the leading edge of violence rather than acting as mere followers. When good guys such as Karl Malone or Greg Maddux do something athletically it makes the newspapers and fades away. But when Tyson and others do something violent and get "slapped on the wrist," it makes the newspapers and stays there. Many of these athletes seem to get away with various forms of violence – and that must send the wrong message to many younger men.

PART VI

Sport and Gender

CHAPTER 23

Sex Equality in Sports

Jane English

What constitutes equal opportunity for women in sports? Philosophers have developed three major positions concerning equal opportunity, but they have focused on fields in which the sexes are either known or assumed to have equal potentialities. In sports, some relevant differences between the sexes, though statistical, do appear to be permanent. All three of the most widely held views on equal opportunity are deficient when applied to this area. Since there may be other permanent differences between the sexes, in such areas as spatial perception or verbal ability, it is useful to examine the problems of equal opportunity in sports.

I

One account of equal opportunity identifies it with nondiscrimination. On this view, if we do not pay any attention to the race of applicants to law school, for example, then our admissions are "color blind" and give blacks equal opportunity. Admission should be based on characteristics relevant to law school, such as intelligence and grades, while irrelevant characteristics such as sex and race should be ignored entirely. Most philosophers have rejected this account as too weak. If women lack motivation because they never see female lawyers on television, "sex blindness" alone will not provide equal opportunity. Although "formal" equality is necessary

for justice, it is not sufficient. These philosophers would permit temporary violations of this ideal, but only in the transition to a just society.

When applied to sports, however, their view proves inadequate. If our sports were made sex-blind, women would have even less opportunity to participate than at present. Given equal incentives and more role models, women would have more interest in athletics, but few would qualify for high school, college, professional and Olympic teams. Statistically speaking, there are physiological differences between the sexes that are relevant to sports performance. Remedial programs and just institutions cannot obliterate all differences in size and strength. So far from being necessary for equal opportunity, sex-blindness can actually decrease it.

A second account of equal opportunity identifies it with equal chances. Oscar and Elmer are said to have equal opportunity to become brain surgeons if it is equally probable that they will become brain surgeons. Most philosophers have rejected this conception of equal opportunity as too strong. If Oscar is a genius with great manual dexterity and Elmer is uncoordinated and slightly retarded, then they should not have an equal chance to become brain surgeons. Our society is not unjust if it encourages Oscar and discourages Elmer from this profession, because these skills are relevant to the job.

When we turn to women in sports, however, the model of equal probabilities seems to have some merit. Sports offer what I will call *basic benefits* to which it seems everyone has an equal right: health, the self-respect to be gained by doing one's best, the cooperation to be learned from working with teammates and the incentive gained from having opponents, the "character" of learning to be a good loser and a good winner, the chance to improve one's skills and learn to accept criticism – and just plain fun. If Matilda is less adept at, say, wrestling than Walter is, this is no reason to deny Matilda an equal chance to wrestle for health, self-respect, and fun. Thus, contrary to the conclusion on the example of the brain surgeon, a society that discourages Matilda from wrestling is unjust because it lacks equal opportunity to attain these basic benefits.

The third account of equal opportunity calls for equal chances in the sense of equal achievements for the "major social groups." Blacks have an equal opportunity to be lawyers, on this view, when the percentage of lawyers who are black roughly equals the percentage of blacks in the population. Like the "equal probabilities" view, this one calls for equal chances, but it interprets this by averaging attainments across the major social groups.

When this third account is applied to sports, it seems to have the undesirable consequence that a society is unjust if less than half its professional football players are women. If we had to provide sufficient incentives or reverse discrimination to achieve this result, it would create a situation unfair to 170-pound males. (They may even clamor to be recognized as a "major social group.") More important, it seems wrong to argue that a low level of health and recreation for, say, short women is compensated for by additional health and recreation for tall women; one might as well argue that women are compensated by the greater benefits enjoyed by men. Rawls and Nozick have argued against utilitarianism by pointing out that society is not a "macro-individual" such that the benefits of some persons cancel out the sufferings of others. But the major social groups are not macro-individuals either. Proponents of the third account have not, to my knowledge, replied to this objection.

Beyond the basic benefits of sport, some athletes reap the further benefits of fame and fortune. I shall call these the *scarce benefits* of sport. The term is not meant to imply that they are kept artificially scarce, but that it is simply not possible for prizes and publicity to be attained equally by everyone at once. Although everyone has an equal right to the basic benefits, not everyone can claim an equal right to receive fan mail or appear on television. For this, having the skill involved in the sport is one relevant factor. In short, I shall maintain that the second account, equal probabilities, should be applied to the basic benefits; whereas the third model, proportional attainments for the major social groups, should be applied to the scarce benefits. And I shall construct an argument from self-respect for taking the "average" across the major social groups in the case of scarce benefits.

II

The traditional accounts of equal opportunity are inadequate because men and women are physiologically different in ways relevant to performance in sports. What is a fair way to treat physiologically disadvantaged groups? Two methods are in common use, and I shall suggest a third option.

One common method is to form competition classes based on a clear-cut physiological characteristic, such as weight or age, well known to be a hindrance in the sport in question. For example, middleweight boxers receive preferential treatment in the sense that they are permitted to move up and compete against the heavyweights if they desire, while the heavyweights are not permitted to move down into the middleweight class.

Sex is frequently used to form separate competition groups. If we apply the boxing model, several conclusions about this practice follow. Women should be allowed to "move up" and compete against the men if they wish. Since sex is not relevant to performance in all sports, the sport should be integrated when it is not. For example, it is probably irrelevant in dressage, riflery and car racing. In other sports, the differences between the sexes may be too small to justify separate classes – as in diving and freestyle skiing. In still others, the sexes have compensating differences. In channel swimming, for instance, men are advantaged in strength, but women profit from an insulating layer of fat. Additional sports could be integrated if the abilities characteristic of the two sexes were valued equally. In many areas, such as swimming, it is simply unknown whether the existing differences are due to permanent physiological characteristics or to cultural and social inequalities. Additional empirical research is needed before it will be known where integration is appropriate.

An objection to the use of groupings by sex is that it discriminates against those males whose level of performance is equal to that of the abler females. For example, if we have a girls' football team in our high school, is it unfair to prohibit a 120-pound boy who cannot make the boys' team from trying out for the girls' team? If we provide an additional team for boys under 140 pounds, does that discriminate against girls under 100 pounds? Against short boys over 140 pounds? It is impossible to provide a team for every characteristic that might be relevant to football performance. The objection has force because the differences between the sexes are only statistical. Our 120-pound boy is being penalized for the average characteristics of a major social group to which he belongs, rather than being treated on the basis of his individual characteristics.

The justification for maintaining separate teams for the sexes is the impact on women that integration would have. When there are virtually no female athletic stars, or when women receive much less prize money than men do, this is damaging to the self-respect of all women. Members of disadvantaged groups identify strongly with each other's successes and failures. If women do not attain roughly equal fame and fortune in sports, it leads both men and women to think of women as naturally inferior. Thus, it is not a right of women tennis stars to the scarce benefits, but rather a right of all women to self-respect that justifies their demand for equal press coverage and prize money.

This provides a justification for applying the third account of equal opportunity to the distribution of scarce benefits. It also explains why the

"major social groups" have this feature, while arbitrary sets of individuals do not. A group singled out for distinctive treatment and recognized as a class tends to develop feelings of mutual identification which have an impact on the members' self-respect. It also affects the respect and treatment they get from others. In an androgynous society, we might be as unaware of a person's sex as we now are of left-handedness. Then roughly equal attainments would no longer be required, on my reasoning, for unequal attainments would not injure self-respect. Conversely, although there is some evidence of late that blacks have physiological traits such as a longer calf that give them an advantage in jumping and sprinting, I do not conclude that we should form separate track or basketball leagues for whites, since the self-respect of whites is not endangered by this modest advantage possessed by blacks.

III

A different method often used to give the disadvantaged equal access to the basic benefits of sport is to group individuals by ability alone. This occurs when we find second and third string games, B-leagues, intramural meets or special matches for novices or amateurs. Groupings by age, sex, or weight are often just attempts to approximate ability groupings in a convenient and quick way. When convenience is the intent, then, it must not be rigidly imposed to keep talented girls off the first string.

Groupings by ability are much easier to justify than groupings by the specific characteristics just discussed. There is no discrimination against less able members of the dominant group. Ability groupings take into account all the traits that may affect performance. Competition with those close to one's own ability usually provides the most incentive and satisfaction, except where style of play is very different. It is imperative to make recreational leagues on all levels of skill available to people of all ages, sexes, income levels, and abilities, because everyone has an equal right to sport's basic benefits.

Groupings by ability must not lead to disrespect for those playing in the lower ability groups, however. Sports is an area in which we have tended to confuse respect with what has been called "esteem." I may have a low (and accurate) estimate of myself as a tennis player without losing respect for myself as a person. Although competition does entail winners and losers, it does not entail disrespect for the losers. Much has been said recently about this among other evils of competition. But competition per se is not bad. It offers fun, excitement, entertainment, and the incentive to perform at one's best. The problems arise when losers are scorned or discouraged from playing, and when winning becomes the end rather than the means to basic benefits. It is ironic that sports, long recommended for building character and teaching how to be a good loser and winner, have often taught aggression and elitism. Experts have become idols and millionaires, while the rest of us watch rather than participate. With effort, the entry of women into sports could foster a reawakening to these values, which are widely shared but have been lost lately in the shuffle of big business sports. Some such reawakening is necessary if ability groupings are to be effective.

IV

So far I have assumed that women are a physiologically disadvantaged group in need of protection or special handicaps. In recent years, women have been making impressive progress in narrowing the gap between male and female performance. But there are apparently some permanent biological differences that affirmative action and consciousness raising will never change: women are smaller than men, they have a higher percentage of fat, they lack the hormones necessary for massive muscle development, they have a different hip structure and a slower oxygenation rate.

Before we conclude that women are permanently relegated to inferiority, however, let us note that what is a physiological disadvantage in one activity may be an advantage in others: weight is an asset to a Sumo wrestler and a drawback for marathon running; height is an aid in basketball but not on the balance beam.

In some sports, women have natural advantages over men. The hip structure that slows running gives a lower center of gravity. Fat provides insulation and an energy source for running fifty-mile races. The hormones that hinder development of heavy muscles promote flexibility. Even small size can be an asset, as jockeys and spelunkers know.

An example of an athletic activity which emphasizes the female advantages is ballet. Some ballerinas can stand on one toe while extending the other leg up into a vertical position where it touches the ear! While admittedly few women can do this, even fewer men can. Men are simply physiologically disadvantaged in the body flexibility that ballet emphasizes. Perhaps the most extreme example of a sport favoring women's natural skills is the balance beam. Here, small size, flexibility and low center of gravity combine to give women the kind of natural hegemony that men enjoy in football.

This suggests a third approach to aiding physiologically different groups. We should develop a variety of sports, in which a variety of physical types can expect to excel. We tend to think of the possible sports as a somewhat fixed group of those currently available. Yet even basketball and football are of very recent invention. Since women have been virtually excluded from all sports until the last century, it is appropriate that some sports using women's specific traits are now developing, such as synchronized swimming.

This method is different from forming handicapped groups or second-string leagues, and it is superior in its impact on the self-respect of the affected groups. It contributes to a woman's self-respect to see or read about the best women golfers. But this pride is tempered by the knowledge that they are "only" the best *women*. The very need for a protected competition class suggests inferiority. The pride and self-respect gained from witnessing a woman athlete who is not only the best woman but the very best athlete is much greater. Perhaps most white male readers have not experienced this sort of identification characteristic of "minority" groups. But it is clearly displayed in the extraordinary interest in gymnastics among adolescent girls inspired by Olga Korbut, and the pride blacks derived from Jackie Robinson.

V

In calling for the development of new sports, I am suggesting that our concept of "sports" contains a male bias. Historically, this is understandable, because sports were an exclusively male domain, probably based on war and hunting, and actually used to assert male dominance. The few athletic activities permitted to women – mostly forms of dance – were not thought to fall under the *concept* of sport, and are still classified as arts or entertainment instead. Speed, size, and strength seem to be the essence of sports. Women *are* naturally inferior at "sports" so conceived.

But if women had been the historically dominant sex, our concept of sport would no doubt have evolved differently. Competitions emphasizing flexibility, balance, strength, timing, and small size might dominate Sunday afternoon television and offer salaries in six figures. Men could be clamoring for equal press coverage of their champions.

Here it might be argued that our concept of sport cannot be altered to make women equal, because speed, strength, and size are inevitable elements of *spectator* appeal. But it is participating rather than watching that is central to sport. Although speed is exciting, so is precision. Nor do audiences always choose to watch the experts. More important, spectator interest is a cultural product, tending to follow rather than lead media attention.

VI

The just society, in my view, would contain a greater variety of sports than we now have, pro-

viding advantages for a wider range of physical types. The primary emphasis would be on participation, with a wealth of local teams and activities available to all, based on groupings by ability. Only where style of play is very different would groupings by weight, age, or sex be recommended. The goal would be to make the basic benefits of health, teamwork, and fun equally available to everyone. Just distribution of the scarce benefits is somewhat more complex. Level of skill, audience appeal, and the self-respect of major social groups all have to be considered.

Current problems of the real world are far removed from such a utopia. Rights to the basic benefits dictate immediate changes in the distribution of our sports resources. Most obvious is the need for equal facilities – everything from socks to stadiums. If this means we must disturb a "Pareto optimal" situation – selling the football team's videotape machine if we are to provide a jogging path for the middle-aged – so be it. More subtle is the need for equal incentives. As well as equal scholarships and prizes, women need peer approval and changed sex-role stereotypes.

In short, I have suggested a division of the benefits of sport into the "basic" and the "scarce" ones. From the assumption that everyone has an equal right to the basic benefits of health and recreation, I have argued that the access to participator sports should not be based upon having the ability to play the sport well. And this ability is only one factor in the attainment of the scarce benefits. Since I believe that the right of women to roughly half of the scarce benefits, overall, stems from the right to self-respect, I have argued that a society which invents alternative sports using women's distinctive abilities and which rewards these equally is preferable to a society which only maintains protected classes for women in sports at which men are advantaged.

CHAPTER 24

Human Equality in Sports

Peter S. Wenz

Issues of social justice are among the most intellectually challenging to both the ethicist and philosopher of law, especially when there appear to be permanent, biologically determined differences of ability and potential among the people and between the groups for whom justice is sought. Such is the case between men and women in the realm of sports. The problem of providing justice in this area has been the topic of popular magazine articles,[1] federal[2] and state[3] legislation, adjudication[4] and philosophical contemplation.[5] But the heart of the matter has yet to be discussed. I will attempt to do this by first reviewing some of the current issues in this area, then exploring the relationship between the use and exchange values of athletic participation, and finally proposing a radical solution which is defended on utilitarian, egalitarian and Rawlsian ethical grounds. The result will be an approach to promoting social justice and equality amongst biologically diverse groups which may be applicable beyond the area of sports.

Contemporary Issues

One of the first issues concerning sex equality in sports was, and still is, monetary. Traditionally, schools have spent much more money on men's than on women's athletic programs. Schools tended to fund a greater number of men's sports in the first place. They also went to the expense of entering more men's than women's teams in interscholastic competition, and gave members of these teams such extra benefits as free laundry service and enlarged coaching staffs. Finally, "men's" sports – those traditionally reserved for male competition, especially football – are the most capital intensive in terms of both the equipment needed to play the game and the facilities needed to accommodate spectator interest. The unsurprising result of these disparities is that women and men were not, and for the most part still are not, afforded equal athletic opportunities at school.

One response to this situation is to attack the monetary issue directly, insist that women's athletic programs be funded at levels equal to men's. But it is unclear what this might mean. If it means that all of the same sports are to be funded for both men and women, and at the same level, there is a problem. One result of sex discrimination in the past is that women have been convinced to take less seriously the desirability and even the possibility of developing their own athletic abilities. One of the worst aspects of social inequality is the internalization of their inferior status on the part of disadvantaged people. The problem this poses for the equal funding of athletics is that there are at present likely to be fewer women than men interested in spending many after-school hours engaged in athletics. So, equal funding of women and men would likely result in greater per capita expenditures for women than men. This may be viewed as unjust.

Also, women and men have been tracked into many different sports, women into field hockey and softball and men into football and baseball, for example. This, too, is most likely reflected in current patterns of participation preferences among men and women so that even if men's and women's programs were funded equally, whether on a per-team or per-capita basis (it's not obvious which it should be), the sports funded would still not be identical. This would cause three difficulties for effecting sex equality in sports. First, the traditionally male sports are more capital intensive, especially when you include the facilities needed to accommodate spectator interest. One might try to circumvent this problem by claiming that because the school stadium is used by women for field hockey as well as by men for football, it is not a football stadium. The capital investment it represents should not, therefore, be attributed to men's as opposed to women's athletics. But this is a sham. The stands could be much smaller and cheaper if designed to accommodate only the number of spectators wanting to see women's field hockey.

The second problem is also a result of disproportionate spectator interest in men's rather than women's athletic competition. If funding is the issue, and that was the issue with which we began, spectator interest in men's athletics can be translated into gate receipts which, it might be argued, could justifiably be spent disproportionately on those sports generating the funds. Rawls's theory of justice might be invoked, improperly I hope later to show, in support of such a position. The disadvantaged – women's field hockey – are treated justly when the advantaged make additional gains, so long as the disadvantaged also gain in the process. So, increased funding of the football program in response to its gate receipts would seem justified, if this was a device used to generate more money for athletics generally, including women's field hockey.

However, further emphasis on traditionally popular men's athletic programs exacerbates the problem of disproportionate spectator interest in men's athletics generally. This is trouble-some not only because it allows the gate receipt argument to be used to justify even greater funding for football (a second round of the same reasoning), but also because it reinforces the pressure in our culture for women to discount their athletic abilities. If the rest of society is interested primarily in men's athletics, perhaps women athletes and potential athletes should be also. Thus, the rich get richer and the poor get pom-poms. For this reason, Rawls, who values self-respect preeminently, would probably abjure the view that increased funding of men's sports is justified when some of the increased gate receipts are given to women's athletics.

In sum, fostering sex equality in sports through changed funding patterns is problematic at best. In some cases it is not clear which changes would be just and which unjust. Finally, funding alone cannot address the problems of motivation, self-concept and self-respect among women that are the legacy of past injustices. This is apparent from the fact that equal funding of men's and women's athletic programs is a "separate but equal" position. It is now normally considered unjustified when applied to different races because separate is considered inherently unequal when applied to groups between whom there is a history in the dominant culture of invidious contrast. Because there is just such a history in the dominant culture concerning men and women's athletics, separate athletic programs for men and women might be inherently unequal. This is illustrated concretely and poignantly by cases of women wanting to compete on men's athletic teams for the increased prestige and competition this would allow.[6]

It might appear, then, that altered funding patterns could be supplemented or replaced altogether by the integration of athletics. The difficulty is that for many sports, including most of those popular in the United States, the biological differences between men and women give men a statistical advantage. These sports include strength and speed and often height and weight among the traits helpful for successful competition. Although some women are stronger, faster, taller and heavier than some men, on the average men are stronger, faster, taller and heavier than women. So some proponents of women's athletics fear that sex-integrated athletic programs will result in even fewer women participants and less funding for and concentration upon the development of women athletes.[7]

In short, given all the variables present in the current situation, the optimal course of action is neither obvious nor agreed upon.

Use Value and Exchange Value in Sports

One philosophic strategy for approaching such situations is the elaboration of an ideal state of affairs which, were it to be realized, would constitute a solution to the problem. The solution is often ideal in the sense that no one knows how its realization might be effectively promoted; aspects of the society which create the problem in the first place might render impractical even *attempts* to directly effect the ideal's realization. Nevertheless, the ideal has an important function. As various policies which are amenable to practical implementation are reviewed and considered, those which would move the society toward the ideal might be preferred to those with an opposite or neutral tendency.

The ideal in this case can be explained by applying to sports Adam Smith's distinction between value in use and value in exchange.[8] The exchange value of a sport to an individual is the fame and fortune he or she derives from participating in that sport. Such rewards result from, but are extrinsic to, the athletic activity in question. The activity itself, the rules in accordance with which it is carried out, the physical qualities and interpersonal cooperation it calls for and so forth, could all be exactly the same whether or not the rewards of fame and fortune are offered for participation. This is because fame and fortune result not from the activity itself, but from the interest others show in one's participation. This interest results in admiration for the participant and a willingness to monetarily compensate him or her for participating. Someone deriving fame and fortune by

participating in a sport under these conditions exchanges his or her participation for these other goods. Thus, they constitute the exchange value for that individual of participating in that sport.

The use value of a sport to an individual, by contrast, is the value to that individual which is intrinsic to his or her participation in that sport. It is dependent on the formal rules of the game, the mores in accordance with which it is played, the qualities of physical coordination and interpersonal cooperation it calls for, and its competitive nature. The values resulting from participation normally include development of motor skills and improvement of bodily health, as well as the enhancement of self-esteem which results from overcoming difficulties. In addition, participation can be character building, teaching the individual to accept criticism, be a good winner and a good loser and, in team sports, a cooperative person. Finally, participation can be fun. Because these goods, which constitute the use value of a sport to a given individual, do not depend on rewards offered by others, they are intrinsic rather than extrinsic to the athletic endeavor.

Though there are exceptions, it will be assumed here that the use value of most sports for most people who voluntarily participate in them is positive. Possible exceptions might include an extremely dangerous sport, like hang-gliding, or moto-cross competition for an epileptic. Generally, however, the use value of voluntary participation is positive.

The aggregate use value of a sport is the total use value of that sport to individuals in a society over a given period of time, such as a year. It is the sum of the sport's use values to all individuals in that society who participated in that sport during that time period. Since the use value of athletics is assumed to be generally positive, the aggregate use value is positively related to the number of people and the time spent by those people participating in that sport during that time period.

The aggregate exchange value of a sport is the total fame and fortune accruing to participating individuals due to this participation. It is positively related to the spectator interest in that sport, because fame and fortune accrue to participants only when others care enough to witness the sport being played that they offer these rewards to participants.

The relationship between the aggregate use and aggregate exchange values of a sport, that is, between the population's interest in playing and watching it, is the topic of the remainder of this section. Generally, people who enjoy participating in a sport come to enjoy watching others play. Having played the sport themselves they can empathize, kinesthetically in some cases, with the players they are watching. Spectators can appreciate, admire and enjoy the players' skills when they have, by playing the sport themselves, attempted to develop and exercise those same skills. They can also better understand and therefore appreciate player strategy and team cooperation if they have played the sport themselves. For all these reasons, it is more likely that someone who has played basketball but not hockey will prefer watching basketball to hockey on television when both are available. Thus, it seems that participation in a sport, its (aggregate) use value in a given population, increases spectator interest and therewith the (aggregate) exchange value of the services of excellent players.

It is doubtful, however, that watching and playing a sport are mutually supporting. I shall argue in the remainder of the section that whereas playing increases watching, watching tends to depress rather than increase the level of participation. I call this the inverse relationship thesis (IRT). Stated fully the thesis is that, all other things being equal, an increase in the use value of a sport causes an increase in its exchange value. But its increased exchange value tends to depress its use value. In this causal direction the use and exchange values are inversely relational. This means that any conditions which cause an increase in the use value of a sport will cause a greater such increase if other conditions operate to prevent the exchange value from increasing as well. More important, it also means that any conditions which cause a decrease in a sport exchange value will, other things being equal, cause an increase in its use value.

This inverse relationship thesis (IRT) is central to the argument of this paper. Nevertheless, I will not claim to have demonstrated its truth in the arguments which follow. Considerable investigation by social scientists is required for its refutation or confirmation. I do claim, however, that the arguments which follow in this section make the IRT exceedingly plausible, and that subsequent arguments from it to further conclusions demonstrate its importance to any consideration of equality in sports.

The first argument for the IRT is that watching can serve as a vicarious outlet for urges to participate, thereby dissipating those urges before they can reach the level at which they would be acted upon. Thus, someone who sometimes plays basketball may find it easier to forego playing if he or she can watch others play. This is analogous to the claim made by those who argue against legal restrictions on the availability of pornography for adults. They claim that watching pornography, rather than inciting people to sex crimes, dissipates the urge to commit such crimes, because it affords people vicarious sexual involvement which serves to replace actual involvement. The evidence gathered to support this claim indirectly favors the view that watching a sport decreases the level of participation.

The same view is supported by a very different consideration. The exchange value of an individual's athletic endeavors is generally directly related to his or her level of proficiency. The function is not linear, of course, but it is generally true that the exchange value increases with proficiency. A society in which the exchange value of participation for those who are proficient is very high is a society in which there is greater spectator interest in that sport. It is also one in which the level of proficiency that becomes normative is very high. As people increasingly watch something done with great proficiency, they tend to think it normal that the activity in question be carried on at that level of proficiency. But as the normative level of proficiency increases beyond what most people are capable of attaining, people are discouraged from participating. Lacking respect for the level of their own attainment, participation is ego-damaging. Conversely, as the norms of proficiency are increasingly established by an individual for himself or herself, or by that individual's peers, participation is encouraged and can be expected to increase. Thus, the exchange value of participating in a given sport in a given society probably varies inversely with its use value.

Another consideration is that as the exchange value and so the level of spectator interest in a sport increases, the organization of participation in that sport tends to become increasingly institutionalized. The reason for this is not hard to find. Spectator interest can be translated into a market demand. In a profit-minded society, people tend to organize themselves and others so as to meet the market demand and gain monetary rewards. What is more, the institutional organization of the sport does not stay at the professional level. It is replicated at lower levels. Professional baseball results ultimately in Little League. Football and basketball are played interscholastically in organized leagues at the grade school level.

It might seem that such organization and institutionalization of a sport might increase its aggregate use value in society as schools and other organizations prompt children to join athletic institutions (organized teams and leagues). The predominant tendency, however, is probably just the opposite. Institutionalized sports notoriously discriminate in favor of the most athletically talented individuals. Development of skills of the less talented is often ignored. The norms of performance of the more talented become normative for the group as a whole, with the consequence that the less talented are not only ignored but dispirited. The net effect of the institutionalization of sports that results from emphasis on its exchange value is therefore predominantly to discourage rather than encourage widespread participation, to decrease rather than increase its aggregate use value in society.

In sum, three reasons have been advanced to support the inverse relationship thesis, the contention that the aggregate use value of a sport ordinarily decreases with an increase in its aggregate exchange value. (1) Watching a sport can serve as a vicarious outlet which dissipates urges

to participate. (2) The norms of excellence increase with a sport's exchange value, discouraging the participation of the less talented. And, (3) as the exchange value increases the sport is increasingly institutionalized, which also puts a premium on talent and discourages the participation of others.

Some examples may be helpful at this point. It is commonly thought, and I have no reason to doubt, that a larger percentage of the American population played baseball in the earlier part of the century than at present. Its professionalization and institutionalization have increased its aggregate exchange value while decreasing its aggregate use value. Jogging, by contrast, is not very institutionalized and has very little exchange value at present. It is not much of a spectator sport. People set norms of proficiency for themselves and engage in the activity informally. Its exchange value is low and its use value high. It is what might be called a folk-sport.

Sports that might seem to constitute counterexamples are golf and tennis. Their use and exchange values have increased simultaneously in recent years, in direct rather than inverse relation to one another. These are sports in which participation is found particularly enjoyable by a large percentage of the people in our culture who are introduced to them. But until recently participation in them was reserved for the relatively wealthy primarily because of the expense, much as is still the case with equestrian events. A major proximate cause of their increased use value, I submit, has been the decreased expense of participating in them.

Since World War II, the percentage of the average family's income spent on food and housing has declined somewhat, leaving more disposable income for recreation of all sorts. More important, the expansion of the public sector beginning with the New Deal has manifested itself in public works projects which include public recreation facilities, among them tennis courts and golf courses. People are paying for these facilities with their taxes, diminishing considerably the differential cost of participation versus non-participation. In addition, tennis was first played on grass, which is very difficult to maintain at the required quality level, then on clay, which also requires considerable mainten-ance. Now, most people play on asphalt, which is much cheaper to maintain. The developing technology of lawn care has made golf course maintenance less expensive also, though the change is less dramatic here. Those develop-ments, I believe, are primarily responsible for the increased use value of golf and tennis. The availability of tennis and golf as spectator sports, especially on television, is a consequence, not a cause, of their increased use value. This is con-sistent with the IRT.

To see this, let us conduct a thought experi-ment. Imagine a dramatic increase of television time devoted to equestrian events. If the cost of participating remained about the same, so, I believe, would participation. Now imagine in-stead a dramatic decrease in that cost. Participa-tion would increase dramatically even in the absence of increased television coverage. Then, of course, responding to increased participation, television coverage would follow suit. This kind of media response is currently occurring in the case of racquet ball. In sum, just as media cov-erage would not be necessary for people to in-crease their participation in equestrian events were their expense dramatically reduced, so media coverage was not necessary for the in-creased use values of tennis and golf.

Finally, consider the case of soccer. It is not a folk-sport in this country, so its use value is so low that its professionalization and institutional-ization can increase that value. (Goodness knows why this is happening. Perhaps it is spurred on by the same folks who want us to think metric, namely, multinational corporations. I suppose they want us to play soccer so that everyone will be able to get along at international-employee picnics. These are only conjectures, of course.) The point is that the use value of sports is great only in folk-sports anyway. Institutionalization holds the level of participa-tion in any sport below that of a folk-sport. So high use value cannot be attained through institutionalization. High use value in a sport occurs only when the culture is allowed to take up its own folk-sports, spurred on by the usual forces involved in cultural evolution. In our country this does involve commercialism,

and producers of jogging shoes and racquet ball racquets have been doing an excellent job of late.

I hope at this point to have made the IRT very plausible. The important part of the thesis is that, other things being equal, a decrease in exchange value will *ordinarily* cause an increase in use value. The qualification "ordinarily" is included because absolute universality is not essential. Only the strong predominance of the tendency for decreased exchange values to in-crease use values is necessary. The usefulness of the IRT for subsequent arguments will not be diminished if an exceptional sport is found not to conform to it. Having made the qualification, I will neglect its reiteration.

Ethical Arguments

Because the exchange value of athletic participa-tion includes esteem from others, it can prob-ably never be reduced to zero. Nor would it be desirable to do so. I will argue, however, that eliminating the *major* source of exchange value, financial rewards for athletic participation, is desirable. What is more, the desirability can be deduced from egalitarianism, John Rawls's theory of justice and the most popular forms of utilitarianism when they are combined with the IRT.

Consider first the ethical view that average utility ought to be maximized. Imagine a society in which, like our own at this time, the monetary aspect of the exchange value of athletic partici-pation is very great for the exceptionally gifted athlete. Because those who reap these scarce benefits are very few, a matter of thousands in a society of millions, these benefits do not con-stitute much of the utility in the society as a whole. This is especially the case because those exchanging their participation in athletics for really large monetary rewards constitute only a small fraction of those thousands receiving any monetary rewards at all. Consequently, the loss of this aspect of the exchange value of sports in society would, taken by itself, have a minute effect upon the average level of utility in the society as a whole. More important from the perspective of average utility would be the effect on spectators. People are spectators, presumably, because they enjoy watching sports. If people are prevented from reaping monetary rewards from athletic participation, it would seem that there would be less athletic competition for would-be spectators to watch, hence a considerable drop in average utility.

If the exchange and use values of athletic participation are inversely related, however, such a drop in average utility would almost surely not occur. The general level of proficiency among athletes whose play is being watched would, on the whole, be drastically reduced. But it is not at all clear that one's enjoyment as a spectator is primarily or even very largely a function of the level of proficiency of the athletes being watched. A close contest, personal acquaintance with the contestants and personal presence at the site of competition are each as significant a determinant of spectator enjoyment as is the level of the contestants' proficiency. And two of these would be increased, for those who chose to be spectators, if athletes were not paid for their participation. By drastically reducing the exchange value of sports, the use value would be greatly increased. This means that many more people would be playing more of the time in more locations. Those who chose to be spectators would more often be able to witness athletic events in person because such events would more often be taking place nearby and the cost of admission would be little (to cover maintenance of the grounds, for example) if anything. And since more people would be participating in athletics, it would more often be possible to view contests among people with whom the spectator is personally acquainted. So there is no reason to suppose that the enjoyment of those who chose to be spectators would be diminished if athletes were not paid.

It is the aggregate of spectator enjoyment which would be reduced, not the average. It would be reduced because fewer people would be spectators as more, if use value is inversely related to exchange value, voluntarily eschew watching in favor of participating. But if, as I have argued, sporting events would be as available and enjoyable for spectators as at present, the predominance of participation would signal that people gain even more enjoyment from participation. This would represent a broad based net gain in utility that would, because it affects so many people, have a greater effect on average utility than all of the preceding considerations.

In sum, the loss of utility to professional athletes would be more than compensated for by the gain in utility on the part of the large proportion of the population who would voluntarily exchange watching for participating.[9] Those who continued to watch would at worst be affected neutrally. So, if the inverse proportionality thesis is correct, the proponent of maximizing average utility should adopt the ideal of a society in which athletes are debarred from being paid for their athletic participation.

Those who, like Richard Brandt and Nicholas Rescher, believe that utilitarian considerations should be combined with egalitarian considerations have a stronger reason for reaching the same conclusion. For this is a case in which utility and equality go hand-in-hand. The gain in utility is broad-based. It accrues to the large number of people who voluntarily exchange watching for participating. The loss in utility, besides being smaller than the gain, includes the loss to those making substantial sums from their athletic participation. There is thus a leveling effect. The relative have-nots gain and the haves lose.

Rawls has an even stronger reason for adopting the ideal of a society in which athletics is de-professionalized. An example will make this clear. Rawls is interested in maximizing the level of welfare of the representative individual from society's least advantaged group. Welfare is gauged in terms of what he calls primary goods, wealth, power, liberty and, importantly, self-respect. Suppose, then, that we group people by sex. (We could get the same results grouping people by age, size or weight.) Suppose, further, that the aggregate of use value and of exchange value accruing to women from sports is less than the corresponding values accruing to men. Finally, suppose that the exchange value of athletic participation for exceptionally gifted individuals in the society is great. These suggestions probably accord well with the actual situation in our society at this time. But this is not essential since the same conclusion can be drawn from plausible alternate assumptions.

On these suppositions women are the worse off group. De-professionalizing sports would result in a greater loss of wealth to men than to women because men have more to lose. But if the inverse relationship thesis and the accompanying utilitarian calculations presented above are correct, utility would be increased by de-professionalization, even for men. The loss to male professional athletes would be more than compensated for by the gain to many more other men in terms of the use value of sports. Rawls's particular emphasis on the primary good of self-respect and his employment of what he calls the Aristotelian Principle both serve to strengthen this conclusion. For the loss among men would be primarily financial, whereas the gain would be, through greater athletic participation, in the realms of self-confidence and self-respect, as these come, in accordance with the Aristotelian Principle, from progressive mastery of skills and development of talents.

A *fortiori*, the position of women would be improved by the de-professionalization of athletics. They have less to lose financially and more to gain in terms of self-confidence and self-respect. So if Rawls advocates maximizing primary values among the most deprived group, and women are the most deprived group (when we group by sex), then he should advocate the de-professionalization of athletics.

The same conclusion would follow were the aggregate exchange value of women's athletic participation equal to that of men. In such a case women would have as much to lose financially as men from de-professionalization. But they would still have more to gain than men in terms of the self-respect that comes from the use value of sports. And even men gain more than they lose by de-professionalization. So women would still be the most deprived group whose accumulation of primary goods would be maximized by banning financial rewards for athletic participation. Like men, they would gain more

in self-respect than they lost financially. Such a ban would, therefore, still follow from Rawls's theory when combined with the inverse relationship thesis.

Conclusion

In sum, if the inverse relationship thesis is correct, the de-professionalization of sports is ethically mandatory from the utilitarian, egalitarian and Rawlsian ethical perspectives. Two conclusions follow from this. First, empirical, social scientific research designed to test the IRT is in order. Second, if the IRT is correct, sex equality in sports is a by-product of and impossible without the more general human equality in sports that results from an emphasis on use over exchange values. This prompts, without in any way confirming, the following conjectural generalization concerning social equality between members of groups which are, as groups, biologically unequal. The equality of the groups can be approached only as a general egalitarianism among individuals, taken as individuals, is approached through a concentration on use rather than exchange values.

Addendum – The Fine Arts Objection

In my discussions with colleagues and students, one objection to the ideas in this paper recurs. There is also a common misunderstanding. I will deal first with the misunderstanding, and then with the objection.

Many people have supposed that if professionalism in sports is disallowed, there could be no professional *teachers* of sports. This is not what I mean, and does not follow from the reasoning that I present in the paper. De-professionalizing sports, as I understand it, involves disallowing anyone from accepting money for his or her participation as a *player* or *contestant*. It does not disallow payment for providing instruction in sports. For example, teachers may still be paid for providing instruction in physical education. Professional instruction in sports, as in other areas, like reading, writing, arithmetic and the fine arts, can broaden participation and improve not only the quality of performance, but also the quality of experience of participation. Aggregate use value is thus increased. If the instruction is inexpensive and widely available, the increase in use value will satisfy egalitarian and Rawlsian as well as utilitarian principles. So the argument in the paper does not imply that *instruction* in sports, or in any other area, should be de-professionalized.

Now for the objection. It is objected that if it is ethically mandatory that sports be de-professionalized, the same should follow for the fine arts. The objector maintains that painters, sculptors, singers, actors and other practitioners of the fine arts should be debarred from receiving payment for the practice of their art. As in the case of sports, de-professionalization would result in a steep decline in the quality of performance. Are we really willing, the objector asks, to have the quality of our fine arts decline precipitously? The objector believes that we should not be willing to experience such a decline. Thus, de-professionalization in the arts is unacceptable. This casts doubt upon the cogency of any reasoning that leads to the view that such de-professionalization is ethically mandatory. The reasoning that leads to the view that *sports* should be de-professionalized is problematic, because it is the same reasoning that is used to show that the arts should be de-professionalized. If the reasoning is suspect when applied to the arts, it is suspect when applied to sports.

The reply to this objection is that sports and fine arts are so fundamentally different from one another that the argument about sports does not suggest that the fine arts be de-professionalized. The arts, unlike sports, are attempts to examine, illustrate and illuminate various aspects of the human condition. They attempt to foster individual and social self-understanding. The quality of fine arts productions is therefore of great importance. A general lowering of quality in the fine arts could easily impede self-understanding and promote alienation on the part of all concerned, artists and non-artists alike. In sum, unlike sports, the benefit that spectators derive from the arts is crucially affected by the quality of the artists' products. If, as seems likely, disallowing payment for such products were to depress their quality (even when professional instruction is allowed) the loss to society would be great. Assuming that this loss would outweigh any gains from de-professionalization, such as increased numbers of participants in the arts, de-professionalization does not satisfy the utilitarian criterion of maximizing the good. If access to the products of professional artists is widespread, there would be no egalitarian or Rawlsian objections to professionalism in the fine arts. In fact, Rawls's view suggests that people with talent in the fine arts be encouraged by the promise of personal reward to develop and employ their talents fully. Everyone, including those who are least well-off, can benefit from the esthetic experience and improved self-understanding that artists make possible.

The argument against professionalism in sports is, therefore, not open to the objection that it leads to the unacceptable conclusion that the fine arts, too, should be de-professionalized.

Notes

1 Rose De Wolf, "The Battle for Good Teams," *Women Sports* 1 (July, 1974), pp. 61–63; in *Sex Equality* ed. Jane English (Prentice-Hall, 1977), pp. 231–238. Ellen Weber, "Boys and Girls Together: The Coed Team Controversy," *Women Sports* 1 (September, 1974), pp. 53–55. Brenda Fasteau, "Giving Women a Sporting Chance," *Ms. Magazine*, July, 1973. Ann Crittenden Scott, "Closing the Muscle Gap," *Ms. Magazine*, September, 1974, pp. 49–55, 89. Mariann Pogge, "From Cheerleader to Competitor," *Update*, Fall, 1978, pp. 15–18.

2 Title IX of the 1964 Civil Rights Act as amended 42 U.S.

3 Michigan, Connecticut, New Jersey, Indiana, Minnesota and Nebraska have statutes providing for the integration of non-contact sports at the high school level.

4 *Hollander v. Connecticut Interstate Athletic Conference*, Superior Court of New Haven Co., Conn., March 29, 1971. *Haas v. South Bend Community School Corp.*, 289 N.E. 2d 495 (Ind. 1972). *Bucha v.*

Illinois High School Association, 351 F. Supp. 69 (N.D. Ill. 1972). *N.O.W. Essex County Chapter v. Little League Baseball*, 127 N.J. Superior, 22, 318A. 2d, 33 (1974).

5   Jane English, "Sex Equality in Sports," *Philosophy and Public Affairs* 8 (Spring, 1978) [reprinted here as reading 23].

6   De Wolf, pp. 232 ff.

7   De Wolf, p. 235.

8   This is similar but not identical to Jane English's distinction between the basic and scarce benefits of sports.

9   More remote effects can be ignored because they are so problematic and might, for that reason, as likely favor one side as another. Also, those which can be counted on, like the losses to promoters of professional athletics, lawyers for professional athletes and others dependent on professional athletics for a living, will largely be matched by gains for those who produce the athletic equipment used by increasing numbers of participants.

CHAPTER 25

Gender Equity and Inequity in Athletics

Robert L. Simon

For a large portion of American history, highly competitive sport often was thought not to be appropriate for women. During a good part of the twentieth century, more formal athletic competition for women tended to take the form of noncompetitive "play days" or participation on teams that received little of the support accorded to men's sports. Although great female athletes such as Althea Gibson, Babe Zaharias, and Mickey Wright flourished during this period, athletic competition was available only in attenuated form for most females in most sports.

Thus, in 1971, slightly less than 300,000 girls participated in high school sports, while nearly 4,000,000 boys participated (8: p. 3). James Michener, in his book *Sports in America*, in writing about the period shortly before passage of Title IX, reported that

> one day I saw the budget of . . . a state institution (a university) supported by tax funds, with a student body divided fifty-fifty between men and women. The athletic department had $3,900,000 to spend, and of this, women received exactly $31,000, a little less than eight-tenths of one percent. On this face of it, this was outrageous. (6: p. 120)

This situation changed radically along with, and surely in great part because of, the passage of Title IX, the federal legislation that prohibited discrimination by gender in all federally funded programs, including athletics. Thus, by 1979, 2,000,000 girls were participating in high school athletics. Similar growth took place at the intercollegiate level as well (8: p. 3).

Although the growth of participation in women's sports on the interscholastic and intercollegiate level has been enormous since the passage of Title IX, issues of gender equity in athletics are still very much with us. For example, in intercollegiate athletics in the United States, less total income is spent on female athletes than on male athletes, female athletes receive significantly less attention from the media than male athletes, and females continue to participate less than their male counterparts. Thus, issues of justice and fairness for each gender remain significant in organized athletics, including at the intercollegiate level.

Title IX lays down the legal criteria of non-discrimination in athletics. Gender equity sometimes is taken as a broader notion having to do with morally fair and just treatment. But how are we to tell when men's and women's athletic programs within the same institution are treated equitably? What are the criteria of equity in this area?

In this essay, I will try to identify and explore some of the major issues that arise under the heading of gender equity in athletics. I will try to sketch out the landscape and indicate where controversies lie. My main focus will be on intercollegiate athletics in the U.S., although the discussion certainly will have broader application, and on some of the important questions of gender equity that arise in such a context.

Gender Equity and Intercollegiate Sport

The general kind of consideration underlying the case for gender equity in sports is that no individual should be deprived of access to beneficial activities or opportunities merely on the basis of gender. Participation in athletics can provide important benefits ranging from what Jane English has called the basic benefits of sport, such as healthy exercise and the opportunity to learn to compete, as well as scarce benefits such as fame and fortune (3: pp. 329–330). In addition, there are what might be called constitutive benefits, that is, goods that are comprehensible only within the framework defined by the constitutive rules of the game and that have no value to those who do not appreciate the nuances of the game itself (5: pp. 175–178). Thus, the pleasure of pulling off a perfect double play in baseball, the faking out of a defender in basketball, or the execution of a difficult fade to a pin cut in the right corner of a well-protected green in golf are all examples of such constitutive goods, which may be virtually meaningless to nonplayers, but which may be remembered for a lifetime by participants and fans. Finally, as Jan Boxill emphasizes in her contribution in this issue [reprinted here as reading 26], sports not only constitute a widely available means of unalienated self-expression but also open doors for other sorts of opportunities in our society. The case for gender equity presupposes that to restrict access to these sorts of goods by gender is unfair and unjust.

However, it doesn't follow from this that educational institutions, particularly colleges and universities, should support athletic teams and engage in the existing practice of intercollegiate sport. Whether colleges and universities ought to support intercollegiate athletics in the first place is a different issue from what counts

as gender equity once such programs are already established. Indeed, many observers are skeptical of the value of intercollegiate sports. (Leslie Francis expresses such skepticism in her contribution to this issue [9].) In part, this may be because of highly publicized abuses in major college athletic programs. Even where such abuses are eliminated, however, skepticism might still arise from concerns about the time athletes are required to commit to their sport, the expenditures on athletics that critics feel might be applied to more central educational concerns, the exploitation of athletes, and the tremendous emphasis on athletic (as opposed to academic) success at some U.S. universities. In other words, intercollegiate athletics are seen to be in conflict with the central academic mission of the university.

While such skepticism cannot be fully assessed here, it is relevant to our concerns about gender equity, since most proponents of gender equity are concerned about equity within the present framework of intercollegiate sports. A more radical approach (which Francis goes some way towards endorsing) would encourage making fundamental changes in the framework itself, or perhaps even eliminating it.

In assessing skepticism about intercollegiate sports as presently constituted, two points do need to be kept in mind. First, it is important to distinguish the high pressure, "big-time" athletic programs of the major intercollegiate athletic powers from other sorts of intercollegiate athletic programs. Division III is the largest division of the National Collegiate Athletic Association (NCAA), and its schools, which do not award athletic scholarships, are explicitly committed to the ideal of the scholar-athlete and to the priority of academics over athletics. In addition, a number of conferences in Division I, such as the Ivy League and the Patriot League, embrace a similar philosophy. Moreover, many of the major athletic powers appear to run "clean" programs and recruit academically successful athletes. Differences among the different kinds of athletic programs clearly can be relevant to the moral evaluation of them.

Second, although a case can be made casting doubt on the educational value of participation in athletics, it is important to remember that much can be said on the other side. Thus, one can plausibly (although controversially) argue that intercollegiate athletics at their best do serve educational functions that are compatible and that may even reinforce the central academic tasks of the university. Effective performance in intercollegiate sports requires commitment, the ability to analyze one's weaknesses and the means to improve them, the capacity to perform under pressure, and the ability to work together with many different sorts of people towards a common goal. Similar values are necessary for academic success. The test of excellence, which constitutes the athletic contest, can be an important educational experience in which the participants learn about themselves and others. Moreover, effective performance by athletic teams can illustrate the values of dedication, coolness under pressure, courage, and intelligence in performance for the entire community within a common framework to which individuals from different genders, religions, ethnic backgrounds, cultures, and academic disciplines can all relate.

Whether such an argument is ultimately justifiable is controversial. However, it is relevant to the question of gender equity in intercollegiate athletics. If the practice does provide important educational benefits to participants, as well as opportunities for recognition and fun, a strong presumptive case exists against making distinctions by gender in cases of access to participation or treatment of participants. Moreover, even if (as Francis claims [9]) intercollegiate athletics is a morally flawed practice that ought to be modified or even radically changed, presumably the benefits it does provide should be available to each gender.

In any case, the discussion that follows primarily concerns the framework of intercollegiate athletics. Because the gross abuses found in some major athletic programs need not be part of such a practice, and in fact violate existing rules of the NCAA and go beyond the scope of gender equity, they are not considered here. Instead, the issues concerning gender equity within intercollegiate athletics, as so constituted, are addressed.

Concepts, Conceptions, and Tests of Equity

It is puzzling when one finds all the parties to an ethical dispute appealing to the same value. Why then is there a dispute? Often, it is because the parties have different and conflicting conceptions of the value in question. For example, two individuals may both profess to believe in equal opportunity in hiring. However, one might understand equal opportunity as requiring simply the hiring of the best candidate as measured by standard meritocratic criteria, while the other may view virtually any set of meritocratic criteria as culturally biased. Such an individual may understand equal opportunity as requiring reasonable representation of disadvantaged groups in the work force. Clearly, although both individuals believe in "equal opportunity," what each considers equal opportunity is vastly different.

A similar point seems to apply to the value of gender equity in athletics. Although conceptual lines have not been drawn very clearly by participants in the public policy discussion, it is far from clear that all are working with the same conception of gender equity or that important conceptual distinctions have been made.

Thus, the Gender Equity Task Force of the NCAA declares that an athletics program is equitable to each gender "when the participants in both the men's and women's sports programs would accept as fair and equitable the overall program of the other gender" (4: p. 3). This account seems related to the idea of role reversal and impartiality in moral theory, but leaves open many of the questions raised by such approaches.

For example, does this mean that members of each gender should assess the program of the other gender using their own values and criteria? Or should they "bracket" those values and criteria and try to view things as if they had the values of the other gender? (Do values differ, even statistically, by gender?) Should they try to view things from some neutral perspective, perhaps behind a Rawlsian veil of ignorance, which would obscure from them the knowledge of just which gender they belong to?

Moreover, even if we could agree on the perspective from which we were to evaluate the program of the other gender, it is far from clear that all those who took that perspective would agree in their evaluation. For example, Jones might believe that coaches in high visibility men's sports work under higher pressure than coaches of the same sports in women's programs and so should be paid more even if all other qualifications are equivalent. Smith, however, might disagree. Such persistent disputes need not be largely factual (Are coaches of men's sports necessarily under more pressure to win than coaches in parallel sports in the women's program?) but may be primarily normative. Jones may see nothing wrong with men's sports getting a disproportionate share of national publicity, since that is what the public wants, but Smith may see the media as having a moral duty to promote more equal coverage regardless of public demands.

Such concerns may not do justice to the intent of the Gender Equity Task Force, because their goal almost surely was not to present a philosophically adequate theory of gender equity. Their account in terms of taking the perspective of the other gender may be quite useful, not as a philosophical theory, but as a ground rule for discussion. Be that as it may, such a requirement is not sufficient to dictate agreement on what counts as gender equity, or whether it has been achieved in a specific context, both because of ambiguity in what counts as taking an alternate perspective and because disagreement may persist even among people evaluating from the same perspective. Thus, even individuals of the same gender often will disagree among themselves when evaluating the fairness of an athletics program.

While disagreement is possible even among people using the same conception of gender equity, disagreement is also possible over which conception should be employed. Even worse, parties to a dispute may not even notice they are using different conceptions of gender equity. Thus, if X identifies gender equity in college athletics with proportional representation of men and women in the athletic program, and Y identifies it with similar treatment of parallel

teams, for example, similar budgets for men's and women's volleyball, then gender equity may exist according to Y's conception but not X's. A genuine issue they need to discuss is whose conception of gender equity is more defensible.

Moreover, we also need to distinguish tests or procedures for discovering what gender equity requires. For example, one might hold that gender equity substantively requires representation of each gender proportional to the gender's representation among the student body. One might justify this by appeal to the test of taking the perspective of the other gender. The latter functions as a kind of role-reversal test at the level of justification, while the former requirement is alleged to be what those who actually do reverse roles would come to agree upon.

Thus a full conception of gender equity in intercollegiate athletics has several levels, including a level of justification that involves procedures or methods of moral evaluation and a level of substantive criteria or requirements that specific programs should satisfy. Conceivably, different justificatory approaches could support the same substantive requirements. It is equally conceivable that those who use the same justificatory approach might disagree about what requirements are justified, perhaps because they apply the justificatory method differently or disagree on factual matters relevant to the argument.

Rather than attempt to distinguish all the possible conceptions of gender equity, it will be useful for our purposes to simplify so as to advance the discussion. Let us say that an athletics program is gender equitable if it makes no unjustified distinctions between the genders. This approach has two advantages. First, it avoids begging key questions by stipulation because it leaves open what a justifiable distinction is. That is to be settled on a case by case basis by discussion, although general principles of justifiability may emerge from the examination of cases. Second, this approach is related to the one used to interpret Title IX that has recently been developed by the Office of Civil Rights (OCR). Thus, relevant aspects of the legal discussion over Title IX can be incorporated into the moral discussion of gender equity.

The OCR's Three-Tiered Test

Sometimes individuals who are frustrated by what they perceive as the lack of equity for women in intercollegiate athletics will express disbelief that progress has been so slow two decades after the passage of Title IX. It is only recently, however, that relatively clear (although still contestable) guidelines for the legal interpretation of Title IX have been promulgated by the OCR. Indeed, prior to special legislation by Congress, the Supreme Court had ruled in *Grove City vs. Bell* (1984) that Title IX only applied to those programs within educational institutions that directly received federal funds. If Congress had not passed special legislation in 1988 overriding that decision, it is unclear that Title IX would have applied to intercollegiate athletics at all since few if any intercollegiate athletic programs receive funds directly from the U.S. government.

The guidelines promulgated by the OCR are of interest both because they specify allowable exceptions to a general presumption of equal treatment and because they raise some interesting problems in their own right. The OCR identifies three major areas of compliance with Title IX: athletic scholarships, accommodation of athletic interests and abilities, and other athletic benefits and awards. We will be concerned with the second area, accommodation of athletic abilities and interests, since it clearly is most fundamental.

The OCR proposes the following three-part test for gender equality in the accommodation of athletic abilities and interests. One must consider

- Whether opportunities for participation in the intercollegiate athletics program for students of each sex are substantially proportionate to their respective enrollments
- If not, whether the institution can show a history and continuing practice of expansion of the intercollegiate athletic program responsive to developing interests and abilities of members of the underrepresented sex
- If not, whether the interests and abilities of the underrepresented sex are "fully and effectively accommodated" by the existing program (1: p. 7).

Legal compliance is established by satisfying any one of the three tests. An intercollegiate athletic program that fails an earlier element might still be in compliance with Title IX by satisfying one of the later prongs. The first is a "safe harbor" in the sense that a finding of proportionality will at the very least establish a strong and indeed virtually overwhelming presumption of compliance. However, failure to show proportionality (it is doubtful if any institutions of higher education in the country now satisfy this requirement strictly construed) is not sufficient to establish noncompliance since the other criteria still might be met.

The three-part OCR test has some important resemblances to the presumptive approach to gender equity. It assumes both genders will be treated equally and specifies some allowable reasons for inequality. Representation of gender in proportion to its share of the overall student body normally will be taken as virtually conclusive evidence of equal treatment. However, if proportionality cannot be satisfied, inequality can be justified by showing compliance with one of the other two prongs of the test. Moreover, in assessing whether the interests of the underrepresented gender have been "fully and effectively accommodated," the assumption is that each gender will be treated equally in the absence of justifying reasons for inequality.

Of course, what counts as a justifiable reason for inequality often will be controversial. Does the past success of the men's basketball team at a Division I institution justify them playing a more nationally prominent schedule than the less successful women's team? What if the athletic director promises to upgrade the women's schedule as soon as the team develops sufficiently to compete successfully at that level? Should a 98-pound female gymnast receive the same daily meal allowance as a 275-pound male lineman when the teams are on the road? Would it be an inequity if the lineman were given a greater allowance because he needs more food? Is it an inequity if the basketball coach of the men's team is paid more than the equally experienced and competent coach of the women's team on the grounds that there is more pressure to win and greater chance of being fired after a losing season in the men's program?

Clearly, all of these questions cannot be explored in one paper. In what follows, I will raise some questions about two fundamental parts of the OCR three-pronged test: proportionality and effective accommodation of interests. Because they are fundamental, exploration of these areas may help shed some light on other important issues of gender equity that are likely to arise as well. I will conclude with some brief comments on suggestions for fundamental change in intercollegiate athletics.

Proportionality

The idea that men and women should be represented in an educational institution's athletic program in proportion to their representation in the student body initially sounds plausible. After all, if participation in athletics provides significant benefits and opportunities, and if there is no reason to favor one gender in the distribution of these benefits and opportunities, then one would expect them to be made available to both genders equally. So if 60% of the student body are men and 40% are women, then in the absence of discrimination one would expect to find that about 60% of the institution's athletes are men and about 40% are women.

However, there are a number of problems with this initial expectation. According to the NCAA Gender Equity Task Force, there currently are 3.4 million male and 1.9 million female participants in interscholastic sports at the high school level in the U.S. (4: p. 5). Clearly, there is a significant disproportion in the representation of each gender in sports at the precollege level. Is it reasonable, then, to expect the proportion of women participating at the college level, which is significantly more demanding than the high school level, to suddenly jump? If not, it seems unreasonable to place so much stress on proportional representation in the first place. Where are the additional female athletes needed to achieve proportionality to come from?

In other words, the argument that each gender should be proportionately represented in the university's intercollegiate athletic program presupposes that the members of each gender have an *equal interest* in participating. It is just that presupposition that critics of proportionality call into question.

Many proponents of proportionality do not find this objection persuasive, however. They reply that females in America traditionally have been discouraged from participating in athletics and are only beginning to overcome the kind of socialization that has inhibited participation. Hence, rates of participation are not adequate indicators of true interest. If colleges and universities will provide additional women's sports, the participants eventually will come.

While this rejoinder does have some force, I think it also raises some difficult questions. First, it is important to remember that questions of distributive justice in intercollegiate athletics arise at least at two levels: distribution of resources within the athletic program and distribution within the university generally. Thus, should colleges and universities be required to increase expenditure on athletics at a time when many academic needs are unmet because of lack of funding, simply to generate purely hypothetical interests that some women would have had or might have had if they had been socialized differently?

Perhaps the answer to this rhetorical question is affirmative. After all, if participation in athletics does have important educational, personal, and recreational benefits, why shouldn't women be especially encouraged to participate? Similarly, shouldn't the university take it as part of its mission to expose students to great literature even though they may have no prior expressed interest in it (and may even desire avoiding it)? Moreover, many more women than those who try out for teams may have an interest in participation in athletics, but may not express that interest due to lack of encouragement.

Be that as it may, is *varsity* athletics the place to cultivate such interest? Perhaps what would be more appropriate are more general recreational programs including club sports and intramurals, at a level of lower competitive intensity, designed to involve large numbers of women in sports. The addition of a varsity team or two hardly fulfills such a role and surely is better justified for individuals already strongly interested in participating. Varsity sports demand a high level of commitment, involve a great deal of competitive intensity, and seem most appropriate for those individuals who already have significant interest in participating in athletic competition.

Advocates of proportionality see it as a means for increasing participation in athletics. Moreover, they point out that institutions need not provide proportional participation by gender if they can meet the other OCR criteria. Thus, proportionality is a "goal" and not a "quota."

However, an additional concern about proportionality is that it can function in ways unintended by its supporters, because there are two different ways to remedy disproportional representation of men. The first is to raise the proportion of women participating. The second is to *reduce* the proportion of men participating.

Suppose an institution is 60% male and 40% female. Suppose further that 70% of its 1,000 intercollegiate athletes are men and only 30% of its intercollegiate athletes are women. The school could, of course, try to raise the percentage of female athletes to around 40%, but it may find it very difficult to do so both because of the expense involved and because of the difficulty of finding interested female athletes. Instead, it could cut male teams and reduce the percentage of men playing to, say, under 50% of all athletes. That is, by cutting sports involving 300 male athletes, the school would be left with 700 athletes of whom 400 would be men, and 300 would be women. Men would now only constitute 57% of all athletes and women would constitute 43%. In other words, by cutting men's sports, the institution could achieve proportionality and a "safe harbor" from further legal action *without adding an additional opportunity for even a single female athlete to participate*.

While this is undoubtedly an extreme case, the provision that proportionality is a safe harbor from legal action can act as an incentive to trim men's programs so as to appear to provide equal access to underrepresented women athletes without increasing opportunities for women. In fact, less visible men's sports teams seem to have

been cut at a number of institutions, quite possibly in part to achieve a more respectable looking ratio of female to male athletes.

Accordingly, the requirement of proportionality may have the unintended consequence in American colleges and universities of decreasing the total number of slots on athletic teams, quite possibly without significantly increasing opportunities to participate for women.[1] Strictly speaking, the incentive to cut male sports arises not from the proportionality requirement taken alone, satisfaction of which is not necessary for compliance with Title IX, but from the additional suggestion that satisfaction of proportionality is a virtual presumption of immunity from further complaint about gender equity.

Perhaps the problem then is not with the proportionality requirement, conceived of as a long-range goal, but with the additional presumption of virtual immunity. It is hard to understand, in any case, why an athletic program that satisfies proportionality may not be deficient in other serious ways (e.g., women being denied equal access to training facilities). Accordingly, a more sensible policy might be to take proportionality as an ideal to be achieved in the long run, indicate what colleges and universities ought to do in the short run to make modest but significant gains in participation in athletics by females, and drop the idea of a "safe harbor" from examination altogether.

To summarize, the requirement of proportionality raises several issues. First, is it unrealistic and unfair to expect colleges to achieve proportional representation by gender in athletics by increasing the number of female participants, when females are significantly underrepresented in interscholastic athletics at the high school level? (Colleges and universities might still be expected to make genuine efforts to incrementally increase the proportion of women participating in intercollegiate athletics, however, without being expected to achieve proportional representation.) Second, should achievement of proportionality count as a "safe harbor" from either moral or legal scrutiny of an intercollegiate athletics program? This provides an incentive for institutions to achieve proportionality, not by enhancing participation for women, but by eliminating opportunities for men, probably in less visible sports without powerful lobbies to protect them. In addition, it is far from clear that a program that achieves proportionality is equitable in other ways, and so it is far from clear that such programs should receive protection from examination or culpability.

Accordingly, the proportionality test is problematic, whether construed as a legal requirement or as a moral standard that intercollegiate programs can be held culpable for failing to meet.

Interests and Equity

Because few if any intercollegiate athletic programs are likely to achieve proportionality in the next few years, most institutions that wish to demonstrate compliance with Title IX will try to show that they "fully and effectively accommodate" the interests of the underrepresented gender, which typically is women. If we turn to the moral analogue of the OCR test, this means that if men are disproportionately represented in an intercollegiate athletics program, colleges and universities ought to fully satisfy the interests of the gender that is least represented. (The case for full and effective accommodation becomes even stronger if the bulk of funding goes to men, which normally will be the case in athletic programs that include football.) This at least appears to resemble the Rawlsian idea that the group getting the lesser share ought to be made as well-off as possible.[2]

Clearly there is a moral case to be made for this kind of approach. Until the passage of Title IX, college athletic programs made little attempt to support the athletic interests of female students, while providing a great deal of support for male athletes. Surely, it is fair and just to require colleges to meet the interests of female athletes, given that so much has been, and is being, done for male athletes.

Nevertheless, the idea that the interests of female student athletes should be "fully and effectively accommodated" raises problems that deserve examination. This is because the

accommodation of interests criterion (AIC) is quite strong. In programs that have not achieved proportionality, and in which females are underrepresented when compared to their share of the student body as a whole, the AIC virtually ensures that the interests of women athletes will be fully accommodated, even when the same is not true for the interests of men. For example, consider a hypothetical institution in which the student body of 1,000 is 55% male and 45% female. Suppose 200 men and 100 women play in the intercollegiate program. In other words, about 66% of the athletes are men and 33% women. Suppose now that a group of women show an interest in having a varsity crew team, a relatively expensive sport. Under the AIC, the women should get the team and the university is inequitable if it fails to provide it for them. Let us review the case for this conclusion.

Roughly sketched, the argument is that because women have had the lesser opportunity in the past and because men receive the bulk of the benefits provided by participation in intercollegiate athletics, equity requires that the position of women be improved. This case becomes even stronger (perhaps, as Leslie Francis suggests in this issue [9], it is comparable to the case for some forms of affirmative action) if we assume the past lack of opportunity for women to participate in intercollegiate athletics was a moral *wrong* or has arisen from moral *wrongdoing*.

What problems does this kind of argument face? For one thing, those critics of affirmative action who tend to focus on individuals as the locus of moral analysis will want to raise individual-group concerns. Although women may have been wronged in the past, it is unlikely that those individual women who would now participate in sports if the program were expanded are the very same individuals who have been wronged in the past. A rejoinder to this criticism is that the point of expanding the women's athletic program is not to provide compensation to individuals. Rather, it may be to improve the status of women, provide future opportunities for women, or enhance the overall fairness of the athletic program by providing equal access to each gender. (Indeed, if we add 16 women to the program by making crew a varsity sport, women are still only 37% of the intercollegiate athletes although they constitute 45% of our hypothetical student body.) None of these goals have anything to do with individual compensation, but instead are concerned with moral improvement of the athletic program in the future.

Some would argue that the concerns of the individualist can be laid to rest by such a reply. In any case, the concerns raised by the individualist cover ground familiar to those who have followed the literature on affirmative action (2). Be that as it may, both the individualist criticism and the rejoinder presuppose that women's interests have not been effectively accommodated in the past. This surely is true if we go back to the days before Title IX when women had few opportunities, let alone equal ones, in competitive athletics. But is it necessarily true of our hypothetical student body if crew is not elevated to varsity status?

Suppose the following were the case at our hypothetical university. Although 200 men participate in the intercollegiate program, 300 have tried out for teams. One hundred were cut either because of lack of ability or because the coaching staff could not work effectively with so many players. Only 15 women who tried out for teams were cut. Thus, 87% of the women who went out for teams secured positions while only 66% of the men who tried out were able to participate.[3] According to a line of argument suggested by these figures, women have had a *greater* chance than men to play varsity sports at our hypothetical institution if we restrict the relevant pool of comparison to those interested enough to try out for teams. In what sense, a skeptic may ask, have women had less opportunity than men to play in the intercollegiate program?

The point here seems to be that in deciding which gender is underrepresented, we need to use the relevant pool of students as our standard of comparison. What is controversial is the specification of the relevant pool. If the relevant pool is not the student body as a whole, but instead it is the students sufficiently committed to try out for teams, it may be debatable whether women are the underrepresented gender. Why then, a critic of the OCR guidelines may ask, should failure to meet the proportionality prong

of the OCR test virtually guarantee women that their interests in varsity athletics will be "fully and effectively accommodated"? Their interests already may be accommodated more fully than those of men.

Something like this line of argument was advanced by Brown University when, after attempting to drop two women's and two men's intercollegiate sports, it was sued by the women athletes who wanted their teams protected from cuts. One line of defense advanced by Brown was that "an institution satisfactorily accommodates female athletes if it allocates athletic opportunities to women in accordance with the ratio of interested and able women to interested and able men, regardless of the number of unserved women or the percentage of the student body they comprise" (1: p. 8).

What might be the grounds for rejecting Brown's argument? The U.S. First Circuit Court of Appeals rejected Brown's argument citing a variety of reasons. For one thing, Brown's proposal places a significant administrative burden on the plaintiffs to a suit since they would have to gather evidence as to the number of "interested and able" male and female athletes. Moreover, would the relevant pool be the present student body, the high school pool the university normally recruits from, or an expanded pool it could recruit from if it wanted to attract a larger number of female athletes?

More important, the court believed it proper to assume that, given equal opportunity and encouragement, women will participate in athletics to the same extent as men. Accordingly, that more men show an interest in participation than women under inequitable conditions of opportunity and encouragement must not be taken as determinative. Moreover, the court concluded that even if regulations "create a gender classification slanted somewhat in favor of women, we would find no constitutional infirmity" (1: p. 10).

These kinds of arguments still leave questions unresolved. For example, what is the relevance of appeal to *administrative inconvenience* to claims of *equity* and *fairness*? Surely, the more convenient and less complex policy is not necessarily the more equitable or fair one.[4] After all, plaintiffs in gender equity suits already have the burden of showing that their gender's interests have not been accommodated, yet that is not considered unfair.

The second and more weighty line of argument maintains that because women are currently in a situation that unfairly disadvantages them athletically, their relative lack of current overt expressions of interest cannot be taken at face value. But even here, problems remain. Does the assumption that conditions are not yet fair beg the issue, since the very point at issue is whether or not women's interests are already fairly accommodated?[5] Again, what if the specific institution in question never itself discriminated against or disadvantaged women athletes? (Suppose it were all male until recently going co-educational.) But leaving these points aside, perhaps a more crucial issue is whether *balancing* is permitted at all. That is, in a college or university that has not achieved proportionality as defined by the OCR and that has no recent history of expansion of the women's athletic program, must the interests of any group of women be fully met regardless of other factors that might be relevant? Or, is there simply a weighty presumption in favor of meeting the women's interests, but one which may be overridden if there are sufficiently strong competing considerations on the other side?

In the case involving Brown University, there may have been no such overriding factors. But suppose that in our hypothetical example a very large number of able and interested male students lack the opportunity to play intercollegiate sports and only a small number of able and interested female students lack the same opportunity. Suppose the interested female students want to play an expensive sport (say, ice hockey), but the administration would rather institute a less expensive sport for women (say, soccer) and use the money saved for scholarships for needy students (who may or may not be athletes). Should the administration have the moral (or legal) discretion to decide whether or not to add a women's sport in such a context? If it must add a sport, does it have the discretion to decide which one to add? Or must it add the sport that will satisfy the interested and able students who are petitioning?[6]

Accordingly, we can conclude that just as the requirement of proportional representation of genders in intercollegiate athletic programs raises problems of significance, so too does the requirement that if proportionality is not achieved (and there is no recent history of expansion of the program of the underrepresented gender), then the interests of the underrepresented gender must be "fully and effectively accommodated." What counts as full and effective accommodation, and how is it to be weighed against other factors that are likely to be highly controversial in many contexts? My own suggestion is that some sort of balancing test, in the context of a presumption in favor of the underrepresented gender, is appropriate. But, how strong the presumption should be, or what sort of factors should be allowed to override it, are difficult to decide *a priori* (at least for me) and are probably best left to emerge from case law and consideration of actual and hypothetical examples in moral discourse.

Reform or Revolution

The discussion so far has focussed on problems that arise within the existing framework of intercollegiate sport. However, some advocates of gender equity may find that the existing framework is itself the problem. That may be because of the emphasis presently placed on high visibility men's sports such as basketball and football, or more general doubts about a "male model" of competitive athletics. Proposed remedies may range from the abolition of intercollegiate athletics as we now know them to major changes in the existing framework designed to produce more gender equity. Additional changes may include diverting some of the income presently going to intercollegiate sports to allegedly more central academic purposes.

Of course, the line between reform and revolutionary change is not a sharp one, and some proposals may be hard to categorize. Thus, is the proposal that teams in some noncontact sports, such as tennis and golf, be co-ed a reform designed to cut costs and minimize gender differences, or is it a revolutionary change in the current gender-conscious way we organize sports? While all major proposals for fundamental change in intercollegiate athletics cannot be considered here, some issues deserve attention.

One important set of issues arises from the predominance of high visibility men's sports, such as football and basketball. Where men's and women's sports are parallel, direct comparisons of equity can be made. Is College X spending as much on the women's volleyball team as the men's? Do they play comparable schedules and have similar access to similar practice facilities? Such questions are relatively easy to answer.

What happens, however, when there is no comparable women's sport? Football, in particular, involves large numbers of participants and disproportionately large expenditures. At most campuses, it, along with men's basketball, receives the bulk of the community's and the media's attention. Although women's basketball has been achieving increasing prominence, both in national media coverage and locally on specific campuses, there is little doubt that the bulk of public attention has gone to men's high visibility sports at the athletically elite colleges and universities. Does the disproportion created in expenditures, participation, and attention by these high visibility men's sports count as an inequity? If so, what is the appropriate remedy?

Defenders of such programs often argue that men's football and basketball are revenue-producing sports. According to this line of argument, the revenue generated by such programs can be used to support less visible sports teams, including women's teams. Where true, this line of argument would seem to implicitly appeal to something like John Rawls's difference principle that maintains that inequalities are justified insofar as they work to the benefit of the less advantaged group.

However, critics are quick to point out that relatively few football programs, even in Division I, show a profit (8: p. 29). Critics are also skeptical about whether profits there actually are used to support women's athletic programs.

While the critics are right to question whether the major men's sports normally are the giant revenue producers they are claimed to be, the issue of revenue production is itself complex. What counts as revenue? Just gate receipts? While studies fail to show that alumni contribute more to winning than to losing teams, would they contribute as much if men's football and basketball were deemphasized or eliminated entirely? What about the support generated throughout the state for schools like the University of North Carolina? Does it lead to more donations, purchase of university paraphernalia, or even favorable consideration from the state legislature? What about the billions paid to the NCAA by the CBS television network for rights to televise the men's basketball championship? Some of the money is used to pay the expenses of both men's and women's teams to participate in national championships sponsored by the NCAA. This is not to claim that men's visibility sports often are revenue producers after all, but only to point out that the assessment of whether they are or not raises difficult questions about what to include or exclude as profits and losses.

In fact, at many (perhaps most) American colleges and universities, particularly those in Division III of the NCAA (the division with the most members), the point of having sports teams is not to raise revenue or provide entertainment for regional or national audiences, but rather the point is to benefit the student-athletes, the campus, and the local communities. At such institutions, expensive sports like football are funded out of general revenues just like any other program. Are women athletes at such institutions treated inequitably simply because football has a disproportionate amount of participants and expenses?

I suggest not, at least if certain other conditions are satisfied. If women's interests in participating in athletics are effectively and fairly accommodated, it is difficult to see how women athletes lose simply because more is spent on football than other sports. (Do philosophy majors lose if more is spent on physics students, perhaps because of the cost of equipment in physics, or are both kinds of majors treated fairly if they are both enrolled in equally strong programs?) Even in high visibility programs, difference in spending alone, whether total or per capita, need not necessarily show an unfair inequality, given equal satisfaction of interests.

The problem, of course, is what happens when women's interests are not fairly accommodated? Then, especially where the Rawlsian argument does not apply, it arguably is unfair for so much to be spent on a men's team when some interested and sufficiently talented women are not given an opportunity to play their sport.[7] In the high visibility programs of Division I, in which over 80 players on a football team may be receiving athletic scholarships, some redistribution to the women's program certainly seems appropriate. (The issue may be complicated, however, if it is true that football players in large Division I programs tend to disproportionately come from less advantaged backgrounds and/or are minority students, while the female athletes are white and come from more advantaged backgrounds.) The issue of redistribution is likely to be very divisive at nonscholarship schools, however, since any transfer will deprive some students who are participating simply for the love of the game of the opportunity to play while providing that opportunity to others. In many contexts, there will be no easy answer as to where opportunities should be cut for some so as to make them more equal for others.

One proposal that deserves attention is to eliminate separate men's and women's teams in parallel sports and have single co-ed teams in each sport. For example, instead of having a men's tennis team and a women's tennis team, have one team with both men and women on it. (Thus, as Francis suggests in this issue [9], mixed doubles could be made part of intercollegiate tennis.)

While this proposal has promise, it also has problems. Is the idea to cut costs by cutting the number of students participating?[8] If so, significantly fewer students will have a chance to participate. Moreover, it is unclear if financial savings will be significant. Some expenses will be saved on coaching salaries and travel expenses, but there will be fewer alumni of such programs in the future to provide support as well. Because many less visible sports, such as tennis, track, and golf, need not be expensive to begin with, especially at institutions that do not offer athletic scholarships, savings may not be significant either.

Moreover, while there may be benefits other than economic, such as promoting greater cooperation and teamwork between genders, there also may be losses. If men and women compete directly against one another in sports in which there are physiological differences between the sexes, women's skills may be eclipsed by stronger and more powerful men. If contests are arranged so players compete only against opponents of the same gender, it is unclear why the consequences will be as different from those generated by separate men's and women's teams under present arrangements.

Some writers have suggested that we place more emphasis on sports, such as gymnastics, in which women are not physiologically disadvantaged, or on other sports in which women might be in a physiologically favored position over men (7: p. 54). While this suggestion has merit, the preferences of most women athletes to play highly popular sports such as basketball, track, tennis, golf, and soccer may not be easy to alter without limiting the athletes' freedom to choose.

Perhaps more important, the suggestion of emphasis placement may presuppose that in sports in which men are physiologically advantaged, the women's game is unlikely to achieve parity of recognition or interest from the general public. I am not sure this is true. It may be far easier to educate sports fans about the nuances of the women's game than radically change the preferences of athletes about what sports to play. Women's tennis has achieved wide fan support, perhaps because the clever volleying game played by women is of greater interest to many spectators than the power game of men. While women's basketball lacks the dunking and highly athletic moves of superstars such as Michael Jordan, it features ball and player movement that also is of great interest. Major contests have filled arenas, and players such as the aptly named Sheryl Swoopes, Dawn Staley, and Jennifer Azzi are wonderful athletes capable of generating plenty of fan support if given sufficient attention in the media. Arguably, the best golf swings in the world are those of female players like Patty Sheehan, who may not drive the ball quite as far as top male players, but who may swing more efficiently. In other words, the assumption that separate women's programs in sports in which men are physiologically favored are of less interest, or that women's games are inferior, is questionable at best.

Why have intercollegiate athletics at all? Wouldn't intramurals be less expensive, involve more students, and serve many of the same social functions? The case for such a view, suggested in Leslie Francis's contribution [9], is of great interest but also faces problems. Intramural sports, by their very nature, are likely to lack the intensity and levels of skill of intercollegiate sport. For those of us who believe intercollegiate sport should (and often does) have a significant educational component, the intensity of the intercollegiate contest, and the preparation that goes into it, provide opportunities for gains in self-knowledge, for enhancing developing skills, and for opportunities to learn to handle pressure. It is doubtful intramurals can match these benefits.

Perhaps another approach is to move intercollegiate athletics as far as possible towards the existing model supplied by institutions in Division III and the Ivy and Patriot Leagues in Division I, in which athletic scholarships are not awarded, and athletics is conducted within the primary academic framework of colleges and universities. In such a framework, the intensity and educational benefits of an intercollegiate athletic program are preserved, although not at the level of the present major Division I programs, and most major problems are, or can be, eliminated. Such a solution promotes gender equity as well, because no team is expected to be a revenue producer, and athletics is funded out of general revenues as are other components of the institution's educational program. Fairness should be easier to achieve in such a context because the often pernicious pressures to win so as to maintain support or enhance revenue can be substantially reduced or entirely eliminated.

Concluding Comment

In this essay, I have tried to identify and sometimes examine many of the major issues connected with the search for gender equity in intercollegiate sports. These issues, as well as others I have not touched upon, are considered from different perspectives by Leslie Francis[9] and Jan Boxill [article reprinted here as reading 26] in their contributions to this symposium. We hope all three articles show that the issues of gender equity raised by intercollegiate sport are complex, of philosophical and ethical interest, and well worth our attention, both as theorists of sport and out of concern that our educational institutions be fair and just to all students.

Notes

1   While this result may not be unwelcome to critics of intercollegiate sports, it surely is not a desirable way of reducing commitments to intercollegiate athletics. It is doubly dishonest, in that it decreases opportunity under the guise of equalizing changes for women and avoids the need to debate the case for cutbacks or radical reform on the merits.

2   Keep in mind, however, that even if the bulk of funds spent on the athletic program goes to men's sports, the bulk of participants also may be men. Whether more is being spent per capita on men than women is a separate question from whether more total funds are being spent on male athletes than on female athletes.

3   This kind of case is not merely hypothetical. At my own institution, which has had outstanding men's and women's basketball teams over the last ten years at the Division III level, the men's program has had to cut sometimes as many as 30 players, even after assignments are made to a junior varsity squad, while the women's program rarely has had to make cuts. The numbers of players trying out for each team are quite different.

4   Perhaps the connection is this. It would be excessive and hence unfair to expect the plaintiffs, who normally would be students, to have the burden of showing a difference in the ratio of interested female to male athletes in the relevant pool, whatever it turns out to be.

5   Thus, in our hypothetical example presented earlier, 87% of the women who went out for teams made them, while only 72% of the men were similarly successful.
6   For a case that has at least some significant resemblances to this example, see *Cook et al. vs. Colgate University* (802 F Supplement 737, N.D.N.Y., 1992) in which a U.S. District Judge upheld the claim of women students that Colgate must elevate the women's ice hockey club to varsity status to accommodate their interests.
7   Again, the issue of gender inequity may be complicated if a significantly greater number of men also are denied the opportunity to participate.
8   In other words, instead of having two tennis teams with 10 men on the men's team and 10 women on the women's team, have 5 men and 5 women participate on one team.

Bibliography

1   *Amy Cohen et al. v. Brown University*. 1993 WL 111514 (1st circuit, RI) April 16, 1993.
2   Cahn, Steven M. (Ed.). *Affirmative Action and the University*. Philadelphia: Temple University Press, 1993.
3   English, Jane. "Sex Equality in Sport." *Philosophy & Public Affairs*, VII (1978) [reprinted here as reading 23].
4   Gender Equity Task Force of the NCAA. *Final Report of the NCAA Gender Equity Task Force*. Overland Park, KS: National Collegiate Athletic Association, 1993.
5   MacIntyre, Alisdair. *After Virtue*. South Bend, IN: University of Notre Dame Press, 1981.
6   Michener, James. *Sports in America*. New York: Random House, 1976.
7   Postow, Betsy. "Women and Masculine Sports." *Journal of the Philosophy of Sport*, VII (1980), 57–58.
8   United States Commission on Civil Rights. *More Hurdles to Clear: Women and Girls in Competitive Athletics*. Clearinghouse Publication No. 63, 1980.
9   Francis, Leslie P. "Title IX: Equality for Women's Sports?" *Journal of the Philosophy of Sport*, XX–XXI (1993–4), 32–47.

CHAPTER 26

Title IX and Gender Equity

Jan Boxill

Title IX is the portion of the Education Amendments of 1972 that prohibits sex discrimination in educational institutions receiving any federal funds. Title IX states:

> No person in the United States shall, on the basis of sex, be excluded from participation in, be denied the benefits of, or be subjected to discrimination under any educational program or activity receiving federal financial assistance. (8: p. 3)

One of the main targets of Title IX has been sports and athletic activities. Before its passage, athletic scholarships for women were nonexistent. Now, there are over 10,000 scholarships for women athletes (8: p. 4). Today, Title IX guarantees equal opportunity in all aspects of education, including sports, covering at least two major areas of high school and college athletics: financial assistance and effective accommodation of student interests and abilities.

Since the passage of Title IX in 1972, great strides have been made in girls' and women's sports. The 1994 Women's Basketball Championship made that clear to me. In an atmosphere usually seen only in the men's "Final Four" games, the women's "Final Four" games were played before a packed Richmond Coliseum in Richmond, Virginia; tickets were sold out months in advance. Also like the men's games, the women's games were nationally tele-

vised. And to top it all, the 1994 Women's National Championship team, the University of North Carolina (UNC) Tar Heels, were treated to a visit to the White House for an audience with President Clinton. All this is a far cry from when I played college basketball in the days before Title IX. The progress has been great, but there is more to be done, for along with the gains have come some losses and a great deal of misunderstanding. The integration of women into the traditionally male domain of sports, as with any integration, is not without conflict, compromise, and confusion. Men tend to see sports as their territory and the mere presence of women in the arena as a violation. But not only can sports benefit from the integration, so too can the men and women who participate. In this paper I will attempt an analysis of the gain, the benefits, the losses, and the misunderstandings of women in sports and will conclude with some recommendations.

With the Civil Rights movement and women's liberation, calls for equality have often been heard. Women and minorities have argued for equal access to education, to economic opportunities, to political opportunities, and to opportunities for social equality. But the meaning of equality in these claims was, and still is, controversial. In education it seems relatively clear that equality means essentially that men and women are treated the same with regards to admissions policies. On the surface, quantitative grades and

Scholastic Aptitude Test (SAT) scores are easy to compare in admissions applications; however, controversy has arisen because these grades and SAT scores do not reveal the possible hidden biases beneath that surface.

In the sports world, women not only have to contend with hidden biases, they also have to compete against the more firmly entrenched biases based on observable physical attributes such as height, weight, strength, muscle mass, and speed – all attributes admired in men. Because sports are seen as activities designed to develop these attributes, women's exclusion from sports was not seen as the result of bias, but as mere fact. As a result, attempting to gain equality in sports requires more than eradicating the hidden biases in how people think about sports; it requires a recognition of the physical differences between men and women and a rethinking of the value of sports. The value of sport is not only about achieving a goal, it is also about determining what that goal should be. I will approach the topic of equality by examining why women want to participate, why they ought to participate, and thus why women ought to have equal access.

Women wish to participate in sports for essentially the same reasons that men want to participate, though this does not necessarily mean they wish to be men. The reasons are closely related to why sports are so pervasive in the United States and the world.

What accounts for the fascination with sports? Sport fascinates for many reasons. Its beauty and its display of morally heroic virtues are just a couple of reasons. Human beings admire the beauty and grace of sport; they are moved by the discipline it requires. Often it is the heroism and the courage in sport we applaud, not the violence that occasions the display of these virtues. Both men and women want to participate for these reasons.

There are further reasons why both men and women ought to participate. Because of the nature and design of sport, it provides a significant moral function both for the individual and for society at large. It does so first because it provides autonomous agents with a vehicle for self-expression – a means to self-respect and

self-development. Sport in this sense serves as what John Rawls (7: p. 523) calls "a social union in a society of social unions, a community of shared ends and common activities valued for themselves, enjoying one another's excellences and individuality as they participate in the activities." These virtues, shared ends, and common activities are not gender-specific; that is, they are not exclusively male.

To understand the issues involved, a working or paradigmatic notion of sport may be helpful. In its paradigmatic form, sport is a freely chosen, rule-governed activity in which one is physically challenged through competition. The first two features certainly are gender neutral; the last two may give us hints as to why sport was traditionally male. Competition is often claimed as a male domain, first because it involves the physical body and second because it engenders a "macho" aggressive image.

Physical challenges are usually associated with the male body. This may explain why there are sports available for almost every male body type. We have been socialized to think that men's bodies are to be developed and challenged to be made strong, while women's are to be admired for their beauty. Indeed when we think of someone as "athletic," we think of this in terms of men's bodies.

One of the most controversial, and perhaps most misunderstood, features of our society is "competition." Competition is seen to be driven by selfish motives and involves competitors treating others as means, as enemies to be defeated, or as obstacles thwarting one's victory or success – all of which are to be removed by any means possible. Competition places an emphasis on winning, leading to the "win-at-all-costs" syndrome. These characteristics are associated with men. On the other hand, cooperation, the unselfish treatment of others as partners sharing in the ends, places no emphasis on winning. These characteristics are associated with women. It has been stated, "Athletic competition builds character in our boys. We do not need that kind of character in our girls"[1] (1: p. 135). This mentality has served to keep women out of sports. And since sports competition has been viewed as preparation for the business world, excluding women from this competition has also served to exclude them from the business world.

While competition can lead to the win-at-all-costs syndrome with all its evils, it need not and most often does not. While we see instances of cheating, injuring others, and steroid use to win at all costs, we more often see fair competitions in which the participants respect each other for the challenge. Examples can be seen in almost all women's competitions, in the Olympics, and in most high school and collegiate competitions. The desire to win is no less strong, but not at all costs. We do indeed see clear instances of the evil consequences of competition, but they are made clear because sport dramatizes the virtues and vices of our society. While virtues and vices are both dramatized, vices are not more noticeable because they are more prevalent, but because they make better headlines.

Athletic competition need not be seen as combat where opponents are viewed as enemies. Rather, one's opponents are seen as challenges to make one better and to achieve excellence. Each agrees to do her best to test herself against her opponent. Each tests her capabilities against the other. The emphasis is not solely on defeating her opponent, but on striving for excellence through a desire to win within the rules of the game. In playing tennis, for example, if I wish to test my abilities, I choose a partner of similar or slightly better ability who has a similar desire to win within the rules. To complete the challenge, competition requires a great deal of cooperation. Indeed competition is a cooperative challenge for each participant. Viewed in this way, sport competitions are neither evil nor "for males only." Rather, sport competitions serve to develop both men and women, with the result that they benefit everyone.

It is true, and perhaps some may say unfortunate, that sport plays a significant role in the social and business worlds. Sport is a means for providing opportunities, jobs, promotions, for understanding society, appreciating both its benefits and burdens. Education also provides these same opportunities, which is why Janice Moulton (5: p. 220) eloquently and effectively argues that everyone deserves a sporting chance. "Like education," Moulton concludes, "sport is

a means, and participation in our civilization is the end. This is why equal opportunity in both is important." This sentiment is the impetus behind Title IX.

I wholeheartedly agree with Moulton but would also like to go further. I maintain that sport is the single most available, unalienated activity that provides autonomous agents a vehicle for self-expression, self-respect, and self-development. An unalienated activity is freely chosen and exemplifies human creativity requiring both the energy of the mind and the body, in accordance with aesthetic standards. It is an activity designed specifically to provide room to express and develop oneself. Though it may serve other purposes, it has as its end the activity itself. It need not have a product nor provide a service. Sports are such activities. Sports are ends in themselves, and as such are included in Marx's "realm of freedom." Both men and women need such activities, and since sports are readily available, they must be made available for both men and women. What is interesting and significant is that different sports are designed to exploit the different bodily excellences that correspond to the different body types of men; this is not the case for females. To achieve this end, females must be allowed access to more kinds of sports. This may require opening traditionally male sports to women, modifying these traditionally male sports, or creating new sports. While this is possible, it raises further difficulties.

One of gender equity's goals is equal access to sports for girls and women. Title IX is the means to that end. Women cannot, as a rule, compete in football or boxing, nor can they compete with men in most other sports.[2] Although there are exceptions, because they are *exceptions*, they reinforce society's prejudices and thus perpetuate the inequalities of opportunities. Therefore, there is a case for developing sport activities that exploit women's body types. In some cases this may simply be done by modifying the rules of existing sports; in other cases it might require the development of entirely new activities.

Some have argued, among other things, to create new sports for women that emphasize traditionally female attributes such as flexibility, balance, and grace (3). This has been done in the Olympic Games with the addition of rhythmic gymnastics and synchronized swimming. Now, while many of us find these appropriate and competitive additions to the Games, many have still heard sarcastic comments that they are not "real" sports. This is not unusual; often when something new is added, in any area, it is not readily accepted. It must be time tested; some new activities make it and others don't.[3] Creating new activities for specific purposes is certainly not new. Basketball was originally created for men to play during the winter months, in between the fall and spring sports, to keep them fit. Interestingly, both men and women participated in the early days of basketball. This testifies to the truth that sport can be a fresh creation made to satisfy definite purposes; so other sports could be similarly created. The rules of the game have changed a great deal over time, but the essential concept of basketball still remains.

This brings us to another avenue of allowing access, namely, modifying established sports specifically for women. This is where we hear the complaints that if women want equality, then they should have to compete using the same rules, standards, and equipment as men. For instance, women should use the same ball as men in basketball and the same tee as men in golf. Why change the rules to suit women? But we might ask, why do we ever change the rules of any sport? And further, if the rules were created to favor attributes men tend to have, why not create rules to favor attributes women tend to have? As I mentioned previously, basketball is a very different game today from when it was first invented by James Naismith. The point is that sport governing bodies modify rules all the time for all kinds of reasons, but the main one is to make the game as challenging as possible for all participants. The college game is different from the professional game; international rules are different from U.S. rules; NCAA rules are different from USABA rules; college rules are different from high school rules; and yes, women's rules are different from men's. Yet it is all competitive basketball. There has been discussion for years about

lowering the height of the basket for women. Given that in general women are shorter than men, it makes sense to consider this proposal. The women's ball is smaller in diameter than the men's ball by one inch to suit the generally smaller hands of women. I believe this rule has improved the game and made it more challenging for the participants, just as the dimensions and design of the basket have been modified to make the game move more quickly and be more challenging.[4] I could mention a great many other modifications, but the point is that sport activities have been modified for all kinds of reasons for men; there is no reason not to accept modifications for women. Some modifications are to permit equal opportunities for all men to participate; we can do the same for women.

Gender equity seeks the equal opportunity for women to participate in the goods of our society. And as in any aspect of our society, we treat similarities similarly, and differences differently. This certainly holds true in sports. The obvious problem is to determine just when this is appropriate. In examining the issues in sports, we see all kinds of different treatment especially designed to promote equal opportunity as well as safety. We don't require the same equipment in all sports; in fact, we don't even require the same equipment within sports. In baseball, different gloves are used for the positions, and all the present-day gloves are significantly different from those used even 20 years ago. Even different bats are used by the players on the same team. Different equipment is used to protect different areas of the body that are vulnerable in different sports. For example, shin guards are worn in soccer but not in football; in football the helmets worn by the linesmen are different from those worn by the place kicker or the quarterback; the catcher's gear in baseball is different from all the other positions. I could go on, but the point is that the different treatment is based on relevant factors. Thus, it makes good sense for men to wear protective cups and women perhaps to wear protective bras.

One might say here that all this is fine, but if women want to compete with men, then they must compete against them on the same level, using the same rules and standards. But, we don't even require this of men. There are many different classifications based on age, weight, and size within men's sports, most specifically in boxing and wrestling, and not only do we not require them to compete against each other, we do not sanction it. For example, a heavyweight boxer may not fight a lighter classed boxer unless the lighter classed boxer promotes the challenge. Again, this is to allow equal opportunity for all male body types to develop and be challenged physically. In general, sports, like everything else, are most satisfying when played among people with similar body types and skills.

Could women simply integrate in the established sports and classes? They could and should be allowed to in some sports (e.g., equestrian, archery), but there are good reasons for gender specific classes or sports, some based on physical differences and others not. There are obvious and significant differences between men and women. Those relating to reproduction are the most obvious, but there are others such as body fat content, strength, and height. These differences may need to be taken into consideration when promoting challenges. It is still unlikely that the UNC women's basketball team, though the NCAA National Champions, could successfully challenge the UNC men's basketball team. Size, strength, and speed differences are too great, although there may be individuals on the team who could successfully compete on a one-on-one basis or for a spot on the team.

The gender equity question is: Should women be allowed an opportunity to play on the men's team? At this time I would argue that until women's sports provide the same opportunities as those available for men, women should be allowed to play on a men's team. If, for example, a female player of any sport is so far superior to any other female and thus has no significant challenges, then she should be allowed to compete with the men. It would be similar to a "cruiser weight" boxer finding no more challenges in his own weight class and thus wanting to be challenged by a heavier weight boxer. As I mentioned previously, the converse is not permitted; that is, a heavyweight unable to compete successfully in his own weight is not allowed to fight a lighter weight.

Title IX is an attempt to provide opportunities for women to develop in activities previously denied them. To integrate sports fully before women have been given full opportunity to develop in the traditionally male sports would be disastrous and would serve initially to reinforce stereotypes and prejudices and worse, would yield fewer opportunities and would discourage women from participating in the activities at all. The hope is that there will come a time when the best athletes, male and female, compete together, but that time has not yet been reached. Thus, a policy of separate but equal is still necessary. The question is: Is separate but equal ever equal?

Traditionally, separate but equal was never equal, and still is not – but it can be. The NCAA Gender Equity Task Force adopts this premise in advocating equal scholarships and budgets for men's and women's sports. While more money and scholarships are given to women's sports today than in 1972, an NCAA gender equity study conducted in 1992 showed that three-fourths of the money spent on athletics nationally goes to men's programs. These figures are not much different today (2).

In the more than twenty years since the passage of Title IX, strides have been made. There are more scholarships, bigger budgets, more women participating, more television coverage, and more role models for young girls. But along with these strides have come some losses. In 1972, 95% of women's sports were coached and administered by women; in 1990, less than 20% were (6: p. 159). Several explanations come to mind. First, prior to 1972, women were paid very little to run their programs. When more money was put into the programs, men became more interested in positions that paid them to coach and administer programs. In addition, men as coaches reinforced the traditional biases.

There is a belief that men know more about sports and are more capable, so they are naturally more qualified to run and coach sports no matter who is playing. Unfortunately, women collude in this belief, as do parents of girls who wish to participate. Further, since the programs became integrated and thus were automatically subsumed under departments run by men, the "old boy networks" took hold. The women who had coached and run their programs did it because they loved it. (They had to love it, since they did it for little or no monetary compensation!) This was taken to mean by many that they weren't really serious. If sports are to be taken seriously, they must be run by men. And since resources are limited, if money is to be distributed, it must go to those who are the most serious.

Another factor that serves to perpetuate male dominance is homophobia. Homophobia serves to prevent women from participating. As Jackie Joyner–Kersee (6: p. 145) put it: "It used to be you couldn't play basketball or any sport without, 'Oh, she's a lesbian.' Now it's a little better. But it's something they do to keep you from playing sports. That's all it's about." This turns participants into sexual beings and misunderstands the whole concept of sports participation. "Homophobia in sports serves as a way to control women, both gay and straight, and it reflects a gross misunderstanding of who women are as physical and sexual beings" (6: p. 145). Thus homophobia undermines the joy of participating. It still takes courage to be female and athletic.

Homophobia also serves to control the resources, and thus, the administrative and coaching positions. As a coach, this was made very clear to me. First of all in recruiting, when talking with parents about their daughters playing basketball for me, almost all of them asked about whether my assistant and I were married, and whether there were lesbians on the team. The first time this was asked of me I was quite unprepared for the question and went away thinking it was just these parents. Little did I know. As married coaches, we were able to allay many of the parents' fears. If they inquired further about the team, we responded that sexual orientation was not an issue with us, and this usually satisfied them.

Homophobia was again made clear to me in a case in which a coach resigned her position in 1985 to go to another school. The administration made it clear that they wanted either a married woman or a man, single or married, for the coaching position. What is more interesting in this case is that the search had been narrowed to three candidates – two women and one man. Both women had been members of national championship teams and were successful head coaches; one was married and one was single. The man was an assistant coach and was single. The first candidate was made an offer which she turned down because it was significantly less than the salary she was making at her current school; further, she was asked to coach not just basketball, but tennis or another team as well. She could not take such a deep cut, so she negotiated for a salary still below her current one, but one she could live with. The administration refused and went to the second candidate with the same proposal; she countered with a similar request and was refused. They then offered the third candidate, the man, even more than the salary the women had asked for and indicated that he would be required to coach basketball only. When asked why they went with a man, the answer was that it had been offered to two women and they both turned it down. This case arguably has both to do with homophobia and with the bias that women either do it for love or the fun of it and are not serious. In either case, money should not be an issue. For men, coaching is a serious career, and thus money is an important issue. Two very good coaches were denied a chance for advancement and even more, women participants were denied the opportunity to learn from positive role models. It also "soured" both women applicants toward college coaching.

Like all the prejudices held about women participating in sports, homophobia will begin to disappear when more women are participating. Both men and women not only can learn more from and about one another but also about themselves as well. Sports can serve to show that many of the old ideas about women are simply prejudices. It is time the established programs realize that women want to gain access to the goods of sports, that women don't want power over men, but instead they want power to participate. Women don't want to be men or even defeat men, although they may want to play with men. "If women's athletic potentialities are taken with as much seriousness as a man's it will become more evident that sport concerns not only *man*kind by *human*kind and deserves to be viewed as a basic human enterprise" (9: p. 228).

Though Title IX has done a great deal toward achieving gender equity, there is still more to do. The debate is quieter than before, but it is no less important. The fact that it is not on the front pages of national newspapers does not mean it is no longer an issue. Ninety-five percent of colleges still do not comply with Title IX (2: p. C1). The push for gender equity has now moved to the legal courts. This is unfortunate because it wastes valuable resources and it serves to make enemies of potential partners.

There is no easy way to settle the issue, but I believe that once we recognize that men and women are partners rather than adversaries, then we can achieve a great deal through co-operative endeavors. One approach may require creating more women's programs and even some women's sports, or modifying others. As already mentioned, we make such changes all the time with no loss to the game. We need to educate all people that sports participation has value, not just for men, but for all of us. It is not simply a male activity. Through education we will come to realize that strength is important in some sports, but is overrated and not the decisive factor in most sports.

Another approach toward achieving gender equity has been to cancel men's sports. But this is both dramatic and causes animosities.

Revenue shifts can be done with less fanfare; digging in one's heels prevents sensible compromise. An approach taken by legislators in Washington state was to commit 1% of the state universities' tuition revenues to achieve equality for women in sports.

That everyone is entitled to self-respect and self-esteem is undisputed. That everyone has capacities that ought to be developed is also undisputed – capacities that include the moral, the rational, and the aesthetic, what many refer to as "uniquely human attributes." What is required for self-respect, self-esteem, and the development of these attributes is a certain kind of activity. A particularly important kind of activity in this respect is "unalienated activity" – activity that is not a means to an end outside itself. For the vast majority of people, sport is the most available form of unalienated activity and consequently is an important way that people develop their uniquely human attributes, their self-respect, and their self-esteem. In this way, sport serves to humanize the individual. Thus, gender equity is essential in order that women may take advantage of this humanizing activity, just as men have for centuries. Providing women with access to sports allows them to participate in the joys and excellences of a significant social activity, and it allows them to share those joys with others. As such, participation serves not to separate the sexes but to integrate them as partners in a true social union.[5]

Notes

1 A judge ruling against allowing a girl to compete on the boys' cross country team made this statement.

2 I asked a hundred tenth-grade girls how many of them would like to play football and not powder puff. All but five said they would.

3 For example, motorball, motorcycle soccer, was added in the Moscow Olympics. It has not caught on and it is unlikely we will see it again in any Olympic Games.

4 The original basket was a peach basket, 15″ in diameter, with a closed bottom. For other changes consult Naismith's original rules (4: pp. 14–15).

5 I wish to thank Bernard Boxill for comments on earlier drafts of this paper.

Bibliography

1 Addelson, Kathryn Pyne. "Equality and Competition." In *Women, Philosophy and Sport*. Metuchen, NJ: Scarecrow Press, 1983, p. 135.

2   Dame, Mike. (1994, August 21). "Many Lawsuits Later, Women Still Not Equal: The Push for Gender Equity Has Stirred Courts – But Not Playing Fields." *Orlando Sentinel.*

3   English, Jane. "Sex Equality in Sports." *Philosophy and Public Affairs*, VII (1978), 269–277 [reprinted here as reading 23].

4   Fox, Larry. *The Illustrated History of Basketball.* New York: Grosset & Dunlop Publ., 1974, pp. 14–15.

5   Moulton, Janice. "Why Everyone Deserves a Sporting Chance: Education, Justice, and College Sport." In *Rethinking College Athletics.* Edited by Judith Andre and David N. James. Philadelphia, PA: Temple University Press, 1991, pp. 210–220.

6   Nelson, Mariah Burton. *Are We Winning Yet? How Women are Changing Sports and Sports are Changing Women.* New York: Random House, 1991.

7   Rawls, John. *A Theory of Justice.* Cambridge, MA: Harvard University Press, 1971.

8   Reith, Kathryn M. *Playing Fair: A Guide to Title IX in High School & College Sports.* (2nd ed.). East Meadow, NY: Women's Sports Foundation, 1994.

9   Weiss, Paul. *Sport: A Philosophic Inquiry.* Carbondale: Southern Illinois University Press, 1969.

CHAPTER 27

Why Women do Better than Men in College Basketball, or "What is Collegiate Sport for, Anyway?"

Nicholas Hunt-Bull

Numerous discussions of women's participation in sports at United States colleges and universities have focused on Title IX of the Education Act of 1972.[1] Whether discussing specifically legal questions, or addressing more general issues of distributive justice, those concerned with women's sport have focused on using legal and political means to eliminate bias in the funding of athletics. Important as justice in the distribution of resources is, a focus on fairness can disguise the subtle, if morally more important, ways in which female collegiate athletes are already outperforming male "student-athletes."

Title IX has enormously improved the economic and social status of women's sports in the United States.[2] Despite such advances, one still frequently hears the complaint that women athletes are short-changed by the lesser amounts of public attention paid to their sports.[3] In those sports such as soccer and basketball where women's and men's teams compete on an equally high level, women tend to get less spectator support, less media coverage, less fame, and less money than their male counterparts at the same institutions. Grand as the Women's Basketball Final Four is, it is still seen as a sideline to the real thing, the famed "Final Four." The Men's College Basketball Final Four does not need all those extra introductory adjectives.[4] College basketball scholarships are now relatively equal, unbalanced in favor of women even at schools which award a maximum

number, but it is still men who predominate (at least while fully clothed) in *Sports Illustrated*.[5]

I participate in an email list of women's basketball fans and this sort of complaint is common. Women athletes, it is asserted, are being cheated of the attention they deserve. As my title, "Why Women do Better than Men in College Basketball," suggests, I think this objection, while factually accurate, is misdirected. That is not because women are not denied equal access to the goods of fame and attention – they are denied those benefits – but rather because those benefits are not worth having. Once we really understand the point of collegiate athletics, we must recognize that women on average do far better than their male counterparts, at least the men in "bigtime" sports at "bigtime" colleges.

The Purpose of Sport

What, then, *is* the purpose of collegiate athletics? Jan Boxill, writing in the twentieth anniversary issue of the *Journal of the Philosophy of Sport*, describes sport as "the single most available, unalienated activity that provides autonomous agents a vehicle for self-expression, self-respect, and self-development." She adds, in an almost Kantian tone, that "Sports are ends in themselves."[6] Her point, presumably, is that sports are activities that are worth doing in and for

themselves, without any regard to their consequences. They are, for example, fun.

While Boxill is surely right that participation
in most sports is good in itself, many sports also
produce other goods as consequences. These
include such valuable things as public acclaim,
$10 million a year to play in the NBA, lucra-
tive endorsement contracts, or a chance political
career. A proper understanding of collegiate
sports requires us to distinguish between these
two distinct classes of benefits produced by
sports for their participants. In this I follow the
late Jane English, who, in her essay "Sex Equality in Sport," distinguished between the "basic"
and "scarce" goods produced by participation in
sports.[7] Basic goods are those which come from
participation itself, such as fitness, fun, enhanced self-respect, and teamwork skills, while
scarce goods are those benefits extrinsic to the
sport itself that tend to go only to the best athletes in the most popular sports. Only these stars
claim such scarce goods as fame and wealth.
English argues, appealing to principles of equality, that women deserve a far larger share of the
scarce goods than they now receive.

Jane English's distinction between basic and
scarce goods has a long and rich history. Adam
Smith, for example, distinguished between the
value-in-use and the value-in-exchange of certain goods. The value to you of participation in
sport is mostly paid in basic goods; the value to
others, its "exchange value," is what others will
give you for it, which for men with a nice jump-
hook or a .285 batting average might be many
millions of dollars a year. Similarly, Aristotle and
his modern follower Alisdair MacIntyre emphasize a distinction between internal and external goods.

For MacIntyre sports are an example of what
he calls a "practice." MacIntyre mentions chess,
portrait painting, and (American) football as
examples of practices. While many practices
are carried out by particular institutions, a practice is any social activity which creates particular
roles, follows an internal set of rules, and aims at
goals that make sense only within the context of
the practice.[8] Thus, for example, the goal of
overwhelming the Sicilian defense against an
experienced player only makes sense within the

practice of chess, and making a triple-double
only makes sense in organized basketball.

As the reader may have guessed, internal
goods are those that are internal to a practice,
such as the feeling of achievement one gets from
excelling in a sport. External goods are those only
contingently connected to a practice, such as the
fame or wealth one might get by being an excellent athlete or world chess champion. Like Socrates in Plato's *Republic*, and most of us in our
better moments, MacIntyre believes that internal
goods are more valuable than external ones. The
basketball player in the best sense of that term is
the one who wants to win the tournament, but
who would rather lose than win by cheating, even
though cheating would gain her all the external
rewards that come with the winner's trophy.
Internal goods are acquired by those who display
excellence, and so, unlike external goods, are
not always claimed by the winners. As Mariah
Burton Nelson elegantly says, athletic competition should aim to be an activity where each of
the participants "seeks excellence together."[9]

College Sports and Internal Goods

Jane English, when she introduced the distinction between what I will call internal and external goods, argued that women deserve more of
the external goods than they are getting. Here
some limited progress has been made: now, for
example, one of the four "Grand Slam" tournaments of professional tennis, the US Open, pays
equal prize money to the male and female
winners. There is talk of extending this parity
to other major tennis tournaments now that
women's professional tennis is overtaking the
men's game in competitiveness and fan interest.
English, however, does not differentiate between professional and collegiate sports, so it is
not clear whether she would demand more fame,
attention, and money for collegiate women's
sports as well as for female professionals. As I
mentioned before, others have explicitly made
such demands on behalf of college athletes, and
some sports like women's basketball have begun to take on the air of big-college football
and men's basketball, drawing huge crowds

and significant television coverage. Here the obvious examples are the women's basketball teams at Tennessee and the University of Connecticut (UConn, pronounced "Yukon"). I believe that supporters of women's athletics are making a fundamental mistake when they seek more external goods for female student-athletes, since, as the experience of male athletics shows, these goods are usually gained at the expense of internal goods.

I believe that we can divide sports into three general categories – which I will call "folk sports," "professional sports," and "school sports" – on the basis of the balance each class achieves between internal and external goods. Folk sports like jogging or in-line skating seek only internal goods like fitness, fun, and personal achievements such as running a 3-hour marathon. Professional sports such as NFL football or Olympic track-and-field aim at the limited external goods of fame and wealth, almost to the exclusion of the internal goods that originally justified their existence.[10] Tennessee school sports fall into an uncomfortable middle place between folk and professional sports, existing both to nurture the bodies and characters of the student-athletes and to draw financial contributions from alumni supporters and television networks while training players for the professional leagues.

Revenue, Non-Revenue, and the Point of Sport

College athletic administrators commonly distinguish between "revenue sports" – football and men's basketball – and "non-revenue sports," which include all women's sports and lower-profile men's sports like wrestling, soccer, and lacrosse. A clear hierarchy exists, with the revenue-generating teams seen as "real" sports while the non-revenue sports are at best a sideshow to football and men's basketball.[11] Given their economic and cultural similarity to the professional sports they emulate, revenue sports predominantly emphasize the acquisition of external goods, even though the players are supposed to be students. Prestige flows to athletes who get promoted to the NFL and NBA and to coaches whose protégés flourish in the professional environment. There would be no reason to object if, as in the minor leagues of baseball, this were the *purpose* of these college sports. It is an unfortunate sociological fact that the training of professional athletes has become the purpose of revenue sports, and this shows their failure as sport – when winning is the only thing, the internal goods of sport are lost. While no one expects professional athletes to play solely for the love of the game, the American public's apathetic response to the recent many-month NBA lockout reflects how cynical we have become about the motives of high-profile athletes. It is hardly surprising that the public was bored by this conflict between tall millionaires and short millionaires.

I believe that it would be a tragic mistake for college women to emulate the quasi-professional status of traditional "revenue-generating" male sports such as football and men's basketball. Those sports seem to show that greater fame and attention (external goods) inevitably undermine the achievement of goods internal to playing sports. If, as Jan Boxill says, teamwork, commitment, self-expression, self-respect, and self-development are the point of athletic participation, then women athletes shouldn't want to be like the football players.

Let me say a little more about the goods internal to participation in sport. Alisdair MacIntyre, from whom I borrow the terms internal and external goods, notes a key difference between them. Whereas "external goods are . . . characteristically objects of competition in which there must be losers as well as winners," internal goods are different because "their achievement is a good for the whole community who participate in the practice" and not the winners alone.[12] Consider some examples: teamwork requires us to subsume ourselves in a goal greater than ourselves. While it has its satisfactions, genuine teamwork undermines each player's ability to stand out and so draw to herself greater external goods. Women's college basketball teams display teamwork in many ways, including playing zone defenses, passing to the open player, and practicing their free-throws. Contrast this with the external-good-oriented NBA, where the zone defense is illegal and each player plays one-on-one to maximize his exposure and wealth. Similarly, college sports allow women to express themselves verbally and physically in an environment where assertiveness and strength are valued. In a sexist culture sports provide a social space where women can safely explore roles, display leadership, and learn to channel their feeling to achieve group objectives. In sports, as in few other areas of life, one has a chance to achieve excellence against an impersonal standard. Such achievements are the essential ground of self-respect and self-confidence. While the comments I have made about the internal goods made possible by sport may seem obvious, two points are worth reiterating: first, before the recent explosion of women's sporting opportunities nurtured by Title IX, most girls and women in the United States were denied access to these internal goods, which had been the birthright only of boys who were allowed to play organized sports; second, external goods seem inevitably to crowd out internal goods once both are available.[13] Asked to choose between achievement and money, human nature is sadly prone to grab the cash.

Given the antagonistic relationship between internal and external goods, the less that, for example, women's college basketball approximates the wealth and popularity of men's basketball the better it is for the women who play the game. Thus, the growing popularity of many women's sports – soccer and ice hockey, for example – may be more of a risk than an advantage to women athletes and women in general. Once we recognize the proper purpose of college sports – developing the bodies and characters of the players – we see that it is the high-profile male sports that are failing and traditional female sports such as field hockey, gymnastics, and volleyball that are succeeding. The objective, for women athletes in colleges and universities, should not be to play like the men on the "revenue-generating" football and basketball teams. Competition for scarce external goods by these athletes causes some of them genuine harm. Think of all the athletes with no degree, few skills, and a bitter sense of failure at not "making it" in professional sports. The wealthy male

sports may be past saving, but that is not yet true of women's sports, despite the efforts of the WNBA. Female athletes who get less public attention and fewer external rewards than some male athletes are not losing out in getting the benefits of sport; rather, they are doing much better.

Two Special Issues

Two further special issues suggest themselves that I will mention in passing. The first is the status of male non-revenue sports. Most of these are more akin to women's sports than to football and men's basketball. They draw sparse crowds but give their participants a sense of achievement, teach them valuable life lessons, and richly reward them with internal goods. At least in some cases they make it possible for poorer students to afford an education. Furthermore, these sports do not require the rare extremes of physical size and weight sought by the revenue sports.[14] While I have presented this argument, partly for rhetorical reasons, as a contrast between men's and women's collegiate sports, my arguments for the moral superiority of female athletics extends to most male non-revenue athletics. It is a striking irony that many of these sports, such as wrestling and cross-country running, are being cancelled by colleges allegedly to comply with Title IX.

The second issue is the value of women's sports for their spectators. While these benefits are extrinsic to the games themselves, they are of significant value for women in general. Women's sports strengthen the self-esteem of women who watch the players as well as the players themselves. While the little girl who watches women play basketball and says, "I can do that too" is an advertising cliché, she is also many real little girls who can now see themselves as point-guards and center-forwards. Here again the contrast with the NBA is instructive. Spectators at NBA games can only watch, they cannot identify with the players. Professional basketball is a veritable freak show where extreme physical specimens do remarkable things the spectators can at best imitate in a video game.

Male fans can only stare up at the stars with awe at their remarkable, and alienating, physical gifts. Since most women athletes are of physically normal size, girls and women can identify with and model themselves upon their heroes.

Conclusion

I began this essay considering the complaint that women's basketball players at American colleges and universities are being cheated out of benefits that go to (at least some) male athletes at those same institutions. In a sense those who make this complaint have the problem exactly backwards. What we should recognize is that most women's college sports are successes, while the highest-profile men's sports are failing miserably. Perhaps the real challenge is to find a way to remake men's athletics so that it too can truly be *sport*, as the women's games already are.

Notes

1   The essential passage reads: "No person in the United States shall, on the basis of sex, be excluded from participation in, be denied the benefits of, or be subjected to discrimination under any educational program or activity receiving federal financial assistance."

2   The number of female student-athletes at US colleges has increased almost five-fold, from 31,000 in 1971 to 146, 000 in 1999, with a parallel increase in number of coaches and level of funding. For a summary discussion, see "Title IX: 25 Years of Progress," published by the US Department of Education in June 1997, available at http://www.ed.gov/pubs/TitleIX/. For 1999–2000 participation data, with a breakdown by gender and sport, see "NCAA News Digest," *NCAA News* 38.23 (November 5, 2001), p. 2.

3   Mariah Burton Nelson, for example, dedicates a chapter to this issue in her *The Stronger Women Get, the More Men Love Football* (New York: Harcourt Brace, 1994), citing (p. 215) a study of elite women athletes whose highest priority was increased media attention and respect.

4   Nor, of course, do *men's* golf, hockey, or lacrosse. In each case men play the game and women play a related sport, such as "women's golf."

5   Burton Nelson notes that only 4 percent of the covers of this prominent magazine, in the years 1954–90, depicted women athletes. An equal number showed swimsuit models, wives of male athletes, or cheerleaders (*The Stronger Women Get*, p. 196).

6   Jan Boxill, "Title IX and Gender Equity," *Journal of the Philosophy of Sport*, XX–XXI, 23–31, p. 26 (reprinted here as reading 27).

7   Jane English, "Sex Equality in Sport," *Philosophy and Public Affairs*, 7.3, 269–77 (reprinted here as reading 23).

8   See ch. 14 of Alasdair MacIntyre, *After Virtue*, 2nd edition (Notre Dame: University of Notre Dame Press, 1984).

9   In a lecture given on December 4, 1998, in Greensboro, North Carolina, at the conference for which this essay was written.

10   While the Olympics are officially *amateur* competitions, that fiction has mostly been dropped over the last two decades, particularly with the involvement of NBA basketball players.

11   Ellen Staurowsky points out that the argument for the special status of revenue-generating sports "subjects the experiences of student-athletes to a unique standard of measurement that has no counterpart in any other area of the academy." That is, these "students" are valued not for the education they gain, but rather for the wealth they bring the colleges, serving effectively as employees in the entertainment/alumni-fleecing industry (Ellen J. Staurowsky, "Critiquing the Language of the Gender Equity Debate," *Journal of Sport and Social Issues*, 22.1, February 1998, p. 18).

12   *After Virtue*, p. 190.

13   Here again the professionalization of the Summer and Winter Olympics is an instructive example.

14   Basketball players well over six feet tall are often referred to as "short," while I once heard a collegiate lineman (somewhat jokingly) described as "a pencil-thin 240 pounds."

CHAPTER 28

Women, Self-Possession, and Sport

Catharine MacKinnon

Since I grew up in pre-Title IX America, the first time it ever occurred to me to identify as an athlete was when I was being given a blood pressure test after a training accident. The nurse put the sleeve on me, made a reading, paused, took it off, put it back on, made more readings, and stopped and looked at me. Is anything wrong? I asked. Well, she said, either you're a football player or you have some exotic disease. Since only men played football then, to my knowledge, it seemed as though this was not my first chance – and probably not my last – to choose whether I was a man or whether I was sick. I mean, she said, are you an *athlete?* I contemplated the five years I had spent two hours a night, five nights a week, at martial arts as a physical, spiritual, and political activity. I told her yes.

The issues of sexual politics in this story are new to none of you. They raise a series of feminist questions on athletic planning, policy, and institution creation, and also connect to women's presence and possibilities in other areas of life, such as the law.

As context for pursuing these issues, I propose for your consideration two different strands of feminist theory. Most work on women in sport (most work on women in anything) comes from the first approach. In this approach the problem of the inequality of the sexes revolves around gender differentiation. The view is that there are real differences between the sexes, usually biological or natural. Upon these differences, society has created some distorted, inaccurate, irrational, and arbitrary distinctions: sex stereotypes or sex roles. To eliminate sex inequality, in this view, is to eliminate these wrong and irrational distinctions. The evil and dynamic of sexism here is the twisting of biological males and females into masculine and feminine sex roles. These roles are thought to shape men in one way and women in another way, but each sex equally. Implicit here is the view that initiatives toward sex equality are limited to or constrained by real underlying differences. "Arbitrariness" of treatment in social life is measured by implicit reference to these differences. This is liberal feminism's diagnosis of the condition of women. The solution that responds to this diagnosis is that we need to ignore or eliminate these distortions so that people can realize their potential as individuals. Liberal feminism does not usually purport to be sure what the real underlying differences are, but its idea is that they are there. The way you know the wrong of stereotyping is distortion is that there is something preexisting to distort. Liberal feminist strategies for change correspond to its critique: ignore or eliminate irrational differences. To the extent that differentiation is irrational, assimilation or integration is recommended. Those things that men have been, psychologically and physically, so also women should be allowed to become. Androgyny as a solution, free choice of qualities of both roles, is also consistent with these politics.

I want to contrast a second view with this. This view doubts that differences or differentiation have much to do with inequality. Sexism is a problem not of gender differentiation, but of gender hierarchy, in which gender differentiation is only one strategy. Nor is sexism gender neutral in the sense that it hurts men and women equally; the problem is instead male supremacy and female subjection. From this second point of view, issues like rape, incest, sexual harassment, prostitution, pornography – issues of the violation of women, in particular of women's sexuality – connect directly with issues of athletics. The systematic maiming of women's physicality that marks those athletic and physical pursuits that women have been forced or pressured or encouraged to do, on the one hand, connect with those we have been excluded from doing, on the other. If you ask, not why do women and men do different physical activities, but why has femininity *meant* physical weakness, you notice that someone who is physically weak is more easily able to be raped, available to be molested, open to sexual harassment. Feminine means violable.

This critique of gender hierarchy, which I identify as the radical feminist analysis, is developing a theory beyond stereotyping, beyond the dynamics of differentiation but including them. It is developing a theory that objectification is the dynamic of the subordination of women. Objectification is different from stereotyping, which acts as though it's all in the head. Stereotyping, as critique, proceeds as though what we need to change so that women will no longer be kept down is women's images of ourselves as victims and men's mistaken views of us as second class. It's not that that wouldn't help. It's just that the problem goes a great deal deeper than illusion or delusion. Masks become personas become people, socially, especially when they are enforced. The history of women's athletics should prove that, if nothing else does. The notion that women cannot do certain things, cannot break certain records, cannot engage in certain physical pursuits has been part of preventing women from doing those

things. It isn't only that women are excluded, it's that even women who do sport are limited. This isn't just ideas or images – or just women, for that matter. When you think, for instance, about the relationship between the scientific discovery of the physical possibility of running a mile in less than x time and people actually running the mile in less than x time, you see a real relationship between images of the possibility of a particular achievement and the actual physical ability to do it. Anyone who trains seriously understands this on some level.

What I'm suggesting is that the sexual, by which I mean the gender, objectification of women that has distinguished between women, on the one hand, and the successful athlete, on the other, has reached deeper than just mistaken ideas about what women can and cannot do, notions that can be thought out of existence by the insightful or the exceptionally ambitious. It is not only ideas in the head that have excluded us from resources and most everything else. It is also the social meaning of female identity that has restricted and contained us. If a woman is defined hierarchically so that the male idea of a woman defines womanhood, and if men have power, this idea becomes reality. It is therefore real. It is not just an illusion or a fantasy or a mistake. It becomes *embodied* because it is enforced.

Radical feminism is not satisfied with women emulating the existing image of the athlete, which has been a male image. Neither with that, nor with the separate and vicarious role of cheerleader, nor with other feminine physical pursuits that have been left to us. Instead, feminism moves to transform the meaning of athletics, of sport itself. I am going to talk about what it would look like to transform sport from a feminist perspective. To do this, I need finally to distinguish this feminist perspective from what I have characterized as the aspiration to the genderless point of view that characterizes liberal feminism. The idea of liberal feminism is that because society and thought are so twisted by sexism, we have to somehow transcend all that in order to have a nonsexist perspective from which to view social life. I think the radical feminist move is exactly the opposite. It says that we need a women's point of view that criticizes all the ways we have been created by being excluded and kept down but that also claims the validity of our own experience. This is not a transcendence operation, whereby we get to act as though we don't have any particular perspective, but instead an embrace of what we have become with a criticism of the process of having been forced to become it, together with a similar dual take on everything we've never been allowed to be.

In the context of liberal feminism, when one asks why don't women participate in athletics or why haven't they participated in athletics, the answer looks like: illusions about women's weakness, notions about femininity, stereotypes. These are all part of it, to be sure. The corresponding solution reveals the limitations on the underlying account, though: challenge wrong ideas so that women can play with the boys. From a radical feminist perspective, if you ask why women have not participated in athletics, you get a much more complicated picture. Women have learned a lot all these years on the sidelines, watching. Not only have we been excluded from resources, excluded from participation, we have learned actual disability, enforced weakness, lack of spirit/body connection in being and in motion. It is not that men are trained to be strong and women are just not trained. Men are trained to be strong and women are trained to be weak. It's not *not* learned; it's very specifically learned. Also, observing athletics as pursuits, we notice that most athletics, particularly the most lucrative of them, have been internally designed to maximize attributes that are identical with what the male sex role values in men. In other words, men, simply learning to be men, learn not only sports but learn those things that become elevated, extended, measured, valued, and organized *in and as sport itself*. Women, simply learning to be women, do not learn those things, do learn the opposite of those things. So it's no news to any of you that being female and being athletic have been socially contradictory and that being male and being athletic have been more or less socially synonymous. Femininity has contradicted, masculinity has been consist-

ent with, being athletic. Women get to choose between being a successful girl and being a successful athlete.

Now I want to extend and deepen the feminist analysis of athletics from this second perspective, which I will call simply feminist. When you look at athletics from the feminist standpoint, the question becomes: what is athletics *for?* Once, when I asked a class of Harvard law students this question, one woman answered: what is *education* for without athletics? Which I thought was very much the point. It was not just that without basketball, she would have had no interest whatever in school, but that physical education was central to becoming an educated person. Keeping this in mind, and keeping in mind that the standard for personhood, in athletics as elsewhere, has substantively, socially, been a male standard, I want to answer the question "what is athletics for?" in two parts: what has it meant to men? and what can it mean to women?

From a feminist perspective, athletics to men is a form of combat. It is a sphere in which one asserts oneself against an object, a person, or a standard. It is a form of coming against and subduing someone who is on the other side, vanquishing enemies. It's competitive. From women's point of view, some rather major elements of the experience appear to be left out, both for men and for women. These include things that men occasionally experience, but that on the whole are not allowed to be the central purpose of male athletics, such as kinesthesis, pleasure in motion, cooperation (and by this I do not mean the male bond), physical self-respect, self-possession, and fun. Because of the history of women's subjection, physicality for women has a different meaning from physicality for men. Physicality for men has meant male dominance; it has meant force, coercion, and the ability to subdue and subject the natural world, one central part of which has been us.

For women, when we have engaged in sport, when we have been physical, it has meant claiming and possessing a physicality that is our own. We have had something to fight and therefore something to gain here, and that is a different relation to our bodies than women are allowed to have in this society. We have had to gain a relation to our bodies *as if they are our own*. This physical self-respect and physical presence that women can get from sport is antithetical to femininity. It is our bodies as acting rather than as acted upon. It is our bodies as being and presence, our bodies that *we* do things with, that we in fact are and identify with as ourselves, rather than our bodies as things to be looked at or for us to look at in preparation for the crucialness of how we will appear, or even to carry our heads around in the world. In other words, athletics can give us our bodies as a form of being rather than as a form of appearance, or death-likeness. In particular, I think, athletics can give us a sense of an actuality of our bodies as our own rather than primarily as an instrument to communicate sexual availability.

If you doubt that we are not allowed to have what I am saying athletics gives us, I suggest that we can tell we've broken some rules when people start calling us what they consider epithets. We all know that women athletes are considered unfeminine. This is integrally related to the fact that women athletes are experienced as having physical self-respect. We also know that women athletes are routinely accused, explicitly or implicitly, of being lesbian. I think that this is directly related to the sense women athletes have of body as self, as acting, as opposed to body as something that conveys sexual accessibility to men, as there to be acted upon. I often find that the allegedly nasty words people use to describe us have truth in them, in that if one asks why they see us this way, we learn some real things. On the equation of woman athlete with unfeminine with lesbian, I wonder: why does women's self-respect and conveyed capacity to act *mean* that we reject male sexual access? *They're* the ones who are telling us that's what it means. What does it say about the relation between sexuality and physicality, what does it tell us in particular about the content of heterosexuality, that when a woman comes to own her own body, that makes her heterosexuality problematic? I think it tells us that the image and in large part the reality we have of female sexuality is equated with and defined as availability to being taken by a man. It's

threatening to one's takeability, one's rapeability, one's femininity, to be strong and physically self-possessed. To be able to resist rape, not to communicate rapeability with one's body, to hold one's body for uses and meanings other than that can transform what *being a woman means*.

Some of you may be thinking that what I have described as the image of weakness, pregnability, vulnerability, passivity, the feminine stereotype, the eternal female, and the ways in which those are antithetical to the image of the athlete, is outdated. You may be thinking that since the passage of Title IX and the new improved image of the woman athlete, it has become more acceptable, hence less stigmatic, for women to be physical. Title IX has been extremely important. But the minute women claim something for ourselves and it is seen as powerful and important, especially if it becomes profitable, it immediately gets claimed and taken over by men. I mean to include everything from the eroticization of the female athlete in *Playboy* to the recent moves by the NCAA.[1]

That comment suggests some institutional consequences, not all of which I have resolved in my own mind. Given what I have said about women's physicality, women's point of view on athletics, and its connections with sexuality and the subordination of women generally, *now* let's ask, what about separate teams? what about separate programs? what about separate institutions? If women/men is a distinction not just of difference, but of power and powerlessness, if power/powerlessness is the sex difference, those questions need to be asked very differently than they have been. For instance, if not participating in male-defined sport does not mean fear or rejection of failure or success, but the creation of a new standard, of a new vision of sport, the problem of pursuing a feminist perspective in an institutional context is not solved, but it is differently posed.

This attempt at a new perspective, in other words, does not simply justify separatism.[2] It is an argument that women as women in a feminist sense have a distinctive contribution to make to sport that is neither a sentimentalization of our oppression as women nor an embrace of the model of the oppressor. As feminists, we are critical of both femininity and masculinity as serving the interest of men, as furthering male power, and as instrumental to male dominance. We are attempting to create a social reality, a social identity, that is bound up with neither. A vision of sport from this standpoint finds ritualized violence alien and dangerous as well as faintly ridiculous, every bit as much as it finds sex-scripted cheering from the sidelines demeaning and vicarious and silly. The place of women's athletics in a larger feminist analysis is that women *as women* have a survival stake in reclaiming our bodies in our physical relations with other people. We need to do this in a way that claims our bodies as ourselves, rather than as an eager embrace of our bodies as nature, or abdication of them to other people as something to be resisted or overcome or subdued.

I hope that what I'm about to say won't get sentimentalized. It is part of a critical analysis of art as well as of sport. I have said that I think women's physicality, or what it could be, has a distinct meaning, a meaning that comes from women's oppression through our bodies, but that means we have something to offer the world of athletics, much as it has something to offer us. I do mean to include men who have been excluded from sports by their rejection of the masculine ideal. But it is not only men who can't make it, and not only women who can, who stand to benefit from a revaluation of sport. Women have a contribution of perspective to make here that is a lot more powerful than either playing with the boys or allowing the boys to play with us. Once when I was talking about this with the same student I mentioned earlier, she reminded me that both men and women have climbed Mount Everest. When asked why, the man said, because it is there. The woman said, because it is beautiful.

Notes

1   The attempt of a male athletic association to take over a women's athletics association is documented in the women's unsuccessful antitrust action, Association for Intercollegiate Athletics for Women v. National Collegiate Athletics Association, 558 F. Supp. 487 (D.D.C. 1983), *aff'd* 735 F. 2d 577 (D.C. Cir. 1984). *Playboy* has begun sexualizing athletic women.

2   As to the law of this issue, American courts have not often considered the legality of institutions or programs that disadvantaged groups such as women have organized to promote their equality, such as separate-sex athletic teams or organizations. Existing law on single-sex institutions is dominated by members of advantaged groups seeking the further advantage of access to the few resources previously available exclusively to disadvantaged groups. For instance, the U.S. Supreme Court found sex discrimination in the exclusion of a man from a public all-women's nursing school. Mississippi University for Women v. Hogan, 458 U.S. 718, 725 (1982). However, it was important that no institution of comparable convenience and quality existed at which the plaintiff could study.

Separate associations, activities, or programs of or for the disadvantaged have sometimes been permitted when equal treatment is thereby promoted by compensating for disadvantages. Mississippi University for Women v. Hogan, 458 U.S. 718, 730 n.16; Califano v. Webster, 430 U.S. 313, 318–20 (1977) (per curiam); Schlesinger v. Ballard, 419 U.S. 498, 508 (1975); *see also* Orr v. Orr, 440 U.S. 268, 283 (1979). Scholars have found the compensatory rationale even more appropriate when applied to women's membership organizations that seek sex equality than when applied to economic benefits, C. Feldblum, N. Krent, and V. Watkin, "Legal Challenges to All-Female Organizations," 21 *Harvard Civil Rights–Civil Liberties Law Review* 171, 215 (Winter, 1986). It would seem that where a women's organization with sex equality goals is a power base and leadership laboratory, is activist or service-oriented or a support system rather than a ghetto, such an organization may be seen to counteract and undermine the inferiority of women that compulsory sex segregation is based upon.

In a context in which women are socially unequal to men, all-women affiliations and activities are often not seen to run the same risks of perpetuating sex inequality that all-male affiliations can. The area of athletics provides examples of all-women groupings seen to further equality goals. By federal and constitutional law, teams for girls must be provided or girls must be given opportunities to compete in athletics programs formerly for boys, with some modifications for contact sports. The Title IX guidelines permit separate-sex teams where "athletic opportunities for members of that sex have previously been limited." 45 C.F.R. 86.41. *See* Yellow Springs Exempted Village School District Board of Education v. Ohio High School Athletic Association, 647 F.2d 651 (6th Cir. 1981); Leffel v. Wisconsin Interscholastic Athletic Association, 444 F. Supp. 1117 (D. Wisc. 1978). Women-only sports have been preserved against sex equality attacks both by exceptional girls seeking to compete on boys' teams when girls' teams were available, O'Connor v. Board of Education of School District 23, 545 F. Supp 376 (N.D. Ill. 1982), and by boys seeking to compete on girls' teams when boys' teams were not available. Petrie v. Illinois High School Association, 394 N.E.2d 855 (Ill. App. 1979). But *cf. Darrin v. Gould*, 85 Wash. 2d 859, 540 P.2d 882 (Wash. 1975).

In this context, courts have concluded that women-only teams are consistent with the sex-equality goal of precluding "a male dominance" of a sport. 394 N.E.2d 857; Ritacco v. Norwin School District, 361 F. Supp. 931 (D. Pa. 1973). "Overall" equality considerations for all girls often justify such results. Forte v. Board of Education, North Babylon Union Free School District, 431 N.Y.S. 2d 321 (Sup. 1980); Hoover v. Meiklejohn, 430 F. Supp. 164 (D. Colo. 1979), even in individual cases of boys who have no comparable opportunities. Mularadelis v. Haldane Central School Board, 427 N.Y.S. 2d 458 (Sup. Ct. 1980). The Ninth Circuit Court of Appeals has similarly held that a boy who was denied admission to a girls' volleyball team was not discriminated against on grounds of sex because girls-only sports further the social interest in sex equality, an interest which admitting boys to the girls' team would undermine. Clark v. Arizona Interscholastic Association, 695 F.2d 1126 (9th Cir. 1982), *cert. denied*, 464 U.S. 818 (1983). Even though there was no boys' volleyball team, girls were seen to retain their equality interest in the single-sex team in the absence of a symmetry of opportunity for boys.

CHAPTER 29

Stronger Women

Mariah Burton Nelson

Boy, don't you men wish you could hit a ball like that!
Babe Didrikson

Laughing, Patrick Thevenard would scoop his wife, Gail Savage, off the floor and carry her around the house like a squirming child. This was early in the marriage, and Patrick, an ecologist from Hyattsville, Maryland, thought it was funny, a joke. Gail, a history professor, didn't like it. Feeling helpless and angry, she would ask to be put down. He would refuse.

Later, Gail became a dedicated runner. Patrick argued that she was running too much, or in the wrong way, or at the wrong times. They would quarrel, and he would yell. Patrick didn't literally lift her off the ground then, but to Gail the sensation was similar: Patrick's criticisms felt like physical restraints, as if he were trying to prevent her from going where she wanted to go.

Patrick says Gail used running as a "weapon" against him, a way "to escape out of our relationship – to literally put physical distance between us."

Gail says running became "the focus of a power struggle over who would control me."

The way Gail gained strength, and keeps gaining strength, is through sports. Women can become strong in other ways, without being athletes, but athletic strength holds particular meaning in this culture. It's tangible,

visible, measurable. It has a history of symbolic importance. Joe Louis, Jackie Robinson, Jesse Owens, Billie Jean King: their athletic feats have represented to many Americans key victories over racism and sexism, key "wins" in a game that has historically been dominated by white men.

Sports have particular salience for men, who share childhood memories of having their masculinity confirmed or questioned because of their athletic ability or inability. Along with money or sex, sports in this culture define men for men. They embody a language men understand.

Women also understand sports – their power, their allure – but often from a spectator's perspective. When a woman steps out of the bleachers or slips off her cheerleader's costume and becomes an athlete herself, she implicitly challenges the association between masculinity and sports. She refutes the traditional feminine role (primarily for white women) of passivity, frailty, and subservience. If a woman can play a sport – especially if she can play it better than many men – then that sport can no longer be used as a yardstick of masculinity. The more women play a variety of sports, the more the entire notion of masculine and feminine roles – or any roles at all assigned by gender – becomes as ludicrous as the notion of roles assigned by race.

Female athletes provide obvious, confrontational evidence – "in your face" evidence, some might say – of women's physical prowess, tangible examples of just what women can achieve.

An avid equestrian as a child, Gail thought of herself as "just one of those girls who loved horses." No one suggested that a girl who trains and competes in equestrian events is every bit as athletic as the boys her age who earn letters in baseball or track. Lately, thinking about her lifelong love affair with sports, she realized that she "was really being an athlete the whole time."

She rode during her first marriage, which lasted thirteen years. She taught riding and spent an inordinate amount of time at the barn, as equestrians do. Her husband did not object, but nor did he ask questions about her teaching, or speak proudly of her to his friends, or take an interest in her career. "What I did was OK because it was not considered important," says Gail. "He never took it seriously."

During her second marriage, Gail's horse grew lame and had to be put out to pasture. She discovered she "couldn't just sit around" so she began running. For three months she was "in agony," then she fell in love with the hypnotic process of landing, step by step, on the earth, as well as the fleeting moments of flight in between. She was forty-two.

At first, Patrick did not object. When her training was occasional, her schedule flexible, he didn't mind. "I was supportive when she started out because she had gotten a little overweight," Patrick recalls. "I was surprised she stuck with it as long as she did."

Gail increased her mileage. She joined a running club, where she learned about interval training, track workouts, and the value of taking one's pulse. She memorized *Runner's World* magazine. She went running for two, three hours at a time. Patrick started to get upset.

He didn't say he was upset, exactly. He said he was concerned. "A woman of your age shouldn't be doing this to her body," he would say.

Rapists also concerned him. "He would try to frighten me into not going out," Gail says. "I

couldn't go out late in the afternoon because it would get dark. I couldn't go out at sunrise; he didn't like that either. It made it more difficult for me to exercise my judgment. It seemed like his conclusion was I should never go out."

Patrick's assessment: "It was a conflict between moral imperative and reality. Gail would say, 'A woman should be able to run freely.' I'd say, 'Of course, but in the real world, you can't.'"

He criticized her tactics, too, charging her with working too hard, risking damage to her joints. "I had been a runner myself," he explains. "I thought she should spend as much time stretching and doing yoga as running. I thought she should take some time off. She didn't."

"When you train hard, you run some risk of injury," Gail concedes. "But it was a double bind. No matter what I did, it wasn't right."

The more she ran the better she felt about herself, and the more she ran the more she believed that she had a right to this time, this pursuit of excellence. "I've always wanted to do everything as best I could, but women of my generation weren't supposed to try hard. That would mean you would sweat, you might make noises, you might fail." Running offered Gail an opportunity to test herself, to find out how good she might be.

The more she ran, the more running became "a lightning rod for the larger issues of who was in charge" in her marriage, Gail says. "Talking about it makes it sound like we sat down and had rational discussions about it. We didn't. Mainly I'd stomp out of the house and run, and he'd give me lectures about how I was hurting my knees and ankles."

As she was lacing her shoes, he would ask, "Where are you going?"

"Out," she'd say.

"When will you be back?" he'd ask.

"Later," she'd answer.

"I was very determined to go out on my own and not tell him where I was going," she admits. "That did exacerbate the conflict between us."

Eventually, after an eleven-year relationship, they divorced.

Now in her late forties, Gail's still running – farther, up to forty-five miles per week, at about an eight-minute-per-mile pace. She competes in 10Ks, recently placing second in her age group. She lifts weights and swims. She has tried orienteering, and is intrigued by the idea of competing in triathlons and marathons. "I seem to enjoy everything I try," she marvels. "I tend to acquire strength fairly easily."

For a woman, especially for a married woman with a controlling husband, running is a feminist act. The athlete's feminism begins with the fact that her sports participation is, in Gail's words, "a declaration of independence." The runner runs on her own two feet, on her own time, in her own way, without male assistance. If a man wants to join her club, trot along next to her, watch her race, and leave a light on for her when she arrives home late, fine. If not, if she encounters male interference, she may not tolerate it. She may prioritize, instead, her own athletic joy. Running raises the possibility that the woman with the aggrieved husband will become the woman with no husband – that, in the process of running, women will run away from men.

Running also raises the possibility that mothers will leave fathers at home to wash dishes and put kids to bed. According to a 1993 Women's Sports Foundation survey of almost 1,600 working women, the more hours women devote to housework, the fewer they devote to sports or fitness. Twenty-nine percent of working women report that their husbands do no housework at all. Married women with children are the most likely to report a decrease in sports or fitness participation in the past five years.[1]

So if a woman runs in the morning while her husband dresses the children, feeds them, and gets them off to school, she tips the balance of power not only within the marriage but within the family. The runner who has no children, no husband, and no boyfriend – who instead carves out a life for herself with other athletes and other women – is likewise committing feminist acts. Her running represents a world in which women are neither running toward nor alongside nor away from men; where men and their ideas about what's too strenuous for women, what's acceptable for women, and what's attractive in women become irrelevant.

Female athletes don't necessarily see it this way. They don't necessarily call themselves feminists. They cycle or swim or surf because it's fun and challenging, because it feels good, because they like the way it makes them look, because it allows them to eat more without gaining weight, because it gives them energy and confidence and time spent with friends, female or male. Many are ignorant about the women's rights movement. I've heard college students confuse feminism with feminine hygiene.

Female athletes have a long tradition of dissociating themselves from feminism. Their desire to be accepted or to acquire or keep a boyfriend or a job has often equaled their passion for sports. Thus athletes have taken great pains – and it can hurt – to send reassuring signals to those who would oppose their play: "Don't worry, we're not feminists. We're not dykes, we're not aggressive, we're not muscular, we're not a threat to you. We just want to play ball." It has been a survival strategy.

It's time to tell the truth. We are feminists.[2] Some of us are dykes. Some of us are aggressive, some of us are muscular. All of us, collectively, are a threat – not to men exactly, but to male privilege and to masculinity as defined through manly sports. By reserving time each day for basketball dribbling, or for runs or rides or rows, women are changing themselves and society. Feminism is rarely an individual's motivating force but always the result: a woman's athletic training, regardless of the factors that lead to her involvement, implicitly challenges patriarchal constraints on her behavior. Sport for women changes the woman's experience of herself and others' experience of her. It alters the balance of power between the sexes. It is daring. It is life changing. It is happening every day.

Feminism is about freedom: women's individual and collective liberty to make their own decisions. For women, sports embody freedom: unrestricted physical expression, travel across great distances, liberated movement. Sports give meaning to the phrase "free time." Women find it, use it, and insist on retaining it. Their time for sports becomes a time when they free themselves of all the other people and projects they usually tend to. They become the person, the project, who needs care. They take care of themselves. For a group of people who have historically been defined by their ability to nurture others, the commitment to nurture themselves is radical.

Sports give a woman the confidence to try new things, including things previously defined as dangerous or unfeminine. "Boys grow up trying lots of new physical activities," notes University of Virginia sports psychologist Linda Bunker. "They develop an overall sense of their ability to handle unknown situations. Ask a male tennis player if he wants to play racquetball; he'll say 'sure,' even if he's never seen a racquetball court. But ask a nonathletic woman to play racquetball, and she'll say, 'Gee, I don't know if I can do it.'"

Several writers have used sports as metaphor, depicting women emancipated by the process of building muscle and endurance. In Fannie Flagg's film, *Fried Green Tomatoes*, a meek and depressed Evelyn Couch (played by Kathy Bates) takes aerobics classes, meets with a women's support group, and develops a deep friendship with an old woman. Soon she has acquired a new persona, Tawanda, who skips up steps, knocks down walls, and asserts herself with her husband. "I'm trying to save our marriage," she tells him. "What's the point of my trying if you're gonna sit on your butt drinking beer and watching baseball, basketball, football, hockey, bowling, golf, and challenge of the gladiators?"

In *Daughters of Copperwoman*, Anne Cameron creates a fictional world (based on the lives of the native people of Vancouver Island) in which prepubescent girls practice sprinting in the sand, running backwards, and swimming while tied to a log "until we were so tired we ached, but our muscles got strong and our bodies grew straight." Finally, after a girl's first menses, she is paddled by canoe out to sea, where she disrobes, dives overboard, and swims back to the village. As she approaches the shore, the villagers "sing a victory song about how a girl went for a swim and a woman came home."[3]

In Alice Adams' short story, "A Public Pool,"[4] a shy, anxious, unemployed woman who feels too tall and too fat and who lives with her depressed mother is slowly and subtly transformed by the process of swimming laps. At first she feels embarrassed to appear, even in the locker room, in her bathing suit. Swimming twenty-six laps, a half-mile, seems a struggle. She feels flattered by attention from a blond, bearded swimmer not because he is kind or interesting – in fact he cuts rudely through the water with a "violent crawl" – but because he is male.

By the end of the story she becomes "aware of a long strong body (mine) pulling through the water, of marvelous muscles, a strong back, and long, long legs." She applies for a job she'll probably get and looks forward to moving out of her mother's house. When she happens upon "Blond Beard" outside a cafe, she realizes that he is a gum-chewing, spiffily dressed jerk. The story ends with his inviting her to join him for coffee, and her declining. "I leave him standing there. I swim away."

No national statistics exist on the association between divorce and female athleticism, but stories are prevalent. The more she goes to the gym, the more he mopes. And the more she goes to the gym, the less willing she becomes to stop going, or to stop growing, to please him. She swims away.

Nancy Murray, an equestrian and public health doctoral student from Houston, Texas, quit riding the day she got married because she thought her husband wanted her to. She also quit graduate school and stopped talking to her friends in the evenings. "I was not a sane person," she recalls. She became ill with a severe thyroid disease that mysteriously cleared up when she started riding again, after eleven years. "It amazed the doctors," she says. Now she competes at fourth level, just below international level, in dressage.

"When I started riding again, I found my power," says Murray. That power transfers outside the ring. She is no longer able, she says, to play the subservient role her graduate school professors expect. Pursuing her dreams takes a toll, though. Murray says her husband now "supports my riding conceptually, but it's hard for him to have my attentions elsewhere." Like many of her married friends, Murray arrives at weekend competitions "blasted" with exhaustion, she says, "because it took so much energy just to leave – to leave our husbands, to get them to take care of the kids."

Traveling around the south to equestrian events, Murray drives a truck with horse-trailer attached. When she pulls of the road, she enjoys men's reactions. "My horse stands 17 hands high and weighs 1,500 pounds. I put a chain around his nose and hold a whip in my hand. He behaves. Men see me coming, controlling this huge beast, and they say, uh-oh." She laughs. She's in control. She's an athlete. She's free.

Feminism is about bodies: birth control, sexual harassment, child sexual abuse, pornography, rape, date rape, battering, breast cancer, breast enlargement, dieting, liposuction, abortion, anorexia, bulimia, sexuality.

Sports.

"The repossession by women of our bodies," wrote the poet and author Adrienne Rich in *Of Woman Born*, "will bring far more essential change to human society than the seizing of the means of production by workers."

As athletes, we repossess our bodies. Told that we're weak, we develop our strengths. Told that certain sports are wrong for women, we decide what feels right. Told that our bodies are too dark, big, old, flabby, or wrinkly to be attractive to men, we look at naked women in locker rooms and discover for ourselves the beauty of actual women's bodies in all their colors, shapes, and sizes. Told that certain sports make women look "like men," we notice the truth: working out doesn't make us look like men, it makes us look happy. It makes us smile. More important, it makes us healthy and powerful. It makes us feel good.

According to the Women's Sports Foundation's 1993 survey, 71 percent of women who exercise said they work out primarily for the physical benefits.[5] The National Center for Health Statistics reports that physical fitness is linked to a general sense of well-being, a positive mood, and lower levels of anxiety and depres-

sion, especially among women. The athlete is more likely than her nonathletic sisters to have a good body image, studies have consistently shown. Female athletes also report that sports reduce stress and enhance self-esteem. And University of Maine psychology professor Richard Ryckman has found that girls in the seventies derived their self-esteem primarily from their physical attractiveness, whereas for girls in the early nineties, physical competence is as essential to self-esteem as beauty.

As little as two hours of weekly exercise can lower a teenage girl's lifelong risk of breast cancer. According to the Women's Sports Foundation, female high school athletes are more likely than nonathletes to do well in high school and college, to feel popular, to be involved in extracurricular activities, to stay involved in sport as adults, and to aspire to community leadership. Female high school athletes are 92 percent less likely to get involved with drugs, 80 percent less likely to get pregnant, and three times more likely than their nonathletic peers to graduate from high school.[6]

Exercise reduces an older woman's chances of developing osteoporosis. Pregnant athletes report a lower incidence of back pain, easier labor and delivery, fewer stress-related complaints, and less postpartum depression than women who don't exercise.[7] And the effects of exercise seem to persist throughout a lifetime. Women who were athletic as children report greater confidence, self-esteem, and pride in their physical and social selves than those who were sedentary as children.[8] If, as a society, we were interested in the health and welfare of women, we would encourage and enable them to play sports.

In a country where male politicians and judges make key decisions about our bodies and all of us are vulnerable to random attacks of male violence, the simple act of women taking control of their own bodies – including their health, their pleasure, and their power – is radical. In a society in which real female bodies (as opposed to media images of female bodies) are unappreciated at best, the act of enjoying one's own female body is radical. It contradicts all feminine training to move, to extend our arms, to claim public space as our own, to use our bodies aggressively and instrumentally, and to make rough contact with other bodies. Temple University doctoral student Frances Johnston interviewed dozens of female ice hockey and rugby players and found that "physicality" was one of the most appealing aspects of the games. "They enjoyed the tackling, the checking, the falling down and getting up, the discovery that they had 'survived' another hard hit or rough game." Besides body contact, they enjoyed "kicking the ball, getting rid of the ball right before a tackle, the power of a well-hit slapshot."[9]

Lunging for a soccer ball, we do not worry if our hair looks attractive. Leaping over a high bar, we do not wish we had bigger breasts. Strapped snugly into a race car, roaring around a track at 220 miles per hour, we do not smile or wave.

While playing sports our bodies are ours to do with as we please. If in that process our bodies look unfeminine – if they become bruised or bloody or simply unattractive – that seems irrelevant. Our bodies are ours. We own them. While running to catch a ball, we remember that.

I coach basketball. My players are girls (nine through twelve), teenagers (fifteen through eighteen), and grown women (twenty through forty). They all have trouble with the defensive stance, and with "being big."

The defensive stance requires a player to squat, low to the ground, her legs wide. Her knees should gape open, farther apart than her shoulders, her hands ready to deflect passes or shots. From this position she can react quickly to any moves an offensive player makes.

Why is this difficult for girls and women to learn? It's the leg spread. It's unladylike to yawn one's legs wide open. Even little girls growing up today are getting this message. I can tell because I tease them, imitating the way they try to squat without separating their legs. "It's OK," I say. "No one's going to look up your skirt." They laugh and I know I've hit the mark. Most little girls don't even wear skirts to school anymore. But their foremothers' skirts still haunt them, even on the basketball court.

My players are haunted, too, by size taboos. They don't like to feel tall, to seem wide, to

make loud noises. They don't feel comfortable inhabiting a big space. Even many young ones talk quietly and act timid. In basketball, you need to snatch a rebound as if you own the ball, as if you're starving and it's the last coconut on the tree. You have to protect the ball, elbows pointed outward like daggers, lest others try to grab it. You have to decide where you want to be, then get there, refusing to let anyone push you out of the way. You have to shout, loudly, to let your teammates know who's cutting through the lane or who's open for a shot. Basketball teaches women and girls to renounce the suffocating vestiges of ladylike behavior and act instead like assertive, honest, forthright human beings. It's about unlearning femininity.

When Sarah Burton Nelson swims, she never follows a linear path for long. My mother will log her twenty laps "crawling" smoothly and efficiently from one end to the other; if anyone joins her, she'll eagerly offer to race. But she never enters a pool without also spending some time flat on her back, face to the sky. She has one of those rare buoyant bodies that, though thin, can float with hands and feet exposed; she wiggles all her fingers and toes, grinning. She likes, from that floating position, to point one leg then the other skyward, pretending she's Esther Williams. She likes to swim freestyle with one arm, then backstroke with the next, so that her body rolls like a spinning river log. She plays in the water the way children play, bobbing, twirling, languishing. Like children, she unabashedly savors the weightlessness, the wetness, the automatic grace granted to swimmers who dare to sink as well as to swim.

Sports offer women a chance to enjoy their own physical natures: graceful, expansive, experimental, joyful, sensuous. The athlete breathes not with the shallow breaths of a woman trying to hold her abdomen flat but with a deep, full sort of breathing that expands the lungs with air, the mind with possibility. The athlete knows movement, sweat, stretching. She knows how to use her body to get what she wants.

This can be scary. "We have been raised to fear the *yes* within ourselves, our deepest cravings," wrote the author Audre Lorde in an essay entitled "Uses of the Erotic: The Erotic as Power."[10] Many women feel vaguely embarrassed by their bodies: their muscles, their fat, their breasts, their hair, their desires. Many women feel uncomfortable about their own perspiration. Their first reaction, upon noticing sweat, may be to get rid of it. They may feel too self-conscious to fully appreciate other sensations – racing pulses, stretching muscles – that arise in the course of jumping, throwing, lifting weights, skating. They may feel embarrassed by public displays of sensuality, too inhibited to turn slow somersaults in a pool.

But the popular sports maxim could aptly be inverted: no pleasure, no gain. Sports require athletes to pay attention to their bodies. It is through this careful attention that athletes improve. Surely it is not gold medals but pleasurable perceptions – two skis caressing a mountain; a hand rolling a heavy ball toward ten pins; the welcome ache of powerful thighs kicking through ocean waves – that keep the athlete returning to her sport again and again despite fatigue, frustration, or grumpy husbands.

Nancy Nerenberg compares the onset of perspiration to orgasm. Nerenberg played basketball for the University of California, Berkeley, in the late seventies. Now a freelance writer and mother of two, she still plays pick-up games with men.

She enjoys sweating. After several trips up and down the court, when her pores open and her skin begins to glisten with moisture, Nancy notices. She's paying attention not only to the ball, to her teammates, and to the opposing team but also to her own physical sensations. "It's like a climax," she says. "It's like a faucet turning on. It's a rush."

Maybe you haven't noticed this. Maybe sweating doesn't feel like orgasm to you. Maybe Nancy Nerenberg is eccentric.

But maybe she's right. Maybe, if we pay attention, we'll notice that sweating feels, for starters, good. Maybe, if we open our minds to new possibilities, sweating could feel, if not like orgasm, at least interesting. Relaxing. Luxuri-

ous. After all, doesn't all personal, physical experience have sensuous, even erotic potential?

Ever since they stopped riding sidesaddle, horsewomen have shared an erotic secret alluded to with smiles, nods, and the phrase "girls love horses." One woman I know had "sensations very similar to the sensations that precede orgasms" while squeezing her legs closed on the adductor machine at the gym. It actually became a problem for her. Afraid of "going all the way" in front of dozens of other gym members, she eventually stopped using the machine altogether.

But sports don't have to feel sexual to feel sensual. They don't have to feel sensual to feel pleasurable. One definition of Eros is "love directed toward self-realization." There's something about physical joy that teaches an athlete who she is. "Sport holds a mirror to a woman's life," LaFerne Ellis Price wrote in *The Wonder of Motion*.[11] The athlete learns to love herself the way we all want to be loved: with eyes open, with forgiveness and enthusiasm. She becomes her own cheerleader. Moving alone, she discovers that physical joy resides in her body, regardless of how pleasing or attractive that body might be to others. Moving in concert with other women, she discovers the beauty of those women, and of women in general. Surely these twin pleasures – personal pleasure and communal female pleasure – go a long way toward explaining the powerful potential of women's sport.

Almost two million girls play soccer. Sixteen million women play softball. College volleyball is second only to football in autumn participation rates. Basketball is the most popular high school and college sport for women. Not gymnastics. Not tennis or golf. Basketball: Big, sweaty, strong, and requiring complex, intricate, intimate teamwork. This is the essence of much of women's athletic joy and much of women's athletic power. Feminism is about female bonding.

Adrienne Rich wrote a poem about a team of women who died during an ascent of Lenin's Peak in 1974. Imagining the leader's thoughts before she froze to death on the mountain, Rich wrote:

I have never loved
like this I have never seen
my own forces so taken up and shared
and given back
After the long training the early sieges
we are moving almost effortlessly in our love . . .
We know now we have always been in danger
down in our separateness
and now up here together but till now
we had not touched our strength.[12]

We're not used to hearing such passionate depictions of love by women, for women – neither by lesbians, who still remain largely invisible in this culture, nor by heterosexual women. When Magic Johnson retired from basketball in 1992, he said he would most miss his "buddies" – his teammates and opponents. Sportscaster Dick Vitale, introducing the cancer-stricken former coach Jim Valvano at the publicly televised "Espy's," the first American sports awards, said of his friend, "I love him." When was the last time we heard a woman publicly declare her love for another woman or team of women? When Chris Evert retired after playing almost two decades of phenomenal tennis, did Billie Jean King or Martina Navratilova or any other woman publicly say, "I love her?" I don't think so. Women finishing college basketball careers or returning from overseas professional careers surely feel the same way Magic Johnson did – affectionate toward and dedicated to their teammates. But these women – Heidi Wayment, Kamie Ethridge, Lynette Woodard – are not household names. No one even asks them whom or what they'll miss most.

Teams can offer women a welcome all-female world devoid of male commentary or competition. This sanctuary is one of sport's delights. "We want to be away from men, playing our sport for ourselves, with ourselves," one softball player told University of Iowa sociologist Susan Birrell. "We have a good time, stay in shape, and share being women – but mostly without men. It's refreshing."[13]

All-female sports participation places women somewhere along what Adrienne Rich calls the lesbian continuum.[14] Which is not to say that women who join sports teams become lesbians.

Most don't; most female athletes, like most male athletes, are heterosexual. But Rich expands the usual definition of lesbian in this continuum to mean "not simply the fact that a woman has had or has consciously desired genital sexual experience with another woman," but also "many more forms of primary intensity between and among women, including the sharing of a rich inner life, the bonding against male tyranny, the giving and receiving of practical and political support." Even heterosexual athletes, especially team sport athletes, could be classified as falling somewhere on this continuum, which is based on love and commitment to women rather than sex. In a society in which "lesbian" is a pejorative used against women who become strong and assertive, the athletic act of enjoying one's female body as it moves with and against other female bodies becomes a feminist act.

Much of male pornographic lore depicts women as having intimidating, insatiable sexual appetites, but Rich says "it seems more probable that men really fear, not that they will have women's sexual appetites forced on them, or that women want to smother and devour them, but that women could be indifferent to them altogether, that men could be allowed sexual and emotional – therefore economic – access to women *only* on women's terms, otherwise being left on the periphery of the matrix."[15]

The lesbian label used against female athletes (and against politicians, pilots, and other women who enter traditionally male domains) becomes clearer in this context: it names male fears of female empowerment. In the case of athletes, there's some truth to the rumors. Some of the best athletes in this nation's history were lesbians, largely because straight women were constrained by husbands or by restrictive definitions of appropriate female behavior. Nowadays, fewer women tolerate male interference in their athletic pursuits. But female athletes still symbolize this threat: women will devote their passions to women. In a significant power shift, millions of women are now becoming "team players" – not with men in corporations, but with women on softball, volleyball, and soccer fields.

Sports are more than games. When they work together toward communal goals, regardless of differences in race, class, physical ability, and sexual preference, women create unity through diversity, laying the groundwork for empowering political change. What if women really bonded against male tyranny? How bonded could we get? What if women truly trusted other women? What if we became comfortable in female worlds, with female leaders? Women are, after all, the majority. The majority rules, usually.

Simone de Beauvoir wrote in *The Second Sex* that the athlete receives from sports a sense of authority and an ability to influence others. "To climb higher than a playmate, to force an arm to yield and bend, is to assert one's sovereignty over the world in general." By contrast, the woman deprived of sports "has no faith in a force she has not experienced in her body; she does not dare to be enterprising, to revolt, to invent; doomed to docility, to resignation . . . she regards the existing state of affairs as something fixed."[16]

Thus the very desire to change the conditions of our lives – to demand the equal rights that are a cornerstone of feminism – may be traceable to our own sense of our physical power. This is supported by anecdotal evidence that many female politicians, business leaders, and other successful women were athletic as children.

This may also explain, in part, how dozens of female athletes have of late developed the chutzpah to sue their universities. Historically, boys and men have been granted more and better of everything athletic: facilities, coaches, travel, training, scholarships. In 1991, women made up more than half (50.3 percent) of the overall college student population but less than a third (30.9 percent) of all athletes. Men received 83 percent of recruiting funds, 77 percent of the athletic budget, and 70 percent of the scholarship money: approximately $179 million more per year in scholarships than their female counterparts.[17] Men now coach 52 percent of the women's teams and 99 percent of the men's teams.[18] Even when women and men coach identical sports, men receive bigger paychecks;[19]

female basketball coaches typically receive $23,000 less than male basketball coaches.[20] At the Division I level, 289 out of 298 athletic directors are men.

Lately, to save money, athletic directors have been cutting programs. Usually they eliminate one men's sport and one women's – or two men's and two women's – despite the fact that men begin with more opportunities, so the cuts detract disproportionately from women. "It's the only time we experience equity – when they're dropping sports," University of Iowa women's athletic director Christine Grant notes wryly.

But the law is on women's side, and they're beginning to use it effectively. Title IX, a 1972 amendment to the Civil Rights Act, forbids gender discrimination in educational institutions that receive federal funds. Most schools and colleges receive federal funds. The Supreme Court's 1992 *Franklin v. Gwinnett County* decision further strengthens the law, enabling plaintiffs to receive monetary damages.

From 1991 through the first half of 1993, at least thirty-four colleges and universities were sued by their female athletes or coaches, threatened with lawsuits, or had complaints filed against them.[21] Judges, juries, and the Office of Civil Rights virtually always ruled in favor of the women. When schools appealed the decisions, they virtually always lost.

Five colleges – William and Mary, the University of Oklahoma, the University of New Hampshire, the University of Massachusetts at Amherst, and UCLA – canceled women's teams only to reinstate them a few months later after women's groups, legal advisors, or judges reminded them that they were violating the law.

The University of South Carolina in 1991 announced a plan to eliminate women's softball but add women's track – a net reduction of the women's athletic budget (then $1.5 million, compared to $18.5 million for the men). Public pressure, galvanized by women's sports organizations, persuaded South Carolina to add track *and* keep softball.

Indiana University in Pennsylvania dropped women's gymnastics and field hockey, along with men's soccer and tennis, in the 1992 season to save $350,000. The football team took over the hockey field for their practices. But U.S. District Judge Maurice Cohill ordered the University to restore funding of the two women's teams, ruling that financial problems were no excuse for sex discrimination.

At Brown University, athletes filed a class action suit after the school cut its women's gymnastics and volleyball programs. A U.S. District Court judge ordered the school to reinstate both sports. University of Texas students also filed a class action suit. In an out-of-court settlement, the university agreed to increase the number of female athletes from 23 percent to 44 percent by 1996.

All of this was mere warm-up for the landmark decision in 1993, when Howard University women's basketball coach Sanya Tyler was awarded $1.11 million by a U.S. Superior Court in Washington, D.C. The 1991 sex discrimination suit claimed that Tyler and the men's basketball coach had identical job descriptions but he was paid almost twice as much and was given more office space and more assistants.[22]

As if to stave off such lawsuits, college administrators have recently given five top women's basketball coaches (Tara VanDerveer of Stanford, Vivian Stringer of the University of Iowa, Pat Summitt of the University of Tennessee, Ceal Barry of the University of Colorado, and Debbie Ryan of the University of Virginia) phenomenal raises – between $20,000 and $60,000 annual increases – to bring their salaries in line with or closer to the men's.

Dozens of girls, too, are suing. A 16-year-old named Jennifer McLeery successfully sued the U.S. Amateur Boxing Association in 1993, overturning their rule barring women from competition. Her goal: to box in the Olympics.

Sometimes athletes flex their political muscles beyond the sporting arena. Run, Jane, Run, which bills itself as the largest U.S. amateur sports competition for women, each year donates more than $655,000 to battered women's shelters, rape crisis hotlines, job training programs, YWCAs, and other women's groups. Women have also organized benefit

runs and walks for breast cancer research and against rape.

A few pro athletes in the post-Billie Jean King generation have become outspoken advocates for women. Golfer Carol Mann, race car driver Lyn St. James, and Olympic swimmers Nancy Hogshead and Donna de Varona have served as Women's Sports Foundation presidents. Zina Garrison has talked openly about a troubling feminist issue: the body/self hatred that in her case led to bulimia. Martina Navratilova has become an outspoken advocate of lesbian rights, supporting the Gay Games and joining a successful 1992 suit against the Colorado antigay amendment.

Many women, particularly women of color, believe that sports participation is an asset in gaining access to the business world. The energy, confidence, and connections that accrue from sports seem to spill over into job success. According to the 1993 survey of working women, about 50 percent of women of color believe their sports participation – not talking about the Dallas Cowboys but actually playing sports – helps them to access decision-making channels outside the office, gain acceptance by co-workers, advance their careers, and tap into business networks. About 36 percent of white women agree.[23]

Women who have played college sports rate themselves higher in their abilities to set objectives, lead a group, motivate others, share credit, and feel comfortable in a competitive environment. Former high school athletes also rated themselves fairly high in these abilities, followed by former youth sport athletes. Women with no childhood competitive experience felt least adept.[24]

Surely sports experience helps women obtain coaching jobs; female coaches are even more likely than male coaches to have played college sports.[25] Men have taken over most women's teams, but a handful of former female athletes are breaking through a cement ceiling to gain men's leadership positions. Meg Ritchie, for example, the first female strength and conditioning coach at a major university with a football program, was a former 1984 Olympic discus thrower. When she arrived for work at the University of Arizona in 1985, she could power clean (a type of lift) 350 pounds, more than any of the football players.

Wanda Oates has coached boys basketball at Ballou High School in Washington, D.C., since 1986. Since 1990, Bernadette Locke-Maddox has served as assistant men's basketball coach at the University of Kentucky. Carol White, a former assistant football coach at Georgia Tech, now works with Tech as a freelance kicking instructor. It's only a matter of time before a woman coaches an NFL team. Only sexism now keeps women from those positions. They needn't have playing experience. Some of the best male coaches have never played the game.

In 1991 Sandra Ortiz-Del Valle became the first female official to call a men's pro game, in the United States Basketball League. In 1992, Constance Hurlburt was named executive director of the Patriot League, the first woman to head a Division I all-sports conference for men and women. Sally John, a Little League coach since 1986, became in 1992 the first woman appointed to the sixteen-member international Little League board of directors. The following year, Kathy Barnard became the first woman to coach in a Little League World Series.

Susan O'Malley serves as President of the Washington Bullets. Joan Kroc inherited the San Diego Padres from her husband. Georgia Frontiere owns the L.A. Rams. Marge Schott owns the Cincinnati Reds (a dubious victory, considering her racist remarks and hiring practices). Marian Illitch of the Detroit Red Wings co-owns the hockey team with her husband, Mike. Ellen Harrigan-Charles serves as general manager of the St. Catharine's (Ontario) Blue Jays, a minor-league baseball team. She has assembled the only all-female front office in professional sports.

In 1993, *The Sporting News* named Anita DeFrantz, director of the Amateur Athletic Foundation and a member of the International Olympic Committee, one of the 100 most powerful people in sports. Women's Sports Foundation executive director Donna Lopiano, U.S. Figure Skating president Claire Ferguson, and NCAA President's Commission chair Judith Albino were also on the list.

Judith Sweet became the first female NCAA president in 1992. Barbara Hedges of the University of Washington and Merrily Dean Baker of Michigan State are the first two female athletic directors at major college programs (Division I-A) that include football. Two African-American women, Vivian Fuller of Northeastern Illinois University in Chicago, and Barbara Jacket of Prairie View A&M, are among the nine female athletic directors at Division I schools. Fuller says of working with sexist men, "The good old boys can ride my train or get off. It's up to them." Where did she obtain such self-assuredness? "I ran track in college."

Athletes are some of the strongest women in America. Perhaps our greatest potential for changing the gender balance of power lies in our strength. Physical power is not the only kind of power there is, but it's an important power: measurable, salient, symbolic, and understood by men. "Violence is the authentic proof of each one's loyalty to himself, to his passions, to his own will," wrote de Beauvoir. "For a man to feel in his fists his will to self-affirmation is enough to reassure him of his sovereignty. Against any insult, any attempt to reduce him to the status of object, the male has recourse to his fists."[26]

Many women don't even know how to make a fist. We weren't raised to fight. As girls, we weren't taught how to scream, run, hit, or kick – in short, how to take care of ourselves. Girls who live near the water are taught to swim, and girls who drive cars are taught to steer and brake. But while verbal, physical, and sexual assaults are common, most girls are not taught to develop the strength and technique necessary to resist attacks. "Don't take candy from strangers," they warned us in school. Big help. Almost 90 percent of rapists are acquaintances.[27]

Denied sports training as well as fighting skills, many women have become physically retarded, literally: slowed or delayed in their physical development. "I've taught black women, Hispanic women, and white women," says karate black belt Susan Erickson of Arlington, Virginia. "What they have in common is they have no sense of their physical prowess."

Women's physical inferiority, and our concomitant fear, is not incidental. It's not natural. If we are the weaker sex, it's because men have denied us the opportunity to build strength. "All patriarchal cultures idealize, sexualize, and generally prefer weak women," writes Gloria Steinem in *Revolution from Within*.[28]

Girls learn that female strength is unattractive to men, and that being attractive to men is paramount. "There are young girls who could be a lot better at taekwondo than they are, but they're afraid of what the boys will think," laments Olympic gold medalist and four-time taekwondo world champion Lynnette Love. "For so long they've been taught that if there's a boy and a girl the same age, the boy must be naturally better. If they do something to assert that they are stronger, then they have to apologize for it. It's frustrating because it takes such a long time to remold that."

Women learned from Billie Jean King's 1973 victory over Bobby Riggs that we can exceed male expectations – and often our own. That we can, brick by brick, dismantle the Gender Wall the men have constructed to keep women out. Relatively, men's upper bodies are usually stronger than ours, even if we are equally well trained. But their legs aren't. We could learn to kick, as Lynnette Love does. She can kick to the chest, the neck, the knee, the groin – anywhere she wants. With a kick to the head, she can kill.

In the film *Necessary Roughness* a college football team, short on players, invites a soccer player named Lucy to be their place-kicker. Team members fear that they'll be the laughingstock of the conference, and they make sexual comments about her body.

But Lucy scores the tying kick in the final game. A player from the opposing team, his sense of masculine dominance clearly threatened, gratuitously and angrily knocks her to the ground, saying, "Welcome to football." Her teammates, by then appreciative of her ability but still ensconced in their mythic man-as-protector role, run toward the guy who had tackled her as if to retaliate.

No need. Lucy can take care of herself. She kicks him in the groin, saying, "Welcome to football."

What interests me about this scene is the kick, this refreshing double-entendre on the word football. When a strong female foot connects with and injures delicate male "balls," it breaks all the rules, not only in the game of football (surely this would be ruled unnecessary roughness) but also in the game of life. Yet the title of the film is *Necessary Roughness*.

Six months pregnant, Amelia Brown[29] was walking along a street in the financial district of a major city, lost in maternal daydreams. It was Saturday; the street was quiet. Suddenly a man grabbed her by the arm, said, "Fuck me, bitch," and pulled her toward an alley.

Brown struck him in the face. It sent him backward. She stepped into him and jabbed his stomach with her elbow. He doubled over. She grabbed him by the hair, yanked his head down, and brought her knee up as if to smash him in the jaw, but stopped short, as if to say, "See what I could do?"

He fell on the sidewalk. Waving her finger in his face, she yelled, "You asshole. Don't you ever, ever do that again."

She felt a little better at that point. "My next thought was, I can't miss my train," she recalls. "I was going to see my obstetrician, and it was difficult to get appointments. So I just left him there."

A legal secretary, Amelia Brown had been raped by her husband's brother one morning in 1987, when she was alone at her house. She had let him in; she had trusted him. For weeks afterward she had been debilitated by fear, unable to stay home alone, to answer the door, or even to answer the phone. At the suggestion of a friend, she began to study and eventually to teach a women's self-defense program called Chimera. That prepared her for the attack, four years later, by the man on the street.

It also prepared her for life at work. Since studying self-defense, Brown deals with coworkers and superiors "from a position of strength. I'm the only legal secretary who'll march into the partners' corner offices and tell them what I really think."

Her physical training transformed Brown's marriage. "Before, when my husband would raise his voice, I'd run and hide. He never intended to threaten me, but occasionally he would get angry, and we couldn't continue the argument because I was frightened. He'd have to reassure me: 'I'm not going to hurt you.' One day we realized that my old fear was completely gone."

Amelia Brown is not alone. Women who study self-defense or otherwise build strength often have previously been assaulted. Their interest in physical power emerges as a direct result of their awareness of their vulnerability and their desire to become less vulnerable.

Psychologists say that the best antidote to depression and helplessness is action. Athletes, with their proud muscles and trained minds, are poised to take those actions, and to provide leadership for women who are sick of living in fear. When asked what she'd do if a man tried to rape her, Donna Lopiano, executive director of the Women's Sports Foundation, replied, "I'd kill him." She did not hesitate. She did not seem to worry that killing him might be unkind or unladylike. She'd kill him. Lopiano played in twenty-six national championships in four sports and was inducted into the National Softball Hall of Fame. Now in her late forties, she's still, she says proudly, "strong as a horse." If a man were foolish enough to attack her, she'd have the means to resist.

Ailene Voisin, a sportswriter for the *Atlanta Journal-Constitution*, was attacked in her own house by an employee of a professional moving company, whom she had recently hired. He returned to her new home the following week, knocked on her door, and asked to use her phone. When she let him in, he grabbed her from behind in a choke hold, lifted her off the ground, and tried to drag her toward the bedroom. Though she was much smaller, she wrestled him across the kitchen, where she was able to activate an alarm. Her sports training, she believes, helped save her life. From years of playing basketball, volleyball, softball, and other sports, Voisin acquired "strength, quick thinking, and also aggression," she says. "In sports, aggression is not only necessary, it's rewarded. It becomes automatic."

Tennis player Chris Thayer, furious about daily harassment from a construction crew near her home, decided to take matters into her own hands one day when walking to her car in a tennis dress. "The more I thought about it, the madder I got," she wrote in a letter to the *San Diego Union.* "Why should I be intimidated every time I enter or leave the place I live? I grabbed my tennis racket as though it were a weapon. I marched from my apartment straight past the construction workers, staring at them with sheer hate in my eyes. Guess what? I got in my car, slammed the door, and drove off without getting so much as a peep!"

Are female athletes, with their quick minds and swift feet, less prone to rape than nonathletes? Researchers have not yet answered – or even really asked – this question. But in one study, University of Arkansas psychologist Thomas L. Jackson found that female athletes reported significantly less rape victimization than has been reported by other researchers studying general female populations.[30]

Our problem is not so much superior male strength, but superior male training, combined with a culture that encourages male violence. Men have culturally sanctioned *rights* to violence. Sports – particularly football, boxing, and ice hockey – train men to use their bodies to injure others. Not only do women miss out on military-style sports training; many of us are actively discouraged from fighting. Amelia Brown says she was "socialized not to be angry. I was always told I was a hothead, I flew off the handle, and that was bad."

What if women became hotheads; what if we flew off the handle?

The Reverend Jesse Jackson, noting the social influence of sports heroes, said of the late great boxer, "Joe Louis taught us we can fight back with dignity and conquer." By "we" he meant African-American people and he seemed to mean primarily men, for whom boxing tends to be a more meaningful metaphor than for black women.

Do African-American women – and other women – know that we, too, can fight back with dignity and conquer? What if we learned that lesson from the story of Amelia Brown? Or from Lynnette Love, who now co-owns the National Institute of Taekwondo and Fitness in Temple Hills, Maryland? Or from our own sports training?

Surely we have discarded that bad, old advice: "If you don't resist rape, you won't get hurt." Since when can a woman be raped without being hurt? Surely it must be appropriate, sometimes, to "act like men." Otherwise we're defenseless against their attacks.

What if we did act as men act? What if women became not merely assertive, but aggressive – or, more precisely, counteraggressive? What if, when attacked, we retaliated? What if, before being attacked, we knew that we could fight back? What if, walking down the street or sleeping in our own beds, we didn't feel so damn vulnerable? Historically, men have used sports training to prepare for war. What if we used sports training to prepare for what Marilyn French calls men's "war against women"?[31] What if female coaches openly encouraged their athletes to transfer their strength, power, and presence of mind into self-defense off the playing fields?

Daily, I walk with Kabir, a big friend of German shepherd ancestry. Men never hassle me. I'm big, too, and that may be part of it. But I think it's mostly the dog. Many men are afraid of dogs, in particular German shepherds, in part because the police commanded the dogs to attack demonstrators during the Civil Rights marches of the sixties. I abhor any police or dog brutality, but what interests me is that many men are wary of dogs the way they're wary of each other. I'd like them to be wary of women, too.

Any athlete knows that smaller is not necessarily weaker. Women are getting strong, and we could get stronger. We could make men wary of us, make them walk a wide circle around us, even if we weren't accompanied by dogs. It won't work, my friend Susan says. Men will only start using more weapons. Or they'll gang-rape more. That may already be happening. Still, I'd like men to know that they can't trust women to be passive, to be victims, to be nonviolent, the same way they can't trust dogs.

We could also team up. Remember: sports teach women how to rely on each other, help each other, trust each other. One-on-one, the average man may win a fight with the average woman. His greater size, upper-body strength, athletic and aggression training, and culturally granted rights to violence give him the advantage. With training, she could fare better. With the help of her sisters, she could win.

Rarely do we hear of women banding together to protect each other or children from male violence. But it could happen, and athletes could lead the way. Wasn't this the appeal (for women) and horror (for rapists) of *Thelma and Louise*? It represented what editor Merle Hoffman called "two women giving the ultimate 'fuck you' to the patriarchy." Male reviewers expressed disgust that women would "act like men," proclaimed the film "toxic feminism" and worried about, in Hoffman's words, "the film's catalytic possibilities for general female revolt."[32]

If athletes lead the way in resisting male violence, those athletes may be girls. A 14-year-old named Hannah Alejandro recently wrote to *Ms.* magazine: "At school today I walked in on a group of my friends, two 15-year-old girls and a 15-year-old boy. The boy was playfully threatening to slap one of the girls. I leaned over to her and said loudly, 'Let me know if he bothers you, and I'll take care of him. I can body slam him, you know.' I made this comment partly to be funny, partly to warn. The boy immediately yelled that 'guys don't like to go out with big strong manly girls.' This is a boy who weeks ago asked me if I took pride in being manly, because I was discussing weightlifting with other boys. (I was forced to break it to him that it is possible to be a woman and strong.)

"I reacted to today's incident with indignation, and I think I've lost him as a friend. (I wonder if it was a loss?)"[33]

We have been ridiculed for throwing "like girls." What does it mean to throw like a woman? Maybe it means to throw hard, imagining oneself playing in the All-American Girls Pro Baseball League of the 1940s and 1950s. Maybe it means to throw with pride, having trained oneself, at age fifty. Maybe it means to throw often and publicly, hoping to inspire young girls. Maybe it means never throwing anything *at* anyone – unless in self-defense.

Sport, by definition, strengthens. Like Gail Savage, we all tend to acquire strength fairly easily. At 5'5", Gail can now bench-press eighty-five pounds and leg-press 325. She knows she's not "a total weakling." No female athletes are. The athlete dedicates herself to women's rights, beginning with her own. The team athlete becomes appreciative of women's bodies, beginning with her own. She cares for women, respects women, and becomes willing to take physical risks for and with women. Sport for women represents autonomy, strength, pleasure, community, control, justice, and power. It disrupts men's attempts to elevate themselves above women. It changes everything.

Patrick Thevenard, for example, has been changed. Thinking back on the times when he would lift and carry his ex-wife despite her objections, Patrick says, "That was years ago. That was before I'd done enough reading and

thinking to understand that it was another one of those nice reinforcements of physical masculine dominance. You can pick up someone and show them to be helpless, but it's all a good joke, ha-ha-ha, so the woman is not in a position to put up much of a struggle. It maintains an underlying physical domination."

He would not, he says, do it again.

Meanwhile, President Clinton moved to Gail Savage's town. I mentioned to her that they're the same age. "I can run faster than Bill," she responded immediately. News reports have described his jogging regimen – about two to three miles a day – as "real slow, not too strenuous." Gail noticed. She added generously, "That's OK for him."

As for herself, she has faster goals, including a 10K at a seven-and-a-half-minutes-per-mile pace. Meanwhile, it's nice to know that already she can outrun one of the most powerful men in the world. It makes her feel good about herself. It makes her feel like running.

Notes

1 Don Sabo and Marjorie Snyder, "Miller Lite Report on Sports and Fitness in the Lives of Working Women" (in cooperation with the Women's Sports Foundation and Working Women), March 8, 1993.

2 Susan Greendorfer, professor of kinesiology at the University of Illinois, Urbana-Champaign, asserts that women's sports are inherently a political act. Susan Greendorfer, "Making Connections: Women's Sport Participation as a Political Act." Paper presented at the National Girls and Women in Sports Symposium, Slippery Rock State University, Slippery Rock, Pennsylvania (February 13, 1993).

3 Anne Cameron, *Daughters of Copperwoman* (Vancouver, British Columbia: Press Gang Publishers, 1981), pp. 101–102.

4 Alice Adams, "A Public Pool," *Mother Jones* (November 1984), p. 38.

5 Sabo and Snyder, 1993.

6 Women's Sports Foundation, Eisenhower Park, East Meadow, New York 11554 (1992).

7 Ibid.

8 L. Jaffee and J. Lutter, "A Change in Attitudes? A Report of Melpomene's Third Membership Survey," *Melpomene Journal* 10, no. 2 (1991), pp. 11–16; and L. Jaffee and R. Mantzer, "Girls' Perspectives: Physical Activity and Self-esteem," *Melpomene Journal* 11, no. 3 (1992), pp. 14–23.

9 Frances Johnson, "Life on the Fringe: The Experience of Rugby and Ice Hockey Playing Women." Paper presented at the annual meeting of the North American Society for the Sociology of Sport (Toledo, Ohio: November 5, 1992).

10 Audre Lorde, *Sister Outsider: Essays and Speeches* (Freedom, California: Crossing Press, 1984), p. 57.

11 LaFerne Ellis Price, *The Wonder of Motion: A Sense of Life for Woman* (Tette Haute, Indiana: LaFerne Ellis Price, 1970).

12 Adrienne Rich, "Phantasia for Elvira Shatayev," *The Dream of a Common Language* (New York: W.W. Norton & Co., 1978), p. 4.

13   Susan Birrell and Diane M. Richter, "Is a Diamond Forever? Feminist Transformations of Sport," *Women's Studies International Forum* 10, no. 4 (1987), p. 401.

14   Adrienne Rich, "Compulsory Heterosexuality and Lesbian Existence," *Signs* (Summer 1980), pp. 631–60.

15   Ibid., p. 643.

16   Simone de Beauvoir, *The Second Sex* (New York: Vintage Books, 1952), p. 331.

17   NCAA Gender-Equity Study (Overland Park, Kansas: National Collegiate Athletic Association, 1992).

18   R. Vivian Acosta and Linda Carpenter, "Women in Intercollegiate Sport: A Longitudinal Study – 1977–1992." Unpublished paper. Department of Physical Education. Brooklyn College, Brooklyn, NY 11210, 718/780-5879.

19   Annelies Knoppers, Barbara Bedker Meyer, Marty Ewing, and Linda Forrest, "The Structure of Athletic Obstacles to Women's Involvement in Coaching." Paper presented at the annual forum of the Council of Collegiate Women Athletic Administrators (Washington, D.C.: September 17–19, 1989).

20   Women's Sports Foundation.

21   Christine Grant and Mary Curtis, "Judicial Action Regarding Gender Equity." Unpublished manuscript (University of Iowa, 1993).

22   Jack Carey, "Sportsline: Cold Cash," *USA Today* (June 25, 1993), p. C1.

23   Sabo and Snyder, 1993.

24   Ibid.

25   Knoppers, Meyer, Ewing, and Forrest, 1989.

26   de Beauvoir, 1952, p. 330.

27   Diana E.H. Russell, *Sexual Exploitation: Rape, Child Sexual Abuse, and Workplace Harassment* (Beverly Hills, California: Sage Publications, 1984).

28   Gloria Steinem, *Revolution from Within* (Boston: Little, Brown and Company, 1992), p. 217.

29   Amelia Brown is a pseudonym, and some of the facts of her life have been changed to protect her identity.

30   Thomas L. Jackson, "A University Athletic Department's Rape and Assault Experiences," *Journal of College Student Development 32* (January 1991), p. 77.

31   Marilyn French, *The War Against Women* (New York: Summit Books, 1992).

32   Merle Hoffman, "Editorial," *On the Issues* (Winter 1991), pp. 2–3.

33   Hannah Alejandro, "Letters," *Ms.* (March/April 1993), pp. 8–9.

CHAPTER 30

The Sports Closet

Liz Galst

At East Stroudsburg University in Pennsylvania's Pocono Mountains, Angee Phong is the big dyke on campus. She drives around in a gold pickup truck that sports stickers supporting gay rights, AIDS activism, and the band "disappear fear," which is fronted by lesbian Sonia Rutstein. Last year, Phong was president of the university's Gay, Lesbian, and Bisexual Student Organization; for two years before that, she served as V.P. She walks with an understated swagger, tends to wear freedom rings, those rainbow-colored necklaces that show support for gay and lesbian rights to those in the know, and T-shirts bearing slogans like "Dykes Rule."

On college campuses across the United States there are thousands of young women like Angee. They're shaving their heads. They're having double women's symbols tattooed beside their belly buttons. Nothing's unusual about how out Angee Phong is, except for one particular fact: Phong is a varsity athlete.

"What she's doing is totally radical," says Pat Griffin, author of *Strong Women, Deep Closets: Lesbians and Homophobia in Sport*. "Angee," she says, "is a pioneer."

And a rarity as well. Though many people assume women athletes are, by definition, lesbians, an out lesbian athlete or coach can be pretty hard to find. This is true in professional sports and especially true on college and university campuses, where closeted coaches are teaching closeted athletes how to play the game: both the one on the field, and the one required of them by administrators who say they don't discriminate, but who fear they'll lose students and money if their women's teams are thought to be made up of lesbians.

Faced with these obstacles, the lesbian sports subculture has developed apart from the larger lesbian subculture. At colleges and universities, where some of the most passionate, open, and radical gay organizing is going on, the overwhelming majority of lesbian coaches and athletes live in a world of silent glances, private parties, and marriages of convenience. It's as if they don't know their activist sisters are out there picketing, kissing-in, and walking arm in arm across campuses with their girlfriends.

Had women's athletics languished in obscurity, as it seemed destined to do only a few short decades ago, open lesbian athletes might have been able to make a go of it. But now women's sports have begun to hit the big time, with two professional basketball leagues and a professional fast-pitch softball league all in their second season, and pro hockey and soccer leagues in the works. In an age of nationally televised women's basketball finals, where aggressive coaches bark orders from the sidelines, tough athletes muscle each other for rebounds, and little girls on their mothers' shoulders wave from the stands, the stigma of homophobia still holds. Olympic softball star Dot Richardson, for example, felt compelled to publish an article in *Sports*

Illustrated's short-lived *Women/Sport* magazine last year asserting she was not a lesbian. (A photo of "date Bob Pinto" accompanied the piece.)

With multiyear contracts, high-stakes endorsements, and whopping TV revenues, nobody wants to bet their money on setting up an openly homosexual athlete as an American icon. Not even tennis great Martina Navratilova could break out of that particular box. For all her brilliance on the court, she was never offered the opportunity to have her picture on a Wheaties carton. "Women athletes are smart. They know that if you want to attract corporate sponsorship and TV revenues, you have to look appropriately feminine" – i.e., straight, says Mary Jo Kane, a University of Minnesota sociologist who directs the school's Tucker Center for Research on Girls and Women in Sport.

Indeed, women's athleticism itself is still suspect. Only in recent years – thanks to Title IX especially – has women's participation in sports been viewed as anything other than a major gender transgression. For most of this century, the specter of the "mannish" lesbian has haunted women's sports in the U.S. "Sports 'belong' to men," notes Kane. "Sports have been seen as their natural, inherent birthright, so women's participation in sports, particularly team sports, threatens the "natural" order of what it means to be a man and a woman." Gender stereotyping plays an intriguing role in all this. An aggressive woman with a physically powerful body goes against the norm of female looks and behavior. So women who look and act this way – or play sports this way – are too much like men; they're "abnormal." "Unnatural" and "abnormal" are the same terms medical science has long applied to lesbians. So it's not surprising that women's athletics has been conflated with lesbianism.

Of course, there was always some truth to the rumors. Starting in the 1920s, women in nascent urban lesbian communities flocked to organized sports leagues. No hard numbers exist, but anecdotal evidence suggests that until Title IX, lesbians were vastly overrepresented in athletics. "They had already transgressed a lot of boundaries," says Pat Griffin, who teaches in the social justice education program at the University of Massachusetts at Amherst. Besides, says Griffin, who played college ball in the 1960s, sports "was an incredible social network for women to meet each other."

Nowadays, on college campuses, where most of women's competitive sports are still played, the stigma isn't so much about being an athlete or a lesbian, but about being both. It is at colleges and universities that young women begin to plan their careers, and that they often first begin to express their sexuality. And it is on those campuses that women athletes get the message to stay in the closet. Many women arrive on campus and see lesbians and bisexuals who possess a new sense of entitlement – women like Angee Phong, filled with self-confidence. They also see that, despite the large number of schools with antidiscrimination policies, lesbian coaches are regularly fired or forced to resign – athletics departments have gotten good at pulling together trumped-up charges. And regardless of their qualifications, these coaches have trouble finding jobs once it's rumored that they're gay. Incoming students also hear constant derision of lesbian athletes, and stories of fellow students who can't even get summer internships, let alone sports-related jobs after they graduate. (Phong, for instance, believes she was turned down for an internship with a women's pro team because her résumé is filled with lesbian-identified extracurricular activities. On the other hand, she finally managed to snag a sports-management internship at another pro team this past summer.)

What happened to Karen Weaver, the former head field hockey coach at Ohio State University, is almost a textbook example of the discrimination faced by female coaches believed to be lesbians. It's a discrimination that is simultaneously blatant and hidden. Hired by sports powerhouse OSU in 1987, Weaver was, without question, the best field hockey coach the university ever had. Only a few years after she arrived, she had pulled her team from near the bottom of the standings into the Division I top twenty – a first for the program. (Division I is the National College Athletic Association's [NCAA] most competitive grouping.) Weaver's 1994 team managed to break into the top five. And the Atlanta Olympic Committee chose Weaver as one of two stadium and broadcast announcers for field hockey at the 1996 games.

None of this stopped some members of the OSU athletics department from attacking Weaver because they believed she was a dyke. Most comments were made behind her back, since the school's policy prohibiting discrimination on the basis of sexual orientation made it difficult to harass her publicly.

"There were all sorts of little remarks about queer coaches, especially Weaver," says a former member of the athletics department who declined to be identified. "Whenever names of people who were gay would come up, there was always a sneer, or an aside." The hostile climate put her at a disadvantage. Says Weaver: "You feel that if you don't fit in, you're not going to get the resources other teams might get that are part of the straight, white culture of college sports."

And certainly the resources OSU offered her didn't hold a candle to those it offered its men's teams, many of which play in facilities even the pros envy. While male athletes often ate steak and eggs for breakfast at OSU's expense, and sometimes stayed overnight at hotels before big games, Weaver had little money for new uniforms or even for hiring an assistant coach, a position all the other teams in her league took for granted. Worse still was the gray-green patch of 25-year-old Astroturf that served as the team's field. Essentially a threadbare nylon carpet stretched over poorly padded tarmac, it was by far the most dangerous field in the league. "We used to have to pour water on it so we wouldn't stick to the turf and blow out our knees," says Kim Bush, who played for Weaver.

Then, in 1996, the department fired Weaver. She says she was fired "for speaking out and pushing for the health and safety" of her athletes. Many of the students and members of the athletics department who worked with her believe she was fired because she was a *lesbian* advocating for her players. Supporting their homophobia theory, they point to the six other women coaches – almost all perceived to be lesbians, although none of them were out – who were forced from their jobs between 1994 and 1997.

One was women's basketball director Nancy Darsch, now head coach of the WNBA's New York Liberty. Darsch was one of college ball's best coaches. But in January 1994, the season after she brought her squad to the NCAA finals, Monica Taylor, a player who'd been dropped from the team, slapped Darsch with a $150,000 civil suit alleging that Darsch "made comments and engaged in actions designed to induce [Taylor] to become involved in and engage in activities of an alternate lifestyle, of which Darsch is a participant." Taylor maintained that when she rejected the alleged advances, Darsch removed her from the team.

Darsch denied the allegations. Despite a strong record (Darsch left OSU with 222 team wins and 109 losses) she soon had trouble recruiting top players, and her teams fell in the standings. She never got support from the athletics department as she tried to repair the damage. In the spring of 1997, she was fired. If it weren't for the start-up of the WNBA, it's quite likely Darsch would have had nowhere to go. Coaches just as talented as she have spent years in the job market. Applicants are regularly subjected to unofficial background checks, made easier by Web sites and e-mail lists that provide the names of suspected lesbian coaches.

Of the coaches fired by OSU, only Weaver filed a sexual orientation discrimination suit – the first at the university. The suit has since been deferred, awaiting the outcome of a gender discrimination and equal pay suit she also filed. At press time, that case was scheduled to go to court in August.

Experts on lesbians and sports say the situation at OSU is typical of most colleges and universities. Administrators at major women's sports schools fear they won't be able to recruit the best athletes or put together top teams if word gets out that a coach is gay. Pat Griffin points the finger at parents who, she says, are loath to turn their daughters over to dyke coaches, as if women's sports really were a giant recruiting initiative for the Lesbian Nation.

So-called negative recruiting plays upon these fears. Athletes say that when they're considering colleges, coaches visit them at home, pop a video about their school's program into a portable

VCR, and then ask the parents (it is almost always the parents who choose the schools their talented progeny attend), "Where else are you looking?" A favorite way to attack a rival school is to say its coach is a lesbian.

"If my name came up," says former Penn State University softball coach Sue Rankin, once the only out lesbian coach in all of Division I and now the coordinator of Lesbian, Gay, Bisexual, and Transgender Equity at Penn, "the other coach would say, 'You don't want your kid to go to that school. She's a lesbian and all her players are lesbians. She recruits players to be lesbians.'"

Rankin says that only in her last few years of coaching at Penn State did any parents ever tell her they appreciated her honesty in coming out. "But they also told me stories of people who wouldn't let their kids play for me. I'm sure I lost recruits because of that." And recruiting – athletics recruiting that is – is the name of the game, especially in the highly competitive Division I.

After she came out, Rankin began having trouble with her evaluations from the athletics department head. They went from "excellent" to "poor," from 1990 to 1991, she says – coincidentally the same time when she was doing battle with Penn State over its failure to respond to the alleged homophobia of its high-profile women's basketball coach, Rene Portland. Some of Portland's former players had told a reporter that her training rules were "no alcohol, no drugs, no lesbians," and Rankin wanted to know what the department intended to do about it. Rankin finally left her job in 1996 before she could be asked to go. She considered bringing suit. "I asked some friends – my very best friends – if they would support me if I brought this to court," she says. The answer was no. "It would have incriminated them," she points out. Luckily, the university's vice provost for educational equity offered her her current job.

It's no wonder then, that most lesbian coaches are in the sports closet. Their strategies vary from deep closet – it's not uncommon for some to marry in order to protect their reputations – to what Pat Griffin calls the "glass closet," where coaches make no claims to heterosexuality

and may even bring their partners to department functions, but never mention their lesbianism specifically. Rarely, though, do coaches come out – even to players they know to be lesbians. Many go to great lengths to avoid being seen in public with other lesbians, including fellow coaches in their own departments.

The result, says Rankin, is a secret society that exists largely apart from the rest of the lesbian and gay world. "Everybody knows about each other within the context and the confines of that coaching network, but nobody ever says anything outside the secret society." Indeed, when *Ms.* asked more than three dozen coaches to participate in anonymous interviews for this article, not one agreed.

Such norms are passed down from coach to student. Lesbian athletes, especially those who want to work as coaches or physical education teachers, or hope for professional sports careers, understand that their future is dependent on not being open. Ronni Sanlo, director of the Lesbian, Gay, Bisexual, Transgender Campus Resource Center at the University of California, Los Angeles (and before that, at the equally powerful University of Michigan), says she's received many a late-night phone call from young women too scared to give their names. At coffee shops far from campus, they talk with her about the fact that they might be gay. They tell her they've heard rumors – many true – of young women who lost their scholarships when they were discovered to be lesbians. One Olympic-caliber athlete came to Sanlo feeling suicidal. "Her terror was that if she made her sexual identity known, or if people discovered her sexual identity, she would be kicked off the team and lose her scholarship," Sanlo says. "If she lost her scholarship, she couldn't afford to go to school, and that way her family would find out. Her life wouldn't be worth living. And that's the mental path many young women tend to take."

Occasionally, Sanlo will find herself accompanying a lesbian athlete to an abortion clinic. "So many girls are trying to deny the lesbian label," she says, "they end up hyperheterosexually active. They end up getting pregnant because they had to somehow get a message out that they're not lesbians."

Sanlo has gotten calls, too, after closeted coaches were fired. "I remember one student saying she wanted to coach, but because this coach was fired, she suddenly got the message that if she were a lesbian, she would be at risk."

"Most lesbian athletes have bought into the idea that being gay is damaging to their team's reputation," says Griffin. "Or, the coach has flat out told them that if you join a lesbian activist group, you're out of here." Some of Rene Portland's former players, for instance, say her antilesbian rule still holds, despite Portland's claim that she's in compliance with Penn State's antidiscrimination policy. And teammates who are uncomfortable around lesbians, or desperate to prove that they're not queer themselves, can up the ante. Current Houston Comets star Sheryl Swoopes left the University of Texas, in part, because she was "bothered by the presence of lesbians on the basketball team," her mother told the Austin *American-Statesman*.

This hostility can start even before the high-pressure world of college. At a high school basketball camp for promising athletes that Joah Iannotta, a 1995 track-and-field all-American from Wesleyan University, attended, someone asked a college player what the rules were on her team. The answer, says Iannotta, was " 'We're not allowed to drink, we're not allowed to party too hard, and there are no lesbians on our team.' The entire gym applauded."

It's no wonder, then, that most lesbian athletes have trouble coming out. And it doesn't help that so many have been pegged as lesbians in the first place. Says Lauren Muser, an Iowa State soccer goalie who graduated this year, "You say you're a phys ed major, and people are like, 'Duh! Well, of course you are a lesbian!' It's almost as if you couldn't do anything else."

And yet, against these formidable odds, a small but growing number of young lesbian athletes – and a few coaches – are bucking the trend, starting to come out, participating in gay pride activities. None of the young women who volunteered to be interviewed for this article are WNBA draft picks. Few plan on working as full-time coaches or phys ed teachers. Most are at schools where sports aren't the reason for living, although a few are at highly competitive programs like East Stroudsburg or Iowa State, where there's a lot to lose. But wherever they are, and whatever they plan to do, these young women say remaining in the closet is unthinkable. "I think that as soon as I knew I was going to step on campus, I was going to be who I wanted to be," says Angee Phong. "The first day I walked into the dorms, I had my freedom rings on."

In fact, sports may embolden some women. "For me," says bisexual Maia Kaplan, of the University of North Carolina fencing team, "being involved in athletics gave me much more self-confidence in who I am. And being out is part of that."

This new visibility is crucial, say the young lesbians arriving on campuses looking for support in coming out. When Maria Cardow, a three-sport varsity athlete, first arrived at the University of Chicago, she "knew there were some lesbians on the team, but they didn't come out. If just one of them had said, 'This is my girlfriend, she's the best thing in my life,' it would have changed so much for me."

Despite the fears of their athletics departments, most of the athletes who have dared to come out have been well received by the majority of their straight teammates. "I made such a big deal about coming out," Maria Cardow says. "I said to the team captain, 'You're going to hear about it!' And she was like 'Yeah, but are you working out?' She couldn't care less who I dated." When Joah Iannotta and her partner held a commitment ceremony, Iannotta's fellow runners served as bridesmaids. And most of Lauren Muser's teammates asked where they could get "ally" pins to show their support for her. "They were ready to march," says Muser.

Iannotta, who now works part-time as a track-and-field coach at a small Division III college in Minnesota, feels safe enough to come out to her students. After being contacted for this article, she told her charges, "Guess what? I'm going to talk to *Ms.* magazine about athletes who are gay and out in college.

Her students' response? "Cool!"

PART VII

Sport and Racial Issues

CHAPTER 31

Racial Differences in Sports: What's Ethics Got to Do with It?

Albert Mosley

In his book, *Taboo: Why Black Athletes Dominate Sports and Why We Are Afraid to Talk About It* (New York: BBS Public Affairs, 2000), Jon Entine presents the evidence for black superiority in athletics and addresses our ambivalence in recognizing this conclusion. The evidence derives from facts produced in the laboratory and, most importantly, on the playing fields.[1] Elite black athletes have a phenotypic edge over athletes of other races, Entine argues, and this edge derives from genotypical differences between the races (p. 18). While Asians comprise 57 percent of the world's population, they "are virtually invisible in the most democratic of world sports, running, soccer, and basketball" (p. 19). On the other hand, Africans, who comprise only 12 percent of the world's population, dominate running, soccer, and basketball.

Superior athletic performance occurs most noticeably where the contribution of cultural and socio-economic factors is least, Entine holds.[2] This is why he focuses on sports based on running. Presumably such sports offer performances that are least dependent on extensive training and equipment. In this, he follows the views of Amby Burfoot (a senior editor of *Sports Illustrated*). Running, wrote Amby Burfoot, "doesn't require any special equipment, coaching, or facilities" (p. 30). Currently, "every men's world record at every commonly-run distance belongs to a runner of African descent" (p. 31). Even given this "fact", Entine warns us that this achievement is not proportionally distributed throughout Africa: "West Africa is the ancestral home of the world's top sprinters and jumpers; North Africa turns out top middle distance runners; and East Africa is the world distance running capital" (p. 31).

Entine believes the refusal to recognize racial differences in athletic aptitude is a derogation of our duty to seek truth. "Measured by fractions of a second, or wins and losses, sport comes as close as we can get to an objective, racially neutral scoring system" (p. 79). In order to dispel the suspicion that acknowledging racial differences is tantamount to endorsing racism, he presents the views of many blacks who have also been led by the evidence to acknowledge the superior athletic ability of black athletes. Thus Arthur Ashe, while militantly anti-racist, was forced to recognize that, in terms of athletic performance, "we blacks have something that gives us the edge" (p. 80). Testimonials of this nature from black athletes are cited to show that acknowledging racial differences is not tantamount to accepting racist explanations of those differences.

In order to account for our fear of acknowledging black superiority in athletics, Entine provides an overview of eugenic thinking in the early and middle nineteenth century, when prominent American intellectuals such as Charles Davenport, Robert Bean, and many others advocated racist beliefs as a matter of

policy. As a result of the work of Henry God-
dard, Lewis Terman, Robert Yerkes, and others,
IQ tests provided a means of ranking human
beings in terms of their cognitive capacity. Citing this evidence, Henry Fairfield Osborn, pale-
ontologist at Columbia University and president
of the Board of Trustees of the American
Museum of Natural History, wrote: "The standard of intelligence of the average Negro is
similar to that of the eleven-year-old youth of
the species *Homo sapiens*" (p. 166). Even European immigrants from East and Southern
Europe were considered inferior races, and in
1924 Congress restricted immigration from
"biologically inferior areas" (p. 167). Steriliza-
tion, miscegenation laws, and segregation were
some of the hygienic racial policies designed
to limit the transfer of bad genes. Such measures were considered necessary for human evolution.

The defeat of Nazi Germany brought about a
repudiation of the ideological basis of racist
views. "Sports became a highly visible way to
demonstrate to the world that Americans took
their government's pronouncements on freedom
and equality to heart", and universities were in
the forefront of putting Negro athletes on the
field to compete on equal terms with the white
athletes (p. 209). The study of racial differences
became tainted by association with the racist
ideology of Nazism, and the very concept of
races differentiated by biological features was
rejected in favor of the notion of "ethnic
groups", differentiated on the basis of cultural
factors. If the Jews were not a race, perhaps
Africans weren't either.

On the other hand, Entine favors recognizing
a biological basis for genuine racial differences.
He surveys polygenecist and monogenecist
views on the evolution of *Homo sapiens*, and
opts for the view that the transformation to
modern *Homo sapiens* occurred in an already
subdivided population, "with one group giving
rise to the modern African and the other to all
modern non-Africans" (p. 92).[3] Entine concludes that "the ancestors of a Nigerian, a Scandi-
navian, and a Chinese have traveled significantly
different evolutionary paths," and that races are
reliable ways of classifying people in terms of the
geographical area they or their immediate ancestors derive from.

After the defeat of the Axis powers, UNESCO
(United Nations Educational, Scientific, and
Cultural Organization) issued a number of studies showing that the concept of race had no
biological validity. But Entine considers the
UNESCO position on race to be an example of
"flawed science" and accuses it of having replaced biological determinism with environmental determinism, in which all relevant differences
are acquired through experience.[4] Nonetheless,
Entine recounts how eminent scientists such as
Sir Ronald Fisher, Professor Henry Garrett, and
Nobel Prize laureates Herman Muller and William Shockley continued to hold that blacks had
less intellectual ability on the average than
whites. In an article published in *Science* in
1962, the past president of the American Psychological Association and chair of the anthropology department at Columbia University
wrote: "No matter how low ... an American
white may be, his ancestors built the civilizations
of Europe, and no matter how high ... a Negro
may be, his ancestors were (and his kinsmen still
are) savages in an African jungle. Free and general race-mixture of Negro–white groups in this
country would inevitably be not only dysgenic
but socially disastrous" (p. 217).

In 1969 Arthur Jensen argued in the *Harvard
Educational Review* that genetic factors rather
than environmental ones (e.g. socio-political
status) were the primary causes of differences in
average IQ among the different races. As recently
as 1994, *The Bell Curve* argued that those who
were least well-off were so because they had
lower intellectual potential while those who
were best off were so because they had, on the
average, higher intellectual potential. It appears
from this perspective that brains vary in inverse
proportion to brawn, and those with least intelligence depend most on athletic performance and
physical labor while those with most intelligence
dominate in intellectual performance and mental
labor.[5] We are led to infer that just as the genetic
makeup of Europeans predisposes them to have
higher IQs, the genetic makeup of Africans and
African Americans predisposes them to greater
manual dexterity and athletic potential.

Of course, attributions of higher and lower intelligence presuppose that we know what we mean by intelligence, and Entine's survey demonstrates that this is not the case. Instead of intelligence being, as Jensen held, a manifestation of a central processing capacity labeled g, others have viewed it as a catch-all term for distinct types of competence: analytic, creative, practical, emotional, linguistic, musical, logical/mathematical, spatial, bodily/kinesthetic, interpersonal, and naturalist. This might suggest the racialist argument that "each group is intelligent in its own special way," but it is also vulnerable to the racist rejoinder that some ways are more important than others: the way Africans think and act may have been valuable in the jungle, but are dysfunctional in the modern world, where the body is routinely surpassed by the machine (p. 245). Entine recognizes that his view might be interpreted as supporting the racist option, but disclaims the inference that "the data that conclusively link our ancestry to athletic skills have . . . anything to say about intelligence" (p. 245). But if athletic skills can be conclusively linked to ancestry, why can't intellectual skills be as well? Conversely, if intellectual skills cannot be conclusively linked to ancestry, how can we be so sure that athletic skills can?

Entine reports the position of prominent social scientists, such as Ashley Montagu and Harry Edwards, who argue that the concept of race has questionable biological validity. They point out that average differences between races is little different from the amount of variation within races. Races, they argue, have a political rather than biological utility, that of continuing a racist agenda. Citing alleged innate differences between groups has historically been a principal justification for supporting existing differences in the distribution of wealth and power. On the other hand, environmentalists typically stress the extent to which black athletic achievement is the result of intelligence, hard work, and the lack of opportunities in other areas. The belief that it is possible to be a "naturally better" athlete "undermines the importance of training, access, early exposure, social reinforcement and the like."[6] By making black youth believe that sport is their natural domain, this belief chan-

nels their energies and talents away from technical and academic areas. In this regard, Harry Edwards argues that sport is a negative image that merely transfers the black male from the cottonfields to the playing fields, and construes him as good for nothing else. The fact that many African Americans have romanticized black athletes as representing the natural potential of the race is no excuse.[7]

But for Entine, stereotypes that portray blacks as naturally better athletes are distillations of commonly recognized truths. And particular stereotypes such as "blacks can't swim" and "whites can't jump" reflect genotypically based propensities of whites and blacks. Entine dismisses the fact that swimming pools and training facilities are in short supply in poor black neighborhoods in favor of "the fact" that blacks have denser skeletons and lower levels of body fat among elite athletes. And while the races may have most genes in common, as environmentalists argue, what matters is not how many genes differ but which genes. Just as different breeds of dogs have distinctive personalities, behavioral tendencies, and afflictions, so the same is true with different races of human beings: "canine stereotypes are both reasonably accurate and critical information for pet-shopping parents" (p. 281). He concludes: "it is not far-fetched to assume we will soon locate alleles for herding and guarding in dogs, as well as faster reflexes or more efficient energy processing in humans" (ibid.).

While Entine raises the question of "why it even matters whether blacks are better athletes" (p. 6), he provides no discussion of it. Yet why it matters is as important as whether it is true. If it is true that "Within the performance range in which most of us fall, the environment may be critical" (p. 8), then why shouldn't most of us be concerned about what might be done to improve the performance of most people? Instead, our attention is directed to the few exceptional members of recognized groups, as if these exceptional individuals were exemplars of the group. Entine commits the common mistake of taking the most outstanding members of a group as ideal types representative of the group, and this allows him to conclude that "when we talk about people such as Einstein and Mozart – or Mark McGwire, Jim Brown, and Pele – genes count a lot" (p. 8).

The belief that black athletic ability is inversely proportionate to black intellectual ability has been used to justify slavery, colonialism, and segregation. And though Entine acknowledges that biological determinism has been used to justify racist social agendas, he does more to reinforce than challenge racist stereotypes of the innate basis of athletic and intellectual performances. While acknowledging white dominance in sports such as golf, rugby, swimming, gymnastics, and tennis, nonetheless Entine stresses the sports in which blacks dominate or in which they are making new excursions, such as bobsledding. But even in sports involving running and jumping, it is debatable whether the evidence so clearly indicates black superiority. He cites the studies of David Hunter, which showed that, when adjusted for body fat, sprint times between similar blacks and whites was statistically insignificant. But, Entine objects, "blacks have much less fat, a tiny physiological advantage that can translate into a huge on-the-field advantage. This difference may be one key variable that provides black males with an advantage in sprinting" (p. 252). But he does not tell us whether it is true that black people generally have less body fat, or whether it is premier black athletes that have less body fat, perhaps because of hard work and training.

Entine glosses over such difficulties, and instead takes these "facts" to show that "sprinters are born, not made," the same holding true of soccer and basketball.[8] Of course, it would be an exaggeration to suggest that, for Entine, Africans take to running the way fish take to swimming. Nonetheless, his conclusion is no less an exaggeration: "Since the first known study of differences between black and white athletes in 1928, the data have been remarkably consistent: in most sports, African-descended athletes have the capacity to do better with their raw skills than whites" (p. 268).

This is an outrageous overgeneralization. Do African and African-descended athletes do better in most sports? Or is it rather that they do best in sports based on running and jumping?

What about sports based on swimming and diving instead of running and jumping? Using swimming as the standard, we might find that black athletes do not perform as well as whites. By choosing running and jumping as exemplary of athletic activities, he is already stacking the deck, and we are predisposed to the conclusion that blacks are naturally better athletes than whites.

As a matter of fact, in many sports blacks are not the superior athletes they are made out to be. Whites continue to dominate in hockey, skiing, bicycling, gymnastics, fencing, and wrestling, as well as track and field events such as the discus, the javelin, the shot-put, and the pole vault. As University of the Pacific sociologist John Phillips argues, if we were to look at all the sports, and not just running and jumping ones, we would see that blacks do not dominate, except in the high-profile activities central to spectator sports.[9] While duly reporting this position, Entine makes no response to it. Instead, he concludes that "the scientific evidence for black athletic superiority is overwhelming" (p. 341). His evidence is black dominance in running, jumping, and boxing. This may be an example of an innocent inductive fallacy, but I would suggest that it is more likely an example of uncritical, stereotypical thinking reflecting an institutionalized racist etiology.

Entine reports that, since 1996, a group comprising 1.8 percent of Kenya's population has produced 20 percent of the winners of major international distance running events. And 90 percent of the top Kenyan athletes come from a 60-mile radius around the town of Eldoret in the Nandi Hills.[10] Entine recounts how, because the men of the Nandi area of Kenya were notorious offenders against colonial authority, they were channeled into athletic games as a way of co-opting their energies (p. 49). But he does not address the question of why this does not remain a plausible explanation for the attention focused on athletic games in the modern world. By diverting the energies of black youth to the least productive areas of modern culture, more lucrative opportunities are reserved for those who are not black. He quotes Brooks Johnson: "The whole idea is to convince black people that they're superior in some areas – sports – and therefore by definition must be inferior in other areas. It's interesting that white people always have the best talent in the areas that pay the best money" (p. 77).[11]

Entine points out that "All of the thirty-two finalists in the last four Olympic men's 100 meter races are of West African descent" (p. 34). But he offers no explanation as to why, if genes rather than training are the crucial variable, no West Africans were among the finalists. And where the finalists were African Americans, he gives no indication as to how he established that they were primarily of West African rather than East African or Central African descent. Entine never attempts to explain why West Africans are not as good as or better than African Americans at short distance running, or why descendants of East Africans have not become dominant in the marathons. In order to make his case, he is forced to ignore such subtleties.

Just as measurements of skull shape (cephalic index) and brain size were once taken as indications of intellectual potential, Entine reports that measurements of body types and physiological reactions reveal the prerequisites for superior athletic performance. Such observations have shown that sprinters are muscular mesomorphic types capable of explosive energy, while marathon runners are slender ectomorphic types capable of endurance over long distances. Entine also cites empirical observations showing that black babies exhibit superior coordination at an earlier age to white babies[12] and that black teenagers have a "faster patellar tendon reflex time – the knee jerk response – and an edge in reaction time over whites" (p. 251).[13] "Facts" such as these, Entine concludes, derive from genetic predispositions that also explain the superior performance of black athletes.

But such "facts" have too often been shown to be artifacts of our social system, reflecting how investigators think things ought to be more than how things are. The conclusion that Africans are naturally better athletes is an unwarranted inductive generalization that reinforces the view that the way things are is the way they are supposed to be. West Africans do not dominate in sprinting, African Americans

do. Africans and African Americans do not dominate in all sports, only some.

The "facts" Entine cites follow a long history of anthropometric studies of Africans, women, and the lower classes. *The Mismeasure of Man* by Stephen Jay Gould and *Myths of Gender* by Anne Fausto-Sterling are but two works that show the extent to which science has not been an objective, value-free enterprise, and how the biological sciences have typically been more instrumental than descriptive: "They do not carve nature at the joints but break it up at places that reflect human needs – the need to control our environment in order to secure food, fiber, health, amusement, and so forth."[14] If ethics is the attempt to secure the good life for ourselves and others, then we must recognize that the facts of biology and athletic performance are instruments we construct to accomplish this.

Entine is best understood in the context of others, like Michael Levin, Nicholas Capaldi, and Louis Pojman, who argue that current racial and sexual disparities in social achievements (athletic and intellectual) are the result of "natural" genetic predispositions. The usual argument has been that European and Asian achievements outstrip African achievements in the sciences and mathematics because Europeans and Asians are naturally smarter than Africans, that is, have a higher IQ. Entine has turned this argument around: African achievements outstrip European and Asian achievements in athletics because Africans are naturally faster and stronger, that is, have a higher proportion of fast-twitch muscle fibers and more efficient metabolic pathways.

But I believe biological determinism of either stripe is misguided. For it defines ideal types for existing groups, and encourages members of that group to actively construct themselves on analogy with those ideals. The exploitation of Africans has been justified by reference to biblical texts, and now by measurements in laboratories and contests. Scientists and judges are supposed to be unbiased, and are supposed to base their pronouncements on fact rather than fantasy. Yet one of the main contributions of the new wave in the philosophy of science is to emphasize the extent to which all facts are theory-laden, and rest on tacitly held beliefs. In this light, "facts" that purport to justify current distributions of opportunities and rewards require special moral scrutiny.

For Entine, the facts prove that Africans and people of African descent are naturally better athletes than whites and Asians. If this is the case, then it makes sense for a mother of African descent to encourage her child to develop athletic skills, and spend less time on intellectual activities.[15]

This line of argument has appealed to many blacks, and even more whites. It is a view that I believe is damaging. It promotes stereotypes that have been developed to justify the exclusions of whole groups of people from opportunities for which they are not considered naturally endowed.

The fact that such stereotypes contain a grain of truth is no redeeming feature. To analogize Entine's argument, short people might be better at entering small holes than people of normal height, and that is something short people might learn to be proud of. Indeed, those that consistently won "entering small holes" contests might be very good at it indeed. Short people might then be encouraged to develop their abilities to compete in "entering small holes" contests because they were naturally better at it than most other people. This might provide great entertainment, but it is counterproductive to the expenditure of time and energy by people of short stature. Other than as entertainment, skill at entering small holes is as unlikely to improve the general social and economic status of short people as running skills are unlikely to improve the general social and economic status of black people.[16]

The odds that a high school athlete will play at the professional level are about 10,000 to 1. Yet a recent survey estimated that 66 percent of African American males between 13 and 18 believed they could become professional athletes, more than double the number of similar white youth. And black parents were four times more likely to believe it than white parents. Athletics is not even a good way of getting a college education. While colleges gave away some $600 million in athletic scholarships in 1997, $49.7 billion was available from other sources.[17]

Encouraging a particular group to cultivate skills of limited utility precludes the group from the full range of opportunities available to the wider population. A commitment to social justice requires that we appreciate the extent to which notions of biological determinism have been used to limit opportunities for people of African descent, women, the poor, and other socially marginalized groups. Ideas are tools that can be used to help or hinder, not descriptions of how God or nature have designed things, and I believe Entine has a special moral obligation to show how his evidence and conclusions are not tools of oppression.

Notes

Another version of this essay appeared in M. Andrew Holowchak (ed.), *Philosophy of Sport: Critical Readings, Crucial Issues* (Englewood Cliffs, NJ: Prentice Hall, 2002).

1   Entine, *Taboo*, p. 4. Further page references to this book are given in the main body of the essay.
2   Where differences of a hundredth or thousandth of a second make the difference between winner and loser, "The decisive variable is in our genes" (p. 4).
3   This is a view he associates with Carleton Coon.
4   "It implied the mutability and perfectibility of humankind. The inexorable forces of evolution and heredity receded into the background, to be replaced by a moral dimension: it was now suggested that prehistoric humans had adapted to austere climates through clever discoveries of fire, clothing, and artificial shelters, not through chance, natural mutations, and the survival of the fittest. Shadowed by the racist ideologies of fascism, common sense was sacrificed to a new ideology: environmentalism" (p. 215).
5   Phillip Rushton, in his book *Race, Evolution, and Behavior* (New Brunswick: Transactions Publishers, 1995), puts it more crudely: brain size varies inversely proportional to genital size (pp. 5, 162, 166–9, 231). Presumably, this makes blacks better at genital sex.

6   Carole A. Oglesby (ed.), *Black Women in Sports* (Reston, VA: American Alliance for Health, Physical Education, Recreation and Dance, 1981), p. 11.

7   John Hoberman, *Darwin's Athletes: How Sports has Damaged Black America and Preserved the Myth of Race* (New York: Houghton Mifflin, 1997).

8   "It appears that for blacks from west Africa, innate ability may be more critical than training in turning out great leapers and sprinters" (p. 256).

9   "If blacks were dispersed across all sports their apparent superiority would largely disappear" (p. 273).

10 He dismisses the idea that it is the town's high elevation that contributes to lung capacity and metabolic efficiency, for many countries have communities living at similar elevations (p. 47).

11 This too is an overgeneralization. Only in the last fifty or so years have Jews been considered white, though they have long been overrepresented in academia, commerce, and professions like law and medicine.

12 Who made the measurements? What was the sample? Was it representative? Instead of raising these questions, Entine accepts these claims as aspects of human nature and gives them to us as facts that need explaining.

13 But he fails to cite Arthur Jensen's evidence that blacks have slower reaction times.

14 Stephen Jay Gould, *The Mismeasure of Man* (New York: W. W. Norton, 1996); Anne Fausto-Stirling, *Myths of Gender: Biological Theories of Women and Men* (New York: Basic Books, 1985); Alexander Rosenberg, *Instrumental Biology, or the Disunity of Science* (Chicago: University of Chicago Press, 1994). And if biology is instrumental, so are psychology, anthropology, and every other science that builds on it (pp. 15–16).

15 Knowing that women have on the average less mathematical aptitude than men, why would a woman not encourage her daughter to enter some aspect of the caring business rather than study math?

16 Following Entine's lead, the fact that there are few small holes a person of normal height is going to be interested in entering is irrelevant to the fact of which group tends to win more such contests.

17 John Simon, "Improbable Dreams. African Americans are a Dominant Presence in Professional Sports: Do Blacks Suffer as a Result?", *U.S. News*, March 24, 1997.

CHAPTER 32

Race and College Sport: A Long Way to Go

Richard E. Lapchick

As America confronts yet another racial crisis in the 1990s, the expectation remains that sport, nearly forty-five years after Jackie Robinson broke baseball's colour barrier, can lead the way. College sport, in particular, has been portrayed as a beacon for democracy and equal opportunity. This perception is taking place at a time when 75 per cent of high school students indicated to public opinion analyst Lou Harris that they had seen or heard a racial act with violent overtones either very often or somewhat often in the previous twelve months.[1] Fifty-four per cent of black high school students reported that they had been a victim of a racial incident.[2] One in three students said that they would openly join in a confrontation against another racial or religious group if they agreed with the instigators. Another 17 per cent, while they would not join, said they would feel that the victims deserved what they got.[3]

According to Harris, the nation's leading opinion analyst, too many of our children have learned how to hate. He concluded:

America faces a critical situation. Our findings show that racial and religious harassment and violence are now commonplace among our young people rather than the exception. Far from being concentrated in any one area, confrontations occur in every region of the country and in all types of communities.[4]

One of the most hallowed assumptions about race and sport is that athletic contact between blacks and whites will favourably change racial perceptions. However, for this change to take place, coaches must be committed to helping guide players' social relations. The *Racism and Violence in American High Schools* survey, conducted by Lou Harris for Northeastern University in 1993, showed that 70 per cent of high school students reported that they had become friends with someone from a different racial or ethnic group through playing sports. Among blacks, a 77 per cent majority reported this result; the comparable majority was 68 per cent among whites and 79 per cent among Hispanics. That, indeed, was encouraging news.[5]

Black Student-Athletes and White Campuses

However, on predominantly white campuses, as in corporate boardrooms, the atmosphere naturally reflects the dominant white culture. Most campuses are not equal meeting grounds for white and black students, whether from urban or rural America.

American public opinion of college sport reached its nadir in the mid-1980s. In an attempt to create meaningful reform, many measures were passed. Among them were Propositions 48, 42 and 16. The wide-ranging debate and protest against Proposition 42 placed the issue of race among the central ethical issues in college sport in the 1990s. Proposition 42 would have prevented athletes who did not achieve certain academic standards from receiving a scholarship. The new debate over Proposition 16 in 1994–5 has again raised the racial spectre in college sport.

The American Institutes for Research (AIR) produced a study for the National Collegiate Athletics Association (NCAA) in 1989 which suggested that there are low academic expectations for black athletes. Only 31 per cent of the black athletes surveyed for the AIR study indicated that their coaches encouraged good grades. The study also suggested that black student-athletes are not receiving the education promised by colleges, since they graduate at a significantly lower rate than whites. They have few black coaches or faculty members to model themselves upon on campus.[6] All of this is drawing attention and public pressure. The Reverend Jesse Jackson founded the Rainbow Commission for Fairness in Athletics to change such imbalances.

While less than 6 per cent of all students at Division I-A institutions are black, 60 per cent of the men's basketball players, 37 per cent of the women's basketball players and 42 per cent of the football players at those schools are black.[7]

All colleges and universities have some form of 'special admittance' programme in which a designated percentage of students who do not meet the normal admission standards of the school are allowed to enrol. According to the NCAA, about 3 per cent of all students enter as 'special admits'. Yet more than 20 per cent of football and basketball players enter under such programmes. Thus, many enter with the academic odds already stacked against them.

The 1989 NCAA AIR study presented a wealth of data. Those familiar with college athletics were not surprised by the study's findings, which indicated that black athletes feel racially isolated on college campuses, are over-represented in football and basketball, have high expectations of pro careers and are uninvolved in other extracurricular activities. However, the results of the NCAA study stood in stark contrast to the findings published by the Women's Sports Foundation.[8] It was the first major study of minorities playing high school sports. It clearly established that, in comparison to black non-athletes, black high school student-athletes feel better about themselves, are more involved in extracurricular activities other than sport, are more involved in the broader community, aspire to be community leaders and have better grade point averages and standardised test scores. Almost all those results contradict the view that most of white society has about the black athlete.

According to Lou Harris, it is apparent that most varsity athletes believe that their participation in high school team sports has helped them to become better students, better citizens and to avoid drugs:

> The value of playing sports in all these areas was significantly higher for African-American student-athletes in particular and for football and basketball players in general. It merits considerable attention by colleges and universities where the experience of African-American student-athletes as well as their football and basketball players is significantly different and appears much more negative.[9]

The primary question which now must be asked is what happens to black athletes, and black students in general, between high school and college that seems totally to change how they perceive themselves. Among other things, many black students leave a high school that is either overwhelmingly black or at least partially integrated. If they are from an urban area, they leave behind a core of black teachers and coaches. If they live on campus or go to school away from home, they leave behind whatever positive support network existed in the community in which they were raised and leave behind possible black role models who are not exclusively athletes.

The student arrives in college to discover that the proportion of blacks at Division I-A schools is approximately 6 per cent. Furthermore, less than 2 per cent of the faculty positions at colleges and universities are held by blacks. Finally, the athletic departments hire just slightly more blacks than the faculty and actually hire fewer blacks than the professional sports teams.

A great deal of emphasis has been placed on racial discrimination in professional sport, especially the hiring practices of professional franchises. In fact, a great deal of the research done at the Center for the Study of Sport in Society is devoted to the publication of the annual *Racial Report Card*. However, a look at the numbers of available employment positions in our colleges and universities indicates that it is less likely for blacks to be hired by higher education than in professional sport.

While the militancy and struggle of the 1960s and 1970s have reduced the negative self-perceptions of most young blacks, the stereotypes still exist for many whites. Those stereotypes come with all the taboos that go with them. White and black athletes can meet on campus carrying a great deal of racial baggage. Their prejudices won't automatically evaporate with the sweat as they play together on a team. The key to racial harmony is the attitude and leadership of the coach.

He must be committed to equality and clearly demonstrate this to the team.* The history of young athletes, and students in general, makes it an uphill task. Chances are that competition at the high school level bred some animosity; usually white teams play against black teams, reflecting urban residential housing patterns. There is virtually no playground competition between blacks and whites, as few dare to leave their neighbourhood.

On a college team, blacks and whites are competing for playing time, while in the society at large black and white workers compete for jobs, public housing, even welfare. A primary difference is that whites are apt to accept blacks on the team, since they will help the team win more games and, perhaps, get them more exposure.

It is easy for white athletes, no matter what their racial attitudes might be, to accept blacks on their teams for two other reasons. First, they need not have any social contact with black team-mates. Sports that blacks dominate are not sports like golf, tennis and swimming, where socialising is almost a requirement for competition. Players need not mingle after basketball, baseball or football. More importantly, black male players need not mingle with white women after those games. Housing on campus and social discrimination through fraternities and sororities further isolate the black athletes. Whether in high school or college, the black student-athlete faces special problems as an athlete, as a student and as a member of the campus community.

Most of white society believed that we were on the road to progress until Al Campanis and Jimmy 'The Greek' Snyder made us challenge our perceptions. Their statements on national television that blacks and whites are physically and mentally different were repugnant to much of the country and led to widespread self-examination. Like many whites who accept black dominance in sport, Campanis believed that blacks had less intellectual capacity. It makes things seem simple to people like Campanis: blacks sure can play, but they can't organise or manage affairs or lead whites. Marge Schott, speaking in private, reopened the wounds in 1992, when her remarks about blacks and Jews again stunned the world of sport. Many people would not see much to contradict this view if they looked to society at large. In 1995, white men and women were twice as likely to hold executive, administrative and managerial positions as black men. At the same time, blacks were twice as likely to hold positions of manual labour as whites. Decades of viewing this pattern could easily reinforce the Campanis viewpoint: whites are intelligent and blacks are physically powerful.

After fifty years of trying to determine the genetic superiority of blacks as athletes, science has proved little. Culture, class and environment still tell us the most. Instead of developing theories about why black Americans excel in sports, perhaps more time will now be spent on the achievement of black Americans in human rights, medicine, law, science, the arts and education who overcame the attitudes and institutions of whites to excel in fields where brains dictate the champions.

Coaches: A Study in Black and White

The coach becomes the black student-athlete's main contact, and the court frequently becomes the home where he is most comfortable. Nonetheless, there are some black athletes who feel that their white coaches discriminate against them and that their academic advisers give them different counselling. This may reflect a general distrust of whites, or a strong perception that racism is the cause of certain events. Even well-intentioned acts can be interpreted by blacks as being racially motivated. Over the years, there have been black student-athletes who have made a series of similar complaints irrespective of where their campus was located: subtle racism has been evidenced in differential treatment during recruitment; poor academic advice; harsh discipline; positional segregation on the playing field and social segregation off it; blame for situations for which they are not responsible. There are also complaints of overt racism: racial abuse; blacks being benched in games more quickly than whites; marginal whites being kept on the bench while only blacks who play are retained; summer jobs for whites and good jobs for their wives.

To say that most or even many white coaches are racist is a great exaggeration. But most white coaches were raised with white values in a white culture. The norm for them is what is important for a white society. If white coaches accept stereotypical images of what black society is and what kind of people it produces, they may believe that blacks are less motivated, less disciplined, less intelligent (53 per cent of all whites believe blacks are less intelligent) and more physically gifted. They may think that all blacks are raised in a culture bombarded by drugs, violence and sexuality, and that they are more comfortable with other blacks. They might believe those characteristics are a product of society or simply that they are the way God chose to make them. They might recognise themselves as racist, disliking blacks because of perceived negative traits. More than likely, however, such a coach views himself as simply trying to

help. But, in any case, if he acts on these images, then his black players are victimised.

In one of the most important scandals of the 1980s, Memphis State University, a 1985 NCAA Final Four participant, fell into disgrace. There were many allegations about the improprieties of the school and its coach, Dana Kirk. One that could not be disputed was the fact that twelve years had gone by without Memphis State graduating a single black basketball player. Like several other urban institutions, Memphis State built a winning programme with the talents of fine black athletes. The fact that none had graduated brought back memories of Texas Western's NCAA championship team which failed to graduate a single starter, all of whom were black. But this failure went on at Memphis State for more than a decade. The NAACP sued the school. Publicity finally led to the dismissal of Kirk.

I do not mean to single out Memphis State. In the ten years since Dana Kirk was fired, I have been on more than seventy-five campuses. The pattern is frequently similar: the academic profile of black football and basketball players and their treatment as students are different from whites and their graduation rate is lower.

Positional Segregation in College

The issue of positional segregation in college is becoming less of a factor. For years, whites played the 'thinking positions'. The controlling position in baseball is the pitcher; in football, it is the quarterback. Everyone loves the smooth, ball-handling guard in basketball. These are the glamour positions that fans and the press focus on and have largely been white positions. College baseball still poses the greatest problem at all positions, as fewer and fewer blacks play college baseball. Less than 3 per cent of Division 1-A college baseball players are black.[10]

However, in a major shift in college football, large numbers of black quarterbacks have been leading their teams since the late 1980s. Between 1960 and 1986, only seven black quarterbacks were among the top ten candidates for the Heisman Trophy and none finished higher than fourth. In 1987, 1988 and 1989, black quarterbacks Don McPherson (Syracuse), Rodney Peete (USC), Darien Hagan (Colorado), Reggie Slack (Auburn), Tony Rice (Notre Dame), Stevie Thompson (Oklahoma) and Major Harris (West Virginia) all finished among the top ten votegetters. In 1989, Andre Ware (Houston) became the first black quarterback to win the award. Florida State's Charlie Ward won it in 1993. In 1994, Nebraska won the national championship with a dramatic Orange Bowl victory behind the leadership of quarterback Tommie Frazier.

Top point guards coming out of college are becoming more and more predominantly black. Recent stars such as Kenny Anderson, Tim Hardaway, Anfernee Hardaway and Jason Kidd are just a few of the more prominent black point guards. Hopefully, this bodes well for an end to positional segregation in college sport in the near future.

Can Black Athletes Speak Out?

The coach is the authority. Historically, athletes have rarely spoken out. This creates problems for all coaches who come up against an outspoken player. When the player is black and not a superstar, he will often be let go. Only the superstars like Bill Russell, Kareem Abdul Jabbar and Muhammad Ali can remain secure, because no one can afford to let them go. But even the greatest ones paid heavy prices for many years after their outspokenness. Muhammad Ali, who had refused to go into the army, knew you had to be at the top to speak out if you were black. Ultimately, Ali had the money and influence to go all the way to the Supreme Court. Most blacks have neither the money nor the influence to make the system work.

In 1992, Craig Hodges spoke out about the Rodney King case in Los Angeles. Hodges was a great shooter but was a peripheral player on the National Basketball Association championship team, Chicago Bulls. He had won the three-point contest at the all-star game. After his remarks, he was cut by the Bulls and not one team picked him up. Tommy Harper's case is also instructive. His contract was not renewed

by the Boston Red Sox in December 1985. The Red Sox said he was let go because he was not doing a good job as special assistant to the general manager. Harper, however, charged that he was fired because he spoke out against racist practices by the Red Sox. Earlier in 1985, he had said that the Sox allowed white players to receive passes to the whites-only Elks Club in Winter Haven, Florida, where they held spring training. (The Sox later stopped the tradition.) Harper sued and the Equal Employment Opportunity Commission ruled that the firing was a retaliatory action against Harper because he spoke out against discrimination. It took him a while to get back into baseball. At the time of writing, he is a coach for the Montreal Expos.

There are positive examples as well. It did not go unnoticed that a group of black athletes at Auburn asked the president of the university to get a Confederate flag removed from a dormitory; it was removed. In 1987, the Pittsburgh basketball team wore ribbons as a protest against their school's investments in South Africa. In 1990, black athletes at the University of Texas at Austin led a protest against racism on campus, encouraged by members of the athletic department. Whether or not this will become a trend is hard to see, but the positive and widespread media coverage of their actions stood in dramatic contrast to early reactions to Russell, Ali and Abdul Jabbar.

In 1969, fourteen black players in the University of Wyoming football team informed their athletic department of their intention to wear black arm bands during their forthcoming game against Brigham Young University. The players' intent was to bring attention to the doctrinal position of the church of the Latter Day Saints, which prevented blacks from holding the priesthood. After hearing of the players' plan, Wyoming's head football coach cited a long-standing team policy which prevented players from engaging in protests of any kind. When the players showed up at his office wearing the arm bands just one day before the game, the coach interpreted their action as a defiance of the rule and a direct threat to his authority. He summarily dismissed all fourteen players from the football team.

Although this incident remained a sore spot in the history of Wyoming athletics for nearly twenty-four years, the university held ceremonies to honour the players on 24 September 1993. The event was the result of the African American studies department working in conjunction with the school's administration to recognise the former players, signalling a new era in communications between student-athletes and the administration.

Note

*The context, I should make it clear, is one of the overwhelming preponderance of male athletics, in terms of recruitment, sponsorship, media coverage, etc.

References

1   LH Associates, Inc. (for the Center for the Study of Sport in Society), *Racism and Violence in American High Schools: Project Teamwork Responds* (November 1993).
2   Ibid.
3   Louis Harris and Associates, *Youth Attitudes on Racism* (October 1990).
4   Ibid.
5   See LH Associates, *Survey of High School Athletes* (November 1993).
6   See AIR, *Studies of Intercollegiate Athletics, Report No. 3: The Experiences of Black-Intercollegiate Athletes at NCAA Division I Institutions* (March 1989).
7   See the National Collegiate Athletic Association, *1994 NCAA Division 1 Graduation-Rates Report* (June 1994).
8   See the Women's Sports Foundation, *Minorities in Sports: The Effect of Varsity Sports Participation on the Social, Educational, and Career Mobility of Minority Students* (August 1989).
9   See LH Associates, *Survey of High School Athletes* (1993).
10 Personal interview with Stanley Johnson of the NCAA (31 January 1993).

CHAPTER 33

Sport and Stereotype: From Role Model to Muhammad Ali

Mike Marqusee

Noam Chomsky, a man always prepared to speak truth to power, confessed he was driven to despair by the addiction of working-class people to a popular phone-in sports programme on local radio. How could they waste so much passion and knowledge on something so trivial?

Chomsky's frustration is in keeping with a long tradition of left-wing hostility to commercial spectator sport. Many have dismissed it as a mere palliative for the oppressed, an opiate of the people. Some Marxists in the 1960s and '70s went further. For them, modern sport was 'a prison of measured time', a model of capitalist alienation. Sport, they argued, is not an escape from exploitation, however fleeting, but a reproduction of it.

For many on the Left, boxing exemplifies all that is iniquitous in modern sport. What could more accurately embody the cruelty of the capitalist order, not to speak of the destructive aggression of patriarchal individualism, than boxing? Could there be a more degrading spectacle than two human beings paid to inflict physical punishment on each other?

And yet, even in these depths, resistance can stir, as a look back at the career of Muhammad Ali will confirm.

Sport, Modernity and Race

Modern, secular, spectator sport – in the forms of boxing, horse-racing and cricket – first emerged from the womb of parochial ritual and folk pastime in mid-eighteenth century England. Its midwives were rapid urbanisation, the spread of market relations and an ambitious elite with both time and money to squander. Rules for boxing were first codified in 1743. Soon after, national champions were recognised. Newspapers advertised the prize fights and employed the world's first sports writers to cover them. Bouts sometimes drew crowds of 10–20,000. They were usually staged under the aegis of aristocrats, who wagered huge stakes on the results. For the elite, the main purpose of modern sport was gambling: the venture capital that fuelled the industrial revolution also fuelled modern sport. Prize-fighting became a pioneer enterprise in the commercialisation of leisure, a trend which has grown to huge dimensions in our own time.

Like cricket and horse-racing (and sumo, an ancient ritual reinvented for popular consumption in the late eighteenth century), boxing remains among the least modern of modern sports. Even on satellite TV, it is easy to see in any boxing match traces of the pre-modern societies out of which it was born. The ancient gladiatorial contests, the village fair slugfests, the tavern brawls: boxing is a modern, regulated descendant of these. It is sometimes argued that sport is a means whereby we keep alive and display in modern societies the physical skills and attributes which industrialisation has made redundant: running, jumping, throwing, etc. In boxing, hand-to-hand combat lives on in a society which otherwise dispenses with it, even in warfare. Despite the Marquis of Queensbury's attempt to recodify the sport as 'a noble art' in keeping with the Victorian ethos, it remains today a rare example (apart from warfare itself) of the resolution of a contest by the overt use of physical violence.

The aristocrats, under whose aegis the world's first sports revolution was wrought, never themselves entered the prize-fighting ring (unlike the cricket pitch). Professional boxers from the beginning were plebeians, performing at the behest of their social superiors. Such was the gulf between patrons and participants that it seemed natural for slave-owners to enter their property into the competition. The first modern black sportsmen were slaves or ex-slaves, trained and groomed by their masters in the same way that they trained and groomed horses.

From the beginning, boxing was a honey-pot for criminals, not least because it was relatively easy to fix the fights. During the nineteenth century, the English aristocrats were replaced in the United States by politicians and newspaper proprietors, succeeded in [the twentieth] century by businessmen, public relations entrepreneurs and satellite and cable television moguls. But the gangsters have been ever-present, expropriating fighters, fans and punters alike. The persistence of gambling and criminality in boxing, despite periodic purges, indicates that capitalist modernisation, far from being an antidote to criminality, can act as a stimulant for it.

In boxing, slavery's ownership of the human body was transmuted with relative ease into a capitalist commodification of it. Boxing today appears highly individualistic but the individuals involved, the boxers, have less power over their bodies and careers than almost any other sports people. Even successful boxers, with few exceptions, are bound like serfs to promoters, managers and satellite TV companies. If they wish to advance towards a title, they must placate a variety of forces behind the scene. Merit is never enough in itself. If they are disabled in action, they are reliant on charity.

No one knows this better than the generations of black boxers who have sustained the fight game at all levels. For a tiny minority of slaves, boxing was a ticket to individual freedom, just as it is for a tiny minority of black working-class people today. This long history has given boxing a special place in black communities. The triumphs and tragedies of black boxers, dependent on elite white power-brokers to make a living in the ring, expected to subordinate themselves to elite white norms outside the ring, have made black boxing a rich, complex, living tradition. If the strangest fact about boxing is that it has not gone the way of cockfighting or bear-baiting, and has somehow managed to survive under the glare of the electronic media, then the next strangest is that it owes its survival in no small measure to the brilliance of black boxers, the people most exploited and brutalised by it.

The Level Playing Field

Jack Johnson became the first black heavyweight champion in 1908. He won the title in Sydney, Australia, because no American city would stage the fight. A white former champion, Jim Jeffries, who had previously refused to fight black boxers and had abandoned the ring rather than face Johnson, now came out of retirement, vowing to put the black man back in his place. Their Independence Day bout was, at the time, the most widely publicised sporting contest in US history, and Johnson's victory was celebrated by black communities across America. White gangs then launched reprisal attacks in the worst racial violence of the decade.

Johnson was the white man's nightmare come alive. Not only did he beat up white heroes in the ring (always sporting his famous grin), he then went off to dally with white women – and made no secret of it. Hated and hounded by the white press, he was ultimately forced into exile to escape a 'morals' conviction trumped up by the federal government. He was without doubt the most famous black person in America at the time and the black masses followed his adventures closely. However, his antics made the tiny black middle class uneasy. Booker T. Washington denounced him and his wretched sport, agreeing with the *New York Times* that

Johnson was a disgrace to his race. In contrast, Marcus Garvey celebrated him and W.E.B. DuBois argued that Johnson's persecution was not the result of his allegedly lax morals but of his 'unforgivable blackness'. In 1915, a weary and demoralised Johnson fought the latest white hope, Jess Willard, in Havana and lost the heavyweight title to him (or, some say, gave it up in a fix) in the twenty-seventh round.

In his recently published autobiography, Nelson Mandela recalls his time as a boxer. In the 1950s, Mandela (a heavyweight) trained regularly at a black boxing club in Orlando, a township north of Johannesburg. The club manager, Skipper Molotsi, would regale his penniless, ill-equipped, passionately dedicated boxers with a round-by-round account of Johnson's defeat in Havana.

'I did not enjoy the violence of boxing so much as the science of it,' Mandela explains. 'I was intrigued by how one moved one's body to protect oneself, how one used a strategy both to attack and retreat, how one paced oneself over a match.' Here, boxing appears as an ideal preparation for long-term political struggle. But, for Mandela, the sport's main attraction resided at a deeper level. 'Boxing is egalitarian. In the ring, rank, age, colour and wealth are irrelevant. When you are circling your opponent, probing his strengths and weaknesses, you are not thinking about his colour or social status.'

Mandela here invokes one of the defining shibboleths of modern sport: the level playing field. Sports lose their meaning for the spectator – and therefore their place in the market – unless everyone plays under the same rules, shoots at the same size goalposts, is timed with the same stopwatch. The level playing field is far more than a moral or ideological cover for a competitive activity. It is the autonomous logic of modern sport. For a contest to be seen as satisfactory, its rules, conditions and conduct must ensure that the result is determined only by the relative and pertinent strengths and weaknesses of the competitors, not by extraneous factors. The objectivity of sporting contests is like the objectivity of a scientific experiment. To the extent that the extraneous is excluded, the test is regarded as valid.

In boxing, the level playing field acquires particular importance. This raw, elemental contest pits one man's strength, stamina and agility against another's – of the same weight. It was recognised early on that a fight between a heavyweight and flyweight was meaningless as a spectacle or a test of individual prowess.

The logic of the level playing field gives sport an egalitarian premise. This is undoubtedly one of the reasons for its enduring appeal to the masses, and especially the most dispossessed among them. The major cliché about race in sport is that sport offers black people opportunities denied them in other spheres. In the autonomous realm of sport, equality reigns.

Of course, the level playing field is enclosed within a society which is anything but level. Access to the level playing field has always been unequal, as has treatment on it, as black boxers have long understood. In 1805, Tom Molineaux, a black American ex-slave, was on the brink of taking the heavyweight title from the legendary English fighter-promoter, Tom Cribb. It was the twenty-sixth round and Cribb was on the floor. The English referee shouted at him: 'Get up, Tom, don't let the Nigger win.' Given four extra minutes to recover, Cribb went on to win the fight. For Molineaux as for Jack Johnson, boxing's level playing field proved an illusion.

It is well to remember that modern sport is a huge commercial enterprise. The level playing field is owned by a capitalist elite and is indeed one of that elite's favourite metaphors. The purpose of the Maastricht Treaty, NAFTA and GATT, we are told, is to create an economic level playing field, to ensure 'fair play' among various nation-states. In reality, these agreements rig global competition in favour of multinational capital and institutionalise the power of the north over the south. There is nothing new in this. By its very nature, the market nourishes and thrives on inequalities. The metaphor of the level playing field is, in fact, a lie about the market, as it is a lie about society as a whole.

But there is a sting in the tail. On sport's level playing field, it is possible to challenge and overturn the dominant hierarchies of nation, race and class. The reversal may be limited and transient, but it is nonetheless real. It is, therefore, wrong to see black sporting achievement merely as an index of oppression; it is equally an index of creativity and resistance, collective and individual. The level playing field can be either a prison or a platform for liberation.

'Uncle Toms' and 'Bad Niggers'

No black fighter was given a shot at the heavyweight title for twenty-five years after Johnson lost it. Jack Dempsey, one of the great American sports heroes of the 1920s, refused to meet black challengers. When Joe Louis came along in the 1930s, his handlers and sponsors (black businessmen from Detroit) were determined not to repeat Johnson's experience. Louis was given lessons in table manners and elocution; he was told to go for a knock-out rather than risk the whims of racist judges; he was told never to smile when he beat a white man and, above all, never to be caught alone with a white woman. Louis was groomed to be the ideal role model for black America.

The symbolic burdens that this would involve became apparent in his first fight in New York City, against Primo Carnera, in 1935. At the time, Mussolini was engaged in highly public preparations for his invasion of Ethiopia. Although neither Louis nor Carnera had said anything about the issue, they were seen by many as representatives of Africa and Italy respectively. Fears that rioting might break out among the fans led to a pre-fight announcement urging all concerned to view the bout solely as a contest between two individuals and nothing more – surely one of the most futile injunctions in the history of sport. Louis finished off the hard-hitting, mafia-backed Carnera in the sixth round.

It was not only Louis's demure behaviour that made him acceptable to the white establishment; it was also the peculiar politics of the times. He won the heavyweight crown in Chicago in 1937, in front of a crowd of 45,000, half of whom were black. But the year before, he had been beaten by a German, Max Schmeling, in a fight that had been hailed by Nazi ideologists as a triumph of Aryan supremacy. The rematch at Yankee

Stadium in 1938 was probably at the time the most widely followed sporting contest in history and a huge event in the life of America's black communities. Louis was made aware by the press, the churches, the president and the Communist Party that knocking Schmeling's block off was his duty to America, the cause of anti-fascism and 'the Negro'. Any remaining doubts were removed when Nazis picketed his training camp. Louis demolished Schmeling in two minutes of the first round.

This time blacks could celebrate without fear of reprisals. Louis may have whipped a white man, but he was a German, and, what's more, a symbol of the Nazi regime. Louis was fighting *for America*, or at least for the liberal America of the New Deal. For once, 'Americanism' and anti-racialism were congruent. Louis was praised everywhere as 'a credit to his race' – not because he had excelled in the ring but because he had vindicated 'the American way' at a critical time. For the American elite, Louis was a means to rally popular support for a war against Germany and Japan. For American Communists, the Schmeling–Louis bout was a classic contest between 'fascism' and 'democracy'. On the night of the fight, Communists organised 'Joe Louis radio parties' in black communities. Both the Communists and the elite emphasised the 'dignity' with which Louis represented his people and with which he had uplifted the sport of boxing, which both had hitherto despised.

The symbolism was not, however, completely arbitrary. It arose from the nature of the sporting contest itself. Here, modern sport's level playing field offered laboratory-like conditions in which to test the theory of Aryan supremacy. Louis's victory, like Jesse Owens's at the Berlin Olympics in 1936, was a 'scientific' repudiation of that theory and was seen as such by millions. The symbolism was intelligible to all, because it emerged from the egalitarian presuppositions of modern sport.

This made Louis the spearhead of a popular front, but it was one within which blacks remained subordinate. Louis did everything the white establishment asked of him and still ended up broke and humiliated. He gave the entire proceeds of one fight to the Navy Relief Fund, even though the navy was widely known as the most racist branch of the services. He enlisted in the army for three years and, though denied permission to defend his title, fought ninety-six exhibition bouts for US troops around the world (all of them still in segregated units) for nothing more than his ordinary soldier's pay. That did not stop the US government from stinging him for back taxes and, at one point, he had to take to the wrestling ring to drum up the cash. He ended up hobbling around Las Vegas, paid by casino owners to greet the high rollers.

The spectres of these two black champions, Johnson and Louis, haunted the black fighters to come. There seemed only these two equally tragic role models: the 'bad Nigger' and the 'Uncle Tom', as they became known in the 1960s. After Louis, boxing was increasingly dominated by black fighters, especially in the upper divisions, but the sport itself was in the grip of white money-men and officials. Sonny Liston and Floyd Patterson, the two heavyweight champions who preceded Cassius Clay, conformed to the old polarity.

Like Mike Tyson, Floyd Patterson came out of the slums of Brooklyn and, like Tyson, he was trained and guided out of juvenile delinquency by Cus D'Amato, a white Svengali who tried to keep both fighters out of the clutches of the crooks. Unlike Tyson, the studiously inoffensive, frugal and churchgoing Patterson became a hero to white America. Having become the youngest man ever to win the heavy-weight title, he was invited to the White House, married a white woman, bought a house in a white neighbourhood, and became a symbol of the integrationist ideal. For several years, D'Amato shielded Patterson from Sonny Liston, widely recognised as the number one contender and the toughest heavyweight on the circuit. D'Amato could get away with this because absolutely nobody wanted Sonny Liston to be the heavyweight champ.

Liston was the most disliked black sports star since Jack Johnson. He was introduced to boxing at the age of 18 in the Missouri State Penitentiary and turned professional soon after his release. In between his early bouts, he pro-vided debt-collecting muscle for local hoodlums. In 1956, he was arrested for assaulting a police officer, following a row outside his house, and was sentenced to nine months in an Illinois workhouse. This not only made it extremely difficult for him to get fights (which, in turn, made him more dependent on the mob), it also made him a marked man for every white cop in the country. By 1962, he had a record of nineteen arrests.

In his new home of Philadelphia, Liston, by now recognised as the leading heavyweight contender, was continually rousted by police, who charged him with a wide array of petty offences, including impersonating a police officer (apparently a woman whom he had approached in his car at night thought for a moment that it was a police vehicle). When he left the city for a new home in Denver, he told the press, 'I'd rather be a lamp post in Denver than the mayor of Philadelphia.'

Sonny was illiterate but quick-witted, and more than prepared to stand his ground against bullies in uniform. Despite his police record and his mob connections, used again and again to deny him a title shot, he was generous and sensitive, as well as prickly and wary. His biographer, Rob Steen, was right to observe: 'All Sonny ever got were cheap shots.' One of the most persistent concerned his date of birth, which was shrouded in mystery. For the press, Liston's inability to produce a bona fide birth certificate was evidence of criminality. In fact, Liston was born among impoverished rural workers, with the aid of a midwife, not a doctor – and he was his father's twenty-fourth child. Not surprisingly, his birth went unrecorded. Liston hailed from America's anonymous lower depths – and he was punished for it. Depicted as sullen, violent, ignorant and menacing, Liston was fair game for journalists, boxing authorities and politicians. Black leaders froze him out. This street-brawler simply did not fit in with their clean-cut, moderate, non-violent image. The NAACP urged Patterson not to give him a title shot.

In the end, however, Liston got his chance, partly because Patterson was embarrassed by the allegations that he was dodging Sonny, but mainly because the promoters and authorities knew that excluding Liston would discredit the heavyweight title even more than giving it to him. The public backed Patterson, but it wanted his supremacy confirmed in the ring.

Thus the scene was set for a fight with almost as many symbolic overtones as Louis–Schmeling. *Sports Illustrated* invoked the Cold War: 'In this day and age we cannot afford an American heavyweight champion with Liston's unsavoury record.' The president of the National Boxing Association made no effort to disguise his bias: 'In my opinion, Patterson is a fine representative of his race, and I believe the heavyweight champion of the world should be the kind of man our children could look up to.' Patterson also received messages of support from liberal icons like JFK, Ralph Bunche and Eleanor Roosevelt. Percy Sutton, then president of the Manhattan NAACP and later a New York Democratic kingpin and millionaire, declared: 'I'm for Patterson because he represents us better than Liston ever could or would.'

In fact, everyone spurned Liston except Malcolm X, who said he hoped Liston would 'shake Patterson up'. Malcolm was angry at remarks Patterson had made about the Nation of Islam and saw him, and indeed all black boxers, as slaves to white money-men. Later, his encounter with Cassius Clay was to change his mind.

As for Liston himself, he seemed resigned to play his assigned role. 'A prize fight is like a cowboy movie,' he said. 'There has to be a good guy and a bad guy. People pays their money to see me lose. Only in my cowboy movie, the bad guy always wins.' Sure enough, Liston knocked out Patterson in the first round. In the rematch six months later, he did it again. The press now declared him 'invincible' – but they still thought someone else should be champion.

What Role? Whose Models?

The origins of the role model lie in the Victorian ideology of amateur sport. The Victorians paid tribute to the level playing field ('fair play', 'may the best man win', etc.) at the same time that they justified the domination of sport by a social and economic elite. Sport's egalitarian autonomy was thus overlaid with the prevailing hierarchies. Competitors were now to be judged by criteria extraneous to sport. Winning under the rules was not enough; one also had to uphold certain social and moral standards.

The role model was and is a means of taming the democracy of sport, of neutralising its sublime indifference to the high and mighty in other realms. The level playing field allowed blacks to become successful at sport; that success had to be confined and modified so that it carried messages approved by the white establishment. Black sports heroes were therefore asked, by both the white and black elite, to act as role models for the rest of the black population. They were required to set an example of proper behaviour – as defined by the elite – on and off the playing field. In this way, the elite ensured that, despite its apparent anarchy, the level playing field mirrored their ideas about the world, including their ideas about race.

Ever since the late nineteenth century, the 'gentlemen's code' deriving from amateur sport has been used to qualify or denigrate black success. West Indian fast-bowlers and Pakistani swing bowlers have both been abused, not for breaking the rules, but for playing the game in a different manner from that established by their former colonial masters. In football, the aggressive and immodest black player, Ian Wright, is compared, unfavourably, to the mealy-mouthed (white) Gary Lineker, though both won fame and lucre by doing more or less the same thing.

Because it is shaped from above, the black role model contains a fundamental contradiction. The purpose of the role model is to provide an example to black people of personal success achieved within the laws and customs of the realm. Yet all but a tiny minority of blacks have no hope of achieving such success within those laws and customs. What is more, the black role models offered are mostly male (in the case of boxing, exclusively so). The female black population is assigned a purely passive role; they are not asked to emulate but merely to admire the role model. In reality, they share this impotence with the vast majority of black males.

The more black sports stars remind people of the oppressive realities of black life (like Sonny Liston), the less they are accepted as a role model for it. More often than not, the duties of the role model have estranged black sports stars from their popular constituency. By radically redefining his duties as a role model, Muhammad Ali changed all that. His evolving politics enabled him to embrace his fans in a new way. Transcending the old stereotypical duality – the 'Uncle Tom' and the 'bad Nigger' – he resolved, however fleetingly, the contradiction of the black role model.

Cassius Clay, Muhammad Ali and Malcolm X

It is hard to believe now, but at first Cassius Clay appeared to many Liston-haters as a 'great white hope'. Certainly he was happy enough in the beginning to join in the conventional role-play. At ringside for the Liston–Patterson fight, he shook Patterson's hand, then looked towards Liston, threw his hands up in mock terror and fled.

Cassius Clay enjoyed a more comfortable and stable upbringing than Liston, Patterson or, indeed, any of the black opponents he was to face in the future. At the 1960 Olympics in Rome, asked by a Soviet reporter about the condition of blacks in the USA, Clay had answered 'To me, the USA is still the best country in the world, counting yours.' In those days he was proud of his Christian name: 'Don't you think it's a beautiful name? Makes you think of the Coliseum and those Roman gladiators.' But when he returned home he complained: 'With my gold medal actually hanging around my neck I couldn't get a cheeseburger served to me in a downtown Louisville restaurant.' Nonetheless, he was sponsored by a consortium of white Louisville businessmen and, thanks to his big mouth and showbiz acumen, quickly became the most publicised fighter in the business. Regarded by many as a vaudeville turn, he was still, broadly, thought to be good for boxing. No one in those days thought this crass comedian would one day become a world-wide symbol of

black dignity. Indeed, the very idea that he might do this without losing his sense of fun and his love of performing violated all the known sports stereotypes. A year before his title fight with Liston, he asked reporters:

> Where do you think I'd be next week, if I didn't know how to shout and holler and make the public take notice? I'd be poor and I'd probably be down in my home town, washing windows or running an elevator and saying, 'yes suh' and 'no suh' and knowing my place. Instead, I'm one of the highest paid athletes in the world. Think about that. A southern coloured boy has made one million dollars.

In other words, the clowning was a way of breaking out of the racist stranglehold. Clay first heard Elijah Muhammad speak in 1959 when he was in Chicago for a Golden Gloves tournament. From the beginning, it was Clay who sought out the Nation of Islam; the Muslims never pursued him. Indeed, only gradually did they realise what a prize had dropped in their laps. The black magazine, *Ebony*, was the first to report the real significance of the emerging Clay story:

> Cassius Marcellus Clay – and this fact has evaded the sports-writing fraternity – is a blast furnace of racial pride. His is a pride that would never mask itself with skin lighteners and processed hair, a pride scorched with memories of millions of little burns.

Nonetheless, it was Liston, not Clay, whose contract barred segregated movie theatres from showing their bout on closed circuit television. And, despite his 'racial pride', Clay was happy to deploy the dehumanising language of the oppressors in the build-up to the fight with the man he called 'that big ugly bear':

> Sonny Liston is nothing. The man can't talk. The man can't fight. The man needs talking lessons. The man needs boxing lessons. And since he's gonna fight me,

he needs falling lessons... After I whup Sonny Liston, I'm gonna whup those little green men from Jupiter and Mars. And looking at them won't scare me none because they can't be no uglier than Sonny Liston... I'm gonna give him to the local zoo after I whup him... I'm young, I'm handsome, I'm fast, I can't be beaten... He's too ugly to be the world champ. The world champ should be pretty like me.

Clay here echoed the worst racist stereotype of the black boxer as an uneducated animal, but he did so with a panache quite foreign to the ethos of boxing's traditional black role models. Clay had already dispensed with the modest self-effacement which all professional sports people, especially black ones, were expected to affect and because of this many in the media wanted him put in his place, even by Sonny Liston. Then, weeks before the bout, Clay and Malcolm X were photographed together in New York. The *New York Herald Tribune* demanded to know if the heavyweight challenger was 'a card-carrying Muslim'. Clay was quick to spot the potential for a role swap and told Liston: 'I make you great. The fans love you because I'm the villain.' Clay may have been amused, but his publicist, Harold Conrad, despaired: 'The whole sales pitch for the fight had been Clay against Liston, white hat against black hat, and now it looked like there'd be two black hats fighting.'

Malcolm's brief encounter with Ali was left out of the Spike Lee film, despite the impact it had on both men's lives. Elijah Muhammad instructed his followers against all sports, especially degrading spectacles like boxing. Malcolm had never even heard of Clay when they were introduced in Detroit in 1962. But he was impressed by the young fighter's seriousness about the Nation of Islam. After all, Clay stood to gain nothing from any association with the Muslims. In his *Autobiography*, Malcolm recalled:

I liked him. Some contagious quality about him made him one of the few people I ever invited to my home. Betty liked him. Our children were crazy about him. Cassius was simply a likeable, friendly, clean-cut,

down-to-earth youngster. I noticed how alert he was even in little details. I suspected there was a plan in his public clowning.

As the Liston fight approached, Malcolm was in rapid evolution – en route to a new revolutionary internationalism and early martyrdom. In his *Autobiography*, he depicts his time in Clay's camp as one of distress and isolation. He had been suspended by Elijah Muhammad for ninety days, following his 'chickens coming home to roost' crack about the JFK assassination. As Clay prepared for his moment of glory, Malcolm was coming to grips with Elijah Muhammad's cult of personality and the danger that his apostasy would place him in.

Elijah Muhammad and his coterie were opposed to Malcolm's presence in Clay's camp. They were as convinced as the white sports writers that Clay, the eight-to-one underdog, would lose and feared that their association with him would be damaging. But Malcolm stayed close to Clay because 'it was Allah's intent for me to help Cassius prove Islam's superiority before the world – through proving that mind can win over brawn'. He fortified Clay to face Liston by talking about David and Goliath. For Malcolm, Liston's whole life and career was proof that the struggle for integration was futile and debilitating. Clay, he felt, could represent something different. 'Clay... is the finest Negro athlete I have ever known, the man who will mean more to his people than Jackie Robinson, because Robinson is the white man's hero.' Malcolm saw Clay's symbolic power more clearly than anyone else at the time, and he helped Clay realise that power in the ring:

'This fight is the truth,' I told Cassius. 'It's the Cross and the Crescent fighting in a prize ring – for the first time. It's a modern crusade – a Christian and a Muslim facing each other with television to beam it off Telstar for the whole world to see what happens!' I told Cassius, 'Do you think Allah has brought about all this, intending for you to leave the ring as anything but the champion?'

Attendance at the fight itself was small but over one million people watched it on closed circuit TV. The *New York Times* reported: 'The general support for Clay seemed to transcend any betting considerations and even the normal empathy for an underdog.' The *Times*' puzzlement brings to mind the lyric written by Bob Dylan at about the same time: 'Something is happening here / But you don't know what it is / Do you, Mister Jones?'

In Miami, Clay danced his way around a lumbering Liston, his speed, footwork and amazing 360 degree ring-vision nullifying the champion's advantages in power and reach. When a bewildered and dejected Liston failed to come out for the seventh round, Clay was jubilant. 'I want everyone to bear witness,' he shouted. 'I am the greatest! I shook up the world!' Nonetheless, many sports writers continued to regard his victory as a fluke. Malcolm was more perceptive: 'The secret of one of fight history's greatest upsets was that, months before that night, Clay had out-thought Liston.' Because of his rejection of the prevailing stereotypes of black sportsmen, Malcolm was able to see in Clay what the sports writers refused to see: a supremely intelligent and inventive boxer inspired by more than just a lust for money.

After the fight, a quiet Clay met privately with Malcolm and Jim Brown, the great Cleveland Browns running back and an early champion of black rights in sport. The next morning, after breakfast with Malcolm, he held a press conference at which he announced:

> I believe in Allah and in peace. I don't try to move into white neighbourhoods. I don't want to marry a white woman. I was baptised when I was twelve, but I didn't know what I was doing. I'm not a Christian any more. I know where I'm going and I know the truth, and I don't have to be what you want me to be. I'm free to be what I want.

No boxing champion, and no black sports person, had ever issued such a ringing declaration of independence. The next day, Clay amplified his views. In place of his usual ingratiating bravado, there was now a steely and even exultant defiance:

> Black Muslims is a press word. The real name is Islam. That means peace. Islam is a religion and there are 750 million people all over the world who believe in it, and I'm one of them. I ain't no Christian. I can't be when I see all the colored people fighting for forced integration get blowed up. They get hit by stones and chewed by dogs and they blow up a Negro church and don't find the killers...I'm the heavyweight champion, but right now there are some neighbourhoods I can't move into. I know how to dodge booby-traps and dogs. I dodge them by staying in my own neighbourhood. I'm no trouble-maker...I'm a good boy. I never have done anything wrong. I have never been to jail. I have never been in court, I don't join any integration marches. I don't pay any attention to all those white women who wink at me. I don't carry signs...A rooster crows only when it sees the light. Put him in the dark and he'll never crow. I have seen the light and I'm crowing.

As Robert Lipsyte observed, Clay was challenging the white establishment's fundamental injunction to all black American sports stars: 'keep our stereotypes in order'. Notice how Clay argued his case. In telling the press that he had never been to jail or court, he was saying, 'I'm no Sonny Liston.' In forswearing white women, he was saying, "I'm no Jack Johnson.' In denouncing integration, he was saying, 'I'm no Floyd Patterson.' In a bizarre fashion, he was adhering to the contours of the role model favoured by the white press. Therefore, he seemed to be arguing, there was no reason they should be threatened by him. Yet the content of the model was utterly transformed – and that posed a major threat to all the white press held sacred, in and out of sport.

Clay undermined his own attempt to paint his conversion as purely religious by his constant references to American racism. Perusing Clay's statements of the time, it is clear he saw the

Nation of Islam as a means of black survival in a hostile racist world. This may have looked like a religious act, but its wellsprings were political. 'I don't believe Muhammad's conversion was a religious experience,' said the born-again Christian, George Foreman, years later. 'I'll believe until the day I die that it was a social awakening ... It was something he needed at the time, something the whole country needed...'

A week after the fight, Clay journeyed to Harlem and checked into the Hotel Theresa, where Malcolm had an office. Later, the two men toured the UN and were photographed together meeting African delegates. On 6 March, Elijah Muhammad announced that the world heavyweight champion was changing his name. 'Muhammad Ali is what I will give him for as long as he believes in Allah and follows me.'

As Ali himself was quick to point out, name changes were commonplace in American sports and entertainment. Joe Louis and Sugar Ray Robinson had done it; so had Edward G. Robinson and John Garfield. But this was different. This was a black man signalling by his name change, not a desire to ingratiate himself with mainstream America, but a comprehensive rejection of it. It was to be many years before he won his battle to force the media to adopt his new name. The *New York Times* persisted in calling him 'Cassius Clay' throughout the 1960s.

In changing his name, Ali was demonstrating what he meant when he said: '*I don't have to be what you want me to be.*' For the first time, here was a black American sports hero who would not allow himself to be defined according to white racist categories. He was seizing back his persona. Johnson and Louis, Patterson and Liston had been endowed with their public identities by the white press; Clay was going to create his own identity and shove it down their throats.

Of course, the only way he could have ever hoped to succeed in this, given the forces he was up against, was with the wind of a great movement at his back. Clay tried to make a virtue out of the Muslims' abstention from active participation in the civil rights movement. But if he chose the Nation of Islam as a means of escaping confrontations with white racism, he was to be sadly disappointed. In the end, Clay would fight all the battles he sought to avoid, and on a grand scale. He would 'carry a sign' by becoming a sign – a living symbol of black resistance to white racism.

Clay's renunciation of the old stereotypes infuriated the establishment, white and black. 'Most of the writers, particularly the older ones, felt more comfortable with the mob figures around Liston than with the Muslims around Clay,' said Robert Lipsyte. Boxing pundit Jimmy Cannon called Ali's ties to the Nation of Islam 'the dirtiest in American sports since the Nazis were shilling for Max Schmeling as representative of their vile theories of blood'. Louisville black churchmen pronounced Ali 'a disservice to his race, nation and the world'. Joe Louis joined in:

> Clay will earn the public's hatred because of his connections with the Black Muslims. The things they preach are just the opposite of what we believe. The heavyweight champion should be the champion of all the people. He has responsibilities to all people.

Acting on a suggestion Malcolm had made before the Miami fight, Ali made a trip to Africa in May 1964. He met Nkrumah in Ghana and Nasser in Egypt. Everywhere he was greeted by huge crowds, who chanted his new name with gusto. On this trip, Cassius Clay was buried and Muhammad Ali superseded him. By now, Malcolm's break with Elijah Muhammad had become public. On his way to Mecca, at a hotel in Accra, he ran into Ali, who snubbed him. 'Nobody listens to Malcolm anymore,' the champ told reporters. According to Alex Haley, 'that hurt Malcolm more than any other person turning away from him'. Ironically, Malcolm was to find that his acquaintance with Ali stood him in good stead on his pilgrimage. In Saudi Arabia, he was often mistaken for Ali ('the Muslim from America'), whose fame was now huge in the Muslim world. For months, the Clay–Liston fight was shown at packed cinemas throughout the Middle East. Ali was becoming a global figure, with tens of millions of supporters outside his native land.

After the Miami fight, Floyd Patterson had declared that, 'as a Catholic', he felt he had a duty to 'reclaim the title for America' from the Muslim Ali. Three weeks later, he was forced to sell his $140,000 house in Yonkers (only a few miles from my own home town) for a $20,000 loss. White neighbours had rejected his attempt at integration, subjecting his family to racist abuse. Nonetheless, Patterson insisted: 'The image of a Black Muslim as the world heavyweight champion disgraces the sport and the nation. Cassius Clay must be beaten and the Black Muslims' scourge removed from boxing.'

Patterson may have initiated the battle of the role models, but Ali met the challenge head on, subjecting Patterson to weeks of verbal abuse.

> Patterson says he's gonna bring the title back to America. If you don't believe the title already is in America, just see who I pay taxes to. I'm American. But he's a deaf dumb so-called Negro who needs a spanking. I plan to punish him for the things he said; cause him pain . . . The little old pork-chop eater don't have a chance.

According to Arthur Ashe, 'No black athlete had ever publicly spoken so disparagingly to another black athlete.' Ali's doggerel was cruel:

> *I'm going to put him flat on his back,*
> *so that he will start acting Black,*
> *because when he was champ he didn't do as he*
>   *should,*
> *he tried to force his way into an all-white*
>   *neighbourhood.*

At the fight itself, Patterson was hopelessly outclassed. Heedless of the outrage of ringside commentators, Ali dragged the fight out to the twelfth round, punishing Patterson with his fists, then stepping back and allowing him time to recover while taunting him, 'Come on America! Come on white America!'

Over the next three years, Ali's attacks on 'Uncle Toms' and their white sponsors became ever sharper. 'People are always telling me what a good example I could be if I just wasn't a Muslim,' Ali observed. 'I've heard it over and over, how come I couldn't be like Joe Louis and Sugar Ray. Well, they're gone now, and the black man's condition is just the same, ain't it? We're still catching hell.'

Did Ali regret not having Malcolm at his side during these difficult years? According to Jim Brown, even before the Liston fight in Miami, Ali knew he would have to reject Malcolm for Elijah. Perhaps he wanted to prove his loyalty, perhaps he also sensed that Malcolm would place too many demands on him and expose him to too many dangers. Perhaps he was aware that abandoning Elijah could be even more dangerous than embracing Malcolm.

'When Malcolm broke with Elijah, I stayed with Elijah,' Ali explained many years later. 'I believed that Malcolm was wrong and Elijah was God's messenger. I was in Miami, training, when I heard Malcolm had been shot to death . . . It was a pity and a disgrace he died like that, because what Malcolm saw was right, and after he left us, we went his way anyway. Colour didn't make a man a devil. It's the heart, soul and mind that counts.'

Ali was openly delighted when the Nation of Islam abandoned anti-white rhetoric for Muslim orthodoxy in the 1970s. He had always had white friends and associates, and his travels had made him aware that oppression comes in many forms on this earth. In the end, Ali came to stand for more than mere black self-assertion; his Muslim allegiance and embryonic pan-Africanism gradually led him, like Malcolm, towards a broader, more inclusive vision of his role.

'I Don't Have To Be What You Want Me To Be'

Ali's refusal to fight in Vietnam made him into a hero in places where boxing was unknown. In reply to those Americans who demanded he 'serve his country like Joe Louis', he asserted a higher loyalty and a broader solidarity. In the process, he became an icon of internationalism.

Initially, Ali was excluded from the draft because he scored so poorly in IQ tests – proof that whatever these tests may measure, it certainly isn't intelligence. But as the US escalated the war, the Pentagon's standards were lowered and, in February 1966, Ali was reclassified 1-A, eligible and likely to be called for military service. When told the news, Ali blurted out, 'I ain't got no quarrel with them Vietcong.' It was a spur-of-the-moment remark, but it became Ali's theme in his long battle with the US government.

Keep asking me, no matter how long
on the war in Vietnam, I sing this song
I ain't got no quarrel with the Vietcong.

Reaction from the political and boxing establishments was swift and hostile. The Kentucky legislature, which had honoured him when he won a gold medal, now condemned him for bringing discredit to 'all loyal Kentuckians'. The state of Illinois banned his scheduled title defence against Ernie Terrell. Miami and Pittsburgh followed suit. Sports writers, including Arthur Daley of the *New York Times*, urged a boycott of Ali's fights, a call taken up by right-wing politicians like Congressman Frank Clark of Pennsylvania:

The heavyweight champion has been a complete and total disgrace. I urge the citizens of the nation as a whole to boycott any of his performances. To leave these theatre seats empty would be the finest tribute possible to that boy whose hearse may pass by the open doors of the theatre on Main Street, USA.

Within days of Ali's remark, 300 theatres across the country pulled out of closed-circuit coverage. The Terrell bout was cancelled. Ali was forced to defend his title abroad. But he would not recant. Instead, he became more vocal and more explicit in his rejection of the war:

Why should they ask me to put on a uniform and go ten thousand miles from home and drop bombs and bullets on brown people in Vietnam while so-called Negro people in Louisville are treated like dogs? . . . I have nothing to lose by standing up and following my beliefs. So I'll go to jail. We've been in jail for four hundred years.

When he finally fought Terrell, in Houston in 1967, his ferocity shocked the pundits. Terrell, a powerful hitter considered Ali's most dangerous opponent since Liston, had made the mistake of calling him 'Clay' during a pre-fight press conference. 'What's my name?' Ali roared again and again as he showered Terrell with punches. 'Uncle Tom! What's my name?' The New York *Daily News* called the fight 'a disgusting exhibition of calculating cruelty, an open defiance of decency, sportsmanship and all the tenets of right versus wrong'. Arthur Daley called Ali 'a mean and malicious man whose facade has crumbled as he gets deeper into the Black Muslim movement'. Another veteran boxing correspondent, Milton Gross, confessed: 'One almost yearns for the return of Frankie Carbo and his mobster ilk.'

Rarely has the hideous hierarchy of boxing's values been so naked. Ali's violence in the ring (and within the rules) was declared reprehensible by the very people who condemned him for not engaging in much more deadly violence in Vietnam. Even the violence of organised crime was considered less discrediting to the sport of boxing than Ali's crime of conscience.

And a crime of conscience it was. The government made it clear that Ali would not be exposed to combat. Like Joe Louis before him, he could box exhibitions and address troops and, in Ali's words, spend his tour 'living the easy life and not having to get out in the mud and fight and shoot'. But he refused all the soft options, including exile abroad.

It has to be remembered that, at this time, opposition to the war, though mounting, was still anything but fashionable. It was to be another year before Bobby Kennedy and the 'liberal' wing of the Democratic Party broke with Johnson. The mainstream civil rights leaders steered clear of the issue. Until the late 1960s, the received wisdom in the white establishment and among many black leaders was that black people would make advances by showing themselves to be 'good Americans'. If they were loyal to their country, their country would be grateful. 'Patriotic blacks', like Joe Louis or Floyd Patterson, were the best blacks. In both politics and sport, the ground rules of Cold War liberalism still applied: if they sought legitimacy, blacks, like trade unions, had to be unequivocally 'on America's side'.

Robeson and DuBois had placed their loyalty to the oppressed of the world before any loyalty to the US government. As a consequence, they were driven out of American public life and ultimately into exile. Now, Muhammad Ali was committing the same heresy for which they had been punished. In 1966, he was one of only a handful of black voices publicly opposing the war. Within weeks of making his 'I ain't got no quarrel' crack, Ali was placed under surveillance by the FBI, which complained, in an internal memorandum, that he had 'utilised his position as a nationally known figure in the sports world to promote through appearances at various gatherings an ideology completely foreign to the basic American ideals of equality and justice for all, love of god and country'.

In fact, Ali was ahead of the established civil rights leaders and more in tune with feeling in the ghettoes, where the real price of the war was being paid. On 29 March 1967, Martin Luther King met privately with Ali in Louisville and then publicly lauded his stand. On 4 April 1967, after much soul-searching, King came out against the war in a major speech in Riverside church in New York City. Three weeks later, Ali reported for induction in Houston. Three times he refused to answer the sergeant's call for 'Cassius Clay'. Then he signed a statement formally refusing induction on religious grounds. Afterwards, he told the press:

> I am proud of the title 'World Heavyweight Champion' which I won in the ring in Miami on February 25, 1964. The holder of it should at all times have the courage of his convictions and carry out those convictions, not only in the ring but in all phases of his life.

Clearly, Ali had radically redefined his duties as a role model. The boxing authorities could not tolerate it. Without waiting for charges to be filed, no less a full trial, they stripped Ali of his title. *Ring* magazine declined to designate a fighter of the year because 'Cassius Clay', the obvious candidate for the award, 'is most emphatically not to be held up as an example to the youngsters of the United States'.

In June, Herbert Muhammad, Elijah's son and Ali's manager, brought together a number of black sports stars for a private meeting with Ali. Some observers were convinced that Herbert wanted the stars to persuade Ali to take the army's deal. If that was so, Herbert had seriously underestimated his fighter's determination. The stars, including football players Jim Brown and Willie Davis and basketball heroes Bill Russell and Lew Alcindor (who later changed his name to Kareem Abdul Jabbar), left the meeting deeply moved by Ali's sincerity and courage. They were also impressed by his ability to break the boundaries within which sports heroes were supposed to act. 'He gave so many people courage to test the system,' said Jabbar, 'a lot of us didn't think he could do it, but he did and succeeded every time.' For Russell, Ali was 'a man accepting special responsibilities'. He told the press:

> I'm not worried about Muhammad Ali.
> He is better equipped than anyone I know
> to withstand the trials in store for him.
> What I'm worried about is the rest of us.

Ali was sentenced to five years in prison and a $10,000 fine. He posted bail and began the three-year process of appeal, which was to take his case ultimately to the Supreme Court. In the meantime, he was forced out of boxing. To make a living, he gave lectures at colleges around the country, winning passionate support among student radicals, despite their disagreements with his homilies on the evils of integration, drugs and sex. 'Damn the money. Damn the heavyweight championship,' Ali told the students. 'I will die before I sell out my people for the white man's money.' Who could resist a pitch like that?

Symbolism and Resistance

Besides inspiring thousands to resist the draft, Ali ignited a wave of protest among black sports stars. During the 1967–8 academic year, black athletes at thirty-seven white-dominated colleges and universities raised demands for more black coaches, facilities, cheerleaders and trainers. Bob Beamon, the future long jump record-setter, was dropped by his university coach for refusing to compete against the Mormon-run Brigham Young University (the Mormon doctrine at the time was explicitly racist). That year, black sports people came together to form the Olympic Project for Human Rights (OPHR), whose first demand was 'the restoration of Muhammad Ali's titles' (second was the removal of the racist Avery Brundage as head of the United States Olympic Committee and third was the exclusion of South Africa and Rhodesia from international competition).

Initially, OPHR advocated a black boycott of the Olympics but, when South Africa was banned, the focus turned to subverting the event from within. The potent symbolism of the Olympic podium – a celebration of individual excellence at the service of the nation-state – was diametrically opposed to the tenets of 'black consciousness' then spreading rapidly among black American sports people. It had to be challenged.

On 16 October 1968, at Mexico City, a supporter of OPHR, Tommie Smith, the 24-year-old son of a migrant labourer, captured the 200 metres Olympic Gold with a world record-breaking run. In third place was another OPHR supporter, John Carlos, a 23-year-old Harlemite. On the winners' podium, they bowed their heads and raised clenched fists during the US national anthem. Tommie Smith explained their gesture:

I wore a black right-hand glove and Carlos wore the left-hand glove of the same pair. My raised right hand stood for the power in black America. Carlos' raised left-hand stood for the unity of black America. Together they formed an arch of unity and power. The black scarf around my neck stood for black pride. The black socks with no shoes stood for black poverty in racist America. The totality of our effort was the regaining of black dignity.

The need to overthrow the old role models had driven Smith and Carlos to invent a complex new symbolism. The rhetoric of individual victory and national glory was replaced by a language of solidarity that amounted to repudiation of the United States and all its works. Thousands of blacks had been lynched for less.

Smith and Carlos were ejected from the Olympic village, banned from the games and vilified at home. The problem for the authorities was that, as far as the public was concerned, Smith and Carlos were the world's number one and number three 200 metres men, just as Ali was the World Heavyweight Champion. They had won these distinctions in open and fair competition. Ali's support grew not only because the tide of opinion swung against the war, but because he could appeal to sport's egalitarian autonomy. Ali was the champ, according to the common understanding of the rules of the game and regardless of what the authorities said. When they staged elimination bouts for his 'vacant' title, Ali warned: 'Everyone knows I'm the champion. My ghost will haunt all the arenas. I'll be there, wearing a sheet and whispering, "Ali-e-e-e! Ali-e-e-e!" '

Ali was 25 years old when stripped of his crown and he spent twenty-nine months – when he was probably at the height of his powers – out of the ring. In June 1970, the Supreme Court reversed his earlier conviction because the FBI had, it transpired, illegally tapped his phone. By this time, many within the establishment had clearly become reluctant to send Ali to jail, but it was a close-run thing. Had it been left to the president, Ali would have served his time. According to Jackie Robinson, a Republican confidante, 'Cassius Clay is Nixon's pet peeve'.

Throughout his ordeal, Ali received little assistance from the Nation of Islam. In 1969, Elijah Muhammad suspended Ali for nine months for saying on television that he would like to fight again. 'Mr. Muhammad Ali has sporting blood. Mr. Muhammad Ali desires to do that which the Holy Qur'an teaches him against. Mr. Muhammad Ali wants a place in the sports world.' And the final insult: 'We will call him Cassius Clay.'

Vindication

Readmitted to the ring, Ali lost to Joe Frazier in March 1971. Officially, Frazier was the champion and Ali the challenger; in reality, as Frazier himself acknowledged, he would not be recognised as the true title-holder until he beat Ali. It was a brutal battle, the first of three they would contest over the next four years.

By now, Ali had mastered both the rhetoric of race and the symbolic power of the ring. He knew better than anyone how to combine the two to mobilise popular support (and sell tickets).

> Frazier's no real champion. Nobody wants to talk to him. Oh, maybe Nixon will call him if he wins. I don't think he'll call me. But 98% of my people are for me. They identify with my struggle. Same one they're fighting every day in the streets. If I win, they win. I lose, they lose. Anybody black who thinks Frazier can whup me is an Uncle Tom.

The irony was that Frazier, who had grown up among the poorest of the black poor in South Carolina, had more genuine street cred than Ali, who treated him with disdain. He called Frazier 'an ignorant gorilla', language which, had it come from a white fighter, would have provoked a bitter reaction among black people.

> Joe Frazier is too ugly to be champ. Joe Frazier is too dumb to be champ. The heavyweight champion should be smart and pretty, like me. Ask Joe Frazier, 'How do you feel, champ?'. He'll say, 'Duh, duh, duh.'

Frazier resented being cast by Ali as another Liston and, these days, is one of the very few people willing to say anything uncomplimentary about Ali in public.

> Calling me an Uncle Tom; calling me the white man's champion. All that was phoneyness to turn people against me. He was helping himself, not black people. Ali wasn't no leader of black people . . . A lot of people went to the fight that night to see Clay's head knocked off and I did my best to oblige them . . .

But this was precisely Joe Frazier's dilemma; the people who wanted him to beat Ali were the diehard racists and the old-guard boxing establishment, both of whom had always resented Ali's uppityness. Frazier was a magnificent athlete whose tragedy was that he came along at a time when his only public profile was as a foil to Ali. His bitter complaint against Ali – that the latter stole his blackness from him – reveals how much had changed since the days of Liston and Patterson, not to mention Joe Louis and Jack Johnson. Blackness had become a positive attribute: a selling point for professional sports figures, a key to success on and off the level playing field. It was a tremendous achievement, and one that belonged in no small measure to Muhammad Ali.

The crown of that achievement was the Ali–Foreman fight in Zaire in October 1974. After losing to Frazier, Ali had been written off, by enemies and friends alike, as a spent force. But his extraordinary resilience enabled him to come back, against the odds, to beat Frazier in another epic, exhausting contest in January 1974. He thus earned a title shot against the new heavyweight champion, George Foreman, widely thought to be the most formidable puncher in decades. Ten years after the Liston fight, at the age of 32, Ali once again found himself a no-hope underdog against a supposedly unstoppable powerhouse.

> This man is supposed to annihilate me, but ten years ago they said the same thing about Sonny Liston. George Foreman don't stand a chance. The world is gonna bow down to me, because the stage is set . . .

Kinshasa was chosen as the venue for Africa's first heavyweight title fight. It became a self-consciously African affair, in keeping with the Africanism then fashionable among the black American middle class. It was also Don King's first venture into heavyweight boxing promotion. The ex-numbers' runner and mafia lackey had capitalised on his blackness to interpose himself between the fighters and the Mobutu government in Zaire. Ali loathed King and, a few years later, Muslim members of his entourage treated the crook to a richly deserved beating. But it was the Zaire fight which gave King his entrée to heavy-weight promotion, a market he was able to corner after Ali's retirement.

Mobutu's purpose in staging the fight was, first, to strengthen his own grip over the country and, second, to promote it as a modern, go-ahead society that welcomed foreign capital. Pre-fight publicity emphasised the city's gleaming new skyscrapers, government buildings and boulevards, as well as the country's mineral wealth (diamonds and copper) and bright economic prospects. David Frost, hired by King to MC the closed circuit TV coverage, invoked the dynamism of technological advance by breathlessly repeating at every opportunity that the broadcast was coming *'live via satellite from Zaire, Africa'*.

Fifteen thousand people turned up just to watch the weigh-in, where Foreman tried to steal Ali's thunder by entering in an African robe. The fight itself was preceded by a lengthy exhibition of state-sponsored 'tribal' dancing. The Mobutu regime presented this as an affirmation of African tradition on the new global media stage; but it was also, like the fight that followed it, a commercial display of black bodies for the entertainment of a largely white television audience. The Zaire fight was one of the pioneer events in the creation of today's global telecommunications-based sports industry. It helped integrate Africa (just as Ali's later bout against Frazier in Manila helped integrate Asia) into the world system of modern sport, but, of course, it was integration as a subordinate. Looking back on the propaganda surrounding the fight, its optimism about the new, post-colonial Africa taking a proud and independent place in the world market seems to belong to another world.

As an Ali fan, I saw the 'rumble in the jungle' (as Ali dubbed it) as a last, probably forlorn, attempt by my hero to recapture past glory. Subsequently, I learned that my feelings were not unique; the fight meant a great deal to many people on the Left. One friend of mine, an Asian community activist with no interest in boxing, came into central London to watch the fight at a cinema because Ali, to him, embodied a 'political concept of blackness'; another friend, a Jewish Trotskyist, did the same – because Ali and Khrushchev had been his boyhood heroes. Reading the sports pages in my furnished flat in Notting Hill Gate, I realised that only the most dedicated wishful thinkers gave the ageing ex-champ and '60s martyr any chance against Foreman. Ali, as always, was quick to exploit the lack of expectations:

> *You think the world was shocked when Nixon resigned?*
> *Wait till I whup George Foreman's behind!*

And so it came to pass. A 62,000 crowd (mostly Zaireans) watched Ali come out attacking in round one. After that, he spent most of his time leaning against the ropes – the 'rope-a-dope', he called it later – and covering his face as Foreman punched away at his body to little effect. Between rounds, Ali led the crowd in its simple deafening chant: 'Ali! Ali! Ali!' Taunting and gabbing to Foreman throughout, soaking up punishment that would have finished off almost anyone else, Ali blunted Foreman's offensive.

It was an astonishing display of total ring awareness. Ali hardly danced at all after the first round, but somehow he managed to lead the ever-advancing Foreman round and round. Even as ringside critics puzzled over his tactics, he was in complete control. At one point, as he took a fearsome pummelling in the ribs, Ali winked at the TV camera. Never was his supreme gamesmanship – holding, clinching, pushing, tying up and frustrating Foreman, while always staying just the right side of the law – better displayed. His blows were fewer than Foreman's, but they counted for more. The punches were swift, economical and accurate. One might almost call them delicate were it not for the telltale swellings on Foreman's face.

With thirty seconds left in round eight, Ali moved out from the ropes and suddenly nailed the tiring Foreman with a perfectly executed left–right combination that sent the champion tumbling to the floor. For a moment, Ali stood over him, bouncing on his toes, fists cocked to deliver more punishment if needed, snarling and supreme, his eyes afire with victory. David Frost was beside himself: 'The most joyous scene in the history of boxing! Muhammad Ali has won! Muhammad Ali has won!'

In Zaire, Ali lived up to and beyond every boast he had ever made. As sports writer Mike Katz said, it was 'the ultimate sports fantasy of all time'. Ali explained its appeal: 'People like to see miracles. People like to see underdogs that do it. People like to be there when history is made.' But there was more to it than that. This was a triumph of intelligence and sheer intensity of personality over impersonal brawn. It was also a triumph for principle and solidarity over expedience and selfishness. Because of that, all over the world, people felt Ali's triumph as their triumph.

In the wake of the Zaire fight, even Ali's old enemies had to admit he was truly 'the greatest'. *Ring* magazine finally named him 'fighter of the year'. *Sports Illustrated* declared him 'Sportsman of the Year'. He was invited to the White House to meet president Gerald Ford in what was widely seen as a symbol of post-Vietnam, post-Watergate national reconciliation. As the wave of protest receded and the black liberation movement stuttered to a halt, Ali seemed a less threatening figure. After Zaire, he became, according to Jim Brown, a 'darling of the media' and 'part of the establishment'.

In 1975, at the Frankfurt Book Fair, I finally saw Ali in the flesh. He was by no means the only celebrity to turn up at the fair to promote a book, but he attracted more attention than the rest of them combined. The publishing crowd does not form one of boxing's traditional constituencies, but they swarmed around the heavyweight champ like star-struck teeny-boppers. This is one of the few times in my life I have queued for an autograph. Like most of the others who surrounded Ali that day, the autograph was only an excuse to get close to the man, a chance to pay him homage. This was just as well, because the next day the autograph itself was pinched from my hotel room.

As I drew closer to Ali, I marvelled at the hugeness of his neck and shoulders. In the midst of what had rapidly become a mob scene, he sat quite still, scribbling his name over and over again. I realised that this must happen to him everywhere. At the time, he was probably the most famous human being on earth, adulated nearly everywhere as 'the Greatest'. Yet he seemed a modest man, bored but patient, accepting the duties of celebrity with good grace. Could it be that the most notorious boaster in the history of sport was, at the bottom of it all, a humble man? Certainly, that is what many of his closest friends have always insisted.

Boxing Damned

Ali's last years in the ring were tragic. Some said he kept fighting for so long to make up for the time lost because of his opposition to the war in Vietnam. Others that his ego would not let him recognise the truth: that he was long past his best and could only tarnish his image. However, no one can doubt that one of the main reasons Ali stayed in the fight game through the late '70s was that he needed the money. He had earned millions, but he had also given away millions. Ali was the original soft touch.

At one point, he even condescended to take part in a gimmick match against a Japanese wrestler. This was primarily a money-spinner, but it was also one of Ali's many efforts to make the 'world' in World Champion mean more than the 'world' in baseball's World Series. It proved an undignified spectacle, a humiliating falling-off from the rigour of true sporting competition. Ironically, here was Muhammad Ali, the man who had remade the image of the black sports hero, reduced to the depths of Joe Louis's wrestling exhibitions or Jesse Owens's races against horses. When Ali was subsequently vanquished by the inarticulate, inelegant Leon Spinks, it was clearly time to end the saga before it turned to farce. Instead, Ali returned to defeat an under-trained, coked-out Spinks in a fight that embarrassed all who saw it. His later come-back bout against Larry Holmes was even worse, not least for Holmes, an Ali devotee who tried his best to keep the 38-year-old former cham-pion going through eleven rounds.

With the rollback of the social movements that had made Ali what he was in the 1960s, his politics lacked focus and became ever more confused. In 1980, president Carter sent him on a mission to Africa to drum up support for the US boycott of the Moscow Olympics. African politicians informed Ali, in no uncertain terms, that they regarded the US position as so much Cold War hypocrisy. Ali came back perplexed and embarrassed. In 1984, he backed Ronald Reagan for president, but was photographed with Jesse Jackson in 1988. In November 1990, he visited Iraq and persuaded Saddam Hussein to release fifteen of the US hostages he was holding in the build-up to the Gulf War. Over the years, Ali's Islam became more conventional and more devout.

Ali now suffers from Parkinson's syndrome, a motor disability which affects his speech and movement (but not, it is said, his intellectual capacities). This is a result of damage inflicted on the brain stem in the ring. If boxing is re-deemed by having given us Muhammad Ali, then it must be damned by what it has done to him.

Ali's Secret Power

Racial, hierarchical symbolism has always been overlaid on sporting contests, especially boxing. This symbolism is imposed on the contestants from outside, by the same elite forces which shape public perceptions in other areas. As we have seen, Ali turned the process upside down. He became the master, rather than the servant, of boxing's symbolism and he did this by seeing himself as the servant of a greater cause.

In 1978, journalist Hunter S. Thompson sug-gested that Ali take on a white South African heavyweight in South Africa. Ali considered the proposal, thinking aloud before rejecting it. His reasoning was revealing. Yes, he would like to undertake the fight, provided that 'on that day

there'd be equality in the arena' (i.e., he would not fight in front of a segregated crowd). Then he added another rider. 'If the masses of the country and the world were against it, I wouldn't go.' He was intrigued by, but also wary of, the symbolic dimensions of such a fight. 'What worries me is getting whupped by a white man in South Afri-ca . . . That's what the world needs . . . me getting whupped by a white man in South Africa.' On the other hand, 'If I beat him too bad and then leave the country, they might beat up some of the brothers.' He concluded: 'I wouldn't fool with it. I'm a representative of black people . . . It's too touchy – it's more than a sport when I get in-volved.'

This insight was the key to Ali's achievements. The politics were not an afterthought. They informed Ali's approach to his fights and ultim-ately his performance in the ring. According to Gary Smith of *Sports Illustrated*:

> Ali understood that in order to be great you need something outside of yourself to flow into . . . If you fight for yourself, maybe it's you against the world and that gives you fuel, but it will never give you the strength Ali had. Muhammad was fighting for more than himself. He fought for God; his mission was huge. And that's why, in places like Manila, he was able to prevail when other men would have lost.

Here is the source of the intense drama of Ali's fights. His whole personality was engaged and, through it, many of the great historical forces of the age made themselves felt in the ring.

The Decline of the Black Sports Star

Surveying contemporary black celebrities, Jim Brown, Ali's old ally, cannot disguise his con-tempt:

> Take a look at black superstars today – Michael Jackson, Richard Pryor, Eddie Murphy – and look at them hiding behind

the bushes with all the power they have. Watch them twist their mouths and make money and pretend, yet do virtually nothing but pay tokenism to black freedom. If Ali was Michael Jackson or Richard Pryor or Eddie Murphy, he'd risk everything for black people.

As for sport, it does indeed seem a steep decline from the days of Ali, Brown and Kareem Abdul Jabbar to those of Mike Tyson, Charles Barkley and Carl Lewis, from the black Olympians of 1968 to the elitist millionaires of the 'Dream Team' at Barcelona in 1992.

One reason for this decline has been the continuing growth of sports as big business and with it the escalation of financial rewards. This has placed an ever greater distance between the black masses and their heroes. Black stars have continued to make advances in sport, while the black community as a whole has suffered one reverse after another. Instead of acting as the cutting edge in the struggle for equality, the disproportionate black presence in major American sports merely reflects the increasing marginalisation of black people in the US economy. In 1992, an NCAA survey revealed that 40 per cent of college football players and 60 per cent of college basketball players were black. However, only 6 per cent of all students were black and 20 per cent of these were enrolled as athletes.

In the USA today, a young black male is murdered every fifty-five minutes. One in three black men aged 14–35 is in prison, on probation or waiting trial. Black communities are gripped by ever-deepening economic and social crisis. At the same time, explicitly racist ideology has returned amid an orgy of victim-bashing. The 1960s have been repudiated and caricatured. In this context, both the white establishment and black 'identity' politicians of various stripes have called on black male sports stars to perform, once again, as patriarchal role models. Accordingly, the heroes of the '90s wrap themselves in the flag and declare their Christian faith, while selling themselves to the highest bidder, Nike or Reebok. Nothing matters but the quest to win. There is no gospel but that of individual success.

Over the years, many black sport stars have emulated Ali's manner, but very few share his mission. We have the shadow of Ali's magnificent arrogance, without the substance of his inspirational rage. Take the black British fighter, Chris Eubank. In his vanity and play-acting, he seems the disciple of Ali, but his insistence that boxing is only a way to make money, and a nasty, unpleasant way at that, has made him something else, a kind of anti-boxer. By declaring openly that he will only fight really dangerous opponents if the price is right, he devalues his own title. In thus exposing boxing for what it is, he may be doing a service, but his message to the black communities is ambiguous. He poses as an English gentleman and the only goal in life he recognises is the acquisition of wealth. Where Ali was generous, Eubank is miserly; where Ali identified himself with the black poor, Eubank wants to be seen as having risen above his racial and class origins. Confronted in a television studio by a number of black youths from Moss Side, Eubank told them the secret of success was to 'be good'. One of the youths replied, 'I can't box. So I can be as "good" as anyone else and still not have a job and still get harassed by police.' Eubank, for once, was silent.

Recently, at what appeared to be a well-rehearsed, pre-fight press conference, the Irish boxer, Steven Collins, accused Eubank of ignoring his roots. Eubank retorted by charging Collins with racism and threatening a 'fight to the death' – an unfortunate choice of words given the brain damage Eubank inflicted on Michael Watson. Eubank may or may not have been trying to rebuild his bridges to the black population, but he was certainly trying to boost interest in the Sky TV-sponsored bout with Collins by invoking the spectre of racial conflict. The stereotypes and role models that Ali shattered and reconstructed have become mere playthings for the likes of Eubank, no different from his monocle and cravat.

Today, boxing is sliding back into the second rank of modern sports. A bewildering variety of title-conferring authorities have stripped any meaning from the designation 'World Champion'. Fights are made for the convenience of promoters and media executives and their quality is often poor. Fighters still run the risk of death and disability. The most important black person in boxing is Don King, a role model embodying the morals of a ghetto crack lord. But it is important to remember that the rapist Mike Tyson, King's prize possession, is as much the creation of those two white gentlemen of the ring, Cus D'Amato and Jim Jacobs, who discovered and trained him, as of the Brooklyn ghetto or Don King himself. As Barbara Koppel's film on Tyson makes clear, his perception of women as commodities, as objects purely for his pleasure, was a product of boxing's big money culture and its glamorisation of individual, male power.

Modern sport liberated physical play from the chains of ritual and religion, but ultimately encased it in another prison, of money and status and the global market-place. If modern sport is not to descend into mere post-modern spectacle, in which a Chris Eubank fight is much the same as an episode of *Gladiators*, then perhaps we need a second liberation, in which the egalitarian premise of modern sport is truly fulfilled. In the struggle for the second liberation, I am sure that much inspiration will be drawn, in the years to come, from the story of Muhammad Ali.

Selected bibliography

A Hard Road to Glory, a history of the African-American athlete (three volumes), by Arthur Ashe Jr, revised edition, 1993.

Black Sportsmen, by Ernest Cashmore, 1982.

Muhammad Ali, his life and times, by Thomas Hauser, 1991.

Sport and the British, by Richard Holt, 1989.

The Autobiography of Malcolm X (with the assistance of Alex Haley), 1965.

Long Walk to Freedom, by Nelson Mandela, 1994.

Sonny Boy, the life and strife of Sonny Liston, by Rob Steen, 1993.

The Great Shark Hunt, by Hunter S. Thompson, 1979.

PART VIII

Sport and Role Models

CHAPTER 34

Do Celebrated Athletes have Special Responsibilities to be Good Role Models?
An Imagined Dialog between Charles Barkley and Karl Malone

Christopher Wellman

CHARLES BARKLEY: "I'm not a role model....[T]he ability to run and dunk a basketball should not make you God Almighty. There are a million guys in jail who can play ball. Should they be role models? Of course not." (*Sport Magazine*, February 1992)

KARL MALONE: "Charles, you can deny being a role model all you want, but I don't think it's your decision to make. We don't choose to be role models, we are chosen. Our only choice is whether to be a good role model or a bad one." (*Sports Illustrated*, June 14, 1993)

There has been a great deal of discussion recently as to whether professional athletes have a special responsibility to be good role models. In my view, this is a deceptively complex matter, and the quotations above by Charles Barkley and Karl Malone capture important parts (but only parts) of the truth. I offer the following imaginary dialog in an attempt to flesh out what I take to be a reasonable position on this issue.

MALONE: Like it or not, we are role models. Because of our prominent and exalted standing, we cannot choose whether or not to be role models. We can choose only what type of role model to be.

BARKLEY: But I'm a basketball player, for crying out loud! I never agreed to be a role model. It's the parents' job to raise their own children.

MALONE: I can appreciate your reaction, but morality is not optional. We have to accept our moral duties whether we like them or not. Just as I could not justify killing you merely by noting that I had never agreed not to kill you, you cannot shirk your responsibility to be a good role model simply because you never agreed to it.

BARKLEY: Of course you cannot justify murder by citing an absence of consent, but the voluntarism I advance is much more plausible than this. I acknowledge that we all have natural duties to everyone else – the natural duties forbidding lying, cheating, and harming others seem like obvious examples – but there is a difference between natural duties (which each of us owes to all others) and special duties (which some of us incur to specific others). The voluntarism I endorse speaks only to special duties; I contend that one cannot incur a *special* duty without one's consent.

MALONE: Although much more reasonable, even this more limited voluntarism is problematic because, while some of our special responsibilities rely upon consent, others clearly do not. Consider samaritan duties to rescue an imperiled person when this assistance is not unreasonably costly. If you come across a child drowning in a shallow pond, for instance, you have a duty to rescue her. This duty to aid does not depend upon your consent; it arises involuntarily as a result of the child's peril and your ability to help at no unreasonable cost to yourself. In my view, your special responsibility to be a good role model is like a samaritan duty: because of your influence over others in contemporary society, you inherit a special responsibility to use that influence to good effect.

BARKLEY: But now your position is implausible; morality is both unfair and excessively demanding if others can simply foist duties on you against your will. Imagine if Madonna started attending all of my games, fell madly in love with me, and desperately wanted to marry me. Would I then have a special responsibility to marry her? Of course not! Because, even though I now have a special influence over her well-being, it is ridiculous to pin the moral responsibility for her welfare on me. In jurisprudence, there is an expression that if a sneeze breaks a glass, you should attribute it to the glass rather than the sneeze. By the same token, when others inappropriately fall in love with me or take me to be a role model simply because I can play basketball, blame them not me!

MALONE: Although entertaining, your analogy involving Madonna is inapt because marriage requires consent only because it is so much more demanding than being a good role model. Whereas marriage is intimate and requires agreement, we *all* have a responsibility to encourage virtue and discourage vice. Conscientious moral agents are not born; they are nurtured and taught.

BARKLEY: Exactly right! Moral agents *are* nurtured, and that is the parents' job; it is *they* who have a special responsibility. I believe in individual responsibility, and thus I think that people should be held responsible for their own actions and for raising their own children to behave responsibly in turn. Just as a scientist is responsible for the actions of a robot she designs, parents are responsible for the children they bring into this world. If you don't want to raise children properly, then don't have any. All I'm saying is that you shouldn't blame *me* if *you* have children, *you* neglect their moral education, and *they* behave irresponsibly!

MALONE: Your commitment to individual responsibility is attractive, but your analogy between a child and a robot is misleading. Whereas robots may have only one programmer, children do not. Parents are typically the primary influence upon their growing children, but they are far from the only one. Occasionally, this is a welcome fact which allows for progress (this is why not all children of racists are condemned to grow up racist, for instance). More often, however, it can be frustrating for conscientious parents who witness their children being corrupted by a variety of unhealthy influences. This is part of the explanation for why each of us has a responsibility to encourage virtue and discourage vice.

BARKLEY: Okay, I'm beginning to become convinced, but it strikes me that your thesis has changed. You now seem to be saying that we *all* have a duty to be good role models. If so, in what sense do professional athletes have a *special* responsibility? Moreover, if anybody has a special responsibility to be a good role model, presumably it would be people like ethics professors, politicians, and religious leaders, since they have voluntarily embraced lines of work which seem more suited to being a good role model. If *I* have any station-dependent special responsibilities, on the other hand, presumably it is only *qua* basketball player. Thus, I might have special responsibilities to my teammates to watch my diet, to avoid dangerous hobbies like skiing where I might injure myself, and to be prompt and cheerful in my attendance of all team meetings.

MALONE: You raise a couple of good points, so let me respond to each in turn. First, I agree that it falls upon all of us to serve as appropriate role models, and so when I speak of celebrated athletes having a special responsibility, I mean only that we have *additional* moral reasons to act virtuously. Thus, I do not claim that we must necessarily behave *better* than others. In short, everyone has moral reasons to encourage virtue and discourage vice, but celebrated athletes have additional moral reasons to behave well.

Second, in suggesting that those who occupy other professions are better candidates to have special responsibilities to serve as role models, you confuse those who *should* have influence with those who *do*. I agree that we would be a healthier society if more of us raised our children to emulate people who could write a graceful sentence, create a beautiful piece of artwork, or construct an elaborate and well-reasoned argument, but that is not the current state of affairs. Despite their being better suited for the job, these people do not have the influence you do, and so they do not have the extra moral reasons to behave well that you do. (Of course, this is not to deny that others may have special moral responsibilities to be good role models for other reasons.)

BARKLEY: By that reasoning, it is the *prominent* and *celebrated* athletes who have these special responsibilities, not all and only *professional* athletes.

MALONE: Exactly! The relatively obscure professional athlete who is not emulated has no special responsibility, but the prominent amateur does. There is nothing intrinsic to athletics which requires its participants to be role models; were it not for the attention we happen to attract, we would have no special responsibilities. Thus, even celebrated high school athletes have special moral reasons to behave in an exemplary fashion insofar as their classmates look up to them. Without exaggerating the influence of athletes in our society, I think it is accurate to claim that the most heralded prep athletes can palpably affect the complexion of a school via their treatment of others. It can make a discernible difference, for instance, whether popular ath-

letes embrace diversity and befriend a wide variety of the school's population or whether they mock and taunt those interested in alternative activities. To take an extreme example, one wonders if the tragic shooting at Columbine High School would have occurred if the varsity athletes there had behaved in a more inclusive and accepting manner.

BARKLEY: Some of what you say makes sense, but your discussion of Columbine High School actually reinforces my attraction to voluntarism and individual responsibility. In my view, the two young men who pulled the triggers are responsible for the tragedy; it's ridiculous to pin the blame on the school's athletes!

MALONE: Let me be clear: I would not for a second try to suggest that the athletes rather than the shooters were responsible for the horrible massacre. Clearly, the blame for any shooting must be attributed first and foremost to those who do the shooting. Still, I cite the case of Columbine High School because it illustrates nicely the twin facts that athletes need not be professional to be influential and that their influence can be of profound importance. My point is simply that, given their prominence, celebrated athletes are more likely to affect the behavior of others, and there are compelling moral reasons for anyone in such a position to try to use this influence to promote acceptance rather than hatred and xenophobia.

Second, I mentioned earlier that by "special" responsibility I mean that a person can have additional moral reasons to behave well, not necessarily that this person must behave better than everyone else. Let me also point out that there is a second way in which my own appreciation for voluntarism and individual responsibility has shaped the position I advance here. Notice that I have consistently spoken of a special "responsibility" rather than of a special "duty." I have chosen my words carefully in this regard because, by "duty," it is common to mean some required action which others may force one to do. To the extent that I share your sympathy for voluntarism, I shy away from asserting that celebrated athletes have a "duty" (in this strict sense) to be good role models. Rather, I use the term "responsibility" in the hopes of invoking something more akin to virtue theory than duty. That is, in suggesting that a celebrated athlete can have a special responsibility to be a good role model, I am alleging no more than that a virtuous person in this position would be sensitive to the additional moral reasons to behave well and that anyone indifferent to this magnified influence would be exhibiting a moral vice. Thus, on my view, if you behaved badly despite your influence on others, you would be blameworthy for your failure fully to own up to the magnified part you play in the moral education of others.

BARKLEY: Okay, now that you have explained your position in full, I'm willing to concede that I have a special responsibility to be a good role model. But now your own arguments show that this responsibility is not so significant, not only because adults are responsible for their own actions but because parents are principally responsible for their children taking me as a moral role model in the first place (since a well-nurtured child would not view me as a paragon of virtue merely because of the things I can do on a basketball court). Moreover, once one acknowledges that athletes have a greater influence on the moral education of our youth than is appropriate, one must admit that we all have a responsibility to amend our society's values.

MALONE: I could not agree more! In arguing that you have a special responsibility, I never meant to suggest that this is the whole story. This issue is extremely complicated, and those who merely sit back and blame you do us all a disservice. Perhaps the most important thing is that parents dedicate more time and energy to raising their children to be sensitive and responsible moral agents, but – as you rightly point out – to stop there is a

pernicious oversimplification. Parents must constantly compete with various influences in society which exert considerable pressure on the development of young people. Given this, we must all be vigilant not only to how society affects *us* but to how *we contribute* to society's values. Do not mistake me: I am not alleging that anyone can single-handedly alter society, but our lack of omnipotence in this regard does not absolve us from our responsibility to make the marginal differences we can. Thus, I ultimately agree that all of us have a responsibility to try to reshape our culture so that when children look for moral exemplars they choose people better suited for the job. In short, everyone should work to construct a society in which children look to professional basketball players as model athletes but look to people like Martin Luther King, Jr., and Mother Teresa as paragons of virtue.

BARKLEY: So, what is the bottom line? Does this mean that I cannot in good conscience accept large contracts and do shoe commercials?

MALONE: Not at all! What all this means is merely that you should recognize that along with the privilege of your exalted standing comes a special responsibility to be mindful of your actions and the heightened influence they have on others. Thus, you have more moral reasons than the average person to take the high road the next time someone tries to pick a fight with you in a bar, for instance, because many of those who admire you for your athletic talents are likely to take their cue from your behavior in other contexts as well. What is more, whenever possible, it would be good of you to use your influence to attract attention to worthy charities and to some more deserving but less prominent voices like Maya Angelou, Cornell West, Toni Morrison, and others who might in turn use their increased influence to further improve society.

CHAPTER 35

Get the Message?

Rick Reilly

My name is Frankie and I'm eight and I wanna be just like my dad.

Like, I used to hate Latrell Sprewell because my dad hated Latrell Sprewell. Dad used to yell at the TV about what a jerk Sprewell was, how the guy choked his coach, and how he never once even 'pologized for it, and how he kept pit bulls, and how one of 'em bit off his little girl's ear and chewed her face, and how he didn't even feel bad about it and even said, "These things happen."

But now Sprewell's on the New York Knicks, and they're my dad's and mine's favorite team, and now my dad yells, "Atta baby, Spree!" and "Take it to the hole, Spree!" And that's what I yell, now, too, cuz the Knicks're kickin' serious booty in the NBA playoffs. And now Spree even has a cool commercial out. In it, he calls himself "the American Dream" and acts like he's almost glad he choked that coach, and I turn the sound up for the commercial because Spree is my dream now, too.

And I seen a man on TV talkin' about Iron Mike Tyson and how things are really lookin' up for the champ cuz, after beatin' the crap out of two guys, he got out of jail early. The judge didn't even care that Tyson'd been to jail before for hurtin' that teenage girl, but like my dad says, "What's she doin' up in his room that time a night anyhow?"

And now the men who run boxin' in Lost Vegas say it's OK for Tyson to fight again, even though they took his license s'pos'dly forever after Tyson went totally mental in the ring, bitin' off a guy's ear like he was Sprewell's dog or somethin'. And the man on TV says that's good because now it looks like Tyson can fight not just once but prob'ly twice this year and make a whole buncha, buncha money, like a hunnert dollars, and it works out good for the boxin' men, too, because he'll prob'ly fight in Lost Vegas, it turns out.

And that's really cool because me and my dad watch a lot of paper view together, which is what best buds do. Like the really cool pro wrestlin' match when the man on TV told us a guy fell 80 feet down from a rope and landed right on the turnbuckle. We couldn't see it on paper view, but I bet everybody there thought it was just another crazy wrestlin' stunt, like maybe he'd lay there awhile and then jump up and eat the mike or somethin', but the guy was really dead. They stopped the show for a few minutes, but then it started up again, and that was cool, because, like my dad said, this was paper view and what're they gonna do, rip off the people?

My mom didn't like that one bit, but she's actin' funny about a lotta stuff lately. Like, after those two high school kids shot everybody, my mom made me throw away almost all of my cool video games like Carmageddon, like it was my fault, because she says they're too violet. I started to complain, but my dad told me to shut up because SportsCenter was just gettin' to the car racin', and there was a cool wreck, and when somebody dies in one of those they stop the race at least half the time.

I like to look over my dad's shoulder when he reads the sports, and just now he asked my mom what kinda gotdamn world is it when a guy like Darryl Strawberry is gonna just get a wrist slap for "doin' Coke and ho's," but I know he doesn't mean it because I saw him with both out in the yard today, and besides he never said anythin' mean about Strawberry when he was a New York Met, which is his and mine's favorite baseball team, acourse.

And sometimes my dad gets tired a me lookin' over his shoulder at the sports, and so now I'm down in my room playin' sock basketball and I'm Chris Webber of the Sacramento Kings, and I see the hated John Stockton of the Utah Jazz come down the lane, and it's only a minute into the game and I do exactly what Webber did, which is I just knock Stockton goofy. That's what my dad says you gotta do to earn a man's respeck, like when pitchers throw the baseball at guys' heads, which is just part of the game and doesn't hurt nobody, except if they're Mets heads, acourse.

And Stockton is layin' there, and Webber don't get kicked out of the game, and I say, "Chris Webber has sent a clear message to the Jazz tonight!" just the way the man on TV did that night my dad and me watched.

OK, I'm only eight, but like my dad says, you gotta send the right message.

Index